This book is to be returned on
or before the date stamped below

The Evolution of British General Practice, 1850–1948

The Evolution of British General Practice

1850–1948

ANNE DIGBY

OXFORD

UNIVERSITY PRESS

OXFORD

UNIVERSITY PRESS

Great Clarendon Street, Oxford OX2 6DP

Oxford University Press is a department of the University of Oxford.
It furthers the University's objective of excellence in research, scholarship,
and education by publishing worldwide in

Oxford New York

Athens Auckland Bangkok Bogotá Buenos Aires Calcutta
Cape Town Chennai Dar es Salaam Delhi Florence Hong Kong Istanbul
Karachi Kuala Lumpur Madrid Melbourne Mexico City Mumbai
Nairobi Paris São Paulo Singapore Taipei Tokyo Toronto Warsaw

with associated companies in Berlin Ibadan

Oxford is a registered trade mark of Oxford University Press
in the UK and in certain other countries

Published in the United States
by Oxford University Press Inc., New York

British Library Cataloguing in Publication Data

Data available

Library of Congress Cataloging in Publication Data
Digby, Anne.
The evolution of British general practice 1850–1948 / Anne Digby.
p. cm.
Includes bibliographical references.
1. Physicians (General practice)—Great Britain—History—19th century.
2. Physicians (General practice)—Great Britain—History—20th century.
3. Family medicine—Great Britain—History—19th century.
4. Family medicine—Great Britain—History—20th century.
5. Medicine—Practice—Great Britain—History—19th century.
6. Medicine Practice —Great Britain—History—20th century. I. Title.
R729.5.G4D54 1999 262.1′0941—dc21 98-51327
ISBN 0-19-820513-9

1 3 5 7 9 10 8 6 4 2

Typeset by Hope Services (Abingdon) Ltd.
Printed in Great Britain
on acid-free paper by
Bookcraft Ltd, Midsomer Norton, Somerset

For Jessica, Naomi
Leon, and Judy

Acknowledgements

THE collegiality of the academic and professional communities has been conspicuously in evidence during the preparation of this volume. Without the generous assistance of many colleagues and friends this extensive project on the history of general practice would not have been brought to fruition. I am also most grateful to the Wellcome Trust for a Wellcome Research Leave Fellowship, to the Nuffield Foundation for a Social Science Research Fellowship, and to Oxford Brookes University for Development Funding.

In the early stages of research I was helped by David Wright who provided me with research assistance in meticulously compiling an archival database. At a later stage, some forty archivists expedited the study by sharing their expertise with me when I visited their archives. The Regional Health Archivists in Scotland were helpful in advising me and, in the case of Alistair Tough and Morag Williams, in supplying me with valuable material. The Librarians at Oxford Brookes University, the Bodleian Library, Cambridge University Library, and the Wellcome Institute for the History of Medicine were also most obliging in enabling me to locate sources.

My colleagues in both universities in Oxford have been extremely supportive, and have provided stimulating comment, as well as source material. And colleagues in the History Department at the University of Cape Town, and in the Humanities and Social Science Division of the Californian Institute of Technology also gave constructive help during very pleasant terms spent at these institutions. At Oxford Brookes University I owe a particular debt of gratitude to the late Colin Pedley, and to John Perkins for facilitating my take-up of research fellowships; to Mary Chamberlain, Jeanne Sheehy, Lori Williamson, and Richard Wrigley for taking over my professional responsibilities during my period of leave; as well as to my other colleagues for tolerating, and supporting my long period of absence from the academic coalface.

My thinking has been clarified by stimulating discussions following papers in Cape Town, Glasgow, Groningen, London, Oxford, and Norwich. I am also appreciative of the input of my students: they have had some ideas tried out on them at an initial stage, and have helped me to refine them. I am especially beholden to colleagues who read some of the chapters. Paul David gave me expert advice on Chapter 1; Carol Dyhouse shared feminist perceptions on Chapter 7; John Horder and Irvine Loudon provided professional insights on Chapter 8; while John Stewart and Charles Webster made perceptive points about Chapter 13. I am also indebted to my colleague, Ian Pope, for his highly developed cartographic skills, which are evident in the splendid maps he provided for Chapter 4.

Dr Granger of Kimbolton, and Mrs Hendry of Nuneaton together with doctors at the Warders Medical Centre, Tonbridge, Kent, and at the Abbey Mead Centre at Romsey, Hampshire, have generously given me access to privately owned documents on the history of general practice. Many other people have been liberal in providing me with material, or otherwise facilitating the progress of my research. These have included: Michael Bevan, Anne Borsay, Nick Bosanquet, Roy Campbell, Melanie Dubber, T. A. B. Corley, Anne Crowther, Rees Davies, Karola Decker, Jennifer Duncan, Marguerite Dupree, Sylvia Dunkley, Carol Dyhouse, C. P. Elliott-Binns, James Foreman-Peck, David Gladstone, Jennifer Hawker, Joy Hendry, John Holden, John Horder, Jean Hughes-Jones, Angela John, Jane Lewis, Glyndwr Lloyd, Jean Loudon, Irvine Loudon, W. F. D. McKinley, Pam Michael, Avner Offer, Margaret Pelling, Denis Pereira Gray, G. S. Plaut, Elizabeth Roberts, C. J. P. Seccombe, Dr Smerdon, Richard Smith, John Stewart, S. R. Turner, Charles Webster, Paul Weindling, and Brenda White.

Oral history has provided an important source for this study. I should like to thank Michael Bevan and Helen Sweet who skilfully conducted interviews. I am also appreciative of the valuable recollections contributed by Dr S. Adler, Dr H. W. Ashworth, Dr H. M. Davie, Dr and Mrs A. F. Granger, Dr B. J. Goff, Dr R. Griffiths, Mrs E. B. Hendry, Dr E. Hope-Simpson, Dr F. E. James, Dr and Mrs R. G. Lilly, Dr A. W. Maiden, Mrs S. Pope, and Dr J. E. Rankine.

My debt to my colleague, Helen Sweet, has been considerable. She has brought a highly developed professionalism to this exploration of the history of general practice, most conspicuously in her exemplary research assistance in the compilation and analysis of a large database of general practitioners. Her enthusiasm, energy, and commitment have played a central role in making this a productive and enjoyable enquiry.

Charles Feinstein has lived with this project for several years, and sustained an active interest in its progress. I warmly appreciate the substantial intellectual input he has made through strategic interventions, discussion of major issues, as well as by attention to minor textual details.

I am indebted for permission to use the unpublished 'Memoirs of Dr William Henry Harding' to his Executors; the unpublished 'Autobiography' of Dr J. Richard to Dr and Mrs R. Scott; the records of the Medical Practitioners Union to the MSF; and the NHI records of their practice predecessors at the Greater Glasgow Health Board Archives, to the present partners in McFarlane, Blair, Short and McQueen. For permission to reproduce illustrations 1 to 8, thanks are due to the Wellcome Trust. For permission to reproduce the cover illustration I am indebted to the Tate Gallery.

Contents

List of Plates, Maps, and Figures

List of Tables

Abbreviations

BHM	*Bulletin of the History of Medicine*
BMA	British Medical Association
BMJ	*British Medical Journal*
CMAC	Contemporary Medical Archives Centre, Wellcome Institute, London
GMC	General Medical Council
GP	General practitioner
LSMW	London School of Medicine for Women
MH	*Medical History*
MO	Medical Officer
MOH	Medical Officer of Health
MPU	Medical Practitioners Union
MWF	Medical Women's Federation
MWFQN	*Medical Women's Federation Quarterly Newsletter*
NHI	National Health Insurance
NHS	National Health Service
PP	Parliamentary Paper
PRO	Public Record Office
RC	Royal Commission
RO	Record Office
SC	Select Committee
SHM	*Social History of Medicine*
SMA	Socialist Medical Association

1

Constructing General Practice

ALTHOUGH general practice provided primary care for the British people its history is much less distinct than that of hospital medicine, and while medical pioneers have achieved fame, the hardworking professional lives and sterling human qualities of general practitioners have remained obscure. Yet the first half of the period has been seen as a time when ordinary doctors 'moved from the margin to the mainstream of social life',[1] and the years covered in this volume as ones 'when the [medical] profession underwent its most meteoric development'.[2] A need for a comprehensive study of the development of modern general practice is apparent. With a few significant exceptions there has been a dearth of work on the general practitioner of the second half of the nineteenth century.[3] General practice within the first half of the twentieth century has received better coverage in relation to selected aspects, with some illuminating specialist work.[4] However, much existing historical work has tended either to focus teleologically on the time immediately preceding and accompanying legislation in 1911 and 1946–8,[5] or has analysed a particular issue such as the national health insurance scheme,[6] or professional organization.[7]

---

[1] J. Harris, *Private Lives, Public Spirit. A Social History of Britain, 1870–1914* (Oxford, 1993), 56.

[2] M. Dupree, 'Other Than Healing: Medical Practitioners and the Business of Life Assurance During the Nineteenth and Early Twentieth Centuries', *SHM* 10 (1997), 81.

[3] M. J. Peterson, *The Medical Profession in Mid-Victorian London* (Berkeley, 1978).

[4] For example, B. N. Armstrong, *The Health Insurance Doctor. His Role in Britain, Denmark and France* (Princeton, 1939); F. Honigsbaum, *The Division in British Medicine. A History of the Separation of General Practice from Hospital Care, 1911–1968* (1979); R. Stevens, *Medical Practice in Modern England. The Impact of Specialization and State Medicine* (New Haven, 1966); D. M. Fox, *Health Policies Health Politics. The British and American Experiences, 1911–1965* (1986).

[5] H. Eckstein, *The English Health Service. Its Origins, Structure and Achievements* (Cambridge Mass., 1964); J. S. Ross, *The National Health Service in Great Britain* (Oxford, 1952); A. Lindsay, *Socialized Medicine in England and Wales. The National Health Service, 1948–1961* (Chapel Hill, 1962); J. and S. Jewkes, *The Genesis of the British NHS* (Oxford, 1962).

[6] N. R. Eder, *National Health Insurance and the Medical Profession in Britain, 1913–1939* (1982); B. B. Gilbert, *The Evolution of National Insurance in Britain* (1966); H. Levy, *National Health Insurance. A Critical Study* (Cambridge, 1944); G. F. McLeary, *National Health Insurance* (1932); J. S. Whiteside, 'Private Agencies for Public Purposes: Some New Perspectives on Policy Making in Health Insurance Between the Wars', *Journal of Social Policy*, 12 (1983).

[7] H. Eckstein, *Pressure Group Politics. The Case of the British Medical Association* (1960); J. Rogers Hollingsworth, *A Political Economy of Medicine: Great Britain and the United States* (Baltimore, 1986); P. W. J. Bartrip, *Mirror of Medicine. A History of the British Medical Journal* (Oxford, 1990).

Rationale

By 1850 the traditional three medical estates of physician, surgeon, and apothecary had been transformed. Ordinary medical care for much of the population was being performed by a doctor, formerly termed the surgeon-apothecary, but now commonly referred to as the general practitioner.[8] During the ensuing century this practitioner's role was to be changed fundamentally by three major pieces of legislation. The Medical Act of 1858 established state registration of qualified doctors and advanced professionalization; the 1911 National Health Insurance Act initiated the state panel doctor scheme for poorer patients, and a mix of public and private finance for their GPs; and the 1946 act laid down a comprehensive, publicly funded National Health Service. On the eve of the NHS there were an estimated ~~17.6 million~~ ✳ general practitioners in England and Wales, and ~~2 million~~ in Scotland.[9] During this century significant changes occurred in the social status of doctors, in their role in relation to the state, in the medical market and, resulting from this, in the social composition of patients and speed of consultations. These developments provided the foundations for modern health care.

British doctors' lives reflected the internal dynamics of a triangular relationship between England, Wales, and Scotland, and these countries form the geographical focus of this study.[10] Amongst the professions, medicine led the way in helping to develop a British identity because an individual's birth, training, or practice might occur in different countries within the British Isles. Doctors' registration under the Medical Act of 1858 operated within an overall British context. Equally, the BMA as the key professional association became a genuinely British structure.[11] In society more generally, however, there was slower integration and a weaker impulse towards a sense of British identity: change was impeded because of firmly entrenched feelings of being Welsh, Scottish or English. Linguistically there was variety, so that in Wales in 1870 two-thirds of the population spoke Welsh as a first language, and in the Highlands Gaelic was the *lingua franca*. In more remote areas cultural integration was long hindered by poor communications. Diversity within and between these three countries therefore persisted so that integration by way of a cross-cultural blending only gradually occurred. Britain was united but not uniform.

---

[8] I. Loudon, *Medical Care and the General Practitioner, 1750–1850* (Oxford, 1986), 1.

[9] C. Webster, *The Health Services since the War. Volume I. Problems of Health Care. The National Health Service before 1957* (1988), 122.

[10] Following the Act of Union of 1800, Ireland became part of the United Kingdom—of England, Wales, Scotland, and Ireland—for two-thirds of the period covered by this volume. Although Ireland is sometimes incorporated in discussions of Britain and Britishness, this usage is not followed here.

[11] L. Brockliss, 'The Professions and National Identity', in L. Brockliss and D. Eastwood (eds.), *A Union of Multiple Identities, The British Isles, c.1750–1850* (Manchester, 1997), 18–21.

✳ On p. 2, the sentence in the first paragraph should read as:

On the eve of the NHS there were an estimated 17,600 general practitioners in England and Wales, and 2,000 in Scotland.

Urbanization and industrialization changed the demographic balance between the three countries. England had more than four times the combined population of Wales and Scotland in 1851 and, a century later, more than five times as many people. And, although Wales had only slightly more than one-third of Scotland's population in 1851, its faster growth meant that Wales had not far short of half of Scotland's population by 1951. Internal contrasts were as striking as comparative ones. There were marked differences between low-density, predominantly rural counties, and others with an enduring high population density. In 1851 one in two of the English population was in Greater London, Yorkshire, and Lancashire, and a century later two in every five inhabitants lived there. Nearly a quarter of the Welsh population was in Glamorgan in 1851, with more than half residing there in 1951. In Scotland over a quarter of the population lived in Lanarkshire and Midlothian in 1851, and a century later not far short of half the Scottish people resided there. In turn general practitioners were attracted to these well-populated areas, and notable medical concentrations were found there.[12]

The British professional landscape was complex. Cutting across national boundaries were medical centres with their own distinctive hinterlands. Liverpool, for example, had a university medical school that recruited substantially from north Wales. The city had Welsh inhabitants, and an even more substantial Irish population. They were treated by Welsh, English, Scottish, and Irish doctors. Regionalization in general practice meant that a geographical 'core and periphery' model had limited applicability.[13] It was said of the Scottish medical profession, for example, that 'the north of Scotland does not know the south or the west'.[14] One characteristic of this intricate medical topography was an upland/lowland dichotomy. A GP with a far-flung practice in the Scottish Highlands had more in common with a North Yorkshire doctor than with one in Edinburgh, while industrial doctors in the valleys of South Wales shared the concerns of Scottish colleagues in the Fife or Lanarkshire coalfields. An even finer-grained spatial articulation was also evident at the local level with diversification of general practice suggesting a typology of country, suburban, and urban practices. Doctors in 'six-penny' or 'panel' practices located in inner-city Birmingham or Glasgow, for example, would have had intensive patient demand, a fast surgery through-put, and standardized medicines. In contrast, country doctors in Merionethshire, Devonshire, or Galloway, for instance, would have had

---

[12] The local lists in *Medical Directories* clearly indicate striking concentrations of doctors in central Scotland, and Greater London, especially.

[13] K. Robbins, 'Core and Periphery in British History', *Proceedings of the British Academy*, LXX, (1984), 283, 290; id., *Nineteenth-Century Britain. Integration and Diversity* (Oxford, 1988), 2, 184, 190; 'An Imperial and Multinational Polity. The "Scene from the Centre", 1832–1922', and E. Evans, 'Englishness and Britishness. National Identities, 1790–1870', in A. Grant and K.J. Stringer (eds.), *Uniting the Kingdom? The Making of British History* (1995), 240–1, 253.

[14] *Special Report from the SC on the Medical Act (1858)*, Q 54, evidence of Professor Struthers on the adequacy of Scottish representation on the GMC.

extensive patient demand, with similar work patterns of long distances travelled in visits to a few patients, perhaps with short intervening periods of relaxation (as when a pheasant was shot for the pot).[15]

Approach

Inclusivity has been an important objective in this study, so that it has been the aim to give as much attention to country GPs as to metropolitan colleagues. Data on the life-styles of general practitioners in contrasting locations, as well as on the character and organization of their general practices were derived from varied sources. Three principal types of material were employed: archival documentation, oral testimony, and printed sources. Quantitative data facilitated analytical precision and qualitative material involved more open-ended discussion. These complementary approaches have provided extremely detailed information on the past development of general practice, as well as shedding some useful light on the ways in which past development has shaped present patterns of primary health care.

A comprehensive survey was made of archival sources of information, but the large amount of relevant material available meant that only a selective cross-section of records was consulted. The bibliography indicates the numerous record offices visited, their selection being dictated not only by the richness of the holdings, but also by the need to be sensitive to local and regional variation, as well as to balance the investigation between different generations of GPs. The documents which general practitioners kept were found to be predominantly functional, so that record-keeping was only partial. General practice documentation had survived unevenly, and retrieval had been imperfect. Relatively little was found on practice organization with the notable exception of legal documents on partnerships, assistantships, and apprenticeships. Archival information on treatment was also slight, because day books usually gave little clinical information. Surviving correspondence between GPs and consultants usefully illuminated the development of a referral system, together with the nature of the interface between generalist and specialist practice. Financial records were both substantial and well preserved. This suggested that economics—although seldom receiving much public discussion—was nevertheless the bottom line in professional survival. Running a small business loomed large in general practice, so that bulky financial ledgers, debt collectors' volumes and, for more recent years, income tax returns, were prominent amongst surviving records. Material on patients was scarce, although correspondence about bills, as well as a few surviving record cards, was enlightening. In addition a variety of ancillary documents (for example on poor-law medicine, cottage hospitals, or club practice) pro-

---

[15] Personal communication from Dr Granger, who practised in Kimbolton, Cambridgeshire.

vided a wider context in which to view the multifarious activities of the GP, as did other material (notably on medical officers of health, midwives, or district nurses) in suggesting the nature of collaboration. After 1911 the greater bureaucratic impulse generated by the national health insurance scheme resulted in some detailed records for panel practice. Professional pressures meant that the doctor rarely had the time to record a personal view on everyday events, although this private dimension of the doctor's life might be revealed retrospectively in a printed autobiography. Parliamentary papers, medical surveys, professional journals, and newspapers were other major printed sources used in this study.

Fresh insights into practice immediately preceding and accompanying the passage of the National Health Service Act came in the form of oral testimony from retired general practitioners, and their families. Oral histories relating to the reconstruction of a complicated past may involve selectivity, telescope periods of less interest to the subject, or reshape memory after the event so resulting in unconscious misrepresentation. An element of self-validation, or of received wisdom from collective professional memory, may perhaps erode past ambiguities or complexities. Despite these possible pitfalls such self-representations and subjective viewpoints have been found to be very valuable, not least when employed in conjunction with other sorts of information.

An important new source exploited for this examination of general practice was the GP obituary published in the *British Medical Journal*. The obituary's distinctive rhetoric and format means that it may be considered an art form but—despite varied styles of presentation and the highlighting of personal or professional attributes—these notices also contained very useful pieces of standardized information. Precisely because of the finite space available in a professional journal, the selective view of a medical life given in an obituary necessarily involved the inclusion of key attributes. These were central items in the compilation of a substantial database of general practitioners.

Obituaries were sampled on a decennial basis, beginning in 1880 when death notices for GPs first began to be published in any quantity, and ending in 1970. The first cohort of those dying in 1880 had to be supplemented with those of 1881, in order to provide a group which was sufficiently numerous to compare with later cohorts, and large enough for quantitative analysis. Obituaries from these ten dates (1880–1, 1890, 1900, 1910, 1920, 1930, 1940, 1950, 1960, 1970), were then reorganized by date of qualification to give successive cohorts of doctors.[16] The first group were those who had qualified before 1850 (but of course practised within the period covered in this book), and the last group were those who had graduated in the years

---

[16] The year of actual death determined inclusion in each decennial cohort, although the obituary notice for a GP dying in late November or December might appear in an issue of the *BMJ* at the beginning of the following year.

immediately preceding 1948 (whose practice spanned the changes brought in by the National Health Service).

As others have noted, 'the distinction between speciality and general practice remains blurred . . . [so that] general practitioners . . . are often invisible' historically.[17] The distribution of practising generalists relative to specialists cannot always be plotted precisely because the boundary was both permeable and changing. Included in the database were all those who were stated to have engaged in general practice at any stage of their lives, even if they also practised as a specialist at some point in their careers. A more intractable problem emerged in that obituaries, even when cross-checked against medical directories, did not always give sufficient information to determine with absolute confidence the kind of practice meant. A selective cull of obituaries was undertaken to weed out ambiguous cases. Beginning with a total of over a thousand obituaries, which at first sight appeared to be those of general practitioners, the total in the database for purposes of analysis was reduced on closer inspection to 961 individuals.

In compiling an electronic database Microsoft Access 2 software was used to create 107 major fields, and these were linked to Excel 7 software in order to facilitate large-scale quantitative analysis on both a longitudinal (time-dimensional), and a cross-sectional basis. Some of the key issues examined in this way were: the place of medical education and training undertaken; the qualifications obtained; the individual's publications; the number of practice areas; the extent of familial-based practice; part-time appointments combined with work as a general practitioner; the numbers of GPs who saw armed service; the organization of the practice (whether single-handed or in partnership); the varied roles GPs took in the local community; practice abroad; and the degree to which active participation in professional associations was undertaken. This enabled an inclusive, rounded picture of general practice to be assembled, which, while indicating general trends, was also sensitive to the characteristics of sub-groups, as well as to the traits of individuals. Those included in the GP database were those who practised in England, Wales, and Scotland. Most had been born there, but a small minority was of Irish or foreign birth. Only those who had been principals, and thus fully engaged in general practice, were included. A pronounced tendency for medical women to practise only as assistants in general practice, before taking posts in public health or municipal medicine, meant that relatively few medical women were in the database.

Unfortunately, there was no *definitive* way of checking the representativeness of the sample in the GP dataset against the total of those engaged in general practice, because *Medical Directories* and the *Medical Register* did not provide separate lists of general practitioners. (Indeed both the *Register* and

---

[17] A. Crowther and M. Dupree, 'The Invisible General Practitioner: The Careers of Scottish Medical Students in the Late Nineteenth Century', *BHM*, 70 (1996), 388.

the *Directory* had their own lacunae.)[18] It is likely that there are some biases in this database, as in other samples, and where possible the nature of these has been explored through cross checking with other sources. A comparison was made between the database of general practitioners, and national totals of *all* types of British doctors, given in the *Medical Register*, as well as those in the *Medical Directory*. This somewhat unsatisfactory test revealed that English and Welsh practitioners were consistently overrepresented in the GP database relative to Scottish ones. Another comparison sought to throw light on whether the database gave undue prominence to the 'medico-politico' type of doctor who was active in professional affairs. This was because the *British Medical Journal*, as the journal of the British Medical Association, might have published obituaries mainly on BMA members, thus constituting a skewed sample of the profession. However, when BMA membership as a percentage of those within the GP dataset, was related to the proportion of the wider profession who were members, the biases to some extent offset each other. This was because there was overrepresentation of BMA members before 1911, but underrepresentation thereafter.

It also seems intuitively likely that obituaries would highlight a subset of the profession with a high public profile, whilst obscurer colleagues in country or panel practice would be less prone to receive a notice. Did this in fact occur? Historically there was a very widespread diffusion of appointments before 1911, which suggests that any disposition towards recording the achievements of only the more active Victorian and Edwardian GP was unlikely to have been very marked. It is possible that this tendency became more apparent during the subsequent period. Certainly, the overall diversity of practitioners is a conspicuous and consistent feature of the database, which gives some confidence that it contains a reasonable cross-section of generalists.

The obituarists in the *BMJ* were a disparate group, and this had the advantage of giving varied professional and personal perspectives. In wartime some general practitioners wrote their own notices in anticipation of death in action,[19] but in more normal circumstances a colleague or friend would supply the obituary. Frequently, the secretary of the local BMA, or the individual's own doctor would organize this. Fellow students, former assistants, present partners, or friends were frequent contributors to the main notice, and the views of patients, hospital sisters or eminent colleagues were also

---

[18] Practitioners were first placed on the *Medical Register* as medical students for the Medical Student List, but then registered again later, at the start of their careers as doctors. Sometimes this occurred immediately after graduation, thus introducing a bias towards Scotland in any national breakdown of practitioners within the *Register*, given the pre-eminence for much of the period of Scottish universities. In other cases registration was delayed until the young doctor was ready to start in practice. The *Medical Directory* did not give an accurate national distribution of practising doctors, because it was dependent on practitioners themselves returning information, and so was unlikely to be completely up to date.

[19] It is interesting to note that such self-written obituaries have been more generally encouraged for the *BMJ* in recent years.

sometimes reported more briefly. In one instance even the prime minister was quoted on his view of a deceased GP who had been an MP.[20] On occasion a notice from a local newspaper or the carefully worded encomium of a Hospital Management Committee was added. The deceased tended to be viewed through the lens of an obituarist from a later generation, so that subsequent concerns might dictate what was selected for comment. Sometimes obituaries showed an inability to empathize with the values of an earlier generation. For example, 'He was a survival of the God-fearing Victorian Englishman in the tradition of Charles Kingsley.'[21] At worst, it was apparent that obituarists had no first-hand knowledge of their subjects, particularly when practitioners lived to advanced ages.

Employing a group biography approach for general practitioners has extended the benefits of prosopography. For the first time a clear picture of the general practitioner has emerged which is quite distinct from the previously undifferentiated view of the profession. In their flexibility, resilience, and frequent change the lives of general practitioners that have emerged from this database analysis contrast strikingly with a received stereotype of family doctors rooted for generations in one locality. Conspicuous in this new study is differentiated generational experiences, contrasting cohort life chances, and varied individual lives.

An Evolutionary Framework

The 1850s marked the beginning of modern general practice. In the period between the Medical Act of 1858 and the inception of the National Health Service of 1948, general practice was transformed in its structures, economic organization, and medical content. Women joined men in the profession, single-handed practices became partnerships, and the use of phone and car enlarged the professional hinterland in which patients could be treated. Fresh sources of income from corporate or state sources enabled the GP to care for a wider sector of the population. Doctors accumulated more information about the causes of illness, the working of the body, and new drugs began to revolutionize the doctor's therapeutic potential. How is this transformation to be explained? For the historian of medicine, evolutionary theory provides a useful approach with which to try to explain some of the many changes in medical practice, and gives a useful framework for presenting the results of extensive empirical investigation.

Fortuitously, the year after the Medical Act saw the publication of Charles Darwin's *Origin of Species,* which interpreted success and failure in evolutionary terms, by focusing on the processes underlying the survival of the fittest. In Darwin's work hesitancies and ambiguities as well as a series of

---

[20] *BMJ* ii (1930), 126–7.   [21] *BMJ*, ii (1950), 420.

'interlinked propositions and ideas' give flexible possibilities for transference into a whole series of ideological positions.[22] Given that Darwin did not systematize his social and political ideas, a veritable intellectual industry has been created on: Darwin; the debt owed by Darwin to earlier thinkers such as Lamarck; on Darwin's putative relationship (if any) to Social Darwinism; on whether Social Darwinism should be termed something else, such as Social Lamarckianism; and on the 'cultural malleability' of a 'diffuse cluster of social theories' involved in the term Social Darwinism—that we continue to use, despite its problematical nature.[23]

It should be emphasized that in this volume evolution is being interpreted very broadly. The following discussion uses Lamarckian evolutionary theory that has been preferred to that of Darwin in looking at the cultural traits or memes of general practice. This is because of the intentional—rather than blind—character of cultural transmission. However, what follows is metaphorically rather than literally Lamarckian, so that genes and practices (memes) are viewed as analogous. The time scale involved is not evolutionary but historical, and the changes implied are therefore relatively dynamic rather than very gradual. One important reason for this faster rate of change is that whereas the individual Darwinian unit is stable, the Lamarckian one is unstable, because adaptable to changes in the environment.[24] Also central to my discussion are general practitioners that acted as the agents for the cultural transmission, or replication, of memes. However, their roles were not restricted to this and, within this wider historical context, a social Darwinistic interpretation is employed to explain the differential success of individual doctors.

In Darwinian thought evolutionary processes involve mutation, selection, and replication. The evolution of general practice over our hundred-year period is interpreted as being an interaction of these three processes: the mutations initiated by various forces acting both within the medical profession and from outside, the manner in which members of the profession responded to them, and their subsequent diffusion through the profession as a whole. We thus need to consider each of these stages in turn. What were these mutations which triggered the process of change, and what were the underlying forces responsible for them? How did doctors initially react to these mutations, and what determined the nature of that reaction? What then

---

[22] M. Hawkins, *Social Darwinism and European and American Thought, 1860–1945* (Cambridge, 1997), 32.

[23] For example, R. J. Evans, *Rereading German History. From Unification to Reunification, 1800–1996* (1997); A. Kelly, *The Descent of Darwin. The Popularisation of Darwinism in Germany, 1860–1914* (Chapel Hill, 1981), 101; Hawkins, *Social Darwinism*, 19.

[24] In constructing this cultural framework I have found the following particularly helpful: R. Boyd and P. J. Richerson, *Culture and the Evolutionary Process* (Chicago, 1985): D. L. Hull, *Science as Process* (Chicago, 1988); J. Mokyr, *The Lever of Riches. Technological Creativity and Economic Progress* (Oxford, 1990); and J. J. Vromen, *Economic Evolution. An Enquiry into the Foundations of New Institutional Economics* (1995.)

served to promote or hinder the rate at which other members of the profession took up changes, and what impact did this have on the character of medicine, and on the fortunes of individuals?

A conceptual analogy is first adopted which uses cultural entities as a substitute for the mechanism of genes. The counterpart to biological mutation in cultural terms is innovation, and innovation across a wide range of medical, socio-political, economic, and technological customs, techniques and institutions is discussed. In some cases these innovations can be traced to developments wholly external to the profession, for example, the availability of the motor car and the telephone. In these cases we can simply accept this as an exogenous change, and need consider only its effects on general practice. In other cases the initial innovation was endogenous, as where the consequences of treatment procedures were critically observed, and then modified in the light of their consequences for the health of patients. For example, the over-complicated, sometimes harmful, mixtures concocted in individual practices gradually gave way to more standardized and effective medicines.

The third, and in some ways the most significant, category of innovations were those which were partly internal, partly external in origin, and thus reflected wider economic, political or social changes. Pharmaceuticals were prime examples of this type of innovation. Medicines had earlier been compounded by individual doctors, but increasingly were supplemented or replaced by new, powerfully effective, pharmaceuticals (such as Aspirin, Salvarsan, Prontosil or Penicillin), that were manufactured industrially. By the end of this period the latter were transforming the GP's therapeutic potential. This mixed category of innovations also included other notable changes in general medicine. One example was the movement of women into general practice, resulting partly from exogenous factors such as the first woman's movement, and partly from the professionalization of medicine. Another striking instance was the changes signalled by legislation, notably the National Health Insurance Scheme of 1911 or the National Health Service Act of 1946. These innovations were in part responding to a complex of wider concerns including those of labour efficiency and citizen's rights, but were also recognition of incipient needs and emerging trends within medical practice. However, the division into endogenous and exogenous factors for the purpose of this hypothesis is itself inherently problematical, because it involves an allocation of factors deemed to be medical or non-medical. This is somewhat arbitrary; the selected framework itself attributes exogeneity, it is not an intrinsic attribute of the factor involved.

What was the response to these innovations in general practice? Response repertoires could involve the agent of cultural change—the general practitioner—making a subjective evaluation of what was rewarding or beneficial in innovation. This process was an evolutionary one but it was one in which the selection mechanism was essentially by trial and error. (Selection processes are further discussed below in relation to social Darwinism.)

Cultural transmission mechanisms for replicating, and thus diffusing new ideas within general practice are also interpreted as working vertically through medical training, and horizontally through professional imitation. This process of cultural replication encompasses a larger population than in a Darwinian transmission from ancestor to descendant, and hence the process implies a greater diffusability. For example, the cultural replication of new ways of organizing general practice—such as partnerships or the employment of the phone and car—helped modernize and adapt it to a changing social and economic environment. In a developmental time-scale the adaptive learning of individual GPs also involved the process of causality in testing old material for its suitability for new uses or contexts. One example of this was the transference and adaptation of patient management from its use in old-style Victorian club practice *in tandem* with friendly societies, to meet the fresh professional challenge of national health insurance practice in partnership with the state after 1911.

Such processes are context-sensitive in taking into account the social environment of the general practice. Adaptation to the environment is central to the biological selection process, whereas in cultural evolution there is manipulation of, or interaction with, the environment. In the history of general practice, between the mid-nineteenth and mid-twentieth centuries, favourable ecological 'niches' developed in which certain kinds of practice could flourish (as when industrialization developed coalfields which assisted the creation of colliery practices discussed in Chapter 10), and adaptive routines then assisted in their survival. In the first half of the period opportunistic strategies by general practitioners produced a growing variety of practice types. Differential rates of replication occurred as between distinctive kinds of practices, as a result of an empirical testing of the utility of their organizational features. Some experiences were generalizable, and were imitated by neighbouring practices, thus having a higher rate of replication, others were not. If disruptive inputs impinged, mistakes occurred, and poorly adapted individual practices failed to prosper, then practice types or their traits might disappear. In cultural as in biological arenas the finiteness of resources was often a key element in this selection and weeding out process. However, practices with some dysfunctional features could survive because protected—by geographical remoteness, for example—from the competition of more functionally efficient practices. At any one time there was thus a range of optimally, and sub-optimally organized practices.

The use of evolutionary insights to map out important cultural correlates results in some interesting insights into the history of general practice. As Hull aptly states, 'The explanatory force in historical explanations comes from the coherence and continuity of the historical entities whose development they chronicle.'[25] But while the concepts of cultural evolutionary theory

[25] Hull, *Science as Process*, 481.

are helpful in explaining certain changes in the practice, analogies with biological evolution are by no means perfect. Problems or disanalogies in cultural applications include the vagaries of socio-cultural selection; the complexity of historical situations (and hence the difficulties in isolating causal factors); and the diffuseness of cultural transmission compared to the verticality of biological evolution. In the evolution of general practice there were also obvious institutional complexities such that changes within a practice involved both a transmitted environment, *and* the decisions of the individual doctor.

Social Darwinistic insights are also employed in this volume in order to look at the selective processes that influenced the survival, success, or failure of individual general practitioners. This is analytically distinct from the practice (or cultural meme), whose selection and survival has so far been discussed. Historically, the two intersected, although it is possible to isolate a maladapted individual within a successful practice type, or vice versa.

The language of Darwinism was, and is, easily appropriated. Social Darwinism has been seen as 'a configuration of interlinked propositions and ideas', or alternatively as a language, a collection of words, which provides a discursive framework for debate.[26] When its concepts are applied to society in attempts to interpret evolution and development in social terms, this has usually involved both fragmentation and problematization. Prominent in contemporary thinking was the use of social Darwinism to defend competitive individualism in Victorian society, and thus to justify attempts to gain advantage over competitors in the race for economic survival or success, as in Herbert Spencer's *Man Versus the State* (1884).[27] As applied in *The Evolution of British General Practice* a social Darwinistic interpretation views competition as playing much the same role in separating the 'success' from the 'failure', as Darwinian natural selection did in weeding out the 'fit' from the 'unfit'. And a discussion of the historical ways in which GPs established and developed their practices is imbued with an analogous notion of fitness. Doctors might appropriate a suitable (or well-fitting) ecological niche within a community to establish a practice, shaping it so that it increasingly was assimilated to—and thus efficiently met the needs of—its neighbourhood. In so doing, doctors might gain patients from colleagues. They might also show their well-developed competitive individualism by attempting to keep out rival practitioners from their practice territory, through monopolizing available appointments. Appointments put the jam on the bread and butter of a medical living, and thus differentiated the economically successful practitioner from the one more likely to fail. This concern with business-like practices was characteristic of a much wider contemporary drive for, and application of, ideas of 'national efficiency'.[28] In its emphasis on the efficient

[26] Hawkins, *Social Darwinism*, 19; Evans, *Rereading*, 137.
[27] G. Jones, *Social Darwinism and English Thought* (Brighton, 1980), xii–xiii, 36, 55–6.
[28] G. R. Searle, *The Quest for National Efficiency* (Oxford, 1971), 54, 92.

character of social institutions which were held to influence the success or failure of the nation state in its international struggle for survival, a complex of beliefs around national efficiency was itself strongly imbued with Darwinian modes of argument.

This 'Spencerian' framework of the 'survival of the fittest' has stimulated examination of the criteria that operated to facilitate selection in general medical practice. Developing a viable practice usually involved an individual doctor's ability to discern a practice niche (as we have seen), the possession of social connection and/or social networking skills to develop it, and some managerial competencies in the allocation of resources to organize it. Ethical aptitude in relating to colleagues, and in adopting appropriate conduct in demarcating professionally from them, was increasingly needed. More fundamentally, the GP needed a medical competence acquired from licensed training, together with highly developed interpersonal abilities with patients (more particularly private patients), such that confidence in the doctor compensated for therapeutic deficiencies, since palliation rather than cure was often the outcome of doctor–patient encounters.

How then can the conceptual frameworks of cultural evolution and of social Darwinism be applied to illuminate the history of general practice?

Chapter 2 argues that in medicine, as in law, there was an oversupply of practitioners in relation to market demand for their services before 1911. An investment in prolonged education by middle-class parents was an international response to a late nineteenth-century demographic transition to smaller families. In consequence, the supply of entrants to the medical profession began to outpace the contemporary growth in the number of professional openings. And, as Chapter 7 indicates, the entrance of women into medicine intensified this problem. In an open medical market this supply involved both 'alternative' and specialist practitioners. Both these groups were poorly differentiated from the qualified general practitioner in terms of legal status, therapeutic power, and popular perception. This is a classic 'Spencerian' evolutionary case—that of population pressure forcing adaptation and differentiation. Later chapters indicate the factors facilitating survival against such fierce competition.

In a cultural evolutionary model education and training should give good opportunities for replication, by which useful professional experiences may be generalizable and transmitted to later generations. In the case of general practice, however, Chapter 3 shows that education was a poor training for later professional survival, being geared to the needs of specialists. This was because of the power of specialists in teaching hospitals, and their dominant membership on the GMC, which was responsible for issuing guidelines for medical education. Strong on academic cramming, but weak on training in the practicalities needed by generalists, medical education gave few clues about how to survive the conditions likely to be experienced after graduation, whilst the lengthy nature of education itself inhibited adjustment to changing market conditions. Growing numbers in successive cohorts of graduates meant increasingly severe professional competition. Survival or success in such conditions would tend towards variety as each larger cohort attempted to find fresh market opportunities to exploit, whether these were non-traditional practice locations or new sources of funding. Later modification of this Victorian and Edwardian trend towards heterogeneity resulted from increasingly good communication about the options available to a GP, whether through medical societies, journals, professional associations, or word of mouth. This was especially applicable for the period after 1911, when initial suspicion of national health insurance practice, and its practitioners, gradually gave way to imitation, and an almost universal incorporation of some panel patients in general practices.

Environmental conditions thus affected cohort behaviour. This is explored in some detail in Chapter 4. Cohort differences were very noticeable during the late nineteenth century in the numbers of places where practice was attempted by a GP before a viable living was secured, as well as in an increasingly wide range of medically related appointments which were sought for income or status. These included prestigious but honorary appointments such as those with hospitals and dispensaries, or the Volunteers. Amongst the main paid offices were those provided by public bodies, voluntary organizations, and also by works, mines, or factories. A hierarchy of esteem was attached to these appointments ranging from the hospital post or government appointment at the peak, to the poor law or club appointment at the bottom. An even more obvious ranking was evident among the types of practices that general practitioners created, and in which appointments played a visible part in building up, or dissipating, reputation and respect. Least esteemed were those practices heavily dependent on income from low-status appointments, whilst the successful old-established practice in a pleasant hospital city, spa, cathedral town, and in pleasant sporting countryside, had distinction and standing. Considerable income variation ensued amongst general practitioners, with the result that one-fifth were struggling to achieve a viable income before the NHI, slightly more than a half were making what was considered to be a satisfactory living, and only about one-quarter managed to achieve what was perceived as a good or very good one.[29]

Competition for income, reputation, or just for professional survival was not confined *within* general practice but, as Chapter 11 argues, medical differentiation meant that competition for patients was also found in relation to specialists, as well as other practitioners such as midwives. The permeability of the professional boundaries between these different types of practice, as well as the plasticity of the environment formed by varied practitioner–patient encounters, signalled that the dynamics of professional survival were both complex and changing.

---

[29] A. Digby, *Making a Medical Living* (Cambridge, 1994), 144.

Survival within a crowded medical market required a variety of opportunistic strategies. It has been suggested that 'ecological niches' within generalist practice were one option. Women-only practices were perhaps the most obvious example of this since, as Chapter 7 discloses, general practices run by medical women were usually limited to women and child patients. Utilizing female networks in seeking out practice situations or partnerships, women operated for most of the period in a semi-detached professional sphere, although a separatist stance was gradually subverted by more assimilationist values amongst later cohorts of medical women. Male fears that women would lower the price of work in general practice were not realized because—as Chapter 5 argues—the medical market was sufficiently segmented to enable different kinds of practice to develop successfully. Female GPs chose to build up patient-focused practices with a low throughput, and a below-average remuneration. At the opposite extreme were the high throughput doctors—including the earlier 'sixpenny' and club doctors—as well as the later 'get-rich-quick' type of panel practitioner.

The medical market stimulated variation in practice types. Chapters 5 and 12 indicate the shifting boundary between private and public practice, with the growth in public appointments, in collective provision, and in social insurance during the late nineteenth and early twentieth centuries. This enabled the creation of distinctive mixes in sources of income, as the specimen types of practices indicate at the end of Chapter 5. Diversification offered opportunity but it also posed challenges, not least in the competitive hazards of choice of practice location, or the risks involved in attempting to exploit the lower section of the market with consequent increased vulnerability to bad debt. Those who were able to adopt good practice—in pricing medical skill rather than medical products, in achieving more efficient time management, or in working out flexible fee schedules—were more likely to survive, and even to make a fair living. Those who failed to adapt were much more likely to make a poor medical living or even to be driven out of the profession. However, initiatives in seizing market opportunities were differentially constrained by the cultural context within which different kinds of general practice operated. Devices such as 'patient-pinching' or a relentless pursuit of patients in debt, were viewed by the more respectable as undesirable money grubbing that should be eschewed. Within general medicine the best practice (typified by the family doctor practice), continued alongside the sub-optimal one (the branch practice). A necessary symbiosis between medicine and business meant that the more efficiently managed practices thrived, whereas the inefficient failed to survive. Attempts to manipulate the environment to ensure professional viability were therefore conspicuous features of the medical market.

Chapters 6 and 10 suggest that general practitioners as agents of change within practices had a chequered record in responding to market challenges through practice reorganization. However, later generations became more flexible organizationally in response to market or clinical opportunities, and doctors with industrial and suburban practices also showed greater innovative capacity in shaping their distinctive environments. But there was a powerful in-built conservatism in the single-handed practice with its cottage-industry style. Here an informal professional partnership tended to parallel the marital one, in which the wives of doctors frequently performed a range of ancillary functions—secretarial, public relations, gatekeeping, nursing, accounting, as well as perhaps supplying financial and/or human capital. This constrained the employment of professionally trained ancillaries. The use of the doctor's house for surgery accommodation also inhibited investment in bricks and mortar for purpose-built accommodation.

Within such an environment it was difficult for the GP to see the practice as an organizational opportunity rather than a custom-bound, personal possession. This made the adoption of organizational change problematic; in particular, the employment of assistants was only gradually adopted. However, assistants were used in new roles, such as running branch surgeries, which indicates that traditional aids were being redeployed in problem-solving ways. This helped financial survival for those attempting to widen the medical market by operating in working-class areas. General practitioners at first viewed partnerships with caution, but the professional consensus moved in their favour, as the development of a wider market within twentieth-century Britain enabled more doctors to practice within a limited geographical area. In these circumstances partnerships were perceived to be sounder economically, as well as being more successful medically. Professional intent was shown in deploying young partners to extend the practice in new directions, or to build up a team of partners with complementary clinical skills. Again, this helped professional survival through diversifying practice potential, whilst at the same time reducing the personal stress and strain that had accompanied single-handed practice, and often had had adverse consequences in sickness or premature death.

In the adoption of the new inventions of phone and car less caution was shown. Although the earliest enthusiasm for the phone was misplaced, after 1900 there was a more general and well-founded readiness to adopt these new inventions so that it was pretty well universal by the end of the period. Urban GPs were amongst the earliest devotees of the cycle, and both town and country doctors soon adopted the motor car. Pioneers saw the potential for transforming the spatial dimension of practices, and others soon imitated those who had already realized these benefits. There was therefore a rapid diffusion of organizational good practice in these complementary technologies.

Clinically, change was much less obvious until the final years of the period. A comparison with the beginning and end of the century under consideration would have isolated few striking developments. Enduring weaknesses in much general practice were imprecise diagnosis (employing a limited range of instruments and with little stress on the examination of patients), a tendency to over-prescribe, under-cultivated prognostic ability, and poorly developed obstetric skills. More positive long-term characteristics included good symptomatic spot diagnoses of common complaints, together with a widespread capability to perform a range of minor surgical procedures. Amongst a minority of GP surgeons there were more highly refined surgical skills. Practitioners also showed an expanding knowledge of disease entities, an increasingly sensitive clinical symptomatology based on an interaction between physical diagnosis and medical technology, and a familiarity with a growing range of signs and symptoms through more intensive scrutiny of the patient's body.[30] By adopting a holistic approach to the whole person of their patients, GPs were attuned to an art of healing in which the personality of the doctor, and the faith of patients in their family doctor, were used as important weapons in a therapeutic armoury which in other respects remained restricted in scope. In prescribing patterns there was a transition from polypharmacy to reliance on stock mixtures. The single greatest clinical advance, which transformed therapeutic potential, was the result of the availability of new and powerful pharmaceuticals—the Sulphonamides during the 1930s, and Penicillin during the succeeding decade. The transformation of the GP's power to deal with puerperal sepsis after childbirth, or with cases of lobar pneumonia was dramatic.

Dissemination of best practice by GPs in the clinical side of general practice was not greatly in evidence, and was in any case—given the isolation of individual practices—achieved less through the imitation of colleagues, than reading journals, attending talks, by going on visits arranged by local medical societies, or alternatively through visits by representatives of pharmaceutical companies. The rate of take-up of improved instrumentation or of novel pharmaceuticals was thus very variable. To some extent GPs had to work within a given clinical environment in relation to the facilities offered by local hospitals, but innovative GPs were able to shape that environment themselves, not least through their foundation of cottage hospitals, and by their own adoption of newly fashioned therapeutic methods, better instruments, or improved record keeping. Sub-optimality within great variety in the range of treatments is testament to the importance of the individual GP's decisions as to what quality of services should be offered to patients. These choices were not free of the constraints imposed by the economic and social context of the individual practice. Good medicine was partly dependent on having a middle-class component in the patient population, whose fees could pay for the required service. The interaction of financial and clinical rationales is well illustrated by the purchase of that state-of-the-art rarity in general practice—the X-ray machine—by the Wantage practice, referred to in Chapter 8. Therapeutic standards and procedures in general practice were ultimately grounded in economics, and thus were class-discriminatory in terms of the

---

[30] I. Galdston, 'Diagnosis in Historical Perspective' *BHM*, 9 (1941), 367–84; L. S. King, 'Signs and Symptoms', *Journal of the American Medical Association*, 206 (1965), 1063–5.

time spent with the doctor, the performance or absence of physical examination, the decision as to whether to make a clinical record, the chances of being referred to a specialist, the type of medicine prescribed (whether stock mixtures or individually dispensed), and even the choice of white or brown paper to wrap the medicine bottle.

Poverty of patient expectation did little to pressurize GPs into making improvements in their practices either in clinical or organizational matters, so that professional survival was largely unaffected by their patchy record in these respects. Pressure by patients took other forms, as Chapter 9 suggests, as in non-compliance with instructions, unpaid bills, or abusive behaviour. Another type of patient pressure is discussed in Chapters 6 and 12, consisting of a growing number of surgery attendances, and requested visits under the national insurance scheme, even though capitation payments did not reflect growing work demands. Economic survival in the teeth of low fees and unpaid bills might be secured before 1911 by a practice operating an informal financial welfare state in the local community, whereby the more affluent paid large bills which cross-subsidized their poorer neighbours, as well as by the provision of lower-cost medicine for the latter. The success of the GP within an individual practice depended not only on objective factors—such as the number of paid appointments held or the size of the NHI panel—but also on more subjective elements. Important here was the individual practitioner's personality which was vital as a healing element in bedside medicine, and which also played a key role in the doctor's role in the locality. When the whole town turned out for the funeral of a well-beloved and respected GP, it was a sure sign that that practitioner had been a prime exponent of the art of manipulating a local environment in order to construct an ecological niche in the community. Chapter 10 provides some detailed specimen-type discussion of a few individual practices, in order to illustrate the linkages and tensions between the public duties and personal lives of general practitioners. These kinds of differentiated practice niches were especially characteristic of the period before 1911.

Chapter 12 examines how, after 1911, the largely exogenous input of the national health insurance (NHI) scheme gradually, but substantially, reduced the variety of practices because the vast majority of them ultimately recruited a sizeable panel of patients. As in biological, so in cultural evolution, the stimulus of a major external change—in this instance in the form of parliamentary legislation—led to a widespread transformation. In providing secure capitation payments, and thus an economic safety net for the previous uncertainties of general practice, the scheme gradually but steadily eroded the huge practice differentiation that the previous desperate search for financial survival had imposed in an overcrowded medical market. Chapters 4 and 6 indicate how it became easier for young doctors to start up in practice with the result that the number of practices GPs engaged in during their lifetime was reduced. Equally, the search for sources of medically related appointments became less intense, and the sources of income within a single practice correspondingly narrower than hitherto. Given the greater security of income arising both from the security of guaranteed public payment, and from a wider medical market involving more working-class patients, it became feasible for more doctors to engage in partnerships. This had some knock-on effects in enabling these larger firms to afford more ancillary support services or better premises, although the social conservatism of practitioners meant that the extent to which this occurred was slower than might have been predicted. Partnerships also enabled (but in the same way did not provide a compelling reason), for a more defined division of labour through enabling a greater specialism—as in a wider spread of clinical, patient, or organizational expertise between partners. Not that all was discontinuity. There were also continuities before and after 1911. For example, as Chapter 7 reveals, the women-and-children practices run by medical women were relatively untouched by these changes, because only a small number of women were early members of the national insurance scheme, and hence there were few panel patients in such practices. And some male GPs stood aloof from panel practice, or had very few panel patients, although by 1939 this had dwindled to a small minority.

Paradoxically, in one highly significant sphere the 1911 legislation involved discontinuity based on a wider transmission of a pre-existing feature. It involved the relationship between the earlier 'club practice' (in which GPs had treated members of friendly societies for a small, and defined annual fee) and the NHI. In 1911 the state was only willing to make a modest capitation payment that, although larger than the previous typical club fee, nevertheless imposed similar pressures on the doctor, and therefore affected the overall quality of medical service. The constraint on an insurance doctor with a large panel of insurance patients to achieve a high patient throughput operated to depress clinical standards by diffusing more widely through the profession the earlier methods of club practice. After 1911 panel practice was characterized by stock mixtures, a restricted range of clinical procedures, and vestigial patient records. The changing environment of increasing patient demand also contributed towards this systematization of the less desirable features of earlier general practice in a trend towards a lower common denominator.

A second major reform of medical services occurred with the National Health Service Act of 1946, which became operational in 1948. Unlike the NHI, with its severe class, age, and gender constraints on eligibility for participation, the NHS was intended to be a socially comprehensive system. The accompanying rhetoric, in part induced by the hopes invested in a post-war welfare state, indicated that this new primary health care system would have optimal standards. Unfortunately, as Chapter 13 argues, the fact that the NHS was a continuation and expansion of the earlier NHI scheme imposed developmental constraints. Path dependency meant that the supposedly optimal modern scheme of 1948 was in fact substantially constrained by the unsatisfactory nature of the preceding 1911 scheme. For patients it had notable results in broadening access to medical treatment, for general practitioners it removed the financial element from doctor–patient relationships which many had disliked, and also radically affected the relationship of GPs and their patients to specialists, and to hospital services. However, if no NHS had been created, so that an invidious two-tier system of health care had been perpetuated, substantial social groups would have been unable to afford the powerful but costly pharmaceuticals then becoming available, and GPs would then have been unable to disseminate the benefits of modern medicine to the community. The tension between continuation and innovation in my analysis of the significance of 1948 thus modifies, but does not destroy, the historical stereotype of the NHS as a fundamental turning point in modern health care.

PART I

Careers

2

Professional Challenge

THE principal challenge faced by general practitioners was an over-supply of regular, trained doctors in relation to effective demand for their services. This was worsened by the competition of specialists, and by large numbers of alternative practitioners of varied kinds. GPs responded to their weak market position by professional strategies, as well as by hoping for ameliorative action from legislation. Both are discussed in this chapter. Later chapters explore how this challenge to survival stimulated varied responses which, within a century, resulted in significant evolution in the nature of general practice, and in its position in British medicine. Responses included diverse career strategies leading to a highly differentiated general practice adaptable to local environments; and cultural adaptation including enhanced qualification, improved organization, and a better take-up of available technology. Not all change was internally derived; the most important changes resulted in 1911 and 1948 from the external stimuli of state intervention in creating the NHI and NHS which extended effective demand for the general practitioner's services through social insurance.

Overcrowded Professions

The history of the British medical profession is often considered in isolation from developments elsewhere, but this chapter aims to place it in a comparative perspective. Trends in professionalization in Europe and the United States offered instructive differences with Britain as well as some striking similarities. Thus an investment in a more prolonged education by middle-class parents was a common response to the late nineteenth-century demographic transition to smaller families, with the result that the supply of entrants to the professions soon outpaced the contemporary growth in the number of professional openings. Problems of professional overcrowding arising from the creation of a young professional proletariat occurred internationally from the mid-nineteenth to the mid-twentieth centuries. The social and economic implications of producing numbers of educated people in excess of the needs of a nation exercised contemporaries. In Britain the existence of the Empire, together with a highly developed industrial economy absorbed some, but by no means all, of the surplus of young professionals, and in the USA an expanding frontier served the same purpose. Continental Europe was in a much less fortunate position, so that young French and German professionals in medicine and law had even more severe problems than in Britain and the USA.[1]

Complaints of overcrowding, of a surplus of supply in relation to market demand, were not confined to this period, similar cries of woe had been heard earlier.[2] Discussion was conducted from the implicit standpoint of the professional élite itself, and was grounded in an implicit assumption that remuneration, and existing differentials were, and should be fixed. Crucially it was also accepted that professions operated largely within a market economy and thus that effective demand—rather than social need—was the key variable in determining whether a surplus existed. An alternative, more socialistic, perspective might well have suggested that, rather than a surplus, there was often a deficit of professional services. Attempting to see how much credence should be given to such self-interested professional shrieks of anguish has led to attempts at quantification. But quantification can be misleading in, for example, giving numbers of law graduates, without also acknowledging that a sizeable proportion may not have practised law but instead gone into government service or industry.[3] Subjective evaluations cannot necessarily be taken at face value, but there is sufficient objective evidence to indicate a basis in reality for powerful professional anxieties. We turn now to a comparative discussion of the situation in Europe and North America to explore the nature and reasons for them in the legal, as well as the medical, profession.

In mid-nineteenth century France a desire for social mobility was beginning to replace an acceptance of inherited status, so that a contemporary commented that while ambition was 'much more common than one thinks, it is creeping into all ranks, all conditions'. Although at that time it had permeated only about half of the middle classes, forty years later 'Everybody is impatient to move out of his sphere and has pretensions to rising.'[4] A youthful society and a notably rapid expansion of the French university sector from the mid-nineteenth century onwards, were producing one of the worst instances of professional overcrowding. Indeed, a favourite theme of Balzac's novels was the overstocked nature of the professions—'There are a hundred lawyers, a hundred doctors for every vacancy.' This was despite a relative expansion in numbers within the liberal professions and civil service relative

---

[1] L. O'Boyle, 'The Problem of an Excess of Educated Men in Western Europe, 1800–1850', *Journal of Modern History*, 42 (1970), 471–95.

[2] R. Campbell, *The London Tradesman* (1747), 4–8, 36.

[3] G. Weisz, 'The Politics of Medical Professionalization in France, 1845–1848', *Journal of Social History*, 12 (1978–9), 28. In France about three-fifths were in this category during the 1860s.

[4] E. Charton, *Dictionnaire des Professions* (1842), Descuret, *The Medicine of the Passions* (1842), and P. Jacquemont, *Professions et Métiers* (1892), quoted in T. Zeldin, *A History of the French Passions, 1848–1945* (2 vols., Oxford, 1993), i, 88, 91, 96–7.

to the increase in population.[5] Between 1900 and 1939 the medical and law faculties continued to grow to such an extent that French student numbers doubled.[6]

In the Prussian medical profession there was also a rapid increase after 1869 when medicine was deregulated as part of a wider commercial reform. An overall growth in university enrolments, as well as the development of social insurance from 1883 were important factors in further stimulating supply. During the 1880s enrolment at medical schools doubled. Numbers of doctors greatly outpaced population growth, and ratios of physicians to population increased from 300 per million in mid-century to 500 per million by 1900.[7] German lawyers were also very conscious of professional overcrowding as a result of a quadrupled enrolment between 1871 and 1906, which resulted in a doubling in the number of lawyers between 1890 and 1911. Whilst the upper echelons of the legal profession continued to make a comfortable income 'a growing minority had difficulty in making ends meet'. Significantly, although three-quarters of law graduates in 1880 had taken major cases in the *Landgericht*, by 1913 less than one-third were involved. A proposal of 1911 to restrict access to the Bar through an additional two-year training period was defeated within the profession, as was a parallel scheme to have a list based on seniority. Meanwhile, the average case load dropped by one-third between 1891 and 1911, and cases per capita continued their decline thereafter, so that in 1939 they were only about one-third what they had been six decades before.[8] Young lawyers were compelled to take poorly paid criminal and poor-law cases while lucrative cases were concentrated amongst an older élite. Thus 'an underprivileged underclass' of young lawyers was created.[9] This generational differentiation was similar to that of cohorts of British medical graduates where young doctors, in the decades before the state national health insurance scheme of 1911 expanded demand, were forced to become low-status 'sixpenny' or 'shilling' doctors.

During the twentieth century professional overcrowding and increased competition in continental Europe led to an orientation towards more bureaucratic strategies, and in Germany this resulted in neocorporatism.[10] A new professionalism emerged which had a more pronounced income orientation, but paradoxically also sought state assistance; German professionals were

---

[5] Zeldin, *History*, i, 105. The increase was from 1.7 to 2.5 millions between 1856 and 1891, whereas the population had grown from 36.2 to 38.1 millions.

[6] Zeldin, *French Passions*, i, 105; ii, 327.

[7] C. Huerkamp, 'The Making of the Modern Medical Profession, 1800–1914: Prussian Doctors in the Nineteenth Century' in G. Cocks and K. H. Jarausch (eds.), *German Professions, 1800–1950* (Oxford, 1990), 75–6; C. E. McClelland, *The German Experience of Professionalization* (Cambridge, 1991), 80–1.

[8] K. H. Jarausch, *The Unfree Profession. German Lawyers, Teachers and Engineers, 1900–1950* (Oxford, 1990), 10–12, 44.

[9] Id., 'The German Professions in History and Theory', in Cocks and Jarausch (eds.), *German Professions*, 15, 20.

[10] Id., *Unfree Profession*, 10–12, 44.

contradictory in wanting both to be free from the state whilst also seeking government protection from competitors.[11] The extent to which German professional associations continued to shape their professions is controversial, although lobbying for sectional interests and construction of ethical codes to restrict competition occurred. More conspicuous was government influence manifested in the state raising entry qualifications, government-controlled institutions giving medical training, state-appointed boards conducting examinations, and official fee schedules regulating the market.[12] A comparison is instructive between this continental top-down professional model where the state was very influential and the autonomous and market-oriented, liberal professional model of Britain and North America. Tensions arose in both cases, since in the latter a desire for economic advantage arising from professional monopoly could endanger ideals, whilst for the state-orientated continental expert, loyalty to the state might challenge morality.[13] Not that professional strategies were mutually exclusive in the two professional models. For example, ethical rules and rules of professional etiquette existed for similar purposes—as in the same prohibition of self-advertisement.[14]

Within the market-oriented group there were significant differences. In the USA the legal and medical professions were much more successful in creating conditions that ensured reasonable opportunities for professional remuneration. In Britain lawyers failed to rise to the new demands of a commercial society as had their counterparts in the USA with their increase in advisory work. Nor did they defend their professional territory sufficiently vigorously against other occupational groups, such as surveyors, valuers, land and estate agents, or governmental officials. Thus there was an invasion of legal territory both by government and by commercial departments in businesses. In contrast in the USA the rise of the law school enabled the profession to decouple its volume of work from its existing professionals, and thus to react to market openings. In Britain the retention of the articled clerk, meant that the profession could not respond sufficiently rapidly to expanding demands, whilst British solicitors' dependence on conveyancing income made them very dependent on economic cycles in property transactions.[15]

In American medicine there was a fiercely contested medical market. Numbers of alternative practitioners grew from about one-tenth of the total medical practitioners in the 1830s to one-fifth half a century later; a position that was maintained thereafter. These rival groups although able to obtain licensing (as did chiropractors and osteopaths in most states), did not gain

[11] H. Siegrist, 'Public Office or Free Profession? German Attorneys in the Nineteenth and Early Twentieth Centuries', in Cocks and Jarausch, *German Professions*, 61.

[12] Huerkamp, 'Medical Profession', 66–7; Jarausch, 'German Professions', 12–13.

[13] D. Rueschemeyer, *Power and the Division of Labour* (1986), 120–1.

[14] Jarausch, 'German Professions', 13–14, 16.

[15] A. Abbott, *The System of Professions. An Essay on the Division of Expert Labour* (Chicago, 1988), ch. 9 *passim*; A. Offer, *Property and Politics 1870–1914: Landownership, Law, Ideology and Urban Development in England* (Cambridge, 1981), 54–5.

access to hospitals or the right to prescribe drugs. The American Medical Association was more successful in regulating numbers of entrants than had been the German Medical Association.[16] It adopted methods used earlier in the Netherlands from 1865 to 1875 in making training more elaborate and thus more expensive, so that numbers qualifying fell.[17] Entry to the medical profession in the USA was made much more difficult in the early twentieth century, and between 1906 and 1913 numbers of medical schools declined by one-fifth. New requirements lengthened the period of study for medical students in any one year from four to eight or nine months, the overall length of the course was extended from two to five and then to eight years, and tuition fees rose in line with this lengthened course. This heightened the opportunity costs of potential entrants to the profession and discouraged admission, so that between 1910 and 1915 numbers of graduates fell from 5,440 to 3,536. In consequence ratios of physicians to population declined from 1900 to 1930, before stabilizing for twenty years.[18] This was part of a wider restructuring of medicine, led by the American Medical Association, which wished to raise the social status of doctor. Table 2.1 indicates the impact that this reform had in raising the population to doctor ratio. In contrast, in Britain there was no such professional strategy and the longer-term implications that this had for a career in general practice were serious, given that the ratio of population to doctor slumped severely. Legislation of 1858 and 1885 also failed to give much help to qualified doctors against their competitors in a notably free medical market, while the expanding numbers of medical graduates resulted in ferocious competition amongst the qualified as well as the unqualified.

TABLE 2.1. Comparative ratios of doctors to population in Britain and the USA, 1850–1950

Year	Population per doctor in Britain	Population per doctor in USA
1850/1	1,205	600
1860/1	1,128	—
1900/1	1574	578
1910/11	1,529	684
1920/1	1,538	729
1930/1	1,341	800
1950/1	1,014	

Sources: C. Webster, *The Health Services since the War, Government and Health Care. The British National Health Service, 1958–1979* (1996), appendix 3.28, p. 827; P. Starr, *The Social Transformation of American Medicine* (1982), 40, 64, 126

[16] McClelland, *German Experiences*, 119.
[17] H. van der Velden, 'The Dutch Health Services Before Compulsory Health Insurance, 1900–1914', *SHM*, x (1996), 54–5.
[18] P. Starr, *The Social Transformation of American Medicine* (New York, 1982), 99, 115–21, 126–7.

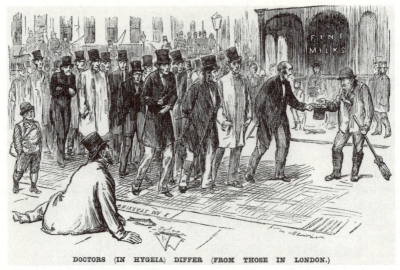

DOCTORS (IN HYGEIA) DIFFER (FROM THOSE IN LONDON.)

1. Doctors differ. *Scene in Dr Richardson's City of Health—Chorus of Medical Practitioners.*
"WE HAVE NO WORK TO DO!"
A group of emaciated physicians lament their lack of work, 1875

Competition in all countries was focused in urban areas. Professionals had to make a living mainly or exclusively from private practice, and thus were heavily concentrated where population was thickest in towns and cities. Rural areas were neglected. French governmental surveys in 1865 and 1881 found that almost five out of six communes were without a doctor or even a less well-qualified *officer de santé*;[19] in Prussia, less than one-third of doctors practised in the countryside although three-fifths of the population lived there;[20] and a study in the early twentieth century showed that there was a high positive correlation between regional levels of *per capita* income and the geographical incidence of physicians in the USA. 'They do business where business is good and avoid places where it is bad.'[21] A similar situation existed in law as in medicine. In twentieth-century Germany both young and old lawyers were concentrated in urban areas, so that even more than in the medical profession there was geographical maldistribution of professionals in relation to clients.[22] And everywhere, legal and medical services for poorer members of society were only very gradually improved through public provision of varied kinds. Complaints of overcrowding by professionals therefore need to be offset by an appreciation of unmet social need.

Anxieties about overcrowding in the professions during the second half of the nineteenth century meant that demands by women for emancipation through higher education and entry to the professions received a hostile recep-

[19] Weisz, 'Medical Professionalization', 6–7.   [20] Huerkamp, 'Medical Profession', 73–4.
[21] Starr, *Social Transformation*, 125.   [22] Segrist, 'Public Office', 56–7.

tion, exclusionary strategies being used by male professionals in medicine and law. For example, by 1918 there were 191 female law students in Germany but it took a Reichstag decree for legal careers to be opened to women in 1922. Even then fierce opposition continued within the profession so that a decade later only one in a hundred lawyers were female. Within the twentieth-century German medical profession women faced a discriminatory quota of only five per cent amongst those applying for certificates to practise, and were seen by others as an inferior part of the profession. Here—as elsewhere—professionals who were married women were scapegoated for the wider economic difficulties of interwar professions.[23] In British medicine institutions operated gendered exclusionary strategies which were countered by women using credentialist and legalistic policies; aspiring medical women attempted to gain access to medical training and thus provide professional credentials, whilst also trying to break a male legal monopoly on practice (see Table 7.1).[24] Female access to British medical training was a long-drawn-out process, the first gain coming in 1879 and the last citadel falling only after the Second World War.[25] Difficulties in gaining qualifications led to a continued reliance by British medical women on MDs at European universities including Berne, Brussels, Montpellier, Paris and Zurich.[26] In the USA access had come earlier in 1848, and the proportion of women increased from 2.8 to 5.6 per cent of the profession between 1880 and 1900. In 1900 there were as many as 7,000 medical women in the USA compared to only 258 in Britain, and 95 in France.[27]

Having looked at professions in a wider geographical context, we now use a narrower, but still comparative, perspective to reflect on law and the church which, with medicine, made up the three old professions within Britain. The early 1870s marked an end of the period of 'high rectory culture' of Victorian England, materially comfortable, culturally self-confident, and parochially active.[28] The ensuing agrarian depression had a severe impact both on rural life, and on rural clerical incomes, such that money incomes halved in the Victorian period.[29] In comparison with other professional groups clerical incomes compared very unfavourably; not only was gross income smaller but outgoings were large, so that net income was pathetically small. In 1893 the young curate—as distinct from the more established vicar or rector—had an average income of only £145.[30] There was contemporary awareness within

[23] Jarausch, 'German Professions', 17–18; Stephenson, 'Women and the Professions', 275–9.

[24] A Witz, *Professions and Patriarchy* (1992), Intro. and ch. 3, *passim*. See also Ch. 7 below.

[25] C. Dyhouse, *No Distinction of Sex? Women in British Universities, 1870–1939* (1995), 12–13.

[26] For example, Elizabeth Garrett qualified at Paris in 1870, Ann Clark at Berne in 1877, Ethel Bentham and Charlotte Brown at Brussels in 1895 and 1896.

[27] Starr, *Social Transformation*, 117.

[28] G. Kitson Clark, *Churchmen and the Condition of England, 1832–1885* (1973), 182.

[29] A decline in the price level of 37 per cent meant that real standards of living did not decline so rapidly, B. R. Mitchell, *Abstract of British Historical Statistics* (Cambridge, 1962), 471–2.

[30] O. Chadwick, *The Victorian Church, Part II, 1860–1901* (1970), 159; A. Haig, *The Victorian Clergy* (1984), 297–8, 302–3. Clergy paid income tax, a land tax, and a local rate, and were not allowed to count their curate's stipend as a professional expense.

TABLE 2.2.   Growth of membership in three British professions, 1881–1911 (thousands)

Year	Lawyers	Percentage increase	Doctors	Percentage increase	Clergymen	Percentage increase
1881	17.4		15.1		33.5	
1891	20.0	23.0	18.9	62.7	36.8	19.8%
1901	20.1		22.5		39.7	
1911	21.4		24.6		40.1	

Note: Clerics and doctors included the retired.

Source: H. J. Perkins, 'Middle-Class Education and Employment in the Nineteenth Century: A Critical Note', *Economic History Review*, xiv (1961), 128–9

the United Kingdom that recruitment to the church was declining in relation to apparently more attractive professional options such as medicine.[31]

Table 2.2 indicates that in Britain it was the medical profession that had proportionately increased the fastest between 1881 and 1911 and which therefore might have been expected to experience the worst economic effects of overcrowding. However, Jeremiahs prophesying doom from professional overcrowding were as plentiful in the British legal profession as in medicine. The earliest crisis hit the Bar when the creation of low-cost county courts in 1846 meant that an oversupply of barristers was immediately proclaimed. 'Until the numbers of the Bar are reduced to some reasonable proportion . . . it will be the most unprofitable and hopeless profession for any man to adopt' lamented the *Law Times* in 1852.[32] In the following year *Punch* took a wry delight in pointing to:

> The Barristers of England, how hungrily they stand,
> About the Hall of Westminster with wig and gown in hand
> With brief bags full of dummies and fee books full of rights
> Result of the establishment of the New County Courts.[33]

Apocryphal stories circulated of barristers keeping confectionery and hosiery shops, or even of running a public house. A growth of mid-nineteenth century legal employment in the civil service, and in business, as well as considerable emigration, reduced the surplus, but the Bar was still considered to be overcrowded in the 1870s.[34] Opportunities in the Empire, although good before the colonies began to train their own barristers, diminished after the 1870s and were said to be poor by the 1890s. In 1897 the ordinary advocate was counselled to 'pause ere he waste his time on a South African adven-

[31] *The Medical Practitioner*, 26 Nov. 1910.   [32] *Law Times*, 19 (1852), 66.
[33] Quoted in J. R. Lewis, *The Victorian Bar* (1982), 41.
[34] The *Saturday Review* in 1873 cited by Lewis, *Victorian Bar*, 109; D. Duman, *The English and Colonial Bars* (1983), 5, 206–7.

ture'.[35] As with élite physicians and surgeons, barristers' career income during the early stages of professional life came in slowly, so that one grumbled that 'the road to business is very long and steep indeed'.[36] A handbook for aspiring lawyers pronounced dryly that 'gentlemen at the Bar do not acquire a practice of any value until they are considerably advanced in years'.[37]

Between the Bar and the solicitor's office there was perceived to be a wide gulf, the former needing both more talent and greater initial financial resources.[38] During the mid-nineteenth century solicitors were much better placed than barristers, however, because the growth of railway business, joint stock companies, life assurance business, and the legal transactions of an increasing population, contributed to buoyant incomes.[39] Through energy and discretion, attention to business and ingenuity a young solicitor could become established more quickly than could a barrister. Even so, there were warnings that it was easier to do the work once the client was there, than to gain the client in the first place, and that 'It takes a good many six-and-eightpences to pay expenses and build up a livelihood.'[40] Anxieties were loudly expressed about overcrowding, and the *Solicitor's Journal* warned articled clerks in 1906 that it was useless 'to think that because they passed the final examination . . . they would be sure to make a living'.[41] Whilst a few solicitors were prosperous and gave an illusion of a buoyant Edwardian profession, economic prospects for many were in decline so that there was professional malaise in Edwardian times. Subjective career expectations were not being modified realistically to take account of objective changes in the market for legal services. In 1909 the *Law Clerk* warned that 'large numbers of men without money or prospects become solicitors carrying on some small apology for a practice in a tumble-down office'.[42] Average earnings were estimated at £200 to £250 for earlier years, with under £300 during the quarter century before the First World War.[43] Professional prospects worsened significantly with a long downward movement in the property market from 1900 to 1917, although a reduction in recruitment during the First World War, and a later revival in the property market, helped restore professional vitality.

The very substantial growth in the medical and legal professions from the mid-nineteenth century onwards meant that an expanded supply of highly educated people impacted on a restricted market in which effective demand lagged behind social need. Whilst contemporaries were aware of 'overcrowding' within their own country, there was little if any awareness of the extent of the situation in Europe and North America. Historical comment has also

---

[35] *Law Journal*, 32 (1897), 550. [36] Quoted in Duman, *English and Colonial Bars*, 95.

[37] J. H. Slater, *A Guide to the Legal Profession* (1884), 8.

[38] Id., *Legal Profession*, 8, 11.

[39] H. Kirk, *Portrait of a Profession. A History of the Solicitor's Profession 1100 to the Present Day* (1976), 88–9.

[40] Slater, *Legal Profession*, 2, 8–11. [41] Quoted in Kirk, *Portrait*, 58.

[42] Cited in Offer, *Property and Politics*, 13. [43] Ibid. 15–17.

focused overwhelmingly on single- or bi-country analyses. Yet the problems of an emerging professional 'proletariat', the professional strategies employed in combating surpluses, as well as resulting generational and gendered and geographical variation, were international in scope.

Competition

In Britain during the mid- and late-nineteenth century the competition given to regular doctors by homeopaths aroused the greatest fear and hostility from general practitioners. Homeopaths followed Samuel Hahnemann (1755–1843), whose ideas were set out in *Principles of Rational Medicine* (1810), and who advocated 'like cures like' (medicines producing pathological effects similar to the disease were interpreted as giving the key to cure); very small doses of drugs (maximizing their effectiveness); and a holistic view of diagnosis and treatment (focusing on the individual needs of the patient). Homeopaths called the regulars allopaths—cure by opposite. By 1853 three hospitals, 57 dispensaries, and 178 doctors in Britain and Ireland were homeopathic, and in addition advice manuals, and homeopathic medicine chests encouraged self-dosing by sufferers. GPs feared this confident advance, not just for the competition it offered in a contested medical market, but because it undercut medicine's claims for scientific legitimacy. Indeed, the original Medical Bill of 1858 reflected their anxieties to the extent that doctors would have been forbidden to pursue any therapeutic system other than those legitimated by approved teaching and licensing bodies. This clause was deleted by homeopathic sympathizers in the House of Lords, who also succeeded in inserting an additional clause that forbade teaching and licensing bodies from insisting on therapeutic purity.[44] The *British Journal of Homeopathy* was relieved that 'the fangs of this serpent that threatened death and destruction to homeopathy have been effectively drawn, and no ingenuity can pervert the Act into an instrument for our suppression or annoyance'.[45]

Hostility by general practitioners continued unabated, with professional strategies to marginalize and diminish the threat posed by homeopathic practitioners, and by eclectics who practised both allopathic and homeopathic medicine. Tactics of 'ostracism, exclusion, dismissal and defamation' followed. After 1858 membership of the BMA was confined to those who were not practising homeopaths, and BMA members were prohibited from referral or consultation with homeopaths. The Royal Colleges of Surgeons and Physicians in Edinburgh and Glasgow followed suit, although thereafter the élite's torpidity in accepting homeopaths as members alienated generalists. Attacks on homeopaths were virulent, and often inconsistent in their attempts to put off potential patients; alleging medicines that were ineffectual but also

---

[44] P. A. Nicholls, *Homeopathy and the Medical Profession* (1988), 134, 144–5.
[45] 'The Medical Act', *British Journal of Homeopathy*, xvi (1858), 530.

poisonous, and practitioners who were either fools or knaves.[46] The hostility felt by orthodox GPs against homeopaths, and their fear of economic competition in a crowded medical market, were exemplified nationally and locally. A local instance of the extent of antipathy was shown in Sussex when a homeopathic practitioner was appointed as MOH for Hastings in 1881. The local medical society circulated other medical societies on the dangers of such appointments, and received a number of sympathetic replies. The society also protested to the Local Government Board as to the legitimacy of the appointment, 'feeling strongly as we do the serious evils that must arise from the want of cordial co-operation between the body of medical men practising in the town and the newly selected Medical Officer of Health'.[47]

By the end of the century the British profession had been successful in marginalizing the homeopath. (Not that local groups of homeopaths necessarily recognized this as, for example, in Lancashire where homeopathic practitioners later sought unsuccessfully to prescribe for their patients under the national health insurance scheme.)[48] This peripheral position of homeopathic doctors contrasted with the situation in the USA where professional convergence and accommodation took place: homeopaths 'won a share in the legal privileges of the profession', but found that this acceptance heralded sectarian disintegration.[49] In Britain also there was a certain irony in that professional ostracism was paralleled by therapeutic inclusion. British allopaths were influenced by the prescribing strategies of the homeopaths in their own renunciation of the heroic doses prevalent during the early nineteenth century.[50]

The Medical Act of 1858 had disappointed the British medical profession in giving them no direct protection against alternative practitioners. In what was substantially still a laissez-faire society the freedom of sufferers to consult whomsoever they chose took precedence over sectional professional interests. The GMC formally recognized that the situation was unsatisfactory in 1908. Their letter to the government stimulated an inquiry into practice by unqualified persons. The inquiry's *Report* stated that:

The General Medical Council being of the opinion that the present Medical Acts do not sufficiently enable 'persons requiring medical aid' 'to distinguish qualified from unqualified practitioners' and that it is contrary to the interest of the public that medical and surgical practice should be carried on with impunity by persons holding no recognised qualifications, request the Government to take steps for the appointment of a Royal Commission to inquire into the evil effects produced by the unrestricted practice of medicine and surgery by unqualified persons.[51]

---

[46] Nicholls, *Homeopathy*, 137–9, 149–53.
[47] E. Sussex RO, AMS 6315/9/9 E. Sussex Medico-Chirurgical Society Minutes, 18 Apr. 1881.
[48] Lancashire RO, Ic La/1/1, Lancashire NHI Committee Minute 30 Feb. 1913.
[49] Starr, *Transformation*, 107.   [50] Nicholls, *Homeopathy*, 157–8.
[51] *Report as to the Practice of Medicine and Surgery by Unqualified Persons in the UK*, PP, 1910, Cd 5422, XLII, 10.

Local MOHs were asked to report on the situation in their own district, and the seriousness with which these doctors treated the inquiry is discernible in the amount of detail each supplied. Taken together they give a revealing insight into the severe competition that registered doctors encountered, or perceived that they faced, from a variety of healers. The report from the MOH for Rhondda Urban District in South Wales is interesting in giving detailed information on what could be discerned of alternative practice, as well as hinting at further unknown dimensions.

Whether increasing [in extent] is difficult to state, but apparently it is, as most of the twenty-six quacks now practising have been established within recent years. Practice by herbalists and botanic specialists, chemists, a bonesetter, an ex-dispenser and others. All give advice and prescribe medicine, and at least eight visit at patients' houses. Suspected abortionists (women garbed as nurses) visit the district.[52]

Thus registered doctors found themselves in a medical market, in which alternative and registered practitioners were poorly differentiated (in terms of advising, prescribing for, and visiting the sick), and where keen competition meant that only the fit survived.

The *Report*'s section on Scotland recognized that it was difficult to draw a line between qualified and unqualified practice, not least because of 'the frequent acceptance by the medical profession of ideas and methods first elaborated by "unqualified persons"'.[53] The degree of appropriation, of mutual accommodation, and of convergence varied, so that relationships between orthodox and alternative practitioners were marked by considerable tension. How distinct were their approaches and practices? Medical groups or sects continued to define their own practices rather than legitimating themselves by reference to orthodox medicine. But whereas in 1850 there had been a parallel set of approaches and practices, by 1900 a professionalizing agenda of making orthodox medicine the dominant partner had had some success in creating a greater sense of medical hierarchy.[54] The *BMJ* stated in 1906 that the term doctor 'conveys an implied compliment that we are, *par excellence*, the depositories of learning and the distributors of its fruits'.[55] This was too complacent since a diffuse, fluid, and heterogeneous medical pluralism still enabled sufferers to choose from other alternatives according to their perceived effectiveness or availability.

Official perceptions of any distinction between the registered doctor and alternative practitioners was not as clear cut as might have been expected, given that one of the privileges gained by doctors under the 1858 act had been a monopoly over public appointments. The *Report* indicated that in some areas Registrars of Death accepted certificates of death granted by unquali-

---

[52] *Practice by Unqualified Persons*, 55.   [53] Ibid. 62.

[54] This paragaph is generally informed by the papers and discussions at the 'Alternative Medicine in Modern Europe Conference', the Wellcome Institute, London, Oct. 1996.

[55] *BMJ*, i (1906), 757, quoted in C. Lawrence, *Medicine in the Making of Modern Britain, 1700–1920* (1994), 68.

fied persons, without any further enquiry being made. From the doctor's viewpoint an ounce of satisfaction (but not the requisite pound of flesh), might have been gained by the fact that these were then entered as uncertified deaths. In other areas school authorities gave the same credence to certificates excusing school attendance issued by herbalists, as to those from registered doctors. Not surprisingly the average sufferer was even less inclined to make an informed distinction as to the degree of official approval of any practitioner, so that it was a popularly held view that the revenue label on bottles of patent medicines implied government sanction. Advertisements utilized this kind of popular credulity, as for example, did one for an abortifacient that read 'My female specifics are reliable "Government Stamped".'[56]

Self-drugging was said to be 'enormous', proprietary medicines being sold very widely by grocers and co-operative stores, while the chemist selling proprietary medicines was perceived by the doctors as the principal rival. The prescribing or counter-prescribing chemist was ubiquitous, and was widely resorted to, especially by the poor. Yet the *Report* made clear that chemists were becoming more than retailers, and in some cases were offering wide-ranging services that rivalled those of the doctor. Some were nascent health centres where chemists—either in the shop, or in the room behind the shop—engaged in consulting, prescribing, minor surgery, dental, and optical treatments. They even visited patients' homes.[57] District nurses and/or midwives were also making inroads into professional territory which doctors might have hoped to see as their own, by running associations and clubs, or even opening shops from which they treated the local community. They were said to be 'rapidly developing into unqualified practitioners' in so far as they might offer their club subscribers 'nursing, surgical and medical attention'.[58]

The *Report* gave a fascinating but complex picture in which the spectrum of practitioners available to consumers varied from place to place. Some alternatives to the doctor were ubiquitous so that counter prescribing was prevalent even in remote places such as Orkney, and itinerants covered isolated country hamlets or farmhouses as well as weekly fairs in towns. In a comment that might have described conditions during the early modern period, it was stated that 'The public are still duped to a very large extent by the methods of the itinerant quack, who travels from market to market, and attracts a crowd by the ruse of extracting the teeth of all comers free.' In remote and thinly populated parts of Scotland it was the alternative practitioner, often the bonesetter, who was often the only help available to sufferers. Interestingly, in Scotland it was reported that other professionals—such as the school teacher or clergyman—might double as an 'alternative' medical practitioner. Regionally, there was some broad differentiation with, for example, alternative practitioners stronger in northern England where registered doctors were thinner on the ground. The dynamics of complementarity are

---

[56] *Practice by Unqualified Persons*, 12, 18.   [57] Ibid. 12–13, 19, 40, 42, 45, 48–9, 54–5, 59, 61.
[58] Ibid. 53, 58.

unclear; registered doctors may have found territory too well held by established alternative practitioners to think it worth competing, or alternative
practitioners may have moved into areas badly served by those with names
on the *Medical Register*.[59]

What was the impact on doctors of this multifarious activity? Delay in
seeking treatment was stated to be the main effect of alternative practitioners, but this restrained kind of statement may have come as much from professional dignity as accurate reporting. To admit that sufferers never arrived
at the doctor because of the efficacy of alternative practitioner's treatment
would have been to muddy the waters, and thus to miss a valuable chance to
promote the registered doctor's cause in an official report. In this context it
was intriguing that the practitioners whom it was admitted actually took over
some of the doctors' territory (as distinct from merely competing with them),
were stated to be female. 'Nurses are now taking much of the work done by
medical men'; or 'midwifery is drifting into the hands of midwives'. Nurses'
activities were apparently much less threatening, and their success less a blow
to male professional dignity, that this could be recognized. Only in Ireland
was the basic underlying economic issue laid bare when it was admitted that
'bonesetters and quacks are employed. Doctors are at a loss in regard to
fees.'[60] Yet the actual impact in constraining the expansion of doctors' practices must have been more substantial than was recognized explicitly in the
inquiry, not least because of the remarkable public confidence that alternative practitioners enjoyed. Bonesetters, for example, had a 'big reputation',
and 'in some districts [they] enjoy a large amount of public confidence'. And
some miner's friendly societies, including the Northumberland and Durham
Miners Permanent Relief Fund, accepted certificates from them 'as equivalent to the certificate of medical practitioners.' In Wales there was a strong
belief that bonesetting was 'a thing apart from the medical man's functions'.[61]
This hinted at a segmented medical market derived from the mental map of
sufferers in which ailments were ranked in a graduated scale of seriousness,
and which had a corresponding sequence of remedies, together with practitioners who might appropriately be consulted.[62]

The doctors who reported to the inquiry on the roles played by alternative
practitioners in their local community occasionally revealed their underlying
hostility by reporting that the 'district [is] much infested by itinerant
quacks',—much as they would have done in filing a MOH report on ver-
min.[63] 'Specialist' was given much the same resonance as 'quack', as in references to 'self-styled specialists' and 'pseudo-specialism':

Pseudo-specialism of all descriptions abounds. . . . Rupture curers and hernia specialists . . . pile specialists, beauty specialists . . . skin disease specialists, including

[59] *Practice by Unqualified Persons*, 29, 62–3, 71–2; Digby, *Medical Living*, 20–4, 64.
[60] *Practice by Unqualified Persons*, 13, 53, 58, 60, 88.   [61] Ibid. 18.   [62] See Ch. 9.
[63] *Practice by Unqualified Persons*, 46.

erysipelas specialists, and others who are described in more or less vague terms as 'Disease Specialists', 'Healing Specialists', or merely 'Specialist'. This form of unqualified practice is said to be 'markedly on the increase'.[64]

Mentioned in the *Report* were others whose field was a narrowly specific, and therefore a specialist, one. These included: those treating venereal disease, the cancer curers, obesity curers, water casters, or consumption curers; as well as electro-masseurs, medical electricians, and magnetic healers; the chiropodists, osteopaths, opticians, and teeth pullers; and the spiritualist healers, Christian Scientists, and faith healers. In addition there were 'wise women' whose 'speciality' was in treating abscesses, burns and scalds with special salves, and the 'native experts' whose treatments included bleeding.[65] The list shows a tension between the resilient competitors who had figured strongly in an earlier age, (such as the water casters and teeth pullers), and those who were later to become more prominent in twentieth-century professional health care (such as osteopaths, opticians, or chiropodists).

Specialists within and without the ranks of those on the *Medical Register* were a growing threat to the economic viability of general practice. In the late Victorian age specialists were few. An authoritative view in 1878 was that they could be limited to ophthalmics and obstetrics, on the grounds that these were the only areas in which 'ordinary men are not capable of lecturing, and which they delegate to others'.[66] However, this dominant generalist medical culture—where hospital consultants were themselves still generalists—was increasingly challenged by a new specialist medicine which originated in, and was informed by, scientific research. By the early twentieth century there were over a hundred specialist hospitals in London offering specialized research and teaching, and the techniques and equipment developed in them then became incorporated into reorganized general hospitals.[67] These developments potentially endangered the survival of GPs because middle-class patients might be sidetracked away from the family care of general practice to specialist outpatient clinics in hospitals. It was only the evolving practice of referral of patients from GPs to consultants that rescued generalists, secured the future of the general practitioner, so attaining what Irvine Loudon has aptly described as the 'symbiotic relationship' of specialist and generalist in British medicine.[68] As Chapter 11 suggests, however, these were permeable categories, so that the outcomes from these conflicts were less straightforward than is usually assumed.

---

[64] Ibid. 53, 29.   [65] Ibid. 30, 40, 42, 44, 53, 58, 71.
[66] *Special Report from the SC on the Medical Act (1858) Amendment Act (No 3) Bill*, PP, 1878–9, XII, QQ. 3764–5, evidence of Ernest Hart, Editor of the *BMJ* (hereafter called *Special Report*).
[67] R. Kershaw, *Special Hospitals* (1909), 28, 43–4, 48.
[68] I. Loudon, *Medical Care and the General Practitioner* (Oxford, 1986), 301.

Registration and Regulation

In a laissez-faire state regulation of the medical profession was problematical:
the first abortive bill was introduced in August 1840, and the successful bill
was enacted in June 1858 as the Medical Act.[69] It set up a General Medical
Council to regulate the profession and to superintend medical examination.
In addition the GMC was to provide a *British Pharmacopoeia* from the three
diverse *Pharmacopoeias* in operation in Scotland, Ireland and England—the
first edition being published in 1864. A *Medical Register* was begun and practitioners could register on the basis of a single qualification in either medicine or surgery. Not until the act of 1886 were qualifications in medicine,
surgery, and obstetrics required. Registration on the basis of a partial qualification also gave only limited advantages: it gave practitioners the ability to
sue for fees; and public appointments were confined to those on the *Register*.
Improved professional self-regulation and the maintenance of standards were
initiated through the GMC's ability to remove registered doctors for infamous conduct, or after conviction for a felony. The act neither outlawed
'quacks' nor regulated druggists, and so disappointed general practitioners.
In the short-term it worsened, rather than improved, the competitive position of the ordinary doctor in the medical market.[70]

General practitioners were anxious to make what limited gains they had
secured from the 1858 act into a reality. The London Medical Registration
Association, which was affiliated to local societies, spearheaded activity.
These might themselves have been active before their affiliation, as had the
East Sussex Medico-Chirurgical Society.[71] In January 1859 it had set up its
own registration committee to review names in the area, and communicated
to the Medical Registrar 'the name of Frederick Thomas, who appears by the
Medical Directory to be practising at Hurstmonceaux, and who is suspected
of assuming titles to which he has no legal right'.[72] Hopes by practitioners
that the Registrar would take legal action against such impostors were to be
disappointed. Activists might initiate a campaign as later did the general practitioner, Robert Carpenter who founded in 1877 the East London Medical
Association, and who carried out over sixty prosecutions against unregistered
practitioners. In most cases he obtained a verdict with costs. But his 'zeal out-
ran discretion' so that his 'passionate desire to promote a particular reform
. . . blinded him to the injustice of the reproaches that he freely scattered'.
This hotheaded GP was unable to persuade the government of the need to
revise the 1858 act so as to make it more stringent and effective.[73]

---

[69] *Special Report*, appendix 3 summarized the bills.   [70] Digby, *Medical Living*, 31–2.
[71] E. Sussex RO, AMS 6315/5/1, E. Sussex Medico-Chirurgical Society minutes 11 Oct. 1859.
[72] Ibid., minutes 17 and 25 Jan. 1859; AMS 6315/9/2 Establishment of Medical Registration
Committee, 1858/9.
[73] *BMJ*, i (1890), 1936. R. H. S. Carpenter, LRCP (London), LSA.

A widespread grievance in the profession was the wording of clause 40 in the Medical Act, which made it a summary offence (for which the maximum penalty was a fine of £20) to pretend registration, rather than as doctors wished, an offence to assume the title of doctor without possession of diplomas. Ernest Hart, Editor of the *BMJ* warned in 1879 that the act did not give adequate protection of the public against false registration, and that cities 'swarm with quacks and extortionate persons, who in most instances take the name "Dr" without possessing any registrable qualification'. He complained that the GMC had failed to initiate prosecutions so as to fulfil practitioners' interpretation of the act's preamble, which had stated that its function was 'to enable the Public to distinguish between qualified and unqualified persons'. The GMC, under the plea of inadequate funds had shown the 'utmost apathy' in Hart's view. It had been left to individuals to initiate legal action so that this had taken place only fitfully and sporadically. The BMA—considering itself to be an ethical and scientific body—had declined to initiate prosecutions.[74]

The GMC's regulatory and disciplinary action was muted, so that by June 1879 only thirty people had been removed from the *Medical Register*, after having been found guilty of infamous conduct. The extent to which the GMC served the interests of general practitioners rather than élite practitioners is doubtful. Although the President of the Council did not think that GPs' interests were neglected,[75] representatives of the BMA disagreed. They argued that the medical corporations were unduly represented: they had good cause to think so because members of the GMC were either nominated by the Queen from the highest echelons of the medical profession, or by the medical corporations and universities.[76] It was not general practitioners but consultants, specialists, and professors who were conspicuous in its membership. Given that the GMC devoted most of its active energies to reforming medical education, it was predictable that the interests of specialist rather than generalist would predominate in this area. This is a central issue for discussion in the following chapter on medical education.

[74] *Special Report*, QQ. 3714–17, 3726–41, evidence of E. Hart.
[75] *Report on the Medical Act*, Q. 1867, evidence of H. W. Acland.
[76] *Special Report*, QQ 1592–6, 3753–5, evidence of E. Waters, President of the BMA, and that of E. Hart.

3

Recruitment, Education, and Training

EDUCATIONAL credentialism was one characteristic of a profession, and in the case of medicine this was shown both in the increasingly structured and full-time character of medical education, and in the growing range of qualifications available. But it is important not to impose too tidy a structure on what remained for a long time a diffuse set of openings into medicine. Continued discussion centred on ways in which additional subjects could be accommodated, on the sequencing of theoretical and clinical work within a British tradition of inculcating good clinical skills for practice, and on a need to accommodate the new scientific thinking associated with bacteriology and germ theory. Medical education and training had the potential to enable professional expertise to be transmitted and generalized to young entrants to the profession, thus facilitating their creation of successful practices. Unfortunately, medical training for general practitioners was vitiated by its gearing to specialist needs. Specialists not generalists usually provided the teaching, while the student's clinical experience was with the serious illnesses of the hospital patient, rather than with the common conditions likely to be encountered in a GP's surgery. Furthermore, an emphasis on factual cramming—instead of the inculcation of habits of careful clinical observation followed by logical deduction—tended to produce a restricted professional outlook. There were only faint echoes in this period of an earlier concern to facilitate a good bedside manner with affluent patients through a liberal education that would give interpersonal skills suitable for a gentleman.

What was the social background of young professionals entering medicine? Recruitment to the Victorian medical profession was from people of modest social backgrounds in comparison with the two other traditional professions of the law or the Church. J. M. Peterson has commented perceptively that Victorian 'medical men were caught in a dilemma of circularity. Their social origins gave them no claim to gentlemanly status; their professional activities were inimical to such claims; and the inferior status of the profession discouraged the sons of gentlemen from entering and thus raising the social standing of the whole group.'[1] Exploding numbers in the Victorian professions had led to a more critically discriminating attitude to them by contem-

[1] M. J. Peterson, *The Medical Profession in Mid-Victorian London* (Berkeley, 1978), 197–8, 204.

poraries, 'Though the professional classes as such have a status, it is doubt-ful whether as a body they occupy relatively the same position in the public estimation as formerly; for, owing to the great diffusion of education in recent times, they have no longer a similar monopoly of culture or learning.'[2] And Lady Warwick pointed out the practical implications of this in that 'doctors and solicitors might be invited to garden parties, though never, of course, to lunch or dinner'.[3] For the more financially successful doctors the possession of homes in more fashionable suburbs, servants, or a carriage might help to assimilate them socially into local élites in provincial towns. These trappings of gentility were important. In 1861, for example, it was stated that 'In our own day an equipage of some sort is considered so necessary an appendage to a medical practitioner that a physician without a carriage . . . is looked upon with suspicion.'[4] However, birth into a good family, private money, and social connection remained the most powerful instrumental factors in attain-ing high social standing; a Victorian medical career appears to have been less a means to become upwardly mobile, than to maintain or consolidate social prestige. Whether practitioners became fully integrated or to some extent remained marginal in the community where they practised varied with the locality.[5]

Germane to the social class of those recruited to the medical profession was its expected rewards. A young graduate who studied in Galway, but later practised in Cardiff, remembered that in the early 1880s he had 'felt confi-dent of having entered an honourable and lucrative profession'.[6] And in 1901 medical students were assured that they could look forward to a 'practically assured livelihood . . . [of] say, £400 or £500 a year'.[7] Significantly, this was well below the £700 earlier thought necessary to maintain a genteel life style, and therefore mirrored contemporary assumptions about the social class of the ordinary doctor. The impact of NHI after 1911 was to significantly increase the size and stability of GPs' income, and this had a knock-on effect on recruitment. During the interwar period Deans of Medical Schools sus-pected that there was a new type of applicant who perceived medicine as 'a safe living' or 'a means of employment with an assured income' rather than a 'vocation' or 'a "call" to become a doctor'.[8] The 'inverse ratio between eco-nomic prosperity and entry to medicine' was shown very clearly at Glasgow, where the medical faculty recruited particularly well in the financially

[2] J. J. Gregson Slater, *Should I Go To The Bar?* (1912), 20.

[3] A. Glynn, *Elinor Glynn—A Biography* (1955), 64.

[4] J. C. Jeaffreson, *A Book about Doctors* (2nd edn. 1861), 8.

[5] Peterson, *Medical Profession*, 197–207; H. Marland, *Medicine and Society in Wakefield and Huddersfield, 1780–1870* (1987), 280–1, 297, 365–7; I. Inkster, 'Marginal Men: Aspects of the Social Role of the Medical Community in Sheffield, 1790–1850', in J. Woodward and D. Richards (eds.), *Health Care and Popular Medicine in Nineteenth Century England. Essays in the Social History of Medicine* (1977), 129.

[6] J. Mulllin, *The Story of a Toiler's Life* (1921), 118.   [7] *BMJ*, i (1901), 513–14.

[8] PRO, MH 77/175, evidence by the Deans of Westminster Hospital, and the University of Liverpool Medical School to the Spens Committee, 1945.

depressed early 1930s. Medicine at this university drew heavily from professional families generally during the interwar years, so that self-recruitment from medical families was less important than had been the case earlier.[9]

This later generation of doctors might hide modest social origins behind a façade of the public school and university they had attended, and in mid-career perhaps acquire status-conferring qualifications. But there is evidence to suggest that amongst the more snobbish the sense persisted that the GP was not of the first rank. One GP ruefully recollected a professional call made to the house of the owner of the local brick works, who had retained the status of a private patient even *after* the NHS. 'Automatically, I went to the front door, and I rang the bell, and I was firmly directed to go round to the tradesmen's entrance. I told them who I was and what I was there for. "Rear entrance, please, doctor", and I had to go round to the back door!'[10]

An important social constraint in medical recruitment was the length of training which resulted in high costs, which might then be further inflated by the need to subsidize the low earnings characteristic of the early stages of a career, more especially if a specialism was chosen. The expense of medical education was increasing everywhere; that obtained in Britain was more expensive than in France or the USA, although cheaper than in Germany.[11] Costs for training (including maintenance) for a general practitioner were very variously estimated, with highest ones for London (because of the cost of maintenance), lower for the provinces (especially when students lived at home), and lowest, whilst training at an extra-medical department at Edinburgh or Glasgow.[12] Additional expenses were also incurred since students often had to retake courses. In Scotland an able but poor individual might obtain the backing of parishioners, who would pay for a medical training so long as the doctor returned to work in the parish.[13] And a developing system of Scottish scholarships, grants, and loans, (especially those from the Carnegie Trust), provided assistance, so that at the end of the period 43 per cent of Scottish students were receiving help, compared to only 11 per cent in England.[14] Other students defrayed their own costs through working through college as did James Sinclair who, having saved up for medical training by working for chemists during a period of eleven years before training,

[9] A. Collier, 'Social Origins of a Sample of Entrants to Glasgow University, parts I and II', *Sociological Review*, 30 (1938), 268, 274. This was based on the years 1926–9 and 1932, together with a comparison of the situation during 1911–13.

[10] CMAC, GP 29/2/49, Donald Gawith.

[11] T. N. Bonner, *Becoming a Physician. Medical Education in Britain, France, Germany, and the United States, 1750–1945* (Oxford, 1995), 228–9.

[12] *S.C. on Medical Education*, PP, 1834, xiii, Q.5908; 'Medical Education', *Westminster Review*, 70 (1858), 141–2; Peterson, *Medical Profession*, 74; C. B. Keetley, *The Student's and Junior Practitioner's Guide to the Medical Profession* (2nd edn., 1885), 116–17.

[13] A. Mair, *Sir James Mackenzie, MD. General Practitioner* (1972), 37. Mackenzie had such an offer but refused it.

[14] *Report of Inter Departmental Committee on Medical Schools* [Goodenough] 1944, 100–1; *BMJ*, 14 Sept. 1946.

then worked at the Edinburgh Medical Mission Dispensary every afternoon and evening during his course, until his final year.[15]

How did this situation compare with that in the legal profession? The full cost of both a solicitor's and a barrister's training was likely to have been much more expensive.[16] An important cost for solicitors was that of Articles, which ranged from £100 to £500, but with £200–£250 being the average during the 1880s, and with a stamp duty of £80 on the articleship.[17] During the mid-nineteenth century an increasing proportion of barristers came from middle-class professional backgrounds, and with a tendency towards recruitment from élite public schools and universities.[18] This trend persisted so that on the eve of the Second World War the Law Society (representing the viewpoint of solicitors) was said to prefer 'the old school tie to the man who got his position solely by merit'.[19]

Apprentices, Pupils, and Unqualified Assistants

During the early to mid-nineteenth century the flexibility of openings into medicine probably encouraged a wider social recruitment to medicine than was the case later. Medical training was often based on individual apprenticeships, pupillage, and unqualified assistantships, succeeded by a period of 'walking the wards' of a hospital. Under the apprenticeship system the master accepted a premium of £100 or £200 and agreed to 'teach and instruct'.[20] Some medical apprentices might also have to do more general household duties, as was the case with a Bideford surgeon in 1809, who privileged duties for his apprentice as household servant in helping in the stable or at table, above work in the surgery in the boy's 'spare time'.[21] Although apprentices disliked the non-craft unskilled duties that might be their lot, they enjoyed watching, and learning from, their master's skilled activities.[22] Periods of

---

[15] National Library of Scotland, Accession 10334, no. 5, 'The Doctor in the Town', the scrapbook of the life of J. D. Sinclair, born 1874, OBE, MRCS.

[16] H. B. Thomson, *Choice of a Profession* (1857), 99–100 quotes £400 for fees and £600 for maintenance. There are similar estimates for the 1918 cost of training and maintenance for a solicitor, B. Abel-Smith and R. Stevens, *Lawyers and the Courts* (1967), 181.

[17] J. H. Slater, *A Guide to the Legal Profession* (1884), 12.

[18] There was an increase from 27% to 42% in this type of recruitment between 1835 and 1885 in a 10% sample of members of the English Bar, D. Duman, *The English and Colonial Bars in the Nineteenth Century* (1983), 19.

[19] *Joint SC to Consider the Solicitor's Bill*, PP, 1938–9., viii, Q. 764.

[20] I. S. L. Loudon, 'A Doctor's Cash Book: The Economy of General Practice in the 1830s', *MH*, 27 (1983), 251.

[21] Wellcome Institute, WMS 7205, apprenticeship indenture of William Ackland (*c*.1793–1867), later in general practice in Bideford. Interestingly, by the time that Ackland himself took an apprentice in 1837, there was reference only to the 'arts, mysteries and professions' of a surgeon and an apothecary.

[22] J. Lane, *Apprenticeship in England* (1996), 76, 78.

indenture varied from the traditional seven years,[23] to an increasingly acceptable five years.[24] Amongst GPs in our database there was a steady decrease in those taking an apprenticeship: 36 per cent (of those qualifying 1820–39); 21 per cent (1849–59); 11 per cent (1860–79); and only 1 per cent (1880–99).

Early careers of three general practitioners drawn from the GP database serve to illuminate a core of common experience, but with interesting variation in the circumstances of individual apprenticeships. William Blackburn, a Nottingham GP was born in 1814, indentured for seven years to Dr Broughton of Dobcross near Oldham, and deputed to look after his master's surgery as well as to attend night confinements in remote hamlets on the edge of Saddleworth Moor. The latter necessitated him travelling miles on foot and by coach to reach the patients' homes. Towards the end of his apprenticeship he attended lectures in Manchester, and after finishing his term, then went to Dublin where he studied at the Rotunda Hospital.[25] Michael Beverley was a later medical apprentice who was indentured to W. B. Francis of Norwich and put to work making pills, compounding medicines, keeping the surgery in good order, and visiting patients in the slum areas of the city or in nearby country villages. He then became a dresser in the Norfolk and Norwich Hospital, studied in London (where he fell under the spell of Lister), and finished his training in Edinburgh and in Paris. Beverley went on to a successful career centred on a series of appointments at the Norfolk and Norwich which lasted for sixty years, and which were run in tandem with a general practice in the city.[26] Lionel Weatherly was apprenticed in 1865 to his father, a Somerset medical man, and dispensed, dressed wounds, and assisted at minor operations. Having obtained a useful introduction to his vocation he then proceeded to the Bristol Medical Infirmary where he acted as a dresser, and finished his formal education at Marischal College, Aberdeen, where he qualified in 1873.[27]

A more detailed view can be gained from the biography of one youthful medical apprentice, Joseph Shrewsbury. However, his early death one month after having completed his articles, imparts a strong hagiographical flavour to the memorial of his *Life*, which was written by his father, a notable Wesleyan missionary and minister. At 16 years of age Joseph had been formally apprenticed to the Bradford surgeon, Thomas Beaumont, for a five-year term, which began in 1844. His master promised to 'receive him as an inmate of his family, grant him free access to his medical library, and afford him every facil-

[23] E. Suffolk R.O., HD/177/DI/3, Indenture of apprenticeship to a surgeon, Robert Anderson of Sudbury, 1812.

[24] D. Van Zwanenberg, 'The Training and Careers of those Apprenticed to Apothecaries in Suffolk, 1815–58', *MH*, 27 (1983), 140. The sample discussed is actually of those apprenticed to the surgeon-apothecaries, later called GPs.

[25] *BMJ*, i (1901), 56. W. Blackburn (1814–1901), MRCS, LSA.

[26] *BMJ*, ii (1930), 500. Michael Beverley, MD (Edinburgh.)   [27] *BMJ*, ii (1940), 340–1.

ity in his power to ensure his future success as a medical practitioner'.[28] At first Joseph remained in the surgery making up medicines. Later he read a lot, including chemistry and anatomy books, although he found anatomy 'desperate hard work for the memory'.[29] By 1848 Beaumont was able to write to Joseph's father that:

his actual attainments, in his elementary knowledge, necessary to a thorough understanding of Medicine and Surgery, are fully equal to my expectations, and although it is not to be supposed that his actual acquaintance with Anatomy, Chemistry, Materia Medica, and the Practice of Medicine, is extensive or profound, yet . . . his actual position in these respects is satisfactory and encouraging. I think also his mind is much directed to *missionary work* . . . [where] the most sound and abundant knowledge of medicine will be not only desirable, but necessary.[30]

The young apprentice enjoyed visiting his patients although his dual motivation in doing so brought out a Wesleyan legacy very clearly in his providential view of patients as a spiritual, as much as a clinical, opportunity. An earlier plan had been to 'perfect his medical studies' by hospital training in London, but later he decided to become a candidate for the Wesleyan ministry. His religious feelings became ever more pronounced. He wrote that 'I am still making it the business of my life to prepare for heaven.' And it was observed of him that 'his professional engagements were to him no drudgery, but a real means of grace'. Joseph's health had long given cause for concern, and consumption was suspected. But it was a shock when, feeling very unwell himself, Joseph insisted on visiting a patient, and died suddenly while engaged on these professional duties.[31]

Pupillage with a hospital surgeon was an alternative to apprenticeship, where the pupil lived in the surgeon's house and accompanied him in his work.[32] A pupil to an infirmary surgeon usually accompanied the medical officer on ward rounds, and might also provide cover for minor injuries during evenings or at night.[33] Edward Copeman acted first as pupil and then as dresser with the Norfolk and Norwich Hospital Surgeons, Arthur Brown and J. G. Crosse, before studying at St George's Hospital and going on to general practice first in Coltishall and then in Norwich, finally becoming a well-known consultant in East Anglia. Another who also served a pupillage with Crosse of Norwich became one of the best-known practitioners in East Anglia—the Ipswich GP, G. C. Edwards.[34]

[28] W. J. Shrewsbury, *Christ Glorified in the Life, Experience and Character of Joseph B. Shrewsbury* (1850), 80.

[29] Ibid. 132.   [30] Ibid. 291.   [31] Ibid. 162, 217, 369–70, 424–5.

[32] Confusingly, the term 'pupillage' was sometimes used interchangeably with an apprenticeship as well as with a clerical clerkship. See, for example, obituaries of W. Pollard and C. Oswin in *BMJ*, i (1890), 697, 929, or C. B. Plowright in *BMJ*, i (1910), 1149.

[33] H. Alford, 'The Bristol Infirmary in my Student Days, 1822–28', *Bristol Medical and Chirurgical Journal*, Sept. 1890.

[34] *BMJ*, i (1880), 382; i (1900), 1508.

Both apprenticeship and pupillage gave a useful preliminary clinical training, although the former tended to be more introductory in character. But
the medical élite viewed apprenticeship as backward-looking, craft-orientated,
limited and, as such, outdated for the aspirations of a profession.[35] It rightly
perceived that too much time was taken in learning too little, but ignored its
utility in giving hands-on experience of practice organization for the future
general practitioner. Later generations had to find a substitute, and a transitional solution was effected by taking an unqualified assistantship before or
during training.

Prior to going to medical school in the 1860s Alexander Blyth went as an
assistant without qualifications to a surgical practice in Aylesbury, where his
duties were indistinguishable from those traditionally done by apprentices—
minding the shop, making up medicines, and looking after poor patients.[36]
Another unqualified assistant from Wales was O. Thomas-Jones who, at the
tender age of 16 years went in 1893 to Dr Grey Edwards of Bangor, and to
similar posts in Llanfairtalhaiarn and Llanberis. Visiting patients in moun-
tainous areas he became an excellent horseman as well as learning much about
the rudiments of country practice, before serving in the South African War,
and only then going on to medical school.[37] Victorian doctors in training
might also take a post as assistant at a local institution, such as an Eye
Infirmary, as did W. T. Griffiths in London during the 1850s or William
Robinson in Newcastle during the 1870s.[38] Not that an unqualified assistantship was necessarily a substitute for other forms of training since occasionally it might be a supplement. Joseph Buck, for example, followed up a
five-year apprenticeship to a Leeds surgeon by becoming an unqualified assistant to another practitioner in the town, simultaneously attending the Leeds
Medical School.[39]

Biographical examples show that preparation for medicine during the
Victorian period was sufficiently flexible for individuals to choose a route
which suited their pocket as well as their social circumstances. Whether
recruits could combine training with employment as an assistant, vitally
affected recruitment to general practice of those from modest social backgrounds. Conan Doyle worked as an assistant during his medical school's
summer break, and even took seven months out to become a surgeon on a
whaling ship, where he earned a useful £50.[40] A few years earlier a young
Welsh student, then studying in London, had two spells as an unqualified
assistant, in order to help out with the cost of medical education. The first
post in 1875, at a salary of £40 per year, was with a practice in a colliery

[35] See, for example, RC into State of the Universities of Scotland, 1831, xii, 67.
[36] Buckinghamshire R.O., Box 5, diary of A. Blyth. See also Digby, Medical Living, 130 for further details.
[37] BMJ, i (1960), 885. O. Thomas Jones, MBE, LRCP and LRCS (Edinburgh).
[38] W. Robinson, Sidelights on the Life of a Wearside Surgeon (Gateshead on Tyne, 1939), 37.
[39] BMJ, i (1940), 281. J. Buck, LRCP and LRCS Edinburgh, LRFPS.
[40] J. Dickson Carr, The Life of Sir Arthur Conan Doyle (1949), 37–8, 41.

village near Newcastle-on-Tyne, where he found he was the third such assistant employed within a short spell of time—a sure sign that the post was no sinecure. Here he began each day at 8.30 a.m. in the surgery, then went on a long country round for the rest of the morning visiting colliers, club patients, and the poor, before returning for lunch at the doctor's house. The afternoon was spent dispensing or doing the books before undertaking more visiting of patients on foot or horseback. Since the doctor was a heavy prescriber, and each mixture contained six or seven ingredients, the evening was spent in even more dispensing by the assistant. Bedtime was 11 p.m., but the night could be disturbed by attendance at confinements. The work was so hard that the assistant soon gave notice. In contrast a second practice in a country practice in north Yorkshire, where he was engaged at the same salary, was very enjoyable because the work was light, and he was allowed—unusually in such situations—to visit better-class patients. Looking back in later life, however, even his first experience was seen as 'of lasting benefit' to him in his own practice.[41]

Working as an unqualified assistant meant that a good grounding in the basics of clinical practice was obtained so that formal education was shorter. However, these routes into medicine were made difficult if not impossible before 1900. In 1892 apprenticeship was abolished by the GMC. Until the 1880s a post as an unqualified assistant to a GP was feasible, since the Medical Act of 1858 had indicated only that the unqualified should not pass themselves off as qualified, and that bona fide medical students could be an assistant with a registered doctor. However, the GMC gradually became more restrictive. In 1883 the council decided that infamous conduct by a registered GP included the employment in certain circumstances of an unqualified assistant, and in 1888 the first practitioner was struck off for this offence.[42] The BMA decided to ban advertisements for unqualified assistants to conduct branch practices apart from the Principal, and also in 1894 outlawed the term 'unqualified' in *BMJ* advertisements for assistants.[43] Practice by the unqualified assistant lingered on, but only a couple of instances were cited in the *Report* on unqualified practice in 1910.[44] In the medical press full-time vacancies advertised were for qualified people only.[45] For the twentieth-century graduate a full-time assistantship after qualification, together with perhaps one or two spells as a *locum tenens*, provided what a mix of apprenticeship, pupillage, and unqualified assistancy had done for their Victorian predecessor. In each case it is significant that practical training for general practice was provided outside the medical school.[46]

[41] 'The Recollections of a Welsh Doctor', *The Welsh Outlook*, xx (1933), 51–2.

[42] R. Smith, 'The Development of Guidance for Medical Practitioners by the General Medical Council', *MH*, 33 (1993), 60.

[43] E. M. Little, *History of the British Medical Association, 1832–1932* (1932), 290.

[44] *Report as to the Practice . . . by Unqualified Persons*, 29, 49, 56. Instances were in Sheffield and Huddersfield.

[45] Ibid. 29.   [46] See Ch. 6 for the qualified assistant.

By 1900 medical education had become a full-time occupation for many students and this therefore demanded greater financial resources. In provincial English, and some of the Scottish universities, where students lived at home smaller expenditures on maintenance ameliorated the situation. A small minority still worked part-time, as did Edinburgh students in the Dispensary.[47] But without the help that part-time employment had earlier given to many more individuals, recruitment became socially skewed to the upper or middle-classes, a criticism made by the East End GP, Alfred Salter.[48]

Recruitment, Numbers, and Provision

Nationally and internationally there was a changing hierarchy of excellence and esteem in medical centres. An earlier generation had studied surgery in the Paris School, as had William Budd, who considered Louis, 'the greatest of authorities, living or dead'.[49] For this period Edinburgh had a sound reputation for diagnostic training but was held in less regard than earlier, whereas London's hospital schools were renowned internationally for their clinical education. The Scottish universities were held to give a more thorough training in the investigation of disease than English ones.[50] While Edinburgh, Glasgow, and Aberdeen were seen as the epitome of this, St Andrews as a university examining for medical degrees but not itself having a medical school, was viewed more sceptically, so that its academic standards had to be defended.[51] A very open market in medical qualifications meant that reputation was crucial, and rivalry between hospital schools or universities was vigorous. In Victorian Glasgow and Edinburgh, for example, there was a very considerable flow of students between the two universities and other centres within Britain and further afield.[52] There was a considerable range of choice for the student by the early twentieth century. In London there were a dozen hospital schools, and outside the metropolis medical education was provided at the universities of Oxford, Cambridge, Durham, Manchester, Birmingham, Liverpool, Leeds, Sheffield, and Bristol. The University of Wales had constituent colleges in Aberystwyth, Bangor, Cardiff, and Swansea. Also needing to be brought into focus, because some of their graduates came to practise in England, Wales, or Scotland were the University of Dublin (Trinity College); the National University of Ireland

---

[47] *Report as to the Practice . . . by Unqualified Persons*, 67.
[48] *Reynolds News*, 12 Apr. 1914.
[49] M. Pelling, *Cholera, Fever and English Medicine, 1825–1865* (Oxford, 1978), 266.
[50] W. Dale, *The State of the Medical Profession in Great Britain* (Dublin, 1875), 65.
[51] See the illuminating discussion in the *Special Report from the Select Committee on the Medical Act (1858) Amendment (No3) Bill*, PP, ix, QQ 112–13 (hereafter *Special Report*).
[52] Ibid., appendix 4; J. Bradley, A. Crowther, and M. Dupree, 'Mobility and Selection in Scottish University Medical Education', *MH*, 40 (1996), 7–11.

with university colleges at Dublin, Cork, and Galway; as well as Queen's University, Belfast. While London, Edinburgh, and (to a lesser extent) Glasgow recruited nationally and internationally, other centres had a more regional or local hinterland. For example, Aberdeen recruited four-fifths of its students from north-east Scotland during the 1930s and 1940s.[53] Thus a strong regional character was superimposed on to national and international flows of students.

The GP database shows a changing take-up amongst medical schools, with an increasing dispersion of medical education within a growing number of centres in Britain. Within this the London hospital schools, and the University of Edinburgh remained the most popular choices. However, the northern universities of Manchester, Durham, Leeds, and Liverpool became increasingly important for recruitment to general practice. Those educated in Welsh colleges were extremely small in number, not least because Liverpool and, to a lesser extent, Manchester appealed to those from north Wales. In Ireland Dublin was the main focus. There was a striking decline in those going to European centres to further develop their medical training.

Arguably failure to control numbers enrolled in medical courses indicated that the economic interests of the medical élite were being privileged over those of GPs.[54] Very high numbers entered the *Medical Register* in the late 1880s and early 1890s before numbers very gradually declined to a low point in 1913.[55] In part this reflected expanding opportunities for higher education. (In the new civic universities—which developed from the 1870s—there was a significant growth in numbers graduating (in all subjects), with about 100 per annum in the 1880s, 200 in the 1890s, and 500–600 in the 1910s.)[56] As far as medical registration was later concerned the exigencies of war led to short term fluctuations, first leading to an expansion in those registering during the opening years of hostilities, then a downturn in the later years of the First World War. During the early peacetime years from 1919 to 1925 a backlog of postwar registrations greatly inflated new entries. A relatively high level of entrants to the medical profession during the interwar period was a reflection of the very buoyant general recruitment to university education at a time when universities were taking a growing role in educating professional people. The trend in numbers of those taking medical courses in the period from 1922 to 1939 therefore showed a close correspondence with fluctuations in general student numbers at British universities.[57] The long-term trend was upwards although there was a dip in general student recruitment, as well as

[53] D., W. D., and C. M. Ogston, 'Origins and Employment of the Medical Graduates of the University of Aberdeen, 1931–69', *BMJ*, iv (1970), 361.

[54] Peterson, *Medical Profession*, 238–9.

[55] Figures for medical registration from 1887 to 1936 are given in *BMJ*, ii (1937), 446.

[56] H. Perkin, 'The Pattern of Social Transformation in England' in K. H. Jarausch (ed.), *The Transformation of Higher Learning, 1860–1930* (Chicago, 1983), 207, 218; M. Sanderson, *The Universities and British Industry, 1850–1970* (1972), 95.

[57] B. R. Mitchell, *British Historical Statistics* (Cambridge, 1988), 811.

in the medical courses taken, during the very economically depressed years between 1932/3 and 1935/6. Although there was some concern in the British profession that 'saturation point' had been reached in terms of these newly registered doctors finding employment, an authoritative view was that the medical profession was 'not so much overstocked as ill distributed'.[58] Similar concerns about overcrowding or maldistribution in the medical market were also being voiced in France, Germany, and the United States of America.[59]

Numbers of applicants for places at prestigious British medical schools rose during the 1920s and 1930s; an increased provision for men largely managed to keep pace with the growth in demand for places, but competition for places for women was fiercer. For example, at University College London, there were twenty applicants for twelve places in the early 1930s, and over a hundred applicants by the end of the decade.[60] Although formal academic qualifications improved in these interwar years, the general calibre of recruits to the medical profession was seen by their teachers as inferior to earlier cohorts because of what was perceived to be a mercenary rather than idealistic motivation. Medical schools were again inundated with applications after the Second World War. During 1946–7, for instance, between two out of five and four out of five applicants were refused at the four Scottish medical schools.[61]

Medical qualifications during the period from 1850 to 1948 showed considerable change, both in their nature, and in the relationship between the licensing bodies. In London the Royal College of Surgeons had examined and licensed since 1800, awarding licentiateship, membership, and fellowship of the college (LRCS, MRCS, FRCS). The Society of Apothecaries had been incorporated in 1815 and had been examining for the Licentiate of the Society of Apothecaries (LSA) since that date. For those engaging in general practice in England and Wales under the Apothecaries Act of 1815, the LSA was legally obligatory. Scottish practitioners thought that this discriminated against them by making it more difficult for them to practise in England and Wales, although they were in possession of what they correctly considered were superior qualifications from universities or corporations in Scotland. A Scottish professor tartly commented that in Scotland 'there are more educated men, and with less of the apothecary about them . . . I know of no country where the general practitioner is better educated than in Scotland.'[62] In addition to the LSA, the LRCS or MRCS whilst technically voluntary was also conventionally necessary.[63]

[58] 'The Medical Profession', *BMJ* 2 Sept. 1933.

[59] For example, *BMJ*, 23 Apr. and 27 Aug. 1932; 27 Apr. and 31 Aug. 1935.

[60] D. M. Smythe, 'Some Principles in the Selection of Medical Students', *BMJ*, 14 Sept. 1946.

[61] *BMJ*, 7 Dec., i (1946), 880.

[62] *Special Report*, Q 83, evidence of Professor Struthers of Aberdeen.

[63] S. Holloway, 'The Apothecaries Act, 1815: A Reinterpretation. Part II The Consequences of the Act', *MH*, 10 (1966), 224, 235.

In 1856, on the eve of the Medical Act, an analysis of entries in the *Medical Directory* found that 55 per cent of those entered had the combined qualification of LSA and MRCS (England). In addition a further 19 per cent had the MRCS only, and another 12 per cent the LSA on its own. This left only 14 per cent who had qualified by an MD or MB, FRCP (4 per cent), Scottish diploma (7 per cent), or Irish and foreign diplomas (3 per cent).[64] The figures from our database of GPs indicated substantial similarity in the dominance of the LSA and MRCS as qualifications. Taking the decade leading up to 1856 44 per cent of the GPs had a combined qualification of LSA and MRCS (England). In addition a further 25 per cent had the MRCS only, and another 6 per cent the LSA only. Three-quarters of the sample of the medical profession as a whole, and of the GP group, thus had qualifications consisting of the MRCS and LSA. However, in the GP group there were some differences in the qualifications of the remaining quarter: a further 8 per cent had only an LRCS; another 2 per cent the Scottish diploma; 2 per cent Irish and foreign diplomas; and 13 per cent an MB or MD.[65]

Practitioners in 1858 had to be qualified in surgery or medicine in order to register; a strategy of occupational closure that restricted the number of registered practitioners. There were twenty licensing bodies, and sixty-one qualifications from medical corporations and universities in Scotland, England and Ireland that were registrable in the *Medical Register*.[66] A minority of GPs who practised in Britain thus had Irish qualifications which included those of the University of Dublin, the Queen's University in Ireland, the King's and Queen's College of Physicians of Ireland, the Royal College of Surgeons in Ireland, and Apothecaries Hall, Dublin.[67] As we have seen earlier another quarter of a century passed before a dual qualification in medicine and surgery (including midwifery), became obligatory under the Medical Amendment Act of 1886. Before this, however, Scotland along with Ireland had led the way in offering a conjoint board for students to acquire a dual qualification in surgery and medicine. It was in 1878 that the Royal Colleges of Surgeons and Physicians in Edinburgh and Glasgow had offered this joint qualification, but it was not until the 1880s that England succeeded in creating a double qualification from the Royal Colleges of Physicians and Surgeons.

There were therefore many qualifying routes to practice. At first, as we have seen, the most popular combination was an LSA taken with a surgical qualification (licentiate, member, or later in the career, fellow) from the Royal College of Surgeons. From the late nineteenth century the GP database

---

[64] C. Singer and S. W. F. Holloway, 'Early Medical Education in England in relation to the Pre-History of London University', *MH*, 4 (1960), 4. The Directory was incomplete, but nevertheless broadly indicative.

[65] Since MDs were usually gained later in life, this figure understated their final incidence, as the figures later in the chapter indicated.

[66] *Special Report*, appendix paper 10 and table 11.

[67] J. F. Fleetwood, *The History of Medicine in Ireland* (Dublin, 1983), 132, 179.

suggests that the MB or BM was displacing the LSA. Qualifications from
the Royal College of Physicians were also sought. In the twentieth century
the B.Ch. or Ch.B., which had previously found limited favour, became a
popular medical degree. From the 1870s and 1880s small numbers took the
BS, as well as some taking the Scottish Triple. A proportion sought an MD;
but although this showed an initial rise in the early nineteenth century to
more than one in two of doctors in the mid-nineteenth century GP cohorts,
the trend from the later Victorian period was one of decline to only one in
seven GPs by the end of the period. This may reflect the more rigorous
examination that had turned it into a higher degree. Figure 3.1 simplifies a
complex historical pattern by portraying those qualifications with a long-
term declining trend amongst our GP cohorts with bar graphs (the LSA,
the MD and the L/M/F/RCS), and those with an upward one by line
graphs (the MB/BM, the B.Ch./Ch.B. and the L/M/F/RCP.) Apart from
the main 'bread and butter' qualifications there were also a few recruits for
more specialist qualifications. In midwifery a very small minority acquired
a Licentiate in Midwifery, and the Bachelor in Midwifery attracted even
fewer. The foundation of the Royal College of Obstetrics and Gynaecology
in 1929 led to a handful acquiring its membership, fellowship, or diplomate
in obstetrics. The dates refer to the year of qualification of successive cohorts
of doctors.

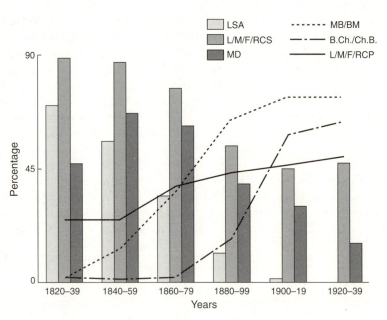

Fig. 3.1. Principal qualifications by GP cohort, 1820–1939

An Evolving Education

In Britain and the USA medical education took place in a liberal and lais-sez-faire environment which facilitated a complex and diffuse structure. This contrasted with the more centralized and regulated models developed within French or German statism.[68] In 1800 key questions still to be decided had included the character of pre-clinical education, the location of medical training (whether in hospital, clinic, university, or through practi-cal apprenticeship), the content of the curriculum, the relationship of surgery to physic, the part to be played by anatomy and dissection in train-ing, and the relationship of bedside medicine to experimental science.[69] By 1850 only a few of these issues had been clarified, with apprenticeship falling out of fashion, and anatomy and dissection having moved more cen-trally within the student's preparation. Before 1850 training had been more practically orientated, and this had distinct advantages for the general prac-titioner, when compared with the later, more academically focused curricu-lum located in universities, which was geared to the production of specialists. During the early nineteenth century London dispensaries had given those aspiring to qualify for the LSA clinical knowledge that had util-ity for the prospective generalist.[70] Also helpful were the public dispensaries that continued to be used for clinical training at Scottish universities until 1948.[71] From mid-century the curriculum of provincial medical schools was beginning to show the increased importance given to academic science in medical education with their endowments and appointments focused partic-ularly on pre-clinical scientific subjects.[72]

Any adoption by Britain of the German model of experimental medicine in training faced considerable impediments. Both teachers and students retained their loyalty to the British tradition of clinical medicine, with its emphasis on applied scientific skills, despite a growing public consciousness of the triumphs of bacteriology in the diagnosis and control of disease.[73] Only gradually was it perceived that the bedside socio-clinical skills of traditional medicine were in fact complementary to laboratory-based insights in modern medicine, and that both were equally necessary for a well-trained doctor. However, this process of assimilation was much less assured than in Germany or the United States. Indeed, the influential critic, Abraham Flexner, con-sidered the early twentieth-century British system still excessively practical

[68] Bonner, *Physician*, 31, 60. [69] Ibid. 59.

[70] S. C. Lawrence, 'Private Enterprise and Public Interest: Medical Education and the Apothecaries Act', in R. French and A. Wear (eds.), *British Medicine in an Age of Reform* (1992), 62–3.

[71] Z. Cope, 'The Influence of the Free Dispensaries upon Medical Education in Britain', *MH*, 13 (1969), 36; G. McLachlan (ed.), *Medical Education and Medical Care* (Oxford, 1977), 60.

[72] S. V. P. Butler, 'A Transformation in Training: The Formation of University Medical Faculties in Manchester, Leeds and Liverpool, 1820–1884', *MH*, 30 (1986), 131.

[73] Bonner, *Physician*, 275, 279.

in nature, and wanted more scientifically orientated courses.[74] One important reason for the conservative stance was the royal colleges' interest in preserving their role in examining, and another was the comparative lack of places in British universities with which to develop new approaches. The Victoria University of Manchester (created in 1881) did something to alleviate this situation since it had separate schools at Leeds and Liverpool, which gained powers to grant their own degrees in 1904. Another obstacle in establishing a more scientific and university-based approach to medical education was the situation in London where there were twelve hospital schools. The Royal Commission on University Education in London highlighted the conflict between hospital clinicians and university scientists, and in its recommendations inclined strongly towards the adoption of the German/US university model.[75] Flexner's highly influential *Medical Education in Europe* (1912) argued that medicine and science were inseparable so that inductive learning by doing was necessary for medical students. But during the interwar years the continuing strength of traditional clinical medicine (focused on the inculcation of observational skills), together with the huge expense involved in developing laboratory medical science slowed the advance of these new approaches in Britain.

Progressing more rapidly in British training after 1850, however, was a change towards a more formal structuring of study. This occurred during the late nineteenth century as a result of the GMC's role in providing guidelines, and which effectively standardized medical education together with the ensuing experience of medical students. The student was to take a preliminary examination showing liberal educational attainment, to spend a minimum of five years in medical study and not to practise before the age of 21 years. The pattern of the undergraduate medical curriculum was firmly established on a pattern of two to three years of pre-clinical studies, and then three to four years of clinical training.[76] In comparison with the precisely structured medical curriculum found in other countries, however, the British models still appeared incompletely articulated.[77] The first two years were spent in the basic sciences related to medical practice, and thus offered a sound grounding for potential general practitioners. During the first year chemistry, physics, and biology, perhaps also *materia medica* (pharmacy) was studied. Those who had had a good scientific grounding at school found this repetitious, but for others it was a hard slog. In the next year, anatomy and the rapidly developing science of physiology, were the main foci of study, often with some histology being taken as a grounding for pathology. Some dissections might be attempted and this brought the students' calling nearer, quickening the appetite for study. The First and Second Examinations followed

[74] Bonner, *Physician*, 'Abraham Flexner as Critic of British and Continental Medical Education', *MH*, 33 (1989), 471.

[75] Id., *Physician*, 295–8.   [76] See for example, *BMJ*, 6 Sept. 1890, for the regulations.

[77] Bonner, *Physician*, 287.

the first and second years, whilst another two and a half to three years—spent in the systematic study of diseases—preceded the Third or Final Examination.[78] Some students found the transition to clinical study a disheartening experience because its abruptness disorientated them, and both the Haldane and the Goodenough Committees made reforming recommendations that the two should be brought into a closer relationship.[79] At the clinical stage students began to interrogate patients, and to use equipment such as the stethoscope, laryngoscope, or otoscope. At this point ward visits and work in the outpatients department were undertaken. Excellent training was obtained through students acting as a dresser, casualty assistant, or clinical clerk. 'At long last it was possible to make contact with the living rather than the dead', recollected one.[80]

Internationally, there was a remarkable similarity in the daily life of the medical student with four to six hours spent in lectures, two to four hours engaged in clinical and dissecting, and then—in theory at least—more private study. As a release from these long hours medical students often sought escape in rowdiness, drunkenness, and debauchery. These aspects of student life were as conspicuous as its brutalizing character was notorious. Even when sport provided an alternative outlet for youthful energy, a focus on work remained unfashionable. 'During my first two years at Barts enjoyment was placed before work' ruefully admitted a student in the 1880s.[81]

An account by one student in the mid-Victorian period is interesting, however, in indicating that even in this comparatively early period some individuals might be sufficiently highly motivated to withstand the ethos of student life. The account was as atypical as that of the apprentice Joseph Shrewsbury, quoted earlier. Yet in its evangelical heart-searching and highly charged motivation William Tyndall Griffith's diary entries nevertheless offer interesting insights into the pattern of a medical student's preparation for professional life. His diary, kept during the years 1855 to 1861, revealed that he saw medicine as God's work:

Let thy Fatherly hand I beseech thee be over me in these my fearful studies . . . and while others have the idle word and the unthinking mind which dares to trifle with that which has been the habitation of the Spirit of God . . . may I be preserved from their tone of levity and profaneness and that my studies may be blessed to the great ends for which God has permitted me to examine the work of His hand. Amen.[82]

Griffith came from Bangor and studied in London, passing the Preliminary Examination of the Society of Apothecaries, and attending lectures at the College of Surgeons and at Apothecaries Hall, as well as at St Bartholomew's

[78] *BMJ*, i (1901), 517–18; M. Foster Reaney, *The Medical Profession* (Dublin, 1905), 11–13.
[79] *Goodenough Report*, 146.
[80] Wellcome MS 5415, Memoirs of M.W. Littlewood (1888–1972), MB, BS (St Thomas's) FRSA.
[81] E. R. Furbes, *London Doctor* (1940), 14.
[82] National Library of Wales, 10209B, Diary of a Medical Student, vol. 2, 1857–9, entry of 14 Nov. 1857.

Hospital. He was keen to develop his surgical skills and 'did bone' (his name for dissections), whenever he had the opportunity. Practical work was undertaken throughout his period of studies. His first hands-on experience occurred at the Bloomsbury Dispensary. Here his work impressed more senior colleagues so that he was offered testimonials by three of them, including Dr Piddock, who promised to assist him in his career, and who hoped he would later apply for the post of resident medical officer at the dispensary. Griffith noted modestly, 'I was astonished to find he took so much interest in me.'[83] Later, he walked the wards at Barts, and (more unusually), also at St Lukes—the hospital which specialized in the care of the insane. Griffith gained further clinical experience by working at the outpatients' department of the Royal London Ophthalmic Hospital where, on 26 October 1857 he noted censoriously that 'they [the patients] were very unruly this morning'. His studious, busy, and upright life—filled with medical study and reflection on the Bible—was a conspicuous contrast to the levity of much student life. Long arduous days ended with self-reflection—'Am I living for eternity?' 'O Lord make me thankful I pray thee for the means of learning the duties of my calling . . . Amen. It is drawing towards 1 o'clock [am] and I feel much fatigued.'[84]

A more serious and committed attitude to medical studies was becoming more generally evident by 1900.[85] By this time students were also older, and faced lengthier periods of training, which may have fostered a more committed attitude to their calling.[86] The advent of medical women could also have reinforced this attitudinal change. At UCL, as at other medical schools, female medical students were highly selected and so—as a male colleague remembered—'the women, of course, were much brighter than the men'.[87] A woman at the Royal Free recollected that 'women . . . got on with the job a bit more. And, of course, we were teased as being blue stockings'.[88] By the clinical stage both male and female students had usually become more focused on their studies. At this point students joined 'the clinic' (in Scotland) or 'the firm' (in England and Wales) of a surgeon or physician, in order to fulfil GMC regulations of being a clerk for six months, and a dresser for the same period. A clinic or firm consisted of a group of up to a dozen people—two physicians or surgeons, one or more house officers, and a small number of students acting as clerks—who each week did a few ward rounds, a couple of outpatients sessions, as well as one or two operating sessions.[89] Students learned their profession, as one remembered, by 'waiting, listening,

[83] National Library of Wales, 10209A, Diary vol. i, 1 July 1856.

[84] Ibid., 10209B, Diary, vol. 2, 30 Dec. 1859, 16 Oct. 1857. Griffith's later career is unknown, but he may have found his calling as a missionary.

[85] *Punch* provided contrasting cartoons of medical students in 1846 and 1886 (*Mr Punch Among the Doctors* 1933).

[86] Bonner, *Physician*, 214, 218, 316–17.   [87] CMAC, GP 29/2/36, Emanuel Tuckman.

[88] CMAC, GP 29/2/15, Vera Gavin, MRCS Eng, LRCP, London 1943.

[89] *Goodenough Report*, 148.

learning, helping'.[90] Unfortunately, the increasing specialism of twentieth-century medicine thwarted many students' need to get a broad experience for a career in general practice.

Training was disrupted during the Second World War. St Thomas's in London was bombed so students did much of their training in Surrey;[91] and at Manchester training was interrupted because students found that departments that had been going to take them for training had been cleared for war casualties.[92] In contrast, anatomical studies were enhanced because there were 'sufficient bodies for you to actually dissect. You didn't have demonstration bits and pieces. You actually had to dissect it out.'[93] Work in the casualty department could involve dealing with a wide range of injuries from bombs; as when a V2 fell on Smithfield and the victims were treated at Barts.[94] In Liverpool medical students had the task of laying out the remains of those who had been killed during the Blitz.[95] Some benefited from the exceptional conditions in that it was now possible to follow accelerated courses, as at Sheffield where a five-and-a-half-year course could be taken in five years. Tuition went from 9 a.m. to 6.30 p.m., so that at the end of the day 'you were fairly knackered'.[96]

Medical teaching naturally varied in its quality and impact. Some teachers were charismatic like Sir John Graham Kerr at Glasgow: 'I sat entranced at the feet of a very great man, who gave me all the enthusiasm, and all the learning, and all the keenness for scientific interpretation of clinical signs in the human body which I have had throughout my life.'[97] Others, like Edmund Lyon of Manchester, socially diffident and therefore unwilling to assume a pedagogic role, must have demotivated the students embarking on his clinical course. He told them that 'It is so foreign to my disposition and habits to appear in the character of a teacher, that I think it necessary to say plainly that nothing short of the most pressing solicitations could have induced me to undertake the task upon which I am now entering.'[98] Most teachers probably fell between the inspirational and the inadequate, being at least didactically competent. But, revealingly, in interviews few GPs seem able to remember much about their pre-clinical teachers. Was this perhaps more a product of intellectual numbness resulting from the factual overload of courses, than a telling verdict on their teachers' skills?

Clinical teaching engendered greater admiration not just for consultants' skills but also for their personal styles. For example, the Manchester cardiologist, Creighton-Branwell's habits in examining a patient had a life-long influence on one member of his 'firm'.

[90] CMAC, GP 29/2/59, Samuel Isaacs.
[91] Ibid., GP 29/2/27, John Evans.
[92] Ibid., GP 29/2/49, Donald Gawith.
[93] Ibid., GP 29/2/22, Jack Ridgwick.
[94] Ibid., GP 29/2/26, Norman Paros.
[95] Ibid., GP 29/2/48, Bertie Dover.
[96] Ibid., GP 29/2/22, Jack Ridgwick.
[97] Dr Morgan of Rochdale (*Hansard*, vol. 422 (1945–6), col. 129).
[98] Manchester R.O., M134/1/2/8, Misc. papers of Edmund Lyon.

He always had a nurse to carry a warm, a hot, bottle, and he said, 'Nurse', and he held it for a moment or two, before he put his hands on the patients . . . And I've always warmed my hands . . . But the thing that stuck in my mind was his . . . care. IIis attitude that these are people, they're not just samples, just stick your hands on it, it doesn't matter what they're feeling. They're people who feel.[99]

This recollection also gives an inadvertent glimpse of the elevated status of the hospital consultant with a typically operatic style of ward appearances, supported by nurses as handmaidens, and students as chorus. It also indicates the contrast between this cardiologist's humane custom and the more usual hospital practice of objectifying the patient, signified in this text as a depersonalized 'it'. Interwar students at provincial medical schools had an especially positive attitude towards their teachers. There was said to be a 'very good' standard of teaching in the early 1930s both at Cardiff and at Newcastle.[100] A strategic reason for this may have been that the relationship between the consultants and the students was a close and durable one. Consultants were inspired by a mix of idealism and self-interest in devoting part of their busy lives to teaching; the pay-off being that later on they expected their erstwhile students to refer their patients to them.[101]

Criticism of the medical curriculum showed a swing of the pendulum from an early concern to add subjects, to a later anxiety to slim down factual content in order to develop scientific understanding. In the nineteenth century midwifery had been the omission most wished to see remedied, while during the early twentieth century preventive medicine, public health, and gynaecology were suggestions for inclusion. During the interwar period the pressure to subdivide the curriculum so as to pay lip service to emerging specialities meant a hopelessly overcrowded curriculum. One GP, Dr C. E. S. Fleming, spoke disapprovingly of the 'exaggerated value on mere knowledge as apart from reason' in medical schools at this time.[102] And in a seminal contribution C. M. Wilson, the Dean of St Mary's Medical School, commented in 1932 on the implications of cramming rather than educating:

The one purpose of students' years, it seems, is not to train and test habits of thought but to collect and store a set of facts as squirrels hoard the nuts on which they hibernate. These facts are his capital, and he must perforce live on it throughout his working life, for he has not been put in the way of adding to his possessions as time passes. Presently it shrinks, and he must needs replace it by a stock of worldly wisdom upon a growing discernment of the ways of human nature, so that soon he is as cunning in the management of man, as he is helpless in the control of their diseases.[103]

[99] CMAC, GP 29/2/49, Donald Gawith.
[100] Ibid., GP 29/2/59, Samuel Isaacs; GP 29/2/8, Frank Boon.
[101] Sir John Grahm Kerr in *Hansard*, vol., 422 (1945–6), col. 117.
[102] G. Newman, *Some Notes on Medical Education*, PP, 1918, Cd 9124, xix; 'The GP and the Curriculum', *BMJ*, ii (1932), 1021–2.
[103] Quoted in *BMJ*, i (1936), 1212.

Three years later the BMA reported that the medical curriculum was needlessly and unwisely specialized, overemphasizing the curative at the expense of the preventive, and thus failing to meet the needs of prospective GPs.[104] The Medical Practitioners Union lamented the absence of a medical curriculum that paid some attention to essential features of general practice, and to panel practice in particular.[105] In 1944 the influential *Goodenough Report* concluded that 'a drastic overhaul of the medical curriculum is an urgent necessity'. General medicine should be the most important part of training and should give greater attention to minor ailments, common and chronic diseases, and rehabilitation as well as enabling the graduate to recognize acute infections, abdominal emergencies, and malignant disease. Surgery should focus on general principles, and on the early treatment of conditions likely to be encountered in general practice, including acute injuries. Social medicine should 'permeate the whole of medical education'.[106] These radical proposals, with their emphasis on health rather than illness, on preventive rather than curative medicine delivered by purpose-trained general practitioners, should have underpinned the nationalized, socialized medical service introduced in 1948. Unfortunately these recommendations were not implemented, due to the power of specialists in teaching hospitals, and on the GMC.[107]

From Medical School to Later Practice

One in three of those starting medical training at Edinburgh or Glasgow had failed to establish a successful medical practice of any kind by 1885, that is within fifteen years of beginning to study. Explanations for this high fall-out rate included ill-health, death, financial problems and failure to complete courses, or to pass examinations.[108] Even those who did graduate were hardly well equipped to succeed. Almost universally taken up at the end of training were a couple of six-month posts in hospitals. Practitioners often looked back with regret at the choices they had made, and thought that obstetrics, and later on, ENT or dermatology, would have had a more practical application in general practice than the more obviously interesting posts they had chosen.

Graduates from medical schools at the end of the period did not think that an adequate preparation had been given for general practice.[109] A long-standing defect was that 'general practice may be summed up as consisting

---

[104] *BMJ*, i (1936), 1212.

[105] Modern Records Centre, University of Warwick, MSS 79/MPU/1/2/2, MPU council minutes 19 Jan. 1928, 16 Apr. 1931.

[106] *Goodenough Report*, 28–9, 31.

[107] N. T. A. Oswald, 'A Social Health Service Without Doctors', *SHM*, 4 (1991), 306–8.

[108] Bradley, Crowther and Dupree, 'Medical Education', 13–23. The Edinburgh figure was 36%, and the Glasgow one was 30%.

[109] CMAC, GP 29/226, N. Paros; GP 29/2/27, John Evans.

of a great deal of medicine, a fair amount of obstetrics and gynaecology, and very little surgery; and yet, the recently qualified man knows his work in the reverse order'.[110] A focus in medical schools on the unusual or serious conditions found in hospitals meant that young doctors could not diagnose the commoner ones found in general practice. Missing in training, as one GP ruefully recollected, was:

all the information, really, about the general range of illnesses that never turn up in hospital . . . that side of things, the undramatic, you never come across in medical training . . . What you didn't see was the other 99 per cent of . . . cases who never went into hospital.[111]

An even more fundamental defect was that, as James Mackenzie shrewdly observed, few teachers in medical school had been GPs and were aware of the problems likely to face the vast majority of their graduates.[112] Whether students were taught by GPs or not varied, but was much more likely at provincial establishments. At the College of Medicine, Newcastle, for example, all the surgeons who taught during the late 1870s and early 1880s were general practitioners.[113]

A crammed curriculum induced rote learning and this had serious consequences because, as more thoughtful commentators observed, one of the purposes of medical education should be 'learning how to learn' so that 'knowledge is essentially progressive'.[114] Those who gave 'Addresses' to medical students were fond of observing that even after graduation their education was only beginning. An eminent member of the profession warned that 'To be a thorough master of the profession in the beginning of his career is out of the question.'[115] He suggested that:

The description of disease, and the rules of treatment, are simplified in lectures and books . . . But you will find hereafter, that disease is infinitely varied . . . Every case that comes before you must be the subject of special thought and consideration . . . There is no profession in which it is more essential that those engaged in it should cultivate the talent of observing, thinking, and reasoning for themselves, than it is in ours. You have not done much more than learn the way of learning. The most important part of your education remains.[116]

Another guru was more encouraging to Edinburgh graduates in suggesting, that 'The books that you have plodded through wearily and patiently will glow with a living interest now when you read them again in the light of the

[110] Reaney, *Medical Profession*, 20.   [111] CMAC, GP 29/2/49, Donald Gawith.
[112] Quoted in Mair, *James Mackenzie*, 47.
[113] William Robinson, *Sidelights on the Life of a Wearside Surgeon* (Gateshead on Tyne, 1939), 45.
[114] W. W. Gull, 'Some Guiding Thoughts to the Study of Medicine', delivered at Guys Hospital 1855–6 and included in *Memoirs and Addresses*, ed. T.D. Acland (1890), 7.
[115] B. C. Brodie, *Autobiography* (1865), 173.
[116] Id., *An Introductory Discourse on the Duties and Conduct of Medical Students and Practitioners* (1843), 15–17.

needs of patients whose health depends upon your management.'[117] But at the end of the period, the ideal for a trained young doctor was a counsel of perfection that few can have achieved:

A general practitioner should possess a scientific foundation for his professional work and a proper outlook on the social aspects of medicine and the promotion of mental and bodily health. He should be competent in diagnosis and treat all simple disorders, including the milder forms of mental ill-health; and should be capable of recognising when a disorder is one with which he is not fitted to deal and of seeking promptly the proper treatment for the patient. Able to observe accurately, reason logically, and assess the claims of new knowledge, he should also possess a sympathetic understanding of people and their environment.[118]

After some years in practice more of these desiderata might have been achieved, but by then other needs might have become apparent. The exceptional GP took pains to address this, as did G. E. Hale who, at the turn of the century, paid a locum for a fortnight each year and went to St George's Hospital to update his knowledge.[119] For most individuals a more formal initiative was required which developed between 1872 and 1895, when the West London Hospital set up a systematic scheme for postgraduate teaching (the first general hospital to do so), as well as in 1899 when the London Medical Graduate College and Polytechnic was founded.[120] In 1935 the Hammersmith Hospital set up a Postgraduate School, which effectively marginalized the West London courses, and a decade later four other institutes joined the Hammersmith to form a Postgraduate Medical Federation.[121] Postgraduate education by this time embodied a number of approaches including general recapitulation and updating of earlier education, instruction in a special branch of practice, and a specialized qualification to enable practice to be pursued along more specialist lines. Amongst specialist diplomas were those in psychological medicine, ophthalmic medicine, in medical radiology and electrology, in tuberculosis, and in laryngology and otology. Those in public health (first established in 1875), and in tropical medicine were amongst the most popular.[122]

The predicament of 'rusty' GPs with a 'restricted outlook' stimulated the provision of short refresher courses during the early twentieth century. Demand usually exceeded supply.[123] In 1932 one Nottinghamshire GP went on a fortnight's course at the Prince of Wales General Hospital in Tottenham,

---

[117] A. R. Simpson, *Address to the Medical Graduates in the University of Edinburgh* (Edinburgh, 1878), 5.

[118] *Goodenough Report*, 39–40.

[119] CMAC, GP 23/5, Notes by Mrs Hale on her husband's practice.

[120] C. Newman, 'The History of Postgraduate Medical Education at the West London Hospital', *MH*, 10 (1966), 339–59.

[121] F. Fraser, *The British Postgraduate Medical Federation* (1967).

[122] *The Lancet*, 'The Conduct of Medical Practice' (1927), 250–6.

[123] BMA memorandum to the Goodenough Committee (*Report*, 220); Nottinghamshire R.O., SO NH 1/6, Finance and General Purposes NHI Sub-Committee (1929–37), minute of 29 May 1929.

but found only one thing of clinical note (an elastoplast method of treating varicose veins) and one of social interest (an ENT surgeon emerging from a Rolls Royce, dressed in the traditional frock coat and top hat which was becoming outmoded after the First World War). Six years later he attended a postgraduate course at Sheffield Medical School which was professionally more stimulating in terms of new pharmacological and therapeutic approaches, including radium treatments.[124]

On a more informal basis medical societies, both general interest and (increasingly) specialist ones had an important role in the 'horizontal' transmission of new ideas and practices between colleagues, and thus in enabling doctors to acquire additional expertise of varied kinds to give them a competitive edge in the medical market. These societies had long had the role of hosting clinical papers that played an important, sometimes the only, part in fulfilling practitioners' need for life-long learning.[125] A substantial proportion of general practitioners belonged to medical societies; over the period as a whole from two-fifths to one half of those in the GP database had such a membership. Professional organizations also held clinical meetings and lectures at the local or regional hospital. Branch meetings of the BMA customarily had lectures on clinical subjects and also meetings in hospitals where the most recent techniques were demonstrated. A well-planned programme of this type was that of the South Wales and Monmouthshire branch which during 1944–5, for example, had lectures on plastic surgery, rheumatism and its treatment, penicillin, industrial medicine, and mass radiography. In addition, there was a visit to the Miners' Rehabilitation Centre at Talygarn, near Cowbridge, and another to the outpatients department of the Royal Gwent Hospital.[126]

The importance of keeping up to date had continuing professional lip-service paid to it, so that in 1944 the *Goodenough Report* recommended that refresher courses should be a recognized feature of general practice.[127] Unfortunately, practical difficulties in finding time or travelling over long distances, together with some dissatisfaction over the utility of these events, continued to make GPs place a low priority on such optional activities. A survey during the early 1950s amongst GP principals found that one-quarter of the respondents never used such facilities for continuous education, while nearly a half used them only occasionally. Rather than the existing format of formal academic meetings, the survey found that there was a desire to improve technical competence through more informal and interactive clinical meetings with consultants based on hospital cases under treatment.[128]

[124] Harding, 'Memoir', 47, 64.

[125] J. Jenkinson, 'The Role of the Medical Societies in the Rise of the Scottish Medical Profession, 1730–1939', *SHM*, 4 (1991).

[126] National Library of Wales. BMA Collection on South Wales and Monmouthshire, Minute book of branch, 1942–52.

[127] *Goodenough Report*, 34.   [128] *BMJ Supplement*, 26 Sept. 1953, 129.

Given low participation in organized events it was left mainly to reading,—particularly of specially written refresher articles—to act as the staple for updating knowledge, with the *BMJ* and the *Practitioner* as the favoured journals. (Not that more than lip-service was always paid to this ideal, so that the examination couch in some surgeries was more likely to be the repository for unopened back copies of the *BMJ* or of the *Lancet* than of any patient being examined.)[129] An informal updating might come from recently qualified assistants or junior partners, whose more up-to-date ideas could transmit modern developments to the more open-minded amongst older practitioners. Also useful were the visits of representatives of pharmaceutical firms with news about new drugs. These were haphazard and uncertain methods through which to update professional skills. It was equally possible that the lines of vertical communication were one way only, so that it was only the assistant or young partner who imbibed practical knowledge from a previous generation, as had the apprentice at the beginning of the period.

Conclusion

In principle medical education was a significant mechanism for the cultural transmission of new ideas into general practice through the 'vertical'—or intergenerational—inculcation of competencies. Licensed training was intended to lead to qualifications attesting fitness to practise, after technical proficiencies within more general capabilities had been acquired. As such it should have given registered doctors an obvious superiority over unqualified practitioners in their treatment of patients. However, in actuality medical schools were geared far too much to the needs of a small minority of potential specialists to provide adequately for the three-quarters of their graduates who would become generalists. Medical schools failed the general practitioner in the delivery of key skills and attributes for competitive practice. Clinical training gave minimal opportunity to study common conditions, to become familiar with the earliest stages of disease, or to develop the interpersonal skills that would be vitally necessary in dealing with patients in general practice. The schools were strong on academic subjects but weak on professional practicalities. Each bias was a weak reflection of wider characteristics in British higher education that privileged the academic above the vocational, and the needs of an élite over the education of the majority. But these proclivities were even more strongly the product of a wider medical culture, where general practice was not regarded as 'an independent clinical discipline but was the sum of a number of other disciplines practised outside hospital and at a more superficial level'.[130] Only later did the concept emerge of general practice as a specialism in its own right dealing with primary care.

[129] CMAC, GP 29/2/61, Anthony Ryle.
[130] D. Pereira Gray (ed.), *Forty Years On. The Story of the First Forty Years of the Royal College of General Practitioners* (1992), 90.

The *Goodenough Report* had criticized medical education because in its organization and conduct 'there is failure to take account of the types of problems that most frequently face practitioners in general practice'. It recommended biasing medical education towards the needs of future general practitioners by giving a broad and liberal education in which fundamental scientific principles and methods would be inculcated, rather than a mass of factual knowledge. It also considered that there should be education in health as well as on disease.[131] The *Medical World* reacted humorously with the headline 'It is Good, but is it Enough', and hinted at the need for general practitioners to teach in medical schools.[132] More conservatively, the BMA commented later that 'With our wider and deeper knowledge of scientific medicine we have tended to lose sight of general principles in a wealth of detail; the individual patient is subordinated to our interest in the disease with which we label him.'[133] In order to further an understanding of each patient as 'a whole' it recommended an end to the teaching of compartmentalized specialisms.

A survey by the College of General Practitioners in 1953 found that only two universities (Edinburgh and Manchester), and two London Schools (Charing Cross and St Mary's), involved general practitioners in their teaching, or provided very short periods of teaching on general practice. It recommended that all medical schools should involve GPs in teaching students general practice; an aim achieved only in 1987. However, movement had occurred before this, for in 1963 a chair in general practice was established at Edinburgh, which was the first such professorship in the world. Within another decade all Scottish universities had followed suit, but only one English university—Manchester. The RCGP *Report on Undergraduate Education* of 1953 had also recommended a syllabus that included ailments seldom seen in hospital, early diagnosis and diagnostic problems, equipment, practice organization, health education together with a consideration of the GPs part in preventive medicine, and the family–doctor relationship. By 1967 the GMC recommended that undergraduates should be systematically introduced to general practice, whilst in the following year the *Report of the Royal Commission on Medical Education* emphasized the need to introduce post-qualification training experience. By the late 1980s the GMC's guidance emphasized the need for more interpersonal and communication skills in the medical curriculum. Some of the difficulties in so doing are shown in an earlier depiction in Plate 2. General practice was thus beginning to be perceived as an integrating discipline within the medical school.[134]

Throughout the period those intending to be general practitioners had undertaken a lengthy training and this meant that adjustment to changing market conditions was inevitably delayed; the examination system in medical

---

[131] *Goodenough Report*, 10, 12, 28.   [132] *Medical World*, 28 Apr. 1944.
[133] BMA, *The Training of a Doctor* (1948), para. 161.
[134] Pereira Gray, *Forty Years On*, 92–107.

CANDIDATE FOR MEDICAL DEGREE BEING EXAMINED IN THE SUBJECT OF "BEDSIDE MANNER."

2. Candidate for medical degree being examined in the subject of 'Bedside Manner', 1914

schools and elsewhere was a notoriously unreliable regulator of labour supply. An overproduction of graduates in Western Europe from the second half
of the nineteenth century caused overcrowding and poor prospects. (This was
overproduction in terms of ability to make a living, rather than of social
need.) 'Addresses' given to medical students from the 1850s onwards reiter-
ated caution about professional prospects. Medicine will yield 'an honourable
subsistence'. 'Medicine, is, I believe, its own sufficient reward. It does not
conduce to wealth, but it rarely fails to secure a competency.' 'At the outset
your practice will probably be for some time largely, if large at all, among the
poor.' 'Diligence will almost invariably secure an honourable competence.'[135]
An authoritative estimate in 1935 stated that 'It is estimated that three-
quarters at least, of those who pass out of medical school become "family doctors" sooner or later. The work is onerous and the income often inadequate;
but it is a full life, rich in human interest.'[136] The varied nature of attempts
to achieve this modest livelihood is the subject of the next chapter.

[135] H. W. Fuller, *Advice to Medical Students* (1857), 5, address given at St George's; T. Holmes,
Introductory Address, given at St George's Medical School to open the 1867–8 session; A. R. Simpson,
Address to the Medical Graduates in the University of Edinburgh (Edinburgh, 1878), 8; C. West, *The
Profession of Medicine. Its Study and Practice. Its Duties and Rewards* (1896), 100, an address at St
Bartholomew's Hospital, 1880–1.
[136] BMA, *The Medical Practitioners Handbook* (1935), 21. However, a study of graduates from
Aberdeen from 1931 onwards found a constant proportion of only about two-fifths opting for general practice. (D., W. D., and C. M. Ogston, 'Origin and Employment of the Medical Graduates of
the University of Aberdeen, 1931–1969,' *BMJ*, iv (1970), 360–1. The percentages were 41.3 (1931–5),
43.9 (1936–40), 44.5 (1941–5), and 40.0 (1946–50).

4

Reinventing Roles

'I SHOULD like to pay tribute to this really great general practitioner. He is one of the many "Unknown Soldiers" who form the backbone of the medical profession', stated one obituary.[1] General practitioners were familiar—yet surprisingly indistinct—figures within British society. An important reason for this was that their defining characteristics were remarkably fluid over time. Why did these mutations occur? Causes included a moving frontier between general and specialist medicine, a growing number of public and private appointments leading to increasing diversification in generalist roles, as well as a changing medical market. There were few, if any, grandiose dreams of ideal medical landscapes to explore and exploit, rather there was an ameliorist agenda of pragmatic responses to everyday challenges in order to yield professional or financial dividends.

During the second half of the nineteenth century the striking increase in the supply of doctors, had led to population pressure and competition within the profession; the resulting compression of income forced adaptation.[2] Overproduction of medical graduates—in relation to effective demand for their services—forced young doctors to adopt a variety of opportunistic survival strategies, and these shaped a developing heterogeneity in practices. A general practitioner's professional viability was facilitated if she or he could discover a local niche for a practice, and progressively exploit the local environment through social networking with key personnel and organizations, thus creating a good ecological 'fit' between doctor and community.[3] A territorial principle operated whereby a doctor tried to monopolize as many of the local professional openings as possible, thus excluding competitors from his or her practice area.[4] Diversification in appointments was necessary for successive cohorts to sustain their income in a competitive environment. A hierarchy of offices in terms of status, income and esteem meant that their number and type marked off the successful, from the struggling, practitioner. Such adaptive routines assisted survival, so that there was a differential rate of replication amongst different sorts of practices.

[1] *BMJ*, i (1941), 178, obituary for Dr B. M. Lewis, qualified 1888, who practised at Pontypridd, Glamorgan for nearly fifty years.
[2] A. Digby, *Making a Medical Living* (Cambridge, 1994), 147.   [3] See Ch. 10.
[4] Digby, *Medical Living*, 108–27.

The immense variation in practices which had been stimulated by the over-crowded Victorian and Edwardian medical market was then eroded by an exogenous shock: the introduction of the national health insurance scheme of 1911. This substituted secure capitation payments for uncertain fee income, thus providing a financial safety net. The vast majority of practices recruited an insurance panel of patients, and so a convergence in practices ensued, not least because the economic stimulus to innovate and diversify had been blunted. During the interwar period the stable platform of panel income meant that general practice was able to absorb a further even larger increase in the supply of young doctors, stemming in part from a general large increase in numbers at university, in part from people returning to complete an education interrupted by the First World War, as well as from men and women attracted by the economic situation of the medical profession.

Peterson has commented that 'The diverse patterns of medical men's careers include not only the fortunate men who studied, qualified and moved directly to a stable and prosperous practice, but also those whose careers are a record of repeated attempts to establish themselves.'[5] But whilst diversity is recognized, its actual pattern is unknown, and it is the purpose of this chapter to help chart and evaluate it. The main source used to explicate the changing dynamics of career development is the GP dataset, the nature—and limitations—of which have been discussed in Chapter 1. It should be noted that in the maps, tables, and figures, the dates refer to the year of qualification of successive cohorts of doctors.

Practices

Obtaining a medical qualification was merely the first of many hurdles to be surmounted in establishing oneself as a GP. A practice could be acquired by purchase, partnership or by squatting (thus trying to build one up from scratch); all three were problematic. The doctor's personal or social character did not always meet prospective colleagues' or patients' expectations. There might be a prolonged period before settling down in a permanent or long-term place of practice.

Where did people have their main practice? Locations were determined from information given in obituaries, supplemented by that in the *Medical Register*, and cross-checked by information in medical directories on locations at a ten-year and twenty-five-year interval thereafter. Cross-tabulations of university of first qualification by place of main practice in Britain are interesting in indicating the strong pull of familiar territory in choosing a prime practice location. A spatial mapping of practice locations has been undertaken

---

[5] M. J. Peterson, *The Medical Profession in Mid-Victorian London* (Berkeley, 1978), 126.

for Scotland, Wales, southern England, and northern England.[6] Cross-tabulations of place of qualification with that of practice have also been undertaken. The period has been divided into three—1820–80, 1880–1910, and 1911–48—to reflect the changing economic conditions. The first sub-period included years of diversification into a range of viable practices; the second covered the time when the most intense competition occurred in an overcrowded medical market; and the third comprised the more financially-secure period of national health insurance.

Map 1 illustrates the fact that in Scotland 'the export of university graduates had long been a feature of Scottish life'.[7] The esteem in which Scottish medical education was held meant that universities drew their students from other parts of Britain, as well as from the Empire and elsewhere. Graduates from Scottish universities did not confine themselves to locations near to their *alma mater*, more going to English practices than Scottish ones. Only around one-third of graduates from the Scottish universities of Aberdeen, Dundee, Edinburgh, Glasgow, and St Andrews succeeded in establishing a practice within Scotland. The other large, and increasingly popular, destination for Scottish medical graduates was northern England—up from one in four to two out of five. A handful went to Wales, only one in seven to southern England, and a declining proportion (down from one in five to one in ten) practised in London.

Maps 2 and 3 show the spatial distribution in their main place of practice of graduates from northern English, and southern English, universities. Map 2 indicates that graduating doctors from Birmingham, Durham, Leeds, Liverpool, Manchester, Newcastle, Sheffield, and York overwhelmingly travelled very short distances before establishing themselves in their main practice location, with four-fifths, later declining to two-thirds, practising in northern England. Very few went north to Scotland, a handful travelled west to Wales, more went to London, but the second most popular destination was one in southern England. Map 3 shows the spatial practice distribution of medical graduates from London and Bristol, and in most respects is a mirror image of Map 2. There is the same concentration on nearby destinations, with doctors choosing to put up their plate either in the capital (from a third to a fifth), or in southern counties of England (from over one third to nearly a half.) Again only a handful of such graduates later established themselves in Scotland, but rather more did so in Wales than had been the case with northern graduates. About the same proportion chose to practise in northern counties, as had been the case with northern graduates selecting either London or southern counties for their practice location. (Numbers with medical qualifi-

[6] Northern England comprised the census divisions of West Midlands, North Midlands, North-Western, Yorkshire, and Northern Counties, while southern England comprised London, South-Eastern, South Midlands, Eastern, and South-Western Counties.

[7] *BMJ*, 14 Sept. 1946.

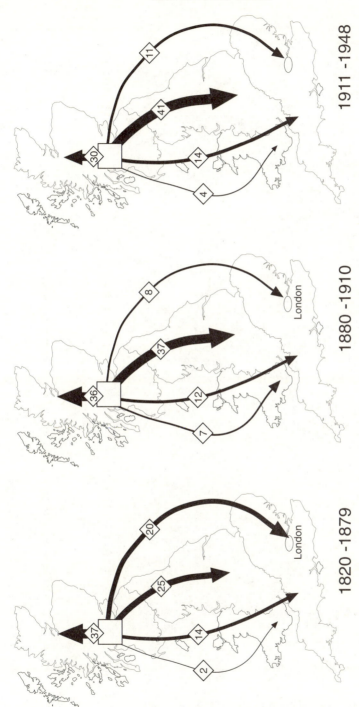

Map 1. Main place of practice for those qualifying in Scotland

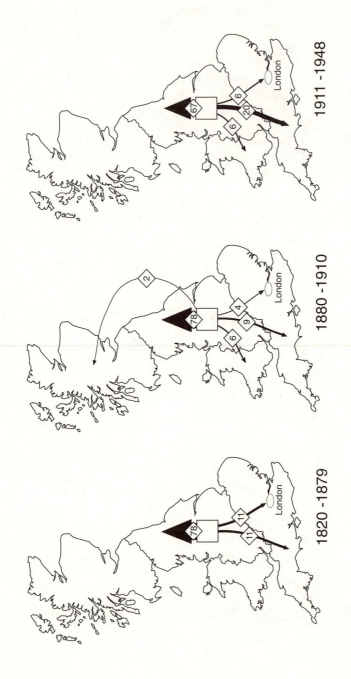

Map 2. Main place of practice for those qualifying in northern universities

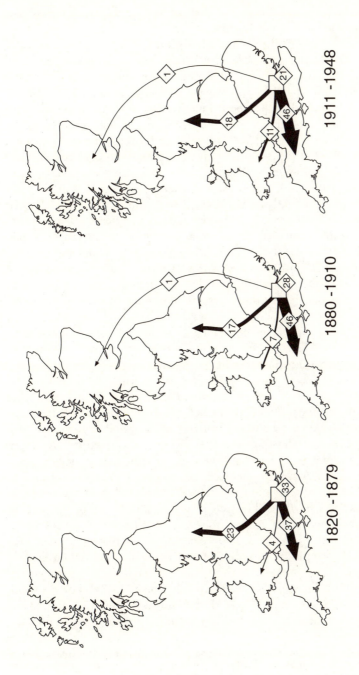

Map 3. Main place of practice for those qualifying in southern universities

cations from the Welsh Universities of Bangor and Cardiff were so tiny that mapping distributions was not feasible.)

Map 4 depicts the overall relationship of place of main practice to area of qualification. In England from around two-thirds to four-fifths were able to practise in the region or country of their medical qualification. This powerful tug of well-known territory in choosing a practice location after training was strongly entrenched. It had been found earlier amongst apprentices, so that in a sample whose careers could be traced, nearly half returned to the English county where they had been apprenticed for their first place of practice.[8] But the figures of general practitioners who had both qualified, and had their main practice location, in Scotland were much smaller, ranging from one-quarter to a half. While this perhaps reflected a greater difficulty in making a medical living in Scotland, it is also likely that some that were educated in Scotland had been born outside Scotland. Map 5 explores this point further by relating main place of practice to area of birth. An extremely strong pull is evident in this spatial distribution. It was potent in Wales and England where more than two-thirds were returnees. A finer calculation based on the county rather than the region indicates that this draw was most powerful in the north of England, where those born in Yorkshire and Lancashire were particularly prone to practise there. It was much less apparent in Scotland where those able to practise in the country of their birth formed a shrinking proportion of GPs. Here a striking decline was evident from two-thirds in 1820–79 to only one-third in 1911–48.

Map 6 reinforces this impression of a strongly localized general practice by revealing the percentage of general practitioners who later located their main place of practice in the region both of their place of birth, *and* of their university. Again a difference between Scotland and England is apparent, with the latter consistently showing a greater degree of correlation. Northern England again stands out, since here the habit of undertaking medical studies at a local university was pronounced. But, interestingly, all areas showed that the coincidence of place of birth, medical school, and main place of practice had weakened over time. This was related to the growth of the medical profession which meant that at least from the 1870s (possibly earlier) formal agencies played a growing role in finding personnel for practices rather than the previous reliance placed on purely personal networks centred on medical schools.[9]

Doctors with qualifications obtained outside England, Wales or Scotland, but who practised there, must be added to an already complex picture. 'They say that in Ireland, medicine always leads to the Liverpool boat.'[10] Certainly,

---

[8] D. Van Zwanenberg, 'The Training and Careers of those Apprenticed to Apothecaries in Suffolk, 1815–58', *MH*, 27 (1983), 147. The sample discussed is of those apprenticed to the surgeon apothecaries, the linear professional ancestors of general practitioners.

[9] See Ch. 6.

[10] GP29/2/44, Thomas McQuay trained in Belfast, and practised in Blackburn.

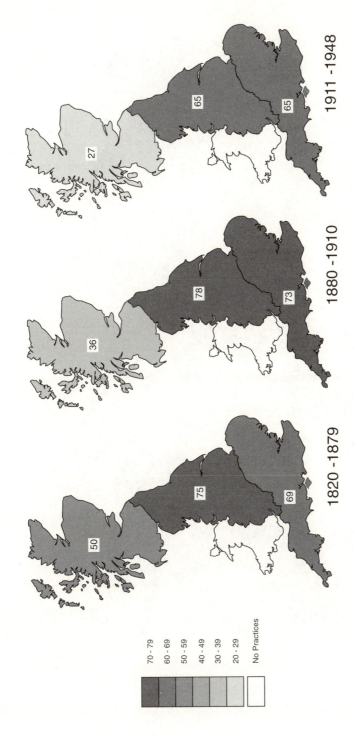

Map 4. GPs having main place of practice in area of qualification in England and Scotland

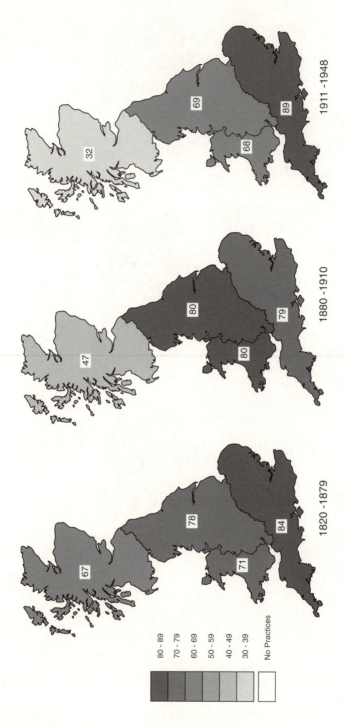

Map 5. GPs having main place of practice in area of birth

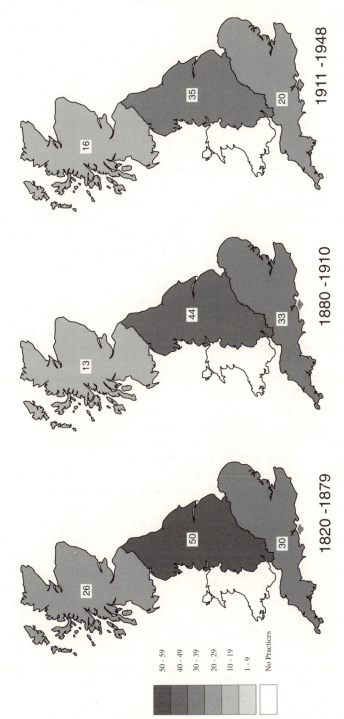

Map 6. GPs with the same area of birth, qualification, and practice

Irish entrants to the profession (like their Scottish counterparts), had a reputation for hard work, and thus for being able to establish a practice in an
area hitherto thought unpromising.[11] And immigrants from a wider world,
notably refugees from Germany and eastern Europe, also had the same characteristic.

Multiple causes operated to influence individual GPs' changes in practice
location. For a minority, health concerns were the deciding factor in mobility. Some found that the workload resulting from the large patient numbers
and fast surgery throughput inherent in an inner city or colliery practice was
not sustainable, as energies diminished in late middle-age, so that a move to
a small town practice ensued.[12] In other cases illness forced a move to a
healthier environment, usually to a practice by the sea.[13] Economic reasons
loomed large: at the start of a career the need to acquire a practice with a
viable income dictated shifts from unpromising to sustainable practices; and
in mid-career, especially, a modest build-up of capital could make possible a
move to a 'better' area, as through buying into a well-established partnership.[14]

One may speculate that the influence of economic pressures of varied
severity experienced by successive generations of practitioners is discernible
in the findings in Table 4.1. This shows numbers of GPs who had more than
one practice location. The early and mid-Victorian period, when almost two
out of five practitioners (39 per cent) had more than one location, was succeeded during the time of a more overcrowded medical market during the
late-Victorian and Edwardian period, by a rise of several points (to 42 per
cent). This then fell back very substantially—during the later more financially
secure conditions of NHI and private practice—to fewer than one in three
(31 per cent). Although up to one-third were involved in a second practice,
those moving for a third time were a small minority, involving less than one
in ten doctors. Professional overcrowding had been at its worst during the
1890s as a result of its hugely inflated graduation figures adding to the already
swollen number from the 1880s. In the *Lancet* a leading article in 1890 commented that 'In every profession there is constantly recurring the cry against
overcrowding, and although it is sometimes asserted that the Darwinian principle of the survival of the fittest must tend toward ultimate improvement,
this lends scant comfort to those who fear being crowded out.'[15] Presumably
driven by the logic of this situation, as many as 16 per cent of this decennial
cohort had three practice locations, and a further 7 per cent had more than
three. For example, after qualifying in 1896 the Scottish-born Dr Thomas
Johnston had six practice locations in the north-east of England culminating

---

[11] As we have excluded doctors not practising in Scotland, Wales, and England from the analysis
it is unclear how many from British training schools went to practise in Ireland.
[12] *BMJ*, i (1930), 844; i (1931), 38.
[13] *BMJ*, ii (1881), 1041; ii (1930), 401; i (1960), 973; ii (1970), 673.
[14] *BMJ*, ii (1930), 759–60.   [15] *Lancet*, 5 July 1890, 28.

TABLE 4.1. Number of GPs with more than one practice location (%)

Locations	1820–79	1880–1910	1911–49
2	29.4	32.2	26.2
3	8.4	10.0	4.5
>3	1.4	<1	<1
Total with more than 1	39.2	42.4	30.7
N	296	369	309

Source: GP dataset.

in a final, extensive practice at Blyth, Northumbria.[16] Even more mobile in this disadvantaged 1890s cohort was Thomas Grey, whose practices took in the length and breadth of England, including the southern locations of Weston-super-Mare, Camborne, Basingstoke, and Fordingbridge, together with Wrexham in the west, as well as two in the north at Corbridge on Tyne, and Newcastle on Tyne.[17] Contributing to the unusually high number of practice locations of this nineties cohort was the fact that almost one-third engaged in military service. Later, amongst those who were advantaged by the availability of income from NHI practice, the proportion of doctors having a third practice halved from ten to five per cent.

Medicine is depicted as being substantially dependent on self-recruitment, with the younger sons of medical families following their father's occupation.[18] General practice is also often conceived in terms of its strong familial character, perhaps because in smallish towns especially, multi-generational family practices of well-known dynasties were conspicuous. For example, five generations of the same family practised in Fishguard in west Wales, and three generations of another were found in Chagford, Devon or Buxton, Derbyshire.[19] But this has helped to create a misleading stereotype that overestimates the incidence of family based practice. The GP dataset does not support an historical interpretation of general practice as a 'family industry'. Before 1910 only one in eight practices (12 per cent) were family practices, defined as having more than one family member. Indeed, few practice areas could then generate sufficient income to support more than one doctor, so that even if a family practice had been desired, it was not feasible. After 1910 family practices increased to one in seven (16 per cent), probably in response to the augmented NHI income which was a major factor in making possible the larger practices that could sustain partnerships (see Table 6.1).

It has become a similar commonplace that medicine 'ran in families'. How accurate was this characterization? Two out of five GPs had another relative

---

[16] *BMJ*, ii (1920), 570; T. F. Johnston, MB, CM (Edinburgh, 1896), MD (1904).

[17] *BMJ*, i (1941), 68; T. C. Grey, MRCS, LRCP (1890), FRCS (1892).

[18] J. M. Peterson, *The Medical Profession in Mid-Victorian London* (Berkeley, 1978), 200, 205.

[19] *BMJ*, iii (1970), 351; ii (1920), 415; i (1940) 154.

within the medical profession during the periods 1820–79 and 1910–49. Interestingly, during the intervening period from 1880 to 1909, only one in three entrants to general practice were related to other doctors. This suggests that during this period an unprecedentedly large intake into medicine extended professional recruitment beyond traditional social confines (see Table 2.2). Also evident was the fact that, even amongst the fortunate minority who did have medical relatives during these late-Victorian and Edwardian years, such familial connections were markedly fewer. This suggests a weakening in the earlier cohesion of an extended 'medical family'. Since the life chances of young doctors at this time were less good in terms of advancing a career, any hope of upward social mobility through the medical profession may therefore have proved hard to achieve. Interestingly, a study of Glasgow University during the interwar years, when numbers aspiring to enter the medical profession also showed a huge expansion, indicated that the amount of 'inbreeding' diminished as it had done during the closing years of the nineteenth century.[20]

Appointments

Especially for those individuals without a medical connection, personal qualities were of paramount importance in achieving success. Coincidentally, the year after the Medical Act of 1858 which marked the beginning of this modern period of general practice, a book was published which focused on central Victorian values that would have proved useful to these struggling young doctors. In *Self-Help* Samuel Smiles admonished his reader that 'Help from without is often enfeebling in its effects, but help from within invariably invigorates.'[21] 'Help from within'—in the sense of self-discipline, strength of purpose and resilience—created the ability to obtain 'help from without' through forging useful networks. These assisted in obtaining the appointments that all too often provided the vital difference between professional success and failure.

To some extent community association came naturally as a by-product of professional activity, but the instrumentality with which such connections might be pursued, reveals one aspect of the mechanics of career development. For example, in the four-generation Ackland family practice located at Bideford in north Devon, W. H. Ackland (1825–98), obtained an élite recommendation—from the Earl of Portsmouth—to the Lord Chancellor for appointment as Justice of the Peace in 1864.[22] This post would have provided a useful social entrée to county families, and hence to the recruitment of afflu-

---

[20] A. Collier, 'Social Origins of a Sample of Entrants to Glasgow University', *Sociological Review*, XXX (1930), 277.

[21] S. Smiles, *Self-Help* (IEA edn., 1996), 1.

[22] Wellcome MS 7208, papers of W. H. Ackland.

ent patients. Three decades later his nephew and successor, C. Kingsley Ackland (1859–1940), exploited this social connection to advance the family practice further, obtaining letters of recommendation from another two members of the Devon bench to support his application for the post of Admiralty Surgeon and Agent. In addition, he used his own medical connections by soliciting the backing of two influential members of the profession—the Professor of Medicine at Kings College in London as well as the Physician to the Devon and Exeter Hospital.[23]

There had been a golden age for surgeon-apothecaries during the eighteenth century when fees were buoyant, and there was another golden age, this time in office holding, for their successors—the general practitioners of the mid- to late-nineteenth century. A growth in public responsibilities, as well as a contemporary medicalization of society, resulted in a proliferation of appointments, giving increased opportunities for GPs to hold part-time offices. An obituary for Dr Mackie, who practised in Fife from the 1850s to 1880s commented, for example, that 'He was most successful in practice, and in possessing many good appointments; among them the surgeonship of the Fife County Prison, besides factory, parochial and insurance appointments, and honorary offices in the Fifeshire Volunteers and Artillery.'[24]

TABLE 4.2. Numbers of non-hospital offices held by individual GPs, 1820–1949 (% of cohort)

Number of appointments	1820–79	1880–1909	1910–49
6 or more	6	7	2
5	5	5	2
4	5	8	5
3	8	11	8
2	18	20	15
1	22	19	22
Total with 1 or more	64	71	54
N	296	369	309

Source: GP dataset.

How important for the general practitioner were appointments outside institutions? The GP database indicates that the majority of general practitioners held an appointment of some kind. Table 4.2 indicates that before 1880 around two out of three did so, in the succeeding thirty years this improved to seven out of ten, before falling back during the more secure years from 1910 to 1949 to little more than one in two. The most widely held appointment was that of medical officer to a poor law union (in England and

---

[23] Wellcome MS 7211, correspondence of C. K. Ackland, letters of 6–7 Oct. 1894 from Phil Wood, Henry Davy, Lionel Beale.
[24] *BMJ*, ii (1880), 34. Obituary of Dr J. W. Mackie, of Cupar, Fife, who qualified in 1848.

TABLE 4.3.   Non-hospital appointments frequently held by GPs, 1840–1939 (% of cohort)

Type of appointment	1840–59	1860–79	1880–99	1900–19	1920–39
Poor law	30	40	28	20	8
Public vaccinator	14	19	20	14	5
MOH	14	24	18	12	5
School	5	7	10	10	2
Police	5	10	10	7	8
Post Office	1	11	12	9	5
Military	8	4	7	6	4

Source: GP dataset.

Wales) or burgh (in Scotland); as many as two out of five in the GP database held such an office in the mid-Victorian years, (see Table 4.3). They were particularly valuable in rural areas because there was not the proliferation of appointments available in towns. In a small minority of cases the post of medical officer to a poor-law district and/or to the workhouse was held alongside an appointment as a public vaccinator.[25] Another key appointment was that of Medical Officer of Health—with about one in four active in this role at its peak of popularity among the cohorts who qualified in the 1860s and 1870s.[26] Selection as a school medical officer offered another career option, and as many as one in ten chose it during the decades from 1880 to 1920. Appointment as Victorian police surgeons or post office surgeons involved a comparable proportion from the 1860s to 1890s. In addition, as many as one in five general practitioners also held what may collectively be termed industrial posts (in factories, quarries, works, mines, and railway or canal companies) during the same years[27] (see Table 10.1).

Although it is possible that the GP dataset showed a slight bias towards the successful and energetic after 1911,[28] these career trajectories suggest that from the mid-nineteenth century general practitioners managed to network themselves firmly into their communities through a huge range of paid and unpaid appointments. Constructing 'ecological niches' in this way helped differentiate practices, while enterprise in discovering or securing medically related appointments enhanced chances of survival. Opportunistic strategies could involve using a practitioner's religious and ethnic background to further practices, more especially in Irish-Catholic or Jewish communities.[29] Initiatives for career advancement might be based on political or military connection, while sporting interests might lead to paid appointments as medical

---

[25] The GP dataset indicated 13 per cent (1820–79); 17 per cent (1880–1909); 6 per cent (1911–48) had joint appointments of this type.

[26] See Ch. 11.   [27] See Ch. 10.   [28] See Ch. 1.

[29] *BMJ*, ii (1960), 471; ii (1910), 666; ii (1970), 547; i (1970), 763. See also Peterson, *Medical Profession*, 109.

officer to a race meeting, a football club, or a racing circuit.[30] Once a single high-profile position was obtained, its public visibility assisted the holder to advance further. For example, a young Paddington general practitioner, Dr Danford Thomas, was elected Deputy Coroner for Central Middlesex in 1874, the following year he obtained the post of MOH for Willesden, and on the death of the Coroner in 1881, Danford Thomas succeeded him. Interestingly he was elected on the basis of an 'Address' that emphasized the importance of medical qualifications for this medico-legal position.

Perhaps, not entirely coincidentally, Danford Thomas was the son of a clergyman who held the socially-influential office of Grand Chaplain of England in the Freemasons.[31] A small minority of GPs was a member of this hidden but powerful group; the GP database suggests that in different periods between 4 and 12 per cent were actually known to be Masons. Membership of an élite association such as this facilitated valuable introductions, opening the way to patronage by affluent households or to appointment in prestigious offices. But even non-élite—but highly visible posts—might also give a strategic impulse to practice development, as in the case of a young ambulance surgeon whose name had become a household word in Liverpool. On the strength of this he built up a successful practice.[32]

Another sign of social integration into a range of groups and activities was the growth of gatekeeping roles by doctors: over one-fifth of practitioners in the GP database did work as a medical referee between 1850 and 1910, a proportion which thereafter declined.[33] Taken together non-hospital appointments provided income for many doctors which made all the difference between professional success and failure. About one-quarter of the income of country practices, and one-fifth in urban ones, was provided by this means during the late-Victorian and Edwardian periods.[34]

In 1884 the Lancet warned that 'the [Medical] Register shows a steady increase in the number of persons registering annually . . . an increase confirmed by the competition in the profession and the obvious excess of practitioners'.[35] Using a dataset drawn from practice sales advertisements my earlier estimates suggested that between 1877 and 1909 the proportion of doctors having income from appointments declined in country practices from two-thirds to a half, and in urban ones from a half to one-fifth. During the twentieth century increasing specialization resulted in the conversion of many part-time posts, formerly held by general practitioners, to full-time appointments, so that by the interwar period GPs were apprehensive about their marginalization.[36] Although the trend to full-time positions was evident in

---

[30] BMJ, i (1940), 237; ii (1950), 895; ii (1960), 870; iv (1970), 593.

[31] George Danford Thomas, MRCS (England, 1871), MD (Bruxelles, 1876); (J. Leyland, Contemporary Medical Men and their Professional Work (2 vols., Leicester, 1888), vol. ii, 224–8).

[32] BMJ, i (1900), 1567. I am most grateful to Mr S. R. Turner for this information on his ancestor.

[33] See Ch. 9 for a discussion of gatekeeping.

[34] Digby, Medical Living, 124.

[35] Lancet, 26 July 1884, 159.

[36] See Ch. 11.

MOH posts, it was less well advanced in the School Medical Service,[37] whilst part-time appointments in the police force, post office, factories and collieries, and works continued to be made available.

Emigration and Immigration

Pressures in the home medical market could be alleviated through using external outlets. A transnational perspective is useful in highlighting the ties of mutual culture and interdependence between Europe and a wider world, and within this between Britain and its Empire.[38] Doctors working abroad, together with those in the armed services, comprised nearly one-fifth of the entries in the *Medical Directory*, and during the interwar years this was almost one-quarter. A substantial number of doctors working in the Empire had been trained in British medical schools (especially Edinburgh), although relatively few on the *Medical Register* provided a colonial attribution (4 per cent in 1921 rising to 8 per cent by 1946). Many colonial doctors read the *British Medical Journal*, or belonged to the British Medical Association; their professional outlook was accordingly coloured by this. Doctors in the South African Cape, for example, saw the *BMJ* as holding 'the mirror up to the profession in an altogether admirable way'.[39] A further internationalist leavening was given by the small minority in the profession who served in the Colonial Medical Service, usually in West Africa but also in East Africa, the Sudan, Fiji, and elsewhere. And those doctors who had been born overseas, or had spent part of their careers within the British Empire, might play an active professional part in strengthening the links between metropole and colony. One such was E. J. Gomez, who had been educated in Trinidad, but who practised as a general practitioner in west Somerset, serving for fifteen years on the Dominions Committee of the BMA.[40]

Doctors were aware that having made a substantial investment in a prolonged training they were locked into their profession, so that they needed to be flexible in responding to the opportunities given by an international medical market. The pull of imperial territories amongst young doctors was strong, more especially amongst Scottish and Irish practitioners. In the second half of the nineteenth century these young medical graduates became disproportionately represented in the Indian Medical Service, the Naval

---

[37] PEP, *Report on the British Health Services* (1937), p.157.

[38] D. Arnold, 'Introduction', in D. Arnold (ed.), *Warm Climates and Western Medicine; the Emergence of Tropical Medicine, 1500–1900* (Amsterdam, 1996), 11–12.

[39] *South African Medical Journal*, V (1898), 267; D. Dyason, 'The Medical Profession in Colonial Victoria', in R. MacLeod and M. Lewis (eds.), *Disease, Medicine and Empire. Perspectives on Western Medicine and the Experience of European Expansion* (1988), 199–200.

[40] *BMJ*, i (1940), 914–15, Obituary of Francis Joseph Gomez (1882–1940), MRCS, LRCP (London, 1900).

Medical Service, and the Army Medical Department.[41] During the difficult economic conditions of the 1890s these three destinations became 'rafts on which groups of men are struggling to exist in the storm'.[42] Buoyant recruitment to the Army Medical Department was interpreted in similar terms. 'Our profession is, in fact, overstocked, and the strife to gain a living is very great. . . . In times of commercial depression young men are wont to enter our profession, and so, of late years, our ranks have been preternaturally filled.'[43]

During times of overcrowding and economic depression during the 1880s and 1890s, and again during the interwar years, there was an increase in the proportion of doctors who worked abroad or took posts as ship's doctors. Allegedly the latter was made up of 'the amateur, the toper, the "dead beat" and the professional. The first is often youthful and enterprising—perhaps a medical student who has just secured his "licence to kill".'[44] Some ship's surgeons went on to establish a practice abroad, as did the young Pembrokeshire man, John Day, who after serving twice aboard ship, set up a practice in Geelong, Australia.[45] For the period 1880–1900 the GP database reveals that the percentage taking posts as a ship's surgeon was 10, whilst for civilian posts abroad it was 12, and for the period 1920–39 ship's surgeons comprised 8 per cent whilst civilian posts made up 16 per cent. More than one in five in these exceptionally large cohorts thus sought an economic livelihood outside Britain, compared with only one in seven in other periods. However, in the years before and after the NHS the number of GPs emigrating decreased to only 4–5 per cent.[46]

Good prospects for those finding it difficult to establish themselves at home because they lacked capital to purchase a British practice were apparently offered by colonial practice in South Africa or Australia.[47] The Cape in South Africa provided an instructive and well-documented example of the economics of such emigration during the late Victorian and Edwardian periods. Incentives to practise there included the fact that squatting rather than buying a practice was well established, that social connection did not have the same weight in creating a practice; and that a moving frontier provided opportunities to build a new practice around an official appointment as a district medical officer. A 'pull' factor was also exceptionally strong in encouraging medical migration since the mineral revolution, with its discoveries of

[41] D. M. Haynes, 'Social Status and Imperial Service: Tropical Medicine and the British Medical Profession in the Nineteenth Century', in Arnold, ed. *Warm Climates*, 210.

[42] 'Notes on the Organisation of the Colonial Medical Service', *BMJ*, 26 Sept. 1896, 864.

[43] Valedictory 'Address' by Sir Dyce Duckworth, *Lancet*, 10 Aug. 1889, 254.

[44] *General Practitioner*, 5 Mar. 1910.

[45] 'John Day: A Colonial Medical Life', *Journal of Medical Biography*, 3 (1995), 99–104.

[46] *BMJ*, iv (1970), 361; B. Abel-Smith and K Gales, *British Doctors at Home and Abroad* (1964).

[47] M. J. Peterson, *The Medical Profession in Mid-Victorian London* (Berkeley, 1978), 126; *South African Medical Journal*, v (1897), 36; *South African Medical Record*, iv (1906), 156–8; D. Dyason, 'The Medical Profession in Colonial Victoria, 1834–1901', in MacLeod and Lewis, *Disease*, 197–9.

diamonds and gold, made the Cape Colony appear as an attractive destination. In the eyes of existing practitioners 'almost every steamer brings with it one more recruit for the grand army of colonial medical practice'.[48] The Second Anglo-Boer War of 1899 to 1902 increased this to the extent that Cape doctors perceived an 'outrageous increase', in numbers of colonial doctors, because 'many hundreds of men were brought to this country in a military capacity, and . . . thinking that it was the El Dorado . . . many of them remained'.[49]

As a result both of medical immigration and of the attractions of the profession to locals, by 1891 the number of Cape medical practitioners was more than double what it had been twenty-six years earlier, whilst by 1904 it had doubled again.[50] During these forty years the Cape population had tripled, but numbers of medical practitioners had quadrupled. By the time of the Union of South Africa in 1910 the range and distribution of medical incomes was, in monetary terms at least, somewhat greater in this colonial situation than in England.[51] Opportunities for making 'first-class' net incomes of more that £1,000 per year were better at the Cape, but this was counterbalanced by one in four Cape doctors who made little more than a bare living, compared to only around one in five in this predicament at home. In real terms the differential at the top was substantially eroded, however, because the cost of living was higher in the Cape than in Britain. Substantial financial risks were therefore involved in the professional opportunities that South Africa offered doctors fleeing from a crowded British medical market.[52]

Inward mobility to the British Isles was also experienced. This was particularly evident during the interwar period when Nazism stimulated waves of German Jewish doctors to come to Britain. By 1939 1,200 German and Austrian doctors were estimated to be in Britain, together with about 800 from Poland, and 200 from Czechoslovakia.[53] By the end of the Second World War it was estimated that there were as many as 3000 such medical refugees in Britain.[54] Attempts by medical refugees to enter Britain took place within the harsh context of generally restrictive immigration policies. Within the medical profession the social and medical conservatism of a London-based élite, the financial anxieties of a provincial rank and file, the professionally protectionist and self-interested policies of the BMA or MPU,

[48] *South African Medical Journal*, v (1889), 21.

[49] *South African Medical Record*, i, (1903), 25: iii (1905), 230–2.

[50] G20–66, G6–92, G19–1905, Cape censuses.

[51] See also the figures given for Victoria for the 1890s which were broadly comparable (Dyason, 'Colonial Victoria', 198–9).

[52] For a more extended discussion see A. Digby, ' "A Medical El Dorado"? Colonial Medical Incomes and Practice at the Cape', *SHM*, 8 (1995), 463–79.

[53] I am indebted to Karola Decker for this information, based on the forthcoming *Dictionary of Medical Refugees* on which Paul Weindling and she have been working.

[54] P. Weindling, 'The Contribution of Central European Jews to Medical Science and Practice in Britain, the 1930s–1950s', in J. Carlebach *et al.* (eds.), *Second Chance. Two Centuries of German-speaking Jews in the United Kingdom* (Tubingen, 1991), 243–53.

together with some endemic anti-Semitism coalesced to produce suspicion, ambivalence, or downright hostility.[55] In 1932 the English licensing bodies acted inhumanely by insisting on medical refugees pursuing two years of medical study, as well as taking formal examinations in physiology and anatomy. And under the Aliens Act students could only study at medical school if, having secured a place, they had adequate financial resources to do so. This ignored the inconvenient fact that individuals could emigrate from Germany only if they did not take their financial assets with them. One saving grace was provided by the liberal attitude of those in the Universities of Edinburgh and Glasgow whose open-door policies—and one-year Scottish diploma—helped a sizeable group of medical refugees to re-qualify for practice in Britain.[56] Another was given by the Society for the Protection of Science and Learning, at first in its aim of assisting scientists, doctors, and dentists to secure career placements overseas, and later through its limited success in implementing its view that British science and medicine would benefit from the expertise of refugees.[57]

The excellence of the clinical diagnosis and therapeutics possessed by many refugees had the potential to enrich British general practice, but this was only realized to a limited extent because not all succeeded in practising medicine. By 1939 200 had been allowed to practise and another fifty were then taking re-qualifying courses. And by 1945 the foreign list of the *Medical Register* gave 243 Austrian and 278 German doctors, of whom 210 were in London, and 265 in the provinces.[58] Also in that year 88 German doctors and 23 Austrian doctors were listed in the *Medical Directory* for London, and a further 30 German and 13 Austrian doctors for provincial practices. One refugee who achieved a successful Edinburgh general practice was the Austrian-born doctor, Ernst Adler. Having qualified with an MD in Vienna in 1924, he spent another six years in specialist clinics before going into general practice in his country of birth, and then was fortunate to be selected in 1939 as one of only fifty Austrian doctors permitted to re-qualify in Britain.[59] In the difficult circumstances of relocation some individuals possessing specialist expertise had to re-establish themselves as generalists. Well placed to forge a new professional identity, because of their relative youth and adaptability,

[55] For anti-Semitism in British society see H. Jones, *Health and Society in Twentieth Century Britain* (1994), 80–1; *BMJ*, ii (1900), 1476, obituary of Dr Taunton; personal communication from Sydney Alder of Brighton, MB, BS (Durham, 1929); obituary of Maurice Papworth (*Independent*, 12 Dec. 1994); CMAC, GP29/2/50, Kathleen Norton on her family's reactions to her taking a Jewish partner.

[56] For example, H. Levy was a refugee from Nazi Germany, took the Scottish Triple, and established a practice in Streatham, London (*BMJ*, ii (1960), 871–2). For a general discussion see K. Collins, *Go and Learn. The International Story of Jews and Medicine in Scotland* (Aberdeen, 1988), 81–97, 133–57.

[57] P. Weindling, 'A Transfusion of Medical Expertise. Medical Refugees in Britain, 1930–1950', *Wellcome Trust Review*, 4 (1995), 43–7.

[58] Id., 'Contribution of Central European Jews', 253.

[59] E. Adler, MD, MRCS, LRCP (*BMJ*, iv (1970), 565).

were women who made up around one in five of all refugee doctors and dentists in Britain.[60] After she had qualified Margarete Samuel, for example, was told by her father, a German lawyer 'There is no future for you here.' She came to Britain relatively early, located her surgery opposite the Jewish Hospital in Manchester, and successfully recruited women and child patients from the local Jewish community.[61]

War and Peace

Temporary relocations were more widely experienced amongst general practitioners since many British-born doctors were involved in a range of overseas conflicts. Such duty to monarch and country was also shown through their activity at home in the Volunteer movement—later the Territorials. Here a depth of commitment was evident, not least because of the considerable personal expense involved.[62] It was said of the Leeds GP, Herbert Howe, that 'volunteering was never a mere hobby; it was a serious duty'. In the course of over thirty years' service he became an Honorary Lieutenant Colonel in the Leeds Rifles, the Seventh Battalion West Yorkshire Regiment, being buried with full military honours.[63] He earned the Volunteer Decoration, as did the Birmingham GP, Thomas Richards, who followed up two decades of service in the Volunteers with a Territorial command of C company in the 5th Battalion of the Royal Warwickshire Regiment. Significantly, in his funeral oration the Bishop of Birmingham commended Richards as a doctor whose 'zeal for his profession had not caused him to forget his duty to God, his duty to the poor, or his duty to his country'.[64] The volunteering service given by late Victorian and Edwardian surgeons went hand in hand with their civilian lives as GPs but, especially for later cohorts, territorial duties alternated with full-time service in the Royal Army Medical Corps, after it had undergone radical reorganization involving formation into an independent unit following the South African War. For example, during the First World War the West Riding practitioner, A. C. Haddow, served in France and Belgium, but then became a keen Territorial and served as MO to a battalion of the Duke of Wellington's Regiment, being given the Territorial decoration with bars. He was later given a command in the 147th Field Ambulance, and finally was promoted to colonel in the 46th Division during the Second World War.[65] In such a fluid, evolving professional context it is interesting to find that comment on regular army doctors (as well as on the efficiency of the RAMC) by erstwhile civilian prac-

---

[60] Weindling, 'Contribution of Central European Jews', 243–53.

[61] CMAC, GP 29/2/62, Margarete Samuel born 1901 in Kaiserslantern, Germany, LMSSA (London, 1931).

[62] H. Cunningham, *The Volunteers* (1975), 59–60; *RC on the Militia and Volunteers*, PP, 1904, Cd 2061, XXV, QQ 13,813–14, 13,824, 14,052–8, 14,085 (evidence of A. Clark and P. B. Giles).

[63] *BMJ*, ii (1910), 297–8.   [64] *BMJ*, i (1910), 970.   [65] *BMJ*, ii (1960), 471.

titioners was so often critical.[66] But both groups shared the experience of find-ing a profound disjuncture between earlier peacetime training and practice, and the imperatives of military medicine in time of war.[67]

Appointments as military officers were held by between 4 and 7 per cent of those in the GP database, (see Table 4.3). To the predictable list of wars where many served (the Crimean, Anglo-Boer, and First or Second World Wars), must be added those where an individual gave active medical service (includ-ing the Indian 'Mutiny', the American Civil War, the Franco-Prussian War, the Russo-Turkish War, the Boxer Rebellion, and the Spanish Civil War). A minority were engaged in more than one armed conflict: most commonly the Anglo-Boer and First World War, but also the First and Second World Wars. Those with longer years of service in the RAMC participated in more military encounters: Dr Johnson, later a GP in Guildford, managed to take in no fewer than five conflicts progressing from South Africa, to Korea, thence to the Boxer Rebellion in China, the First World War (where he won the DSO for service at Gallipoli), before retiring in 1933. He later rejoined the RAMC, becoming MO to the Royal Arsenal, during the Second World War.[68]

Numerically, the medical contribution to the war effort was important; from one-third to two-thirds enrolled in the armed services amongst general practitioners qualifying between 1880 and 1939. As would be expected, the generational impact of war was highly differentiated. Amongst those qualify-ing in the 1910s and 1930s almost two-thirds of doctors in the GP database underwent military service, more than one half amongst those graduating in the 1900s, while nearly one-third of the 1890s and 1920s cohorts also served. An impressive number of decorations were won for GPs' medical services in wartime, with awards for tending the wounded under fire especially notice-able. Henry Sylvester won one of the earliest Victoria Crosses for his Crimean War service—'For going out under heavy fire . . . there to dress the wounds of Lieutenant Dynely.'[69] Other instances included Ivor Ridge-Jones who was awarded the Military Cross for 'conspicuous gallantry tending the wounded under heavy fire' in Mesopotamia during the First World War; and the South African born Lancelot Bourdillon, who gained an MC for his medical gal-lantry on the Western Front. A colleague recorded that he 'remained quite unruffled in the most-hair-raising situations'.[70]

[66] Clwyd RO (Hawarden) D/DM/337/15, letter from Dr Hughes to Dr Morris, 4 July 1917; National Library of Wales, D.G. Morgan papers, diary entry for 20 Oct. 1938. See also J. M. Winter, *The Great War and the British People* (1986), 158, 165.

[67] Unpublished papers, I. Whitehead, 'The British Medical Officer on the Western Front', and J. Bennett, 'The British Army Medical Officer, 1900 to the Present Day', Conference on Medicine and the Emergence of Modern Warfare, Wellcome Institute (London, July 1995).

[68] *BMJ*, ii (1960), 1316. J. T. Johnson, MB, BS (Durham, 1899), MD (1903), DPH (1903).

[69] *BMJ*, i (1920), 456. H. T. Sylvester, later a GP in Westminster, MB (Aberdeen, 1853), MD (1855), LRCS (Edinburgh, 1853), LSA (1869).

[70] *BMJ*, i (1950), 255. L. G. Bourdillon, later a GP in Goring, MB, BS, DPH (St Thomas's Hospital, 1923–4); *BMJ*, i (1940), 714; I. Ridge-Jones, later a GP in Maker, MRCS and LRCP (St George's and UCH, 1912).

Service in time of war was of a multifarious character. In the theatre of war doctors were active with casualty clearing stations, field ambulance units, field hospitals, or hospital ships. GPs might find themselves in extraordinary situations, as did the Bridgend doctor, R. J. Phillips, whose interest in psychiatry led to him becoming a consultant psychiatrist to the British Second Army. In this role he was one of the first British Medical Officers to enter the concentration camp at Belsen, and subsequently was awarded the MBE for these services.[71] On the home front during the Second World War, general practitioners made a very useful contribution through performing duties which ranged from the extension of normal medical functions to wartime exigencies (such as acting as superintendent of an Emergency Medical Service hospital, serving on a Local Emergency War Committee looking after the interests of unaccompanied child evacuees, or sitting on medical boards to examine recruits); to the more distinctive features of the home front (acting as MO to the Home Guard, serving in a base hospital, organizing a first-aid post, or providing an ARP casualty service—with heavy duty during and after bombing raids). Even elderly doctors volunteered to play their part, as did Horace Potts who, although then over 70, found his finest hour through volunteering to run his general practice from Great Yarmouth General Hospital, whilst additionally doing the work of the two house surgeons who had enlisted.[72]

Although the war disabilities of some gave sufficient cause to remember military service, others resumed civilian life pragmatically where they had left it several years before.[73] 'Once again I settled down to civilian life', laconically wrote a young Devon general practitioner, after experiencing a very active war on several Fronts.[74] He was fortunate in 1918 in being able to rejoin a viable practice run by his uncle, whereas single-handed doctors had to start afresh, because no national system of safeguarding practice then operated.[75] A few doctors in a partnership could share, and thus minimize, disruption to their professional livelihood as did three partners in a Wisbech practice who agreed to do rotational service of six months duration each.[76] During the First World War the profession in Scotland was first off the mark in creating a Scottish Medical Service Emergency Committee to supervise substitution arrangements for doctors who had enlisted. By 1915 the BMA had assembled an equivalent body for the rest of the UK. This advised the War Office on priorities for recruiting practitioners to the RAMC; placing salaried public doctors first, panel practitioners second, and those in private practice last. By 1915 voluntarism coupled with professional pressure had led to one-quarter of the medical profession enlisting, well above the average for

---

[71] *BMJ*, iii (1970), 352. R. J. Phillips, MBE, MB, B.Ch. (Welsh National School of Medicine, 1933).

[72] *BMJ*, i (1950), 1377.   [73] See Ch. 10.

[74] Wellcome MS 5415, 'Memoir' of M.W. Littlewood (1888–1972).

[75] e.g. *BMJ*, ii (1940), 341.

[76] F. E. Lodge, 'Reminiscences from a Fenland Practice', *BMJ*, 289 (1984), 1761.

occupations overall. Doctors expressed concern that there were not enough practitioners left to deal with the needs of the home population, although also recognizing that they must defer to the 'paramount needs of the military situation'.[77] As a result of doctors' military service it has been estimated (on the basis of doctor to population ratios), that one-fifth of the population was left without adequate medical care, although ironically there was a major increase of life expectancy at this time.[78] However, a suggestion from the Medical Women's Federation that female doctors could substitute for men in depleted civilian posts encountered 'stubborn male resistance'.[79]

During the Second World War the profession protected the practices of those doctors who were in the armed services. Doctors, now too elderly to serve had to take care of the interests of younger doctors in the forces, and might work day and night in order to do so.[80] But, even given these more favourable circumstances, a GP who undertook military service almost invariably returned to a smaller practice because older patients had died, others had moved away, and no new patients had been recruited. And, for those who had qualified just before—or during—this war, but had not yet acquired a practice, demobilization was followed by a period of uncertainty as negotiations over NHS arrangements dragged on. This meant that some young doctors went into salaried posts in public health, rather than pursuing a career as an NHS general practitioner.[81]

Conclusion

Fluctuations in the supply of medical graduates varied the life chances of different cohorts, and the exigencies of war impacted heavily on the lives of individuals. Expanding numbers of part-time appointments at first increased practice differentiation, but the exogenous shock of the national health insurance scheme later reduced it, as convergence was stimulated by the transformed economics of practice. Through illustrating the complex dynamics of changing careers, and the interaction of individuals with their practice environments, the numbers and narratives in this chapter have revealed the striking metamorphoses and reinvention of roles that occurred in general practice during the century before the NHS. The financial dimension of these options was crucial to doctors' survival or prosperity in these competitive circumstances, so that the next subject for discussion is the medical market.

[77] Essex RO (Southend), DZ/60/1, Southend NHI Committeee minutes 1 Feb. 1916, 1 May 1917.

[78] Winter, *Great War*, 154–7, 161, 165, 186–7.   [79] Ibid. 171. See also Ch. 7.

[80] *BMJ*, i (1950), 1438.

[81] J. Hewetson, 'Before and After the Appointed Day', *BMJ*, 287 (1983), 1271–2.

PART II

In Practice

5

The Medical Market

Enough disease my wish would say
To keep me going well by day
Roll on then kindly sweet new year
Fill my purse without a tear.[1]

THIS piece of doggerel, composed in 1862 by a struggling Glaswegian doctor, expressed with unusual honesty the business sentiments that were the bottom line for survival in general practice. The gentlemanly pretensions of the British medical profession meant that these were seldom articulated; elevated medical ideals were seen as respectable aims, but mercenary realities as shameful, even dishonourable objectives. 'Needy men . . . void of professional and gentlemanly feeling . . . [whose] commercial spirit . . . is . . . strong within them' were viewed as having created an overcrowded and beleaguered profession in late-Victorian England.[2] Financial goals by themselves were seen as insufficient motivation for a doctor. A senior member of the profession counselled a young cousin who was contemplating entering medicine in 1914, 'Don't set out to practise simply with the idea that you are going to make sufficient to live upon, but try, if possible, to advance medicine by your own observations.'[3] Practising medicine and making money thus coexisted in an uneasy—if necessary—symbiosis.

Medicine as Business

Medicine—like other professions—responded to the market, and also attempted to control it, through creating monopolies.[4] Historically, markets also increased the heterogeneity of practitioners through a two-tier occupation. Elite members, such as specialist physicians or surgeons and barristers,

---

[1] Royal College of Physicians and Surgeons of Glasgow, 1/10/6 Pocket Journal of Patients Visited by Dr E. W. Pritchard, 1862 (MRCS, Eng., 1846, LSA, London, 1858). This showed very small numbers of patients.

[2] F. H. Alderson, *The Wants of the General Practitioner of the Present Day* (1886), 8–9.

[3] A. Mair, *Sir James McKenzie, M.D.* (1973), 325.

[4] R. L. Able, *The Legal Profession in England and Wales* (Oxford, 1988), 4; Digby, *Medical Living*, ch. 4.

created a professional monopoly by strong educational credentialism, with high standards of entry and long training. The much larger group of rank and file members, such as GPs or solicitors, suffered the consequences of an inability to regulate their numbers. In medicine this two-tier structure was reinforced during the late nineteenth and early twentieth centuries by the development of a process of referral, whereby generalists recommended patients needing specialist treatment to consultant physicians and surgeons. Whilst the élite were typically concentrated in the metropolis, the majority were geographically more dispersed, being strongly entrenched in provincial practice. Economic diversity amongst this rank and file increased before 1911 because a growth in appointments and in forms of collective medical provision resulted in a highly competitive struggle to seize these professional opportunities. After 1911 public payments from the NHI scheme provided a common underpinning of general practice which resulted in greater convergence.[5]

The distinctive economic features of medical practice are seen clearly once a comparison is made with law. In medicine it was usual to bill retrospectively for services rendered, on the basis of the doctor's individual assessment of the sum to be charged, whereas in private legal practice it was very common for a client and attorney to reach an agreement as to the inclusive fee in advance of the work being undertaken.[6] Items of legal service were more uniform, and thus could be charged more easily in a standard form according to schedules, whereas although medical fee schedules existed, these were often adapted or ignored by individual practitioners. Interestingly, an editorial in the *BMJ* in 1872 suggested that doctors should imitate lawyers in fixing fees according to the difficulties of the case.[7]

After 1883 a very important source of legal income in the form of conveyancing fees was regulated, and solicitors thereafter had less freedom than doctors did to operate flexibly in the market.[8] This system tended to multiply legal documents in much the same way that an earlier medical system of billing for items of medicine had increased the amount of physic prescribed. It also produced a similar criticism that the method of charging did not relate accurately, and thus appropriately, to the level of skill and time involved. Although the GP was better off than the solicitor in having greater elasticity in fixing charges, legal professional associations had more success in hindering price competition between practitioners, as well as in imposing restrictive practices that benefited practitioners at the expense of clients. Both GP and solicitor, however, had to deal with the same problem of extending credit to

---

[5] R. Collins, 'Market Closure and the Conflict Theory in the Professions' in M. Burrage and R. Torstendahl (eds.), *Professions in Theory and History* (1990), 24–43; T. J. Johnson, *Professions and Power* (1972), 59, 86.

[6] Turner, *Solicitor's Office*, 91–2.   [7] 10 Aug. 1872.

[8] The percentages fixed then in Schedule 1 were raised by one-third in 1918 and by a half in 1944. Schedule 2 related to the items of service in the form of letters, consultations and phone calls that could be billed (B. Abel-Smith and R. Stevens, *Lawyers and the Courts* (1967), 377–8.

the patient or client.[9] All in all doctors had more market opportunities but, at the same time, were economically more insecure than their legal counterparts.

At the beginning of the period many GPs gave a low priority to keeping their books, and this inefficiency could impact adversely on income. In law, by contrast, the fact that solicitors necessarily had to deal with large sums of money belonging to their clients soon moved accountancy to a more central place in office management as well as in professional ethics.[10] Whereas book-keepers were at first to be found only in the larger medical practices, many solicitors were employing experienced book-keepers before the end of the nineteenth century and, a few years later, book-keeping examinations for articled clerks were introduced.[11] Interestingly, although the business relationship between doctor and patient was usually relegated to a somewhat embarrassed afterthought in professional manuals, in law it was stated that 'foremost among the points of contact between a solicitor and his client is money'.[12] Solicitors were supplied with sets of forms with very detailed instructions and manuals for their use.[13] Even in medicine, however, the characteristic semi-chaos of so many ledgers gave way to more systematized accounts, not least because of the later part-time employment of book-keepers and accountants.

The evolving state of the medical market was shaped by major demographic transition, economic transformation, and a shifting boundary between individual and collective health-care provision. A trend towards a more urban society was obvious, although this was most apparent in England. Here one out of two were town dwellers in 1851 but four out of five by 1901. In contrast Wales still retained one-third of its population in the countryside in the twentieth century.[14] The rural practice that, in an earlier period had been dominant, thus became less numerically important, while its economic viability was threatened by suburban doctors who used car and phone to colonize surrounding villages. New forms of transport helped create suburban areas. Doctors were quick to follow, moving their residences and their practices to accompany this dispersion of affluent patients.[15] City-centre practices then became more uniformly working class, and of a cash and/or panel type. The latter also characterized industrial areas although, in heavy industrial and mining areas, doctors were often employed by firms to look after their workforce in a distinctively industrial type of practice. Expanding industrial and mining areas such as the South Yorkshire coalfield offered new opportunities for turn-of-the-century young doctors.

[9] Turner, *Solicitor's Office*, 80.

[10] The Solicitors Acts of 1933 and 1945 underlined the necessity to keep the money of client and solicitor separate.

[11] G. Sheffield, *Simplex System of Book-Keeping* (1897), 1. Sheffield was a law accountant.

[12] E. F. Turner, *The Organization of the Solicitor's Office* (1886), 48.

[13] For example, J. M. Woodman, *Manual of Book-Keeping for Solicitors* (1888, 1906).

[14] D. C. Marsh, *The Changing Social Structure of England and Wales 1871–1961* (1958), 108–9.

[15] Marland, *Medicine and Society*, 287–9.

This diversification of practices provided both opportunity and challenge. Late nineteenth-century entrants to the profession were more aware of the hazards posed by the medical market than their predecessors had been, although their strategies for dealing with the situation varied. In 1882 one young doctor walked through Southsea and inserted existing doctors and empty premises on a map, so that he would know both where there was competition, and where there was an opening for him to set up a new practice. He settled on an under-doctored area, in a house next to a hotel on a main road, behind which was a large area of terraced houses with artisan and tradesmen residents—all offering a good potential for custom from the well-publicized attendance at a street accident, through passing trade, to a good working-class residential clientele. His name was Arthur Conan Doyle.[16] Eleven years later a young man set up in Eton (a choice dictated by the fact that his father was a house master at the College), but found the area so well-doctored that in the first two years he had to subsist mainly on an appointment as medical officer for the local board of guardians, and a related contract for vaccination. He managed to expand his practice by setting up a surgery in nearby Datchet (where there was no resident doctor), taking on club work and any other appointments available, and through social contacts gradually extending the range of his practice beyond Slough. Although tripling his income within a decade his constant overwork may have contributed to an early death at the age of 38.[17] Another entrant to general practice found that Cardiff had one of the lowest doctor-to-patient ratios in the *Medical Directory*, obtained a map of the town, and pinpointed 'a central spot adjacent to tramlines where a 1*d*. fare made it accessible to other parts', took a small shop and turned it into a surgery. This proved to be the foundation of a successful practice.[18] Careful preparation did not necessarily ensure success as the young doctor in Southsea waited six days for his first patient, and never made more than £300 p.a. in the eight years he practised there.[19]

A later guide on *How to Start in General Practice* warned that 'any district is hazardous, as the profession is overcrowded'.[20] One of the hazards of overcrowding was the hostility to a newcomer by existing members of the profession in the locality. On occasion it appears that this old guard tried to use a professional association to make life difficult for a young doctor whom they regarded as an interloper. In Ammanford local doctors tried in 1907 to dissuade J. V. Rees, a local lad, from setting up in his first practice. Opinion

[16] A. E. Rodin, *Medical Casebook of Dr A. Conan Doyle* (Florida, 1984), 35; G. Stavert, *A Study in Southsea. The Unrevealed Life of Dr Arthur Conan Doyle* (Portsmouth, 1987), 17–18, 24–5. A. C. Conan Doyle, MB and CM (1881), MD (Edinburgh, 1885.)

[17] CMAC, GP 23/1 Obituary notice in local press of G. E. Hale; GP 23/2–3, practice cash books, 1893–1904; 23/5 later notes by wife about the practice. See also, G. Hale and N. Roberts, *A Doctor in Practice* (1974), 1–2.

[18] J. Mullin, *A Toiler's Life* (1921), 158–62. James Mullin, MD (1880), M.Ch. and LM (Queen's College, Galway, 1881).

[19] Rodin, *Medical Casebook*, 37, 39.

[20] I. G. Briggs, *How to Start in General Practice* (1928), 17.

in the local BMA was split as to whether Rees was just offering 'honest competition' or, as his rivals asserted, accepting dishonourable conditions in contract work with miners. Within the bitter contest then being fought between organized labour and the BMA in South Wales, it appears that the professional organization was in danger of being successfully manipulated into deploying restrictive practices by attempting to force the young man out.[21]

The risks involved in general practice meant that in the struggle for survival some fell by the wayside. In some cases doctors became impoverished because ill health or disablement prevented them from carrying on the strenuous lifestyle of the general practitioner.[22] The creation of growing numbers of medical benevolent societies to relieve members of the profession and their families indicated that, as one commentator phrased it in 1901, 'in the battle of life but too many practitioners come to grief'.[23] Uncertainties increased during the latter part of the nineteenth century as the growing numbers coming out of medical school forced young entrants to the profession to set up in non-traditional areas. In working-class practices the scale of bad debts might trap an unwary doctor who had not adjusted to new circumstances by running a cash-only regime. But even in these more difficult years formal bankruptcies in the medical profession were rare, a state of affairs which might at first indicate that professional survival was easier than was in reality the case. However, by investing in their own skills, failure involved not so much financial liabilities leading to bankruptcy, as a less than public waste of human capital with its associated private misery.[24] The downfall of legal financial failure represented only a small fraction of the actual incidence of defeat in the competitive strife for professional survival; a better index of general professional viability were the more numerous sale advertisements of obviously non-viable practice nuclei in the medical press. And even after the NHI scheme had made medical practice economically much easier, during the decades after 1913, financial worries were not necessarily absent. Indeed, an upturn in the numbers of medical graduates during the 1920s and 1930s meant that competitive pressures might again become pressing concerns. Revealingly, the Spens Report commented in 1946 that 'we have no doubt that low incomes have, in fact, been a source of grave worry to many general practitioners'.[25]

General practice required distinctive entrepreneurial and organizational skills if opportunities were to be realized, and these often involved professional

---

[21] National Library of Wales, BMA Collection of South Wales and Monmouthshire correspondence 23 Jan. to 20 Feb. 1907.

[22] Marland, *Medicine and Society*, 293; I. Waddington, *The Medical Profession in the Industrial Revolution* (1984), 35–6.

[23] N. H. Hardy, *The State of the Medical Profession in Great Britain and Northern Ireland* (1901), 15.

[24] Digby, *Medical Living*, 162.

[25] *Report of the Inter-Departmental Committee on the Remuneration of General Practitioners*, PP, 1945–6, Cmd. 6810, XII, para. 9.

adjustments that GPs were slow to implement. At the beginning of the period
an important transition was already being made from doctors selling a product—medicines—to charging for their skill, and patients had to be educated
that they were now buying the doctors' professional expertise.[26] GPs also had
to school themselves to appreciate that another crucial element involved in
transactions with patients was their own time, and that their pricing policy
needed to reflect this. An early instance of a general practitioner who grasped
that time represented money, was William Noot of Cardigan in west Wales.
His ledger for 1876 included the entries 'detained a quarter of an hour',
'detained there 1 hour', or 'waited there an hour', and he made his charges
higher because of this loss of a valuable resource.[27] Another example was
Hugh Parry Jones who was careful to map his journeys in Anglesey so that he
would visit a cluster of patients.[28]

Time-discipline was also implicit in the profession's late nineteenth-
century adoption of branch surgeries in order that poorer patients would
expend time in coming to see doctors, rather than doctors travelling to visit
patients. After 1911 NHI doctors came to appreciate that they needed a rapid
surgery throughput to cope with the greater demand for treatment by panel
patients, and applied time-discipline within the surgery. The lesson of stringent time-discipline was one that non-panel doctors were much slower to
learn, since rigidities in working practices persisted well into the second half
of the twentieth century. This conservative reluctance to effect change
impacted adversely on income.

Attitudes to time had an important influence on the way in which an individual GP was able to cope with professional pressure, notably that arising
from practice size. Surveys made after list sizes had been formalized under
the NHS indicated that both personal preferences and practice constraints
influenced the very different numbers of patients for whom an individual
doctor cared. Rural doctors thought 2,000 the maximum desirable, whereas
in the geographically more compact urban practice 2,500 was preferred by
most, 3,000 or even 4,000 by others. In fact 2,000 to 3,500 patients was the
norm.[29] Practitioners' comments on list size were interesting. The optimum
size is 2,500, stated one and 'beyond this number one would have to be a
"business man" doctor'.[30] Rather than being typical, the implication was that
the business-man doctor was a special type of doctor. This gives a revealing
insight into medical attitudes, suggesting that British general practitioners
were less economically focused than contemporary solicitors.[31] One crucial
area in medical practice where this was evident was in *creating*, rather than

[26] Digby, *Medical Living*, p.151.
[27] National Library of Wales, MS 12540, ledger, 1876, folios 102, 132. W. M. Noot, MRCS, Eng.
and LSA (1870, Middlesex Hospital).
[28] National Library of Wales, NLW MS 21759D, daybook, 1880.
[29] *BMJ Supplement*, 26 Sept. 1953, 151, 703.   [30] Ibid. 127.
[31] R. Able, *The Legal Profession in England and Wales* (Oxford, 1988), 19–21.

in responding, to demand. Doctors were the beneficiaries of a number of factors that stimulated demand for their services, but their active involvement was not always an enabling factor. The financing of medical services through social insurance after 1911 was the most notable instance of doctors benefiting from the creation of additional demand for medical services, whilst at the same time giving less than enthusiastic initial backing for it.

The medical profession congratulated itself that it was becoming indispensable in society.[32] Would sufferers and patients have shared this perception? An expansion of public appointments certainly gave the doctor a higher social profile, and an increase in third-party payers for medical services, particularly assurance and compensation work, pushed up the demand for medical services. During the next three or four decades the profession's enhanced technical competence also became obvious in such areas as surgery, vaccination, and immunization, public and child health, as well as in their prescription of new and powerful pharmaceuticals. A scientific authority was lent to the medical profession, changing cultural perceptions of doctors' capabilities, and a growing public confidence in the efficacy of the treatment they offered, seem likely to have stimulated demand for GPs' services. Competition from outside the profession remained strong, however, and this kept down medical fees. Self-diagnosis and self-treatment were resilient: household remedies were a first resort—especially for the minor or self-limiting ailment—whilst patent medicines offered a seductive option for the ambiguous, embarrassing or incurable complaint. We have seen that those without the formal medical qualifications that ensured registration under the 1858 act continued to flourish.[33] Whilst these were particularly evident in remote, rural and under-doctored areas, their more general appeal to sufferers from chronic complaints—for whom general practitioners might evince little interest—must have sustained a substantial clientele in many other localities.

The general practitioner could offer distinctive, because effective, help to sufferers from acute or infectious medical conditions, to those needing surgical intervention and, to a more limited extent, to people in need of preventative work, especially women (for ante-natal care), and children (for vaccination/immunization). Some expansion of the market accompanied popular appreciation of this, although it is problematic how many GPs *consciously* formulated strategies of demand creation to exploit this situation. Some doctors were aware of ways in which demand for their services could be increased. Thus practice advertisements might suggest that 'practice could be increased if guinea midwifery were undertaken' instead of the fewer cases of two guinea midwifery currently then being undertaken.[34] Enterprising individuals were mindful of economic opportunities in developing market niches such as suburban practices or branch surgeries. However, a professional ban on personal

---

[32] *Lancet*, i (1878), 19 Jan. 1878.   [33] See Ch. 2.   [34] *BMJ Supplement* 19 Apr. 1899.

advertising (other than the brass plate outside their residence or the notice of
a change of address), meant that doctors had to work hard to enhance name
recognition as a way of developing their client base. For young practitioners
favourable publicity following a street accident they had attended was probably the best that could be hoped for.[35] For more established doctors,
appointments at dispensaries or hospitals, secular positions in the local community, or membership of influential groups such as the Masons, served to
network them into influential circles, as well as keeping their name in the
public domain. But obtrusive financial self-interest in medical activity could
result in criticism and a loss of prestige, in contrast to the steadfast virtues
of professional dedication and disinterested concern for patients which had
widespread appeal. Revealingly, these steadfast virtues were popularly
ascribed to country doctors, and to 'family' doctors; both categories being
increasingly mythologized as their numerical importance decreased.[36] The
cultural context in which doctors practised thus constrained, but by no means
proscribed, responsiveness to market opportunities.

Sources of Income

Awareness of the need to stop increasing numbers of doctors from competing amongst themselves, to the point where they drove down fees, was particularly evident from the 1870s when there was a concerted attempt to
restrict competition within the profession by means of fee schedules.[37] The
initiative of a local branch of the BMA in issuing a fee schedule in 1870
(updated in 1874, 1879, and 1889), was endorsed by the national organization. Given the emphasis on the autonomy and freedom of the professional
member this came only as a matter of recommendation rather than of prescription.[38] In these schedules there was a systematic correlation of fees with
house rentals, which were used as a proxy for income. The lowest rentals
used were those of £10 to £25 per year. For people paying less than an
annual £10 rental doctors assumed that medical needs would be met by collective provision through friendly societies or the poor law.[39] And general
practitioners' appointments as medical officers or surgeons to these organizations meant that salaried office substituted for fees for this part of the population. Those paying less than ten pounds in rent comprised about half the
population in 1871 (54 per cent) but around a quarter (27 per cent) thirty

---

[35] Rodin, *Medical Casebook*, 37–8.

[36] I. Loudon, 'The Concept of the Family Doctor', *BHM*, 58 (1984), 347–62.

[37] Earlier fee schedules had also appeared in economically depressed years—1819, 1830–1, and
1842 (Digby, *Medical Living*, 149).

[38] *A Tariff of Medical Fees Recommended by the Shropshire Ethical Branch of the BMA*
(Shrewsbury).

[39] The £10 rental was conventionally taken as the lower limit for liability to pay the poor
rate.

years later.[40] Some medical fee schedules acknowledged this change by raising the lowest rental against which they charged a standard fee.

A change in income distribution had occurred which gave a new market
opportunity for more businesslike doctors to target those in the lowest rental
band in the fee schedule through creating branch surgeries.[41] These 'shilling'
or 'sixpenny' doctors—as working people called them—charged extremely
low fees. 'Four pence for the medicine, sixpence if I examine you' was the
refrain of one inner-city Birmingham doctor.[42] A colleague recollected,
'Competition was keen and charges much too low, as little as sixpence for
advice and medicine.'[43] As the alternative to visiting the doctor for these
patients was the free out-patient clinic at the local hospital or dispensary, the
GP had to treat at rock bottom rates. He did so for cash payment only, thus
cutting out bad debts. The sixpenny doctor thus adopted an economically
rational strategy in maximizing numbers through having a fast throughput at
a low fee.

Elsewhere in the market minimum fees for doctors' visits were also low,
and two-thirds of such fees remained at 2s. 6d. or less. Attempts to compensate for this by raising the maximum fees charged to more affluent patients,
were not very successful overall since, at the turn of the century, three-fifths
of visiting fees remained at 7s. 6d. or less.[44] In suburban practices, however,
flexibility in the fees charged seems to have been more successful in raising
upper limits to 10s. 6d. General practitioners here were able to exploit the fact
that in new residential areas they were neither constrained by the fixed expectations of patients as to what was a 'proper' fee for a procedure, nor inhibited by the customary fee schedules in operation locally from established
doctors. More appropriate than fee changes in the countryside, by contrast,
was a conservative, long-term strategy in which there was a gradual aggrega-
tion of appointments in order to achieve a local monopoly, as occurred in the
Wantage practice described at the end of the chapter.

Given that competition from within and without the medical profession
remained keen, the standard monetary fees for a patient's surgery attendance
or for the doctor's visit showed little if any upward movement. Indeed, the
degree of stability is remarkable in fee levels between the 1850s and 1940s in
the accounts of GPs that I have examined. Midwifery was usually charged at
15s. to £1 for working people, but with graduated fees for more affluent
patients of three, five, or sometimes ten guineas. Fees for the annual care of
members, negotiated collectively with friendly societies or clubs, also showed
the doctor's weak market position, since undercutting by colleagues meant

[40] *H.M. Commissioners of Inland Revenue;* Digby, *Medical Living*, 150.
[41] Ibid., note to table 5.4.
[42] Royal College of Physicians, MS 84, folio 102, Letter of M.B. Webb, Nov. 1908.
[43] H. W. Pooler, *My Life in General Practice* (1948), 59.
[44] Digby, *Medical Living*, 152–3.

that a GP would accept from three to five shillings.[45] Although the 'club question', later termed the 'battle of the clubs' resulted in exhortations not to undercut colleagues, a weak market position meant that low fees continued. Lack of improvement in monetary fees paid also meant that in real terms the doctor's income remained more or less stable.

Doctors found it possible to charge a higher fee for occasional, rather than standard, duties or procedures. In this category were consultation charges at two guineas; assurance examinations at one guinea (but with some standard variations depending on the value of the premium), and certification of lunatics at one or two guineas. An alternative strategy for raising additional revenue was for the doctor to separate out more technical areas of work in order to bill these as discrete items. Thus the fee schedules of the 1870s and 1880s listed operations with recommended charges, so that a caesarean was charged (depending on the patient's income), at from 10 to 30 guineas.[46] And, in individual ledgers, there were higher charges for difficult instrumental labours. For example, 'Confinement, applied forceps £2–2–0' stood out from the usual midwifery charge of one guinea.[47] These charges for unusual procedures were but icing on a financial cake whose main ingredients were ordinary fees. Two-thirds of the late-Victorian and Edwardian doctor's income came from private fees, one-fifth to a quarter from appointments, and the remainder from midwifery.[48] Although payments from social insurance after 1911 supplemented fee income, fees still remained quite important so that competition between doctors remained fierce. Even after 1948 the legacy of the competitive conditions of pre NHS practice meant that in certain areas doctors 'did not speak to each other and averted their gaze if they passed in the street'.[49] In other areas it was impossible to induce cooperation amongst early NHS doctors as, for example, in establishing a rota of medical cover for weekends, because of the continuation of an 'intensely competitive atmosphere'.[50]

The implications of economic competition for professional behaviour are an interesting area involving professional ethics. Canvassing for custom amongst other doctors' patients with undercutting of fees might result in expulsion from the BMA, as happened to two practitioners in South Wales in 1906, after their behaviour had been scrutinized by the association's cen-

---

[45] For example, Cambs. RO (Huntingdon), Accn. 2786/Q/8/23, Oddfellows, Wansford Lodge, charged 4s. 0d. in 1849 and 5s. 0d. by 1864–85; William Robinson was paid only 3s. 0d. by Oddfellows in the early 1880s (W. Robinson, *Sidelights on the Life of A Wearside Surgeon* (Gateshead, 1939)), 51–2: Oxfordshire Archives, Misc Sq XI/2, the Lockington and Ardington Friendly Society raised their rates to 4s. 0d. from 3s. 6d. in 1906.

[46] *Medico-Chirurgical Tables issued by the Shropshire Ethical Branch of the BMA* (Shrewsbury, 1874).

[47] National Library of Wales, NLW MS 12540, folio 167, 15 June 1876.

[48] Digby, *Medical Living*, ch. 5.

[49] C. Elliott-Binns, *The Story of a Northamptonshire Practice, 1845–1992* (Northampton, 1992), 37.

[50] R. E. Stewart, *Out of Practice. Memories of General Practice during the 1950s* (Southport, 1996), 43.

tral ethical committee.[51] 'Patient-pinching' was an unpleasant fact of life, although less often proved than alleged. Accusations multiplied whenever economic depression pressurized income, as during the interwar period, or when a change in the state's relationship to medical practice opened up new possibilities of practice expansion. The NHI of 1911 and the NHS of 1948 gave opportunities for the unscrupulous to disregard the advice of their professional association, to sign up patients quickly, and hence to be regarded by their colleagues as poachers. In St Helens, Lancashire, resentment at the Irish 'early birds' who had caught the worm in 1948 resulted in their professional ostracism during the 1950s. A new colleague was instructed that 'here is a list of doctors that, even if their wives come and bring their visiting card, you must never even say "good morning" '. Nor was conversation permitted with them at the St Helen's Medical Society![52]

Appointments diversified income and helped insulate doctors from market forces by making them less vulnerable to the economic fluctuations that resulted in variation in private fee income and an increase in bad debts. But certainty of payment had to be offset against low remuneration and, in some cases, against a possible loss of public esteem when the office had low social status, as was increasingly the case with poor law or public assistance work. Nevertheless, practitioners found appointments a useful source of income: young doctors found a public office a convenient foothold in setting up a practice in a new area; and older doctors, especially those in country areas, tended to preserve their natural monopoly by aggregating as many offices within 'their territory' as possible in order to prevent such an eventuality. It was only the established and socially well-connected practice that eschewed appointments, because they lowered social cachet and hence reduced the recruitment of the affluent.

Table 5.1 illustrates the fluctuating importance which corporate income of different kinds played in a selection of individual practices which had good surviving financial records. It is possible that their experience was not representative, although it fits more general historical trends remarkably well (see Tables 4.2 and 4.3). The experience of general practices in Table 5.1 reflects the lack of appointments during the mid-nineteenth century, the growth in local and central government appointments, as well as an increase in collective provision of medical schemes in the private sector during the late nineteenth and early twentieth centuries. Interestingly, the table suggests that after the inception of the national insurance scheme in 1911, there may have been less financial pressure on doctors to look for a range of appointments. This was fortunate because professionalization had reduced their availability because of a conversion of some part-time, to full-time, posts.

Doctors envisaged that the regular payments promised by public appointments and third party payers would be an attractive alternative to the

---

[51] National Library of Wales, BMA South Wales and Monmouth correspondence.
[52] CMAC, GP 29/2/34, Jean Hughes-Jones.

TABLE 5.1.   Sources of non-fee income in selected practices, 1850–1948

Income source	I	2	3	4	5	6	7	8	9
Admiralty					*				
Army/Territorials			*	*	*	*	*		
Assurance referee			*		*	*	*	*	*
County constabulary		*				*	*	*	
Dependants of NHI members				*	*				
Dependants of club members				*	*				
Colleges									*
Education (County Council)							*		
Emergency scheme						*	*		
Friendly societies			*	*	*		*		
Home Office						*	*		
Industrial companies				*					
NHI				*	*		*	*	
Poor law	*	*				*	*		
Post office				*	*		*		
Private schools							*		*
Religious organizations.							*		

Notes: 1 = Ingham, 1855–61; 2 = Parry Jones, 1880; 3= Speirs, 1896–1899; 4 = Edwards, 1904–20; 5 = Hamill, 1915–20; 6 = Griffith-Williams, 1906–48; 7 = Birt/Kennedy/Squires, 1900–48; 8 = Meikle, 1922–33; 9 = Pritchard, 1928–48

uncertainties of fee income, but found that this was not necessarily the case. The problem of actually achieving an appointment, which had been promised in an advertisement for the sale of a practice, was well known. Another difficulty could arise with a general practitioner who moved to another area, as did Dr Wyke-Smith whose earnings as Vaccination Officer to the Bicester Union went unpaid, once he had gone to a Dorset practice.[53] The more experienced doctor thus took care to get in his public (as well as private) debts before leaving. Some new sources of income from third party payers augured well but were also difficult to realize financially. At the beginning of the period there had been dissatisfaction about assurance societies not paying fees for doctors' assessment of patients.[54] The Shropshire Medical Association had made a stand in 1843 that members would not answer the enquiries of insurance offices, without payment of a one guinea fee.[55] By 1849 only a dozen insurance offices were listed that *did* pay such fees.[56] Twelve years later the medical directory listed 122 assurance companies but, amongst the half that advertised their services there, only two out of five specified that they

[53] Bodleian Library, Oxford Dew MSS, uncatalogued offical papers, letter from W. Wyke-Smith to P. Nash Esq, 15 Nov. 1873.
[54] For example, *Lancet*, ii (1847), 81–2.   [55] Ibid., i (1842–3), 630.
[56] Ibid. (1849), 47.

gave fees to medical referees. By the end of the century such payments were made across the board, and the interwar growth in life assurance showed that it had been an economically worthwhile battle for the profession to win. In contrast, another source of income—available from 1897—which arose from workers' compensation for injury during employment, proved less difficult to realize. The standard fee was one guinea for certificates issued in connection with such cases,[57] but some practices made much more from appearing in legal actions.

During the four decades before 1911 my earlier estimates suggested that between one-fifth and one-quarter of GPs income came from appointments of different kinds. However, the inability to impose supply control on the number of medics graduating meant that numerically the proportion of doctors holding such offices declined. There was a particularly dramatic fall in urban practice, whereas in rural practice district poor-law appointments kept the situation more stable.[58] The National Health Insurance Scheme of 1911 therefore provided a timely helping hand for hard-pressed doctors.

Apart from income from fees, appointments and social insurance, there was another source of income that is impossible to quantify but easy to overlook. This was the gift by a grateful patient, which was usually of a non-monetary kind, and ranged from flowers to eggs, joints of meat, or game. On occasion, a valuable gift—such as a set of ivories—was given.[59] Gifts could involve reciprocity; an implied conditionality of future benefit from the relationship differentiating presents from more mundane financial transactions.[60] There might also be a subtle difference between a material and a cash gift; the former having an individual quality that made it personal to the doctor concerned. Named legacies were unlike most cash transfers in being in this personalized category. This was recognized explicitly in a Nottinghamshire partnership agreement between William Henry Hill of Basford, Surgeon and Alfred Lewis Barham of Bulwell, Surgeon, 1908. This stated:

All fees and presents of money paid or given to either partner for professional services or the emoluments (whether by fees, salary, or otherwise) of every professional office or appointment now or hereafter held by the partners or either of them during the said partnership term to be partnership property but legacies (whether pecuniary or otherwise) and gifts of specific chattels shall be retained by and shall be the separate property of the partner to whom the same shall have been given or bequeathed.[61]

A provision in a London partnership agreement of 1933 made the same distinction, but went on to state that it was only the individual partner's

[57] Ibid., 7 Jan. 1899.   [58] Digby, *Medical Living*, 151.
[59] CMAC, GP/29/2/50, Kathleen Norton, practised in interwar Kennington, London; CMAC, GP/29/2/20, Margaret Hallinan, practised in Rotherham.
[60] A. Offer, 'Between the Gift and the Market. The Economy of Regard', *Economic History Review*, l (1997).
[61] Nottinghamshire RO, DD/BW/215/26, clause 11, articles of partnership.

property provided that the legacy or gift was not 'in satisfaction in whole or in part of money owing to the partnership'.[62]

Gifts were a bonus whereas payment in kind was a substitute for money. Particularly in rural areas payment in kind endured throughout the period, and beyond.[63] This was usually a patient initiative but—as the account of Dr Ingham's practice in the final section of the chapter suggests—it was not invariably so. In Ingham's case payment in goods minimized bad debts. Medical altruism may also have served the same function for customary social groups including widows, or impoverished professionals, such as clergy or teachers. Some Victorian doctors, such as W. L. Noot, were conspicuously tender-hearted, and thus set aside bills with 'no charge, excused' or 'I don't charge', or else reduced the amount owed because of 'many children'.[64] This tradition continued into the interwar years, as with one Preston doctor, whose reputation for sending no bills to his poorer patients, was confirmed after his death, when boxes of unsent bills were discovered.[65] One could speculate that in some other cases doctors were forced to be altruistic because they had been inaccurate in gauging the market, by setting charges too high or visiting too often, with the result that the patient could not pay the high bill that ensued. If doctors were not altruistic then the alternative was to list the unpaid bill as a bad debt and take appropriate action. Medical altruism was thus the smiling face, and bad debt the frowning face, of the same predicament. Strategies for the latter are discussed below in the final section of the chapter on individual practices, whilst the dimension of the problem is outlined in the succeeding section on medical expenditure.

Expenditure

Surviving practice accounts of Dr G. E. Hale in Eton and Datchet (Berkshire), Drs Martin and Matthews in Crawley (West Sussex), Dr Sparke Welton in Abermorddu (Clwyd), and Dr Pearce and partners in Diss (Norfolk) indicate very different patterns of expenditure in four rural or suburban practices between 1895 and 1946.[66] These show clearly that the doctor's and, later, the accountant's categorization of items of expenditure between professional and private differed both over time and between the practices. One important reason for the growth of practice expenses between

---

[62] CMAC, GP 23/6, clause 4, partnership agreement between F. E. L. Phillips and G. Hale (1933).

[63] Personal communication, Dr Maiden.

[64] National Library of Wales, MS 12539, ledger of 1870, folios 58, 71, 95.

[65] Personal communication from Dr Elizabeth Roberts.

[66] West Sussex RO NP 2011, accounts of Crawley medical practice, 1895–1903; Clwyd R.O (Hawarden branch), D/DM/400/2, papers of Dr H. Sparke Welton; Norfolk RO, BR 218/6, Dr Pearce statements of accounts, 1925–46; BR 218/1, Pearce deed of partnership mentions the cost of employing a dispenser.

the late nineteenth and mid-twentieth centuries was the growing inclusive-
ness of expenditures deemed to be professional.

Transport was an important element in medical expenditures, but the class
of the practice influenced just how important, since Dr Hale's modest bicycle, supplemented by a cab in bad weather, cost far less than the horse and
coach of Dr Martin, with his upper and middle-class clientele, whom he
believed would be impressed by a stylish show, which included a coachman
in livery. For Martin, as for Welton and Pearce, in the succeeding motor car
era, expenditure on transport was the single most important item. By the
interwar era when more middle-class patients visited doctors in their homes,
the need to employ a well-turned out servant became a matter of concern,
and expenditure on maids by both the Welton and the Pearce practices
reflected this trend. Whether the practice was a dispensing or non-
dispensing practice was a major determinant of patterns of expenditure. For
the young Dr Hale, with a non-dispensing practice, the cost of a good
chemist dispensing his drugs meant that this became the single most important item in his expenses. Whether dispensing or non-dispensing the cost of
drugs and appliances showed an upward trend as a proportion of medical
expenses, indicating an increasing range of pharmaceutical products available.
In contrast, expenditure on the practice surgery (rates, rent, heating, light-
ing) remained low. This is hardly surprising in relation to the poor quality
of much surgery accommodation. The expenses of the four individual practices fit reasonably well with estimates for general practice. Dr Hale's 18 per
cent for a club, poor law and private practice, and Drs Martin's and
Matthew's figure of 27 per cent for a middle-class pre-1914 practice relate
well to an estimated expenditure figure of 16 or 25 per cent respectively for
working- and middle-class practices in 1913, by the distinguished statistician,
A. L. Bowley. Dr Sparke-Welton's expenses of 36 per cent for 1931–44 were
the same as the BMA's 1937 calculation for a dispensing practice such as this
was. But, with expenses averaging 27 per cent during the 1920s, and 29 per
cent during the 1930s, the expenses ratio for Dr Pearce's practice was well
below the BMA's interwar estimates for a dispensing practice of 33 to 36 per
cent, suggesting either a thrifty establishment or the employment of a firm
to do income tax returns which had only limited powers of creative accountancy.

Table 5.2 shows more general estimates for the period, and from these it
is evident that the estimated ratio of expenses to gross income increased
notably between 1914 and 1945. This may perhaps suggest that more doctors
had become efficient at keeping accounts, and in assembling data on which
more accurate estimates of medical expenditures could be made. The figures
are interesting both in indicating the range of expenditure (from one-sixth to
more than two-fifths of gross income), and some of the causes of this variation. In contributing to this differentiation the social class of the patients was
important, in that a working-class or industrial practice would spend only a

TABLE 5.2.   Expenses as a percentage of gross income per principal (%)

Source/date	All	Insurance	Middle class	Mixed	Dispensing	Non-dispensing	With assistant	Without assistant
Bowley/ BMA								
(i) 1913/14	—	16	30	26	—	—	—	—
(ii) 1924	—	—	—	—	33	25	—	—
BMA 1937	—	30 (non-dispensing)			36	30	—	—
Bradford Hill,								
(i) 1936–8)	—	—	—	—	—	—	42.6	36.3
(ii) 1945	37.5		—	—	—	—	—	—

Sources: BMJ Supplement, 5 Jan. 1924, 29 May 1937; A. Bradford Hill, 'The Doctor's Pay and Day', *Journal of the Royal Statistical Society* cxiv (1951)

small proportion of its income on very basic surgery facilities, whereas a middle-class practice might well spend almost double this proportion in terms of good transport and wages of servants or support staff. Also significant in practice expenditures was whether the practice dispensed, because this entailed substantial expenditure on a dispenser's salary, as well as the purchase of drugs and bottles. If the practice employed an assistant, as was particularly the case in industrial practices or larger panel ones, then the assistant's wages would also very considerably inflate expenditure because typical wages for an assistant were £250 to £330 in 1914 and £300–£450 by 1939.[67]

Bad debts as an item in expenses were seldom discussed. Victorian and Edwardian doctors were reluctant to distinguish between good debts (which they had some hope of realizing as income), and bad debts (which more realistically should have been written off). An important reason for this was the cost in time that such an exercise would involve in going over ledgers and day books. More business-like doctors avoided the book-keeping difficulty because they kept separate books for different kinds of patients including one for free treatments. Others, with a mixed social clientele, circumvented not only the accounting but also the bad debt problem, because their affluent patients paid for what the poor were unable to afford.[68]

During the 1880s and 1890s GPs began to use accountants, who tried to educate their GP clients on the importance of this distinction. A letter to Drs Martin and Matthews read:

[67] Digby and Bosanquet, 'Doctors and Patients', 83.
[68] H. Morris-Jones, *The Country Doctor of Fifty Years Ago* (1961), 22.

As pointed out to you by our representative, we have, in compiling these accounts, assumed that the whole of the entries in your ledgers . . . (with the exception of some three or four actually marked 'bad' and which therefore we entirely ignored) are healthy accounts, which it is fair to treat, at present, as likely to be paid. If on the other hand you have grounds for believing that certain of these accounts may never be paid there arises the question—to which we particularly draw your attention—of treating these and all similar accounts in succeeding years as *Bad Debts* or writing them off to the debt of Profit and Loss account year by year otherwise the Accounts will present an incorrect statement of your profits. This clarification of the debts due to you can only be arrived at by your own knowledge of the circumstances and we should be dependent upon you for the necessary information.[69]

The doctors were slow to get down to the complicated task of analysing their ledger to clarify this, so that another letter followed. 'Seeing that so small an amount has been written off for bad debts we doubt very much whether your accounts show the true profit made. It is probably considerably less in reality.'[70] Very large sums were then deducted for bad debts in the accounts for 1901 and 1902, amounting respectively to 33 per cent and 19 per cent of expenses. Taken more realistically, however, as an average for the eight years from 1895 to 1902 for which there are accounts, bad debts averaged 9 per cent of expenses in this practice. This was not untypical, as other evidence suggests.

The Plender Report gave 6 per cent, with a further 2 per cent for collection, as their general estimate for bad debts in 1910–11.[71] An interwar London practice in an economically declining area found it necessary to write off one hundred pounds a year.[72] A rough calculation suggests that this represented about a month's visits to patients, or 8 per cent of gross income, which is rather higher than the Plender figure. The Medical Practitioners Union cited an even higher figure of 20 per cent.[73] The BMA later thought the Plender Report's estimate was too low to give a representative picture, both because 1910 and 1911 were years of good trade and employment, and because the practices surveyed were middle-class ones. It suggested that a 'much higher figure' would be appropriate for the 1920s.[74] Predictably, the approved societies gave a contrasting number of 5 per cent, which they acknowledged was a 'very conservative' one.[75]

The fact that doctors during the late nineteenth and early twentieth centuries had targeted working-class areas as an important area for professional expansion undoubtedly increased their vulnerability to bad debts. GPs could

---

[69] W. Sussex RO, NP 2011, Crawley practice accounts, letter of 24 Oct. 1898 from Seear, Hasluck and Co., chartered accountants, to Drs Martin and Matthews on their accounts for 1895 to 1897.

[70] W. Sussex RO, NP 2011, Crawley practice accounts, letter of 18 Nov. 1901 from Seear, Hasluck and Co. to Drs Martin and Matthews.

[71] *Report of Sir William Plender in Respect of Medical Attendance and Remuneration in Certain Towns*, PP, 1912–13, Cd 6305, lxxviii, 679.

[72] CMAC, GP29/2/50, Kathleen Norton.

[73] *Medical Practitioner*, 19 Nov. 1910.   [74] *BMJ Supplement* 5 Jan. 1924, 22.

[75] Ibid., 26 Jan. 1924, 35.

therefore expect to treat between one in ten and one in twenty patients without remuneration. It was no wonder that 'cash down' became the rule in branch surgeries catering for poorer patients. And some late Victorian doctors got in their debts by pocketing their professional pride and taking their ledger to the place where workers had their wages paid, as did all the other local traders.[76] Interwar doctors tried hard to reduce bad debts, not least through emulating the hard-nosed attitudes pioneered by colleagues in industrial or urban areas. During these economically depressed years even a rural Norfolk practice employed the Norwich and East of England General Traders Protection Society, which obtained quarterly instalments from patients, with the entire sum taking as much as two or three years to be paid.[77]

The extent of voluntary and involuntary medical altruism was therefore considerable.[78] How did this compare with doctors' prime reference group—lawyers? There was only very limited legal aid provided from 1875 by the state in civil cases, and consequently a continued shortage of barristers and solicitors prepared to take on such work because of the low remuneration. Effectively the Poor Person's Procedure was rationed according to the numbers of altruistically minded lawyers prepared to take it on.[79] In both law and medicine wider access to free medical care came only after the Second World War. In 1948 the NHS provided a free and comprehensive health service, and in the following year the Legal Aid Scheme gave better access to free legal services.

Income and Capital

To read in an obituary notice that Dr Hitchens 'had worked up a good practice' suggests financial success without any breach of professional discretion,[80] but also hints at a central problem for attempting work in the economic history of medicine—that of getting precise information on income and capital. Estimates of doctors' incomes have to be constructed painstakingly from a variety of sources. Elsewhere I have given estimates of medical incomes, so I will only briefly comment here.[81] Figure 5.1 on the structure of gross incomes in general practice between the 1870s and 1900s indicates that before the NHI the majority of general practitioners had only modest incomes. It must be remembered that anything up to a quarter of that nominal income also needed to be deducted to cover expenses. The rise in the proportion of low incomes in 1899, which is highlighted in the figure, also suggests that GPs

---

[76] W. Robinson, *Sidelights on the Life of a Wearside Surgeon* (Gateshead, 1939).

[77] Norfolk RO BR 218/11 cash receipt book, 1936–9.

[78] Digby, *Medical Living*, 249–53.

[79] B. Abel-Smith and R. Stevens, *Lawyers and the Courts* (1967), 135, 159, 164.

[80] *BMJ* i, 1910, 1208, obituary of F.C.Hitchens, MRCS, LRCP (1897, Guy's Hospital).

[81] Digby, *Medical Living*, ch. 5 and Digby and Bosanquet, 'Doctors and Patients', 74–94.

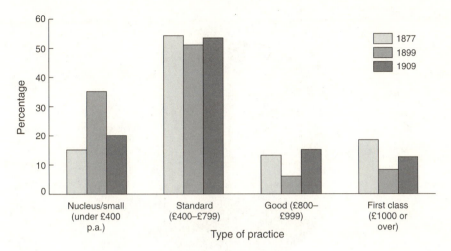

Fig. 5.1. Income differentiation in practices, 1877–1909

were vulnerable both to economic fluctuations in the general economy, and to problems arising from the medical profession's failure to control numbers of entrants. The *Spectator* aptly summarized the situation in 1911:

The profession of medicine in this country is unfortunately one which, as a whole, is distinctly ill-paid. Of the general condition of the profession it is scarcely too much to say that it is hard and precarious. The struggle for life is very fierce among the doctors.[82]

From this precarious situation most GPs were rescued by payments from the national health insurance scheme which came into operation in 1913. Payments from social insurance were important in improving their situation by 1936–8. While one in five amongst single-handed principals engaged in general practice got less than one-quarter of their income from panel payments, seven out of ten received between a quarter and two-thirds of their income from the panel, and the remainder (one in twelve), obtained around two-thirds or more of their income in this way.[83] See Figure 5.2. Turning from distributions to averages, Figure 5.3 shows the make-up of average incomes for three dates within the period from 1913 to 1938. This demonstrates the importance of social insurance payments in raising total income, while emphasizing the growing significance of private fee income. Diversity in total income amongst general practitioners remained, and some still struggled financially.[84]

[82] Editorial, 2 Dec. 1911.
[83] Bradford Hill, 'Doctor's Pay and Day', *Journal of the Royal Statistical Society*, cxiv (1951), 23.
[84] *Report of the Inter-Departmental Committee on Remuneration of General Practitioners*, PP, 1945–6, XII, Cmd. 6810, para. 9.

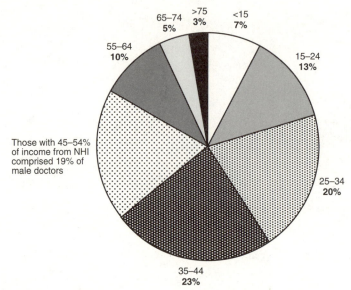

Fig. 5.2. Proportion of income of male GPs from NHI, 1936–38

A doctor needed to have achieved 'a good competence' during a working life before retirement could be contemplated.[85] A comfortable old age could then ensue from savings, along with what the sale of the practice realized in capital. Two 'snapshot' figures of capital accumulated by members of the medical profession are available; the first near the beginning, and the second towards the end, of our period. These were derived from probates for the years 1858 and 1940–1.[86]

Capital included moveable property (such as goods, furniture and stocks and shares), as well as immovable assets (such as land, or houses), but intangibles such as goodwill was excluded, except to the extent that this was reflected in the value of a practice that could be sold. Neither source disaggregated the origins of wealth, so that it is possible that a good marriage, a fortunate inheritance, or other capital from a non-medical source was included in the estate. Nor did the figures differentiate between the small numbers of élite specialists and consultants (who on average were likely to leave larger estates), and the much more numerous 'rank-and-file' general practitioners (who on average would have had lower earnings and therefore were likely to leave smaller estates).

A detailed view of the comparative rewards of the three traditional professions—law, medicine, and the Church—can be obtained from probates pub-

[85] Obituary of Dr Griffith, *BMJ*, ii (1881), 501.
[86] L. Hamilton, 'The Distribution of Capital Among the Medical Profession in England and Wales, 1940–1', *Bulletin of the Institute of Statistics*, Oxford, 12 (1950), 1–6.

lished for 1858. The medical estates included both specialists and generalists, élite, and rank and file members. The distribution of probates indicates that the median for medical estates was lower than that for law or the church, falling in the one to two thousand pound range rather than the two to three thousand one.[87]

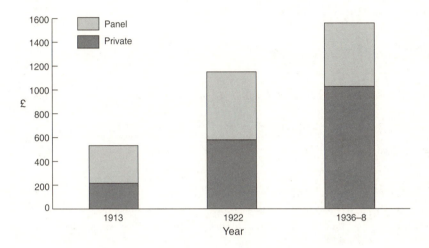

Fig. 5.3. Average gross income from private sources and NHI, 1913–38

The second investigation into doctors' capital was prompted by the observation that a large proportion of wills of more than £20,000 published in *The Times* in 1945 appeared to be those of medics. However, an investigation into medical probates for 1940–1 disproved this casual impression, because only 3 per cent of medical probates were found to have been in this range. Table 5.3 suggests that the amount of capital possessed by different age cohorts in the medical profession differed markedly, with a range from two to thirteen thousand, and a mean of five thousand pounds. In both monetary and real terms this was a very considerable improvement on the position in 1858. There was a broad but fluctuating trend of growing amounts of capital with advancing age, but this was held only up to the age of 75. Thereafter, doctors lived off their capital thereby lowering the amounts of capital they bequeathed. As to the fluctuations in the capital owned at various ages, the increase in capital owned in the 35 to 44 age group may have been inflated by inheritances from parents, and that in the early 70s by the sale of practices. Of course, in comparison with the general population, doctors had much more capital, as befitted a middle-class professional group. However, if we exclude that proportion having capital of £100 or less (11 per cent of

---

[87] *22nd Report of the Registrar General*, PP, 1861, xviii, 231.

TABLE 5.3.   Distribution of capital in medical profession, 1940–1*

Age	No. medical practitioners	% medical practitioners	Amount of capital (£000)	% distribution of capital	Average capital £
25–34	17,505	38.5	36,900	14.9	2,108
35–44	12,503	27.5	70,100	28.4	5,607
45–54	5,229	11.5	40,000	16.2	7,650
55–64	5,001	11.0	41,400	16.7	8,278
65–69	2,364	5.2	21,600	8.7	9,137
70–75	1,637	3.6	22,200	9.0	13,561
75 +	1,228	2.7	15,100	6.1	12,296
N	45,467**	100.0	247,300	100.0	Av. 5,439

Note:
   * These are estimated numbers for 1941 (when no census was taken) derived from projections from the 1931 census.
** The *Medical Directory* for 1941 gave 42,451 members of the medical profession.
Source: L. Hamilton, 'The Distribution of Capital Among the Medical Profession in England and Wales, 1940–1', *Bulletin of the Oxford Institute of Statistics*, 12 (1950), 1–6.

medical practitioners and 77 per cent of the general population) in order to look at the distribution of wealth amongst property holders, then Figure 5.4 indicates very clearly the much greater opportunities to cumulate capital amongst doctors.[88]

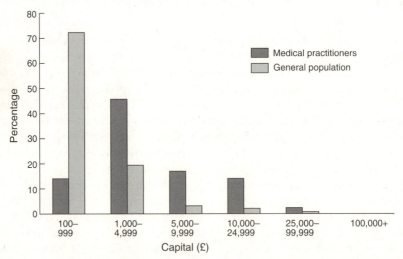

Fig. 5.4. Capital of medical practitioners (1940–1) compared to the general population (1924–30)

Note: Amongst doctors 0.2 per cent and in the general population 0.02 per cent, had capital exceeding £100,000.

   [88] G.W. Daniels and H. Campion, *The Distribution of National Capital* (Manchester, 1936); Hamilton, 'Distribution of Capital', 3.

Contrasting Practices

Three practices are discussed which span the period from the mid-nineteenth to the mid-twentieth centuries which, taken together, indicate a remarkable expansion in the economic opportunities available to GPs. The first two practices were situated in industrialized North Wales. They illustrate the difference between a practice at an early stage in a medical career, and that which had been developed for some years. The third practice, in southern England, suggests the extent to which a practice was able to aggregate a range of appointments, and to exploit a variety of financial openings. All three practices exhibited a strong business character.

Dr George Ingham set up in practice at Ruabon, a small country market town in an area rich in coal and iron. Although Ingham was listed as one of four surgeons in the town in 1856 he had not been included in an earlier directory for 1850.[89] It is likely that the ledger which is used to reconstruct the economics of his practice from 1855 to 1861 was his first practice ledger; not least because very neat handwriting at the beginning deteriorated later, while midwifery was absent until 1857 when his local reputation as a doctor emboldened mothers to book their confinements with him.

About one-third of Dr Ingham's patients had their occupation recorded, and from this it is apparent that he treated people from all parts of the community. His patients included servants; labourers; farm workers; artisans; small trades people; the emerging lower middle-class (such as a policeman, excise man, stationmaster or postmaster); farmers; and a few members of the gentry. The doctor operated in an egalitarian way, rather than being attuned to market possibilities, in so far as his modest charges were standardized, and did not differentiate according to social rank and ability to pay (see Table 5.4). However, this constraint was likely to have been the result of local convention in the charges of competing practitioners, rather than of his own preference, since in some other respects he was remarkably business-orientated.

Where Dr Ingham was especially attuned to economic pressures was in attempting to get in the money that his patients owed him. This was a response to the nature of the practice which had very few corporate clients, and so was overwhelmingly dependent on fee income from individuals.[90] Ingham first sent in a bill stating that 'An early settlement will oblige.'[91] Payment then followed for quite a high proportion of patients. For an additional few patients, who were local artisans or traders, Ingham was able to capitalize on the local economy to achieve settlement of accounts. For a few

---

[89] *Slater's Directory and Topography of Cheshire, Lancashire, Shropshire and N. Wales* (Manchester, 1850 and 1856).

[90] The Wrexham Poor Law Union was the most substantial of these.

[91] For example, Clwyd RO (Hawarden), D/DM/301/3, ledger of Dr Ingham, folio 358.

TABLE 5.4.   Dr Ingham's fees, 1855–61

Payment for:	Amount
Journey*	2s. 6d.
Visit	1s. 0d.
Consultation	1s. 0d.
Night journey	3s. 6d.–5s. 0d.
Mixture	2s. 0d. –2s. 6d.
Liniment	1s. 6d.
Box of pills	1s. 0d.
Ointment	1s. 0d.
Lotion	1s. 6d.–2s. 6d.
Dressing	1s. 0d.–2s. 0d.
Minor surgical procedure	1s. 0d.–3s. 6d.
Vaccination	2s. 6d.**
Injection	4s. 6d.
Reduction of fracture	10s. 6d.
Confinement	1 gn [21s. 0d.]

Note:
   * The fee for a journey was in addition to con-
sultation, medicine, etc.
   ** Fee charged only if the vaccination was suc-
cessful.
Source: Clwyd RO, Hawarden, D/DM/301/3,
Dr Ingham's Ledger, 1855–60.

bills payment was in kind: a debt of £2 19s. 6d. by Mr Lloyd was 'Paid in
full by Nails'; and a large sum of £6 15s. 0d., owed by William Jones since
1855, was progressively set off against Jones's later deliveries of coal to the
doctor's household. Alternatively, the doctor deducted his medical charges
from his payment of tradespeoples' bills, as when the debt of the local gro-
cer's wife was deducted by Ingham from his payment of the grocery bill.[92]
More generally, however, when no money was forthcoming, a sequential
process was set in motion. Collectors were first employed to pressurize for
instalment payments. (One collector was a John Ingham, so it is possible that
there was also a family interest in this course of action.) Where the doctor
judged that a patient was doing his or her best to pay him by recurrent small
instalments, then an outstanding debt produced no further action. But when
no payment at all was forthcoming from those it was thought could afford to
pay the doctor, a later threat of court action was made. Typically, the ledger
recorded 'If not immediately settled legal proceedings will be taken.'[93] If even
this did not produce a response, then a court action was instituted.

   [92] Clwyd RO (Hawarden), D/DM/301/3, ledger of Dr Ingham, fo. 486, 504, 138.
   [93] Ibid., fo. 236.

In taking legal action against recalcitrant non-payers, the Ruabon practice provided an early example of the tougher economic stance adopted by more business-focused Victorian and Edwardian doctors. There were more legal actions recorded in Ingham's ledger than in any other I have encountered. Interestingly, Dr Ingham must have been a very early member of the medical profession to appreciate the potential, and therefore to use, the small claims facility authorized by recent legislation. An Act of 1847 had made it possible to reclaim debts of under £50 in a county court, and Ruabon was within the 29th circuit where a court was held every six weeks. In August 1855 Mr Williams, who owed Dr Ingham 16s. 6d., had his account 'settled through C. Court', and also had to pay costs of 10d.[94] Ingham was less precipitate with more influential members of the local community but, even then, he was not prepared to wait indefinitely. The account of Mr Tudor of Chapel Farm, Newbridge read:

> Owed £5–4/- July 1855
> P[ai]d £2 Oct. 1857
> Pd 5/- on account Sept [1858?]
> Pd 6/- 27 Feb. 59
> Pd 10/- Mar 59 by C. Court
> Pd 5/- July 16 [1859][95]

As a result of this methodical process there were remarkably few 'bad debts' recorded, and these were usually of people who had moved away from the district.[96] Local people must soon have become aware that if they consulted Dr Ingham then there was a fee to pay; medicine meant business in this practice.

Medicine as a business enterprise was even more evident in the early twentieth-century practice of Drs Edwards and Trubshaw, located in Mold, a town fifteen miles to the north-west of Ruabon. The practice was situated in an urbanized, industrial part of the county where leadmining, tinplate manufacture, and smelting gave significant employment.[97] The practice was very similar to that of Dr Ingham; notably, in the way it recruited patients right across the social spectrum and in the extent to which Edwards, like his colleague, was dependent on collectors and legal action to bring in his outstanding accounts. These were itemized in a ledger even larger than that of Dr Ingham. Edwards's accounts for the years 1904–12 were kept in a volume with 1,200 pages that weighed 28 pounds![98]

The Mold practice was a partnership rather than a single-handed practice, as in Ruabon. It was also distinctive in being less dependent on individual patients' fees, because it had built up a number of collective agreements, such

---

[94] Ibid., fo. 38.   [95] Ibid., fo. 30.   [96] Ibid., fos. 563, 700, 791.

[97] J. R. Thomas and M. Griffiths, 'Industrial Railways and Tramways of Flintshire', *Archives*, 14 (1997), 35–45 has a good account of the collieries, tramways, and railways of Mold.

[98] Clywd RO (Hawarden), D/DM/63/33, ledger of Drs Edwards and Trubshaw, 1904–12.

that nine mining concerns and fourteen friendly societies, clubs, and tontines, were now 'on the books'. The latter had small memberships so that each made a modest subscription of from £1 to £15 per year for the medical care of members and their families. Together with a small payment that the practice received from the Post Office, these sums amounted to £123 in 1911— a useful, if minor, contribution to the practice's income. Financially, the mining companies made a larger addition to the balance sheet, amounting to £411. These companies varied considerably in size, so that the smallest paid a subscription of only a few pounds a year, and the largest £200. After the NHI Scheme the practice set up clubs for the non-insured former members of these schemes,[99] and collieries continued to run their own schemes for insured workers.

About one in ten individual patients had their occupation listed and, from these entries, it is apparent that the practice was efficiently recruiting both from traditional occupations (such as artisans, together with rural, industrial and transport workers), as well as from newer and expanding white-collar and service sectors. Unlike Dr Ingham earlier, the fees charged were differentially graded according to social status and presumed income, with fees of from 1s. to 4s. 6d., and with confinements charged from 10s. 6d. to £3 3s. 0d.[100] Although most of the fees were modest ones, the Mold doctors found, as had Ingham before them, that collectors and court actions were necessary in order to bring in the money that was owed. Included in the day book for 1911–12 was a copy of the profession's favourite poem, 'God and the Doctor', which ironically depicted the patient's short memory:

> GOD and the DOCTOR we alike adore
> But only when in danger,
> The danger o'er, both alike requited
> GOD is forgotten, and the DOCTOR SLIGHTED.

If a patient did not pay his or her account within a year, a collector was brought in to try to get the sum owing through instalments. The practice employed a local firm of solicitors to act as collectors who took 10 per cent of the fees collected as commission. During the year 1912–13, for example, they collected £112, and in 1913–14 another £129, from ninety-four patients. Unfortunately, the number of court cases brought against patients is not given. But patients were very anxious that this final sanction was not incurred. One couple who had fallen on hard times, but who owed 17s., received a solicitor's letter threatening legal action and wrote to their doctor:

Dr Edwards, Sir, I am sending you a line to tell you that we will come down week next Saturday as we are afraid for you to put a cost on us. Please will you kindly wait

---

[99] Ibid., D/DM/63/39, correspondence of Dr Edwards, 1913–20.
[100] Ibid., D/DM/63/1/32, day book, 1911–12.

until we come there as it is very hard on us now after such a strike on us. I am your obedient servant. Mr and Mrs John Hughes.[101]

Presumably on the condition that instalments were paid, the couple were not brought up in court, and within seven months had managed to pay all but six shillings of the outstanding amount. However, the ledger makes it clear that this was exceptional, and that strict accounting was the rule. 'No good, practically a pauper', or 'this man became a bankrupt, no assets' were amongst the few extreme cases where the pursuit of debt was actually given up.[102] There was remarkably little medical altruism because Edwards and Trubshaw perceived no conflict between making money and practising medicine. The same was true of the Wantage doctors.

The Wantage practice had been set up in the mid nineteenth century, and for most of the period until 1948 it was run as a partnership, usually with two partners, although with as many as four. The founder of the practice was W. R. H. Barker (1810–89), who left London in the mid-1830s to settle at Wantage, and the senior partner at the end of the period was F. V. Squires, but altogether nearly a dozen doctors were involved. Remarkably, given these changes in personnel, continuity in financial strategy as well as professional vitality was maintained. Wantage was a small market town serving the surrounding agricultural area. The town had as many as half a dozen doctors at any one time, but latterly settled down to two practices, the smaller Newbury Street Practice and the larger Church Street Practice with which we are concerned here. They seem to have worked together reasonably harmoniously (as in running the cottage hospital set up in 1886), although there was always keen local competition for patients, whilst appointments were eagerly sought and jealously guarded. Later, under the NHS, when economic pressures were felt less keenly the two local medical partnerships divided certain public appointments on a six monthly rota, and eventually cooperated in running a Health Centre that was linked to the cottage/community hospital.[103]

The Church Street Practice served all social classes from paupers in the workhouse to members of the gentry. Whereas the Newbury Street Practice was perceived to be a church-going establishment that recruited clergy families as patients, the Church Street Practice did well with other professional families. The latter also prospered because it was prepared to visit over a much wider geographical area than its rival practice. The staple of the Church Street Practice was, however, the day income that came from patients' visits to the surgery, supplemented where necessary by the doctor's home visits. Before the First World War surgery visits were charged on a

[101] Ibid., D/DM/63/33, ledger of Drs Edwards and Trubshaw, 1904–12, folio 404, letter dated 20 August 1912.
[102] Ibid., fos. 422, 420.
[103] Personal communications from Jean Loudon and Irvine Loudon; the latter joined the Church Street practice in 1954, and rose to be Senior Partner. CMAC, GP/29/2/1, J. K. Hawkey, MB, BM, BCH, MRGCP, DObSt, RCOG, in practice in the Newbury Street Practice, Wantage from 1949.

scale that went from 6*d*. to 5*s*. but with most patients being charged 2*s*. or 2/6. Signing certificates of sickness earned from 6*d*. to 2*s*.[104] Towards the end of the period greater flexibility in relating surgery fees to patients' incomes was adopted so that the fee scale went from 1*s*. to as much as 10*s*. 6*d*.[105] Midwifery entries are not mentioned in the day accounts before 1914, presumably a record was being kept in a book that has not survived. More detail on fees, including that for midwifery was available for 1941 and shows that the commonest midwifery charge was one and a half guineas, but more affluent patients were being charged up to three or four guineas. A financially astute, but unusual, policy was adopted in that each quarter the collector extracted instalments of five shillings from mothers-to-be.[106] (This practice was more usually found in dispensaries).[107]

Before the First World War the doctors' appointments were estimated by the book-keeper as amounting to a steady income of £600 per annum. Entries in the day account books of the practice enable two-thirds of this income to be accounted for by annual payments from public and voluntary bodies. Salaries of £55 and £88 respectively for Drs Birt and Kennedy were paid for acting as Poor Law Medical Officers for the Wantage District and Workhouse, and for the Vale District in the Wantage Union. As Public Vaccinators for these districts they received further sums. In addition, they acted as medical officers for a number of institutions run by the Sisters of the Anglican Community of St Mary the Virgin: St Katharine's boarding and day school for the daughters of tradespeople (about £60 p.a., depending on the number of pupils examined), St Mary's School for the daughters of gentlemen (about £60 p.a.), and St Mary's Training Home for Girls (about £75 p.a.). The practice was later successful in replacing variable periodic payments from institutions by an annual fixed payment.[108] Contract practice with local friendly societies supplied medical help on a customarily poorly paid capitation basis. For a local society such as the Locking and Ardington Society the practice had rock-bottom rates, only raising the three shillings annual capitation fee to four shillings in 1906.[109] For branches of national or county organizations a higher annual rate of 8*s*. 6*d*. was charged, which later developed into payment per item of service (see Table 5.5 below). Clients included the Sparsholt branch of the Berkshire Friendly Society (£8 p.a.), the Oddfellows (£21 p.a.), whilst the Wantage Lodge of the Foresters paid larger sums.

Medicine as practised in the Church Street partnership was a small business in which a large number of small items from both private and public sources cumulated into a respectable part of the partners' professional

[104] Oxfordshire Archives, Misc Sq VII/1, Squire Practice Medical Practice Ledger, 1914–16.
[105] Ibid., 1941.   [106] Ibid.   [107] *BMJ*, i (1909), 1263–4.
[108] Oxfordshire Archives, Misc Sq VII/14.
[109] Ibid., XI/2, 12 Mar. 1906, meeting of Lockington and Ardington friendly society unanimously agreed to raise capitation fee.

TABLE 5.5.   Fees authorized by Wantage Foresters Medical Association, 1945

Type of medical service	Payment authorized
Visit and medicine for 2 days	3s. 6d.
Each intermediate visit in dangerous cases	2s. 6d.
If beyond 2 miles, outward per mile	1s. 0d.
Attendance at surgery and medicine for two days	2s. 6d.
Fresh supply of medicine for 2 days	1s. 6d.
Visit in urgent or dangerous cases between 8 p.m. and 8 a.m., with medicine	5s. 0d.
Sick certificate when no medical fees are claimed	1s. 0d.

income. Notifications of infectious diseases such as tuberculosis brought small payments of a half a crown which together added up to several pounds per year.[110] Certification of lunatics at ten shillings a time was probably poor recompense for the trouble involved. Other legal and police work included acting as police surgeon, attending at the prison, being a witness at the county court, or attending inquests. As an expert witness the doctor's services were well remunerated since one guinea was paid for each attendance, later increased to a guinea and a half. Dr Woodhouse was Surgeon to the Berkshire County Constabulary and Dr Birt acted as a Certifying Factory Surgeon for the Home Office.[111] The practice examined employees of the Post Office, and also recruits to the Berkshire Imperial Yeomanry, later the Berkshire Territorial Association.

In addition to this semi-official work the partners did work for numerous assurance and life insurance companies including the Atlas, Pearl, Prudential, Royal Liver, Refuge, and Sun Life. For example, in 1902 the Pearl appointed Drs Emerson and Woodhouse as medical referees and agreed to pay two guineas for a life insurance proposal of £100 and upwards, one guinea for one of £800–1000, and 10s. 6d. for a policy of under £800.[112] A steady trickle of these examinations brought income of nearly ten guineas a year before 1914. However, the growth of life insurance during the economically troubled interwar period was far greater than that in the more stable years before 1914.[113] Doctors benefited from this general growth in assurance, and the

[110] The Infectious Diseases (Notification) Act of 1889 and the later Public Health (Tuberculosis) Regulations of 1912, made mandatory the notification to the MOH of diseases including smallpox, diptheria, erysipelas, scarlet fever, and tuberculosis. It resulted in small payments to the doctor of half a crown (12.5p).

[111] Under the Factory and Workshop Act of 1901 and the later Factory Act of 1914, doctors were employed to certify fitness for the employment of children and young persons; to investigate and report on cases of poisoning, toxic jaundice, or anthrax; and to examine any cases of injury reported to them.

[112] Oxfordshire Archives, Misc Sq XI/2, letter of 4 Mar. 1902.

[113] B. Supple, *The Royal Exchange Assurance. A History of British Insurance, 1720–1970* (Cambridge, 1970), 432.

Wantage practice's annual income from this source doubled.[114] From 1913 NHI work enabled the panel doctor to receive a substantial quarterly payment. Like the remuneration from appointments it was a reliable income; it is significant that NHI payments brought in almost as much as the appointments that had taken generations of doctors to build up. During the interwar years new voluntary and public clients were recruited including the Wiltshire Friendly Society, the Lyford Almshouses, and the Berkshire Education Authority. For several years a patient-lodger was also taken at 3 guineas a week.[115] War posed fresh challenges in 1939: services were rendered to the Oxfordshire Bureau for Evacuees together with the Public Medical Service.[116] And, while Dr Squires served in the RAMC, Dr Dawson, a string of locums of variable quality, and an experienced dispenser/book-keeper kept the war-time practice afloat.

Before the First World War the practice employed a firm of chartered accountants (Wenn and Elsom) to act as book-keepers and debt collectors. The collectors got in sums that patients owed through collecting instalments. As a last resort patients deemed recalcitrant—who were those whom the doctors thought were capable of paying their bills—were 'county courted'. For example, the collector recorded that Alfred Evans 'paid me 9/- on account of his bill—he was county courted for 8/6 and judgement was given for 6/6 and 2/- costs—which he has paid'.[117] This was an unusual custom for a non-industrial or mixed practice to adopt, because the conventional professional wisdom of the day was that a practice that adopted over-legalistic, mercenary procedures would thereby alienate potential middle-class or genteel patients. In the Church Street practice, however, middle-class patients were not exempt from this kind of public indignity. One owed the practice £50 for attendances during 1912–14 but, even in the autumn of 1915, offered the prospect of no more than instalments:

I owe you an apology not only for the non-settlement of your account but for having treated it with scant attention and common courtesy. I have, however, been terribly overworked . . . I will send you an instalment of £2 or more each month until the account is settled but a judgement may upset everything.

He signed an admission of his debt before the county court at Portsmouth (where he was now living) but wrote asking 'you not to press me further by legal process', and enclosed £2.10s.[118]

As a result of a combined strategy of gradually first aggregating—and then consolidating—the economic openings obtainable in a relatively prosperous

[114] Oxfordshire Archives, Misc Sq VII/14, ledger Jan. to Oct. 1941.
[115] Ibid., XI/1–2, correspondence with patients, 1920 and 1921.
[116] Ibid., VII/14, Squire practice ledger.
[117] Ibid., XIX, list of accounts inadvertently included with a partnership document.
[118] Ibid., X/1, bundles of invoices and receipts, letters by W. S. Harrison, 9 and 13 Oct. and 3 Nov. 1915.

area the practice grew steadily in value. A partnership document of 1919 indicated that the practice produced an income of £3,000.[119] But that was after the annual addition of more than £500 from national insurance work. This would put the Wantage practice's pre-First World War income at slightly more than £2,400. We can check this figure by an indirect calculation. Between 1907 and 1912 the Wantage appointments were valued routinely at £600. Typically one-quarter of the income of a rural practice came from appointments, and this nicely corroborates the estimate of £2,400 as the pre-war gross income.

'Surgery expenses' were given in the surgery day accounts. Such expenditures were estimated by the statistician, A. L. Bowley, as making up two-fifths of the expenses of a pre-war general practice. This would give total expenses at about £1,000, or one-third of the Wantage practice's gross income. This was an elevated figure since Bowley reckoned total expenses as a quarter of income for middle-class practices. Transport costs of a rural practice were usually high, and the expenses of a dispensing practice also pushed them up, these two factors may have inflated the expenses figure towards the sort of proportion more generally associated with the interwar period.[120] This expenses figure of one-third is consistent with Drs Birt and Kennedy's income tax returns for 1917–18, which give taxable or net incomes of £1,000 per principal, out of a total gross practice income of £3,000.[121] The partnership's later known strategy of taking out the local tax inspector to an excellent lunch, and then personally handing over the accounts at the end of a rich and bibulous meal, may have played a crucial role here, in making high expenses acceptable to the Inland Revenue!

Practice finances also indicated that later Wantage partners adopted an even more pronounced capitalist stance. Indeed, the Church Street partnership under Drs Squires and Birt was notorious locally for itemizing every possible item of service. 'If Dr B. said "Happy Christmas" to you he put it on the bill', and 'if he sent a wreath to a deceased patient there was a service charge of 50 per cent in addition!' Not only were the partners vigorous in their pursuit of every economic opening, but a very efficient Scottish dispenser/book-keeper, 'Jock' Stewart, was employed. He was meticulous in lovingly recording—in beautiful script—the earnings of the practice, and in ensuring that what was earned, was very largely realized monetarily, in contrast to many other practices where notional and actual income were widely different.[122] Between 1919 and 1946–7 the practice had increased its income

[119] Oxfordshire Archives, Misc Sq XIX, revised partnership document for Drs Birt and Kennedy, 1919.
[120] BMJ Supplement, 5 Jan. 1924.
[121] Oxfordshire Archives, Misc Sq X/1–2, Squire invoices and receipts.
[122] I am indebted to Irvine Loudon for these personal insights into the practice.

two and a half times, in real terms.[123] This was a substantial rate of growth but by no means unique.[124]

On the eve of the NHS, and at the end of a long period of mixed private and public medicine, the partners were benefiting not just from the fruits of their own labour, but from the cumulative hard work of their predecessors, which had succeeded in concentrating many of the economic opportunities of a locality within a single practice. Before the NHS, mercenary attitudes in the Church Street practice in Wantage had dictated a single-minded pursuit of money, through grasping at every job and charging as much as the market would bear.

The medicine that was practised in Wantage, as in Ruabon and Mold earlier, was as much a product of the doctors' financial preferences as of their professional credentials and capabilities. How representative such practices were is a difficult question, but it seems likely that they were amongst the more extreme examples of medicine conducted as business. As in business history more generally, the incidence of surviving records is biased towards successful enterprises. In contrast to many general practices, these three practices had well-kept, plentiful financial records, which in themselves attested to the importance with which these doctors regarded the economic outcome of their work.

Conclusion

General practitioners as a class appear to have been reluctant to adopt more efficient financial management in their practices. The cultural ethos doctors themselves had helped to foster—in attempting to distance themselves from 'trade' and therefore try to establish themselves as professionals—had involved separating their services from immediate payment, which itself then contributed to patients' belated recompense of their doctors. During the mid-nineteenth century easier conditions in the medical market seem likely to have enabled practitioners to give a higher priority to the clinical, compared to the economic, aspects of their practice. But during the late nineteenth century an unregulated growth of medical graduates, and a continued competitive struggle with other suppliers of health care, made it harder to make a medical living. American doctors, when faced with similar problems, made a more organized response through medical societies setting up business bureaux to advise members on book-keeping or the collection of bills, and

---

[123] A trebling of the annual gross income in monetary terms needs to be offset by a rise in the price index of some 36 per cent. In 1919 the price index for consumer goods and services stood at 223 (1913 = 100), and in 1947 it was 304. (C. H. Feinstein, *Statistical Tables of National Income, Expenditure and Output of the U.K. 1855–1965* (Cambridge, 1972), T 132–3).

[124] For example, the High Wycombe practice of Craig and O'Connor doubled its monetary income between 1935 and 1947 (CMAC, GP 5/4, annual income, 1935–59).

also by keeping lists of non-paying patients.[125] In Britain little organized interest in business methods was evinced by the profession. It was also unusual for an individual GP to be known, as was the Scottish-born James Goodfellow, as 'very skilful' in business and legal affairs, and keen to introduce new methods in the management of his practice.[126] Particularly before 1911 colleagues were stimulated by the competitive struggle for survival in the market to adopt a more economically focused outlook in pricing medical skill appropriately, developing flexible fee schedules, exploiting market niches (such as branch surgeries or suburban practices), and adopting sterner methods of debt reclamation. Because doctors later became less dependent on private fees for their incomes—as a result of a growth in public appointments, in third party payers, and more particularly after 1911, in social insurance payments—financial pressures became less insistent. In a discussion of the profession of medicine after twenty years of the National Health Insurance Scheme the *BMJ* commented that now 'medicine holds out the prospect of a fairly certain income'.[127] The cumulative impact of these changing influences on the organization of a general practice as a small business is discussed in the next chapter.

[125] J. S. Haller, *American Medicine in Transition, 1840–1910* (Urbana, 1981), 245–6.
[126] Obituary, *BMJ*, i (1950), 1145. Goodfellow practised in Chesterfield.
[127] *BMJ*, ii (1933), 412.

6

Organizing A Practice

'I ALWAYS felt I was like someone trying to get on a bus that was going, and . . . you never quite get both feet on the platform at the back. You were just chasing yourself all the time.'[1] This chapter discusses whether limited time horizons and acceptance of traditional constraints characterized doctors' management of general practice, or whether there were more strategic, and entrepreneurial considerations that shaped the development and survival of practices through economically rational choices about staffing, accommodation, and technology. Much of the scattered evidence on this subject would suggest the dominance of a short-term approach in which the sheer burden of everyday work and patients' expectations militated against a longer-term vision. Several important underlying factors were also responsible for an in-built conservatism that tended to preserve the *status quo*. Throughout the period medical education—which might have been expected to give a wider perspective—was geared to the production of hospital clinicians, rather than general practitioners, so that training was focused on the scientific, rather than the organizational, features of professional life. Practicalities were learned during a series of locums and assistant's posts after qualification; this gave a limited 'apprenticeship' and a necessarily restricted focus. After setting up in medical practice the GP frequently worked single-handedly and, to a considerable extent, in professional isolation. Yet despite conservative influences perpetuating inherited methods of working, some doctors were able to respond to changing professional opportunities by achieving stronger practice organization, exploiting new technologies, or adopting more efficient time management. Within a century the single-handed, 'horse and buggy' doctor of Victorian times was being transformed into a purposive professional, frequently working in partnership and running a mixed practice of privately and publicly funded health care.

---

[1] CMAC, GP29/2/27, John Evans, MA (Cantab.), MRCS Eng, LRCP (London, 1946), MRCP (London, 1953).

Assistants

Assistantships offered a convenient way to develop a general practice. The viability of a general practice, whether run single-handedly, or in partnership, was often dependent on low-paid assistants assigned humdrum duties. This section focuses first on the practitioner's reasons for employing an assistant, before turning to the rationale for the assistant.

One young assistant, Alexander Blyth, described his day in a dispensing practice in a country market town:

14 October 1864: Came downstairs—had breakfast—dispensed—the new boy [apprentice] has come—. . . I must teach him to dispense . . .—beat it into him if necessary . . . luncheon at 1—after that went and saw some paupers etc. . . . nothing particular. . . . No interesting case, most of them old people—coming home dispensed again—then dinner at 6—after dinner dispensed—then after tea [at 8 p.m.] sat with Mr J. Ceely [one of the two principals in the practice].[2]

In this practice the assistant was assigned low-status duties visiting the workhouse, the gaol and any patients living in the slum areas of the town. This then freed the two principals to look after high fee-paying private patients, and to pursue their duties at the county infirmary.

Those GPs who were appointed as a district medical officer under the poor law, as were the Ceelys, hired an assistant or, if they did not, were instructed to do so. Thus, in the Bicester Union, 'Frederick Gee begs leave to name James Adams Poole, MRCP and LSA as his substitute'.[3] The assistant could 'mind the shop' and, amongst multifarious duties, take messages from the relieving officer authorizing medical treatment for a sick pauper. The Bicester district medical officers had two or three such requests each week, thus necessitating much travel over a large country medical district.[4] Without such a substitute a medical officer might incur an official censure for neglect of a pauper patient, if delays in treatment arising from a difficulty in contacting the doctor led to death.[5]

Practices also employed assistants as a means of accommodating short-term change. A single-handed GP could employ an assistant during the busy winter months, during the principal's long-term illness, or as compensation for failing energies as advancing years took their toll. In the latter case the assistant's post might be advertised 'with a view' to partnership, if both parties were agreeable to a more permanent arrangement. An assistantship could also give flexibility when change apparently justified expansion, but did not yet justify taking on a permanent partner.

[2] Buckinghamshire RO, box 5, diary of A. Blyth, 14 Oct. 1864.
[3] Oxfordshire Archives, PLU2/G/1A16, Bicester Union Medical District Officers Returns, 1846.
[4] Ibid., PLU2/RL/2A4/1–2, Requests to Medical Officers for Medical Attention to Paupers, 1876–7.
[5] A. Digby, *Pauper Palaces* (1978), 168.

Another rationale for the practitioner's employment of an assistant was the desire to expand practice in what were perceived to be socially and/or clinically unappealing, yet financially rewarding, sectors—such as NHI work, industrial contract practice or poor-law work. This then enabled the principal to concentrate on the more rewarding or interesting aspects of practice, leaving the assistant to shoulder heavy, but routine aspects. Assistants could be assigned all the night work and midwifery.[6] And in industrial practice, especially in South Wales, abuse of the system of assistantships occurred through 'farming' out the practice to several assistants, whilst the principal did little if any of the work of running the practice. After 1911 an assistant was often taken on to run a branch surgery for the new working-class patients in a large panel practice.

In 1935–7 Bradford Hill's invaluable statistical inquiry into general practice found that 18 per cent of practices employed an assistant. Significantly, their employment was heavily concentrated in the financially more successful practices. Whereas only 2 per cent of practices with incomes under £1,000 employed them, 6 per cent of those in the income band £1,000-£1,499, 14 per cent of those earning £1,500-£1,999, and a striking 40 per cent of those with incomes over £2,000, had assistants.[7] Was the employment of the assistant the cause or result of this financial success? In some cases it was a significant cause, as for example, in the case of Dr Arthur Owen of Birkenhead. He employed an assistant in 1926 in order to expand his NHI practice substantially from 2,000 to 3,500 patients, thus developing a much larger panel practice than any of his colleagues. As a result his NHI income increased from around £900 to between £1,400 and £1,700 per annum.[8] Typically, those employing an assistant were reaping economies of scale. They achieved this by increasing the panel list of patients (by between the 1,000 and 1,500 additional patients that different localities permitted if an assistant was employed), and thus the capitation payments of around 9s. 0d. per patient. This was a larger amount than they were paying out for an assistant's salary, and the associated costs of taking on more patients.[9]

What of the applicant's purpose in seeking the post of assistant? Here the discussion is focused on the trained assistant (as distinct from the untrained or unqualified assistantships taken up before, or during medical school in the earlier part of the period).[10] Four reasons stood out as being important in taking such a post: to build up capital in order to buy a partnership; to make a decision as to whether general practice was the right career choice; to select

---

[6] Practice advertisement, *BMJ Supplement*, 13 Oct. 1877; C.B. Gunn, *Leaves from the Life of a Country Doctor* (Edinburgh, 1947), 47–8.

[7] A. Bradford Hill, 'The Doctor's Pay and Day', *JRSS*, civ (1951), 23.

[8] A. G. W. Owen (BA Wales, 1903, MB, ChB, Liv. 1909, MD, Liv. 1911). Cheshire RO, NIB 9/1–2, Birkenhead NHI Committee register of payments to practitioners, 1924–30 and 1930–4 and NIB 10, Birkenhead National Insurance Committee register of sums credited to practitioners, 1914–19.

[9] Digby and Bosanquet, 'Doctors and Patients', 83.   [10] See Ch. 3.

by trial and error which kind of general practice was wanted; and to gain the practical experience which medical school and a year's post in a hospital had not given. The need of recently qualified young medics for the latter was very obvious because, as the *Practitioner* commented, 'They are usually very inexperienced, often almost comically so.'[11]

Young entrants to the medical profession might discover that getting the post of a qualified assistant was not a walkover or, that once having obtained it, then a natural progression to independent practice did not necessarily follow. This was most obvious in times of graduate over-supply, as in the late nineteenth and early twentieth centuries. James Hill, for example, thought it necessary to produce six testimonials from his teachers at Glasgow University in applying for such a post in 1890.[12] Problems resurfaced during the economically depressed interwar years, when once having achieved an assistant's post and salary the young doctor could stay there for several years.[13] And concern was also expressed about an unprecedentedly large number of applications for assistantships in the period of uncertainty immediately preceding the NHS.[14]

Three examples of young assistants are described here to indicate some of the extensive range of experience. Working as an assistant for two years in the Welsh valleys, where he found most night work unnecessary, the doctor's services flagrantly abused by patients under colliery schemes, and the colliers thinking 'Are we not his master?', James Mullin decided against an industrial practice preferring to practise in Cardiff.[15] Three decades later Peter Clearkin's reasons for becoming an assistant were not only to decide which sort of general practice was appropriate, but also to see whether this kind of medicine was what he wanted. Significantly, the Welsh valleys had by now become so notorious that he did not even consider a post there:

I scanned advertisements for vacancies, avoiding those from Wales and finally accepted a post as Assistant to a general practitioner in the North of England, salary £125 a year with half the midwifery fees. This was a change from hospital practice, my principal was an Irishman from the West, and he impressed me at once with his practical knowledge of medicine. He explained that there was no time to carry out the meticulous examination of every patient as in hospital; one had to cultivate the faculty acquired only by practice to decide at a glance if a patient was seriously ill, and to reserve detailed examination for those who really required it. The bulk of the work consisted of colds, coughs, bronchitis, pneumonia, with an occasional case of measles, chickenpox, and the inevitable maternity case. Though the practice was a colliery there were few injuries but one had to be prepared for accidents in the pit . . . Work was heavy in winter especially with childhood ailments and I soon decided

[11] *Practitioner* 23 July 1910, 365.
[12] Greater Glasgow Health Board, HB 60, testimonials of James Hill, MB, CM (Glasgow,1890), MD (1895).
[13] *BMJ*, 12 May 1928.
[14] *BMJ*, 17 Aug. and 7 Dec. 1946.
[15] Mullin, *Toilers' Life*, 152.

that general practice was not my life's work, so applied for information about the Colonial Medical Service.[16]

The third assistant reviewed here, James Mackenzie, was motivated by the need to gain hands-on experience, having found that his medical education had not given him the ability to diagnose the complaints of patients. He began to make detailed notes of his work during a trial twelve-month period as an assistant to two Burnley GPs in 1879. At the end of the year he was offered a one-third share in the practice as a partner.[17]

Partners

By the interwar period assistantship with a view to partnership had become the standard route into general practice, although the aspiring young practitioner had to take care that the 'view' did not metamorphose into a 'mirage'.[18] This contrasted with the mid-nineteenth century situation when the norm in medical organization was a single-handed practice. Victorian doctors were unlike Victorian solicitors where partnerships developed earlier, because opportunities for specialization gave them a more obvious rationale. Despite this, the young Victorian solicitor was counselled that 'the partnership relation is always difficult, often supremely uncomfortable, and occasionally disastrous'.[19] Equally, the *General Practitioner* warned in 1910 'A medical man who has one or more good partners . . . is possessed of a great blessing, but when one sees all the trouble and mischief that arises from partnerships one is inclined to think that he who is without a partner is better so.'[20] Given that conventional professional wisdom counselled caution or abstinence, it was predictable that partnerships in general practice advanced slowly. Advertisements of practices for sale from the 1870s to 1900s indicate that more partnerships were of two people than of three, and that it was rare to have four. This situation had not changed much by the 1920s, when tax-derived statistics indicated that there was an average of just over two persons per partnership in medicine and dentistry. This was the lowest in any occupational group.[21]

Table 6.1 is based on the GP dataset and indicates a rise in those becoming partners from one in five (amongst those qualifying at the beginning of the period), to one in two (of those qualifying by the end of our period.) This does not, of course, give information on precisely when, in the course of a career, a doctor went into partnership. However, the trend corresponds to that given elsewhere. My earlier estimates, based on advertisements of the

---

[16] Rhodes House, Oxford, MSS British Empire, 4/1–3. P.A. Clearkin, OBE (1945), MB, BCh, BAO (Belfast, 1912), DPH (1923), MD (1930).

[17] Mair, *Mackenzie*, 47–9.   [18] *BMJ Supplement*, 6 Sept. 1953, 143.

[19] E. F. Turner, *The Organization of a Solicitor's Office* (1886), 55.

[20] Editorial, *Practitioner*, 10 Sept. 1910, 473.

[21] G. D. N. Worswick and D. G. Tipping, *Profits in the British Economy* (Oxford, 1967), 150.

TABLE 6.1.   Incidence of partners in general practice, 1820–1939

Decades for qualification of cohort	Nos. of Partners	% of Cohort
1820–39	10	19
1840–59	22	21
1860–79	34	25
1880–99	62	26
1900–19	107	46
1920–39	90	54

Source: GP dataset.

sales of general practices, indicated that by the beginning of the twentieth century one in five practices were partnerships. A precise calculation based on tax returns for 1928–9 indicated that nearly one in four of those in medicine or dentistry were partners. By this time the possibility of secure income from the NHI, and an expansion of the private medical market, made it much more feasible for several GPs to practise in a confined geographical area. And by the early years of the NHS, more than half of all early NHS principals in general practices had partners.[22] Organizational changes surrounding the NHS had not in themselves contributed to any dramatic increase in partnerships, since only 8 per cent of practices took on either a new partner or an assistant as a result of the new service.[23] Interestingly, one instance amongst these came when four doctors in an industrial town, formerly in 'opposition' to each other, joined together in order to 'grapple with the problems introduced by the NHS'.[24]

The incidence of partnerships amongst types of practices varied, as did their frequency in different geographical locations. The few surviving historical partnership documents are concentrated mainly in urban, suburban and industrial practices, but by 1951–2 there were more partnerships than single-handed principals amongst *both* rural and urban practices. Amongst 17,916 NHS principals, 35 per cent were in single-handed urban, and 12 per cent in rural single-handed practice, whereas there were 37 per cent in urban, and a further 16 per cent in rural partnerships.[25] Earlier, rural practices had often been considered too small to give a medical living to more than a single doctor on a permanent basis, and in this context it is interesting to find that amongst ninety Denbighshire practitioners enrolled in the National Health Insurance Scheme in 1911 the six partnerships in the county were all concentrated in towns.[26] However, more finite partnerships of a bridging nature

---

[22] Digby, *Medical Living*, 132; Worswick and Tipping, *Profits*, 155; *BMJ Supplement* 26 Sept. 1953, 104. The growth of practices was not an even geographical process since as late as 1937 only one in five London practices were partnerships (PEP, *Report*, 143).

[23] *BMJ Supplement*, 26 Sept. 1953, 702.   [24] Editorial, *BMJ*, 26 Sept. 1953, 717.

[25] *BMJ Supplement* 26 Sept. 1953, 104.

[26] Clwyd RO, Ruthin, NTD/741, List of NHI medical practitioners in Denbighshire, 1911.

were found in rural as well as in other kinds of practice. In this kind of arrangement there was an assistantship with a view to partnership, and then the retirement of the senior partner a couple of years later. This highlighted another important feature of partnership in general practice that was its frequently short-term character.

An important reason for partnership was the need to bring in new stocks of human and/or financial capital in a practice with an ageing principal. Running a successful general practice single-handedly in one's late middle years might prove physically taxing, so that a young partner who would do the more routine doctoring might seem appealing. During the next few years the progressive amounts of premium paid for an increasing share of the practice could then assist in the ultimate retirement of the senior partner, although decisions as to retirement would be predicated on the existence of prior savings that would provide the main income in retirement. Premiums in the late Victorian and Edwardian eras varied from less than one-third the annual practice income (for a precarious practice nucleus), to one and a half or even twice (for desirable, unopposed country practices or old-established urban ones).[27] After the NHS had ended the sale of practices a different arrangement ensued. Standard terms given in partnership vacancies in a Manchester Agency were to work for a one-third share for five years, another five years for a half share, and then achieve parity.[28]

Particularly as the medical market expanded, with the late nineteenth-century development of industrial and urban working-class practices, another kind of partnership became more common, where a younger 'workhorse' partner was recruited to look after a branch surgery, a works, or a NHI panel. William Henry Hill, for example, had carried on a 'surgical and general medical practice' at Basford in Nottingham for 'many years' but in 1901 decided to establish a branch surgical and general medical practice in neighbouring, and increasingly suburban Bulwell. That this was a deliberate step to expand the practice was shown by his later decision in 1908 to take on a surgeon as partner. Alfred Lewis Barham, the new partner, was to operate in Bulwell so as to develop further the new practice area.[29] It is likely that there was a degree of economic exploitation involved in many such agreements, since the 'value-added' from the additional work was more than the share of the partnership income that the new doctor received. For example, the young Dr William Harding accepted a partnership in 1925, 'although this meant doing at least half the work of the practice, and only receiving one third of the income'.[30] A young doctor would find this acceptable in the short-term, knowing that higher earnings would offset this later, when he had purchased a larger share of the practice. The national health insurance scheme offered

[27] *BMJ Advertiser*, 1877, 1899, 1909.
[28] CMAC, GP29/2/44, Thomas McQuay, MB, BCH, BAO (Belfast 1945).
[29] Nottinghamshire RO, DD BW/215/26, articles of partnership of Hill and Barham, 1908.
[30] Unpublished 'Memoirs of Dr William Henry Harding', 29.

even more obvious possibilities for practice expansion through partnership. An interesting instance of this occurred in Workington, Cumbria, in 1920. Here Adam Brown had worked as an assistant to John Dudgeon for seven months being engaged in looking after the panel patients. He then bought the panel part of the practice, together with the 'club' part which consisted principally of St Helen's Colliery, the Camerton Colliery and Brick Works, and the Seaton Lifeboat Club, which he ran from Seaton. This left his more established Workington colleague to deal only with private patients, until his retirement eight years later.[31]

Another factor that encouraged partnership formation was the expansion of mixed practices with a strong middle-class patient population. Taken singly, none of the following reasons was particularly strong but, as mutually reinforcing influences, they may have tipped the balance in favour of change. Economies of scale were likely to have been only marginal, as in purchasing an expensive piece of equipment (such as an X-ray machine) that was not possible in a single-handed practice. But, given the low investment in medical technology in general practice, this factor was likely to have been unimportant. Patient preference in an expanding practice might also have led to an additional partner being recruited, since an assistant could not be sent to an affluent patient, whose high fees could be justified only by contact with a more experienced partner. An injection of capital through expanding the numbers of partners may also have facilitated improved premises, but this only served as a means to expand a few progressive practices.

General predisposing influences for changes in organization included the ability to discuss difficult cases or to get a second opinion within—rather than hitherto—outside the practice. Equally important was the opportunity to develop a special interest, accept a hospital appointment,[32] or take a postgraduate course. Within a 'team' of doctors it was easier to envisage the kind of complementary professional and clinical talent that would be useful in enlarging a practice. Certain key attributes were important including attitudes to patients, the clinical nous 'to pick out the wheat from the chaff' or select out patients needing further investigation, and the physical fitness to cope with the workload.[33] And, as leisure preferences became stronger, so too did the appeal of a partnership rota that would permit a regular midweek afternoon at the golf course, a Sunday that was a break from a heavy workload, or the freedom to go on holiday without the worry of leaving the practice with a locum.

Diversification in practices during the period tended to increase partnership formation but the human problems of finding suitable partners who would fit into the distinctive nature of the practice inhibited swift expansion.

[31] Cumbria RO (Carlisle branch), DX 848/4, transfer of panel practice in Workington, 1920. Dr J. H. Dudgeon, LM, LRCP, LRCS; Dr A. Brown, OBE, MB, ChB.
[32] *BMJ Supplement*, 26 Sept. 1953, 143.
[33] CMAC, GP29/2/22, Jack Ridgwick, MRCS, Eng., LRCP (London, 1946).

Earlier, in the more intimate medical world of the mid-nineteenth century the issue of social recruitment was less difficult, because partners might be recruited from erstwhile apprentices, or recommendations of likely personnel were made by colleagues from local medical schools who knew the practice and its principal. But, as the supply of medical graduates later increased, and the number of practices also grew, recruitment became less a matter of personal social networks, and more a matter of utilizing impersonal agencies, with a consequent heightened risk. Advertisements for partners indicated an overwhelming concern to recruit the 'right kind of man' by prescriptive restrictions in terms of class, education, race, and religion. For instance, a conservative, church man might be requested for an English south coast practice, a Welsh speaker for a mixed practice in North Wales, or someone 'of good address' or 'used to good society' in suburban or country practices. Negotiations could founder on belated discoveries—such as that an aspirant partner was Roman Catholic or Jewish—and was thus seen as not fitting into the social arrangements of the practice.[34]

This kind of prejudicial discrimination was related to the difficulty that many practitioners had in perceiving their practice as an organization rather than a private creation. For example, one objected to the very word 'partnership' because it 'savoured of commercialism', whilst another thought of partnership less as a legal document than 'an agreement between gentlemen'.[35] Anxiety about possible problems made many doctors reluctant, even suspicious, of entering into partnerships. The length of legal agreements, and the prolonged period of negotiation, reflection and re-negotiation in drawing them up, revealed the difficulty of the enterprise. Partnership agreements might be drafted which never came to fruition, as in the case of the Hove doctor, D. C. B. Griffith, and the Brighton surgeon, A. P. Wells who contemplated a partnership in 1882, but then decided against it.[36] A common fear was that partners would not pull their weight, so that there was a standard clause urging each partner to be 'just, and faithful to the others'. Some later legal documents attempted to ensure this commitment by detailing, for instance, that each partner shall 'at all times during the partnership devote the whole of his time and attention to the said partnership and diligently and faithfully employ himself . . . for the greatest advantage to the partnership'.[37] Thus the time devoted to the practice became an issue; the distance from the surgery that a doctor could reside was often specified, as was how much holiday each principal could take. Predictably, it was the economic dimension which comprised the heart of a partnership document through a careful list-

[34] BMJ, ii (1900), 1476, obituary of Dr Taunton; personal communication from Sydney Alder of Brighton, MB, BS (Durham, 1929). See also the obituary of Maurice Pappworth for evidence of more widespread anti-Semitism in the medical profession (Independent, 12 Nov. 1994).

[35] BMJ, i (1960), 1817; ii (1950), 420.

[36] Essex RO, D/DDW B9/4, draft article of partnership, 1882. D.C.B. Griffith, MRCS, LRCP, LM (1876), MRCP (1879): A. P.Wells, LRCP, and LRCS, Ed. and LM (1882).

[37] Essex RO, D/DDW B9/4, Griffith and Wells, draft partnership, 1882.

ing and valuation of assets, specification of legitimate expenses, instruction as to what was to be provided by an individual doctor, such as instruments, and, of course, the precise allocation of shares in net income over time. Fear of dishonest accounting also led to the standard provision that 'proper books of account' should be kept, and that these should be open for inspection by all the partners.

An increasingly tightly drawn set of provisions in later contracts is well illustrated by one drawn up in 1936 to provide for an additional partner in a Norfolk practice. The central focus in the legal clauses was a traditional economic concern but, interestingly, fresh problems of indemnity loomed large. The new partner was to become a member of the Medical Defence Union, was to be personally liable and to indemnify the partnership against damage or compensation relating to negligence or misconduct. In addition, there was an attempt to envisage the problems of later life chances. There were agreed courses of action in case of death, illness, retirement, or call-up to HM forces.[38] But on the subsequent retirement of this additional partner a decade later, the eventuality to be accommodated was now not war but the NHS; the financial implications of varied levels of compensation that might be paid by the state produced a clause on possible compensation to the new entrant if that compensation was less than his premium.[39] In fact nothing in the NHS legislation rendered anything unlawful in existing partnership agreements; a Legal Committee on the subject stating that 'there should be as little interference as possible with the continued operation of existing partnerships'.[40]

A dilemma was posed in the partnership contract by a tension between its potential for expanding opportunity on the one hand, and its inbuilt, legalistic constraints on the other. This focused minds not only on the issues of creating, but also of ending, such an arrangement. Partnership agreements could not survive a decisive change in professional direction on the part of one principal. For example, an agreement between two GPs in Barry, South Wales ended, when one practitioner wished to join the NHI and the other did not.[41] Significantly, most partnerships had a clause for terminating the partnership after a number of years, even without the consent of the other party.[42] Even within continuing partnerships tensions could arise, especially over the division of workload, which might lead to an occasional audit of visits and surgeries undertaken by each partner. Presumably because of a fear of being constrained within a legal agreement which had ceased to operate satisfactorily, there were many 'partnerships' that operated informally *without* a legal contract. Indeed, it is interesting to discover that even at the end of the twentieth century a substantial number of partnerships are estimated to be in

---

[38] Norfolk RO BR 218/1, Deed of partnership of Pearce, Robinson and Bowes, 1936.

[39] Ibid., 218/5, Supplemental deed of partnership, 1947.

[40] *Report of the Legal Committee on Medical Partnerships*, PP, 1948–9, Cmd. 7565, xvii, para. 3.

[41] J. H. Williams, *GPs of Barry, 1885–1979* (Barry Medical Society, 1979), 11.

[42] Editorial, *Practitioner*, 10 Sept. 1910, 473.

this category, with family-based groups likely to be prominent amongst them.[43]

Despite the reasons that have been adduced for a more positive attitude towards partnership, a sizeable minority of general practitioners continued to operate single-handedly. A complex of economic, organizational and personal factors underpinned this preference for the *status quo*. Creating trust in the doctor within a local community may have been easier when only one reputation was involved. The state of the medical market in some thinly populated areas would not financially support more than one doctor. 'The chaos which characterizes the organization of the average practice',[44] could also have prevented a partnership that was predicated on an ordered set of arrangements. Of greatest weight, however, was personal preference. It had been common for doctors to assert that their predilection was to work on their own. One medical woman reflected that she was too bossy and perfectionist to work in partnership, while a colleague thought that he was temperamentally happy working single-handedly. 'You're responsible for yourself. You make your own decisions and you have the profits.'[45]

Although opportunities for specialization within general practice remained fairly limited, and thus the central dynamic driving other professions towards partnerships was missing, nevertheless by the end of the period a subtle change in professional attitudes in general medicine was taking place that favoured the growth of organizational change. As the state's incursion into health care, first with NHI and then with the NHS, reduced the financial risks of practice, the attractions of partnership grew in terms of shared responsibilities and workload. During the period professional opinion therefore changed over the balance between the perceived problems and likely benefits of partnerships. Experience had built up a reasonably effective system of checks against earlier abuses in partnership, while the advantages of professional cooperation appeared more compelling. Accompanying the NHS was a change in professional ethos that was particularly strong amongst those joining the service as young entrants, and in which a shift towards professional solidarity, and away from earlier extremes of entrepreneurial individualism, contributed to a more rapid shift away from the cottage industry of single-handed practice.

A Cottage Industry

General practice was frequently referred to as a cottage industry, but the full significance of the metaphor was seldom explored. As in a pre-industrial economy, many practices were still rooted in the household, with professional

[43] CMAC, GP 29/2/50, Kathleen Norton.
[44] J. Collings, 'General Practice in England Today' *Lancet*, 25 Mar. 1950, 558.
[45] CMAC, GP 29/2/62, Margarete Samuel, LMSSSA, London, 1931; CMAC, GP29/2/44, Thomas McQuay.

and domestic activity carried on side by side. This then gave a central importance to the activities of the wife in bridging the management of resources at
the interface between the domestic and professional activities of the household economy.[46] Whilst earlier GP's obituary notices frequently underplayed
this in their brief and ritualistic references to a 'devoted wife', oral testimony
indicated clearly the activist role of the spouse in the management of the
practice, and her part in networking—and thus expanding—its activities in a
wider community.[47] In some respects she might anticipate the functions of
the late twentieth-century practice manager, but less as an overt figure of
authority than as a guiding 'hidden hand'. If one examines some of the standard features of general practice it is obvious that there must have been an
intimate connection between public and private activity, and that the wife
managed this. At the domestic end of the spectrum pupils, apprentices, and
live-in assistants needed to be looked after, as did also the occasional paying
sick guests taken in to supplement fee income, whilst at the more public end
of the spectrum of wifely activities, there was the role of social hostess for an
ambitious husband who might give tennis parties for colleagues, including
consultants.[48]

Increasingly, in larger or more successful practices the wife's role was supplemented by paid assistance. But, although doctors had been professional-
ized themselves, their support staff—with the exception of accountant or
dispenser—were often untrained, so that commitment had to compensate for
any deficiency in skill. From at least the 1870s additional outside professional
services were increasingly paid for from medical agencies, solicitors, and
accountants. A growing number of agencies assisted in finding partners, assistants, or locums, in buying and selling practices, and keeping the books or
collecting debts.[49] Their extensive role has perhaps not been sufficiently
appreciated. One proclaimed in 1909 that 25,000 practitioners had consulted
the agency in the thirty-four years since its inception.[50] That doctors, in a
larger and thus more impersonal medical world, were turning to agencies in
such numbers itself speaks volumes about their increasingly business-like
outlook. Larger medical practices employed firms of accountants to look after
their books and act as debt collectors, or in later years, to prepare statements
for the Inland Revenue.

Within the practice the more successful employed a coachman, later a
chauffeur, to take the load off the principal during extensive visiting. From
the late nineteenth century part-time book-keepers, and book-keeper–
dispensers, were taken on, and dispensing practices might also employ a
trained dispenser, whose ancillary function could include compiling patients'

---

[46] See Ch. 10.
[47] Personal communications from Mrs Granger of Kimbolton, and Mrs Lilly of Long Buckby.
[48] D. G. Greenfield, MB, BS (London, 1901), MD (1902), FRCS (1903), obituary in *BMJ* i (1950), 193.
[49] Digby, *Medical Living*, 141.
[50] *BMJ Supplement*, 27 Nov. 1909, advertisement by Percival Turner.

accounts, or doing secretarial correspondence.[51] By the early twentieth
century more economically successful practices could employ a part-time
receptionist to organize patient throughput, answer the telephone, and type
letters. Large, and successful practices employed more personnel. In a panel
and private practice in Stepney the radical doctor, Harry Roberts, employed
two resident dispensers, secretaries, a dentist, and a medical masseuse.[52] And
in a successful interwar industrial practice in Treorchy in the Rhondda, Dr
Armstrong and partner employed two dispensers and a trained nurse.[53] Even
small rural practices found it necessary to draw on outside help: a boy would
wrap and deliver medicine bottles, or ride with the doctor and open field
gates; while the village postman or bus driver would deliver urgently needed
medicines.[54]

A central but neglected area in practice management was that of record
keeping. During the period before 1914 the central record was a bulky ledger,
which also gave a brief account of each item of treatment given to a patient,
so that these could be billed later. In the interwar period many doctors
switched to a visit and surgery attendance day book which merely outlined
the 'V' or 'A' on a given day. A parallel account book or ledger was then
employed to translate the treatment into bills to be sent out. The central
records of the general practitioner were therefore business oriented. Clinical
records, if they were kept at all, were subsidiary. A Victorian doctor sometimes kept a prescription book that gave an account of his dealings with the
local chemist. In addition, there might be correspondence with consultants
over a very small minority of patients. And a few GPs—with a special interest in midwifery—kept a record of obstetric cases. After 1911 the NHI
Commissioners instructed panel doctors to keep individual clinical records
for panel patients, although these regulations were usually observed more
often in the breach than the observance. Better kept were the books and
returns required by the poor-law authorities on the part of general practitioners employed as district or workhouse medical officers, as were also the
certificates required by friendly societies for those doctors who acted as lodge
surgeons. The stark contrast between the typical doctor's minimalist recorded
entries for his own individual purposes, and the standardized format and
detailed entries of the heavily bureaucratized records of collectivist bodies,
indicated some of the sins of omission in practice management. Given that it
was often the doctor (weary at the end of a long working day), who had to

---

[51] Squire practice, Wantage (Oxfordshire Archives, Misc. Sq. vii/1 and 14, Squire practice
ledgers); Pritchard practice in Cambridge (Cambridgeshire RO, uncatalogued records of Dr S. H. de
Pritchard, 1928–48); Guy Dain practice in Selly Oak, Birmingham (BMA Archives ref. 2054).

[52] W. Stamp, 'Doctor Himself.' An Unorthodox Biography of Harry Roberts, 1871–1946 (1949), 75,
78, 85.

[53] A. D. Morris, 'Two Colliery Doctors. The Brothers Armstrong of Treorchy', in J. Cule (ed.),
Wales and Medicine. An Historical Survey (Cardiff, 1975), 209.

[54] Personal communication from Dr Lilly of Long Buckby, Northamptonshire; J. Rankine, 150
Years in Country Practice (Romsey, 1982), 5.

make a record in the ledger or day book, the basic functionality, and priori-
tizing of financial over clinical detail was predictable.

Before the end of the period some non-industrial practices attempted to
keep clinical records of patients, but had inadequate clerical help to do so,
because of insufficient money.[55] Additional clerical resources for the
inputting of this routine material would, however, have enabled the doctor to
stand back from the minutiae of everyday detail, consider more strategic management issues of the optimal allocation of time between visits and surgery
attendance, decide how best to deliver clinical care (given the growing
resources of cottage hospital, district nurse and trained midwife), or reflect
on whether improved accommodation was desirable.

Accommodation

Relatively little professional interest or investment in accommodation was
apparent, although by the end of the period there was some appreciation that
better facilities could enhance patient recruitment. But only in a handful of
self-consciously progressive practices in the early twentieth century was
accommodation a professional priority. The location of premises was perceived to be more important, so that prominent locations were frequently
passed down through generations of doctors. In urban or suburban practices
a house and surgery on 'a capital corner plot' was advantageous since it drew
in passers-by as patients. 'Commanding house on highway' or 'excellent corner house' were therefore seen as prime assets in selling a practice.[56] And
well-established country practices, located in market towns, would aim to
have premises on—or very near—the central market square, as did the Ceely
practice in Aylesbury.[57]

Many Victorian GPs carried out their work from home with little accommodation for their medical tasks, except for a small room that might have
served earlier as the surgeon-apothecary's shop. In 1821 George Eachus and
Thomas Spurgin of Saffron Walden in Essex, for example, described their
profession as 'surgeon and apothecary' and carried this out 'on and around
the Shop and Premises'.[58] By the mid-nineteenth century 'the shop' was losing its retail function and becoming a working surgery/dispensary where
medicines were dispensed, or minor surgery was performed. Until the early
twentieth century, however, some surgeries were more like shops than consulting rooms, and the doctor stood behind the counter dividing the waiting
area from the dispensary.[59]

---

[55] *BMJ Supplement* 26 Sept. 1953, 701.
[56] *BMJ Supplement*, 1 July 1899; *Medical World*, 14 July 1944.
[57] Buckinghamshire RO, box 5, diary of A. W. Blyth, entry 2 Oct. 1864.
[58] Essex RO, D/DWm T 39, Partnership document between George Eachus and Thomas
Spurgin, both described as 'Surgeon and Apothecary'.
[59] CMAC, GP/29/2/71, Eric Grogono described his father's East London surgery at Stratford in
these terms. The surgery was only modernized in 1919.

As part of the professionalization of medicine provision of dedicated space for their medical activity seemed desirable for doctors' own convenience, and to alter public perceptions. During the 1850s, however, only a few provincial practitioners appear to have had a 'consulting room' where patients were seen, as did the Merionethshire surgeon, Owen Richards.[60] Provision of dedicated space for medical activities grew, as was shown by advertisements of practices for sale from the 1870s. By 1909, for example, a Midlands practice had 'corner house, surgery entrance', a country practice proclaimed that it had a 'good house built for a doctor. Separate surgery etc.'; and a Manchester working-class practice had 'surgery, waiting, dispensary and consulting rooms. Separate entrance.'[61] In general, however, little investment went into the improvement of facilities. A rural doctor at Ashton-under-Hill in Gloucestershire although having a consulting room, had very primitive facilities, using a roadside standpipe for his surgery's water supply, while his sink drained into the roadside ditch.[62]

Purpose-built accommodation away from the doctor's residence was not a common feature of general practice until the late 1960s and 1970s. Doctors operated from their homes. When a Flintshire general medical practitioner, John Owen Jones of Holywell, took a partner in 1920 he had to specify that his new partner, Charles Morris, 'a physician and surgeon' could use the 'surgery and consulting room', part of his private house and stables.[63] Even within the doctor's house specialist accommodation was limited so that, if a private examination of a patient was required, this would have to be done in the patient's own home. Even more deficient was the provision of adequate-sized waiting rooms for patients so that working-class patients might have to queue outside in the yard or street. The novelty of the panel doctor's surgery is revealed in Plate 3. In contrast, middle-class patients found themselves ushered into the doctor's dining room to wait for their appointment.

From the 1870s (possibly even earlier), a significant development was the branch surgery, and the lock up. For example, 'cash surgery—could easily be used as a lock-up'.[64] In 1911 the creation of NHI practices increased the use of branch surgeries, although it did little to improve their level of amenity, as a survey in the early 1920s indicated.[65] Until the 1920s adequate accommodation had been assumed but not specified in the contracts of insurance practitioners. Under NHI terms of service practitioners were 'to provide proper and sufficient surgery and waiting accommodation for his patients,

---

[60] National Library of Wales, NLW MS 7519B, Memoranda and diaries of Richards family, entry 12 Mar. 1852.

[61] *BMJ Supplement*, 22 May 1909, 19 June, 14 Aug. 1909.

[62] F. Archer, *The Village Doctor* (Gloucester, 1986), 54.

[63] Clwyd RO (Hawarden), D/DM/337/12, articles of partnership of John Owen Jones and Charles Edward Morris.

[64] *BMJ Supplement*, 25 Sept. 1905.

[65] PRO, MH62/151, replies from NHI Committees, 1923.

AT THE PANEL DOCTOR'S.

Gentleman (who has been steadily reading for the last hour). "YOU GO NEXT, MA'AM; I'VE ONLY COME HERE TO FINISH A STORY I STARTED LAST WEEK."

3. At the panel doctor's surgery, 1915

having regard to the circumstances of his practice'.[66] This was only an exhortation. Not surprisingly surgeries were overcrowded, with long queues, so that extra surgery hours had to be instituted to solve the accommodation problem.[67] An enquiry and inspection of premises in which NHI patients were treated found pretty basic accommodation, although surprisingly few lock-up surgeries. In some areas equipment and telephones were deficient.[68] An official campaign to improve facilities had a positive, if limited, effect.[69]

Branch surgeries were different in objective, although not in immediate function, from the way-stations that country doctors had been accustomed to use. The surgery was usually a new and expansionist device designed to 'capture' new areas of working-class patient demand for medical services, whereas the way-station was an additional convenience for both doctor and patients within an existing medical market. The way-station—effectively a staging post—might be a front room in a cottage used for a couple of hours on, say, Tuesday and Thursdays, according to the doctor's rotation of visits round the practice hinterland. A nominal sum to the villager would secure this

---

[66] *BMJ Supplement* 5 Jan. 1924, 6.

[67] *Burnley Express*, 10 Dec. 1924.

[68] PRO, MH 62/151, Court of Enquiry into Insurance Practitioners Remuneration, 1923 included NHI Committees replies on panel surgery accommodation.

[69] Nottinghamshire RO, SONH 1/10, Nottinghamshire NHI Medical Benefit Sub-Committee minute 1 Nov. 1922.

accommodation, the doctor would also put in a telephone line, and thus gain
the facility of a telephone service, where late or urgent calls could add to the
day's round of visits. Interestingly, by the interwar period some more enterprising suburban doctors were also colonizing rural territories more intensively, such that they established what they themselves termed rural 'branch
surgeries', each run by one of a growing number of partners.[70]

In 1924 Flexner described the typical urban doctor's accommodation. '[It]
consisted of two rooms, one for waiting and the other for consultation. There
was little to indicate which was which.'[71] In Dr Eurich's surgery in Bradford,
for example, a cupboard washstand had been fitted in 1896, but without a
supply of running water, so that a tank supplied any water, which was then
collected in a pail underneath the basin. Despite the success of the practice
this make-shift arrangement continued in use until the doctor's retirement in
1937.[72] New accommodation was built in areas where practice was expanding, as in a 1927 purpose-built doctor's house with two consulting rooms,
waiting room and dispensary at Blidworth, Nottinghamshire where a new
colliery was being developed.[73] Only the more progressive, successful or
expansionist practices put much effort and money into improving facilities
through bricks and mortar. Thus, in 1921 Dr Bone—who described himself
as the senior practitioner in Luton, the senior surgeon at the hospital, as well
as having a private practice—spent an exceptional £3,000 in reconstructing
accommodation. His centrally heated surgery had 'two large waiting rooms,
with seating accommodation for about 50 people, 3 consulting rooms, a dispensary, an office, and a pathological laboratory'.[74] Setting up in a country
practice, the idealistic young Dr A. W. Maiden mortgaged himself to the hilt
in building up-to-date accommodation, when he set up in Saxilby,
Lincolnshire in 1935. His house had a purpose-built surgery with a waiting
room at the rear.[75]

Even at the start of the NHS there was a general lack of purpose-built professional accommodation that Collings highlighted in his survey of fifty-five
practices. Industrial practices had surgeries located in, or above, a former
shop, and none were purpose-built. Premises consisted of two rooms—a waiting room that was too small for the numbers of patients, and a consulting
room in which a lack of soundproofing made the interview audible to those
in the waiting room. Dispensing took place in a separate small room or, on
occasion, in a cupboard. Some country practices were found to have used the

[70] For example, Essex RO, D/DT B4, articles of partnership of 1926 between Francis, J. B.
Battersby of Rayleigh, James E.J. Jameson of Rayleigh, and Alexander L. Dobbyn of Hockley. The
partnership was unsuccessful since by the mid-1930s the three doctors had all moved away from Essex
and were practising individually in Malmesbury (Wiltshire), Moreton in the Marsh (Gloucestershire)
and Bournmouth (Hampshire)!

[71] A. Flexner, *Medical Education* (1925), 9.   [72] M. Bligh, *Dr Eurich of Bradford* (1960), 80.
[73] Unpublished 'Memoir of Dr William Henry Harding', 37.
[74] BMA archives, reference 2054, Dr J. W. Bone (qualified Edinburgh, 1891).
[75] Personal communication, Dr Maiden of Saxilby.

same premises for over a century. In many of the suburban practices the front part of the doctor's house had been made over into a waiting room and a consulting room, and these were substantially and pleasantly furnished. Only a few practices provided specialist accommodation, as in a suburban practice where three rooms had been built: a 'commodious, well furnished' waiting room, a 'well laid out and well equipped' consulting room, but where a third room had been relegated for use as a store.

Hadfield's survey of 200 practices in 1951–2 gave a less critical impression, because he focused less on industrial and working-class practices.[76] One in three practices were found to be sub-standard; 10 per cent of premises were 'inadequate', while a further 24 per cent had only 'fairly adequate' premises. Nine out of ten practitioners had 'the full range of essential equipment', which comprised instruments for minor surgical procedures, treatment of wounds, and accident and diagnostic instruments, including urine testing apparatus. Only a 'few' practitioners lacked an appreciation of the functional value to their patients and themselves of 'clean, cheerful and suitable premises'. But, significantly, only 17 per cent of premises were found to be 'well above what may be considered adequate'. What was adequate in this context? This was defined in functional terms as being 'reasonably comfortable for doctor and patient, with no hindrance to the satisfactory conduct of the doctor's work and with reasonable warmth in both waiting-room and consulting-room'.

Doctors were engaged in a service industry, however, and might have been expected to have been economically responsive to the demands of potential customers. Yet it is clear that in the accommodation provided for patients, GPs devoted little money, and even less thought, to improvement. Would additional investment have paid off? Amongst working-class patients there was a general poverty of expectation as to what the doctor should offer, and also a high elasticity of demand in relation to the levels of fees charged, more particularly by a 'sixpenny' or 'shilling' doctor. Thus, any improvement to branch surgeries that then led to a raising of charges to pay for it could only have been counterproductive in terms of patient recruitment or retention. Only under a different payment system could cultural expectations be raised, as provision of municipal health centres indicated. Doctors thus intuitively understood that, although their patients might have liked better facilities, the great majority were not prepared to pay for them. 'He had inherited [this accommodation] and never thought to change, and the patients never complained.'[77] For middle-class patients in mixed practices investment in dedicated accommodation was also likely to have been unnecessary, since encounters within the doctor's own home served positively to reinforce relationships between people of similar social status. It was thus in expansionist

[76] J. S. Collings, 'General Practice in England Today. A Reconnaissance', *Lancet*, 25 Mar. 1950, 555, 557, 559, 562–4, 566; *BMJ* i (1953). See fn 15 on p. 189.
[77] Personal communication from Mrs Sue Pope about her father's Faringdon practice.

suburban practices, where affluent but as yet unknown individuals and families might be attracted to a fresh doctor in their new residential area, that some strictly economic returns might have been hoped for from investing in better facilities.

A more general improvement in the accommodation and facilities offered to patients waited on three later developments. The first was the creation of a health service in 1948 with a more socially inclusive patient population to replace the class-stratified clients of the preceding era of private and public health care; their needs could be met by uniform facilities. The second necessary pre-condition for change was public investment in the physical infrastructure of a health service that occurred in 1966. This had apparently been beyond the limited financial resources of general practitioners. Finally, health centres that served a wider geographical area were facilitated by the spread of car and telephone ownership amongst patients.

Technology

The impact of new technology on the organization of medical practice was not as marked in Britain, as it was in the USA where distances between doctors and patients were greater thus providing more incentive for innovation. In the USA take-up of the telephone occurred from the late 1870s,[78] whereas in Britain it appears to have occurred during the 1880s. But the earliest subscribers incurred certain costs because they might find that there were so few others with telephones that it was not much use, as did Dr Gunn, who was the first telephone subscriber in Peebles in 1888. He then disconnected the telephone until 1900, when—like other colleagues—he found it more useful, because telephones had been more widely adopted.[79] There was another start-up problem in that the post office provided no telephone night service in certain areas.[80] However, those who persisted with this new device found it of increasing use, as did Dr Williams in Denbighshire during the early nineties, as was shown by the increasing sums billed for his telephone.[81]

The telephone became a useful professional tool. Figure 6.1 is based on the GP dataset and suggests that the telephone's increasingly widespread adoption amongst doctors began to occur mainly after 1900. There was a fairly steady rise in the rate of take-up of successive cohorts of GPs, although diffusion tended to be slowed by the exigencies of war. Although fewer than two-fifths of those qualifying in the 1880s had adopted the phone, even after 25 years of practice, 95 per cent of the cohort qualifying in the 1930s had

---

[78] P. Starr, *The Transformation of American Medicine* (1982), 69–71.
[79] C. B. Gunn, *Leaves from the Life of a Country Doctor* (Edinburgh, 1947), 18; H. Morris Jones, 'The Country Doctors of Fifty Years Ago', *Country Quest* (Autumn 1961), 22.
[80] Scottish RO, HH 3 6/6, Minutes of Fife NHI Finance Subcommittee minute, 25 June 1915.
[81] Clwyd RO, (Ruthin), DD/HB/1959, miscellaneous accounts.

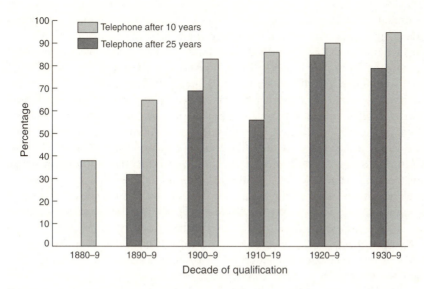

Fig. 6.1. Ownership of telephone by GP cohort, 1880–1939

done so at an equivalent point in their careers. And it is possible that the dataset slightly understates the figures since they suggest that in the early NHS era telephone usage was not yet quite universal amongst general practitioners.

Doctors found the phone useful for professional contacts of varied kinds. Professional opinion differed, however, over the advisability of a telephone consultation. Whilst one interwar country doctor, Dr Meikle, gave advice to patients by telephone, another saw this as a last resort which compromised standards of medicine.[82] Other uses included liaising with the cottage hospital over an admission, arranging for a consultation, or contacting the district nurse. It was also important in reducing the professional isolation of the doctor through increasing contacts with a range of medical and health-care professionals. The phone also contributed to the process by which rural practices became less geographically compact, because the telephone enabled enterprising urban or suburban doctors to capture patients in country areas, thus further increasing the economic problems of running a rural practice.[83] Telephone ownership by patients also gradually inflated the doctor's workload, not least through increasing the number of requests for a night visit.[84]

'A medical man can often ride into a practice more quickly than he can walk into one' commented a professional guide.[85] During the nineteenth

[82] Oxfordshire Archives, Misc Savil, I/i/i medical diary and visiting list of R. W. Meikle MB, CM (Glasgow, 1898); letter from S. A. Forbes of S. Croydon (*BMJ*, 15 Apr. 1933).

[83] Digby and Bosanquet, 'Doctors and Patients', 84.

[84] Id. 'Doctors and Patients', 85.   [85] J. de Styrap, *The Young Practitioner* (1890), 16.

century the horse was the doctor's main form of transport. Indeed, doctors
practising in difficult, hilly terrain used their horse to visit outlying patients
throughout the period.[86] In remoter country areas a variety of devices might
be used including sleds and stilts; in the Highlands and Islands boats were
used frequently, and in a north Devon practice doctors needed to contact the
Admiralty to charter a steamer for them to visit patients on Lundy Island.
Relatively little impact on their own means of transport was felt by GPs as a
result of the mid-nineteenth century railway revolution, although a few doctors might utilize a new branch line to visit a more distant patient, often by
making a special arrangement with the guard for the train to make an
unscheduled stop.[87] Where rail impinged on general practice more substantively was in shifting referral because of the ease with which consultants could
travel longer distances to give their second opinions—thus restricting opportunities for GPs to be called in for a second opinion.

By the 1880s a horse, or a horse and dogcart were being supplemented or
replaced by a cycle by some enterprising young town doctors.[88] This lowered
the costs of practice considerably because, instead of the high costs of horse,
hay, stabling and coachman, the doctor had only the initial purchase price of
a two-wheeled steed to pay. However, for tired country doctors returning at
night from distant visits, a horse which knew its way home, had a value which
a bicycle or car did not possess. During a transitional phase practitioners
might see different forms of transport as complementary rather than competitive, as in the case of a rural practitioner with a far-flung practice who
used his bicycle for nearer visits before breakfast, thus saving his horse's
energies for the long visits afterwards.[89] With the bicycle came a bowler hat,
tweed coat and knickerbockers that replaced the traditional frock coat and top
hat, thus symbolizing the GP's greater accessibility to a broader social range
of patients.[90] Some town doctors also deliberately always went on foot,
eschewing bike or car, so as to maximize their personal contacts, and so
heighten their social profile.[91]

Changes in transport were an important factor in doctors' attempts to
respond to increasingly severe competition. A small number of young doctors embraced the motor bike for their rounds (often because of economy),[92]
but many more turned to motor car from the 1890s. Progress occurred at different speeds: one Birmingham doctor had given up a horse and gig for a car

[86] Swaledale Folk Musem, Reith, North Yorkshire for display on Dr Speier of Swaledale; J. H.
Williams, *GPs of Barry, 1885–1979* (Barry Medical Society, 1980), 14; Obituary of John Cockcroft
of Middleham, Yorkshire (*BMJ*, ii (1930), 502).

[87] Wellcome Institute, WMS 5415, Littlewood Memoir, 46: Archer, *Village Doctor*, 4.

[88] *BMJ Supplement*, 7 Oct. 1899.

[89] D. Huskie, 'Impressions and Experiences of a Country Doctor in the 'Nineties and After',
Transactions of the Medico-Chirurgical Society of Edinburgh (1938), 6, 9.

[90] J. Pemberton, *Will Pickles of Wensleydale* (1970), 30.

[91] For example, Dr George Irvine of Barry (Williams, *GPs of Barry*, 14).

[92] *BMJ*, i (1901), 154–5; Wellcome Institute, WMS 5415, Littlewood 'Memoir', 13.

before 1900, but a rural Yorkshire practitioner began by walking his rounds, then bought a gig with two horses, and only purchased a car in 1911.[93] The earliest medical motorists were those owning a car before the end of the nineteenth century, and such enthusiasts were to be found in urban, suburban, and country practices.[94] What distinguished them, apart from their mechanical enthusiasm, was their busy and energetic lifestyle. For example, 'He was seen to go from patient to patient at great speed, believing that the less time spent in travelling the more time could be devoted to the patient.'[95] Country surgeons found the car especially useful through their enhanced ability to transport a portable operating table, surgical equipment, and a nurse to the scene of an accident or an urgent operation.[96] Others enthused over its economical and efficient performance, 'I have run sixty miles a day for three days in one week, and have often made twenty or thirty calls in a day in it. The cost of running varies from 1s. 2d. to 1d. per mile according to size and gradient.'[97] Another colleague made a comparative assessment of old and new forms of transport in commenting that a car removes the 'fear of knocking up your horses or having them catch cold while waiting'.[98]

Although GPs were amongst the earliest purchasers of cars, the *BMJ* did not feel able to endorse them as a sound investment until 1904.[99] However, practices for sale soon began to advertise quaintly that they had a 'motor house' as part of the premises.[100] A few doctors substituted a 'motor boy' for their previous groom, although the boy might be less reliable; one doctor found that the boy was making holes in the car radiator so that night calls couldn't be answered, and his sleep be undisturbed.[101] By the interwar period the car came to be seen as 'an absolute necessity' for the 'proper conduct of medical practice'.[102] Mileage per practice varied enormously, with figures of 3,000, 6,000, or 8,000 miles per annum being cited.[103] In the medium term the car was to transform most practices; economizing on time, and giving added flexibility to the geographical limits of practice. Hard-pressed doctors with large numbers of patients were alleged to have driven their cars from the running board, never actually sitting down in the car between patients.[104] Rural doctors seized the opportunity to utilize hospital facilities in neighbouring towns more intensively, through employing the motor ambulance for

---

[93] H. W. Pooler, *My Life in General Practice* (1948), 59; B. H. English, *Four Generations of a Whitby Medical Family* (Whitby, 1977), 108–10.

[94] *BMJ*, ii (1930), 450–1; ii (1910), 1895; ii (1960), 1606; i (1940), 154, 236.

[95] *BMJ*, ii (1960), 1812.   [96] *BMJ*, i (1910), 549–50.

[97] *BMJ*, i (1897), 895.   [98] *BMJ*, ii (1897), 1770.

[99] Bartrip, *Mirror of Medicine*, 152–3. Until the Finance Act of 1925 any wear and tear on a doctor's car could not be claimed against income tax.

[100] *BMJ Supplement*, 17 Apr. 1909.

[101] Dr Tylor's letter of recollections in Lodge, 'Reminiscences'. M. F. Tylor (1875–1903), qualified 1903 (Oxford and St George's, London), retired 1936.

[102] *BMJ Supplement*, 29 Mar. 1937, 315, 334.

[103] Ibid. 5 Jan. 1924, 20; 29 May 1937, 328.

[104] CMAC, GP/29/2/71, E. B. Grogono.

their patients. And motor transport facilitated closer professional contacts by making it easier for colleagues to attend medical societies, thereby updating their knowledge, and engaging with medico-political issues. Taken together, the car and phone had the potential to transform perceptions of space: distance could be conquered in order to exploit a wider medical market.

If distance might be conquered, time needed to be managed. In 1851 James Simpson had given wise advice to medical students that 'The two great commodities which the physician carries into the mart of the world to barter for the goods of life, are his professional knowledge and his time.'[105] Doctors' appreciation of the value of the latter was enhanced as medical schools turned out high numbers of medical graduates. A downward pressure of fees ensued so that a new urgency was imparted to the need efficiently to allocate time if doctors were to make an adequate living.[106] A very significant shift from the doctor visiting the patient, to the low fee-paying patient attending the surgery was the logical result. As we have seen earlier, the first most visible sign of the new realities of general practice was the development of the branch surgery in urban and industrial areas with a large working-class clientele. The NHI strengthened this trend after 1911, since there were clear economic incentives to build up a large panel of patients who attended the doctor's surgery.[107] 'I could see three patients in the time it takes to do one call.'[108] For mixed practices of panel and private patients, and for doctors with rural practices, the imperatives were less obviously towards a pattern of surgery attendances rather than visits.

Rural doctors made many more home calls relative to surgery contacts than did town ones; because transport for country patients was lacking. Equally, these visits took longer than those of the urban practitioner. The traditional contact by letter also continued, especially in country areas, where repeat prescriptions with accompanying advice might be sent by post.[109] In rural practices the doctor made regular visits to outlying areas,[110] and under informal but long-standing arrangements (which often dated back to which practice held an area under the Victorian poor law),[111] adjacent practices divided up the country hinterland around the market towns where practices were located, so that patients were taken on only if they lived near the doctor's regular visiting stations.

When judged by the standards of late-twentieth century general practice both town and country doctors made many visits in the era before 1948. A

[105] J. Y. Simpson, 'On the Duties of Young Physicians', in J. Y. Simpson, *Physicians and Physic. Three Addresses* (Edinburgh, 1851), 19.

[106] Digby, *Medical Living*, ch. 5 *passim*.

[107] Digby, 'The Economic Significance of the 1911 Act', in K. Waddington and A. Hardy (eds.), *Financing British Medicine* (forthcoming, Amsterdam, 1999).

[108] CMAC, GP 29/2/66, Walter Shaw.

[109] Norfolk RO, BR 224/11, Dr Speirs' Day Book, 1896–9, fos. 8, 900.

[110] Kelly's *Directory of Essex* (1933).

[111] R. G. Lilly, *An Account of Rural Medical Practice from the 18th Century Onwards in Long Buckby, Northamptonshire* (Dunton Bassett, 1993), 85–6.

significant reason for this was that clinical need dictated frequent visiting. Serious conditions such as pneumonia, as well as ailments in babies and young children, demanded a prudent routine of recurrent contact. The expectations of private patients also contributed to a high rate of visits to their homes. Even panel patients might expect a visit where a present-day sufferer would not. 'If they had a temperature, they'd stay in bed and send for you.'[112]

General practitioners made themselves very accessible, and were seen as being at the service of their patients. 'Twenty four hours of the day and seven days of the week', commented a member of the family of one GP.[113] Doctors' day books are revealing in showing how, even on Christmas Day, the medic was called out several times to visit patients. General practice was certainly not for the faint-hearted or lazy. During the first half of the twentieth century GPs typically had two, or even three surgeries daily, with one or two surgeries on Saturday, and a further one on Sunday morning. Even in a rural practice where more patient contact came through home visiting, doctors maintained morning and evening surgeries. For example, on the eve of the NHS Drs Ellis and Granger of Kimbolton had two surgeries daily on weekdays (one from 9 to 10 a.m., and another from 6.30 to 7 p.m.), with an additional one on Sunday mornings from 9.30 to 10 a.m.[114] There was, of course, seasonal variation in the demand for doctors with much greater pressure from January to March than in the rest of the year, mainly from respiratory cases.[115] Equally, there was a weekly rhythm so that Mondays, and Saturdays in the earlier part of the period, and Mondays and Fridays towards the end, were the busiest days, with midweek being much less frenetic.[116]

Table 6.2 indicates that there was an equivalent rate of increase in visits and surgery attendances during the period of the NHI, although there were three surgery attendances made by panel patients to every one doctor's visit. In responding to a notably increased demand for health care during the interwar period, doctors were therefore either unable or unwilling to shift the pattern of contacts with patients towards surgery attendances, as economic rationality would have suggested.

Before 1948 appointments were seldom used except for paying middle-class patients. Appointments systems came into more general use only from the 1950s. At the same time the number of surgeries was cut, when many doctors abandoned their Sunday surgery.[117] One reason for fewer surgeries was that patient demand at weekends lessened. The regularity of the NHS cheque meant that doctors felt able to take a less economically driven view, whilst at the same time new drugs reduced clinical pressure, by making

[112] CMAC, GP29/2/59, Samuel Isaacs.

[113] *Hansard*, 472 (1950), col. 962, Iain McLeod, the son and grandson of doctors.

[114] Private archive, Kimbolton practice of Dr Granger.

[115] Bradford Hill, 'Doctor's Pay', 13; CMAC, GP/29/71, E. B. Grogono.

[116] Bradford Hill, 'Doctor's Pay', 11, Norfolk RO, BR 224/11, Dr Speirs's day book, 1896–9; GP 29/2/59, Samuel Isaacs.

[117] CMAC, GP/29/2/71, Eric Grogono.

TABLE 6.2.　Patient contact with panel doctors, 1922–36

Year	Visits	Attendances	Visits and Attendances
1922	0.99	2.76	3.75
1925	1.32	3.37	4.69
1926	1.34	3.54	4.88
1927	1.4	3.63	5.03
1928	1.31	3.54	4.86
1929	1.37	3.65	5.03
1930	1.22	3.54	4.77
1931	1.29	3.46	4.75
1932	1.28	3.73	5.01
1933	1.4	3.88	5.29
1934	1.3	3.68	4.98
1935	1.34	3.77	5.11
1936	1.33	3.8	5.13

Source: *BMJ Supplement* (29 Mar. 1937), 315, 329.

frequent visiting less necessary. Interestingly, however, 'rigidities' in work practice remained; older doctors, as well as those in single-handed practice, spent more of their time visiting, and worked longer hours as a result, according to a survey in 1966. This also indicated that country doctors were still seeing twice as many patients at home compared to town doctors.[118]

General practitioners needed to allocate their time efficiently between different groups of patients if they were to maximize their professional effectiveness. Before 1948 there were two issues: first, the relative allocation of time between private and panel patients and, secondly, the pricing of time for visits as against surgery attendances on a fee scale. It is clear that doctors should have charged much more for visits than for surgery attendances if their time was to be appropriately remunerated. In reality, there were two schools of thought on this issue; some charged more, some charged precisely the same.[119] Even where there was a differential, however, it is clear that the better financial recompense was not an adequate reimbursement for the additional time spent in visiting. Depending on the nature of their practices doctors probably took half as much time on surgery attendances as on visits, but their surgery charges were not 50, but 70 to 80, per cent of the charges for visits.[120] Estimating the time-value of medical work was therefore an imprecise art rather than a professional science, but its inexactness had serious implications for practice income. Even the government recognized that a public subsidy was necessary to compensate for the unremunerative nature of

[118] T. S. Eimert and R. J. C. Pearson, 'Working Time in General Practice: How General Practitioners Use Their Time', *BMJ*, ii (1966), 1549–54.

[119] *BMJ Supplement*, 13 Mar. 1920, 71 (evidence of Dr Stamp).

[120] Ibid., 67; 26 Jan. 1924, 84.

lengthy and time-consuming rural visiting in insurance practice and a rural mileage allowance was given to country panel doctors from 1914. In addition, a decade later the government provided an annual sum of £10,000 for 'unremunerative practice' payments to assist with telephone, branch surgeries, payments for locums, and travel costs in sparsely populated areas.[121] By legislation of 1913 and 1929 a Highlands and Islands Medical Service Fund was established under which doctors could be recompensed if they modified fees for patients, so that the costs arising from long distances travelled by the practitioner did not lead to such high fees as to disqualify poorer people from seeking medical assistance.[122]

Turning now to the allocation of the doctor's time between different social classes of patients, a disproportion between time spent, and income received was evident. That there was a general social awareness that time was money for the doctor was shown in contemporary humour. In the *Punch* cartoon, 'The Early Bird catches the Worm', for example,[123] the doctor finds that female patients are taking up too much of his time, rings the bell and tells his servant that when Mr Gladstone arrives he is to be put in the breakfast room to wait a little while.

Pricing inefficiency was endemic in general practice. Implicit in agreements on insurance remuneration during the interwar period was the assumption that insurance doctors would spend less than one-third of their time on their panel patients, yet receive half their income from NHI.[124] Either this meant that public money would compensate for the under-employment of doctors in private practice,[125] or that private patients received a disproportionate amount of time from doctors, in terms of the fees that they paid for their attention. The alacrity with which, after the NHS, a number of doctors with erstwhile mixed practices of private and insurance patients, jettisoned their private patients, indicated that doctors were aware that their time had not been spent optimally. Revealingly, one said, 'I didn't mind wasting my time with these people before the [National Health] Service started, but they're not worth it any more.'[126]

Conclusion

This chapter has indicated that principals in general practice exhibited a patchy and uneven response to professional challenges in their practice organization. In part this was the result of individual preferences and expectations

[121] *Sixth Report of the Ministry of Health*, PP, 1924–5, xiii, 118; *Seventh Report of the Ministry of Health*, PP,1926, xi, 135–6.

[122] PEP, *Report*, 364. The scheme also provided funds for improving doctors' houses and for the employment of locums.

[123] *Punch*, 20 Nov. 1875.

[124] Digby and Bosanquet, 'Doctors and Patients', 82.

[125] *BMJ Supplement*, 5 Jan. 1924, 21.

[126] Quoted in Collings 'Report', *Lancet*, i (1950), 569.

which helped shape professional life as well as the more objective pressures of the medical market. Those doctors who saw their life more in terms of a 'calling', or who embraced the more leisurely lifestyle of the country prac- tice, were less inclined to seize the opportunities for practice expansion offered by changing patient demand. There were also important generational differences. Later cohorts of young doctors considered professional choices more carefully, and thought strategically about career options and their implementation. Responding to the uncertainties of their situation meant that from the 1880s younger entrants to the profession were frequently more con- cerned with the exigencies of professional survival, and thus more market- orientated in their view of medicine than their older, well-established colleagues. They were therefore more effective in responding to the options of practice in a rapidly changing society.

Inner city and industrial practices embodied intensive patient demand, and thus offered a simple opportunity for positive practice development and inno- vation. The employment of an assistant and/or the provision of a low-cost branch surgery promised a good return on a relatively small financial outlay. But general practitioners were quicker to adopt the branch surgery than to employ the assistant, and thus did not fully realize the economic potential of this new medical market.

How effectively did they respond to the more extensive and differentiated patient demand of a rural, suburban or mixed practice? This could be devel- oped by the creation of a partnership which gave added flexibility in the use of resources to develop different sectors in an evolving mix of privately and publicly funded health care. Growth in partnerships during the twentieth century indicated that GPs did respond positively to these options as, for example, when a younger partner specialized in the public part of the mixed practice, taking panel and club patients, whilst the senior partner concen- trated on private patients. However, the financial cushioning which national health insurance payments brought to many practitioners after 1911 probably slowed the rate at which partnerships were created. In any case these were still regarded as easier to enter into—than to withdraw from—if difficulties ensued, whereas more adaptable innovations such as the telephone or motor car were both easier to assimilate as well as to change. Reliance on the motor car and telephone increased the capability of the GP to exploit an increas- ingly complex medical market, through greater personal mobility and improved information. The steady and widespread take-up of this modern technology indicated a forward-looking attitude to meeting the challenges of an expanding demand for health care.

In contrast, there was only a limited appreciation of the need to review time-management in the allocation of the doctor's day as between surgeries and visits to patients' homes, in order to economize on vital but scarce pro- fessional resources of time and energy. A conspicuous failure by all but a few suburban or progressive practices to invest in bricks and mortar was probably not too damaging, given the poverty of patient expectation. But it did highlight some doctors' tardiness in appreciating the growing importance of the surgery as a means of increasing patient throughput, and thus of maximizing revenue. Equally, there was minimal provision of support staff of different kinds, so that many GPs continued to operate in a cottage-industry environment. It was thus in everyday management, in decision-making about scarce resources, that many general practitioners were less than effective. Paradoxically, a failure to do so then set up a vicious circle in which a consequent lack of revenue inhibited developments that would themselves have generated additional income to finance improvement.

A comparison of general practice in the mid-Victorian era with that on the eve of the NHS, reveals familiar features such as the mobility of the doctor, the long working day, and the entrepreneurial nature of a small business. But new dimensions in individual practices were also discernible, in the greater incidence of partnerships, a few purpose-built premises, some substitution of surgeries for more time-consuming visits, and an increased throughput of patients. Most strikingly, an increased differentiation in practice type had developed with the aid of combinations of partners with a new breed of assistants, who were assisted by new technologies. This indicates that some GPs—mainly those in urban, industrial, and suburban practice—had responded positively to the entrepreneurial openings of an expanding medical market, and had made some strategic decisions in exploiting a market niche. In rural, and in mixed practices organizational innovation was less conspicuous, not least because the complexities of patient demand meant that it was difficult, if not impossible, to formulate a coherent response. Even here, however, there had been an adoption of new technology, and of partnerships.

In modernizing their practices through selective response repertoires general practitioners had attempted adaptation in order to ensure their survival. They had shown context sensitivity in their innovative reactions to increasingly urban and suburban practice environments. And, as a result of their initiatives (or a lack of them), general practitioners as agents of cultural change had experienced differential rates of success. One consequence was that variation in types of practice had notably grown. Although general practice might justify its label 'general' in clinical terms, in their social profile individual practices increasingly had a varied composition. In some cases their make-up might be quite restricted, as was evident in the women-and-child practices of the medical women—the subject of the following chapter.

7

Women Practitioners

THE history of women in general practice is that of female practitioners operating in a semi-detached professional sphere. This was in part the product of gendered cultural values, but was also the result of the medical market whose congested state was worsened by the entrance of women themselves. This highly competitive situation encouraged ecological practice niches, where female GPs developed distinctive career paths and patient constituencies. As the period advanced, the forces making for a gendered separatism became weaker, so that medical women became more assimilated.[1] Increasingly women did not wish to see themselves as a separate group: their self-perception became one of themselves as doctors in their profession, but as women in their private lives.[2]

Access and Training

Evolutionary theory informed debates on the suitability of women to enter higher education and study medicine.[3] Male doctors claimed the authority to prescribe conditions of female lifestyle, and in which medical 'knowledge' would enable an optimal interaction of woman's body with its environment. In this way harmful changes to the physiology of the individual would be impeded, the degeneration of the race be prevented, and evolution be advanced. Unusually, a male doctor such as the Darwinist, Lawson Tait, might argue that an exceptional woman who had 'the fitness for survival' had the right to enter the 'great struggle of life' in the ranks of the medical profession.[4] Feminists, who included early women doctors, framed their

[1] I have found two theses especially helpful in providing a general contextual framework for women within the wider profession: Mary Ann Elston, 'Women Doctors in the Health Services: A Sociological Study of their Careers and Opportunities' (unpubl. Ph.D., University of Leeds, 1986); Diana Palmer, 'Women, Health and Politics, 1919–1939. Professional and Lay Involvement in Women's Health Campaigns, (unpubl. Ph.D., University of Warwick, 1986).

[2] P. Jalland (ed.), *The Autobiography of Octavia Wilberforce* (1989), 99–101.

[3] The insights of the thesis by K. J. Rowold, on ' "The Academic Woman": Minds, Bodies, and Education in Britain and Germany *c.*1860–*c.*1914' (University of London Ph.D. thesis, 1996), informs this paragraph.

[4] L. Tait, 'The Medical Education of Women', *Birmingham Medical Review*, 18 (1874), 84. Tait later changed his mind on this issue.

responses within the evolutionary context of these contemporary medical and scientific pronouncements on the relationship of gender to social organization. A prominent pioneer, Dr Elizabeth Garrett Anderson, suggested that in the long term the natural order could take care of itself, but that in the short term liberal beliefs on equality could offer a guide to women's emancipation. She also provided effective arguments on woman's capacity to stand up to the rigours of secondary and college education. Those in Britain's first women's movement skilfully employed Darwinian and Lamarckian insights on the changeability of human characteristics by arguing during the 1870s that medicine was a 'natural' occupation for women through its use of characteristically feminine natural instincts in caring for others. In addition, it was asserted that female doctors could address female ill health more effectively than the male doctor, therefore assisting women in their important reproductive role. From the 1880s feminists' emphases changed from a short-term focus on biological changes in contemporary woman, to a longer-term preoccupation with the formation of minds and bodies in relation to future evolutionary development. As ideas of degeneracy became more prominent, female campaigners deployed evolutionary theory to argue that, just as women's mental capabilities had been shaped by the past in being subjected to men so, given this mutability, they could be influenced positively to benefit not just women but also men in the future. Some, like Olive Schreiner, argued that women's emancipation and, crucially, their entry to the professions, were evolutionary necessities. Debates about women's rights were therefore increasingly integrated into mainstream evolutionary discussions on improving the biology of the race. In these discourses women were themselves both object and subject.[5]

It was significant that it was strong opposition by medical faculties which was prominent in delaying the admission of women students to universities. Though seldom articulated, sectional professional apprehensions and material concerns informed rhetoric. These anxieties resulted from an acute awareness of a congested profession, in which the prospect of competition from women practitioners, more particularly for female patients, was viewed with dismay.[6] 'One of the roots of the medical prejudice against women doctors is the fear that they should lower the price of medical work', stated Elizabeth Garrett Anderson.[7] And a feminist voice from outside the profession, that of Frances Power Cobbe, denounced male doctors for their 'public manifestation of trades-unionism' in attempting to keep ladies 'out of the lucrative profession of physician'.[8] Whilst there were a few progressive voices in

---

[5] Rowald, ' "The Academic Woman" ', 115–23, 133, 163–5, 189–93, 200, 206–7, 444–5, 449.

[6] A. B. Shepherd, *Introductory Address delivered at St Mary's Hospital* (1873), 12; *Correspondence on the Medical Registration of Women*, PP, 1875, lviii; W. Dale, *The State of the Medical Profession in Great Britain and Ireland* (Dublin, 1875), p. v; J.H. Aveling, in *Transactions of Obstetric Society of London*, 16 (1875), 75; C. West, *Medical Women* (1878), 31.

[7] Quoted in P. Levine, *Victorian Feminism* (1987), 46.

[8] F. P. Cobbe, 'Medicine and Morality', *Modern Review*, 11 (1881), 323.

medicine,[9] male prejudice persisted although its strength fluctuated with the state of medical employment.

Within this socially conservative climate of opinion concessions on the entry of women to professional bodies and élite medical institutions came very slowly (see Table 7.1). A sign of a more general change in society's opinion towards women's entry to medicine, however, was indicated by a sympathetic tone in the non-medical press. The refusal of the petition for female membership by the Royal Colleges of Physicians and of Surgeons in 1895 was termed 'reactionary obstinacy' in the *Daily Graphic*, because it considered that public opinion was already supporting the 'accomplished fact' of woman doctors.[10]

Given the brutalizing environment in which medical studies were then conducted, the earliest argument advanced against women in medicine was that delicacy should prevent women studying medicine at all.[11] Later this stance was modified to hostility towards a possibility of men and women studying medicine side by side. Both separatist and integrationist tendencies operated to complicate the British pattern of university admission and of medical qualification. Some of the earliest opportunities for women to achieve a first qualification in Britain thus came through the conjoint examinations offered by licensing bodies outside the universities.[12] Obduracy by some British universities (especially the closure of a route to a medical qualification at the University of Edinburgh between 1869 and 1873 for Sophia Jex-Blake and her fellow students), also led to a continued reliance by medical women on MDs at European universities including Berne, Brussels, Montpellier, Paris, and Zurich.[13] Jex-Blake's belligerence and impetuosity at Edinburgh had made it much more difficult for other women with a more long-term strategy to implement their preferred option of development through quiet incrementalism. Despite precedents in France or Switzerland—where men and women studied side by side—British feeling against co-education remained very strong on grounds of decorum, so that much of the earliest provision for women's medical education followed American precedent in being located in private institutions. This made provision easier than in countries such as Germany where a situation where the state controlled higher education, delayed women's entry to college, and thence to professional employment.[14]

The most successful separatist initiative in Britain was the London Medical School for Women (LMSW), which opened in 1874. Its students had clini-

[9] S. Gregory, *Female Physicians* (1864), 1; A London Physician, *Men-Midwives and Female Physicians* (1864), pp. i–v.

[10] *Daily Graphic*, 9 Nov. 1895.

[11] T. N. Bonner, *Becoming a Physician* (Oxford, 1995), 209–10.

[12] Bonner, *Physician*, 259.

[13] For example, Elizabeth Garrett qualified at Paris in 1870, Ann Clark at Berne in 1877, Ethel Bentham and Charlotte Brown at Brussels in 1895 and 1896.

[14] Rowold, '"The Academic Woman"', 437–8.

TABLE 7.1. Women's progress within the medical profession

Date	Institution or society	Form of closure or of recognition
1859	Medical Register	First woman, Elizabeth Blackwell registered
1865	Society of Apothecaries	Closes loophole by which women could qualify. (Action taken after E. Garrett qualified.)
1874/92	British Medical Assocation	Inadvertently elects first woman member (E. Garrett Anderson); plebiscite 3 to 1 against admission of women in 1878; female members banned 1878–92, readmitted 1892
1877	King's and Queen's College of Physicians of Ireland	Opens final examination to women
1878	University of London	Opens medical and other degrees to women
1885	Irish College of Surgeons	Opens qualifications on same terms as men
1886	Colleges of Physicians and Surgeons of Edinburgh and Glasgow	Opens qualifications on same terms as men—especially the 'Scottish Triple'
1908	Royal College of Physicians (London) and Royal College of Surgeons (London)	Admits women to examinations (Conjoint diploma). The first petition to try to achieve this had been in 1895
1910	Royal Society of Medicine	Elects first woman
1910	Royal College of Surgeons	Elects first woman fellow, Margaret Basden, a graduate of LMSW
1915	Physiological Society	Elects first woman
1920	Royal College of Surgeons of Edinburgh	Admits women on same terms as men
1925	Royal College of Physicians of London	Women eligible for fellowships
1934	Royal College of Physicians of London	Elects first female fellow—Helen Mackay

cal instruction in the wards of the Royal Free Hospital after 1877.[15] The first students took the licentiate examination of the Irish College of Physicians and

[15] This was later called the London (Royal Free Hospital) School of Medicine for Women, and then the Royal Free Hospital School of Medicine but in this chapter will, for the sake of clarity, continue to be referred to as the LMSW.

the Queen's University of Ireland which qualified them for entry to the *Medical Register* and hence for practice. After 1878—despite the opposition of the medical faculty—they became eligible for medical degrees at the University of London.[16] Although segregated facilities left room for the argument that 'different meant inferior', a belief in 'different but equal' meant that students and graduates were proud of their school. Their teachers were perceived both as role models and heroines, so that one spoke of the Dean of the School, Elizabeth Garrett Anderson, as 'our beloved chief'.[17] Initially the School recruited slowly despite the fact that, in order to encourage access, the cost of a five and a half-year medical training was made cheaper than for a man.[18] The main problem in recruitment was that academic prerequisites at first inhibited the flow of applicants. Later, the School became sufficiently successful to need substantial enlargement in 1897–9 and again in 1914. Demand for places continued strongly into the interwar period and, by 1936, was so great that the School could not accept all that applied.[19] The LMSW dominated the early output of female medical graduates in Britain, and the *Reports* of the School indicate that the majority of female practitioners before the First World War had had all or part of their training there. In Scotland there were similar pioneering initiatives. Jex Blake's School of Medicine in Edinburgh was more short-lived than the LMSW, since it operated only between 1886 and 1898. Much more successful, however, was Queen Margaret College, which became part of the University of Glasgow six years after its foundation in 1889, and had over one hundred students by 1914. It managed to attract women from less affluent backgrounds than did the LMSW, not least because of the availability of Carnegie tuition grants after 1901.[20]

Side by side with separatist establishments came co-educational advances. Dublin's extra-mural school's precedent in having men and women taught together was imitated in Scotland, and in English civic universities. By 1900 Cork, Galway, Aberdeen, St Andrews, Durham, and Manchester offered medical co-education, as did Bristol, Leeds, Liverpool, and Sheffield a decade later. But a mixed institution did not necessarily mean mixed classes. Opposition at the Royal Free Hospital, for instance, delayed mixed medical classes until 1924.[21] Other formidable strongholds remained exclusively masculine. London medical schools did not relax their restrictions on female recruitment until a shortfall in male recruitment occurred during the First

---

[16] T. N. Bonner, *To the Ends of the Earth. Women's Search for Education in Medicine* (Cambridge, Mass., 1992), 133.

[17] Malleson, *Murdoch*, 212.

[18] *Daily News*, 6 July 1910. The cost of medical training was estimated as being just under £700, of which nearly two-thirds went on the cost of living.

[19] *Manchester Guardian*, 10 Sept. 1936.

[20] W. Alexander, *First Ladies of Medicine* (Wellcome Unit for the History of Medicine, Glasgow, 1987), 5–6; Bonner, *To the Ends of the Earth*, 134–5.

[21] *BMJ* 8 Oct. 1910, 1027–9; M. Thorne, 'The Royal Free Hospital', *Medical Women's Journal*, Apr. 1924, 93–4.

World War.[22] This liberalization was effectively 'for the duration only' since it had been virtually reversed by the end of the 1920s.[23] Accurately reflecting the contemporary situation was a newspaper headline, 'Sex Rivalry in Medicine', which reported the decision of the London Hospital in 1922 to exclude female students.[24] The National Union of Societies for Equal Citizenship protested,[25] while Dr Edith Summerskill attributed exclusion to the schools' anti-feminism, in which pride in their traditional sporting prowess played an important part.[26] One interwar female medical student at St Mary's recollected that 'some of the staff did not like women at all', and that male students wanted more males 'so that they could play rugger'.[27] This interwar exclusion of women from clinical studies in most London hospital medical schools,[28] and also at Oxford and Cambridge, was important in perpetuating negative attitudes within the profession. It contrasted with the situation in the rest of the UK where co-education was by then the rule.[29] In 1938-9 the percentage of women in training in London was much lower than in other parts of Britain.[30] Continued difficulties for women in gaining access to a medical training, as well as publicity on the problems in earning a medical living, meant that recruitment of women students was less buoyant than that of men during the interwar period.[31]

In 1944 the *Goodenough Report* concluded that coeducation was the 'normal practice' in medical schools and that there was what they termed a 'reasonable number' of women students admitted. The inquiry had found that well-qualified women had been turned away from interwar medical schools, and so it recommended that *all* post-war medical education should be co-educational and that there should be 'no sense of inferiority or of privilege'.[32] The University Grants Commission's subsequent denial of grants to single-sex medical schools meant that all the London hospital schools were co-educational by 1947. The *Goodenough Report's* desire to see the proportion of men to women as one to four was also soon achieved since, within a decade, the 1 : 5.7 of 1938-9 had become 1 : 4 in London and 1 : 3 outside the capital.[33]

---

[22] *School and Society* 4 (1916), 741-2.

[23] The following ceased to admit women: St George's (1919), London Hospital (1922), St Mary's (1924), Westminster (1928), King's (1928), Charing Cross (1928). UCH (1919) imposed a narrow quota.

[24] *Daily Mail*, 4 Mar. 1922.   [25] *BMJ*, 12 May 1928.   [26] *Star*, 17 Sept. 1935.

[27] CMAC, GP/29/2/50, Kathleen Norton, MA (Oxon, 1926), BM (1926), MRCS (Eng)., LRCP (London, 1925).

[28] University College (with a quota) and King's accepted women.

[29] *BMJ*, 3 Sept. 1932.

[30] Scottish (exluding extra mural departments), English provincial, and Welsh, University Medical Schools had one in five female students compared to only one in nine in London Schools (*Goodenough Report*, 98).

[31] *BMJ*, 1 Sept. 1934, 14 Sept. 1946.

[32] *Report of Inter-Departmental Committee on Medical Schools* (1944), 99.

[33] *BMJ*, 7 Oct. 1950.

The second major hurdle for aspiring medical women, and one that took longer to overcome than entry to a first medical qualification, was a difficulty in getting hospital positions to gain initial clinical experience. Women and Children's Hospitals and Dispensaries thus played a vital early role in supplying this need. Particularly important here was the New Hospital for Women, founded in London in 1861, and perceived as 'a valuable training ground for . . . the responsibilities of practice'.[34] For most of the period prejudice continued to operate in making permanent appointments in other hospitals. In 1904 Dr Ethel Vernon, a GP with an extensive practice amongst local women and children, had a post as an attending officer at the Westminster Dispensary terminated in favour of a male candidate. This ignored the fact that she had successfully undergone a probationary period, that the male candidate had no prior experience of practice with women and children, and that the post was concerned with their treatment.[35] In 1910 the Manchester Infirmary Board decided to exclude women from candidacy for the post of Resident Medical Officer. Revealingly, the *General Practitioner*, approved this decision as 'wise', although letters to the non-medical press considered the decision unjust, and a critical leading article in the *Manchester Guardian* spoke of 'prejudice which has no justification in reason, and will be strongly and justly resented'.[36]

In the face of this male hostility some women responded by using their own networks to ensure that suitable people were appointed to junior posts. Mary Murdoch, a graduate of the LMSW, held a post as House Surgeon at the Victoria Hospital for Children in Hull, and made sure that house surgeons and physicians were appointed from her own medical school. Murdoch believed strongly that the 'loyalty of woman to woman *must* be the order of the day'.[37] But men deprecated the tables being turned upon them when women's and/or children's institutions preferred to appoint women, rather than men to resident posts.[38] And senior medical women gave stern advice—women *must* be good enough to compete with men. 'If women are going to compete with men they must be equally efficient . . . If you are good at your work you are certain to succeed, and if you are not, you are certain to fail.'[39]

During the First World War entry to hospital posts was easier, because many medical men were in the forces, so that women for a time were taken on the staff of the London Hospital.[40] But perceived overcrowding after the war renewed a climate of opinion that was hostile to women, with a *Times* headline encapsulating current thinking—'The Case Against Woman

---

[34] Marie Scharlieb in *Queen*, 20 Apr. 1889.

[35] *Morning Leader*, 24 Feb. 1904, *Daily Chronicle*, 24 Feb. 1904, *Morning Leader*, 24 Feb. 1904.

[36] *General Practitioner*, 22 Jan. 1910, 44; *BMJ* 11 Dec. 1909, reporting reactions to the decision.

[37] H. Malleson, *A Woman Doctor. Mary Murdoch of Hull* (1919), 41, 221.

[38] *Lancet*, 22 June, 3 and 22 Aug. 1872.

[39] 'Address' by Marie Scharlieb at LMSW, 1908 quoted in B. Evans, *Freedom to Choose: The Life and Work of Dr Helena Wright: Pioneer of Contraception* (1984), 65.

[40] *Women's Medical Journal*, Feb. 1917, 40.

Doctors'.[41] Prospects for both men and women remained poor in a situation where there was an excess supply of doctors and where competition for hospital appointments was particularly fierce because financial rewards from an institutional appointment compared well with one in general practice.[42] In 1925, for example, as many as seventy-eight women applied for a minor hospital post.[43] Internationally, medical women also encountered discrimination. In Germany where prejudice against women had delayed their qualification as doctors even longer than in Britain, medical women faced quotas, whilst married women became scapegoats for economic difficulties that had structural as well as gendered causes.[44] In Britain a continuing difficulty in getting posts in male-administered hospitals meant that the five general and eight specialized women-run hospitals in Britain retained their importance in the clinical training of women during the 1930s.[45] But, despite these difficulties, experienced women continued to make professional advances—more particularly at the local level—so that by the 1930s nearly one in three women GPs held appointments in hospitals.[46]

Numbers of medical women on the *Medical Register* and in practice grew slowly until 1900 and then more rapidly (see Figure 7.1). By the mid-1930s

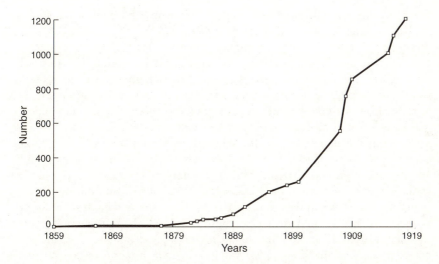

Fig. 7.1. Numbers of medical women on the Medical Register, 1859–1918

[41] *The Times*, 10 Mar. 1922.

[42] The average income of a GP was estimated to be lower (£220) than that of a salaried hospital appointment (£220–£300) in the *Daily News*, 6 July 1910.

[43] *Medical World*, 13 Feb. 1925.

[44] Bonner, *Physician*, 313; J. Stephenson, 'Women and the Professions in Germany, 1900–1945', in G. Cock (ed.), *German Professions* (Oxford, 1990), 279.

[45] *Medical Women's Journal*, Feb. 1931, 45.   [46] *Lancet*, 13 June 1936.

10 per cent of those on the register were women.[47] However, the entry of women to the medical profession during the late nineteenth and early twentieth centuries took place under difficult conditions where a competitive market served to strengthen long-standing ideological prejudices against female practitioners. Senior medical women worked hard to keep up the morale of existing and intending female practitioners,[48] and treated even well-publicized setbacks with exhortations to women to improve their qualifications for a post.[49] Arguably, all medical women remained conscious that they needed to be better than the average male if they were to succeed. Female medical students were advised that in general practice 'The world in general is in a position to criticize the smallest error with severity . . . If you choose this exacting branch of practice you will need a sound medical education, good health, much wisdom and all the virtues.'[50] This was a rather different situation from that of the male entrant to general practice, whose position hardly merited discussion by his teachers, since attention was concentrated on the future specialist rather than the generalist.

Careers

After training and an initial house appointment in a hospital or dispensary, medical women had four main career choices—a clinical post in a hospital, a public appointment in the community, a post abroad, or general practice. General practice was by no means the most attractive option. For the earliest medical women practice overseas with women in medical missions in India, and to a lesser extent, China, and even Borneo had great appeal, not least because missionary societies gave grants to those in training who were willing to work in medical missions after graduation.[51] Indeed, society's anxieties about female entrants to the medical profession were calmed to some extent by the perception that medical women would work in zenanas in India and hence not provide any competition at home. Before the First World War about one in three women lived and/or practised abroad and during the economically depressed interwar period there was renewed interest in foreign posts. Women were admonished by the *BMJ* that 'It is desirable that women . . . should reflect carefully on the keen competition for posts . . . and . . . consider the wisdom of seeking a wider field than hitherto in general practice and specialism. There is a large field opening in India.'[52]

[47] J. G. Neill, 'Married Women Doctors', *Royal Free Hospital Journal*, xxvi (1964), 140.

[48] See, for example, Elizabeth Garrett Anderson (*Gentlewoman*, 5 Jan. 1901) or Jane Walker (*Daily Sketch*, 11 Aug. 1913) for a resolutely upbeat tone.

[49] Elizabeth Garrett Anderson's address to students at the LMSW in 1902 (after the notorious Murdoch Clark case at Macclesfield discussed below), counselled them to go out and gain further experience rather than 'be for ever mediocrities' (*Magazine of London*, 1902, 854).

[50] Frances Ivens, 'Some of the Essential Attributes of an Ideal Practitioner', Inaugural Address, Oct. 1914 in *Magazine of London*, ix, (1914). Ivens, MB, MS, Lond. practised in Liverpool.

[51] Bennett, *Medical Women*, 49–50.   [52] *BMJ*, 1 Sept. 1923.

Victorian girls were indoctrinated by their upbringing and schooling to have high ideals of service to others,[53] and these ideals were reinforced by their medical training. The first medical woman in Britain, the American-born Elizabeth Blackwell, stated that 'we must not enter upon medicine as a trade for getting money, but from a higher motive', and went on to say that 'blind imitation of men' was an insufficient guide, but that 'subordination of self to the welfare of others' was of the utmost importance.[54] Conscious of a double moral imperative, derived both from their status as women and as doctors, early medical women often went into *public* appointments—those in the school medical service, or public health being particularly popular. They were also attracted into medical missionary work abroad, and into appointments in women's and children's hospitals at home. An international survey of medical women in 1949 found that the most frequent career choices of women were paediatrics, psychiatry, obstetrics, gynaecology, public health, and general practice.[55]

The medical élite were divided as to the suitability of women for general practice, not least perhaps because they lacked first-hand knowledge of what such a career entailed. Within the space of three months women at LMSW were informed by male visiting speakers first that 'the rough and tumble . . . of general practice makes it much less suitable as a general rule for women than for men', and three months later that there was 'no sphere of work in which women were more likely to come into their own'.[56] Women themselves tended to see general practice as one involving 'individuality and initiative' and hence as a career in its own right.[57] 'I feel that it is a role for which women are peculiarly well-fitted, and where they can find a useful and satisfactory career not as a stepping stone to specialism but as a career in itself.'[58] General practice was a popular choice amongst Glasgow's graduates where nearly one in four medical women opted for a career as a GP during sample years in 1898–1900 and 1908–1910.[59] During the 1920s numbers of women in general practice were said to be increasing.[60] In 1936 two out of five (38 per cent) of a sample of medical women were found to have become GPs. This finding was based on a survey of female graduates of St Mary's Medical School between 1916 and 1924.[61] In 1945 fewer than one in three women

[53] A. Digby, 'New Schools for the Middle Class Girl' in P. Searby (ed.), *Educating the Middle Classes* (1982), 18–19.

[54] E. Blackwell, *The Influence of Women in the Profession of Medicine* (1889), 3, 7, 8.

[55] D. Odlum 'The Medical Women's International Association', *Journal of the MWF*, Apr. 1958.

[56] *Lancet*, 9 Oct. 1926 (address to students by the Secretary of the Medical Research Council, Sir Walter Fletcher); *BMJ*, 11 Dec. 1926 (speech at annual dinner of LMSW by Sir John Rose, President of the Royal College of Physicians).

[57] Ivens, 'Ideal Practitioner', 154.   [58] *MWFQN*, 26 July 1926.

[59] Alexander, *First Ladies*, 49.

[60] *BMJ*, 6 Sept. 1924, 5 Sept. 1925, and 11 Dec. 1926. However, in 1934 the BMA estimated that 13 per cent, or rather less than one in eight, women were general practitioners (reported in *MWFQN*, Oct. 1934).

[61] *Lancet*, 13 June 1936.

(2,000 out of 7,000) on the *Medical Register* were engaged in general practice,[62] but this apparent reversal of the previous trend is probably explained
by the atypicality of the war years.

Among early medical women motivation for different careers in medicine
formed a counterpoint around a central theme—the desire to serve other
women. Edith Huntley, a student at LMSW argued passionately that it was
not ambition, nor a desire to compete with men that inspired her (and her
colleagues) to study medicine. Rather it was to 're-establish a natural claim
of their own sex, which was recognized in old time, and has since fallen into
abeyance' for women to have 'the opportunity, if she will, [to consult] a qualified member of her own sex.'[63] Some pioneers, like Christine Murrell,
thought that medicine was such an all-consuming vocation that it precluded
marriage, whilst others, such as Elizabeth Garrett Anderson saw the two as
compatible.[64] Individual aspirations within this general climate of opinion
were diverse. For example, Emily Thomson saw Dr S. Jex-Blake's plate from
the street, on impulse knocking on her door, and was inspired by her enthusiasm for the profession to follow her into medicine.[65] Catherine Chisholm
accompanied her father, a GP, on his rounds in a horse-drawn buggy, and
for the first decade of her career was a general practitioner in Manchester
before beginning her distinguished career as a paediatrician.[66] Data on the
occupational background of medical women is fragmentary but social origin
appears to have been quite varied, with strong recruitment from professional
(including medical) or commercial backgrounds.[67]

Many early medical women were as ignorant as their male counterparts
about the 'nuts and bolts' of starting in general practice. An aspirant female
GP wrote:

We need advice on the best way to begin, whether in rooms or with a house; on the
minimum amount of money necessary, on the kind of apparatus to collect. Then, having settled that, how far is it right for women to ignore the professional etiquette
about setting up a plate near other doctors? The procedure as to calls on other doctors . . . is all a matter of anxiety to a beginner.[68]

[62] *MWF Quarterly Review*, Oct. 1945, 11–18.

[63] E. A. Huntley, *The Study and Practice of Medicine by Women* (Lewes, 1886), 26, 49. Edith
Huntley, LRCP, S.Ed., MD, Brux, became MO to the Women's Wing of the Salvation Army, before
serving in India and Kashmir.

[64] St John, *Murrell*, 117; J. Manton, *Garrett Anderson*, 213.

[65] Greater Manchester RO, Q 217/1, MWF Scrapbook, obituary of Emily Charlotte Thomson
(1864–1892), MB, CM Ed., LRCP, and S Ed., LBFPS, Glasgow, general practitioner in Dundee
from 1892 to 1922. This large scrapbook (compiled by Dr Edith Parkinson in 1954 from material
supplied by MWF members) gives an excellent insight into the varied activities of the MWF and its
members.

[66] Greater Manchester RO, Q 217/1, MWF Scrapbook, 212, Obituary.

[67] Alexander, *First Ladies*, 12–15; A. H. Bennett, *English Medical Women. Glimpses of Their Work
in Peace and War* (1915), 44.

[68] Letter from Kathleen M. Tillyard, *MWFQN*, Nov. 1923.

Those women wanting to go into general practice found not only the problems faced by their male counterparts, but also an awareness that what they
did, or did not do, had a higher profile amongst their (largely male)
colleagues. For example, Drs Helen Boyle and Mabel Jones, on setting up
practice together in Brighton in 1897 called upon resident (male) doctors, got
a courteous if unwelcoming reception, and were warned that no female
patients hitherto had expressed a preference for being treated by one of their
own sex.[69] Medical women were thus alerted to the need to maintain a strict
medical etiquette with colleagues.[70]

How were these kinds of professional difficulties to be overcome? An assistantship was advised as one way of gaining clinical and financial experience
(and not necessarily only for a career in general practice), because 'only by
dealing with people in actual practice can they arrive at the best methods of
managing their patients'.[71] Whilst some succeeded in getting an assistantship,[72] others struggled to reach even this staging post. Economic difficulties
in interwar practice reinforced a prejudice against women in general practice,
so that women might accept either a very low salary or room and board
only.[73] A post might even be envisaged as a kind of all-purpose auxiliary, as
in a notorious advertisement for 'Lady Assistant . . . willing to assist in light
household duties.'[74] Women also became scapegoats for economic conditions
and thus were criticized for holding assistantships for several years, rather
than the traditional six month period.[75] An assistantship did not guarantee a
future independent livelihood and this fact was confirmed by a MWF survey
in 1944, which revealed that one in five female assistants saw themselves as
being devoid of prospects.[76]

In 1922, following a number of callers requesting information on suitable
openings, the Medical Women's Federation (MWF) created a Vacant Posts
Bureau. The MWF's *Quarterly Newsletter* also accepted notices of posts and
practices wanted, as well as a few advertisements of practices for sale. An
example of the latter read, 'Medical woman's practice for sale, in London,
central good class district. No night work. Honorary appointments might be
transferred.'[77] Amongst those with more capital some bought their practices
from well-established medical women and, at the end of our period, this

[69] Bennett, *Medical Women*, 98.   [70] *MWFQN*, July 1926.   [71] Ibid., Nov. 1923.
[72] At the turn of the century, Miss Stewart worked as an assistant to a GP in a Stafford practice
and Miss Gowdey to a Lincolnshire one (Royal Free Hospital Archives, LMSW *Reports*, 1899–1900).
The distinguished career of Marion Gilchrist, Scotland's first woman medical graduate and later eye
specialist, also began with an assistantship in general practice (*Inverness Courier*, 9 Sept. 1952; *Glasgow
Herald*, 8 Sept. 1952).
[73] *BMJ*, 7 Apr. and 12 May 1928; *MWFQN*, July 1928, 85–6; *Liverpool Echo*, 26 Nov. 1957 (Dr
Doris Odlum, President of the MWF).
[74] 'The Medical Women's Federation, 1917–67', *Journal of MWF*, 49 (Oct. 1967), 214–15.
[75] *BMJ*, 12 May 1928.
[76] *MWFQN*, Oct. 1945. The survey was vitiated by a low return rate.
[77] Ibid., Feb. 1922.

amounted to about half the women entering general practice.[78] Alternatively, they were encouraged to set up a new practice since the demand for medical women exceeded the supply. 'To women willing to take a room . . . and to start practice with a few introductions an interesting and useful career is always open.' They were also advised to take up a minor hospital post to gain experience, while their practice was still small.[79] 'The first year of your practice is generally fairly satisfactory, as friends help you. The second year is an aftermath of the first. The third is the testing year. It was in that year that I made my minimum of 5 shillings for three weeks work.'[80] This statement was by Jane Walker, by then a Harley Street consultant, recalling her earlier struggles as a general practitioner as a 'nerve-wracking experience'. She considered women bore financial anxiety 'rather badly' and that this inclined them to take 'safe jobs under the local authorities, rather than putting up their own plate'. It needed considerable determination to enter general practice single-handedly as a female GP. One described her turn-of-the-century struggles to build up a practice in Kilburn as 'an uphill trek', and so took up a full-time appointment in the school medical service.[81] A more successful contemporary counselled that 'From the day you put up your brass plate never refuse a piece of work.' Within four years she had enough work to take on first an assistant and then a partner, and to open consulting rooms in a neighbouring town.[82] The MWF helped entrants to the profession by giving loans to assist those starting up in general practice. Hilda Cantrell borrowed £100 without interest for a year in 1928, and together with savings from her earlier salaried posts, bought a house and put up her plate in Liverpool. Seven years later she was earning £650 per annum.[83]

Octavia Wilberforce begged, borrowed and saved, bought premises for £2,900, and in 1923 set up her plate in Brighton. Later, she was interrogated on whether it was 'rather interesting trying to push your way up,' and asserted that 'if you buy a practice you are more limited as it's not generally considered wise to buy a man's practice.' Whilst building up her private practice she took up a position as Clinical Assistant at the New Sussex Hospital for Women.[84] During her first year she made only £304, but was gradually able to enlarge her practice so that it gave an adequate medical living.[85] In

[78] In 1923 Kathleen Lander, Cicely Phelps, and Madeline Baker (together with Ina Clarke), bought London practices from Esther Harding, Mary Mears, and Dorothea Tudor, respectively (*MWFQN*, July 1923); Survey reported in ibid., Oct. 1945.

[79] Mary E. H. Morris, MD, 'A Plea for General Practice', *MWFQN*, Nov. 1923.

[80] Dr Jane Walker in the *Manchester Evening News*, 20 Jan. 1936.

[81] Obituary of Elizabeth J. Moffett (*BMJ*, ii (1960), 1244).

[82] Malleson, *Murdoch*, vii, 31, 155.

[83] CMAC, GP29/2/37, Hilda Cantrell, MB, ChB (Liverpool, 1923).

[84] Wilberforce was later made Assistant Physician, Secretary to the Medical Committee, elected to the Board of Management, and finally was appointed Physician to the Hospital (Jalland, *Wilberforce*, 153–4).

[85] Jalland, *Wilberforce*, 142, 148, 152–3, 166. The probing question came from Hagberg Wright, the brother of the notoriously anti-feminist, Sir Almoth Wright, of St Mary's Hospital.

this she was helped by the presence of the woman's hospital nearby as well as by her extensive social networks locally and in London. A friendly letter from a hospital consultant under whom she had worked previously also comforted her. 'We all tend to be over anxious about the mere business of making money. In reality the rewards of practice are of a different kind and you will find they go far to mitigate the worry inseparable from an uncertain art.'[86] But beginning a practice in less propitious circumstances might be a strain, more particularly for the very first medical women. Starting up in the 1890s amongst the Irish mill girls in Dundee, Emily Thomson found it a 'very hard struggle' since 'women doctors were looked on with considerable suspicion'.[87]

Typically, practices were founded in locations that offered a promising patient constituency, with a sufficient concentration of women and children. Those that also gave an opportunity for appointments at hospitals and other institutions were at a premium. In this context the topographical lists published in the *Reports* of the LMWS are interesting in showing the overall distribution of the School's graduates. These indicated an overwhelming concentration of medical women in London, with very much smaller groupings in large cities; county, hospital, or cathedral, towns; watering places; and seaside resorts. Female GPs fitted neatly into this pattern. Cities proved attractive with, for example, Ethel Williams setting up in Newcastle in 1892, Mary Murdoch in Hull in 1896, and Mabel Ramsey in Plymouth in 1906. County towns and watering places also had appeal so that Sarah Gray put up her plate in Nottingham in 1890, Grace Billings in Cheltenham in 1899, and Ruth L. Bensusan-Butt in Colchester in 1907. In contrast, women pioneers were very few on the ground in heavily industrialized areas, although they were more likely to be found there, if female employment was significant,[88] or if they were in partnership with their husbands. An 'Address' at the LMSW in 1914 drew attention to the need for more medical women in the great industrial towns, and offered the prospect of ample scope for doing well in practice.[89] Occasionally the more intrepid individual did manage to build up an industrially based panel practice, and even to win works patients from male colleagues.[90] A few enterprising women found a practice niche in rural areas—as in the Highlands and Islands—which had been found economically unattractive by their male colleagues.[91] And, by the 1930s, the demand for women practitioners was said to be sufficiently strong for them to be able to practise in some other rural areas, whereas previously these had been

---

[86] Jalland, *Wilberforce*, 147, letter from Dr Wilson (later Lord Moran) then at St Mary's Hospital.

[87] Greater Manchester RO, Q 217/1, MWF Scrapbook, 70, obituary of Emily Charlotte Thomson (1864–1952).

[88] Hilda Swinburne-Jones in interwar Burnley (*BMJ*, iv (1970), 692).

[89] Miss Ivens's address to the autumn session of the LMSW in 1914 (Bennett, *Medical Women*, 51).

[90] Jalland, *Wilberforce*, 148.

[91] Amy Macdonald, neé Galloway, who practised in Stornaway (*BMJ*, ii (1910), 1830).

considered to be hopeless locations.[92] A comparison of surveys undertaken in 1907 and 1934–5 suggests that there had been a dispersion of female GPs away from the early concentration in the capital.[93]

Women—like men—utilized social and professional networks in order to establish a viable practice. Some women entered into partnership with female colleagues although, as with male partnerships, the data on this is fragile. It is clear, however, both that women entered into all-female partnerships from the earliest years of women in general practice, and that by the 1930s medical women in partnership were a well-established phenomenon.[94] Unusually, some went into partnership with their sister.[95] One female partnership in general practice was formed with Elizabeth Fraser by Miss Murdoch Clark after her notorious blackballing by male colleagues in relation to a house post at Macclesfield Infirmary in 1901. The press commented that in Macclesfield she would 'get as much practice as she and her partner can cope with', while the *BMJ* later reflected that 'there can be few instances where a doctor has found such a practice ready made and unbought'.[96] Shortly afterwards, in 1903, Christine Murrell set up in partnership with Honor Bone in Bayswater, a career move which involved them each in a down payment of £1,000. They made only £87 in their first year in practice; receipts caught up with expenses during their second year; four years later they were earning their living in practice; and the practice eventually sustained as many as four medical women.[97] This was in line with the result of a survey in 1934–5 that reported medical women as stating that it took about five years to establish a general practice.[98] By the interwar period women's role in general practice was sufficiently assured for some women to join men in partnership,[99] and a few also worked with their fathers or brothers as partners.[100]

---

[92] Contrast Miss L. M. Brooks, Warden of LMSW in *Morning Post* 7 Mar. 1933 with R. Wilson, *Ausculapia Victrix* (1886), 26 later reprinted in the *Fortnightly Review*, Jan. 1886.

[93] At the earlier date the 389 women practitioners in England and Wales were distributed so that 44 per cent were in London and a further 17 per cent in nine large provincial cities. A quarter of a century later, amongst a small sample, only 29 per cent were in London, 65 per cent in the provinces, and 6 per cent abroad (*Lancet*, 13 June 1936).

[94] *Manchester Guardian*, 5 Oct. 1932. Women-only partnerships in 1892 included Emily Thomson and Alice Moorhead in Dundee; Ethel Williams and Mona MacNaughton in Newcastle; Agnes Swanson and Evelyn Pakeman in Golders Green, north London from 1907 although the partnership covered only part of the 40 years that Swanson was there; Lillian Blake and Mary Deacon in Colwyn Bay in 1911; Alice Sanderson Clow and Eveline Cargill in Cheltenham from 1914; and Dame Barrie Lambert and Elizabeth Patteson in interwar London. (*Inverness Courier*, 9 Sept. 1952; *Glasgow Herald*, 8 Sept. 1952; Greater Manchester RO, Q217/1, obituaries 112–13; Clwyd RO at Ruthin, NTD/741, List of NHI Medical Practitioners in Denbighshire, 1911).

[95] Drs Kate and Julia Mitchell took over Mrs Chaplin Ayres's practice in Sloane Street, London in the mid-1880s (*Queen*, nd, *c.*1886 (in Press Cuttings book of LMWS, vol 1). Kate Mitchell studied at the LMSW, Dublin and Paris, and gained in 1882 a Licentiate of the Royal College of Physicians of Ireland and a Licentiate of Midwifery.

[96] *BMJ*, ii (1930), 983; *Daily Express*, 14 Jan. 1902.

[97] C. St. John, *Christine Murrell. Her Life and Work*, (1935), 37–8.   [98] *Lancet*, 13 June 1936.

[99] For example, Dorothea Blunt went into partnership with Conroy Morgan in Hastings in 1929 (*BMJ* ii (1950), 1500).

[100] Barbara Hick joined her father in partnership in Bridlington (*BMJ*, ii (1970), 673).

The position of the woman in a professional partnership that was also a marriage is difficult to decipher. In 1898 E. Garrett Anderson stated that 'A good many medical women marry after graduation: their husbands are generally medical men, and the wife, as a rule, both practises independently after marriage, and helps her husband.'[101] But this leaves open the issue as to whether a legal partnership was necessarily established in these circumstances. Some married couples did establish partnerships, including Florence Orford in Pontefract in 1891, and Catherine Monro in Barrow during the late 1920s.[102] Existing prejudice against married women having an independent economic existence was strengthened during the 1920s and 1930s. Women had to resign their appointments on marriage in the civil service, and in certain local authorities including the City of Glasgow, and the London County Council.[103] This resulted in a limited movement by women from public positions into general practice, and more particularly into acting as locums for women GPs.[104]

As for the proportion of medical women who married—and who might therefore find themselves confronted by a marriage bar—estimates based on small samples differed considerably so that overall trends cannot be established with any degree of confidence. Half the medical women from Glasgow who had graduated in the two sample periods of 1898 to 1900 and 1908 to 1910 married. More generally, rather lower percentages were recorded during the interwar period (30 to 43 per cent), but higher (80 per cent), during the 1940s.[105]

Income

'In nearly all our large provincial towns are to be found medical women in good practice.'[106] But what did women consider to be a good practice? Service rather than remuneration was certainly the more prominent element in discussions of female general practice. One pioneer woman doctor wrote:

Please accept my best thanks for such a prompt settlement of my account. . . . it is a great trial to me to have to send you a bill at all. The world is wrong somehow— it seems a very dreadful thing to live off the sufferings of others. It is a real pleasure to relieve pain, when one can, but then the hateful money question comes in.[107]

[101] Letter to the *Medical Press and Circular*, 23 Feb. 1898.
[102] Florence Orford, qualified at the Royal Free in 1888 (Greater Manchester RO, Q 217/1, MWF Scrapbook, 44–5, Obituary); J. H. Williams, *GPs of Barry, 1885–1979* (Barry Medical Society, 1979), 2.
[103] *MWFQN* Feb. 1921, 9; July 1921, 8–10; Mar. 1925, 23–6. London lifted the ban in 1936 (*Manchester Guardian*, 19 Sept. 1936).
[104] *BMJ*, 11 Dec. 1926.
[105] Alexander, *First Ladies*, 39; *The Times*, 2 Oct. 1923; *Lancet*, 13 June 1936; J. G. Neill, 'Married Women Doctors' *Royal Free Hospital Journal*, xxvi, Mar. 1964.
[106] Dr Arabella Kenealy, LRCP 'How Women Doctors are Made', *Ludgate*, 1897.
[107] Malleson, *Murdoch*, 46.

Yet even medical women had to acknowledge that the economic side of a practice was the bottom line that permitted practice. So what kind of fees did women charge their patients? An authoritative judgement at the end of the nineteenth century was that medical women in London 'ask and get both in consulting and family practice the fees ordinarily charged by medical men of good position'. Women therefore did not underbid their male colleagues, unless, by 'curing them more quickly or by requiring them to pay fewer visits'![108] The income cited as the norm for an experienced female GP in a provincial city at about this time was £200 per year, with two-fifths of the private patients being obstetric cases.[109]

A detailed source of information on medical women's incomes came in 1938 when the BMA sent out questionnaires to GPs asking for details of their income during the preceding two years, and received 331 returns from medical women.[110] The strength and pattern of earning power by medical women differed from that of men. Figure 7.2 portrays the relationship between gross income per annum and the ages of female GPs. Earnings by female principals peaked by their early forties, in contrast to the late forties and early fifties of men. Why they did so remains a matter of speculation. After years of professional self-discipline and devotion to career, the achievement of modest prosperity may have meant a conscious reorientation by women towards a more balanced lifestyle. Being often without dependants a sufficient livelihood may well have come earlier for single women. Even for a married woman joint household earnings meant that a smaller medical income could sustain family expenditures than was the case with a male colleague whose sole earnings sustained his household. Given that they had sufficient income for their needs, medical women may have made a decision to take on less work during their menopausal years. In the later part of their career, female earnings tapered off more gradually than that of their male colleagues, although this decline was from a lower peak.

A major contrast lay in comparative mean income levels since women had little more than half the earning power of men. We may speculate that this situation was caused by a number of factors, including women having smaller practices, fewer paid appointments, and less national health insurance work.[111] In the 1920s one in five women GPs had a panel, although this rose to nearly two out of five in the 1930s and nine out of ten by the 1940s.[112] Lower incomes may also have resulted from a clientele of female and child patients, since it seems likely that these were charged lower fees. Ironically, however, the workload caused by female and child patients was greater than

[108] Letter from Elizabeth Garrett Anderson to the *Medical Press and Circular*, 23 Feb. 1898.

[109] Wilson, *Aesculapia*, 25.

[110] *Report of the Inter-Departmental Committee on Remuneration of General Practitioners*, PP, 1945, xii, appendix II.

[111] In Birkenhead payments to women panel practitioners during the 1920s and 1930s were few in number and small in scale (Cheshire RO, NIB 9/1–2).

[112] *Lancet*, 5 May 1923; MWF survey, reported in *MWFQN*, 1945.

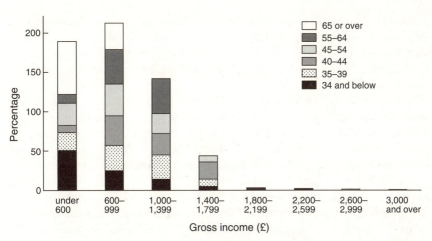

Fig. 7.2. Distribution of medical women's gross incomes at different ages, 1936–8

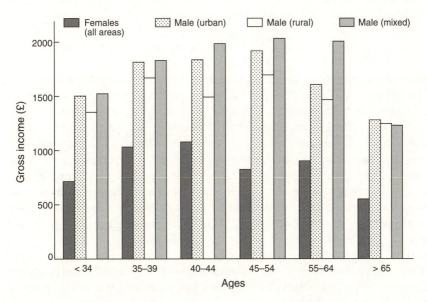

Fig. 7.3. Gross incomes of female GPs compared to male GPs, 1936–8

that of male patients, so that medical women incurred a double penalty (see Figure 7.3).

Within these generally lower female income levels there was a considerable range in incomes. Three-quarters of the sample made under £1,000 gross. This was made up of 9 per cent with fewer than £400, 35 per cent between

£400 and £800, and 31 per cent between £800 and £1,000. Above this 22 per cent earned between £1,000 and £2,000 and a further 3 per cent over that amount. Contemporaries regarded medical incomes for women as relatively good. 'Medicine today [1933] is one of the best-paid professions open to women.'[113]

A pattern of women earning half the mean gross male income was in line with the historical ratio of female to male wages. And once professional expenses were deducted the average medical women's net mean income was little more than half of her gross income. (This was a considerably worse economic situation than that experienced by men whose expenses as a proportion of a larger income amounted to between 33 and 44 per cent of gross earnings, and with the higher proportion tending to be concentrated amongst lower earners.) The end result, as Figure 7.2 suggests, was that relatively few medical women had net incomes of over £500, whereas it was only the elderly, or country, male doctor who made less than £1,000 per annum. Indeed, in order to retain recruitment of 'able men', the Spens Committee of 1946 recommended that 'between forty and fifty years of age approximately three-quarters of general practitioners ought to have achieved a net income of over £1,000 per annum and the remainder even more'.[114]

Medical Women

We have noted that women were deeply committed to the principle of the care of female patients by practitioners of their own sex. 'My dream . . . is, that it will be looked on as one of the barbarisms of a past age that a medical man should ever have attended a woman.'[115] One problem with this ideal was that women in Britain did not necessarily show a preference for being attended by a woman doctor; fashionable women and many middle-class women continued to be attended by men so that it became apparent that industrial workers, professional women and poor women were becoming the main clients of the medical woman.[116] Dr Eliza Dunbar, in practice in Bristol and giving attendance at a dispensary, had poor women consult her 'from all parts of Bristol, from the neighbouring villages, and even from other towns. They express themselves in the warmest terms of the gratitude for the opportunity of consulting a lady.'[117] The pace was therefore slow in constructing women-only general practices:

[113] Miss L. M. Brooks, Warden of LMSW in *Morning Post*, 7 Mar. 1933.
[114] *Report on the Remuneration of Consultants and Specialists* [Spens], PP, 1947–8, xi, 424.
[115] Malleson, *Murdoch*, 178.
[116] Miss Billington, 'How Can I Earn My Living?—As a Doctor', *The Young Woman*, Nov. 1893; Miss Brooks (Warden of LMSW) in *Pall Mall Gazette*, 12 Dec. 1914; *Manchester Guardian*, 13 Sept. 1923.
[117] Letter from Lucy Read in *The Times*, 10 May 1878.

Women are making their way steadily and surely. Fifteen years ago it required considerable courage on the part of a woman to consult a medical woman (except without the knowledge of her friends); now it has almost ceased to be thought anything exceptional to do so. Women are consulted, if they have a good reputation for skill and judgement, almost as naturally as men are. It has become increasingly evident, that to women of all ages, but especially to young and unmarried women, the opportunity of being able to get medical advice from a qualified woman is in many cases of real value.[118]

Whether female doctors should accept male patients was controversial. A wife of one of the colleagues of Ruth Bensusan-Butt, the earliest female doctor in Colchester, visited her and 'said that the male doctors thought it disgraceful that a woman doctor should accept male patients'. Bensusan-Butt retorted, 'I'll give up all my men patients if your husband will give up all his woman patients.'[119] Contentious episodes under the national insurance scheme over the desire of women panel members to retain women-only practices and also over the initially smaller payments to practices where there was a patient list of only one gender, were defused by tactful discussion.[120] (It is worth noting that some male panel doctors refused to accept women patients on their panel, possibly because the higher service demands of the typical female patient did not receive adequate compensation from the capitation system.)[121] Some medical women were gradually won over to the acceptance of men on their panels,[122] and it is possible that economic pressures on interwar general practice were responsible for this. It was estimated that there were equal numbers of women-only practices and practices where women doctors accepted male patients.[123] However, it seems likely that, although these mixed practices had some male patients, most were centred on women and children. Even at the end of the period women practitioners had considerably more female than male patients. Medical women might be suspicious of male applicants for their lists, fearing—at best—potential prostate trouble or—at worst—personal or psychiatric abnormalities. They therefore tended to refer men on to their male colleagues.[124]

Young women starting out in practice were cautioned that they must expect constant scrutiny from patients and public:

Patients and their anxious friends are keen observers. They quickly detect an unbusinesslike or inefficient discharge of our duties, while they fully appreciate a quiet

[118] *Report of RC to Enquire into Medical Acts*, PP, 1882, xxix, app. 2, 941–2, evidence of E. Garrett Anderson.

[119] Greater Manchester RO, Q 217/1, MWF Scrapbook, Obituary.

[120] *Lancet* 14 May 1921, 1 Oct. 1921: J. Cockram, 'The Federation and the BMA', *Journal of the Medical Women's Federation*, Jubiliee issue (1967).

[121] *MWFQN*, Dec. 1921, 15.

[122] One instance was that of Beatrice Lovibond who practised in Greenwich (*BMJ*, ii (1940), 920).

[123] *MWFQN*, Dec. 1921, 15. The *BMJ* of 28 Dec. 1940 reported only a minority of women doctors refusing male patients.

[124] S. Taylor, *Good General Practice* (Nuffield Hospitals Trust, Oxford, 1954), 51–2; CMAC, GP29/2/50, Kathleen Norton.

methodical manner, an easy familiarity in the use of instruments, and the value . . . of the notes . . . of their cases. Always examine your patients on some well-known plan—organ by organ, system by system—else some important point will be omitted . . . In the evening, or the first leisure time, read up the subject in the textbooks; consult the best monographs, and think over the whole matter.[125]

In practice women GPs did establish a reputation for many of the qualities in this exhortation. Sir Thomas Barlow wrote of Anne E. Clark, a pioneer woman doctor, for whom he had acted as a consultant in these terms. 'She belonged to the best type of conscientious family practitioner—an accurate observer, practical in treatment, exact in detailed instructions, and a staunch and faithful friend to both parent and children.'[126]

Medical science complemented the art of successful practice. Women seem to have been particularly conscious that they drew on their personal and caring qualities in their role as healers. Mary Murdoch wrote that 'It is the doctor's business to take away pain. It has often been my privilege to remove the look of trouble from people's eyes. I can but go on inspiring her with hope every day, and that goes a long way towards ultimate recovery.' And a colleague of Christine Murrell's testified to 'her powers to heal the broken-hearted, and to inspire those worn by the stress of life'.[127] Patients saw the healing qualities of medical women as distinctive. The mother of a patient of Murdoch's wrote that she had 'an extraordinary capacity for always appearing to have plenty of time . . . she would play with my boy and let him ask questions as if she had nothing to do in all the world'.[128] And one of Murrell's patients reflected that she 'poured out a living stream of sympathy and understanding which comforted and healed'.[129] Octavia Wilberforce's later autobiographical writings also give an interesting insight into the professional work of a general practitioner. Like Murrell (and some other colleagues),[130] she gave unusual importance to the psychological state of her patients since she believed that 'a patient's anxiety over personal difficulties of all kinds were the contributing, if not the sole cause, of the indigestion, insomnia, irritability which was so hard to control or cure'. Hence she helped set up a convalescent and rest home. Wilberforce viewed preventive, rather than curative, medicine as the more important element in her work. She was very conscious of her limitations in practice. 'My job is nearly all either patching or regretting that God hadn't asked my advice! Much of practice is therefore spent in being humiliated.'[131]

Clinical work was focused particularly on children and on women. Papers to international congresses were on topics such as maternal mortality, abor-

---

[125] M. Scharlieb, *Seven Lamps of Medicine* (Oxford, 1888), 8.
[126] *BMJ*, 15 Mar. 1924, 502–3. Anne E. Clark MD (Berne 1877), MKQCPI (1883), physician to the Women's and the Children's Hospitals, Birmingham.
[127] St John, *Murrell*, 112.   [128] Malleson, *Murdoch*, 39.
[129] St John, *Murrell*, 39.   [130] For example, Jessie Murray (obituary, *BMJ*, ii (1920), 723).
[131] Jalland, *Wilberforce*, 99–101.

tion, cancer in women, diseases in pregnancy, or the effect of housework on women's health.[132] Female GPs chose areas with a high concentration of women (as we have seen that Thomson did in Dundee), because of an interest in obstetrics and gynaecology. Others founded the first baby clinics or hospitals in their towns, including Bensusan-Butt in Colchester, Chisholm in Manchester, and Murrell in St Marylebone, London. The growth in contemporary concern for maternal mortality and for infant care thus benefited the practices of female GPs. Lady doctors also held child welfare clinics as did Grace Billings in interwar Cheltenham. Whilst both men and women went in for 'kitchen table surgery', within their particular remit of caring for women, medical women tended to supply gynaecological assistance in this manner, as did Billlings with D and Cs (dilation and curettage.) Research on neglected 'female problems' was part of their contribution, so that Alice Sanderson Clow, a Cheltenham GP, did research on the hygiene of menstruation.[133] And, while their male colleagues seem often to have ducked the need to give contraceptive advice,[134] medical women such as Billings provided it.

At the start of the NHS female general practice still had many of the traits that had characterized it for the previous seventy years. It was made up of a large amount of paediatrics, an average amount of obstetric work, a substantial demand for birth-control advice, and a considerable amount of gynaecological work. There was also said to be an unusually large quantity of minor surgery, and a substantial amount of neurosis to be treated amongst female patients. One may be forgiven for thinking that the latter may well be a masculinist assumption about women patients, given a later patriarchal comment about medical women's facility with minor surgery. It was stated that 'They do it extremely efficiently, with the neatness, aplomb, and expertise which might otherwise go into dressmaking and embroidery.'[135] (There is a revealing silence on the transferable skills that male general practitioners may have brought from their field sports to the surgery!)

Some women were driven by a strong social conscience to practise in a very poor area. Because these were traditionally under-doctored locations it was also possible to build up a practice by 'squatting' there. Caroline O'Connor created a big practice in Stratford and Bow between 1915 and her death in 1923:

Out in all weathers, by day and night, she carried comfort and hope into the dreary districts . . . Her most telling epitaph might be found in the many ill-spelt touching

---

[132] D. Odlum, 'The Medical Women's International Association', *Journal of MWF*, Apr. 1958; *Scotsman*, 16–17 July 1937.

[133] Alice Sanderson Clow (1876–1959) was a GP in Cheltenham from 1920 to 1938 (Greater Manchester RO, Q 217/1, MWF Scrapbook, 143, Obituary).

[134] The problem may have been inability to give advice through ignorance, since birth control was not taught in medical school, rather than reluctance to offer it (R. Porter and L. Hall, *The Facts of Life. The Creation of Sexual Knowledge in Britain, 1650–1950*; D. Gittins, *Fair Sex. Family Size and Structure, 1900–39* (1982), 42).

[135] Taylor, *Practice*, 52–4.

letters sent by members of the working women who crowded her surgery: 'She never thought of herself, we all feel we have lost a friend'.[136]

Medical women were less hierarchical in their work: they did things *with* their patients not *to* them. As Sarah Gray remarked, 'Patients are mostly not idiots . . . doctors help best when they respect them.' Thus doctors should listen to patient's accounts of themselves, should explain why they were not giving treatment (if this seemed appropriate), and should also advise on the general conduct of a healthy life.[137] Lady doctors felt that they had a 'cast of mind' that enabled them to 'deal with individuals, specially with children and the infirm'.[138] Indeed, children might become so habituated to lady doctors that if a male doctor was called in during a holiday illness, the child's response was 'That's not a doctor, that's a man!'[139] They were also perhaps rather less prone than their male colleagues to demarcate a 'medical' from a 'social service' concern for their patients. They did not just diagnose and prescribe but found themselves, as did Agnes Swanson, obtaining domestic help, or giving advice on diet. She remarked that 'If only, if only my work was *purely* medical, then I *could* get through it, but it is the other complications that really take up most of my time.'[140] This illustrated a more client-centred method that characterized not only medical women but also women councillors at this time.[141] It was an approach that Elizabeth Blackwell had seen earlier as the ideal of female practice:

The department of medicine in which the great and beneficent influence of women may be especially exerted, is that of family physician; and not as specialists, but as the guides and wise counsellors in all that concerns the physical welfare of the family.[142]

Public Roles

Conscious of a need for women's autonomy, and for a recognition of women's potential, early medical women were often liberal feminists and keen supporters of the campaign for the suffrage.[143] LMSW students were urged by one committed feminist doctor that:

If you don't belong to a suffrage society join one to-morrow, because if you are not represented in the affairs of your country your work is not of much value, and it is

---

[136] *MWFQN*, 23 Mar. 1923.   [137] Inaugural Address to LMSW (*The Times*, 2 Oct. 1907).
[138] *MWFQN*, 26 July 1926.   [139] Mary Sturge (MD London), in *Friend*, Oct. 1904.
[140] Greater Manchester RO, Q 217/1, MWF Scrapbook, 112.
[141] P. Hollis, 'Women in Council', in J. Rendall (ed.), *Equal or Different. Women's Politics 1800–1914* (Oxford, 1987), 201.
[142] Blackwell, *Influence*, 27.
[143] It is instructive that when Jane Scott-Calder wrote an anti-feminist letter to the *BMJ* in 1943, it provoked 25 letters, and of the 9 that were published all were highly critical (*BMJ*, i (1943), 229–330, 393–4, 428–9, 461–3).

only when men and women co-operate in the work of the nation that that nation really succeeds.[144]

Suffragist ranks included Kate Mitchell, Mabel Ramsey, Emily Thomson, and Mary Murdoch. Amongst the more militant suffragettes were Marion Gilchrist,[145] Winifred Patch, and Ethel Williams. The latter called herself a 'fighting pacifist', was a stalwart in her battle for the equality of the sexes, having a reputation as a 'champion of woman's independence'.[146] Winifred Patch believed in no taxation without representation and had her belongings distrained three times for failure to pay her taxes.[147]Christine Murrell's membership of the Women's Social and Political Union was motivated by a keen sense of justice and she addressed meetings, went on deputations, and marched in processions for 'the cause'. Both she and Flora Murray gave medical advice to suffragettes during their imprisonment, and helped hunger strikers after they had been released under the horrific 'Cat and Mouse' Act.[148]

With such strong views on their right to participate in public life, it was predictable that medical women should play an active role in the local and national community. Ruth Bensusan-Butt was the first woman councillor (and a Labour councillor at that), in the Tory town of Colchester, serving on the education committee and ending her public career as an alderman. Dame Barrie Lambert gave distinguished long-term service as a Tory alderman on the London County Council.[149] Others were justices of the peace.[150] Mary Esslemont of Aberdeen was the first woman member of a University Court, while Ethel Williams was the first woman on the Senate of the University of Durham.[151] Ethel Bentham was the first medical woman to become an MP in 1929, after practising in Newcastle and Kensington.[152]

These were signs of public acceptance and recognition. But it was entry to the *Medical Register* that was the foundation stone on which later achievements were built. At the School of Medicine for Women the Association of Registered Medical Women was founded in May 1879. The title—with its emphasis on register—gives us an important insight into the rationale of this group, since the necessity of achieving an entry on the *Medical Register* was a pre-condition for practising medicine. The association was a metropolitan

[144] Mary Murdoch, 'Practical Hints to Students', *LMSW Report*, Oct. 1914.
[145] *Inverness Courier*, 9 Sept. 1952; *Glasgow Herald*, 8 Sept. 1952.
[146] Mabel Rew, 'Looking Back', *Jubilee Issue of the Journal of the MWF*, 1967.
[147] *Islington Daily Gazette*, 16 Aug. 1924.
[148] St John, *Murrell*, 53–70; Flora Murray, CBE, MD, BS Durham, DPH Camb, was a Kensington GP. (*MWFQN*, Nov. 1923, 42–3).
[149] Greater Manchester RO, Q 217/1, MWF Scrapbook, 113.
[150] Mary Esslemont in Aberdeen, or Mona MacNaughton in Newcastle.
[151] Obituary of Mary Esslemont, MA, BSc, MB, ChD, DPH, JP, hon. LL D (*Scotsman*, 10 July 1954).
[152] She qualified in 1894 at the LMSW and the Rotunda (Dublin), before gaining an MD in Brussels the following year. She was a keen suffragist and member of the Woman's Freedom League (*The Times*, 20 Jan. 1931).

focus for medical women, acting as a forum for presenting clinical, educational and professional papers, for organizing political action (such as sending memoranda to policy-making groups), as well as for decorous social events. As medical women moved to posts and practices outside the London area they organized regional groups.[153] From 1913 there was discussion of the need for a national network, which found its resolution in the Medical Women's Federation of 1917.[154]

The MWF was of central importance to many medical women, more especially in the earlier part of the period. In 1953 2,300 out of 9,000 women on the *Medical Register* were members of the MWF.[155] Its founding memorandum and articles of association stated that its three objects were:

To promote the medical and allied sciences, and to maintain the honour and interests of the medical profession.

To further the cooperation, and to promote the general interests of those women engaged or interested in the practice of medicine or allied sciences, including medical research.

To advance among women . . . the study of medicine.[156]

Two of the sixteen presidents of the MWF were GPs before 1948, and another two spent part of their careers in general practice.[157] As with male colleagues such an organization built professional solidarity, and its events brought colleagues together socially. The Medical Women's International Association had a comparable but wider role. It was founded in 1919 and within twenty years had twenty-five branches and a membership of nearly 4,000. Biennial meetings were held with those in 1924 and 1946 being held in London, and that of 1937 in Edinburgh. Not only were these important to medical women for the educational value of the clinical papers but their use for social networking was also important.[158] Imposing gatherings and attendance by invited dignitaries from government, the medical profession or from academe also helped make an important public statement about the established status of women in the profession. Whether at international congresses or at regional dinners and buffets medical women were enabled to build formal and informal professional networks. Photographs of happy,

[153] In 1919 there were associations in eastern Scotland, in London, north-west England, northeast England, Yorkshire, and in the Birmingham area.

[154] R. E. M. Bowden, 'The Medical Women's Federation, 1917–87: Its Antecedents, Past Present and Future', *Medical Women*, 6 (3) (1987), 4–12.

[155] *Birmingham Mail*, 17 Sept. 1952.

[156] Greater Manchester RO, Q 217/1, MWF Scrapbook, 'Memorandum and Articles of Association of the MWF', Feb. 1917.

[157] Mabel Ramsey (1932–4) was a GP in Plymouth, and Ethel Williams (1934–6) a GP in Cheltenham, while Jane Walker (1917–20) had begun her distinguished career in general practice before undertaking specialization in TB, and Catherine Chisholm (1928–30) had been in general practice before specializing in paediatrics.

[158] E. P. Lovejoy, and A. C. Reid, 'The Medical Women's International Association: An Historical Sketch', *Journal of the American Medical Women's Association*, Jan. 1951.

relaxed faces at these events vividly suggest how much these events met the participants' need for release from a heavy work load with a constant burden of social expectation.

Women worked under the scrutiny of their male colleagues whose attitudes towards them had been fostered first by separate training, later reinforced by the difficult financial conditions of the interwar years. Thus, professional solidarity with male colleagues was emphasized in the context of the economics of medicine.[159] In 1921 Mary Sturge stated that:

> On entering economic life, one of the first things that women have to learn is to stand shoulder to shoulder with men . . . Medical women of the earlier decades kept a clean record in this matter, both by their refusal to under-bid men for particular posts, and their determination not to under-sell their neighbours in private practice.[160]

Men were equally concerned that they should not be undercut by women through their accepting lower remuneration, so that this provided an excellent opportunity for joint action.[161] Collective action with fellow members of the British Medical Association was helpful in breaking down male prejudices against female colleagues. However, the *Lancet* commented in 1927 that 'We have only to look below the surface of things to find that sex antagonism has still to be reckoned with.'[162] As late as 1952 the female secretary of the branch in Birmingham commented that 'Our brothers, I think, now find us quite reasonable.'[163] The 'now' is indicative of the late recognition of women as equal and valuable colleagues. This more relaxed attitude may be attributed partly to the important role of medical women during the Second World War. It was also due to the fact that some medical women 'worked their passage' as officeholders within the BMA.[164] 'There is nothing to hinder us from taking our proper position in the BMA, if only we are prepared to sacrifice the necessary amount of time and energy', stated one. Christine Murrell heeded her own admonition and in 1924 was the first woman elected to the Council of the BMA. She would also have had the honour of becoming the first female member of the General Medical Council, but died before she could take it up.[165]

Recognition for medical women's earlier efforts during the First World War was largely conspicuous by its absence. Offers to equip and staff women's hospitals were refused by the War Office, but accepted gratefully abroad. Thus a Scottish Serbian Women's Hospital Unit was set up under Dr Inglis and Dame Louise McIlroy; Louisa Garrett Anderson's offer of a

---

[159] See the annual statement in the *BMJ*, 6 Sept. 1924 and 5 Sept. 1925. Also Dr Jane Walker in *Manchester Guardian*, 10 Sept. 1936.

[160] Mary D. Sturge, 'The Medical Women's Federation: Its Work and Aims', *MWFQN*, Dec. 1921.

[161] *MWFQN*, Dec. 1921.   [162] *Lancet*, 8 Oct. 1927, 831.

[163] *Birmingham Mail*, 17 Sept. 1952.

[164] Grace Griffith was chair of the W. Suffolk BMA (*BMJ* iv (1970), 373); Jessie Smailes, chair of the Huddersfield division and president of the Yorkshire branch (*BMJ*, i (1971), 237).

[165] St John, *Murrell*, 78–9.

fully equipped British Woman's Hospital was accepted by the French Red Cross for Paris and Royaumont, whilst another British Women's Hospital operated under the Belgian Red Cross in Antwerp. Only much later were some medical women grudgingly permitted to assist at a British government hospital in Malta. They were also attached as medical officers to the women's services, initially the QMAAC, and in 1918 the WRNS and WRAF. Important work by Letitia Fairfield, Jane Turnball, and Mona Chalmers followed on the health and hygiene of forces women. But the privations of wartime were compounded for medical women by humiliation inflicted through a non-recognition of professional status. As civilian officers under yearly contract, women in the services were denied uniform or badge for several years, and were never given commission, rank, or officers' allowances. Thus, medical women who were senior consultants in civilian life remained junior to the newest male officer. All female doctors in France, for example, had to travel third class as 'nurses'.[166]

As civilian medical practitioners on the home front during 1914 to 1918 women were on a par with their male colleagues. Media coverage of medical women was extremely positive with headlines such as 'Women's Kingdom', 'Women's Chance', 'Women's Opportunities', or 'Women's World'. The demand for lady doctors—to act as locums for male GPs who had been called up—vastly exceeded the available supply.[167] During both wars women gained invaluable experience which enabled them to get access to posts that otherwise would have been difficult if not impossible to attain.[168] During the Second World War medical women operated flexibly on the home front, doing sterling, if largely undramatic work, in the Emergency Medical Service, operating mobile clinics, giving first aid lectures, providing medical care for evacuees, acting as medical officers to the deep tube shelters as did Dr A. E. Beryl, or treating casualties during the Blitz as did Miss Louden. For Kathleen Norton, her wartime work was such a high point in her professional career that she considered her work in the ARP 'justified my existence'. Wearing a Churchillian style siren suit she called her 'bomb rompers' she crawled through the rubble to find people injured after an air raid on London.[169] Medical women took on erstwhile male roles as colliery doctors or police surgeons, after male colleagues had enlisted. They also gave assistance to regular commissioned officers in the forces, and were employed in clinics, hospitals and on recruiting boards. In the ATS their primary importance was in giving hygienic knowledge to women training to be in the armed

[166] Letitia Fairfield, 'Medical Women in the Forces. Part 1. Women Doctors in the British Forces, 1914–18 War', Jubilee issue of *Journal of MWF*, 99–102; *Daily Mirror*, 22 Oct. 1914; *Observer*, 11 Oct. 1914; ibid., 18 July 1937; *Medical Women*, 6 (1987), 4–12.

[167] *The Times*, 25 Jan. 1915.

[168] For example, Cecilia Williamson of Ipswich, whose maternity work during the First World War led to a later appointment at the local hospital (*JMWF*, 47 (Oct. 1965), 260).

[169] CMAC, GP 29/2/50, Kathleen Norton.

forces, while in the WRAF women doctors worked in RAF hospitals and stations at home, in India and in the Far East.[170]

Public and Private Faces

In peace rather than war female general practitioners had, and felt themselves to have, a high public profile. Sarah Gray, for instance, was a well-known figure driving to visit her patients in an open victoria round the Nottingham streets.[171] Beatrice Lovibond was a familiar figure—'the little lady in black with long skirts and a large black bag'.[172] At the very least there was a curiosity element in the sight of an early medical woman, although this later ripened into respect for professional prowess, and affectionate regard for personal attributes. Medical women might enhance this visibility by their personal style but, since the parameters of expected behaviour were narrower for the female than the male doctor, their idiosyncrasies might be perceived as eccentricity. One medical woman was renowned for going round corners on two wheels in her motor car; while another belied gender stereotyping by having a mechanical aptitude, and thus was frequently found *underneath* her car.[173]

Having lived very active lives in their profession and community the prospect of retirement for most medical women was a mixed blessing. A reluctance to retreat into private life was a recurring motif. 'I would rather wear out than rust out', said one redoubtable woman doctor.[174] Given the low earnings of many medical women hardship could strike *if* they retired. And, granted the attitudes of Benevolent Medical Societies, financial assistance was not necessarily forthcoming. After procrastinating since 1911 the Bishop Stortford Court of the Essex and Hertfordshire Medical Benevolent Medical Society decided to accept female members in 1920, thus giving medical women the right to future benefits. But, revealingly, their Colchester members dissented from this decision, and stated that their admission was still 'undesirable'.[175]

Women in general practice, like their male colleagues, might fail to reach retirement. Pioneers were prone to wear themselves out by their heroic efforts, and thus to succumb to what should not have been a terminal illness.

[170] L. Fairfield, 'Medical Women in a Combatant Country', *Journal of the American Medical Women's Association*, Nov. 1946; Greater Manchester RO, Q217/1, Scrapbook, 24–5, A. E. Beryl Harding, 'Work done by Medical Women in General Practice'.

[171] Greater Manchester RO, Q 217/1, Medical Women's Scrapbook, Obituary.

[172] Obituary in *BMJ*, ii (1940), 920.

[173] Greater Manchester RO, Q 217/1 Scrapbook, 154, Obituaries of Grace Billings and Ethel Williams.

[174] Ibid., Scrapbook, Obituary. Bensusan-Butt was a GP from 1907 to 1950.

[175] Essex RO (Chelmsford), D/2 15/6 and 15/12, minutes of Benevolent Medical Society for Essex and Hertfordhire, 10 June 1911, 1 and 8 June 1920.

An account of Mary Murdoch's incessant professional commitments suggests that physical strain contributed to her early death at the age of 52. She might drive out twenty miles from Hull to operate on a country patient before coming back for her morning town round from 10 a.m. until noon, taking an afternoon surgery, and then starting the evening round, returning home at 9 or 10 p.m. Apart from the forty or so patients from her own practice seen daily, on some days she also coped with as many as 200 out-patients at the hospital. Murdoch wrote that 'On Sunday I did sixteen hours on end, with ten minutes at 4 p.m. for a rushed dinner. The week-days are worse. Time becomes an increasingly diminished factor in my life. Eternity will perhaps be a rest.' But, in relation to one of her many radical reforming causes, she also stated that she wished 'to die in harness'.[176] Through the extent of their commitment to poor patients, others caught diseases that proved fatal, as did Mary Royce. Having run a mission in Leicester for many years she qualified as a medical practitioner 'that she might be of more service in her visiting of the sick and poor families', and then built a medical mission at her own expense, which she operated single-handedly. Here she was as much nurse as doctor to the poor women of the area, refusing payment for her services, and not sparing herself in her devotion to them. She only took a holiday on one occasion (and that on her doctor's orders) in the twenty-five years she ran her missions. Shortly after becoming medically qualified, she was elected a poor-law guardian and—when visiting the Infirmary—caught erysipelas from a woman, dying at the early age of 46.[177]

Obituaries of male and female GPs give an interesting insight into the gendered ideals that informed them. One of the first obituaries in the *BMJ* of a medical woman was that of Elizabeth Blackwell in 1910. Here this doughty pioneer is presented to a predominantly male readership as a 'womanly woman' much of whose medical career was explained away by a series of almost accidental circumstances.[178] Obituaries written by women often adopted a less restrictive professional formula, being more informal in tone, bringing the personal as well as the professional aspects of their subject into focus, and emphasizing relationships with patients. Dr Orford was saluted for her 'success in combining domestic and professional duties. Her solution to the worry of medical practice was an hour or two's cookery'.[179] Dr Ramsey was thanked by her obituarist, Dr Annie Bryce. 'She was a steadfast friend to the young and newly qualified, and I have many grateful memories of her kindness to me when I timidly started out in general practice thirty years ago.'[180]

What of the professional satisfactions of women in general practice? A non-mercenary element was conspicuous, as this comment indicates:

---

[176] Malleson, *Murdoch*, 31–2, 34, 87. (The comment was about the female suffrage).
[177] *Midland Free Press*, 5 Nov. 1892. She qualified LSA at the LMSW in 1890 and died in 1892.
[178] *BMJ*, i (1910), 1523–4.
[179] Greater Manchester RO, Q 217/1, Scrapbook, 44–5, Obituary.   [180] *BMJ*, 22 May 1954.

Those people who enter medicine with the idea of making money may make a success, but they never realise the full happiness it can bring. There is such a vast amount more in it than merely making money.[181]

And a plea for women to take up general practice suggested that 'When she comes to render an account at the last of the suffering she has been privileged to prevent or relieve one can wish for no better epitaph than "she hath done what she could." '[182] Obituary notices give us a good insight into this central, yet private, area of professional satisfaction as a comparison of two from the MWF *Newsletter* of 1924 indicates:

Dr Stephens was an ideal general practitioner, possessing good judgement, sympathy, tact and a winning manner which endeared her to all who knew her.

[Dr Patch] was the ideal general practitioner, an able physician and good surgeon, keeping up with medical progress and new methods, and putting all her powers of head and heart at the service of all who sought her.[183]

The early parts of both notices could have come from the obituaries of male colleagues in the *BMJ*, but their later references to the 'sympathy, tact, and a winning manner' of Dr Stephens, and to the power of the 'heart' of Dr Patch suggest that medical women were more open in recognizing the importance of psychological and emotional factors in their work.

One medical woman attempted to draw up a private balance sheet of the satisfactions and drawbacks of her life:

Very rarely I considered whether this medical life was indeed the life of coveted independence I fought so hard to gain—a life of comparative slavery, it could be argued to any Tom, Dick or Harry for twenty-four hours a day. And yet I maintain now, a life . . . of the greatest happiness, however hurtful it might be to fight at times a losing battle against death; a life of great rewards, of incessant striving, of always being a learner at the foot of nature but, through it all, a life which gives a freedom, an independence of spirit . . .[184]

Conclusion

During the period generational differences were apparent amongst successive cohorts (see Plate 4). Culturally, the change was visible in an evolution in the terms of popular description from 'medical women', to 'lady doctors', and finally 'women doctors.' To the early women, like Marie Scharlieb, 'our profession must be to us a sort of religion: a golden band binding together all

[181] Comment by Dr Mabel Ramsey (the second female Plymouth GP) reported in the *Western Morning News*, 11 May 1954.

[182] Mary E.H. Morris, 'A Plea for General Practice', *MWFQN*, Nov. 1923, 24.

[183] Obituaries of Dr Henrietta Stephens, MB Royal Free, London: Winifred Patch, MD, BS, BSc, London. Patch was in general practice for nearly 20 years, first in the Holloway Road and then in Highbury Place, London (*MWFQN*, Nov. 1924, 60).

[184] Jalland, *Wilberforce*, 158–9.

WOMAN'S TRIUMPH IN THE PROFESSIONS.

MEDICINE.

First Lady Doctor. "HE IS SLEEPING NOW, AND IS CERTAINLY RECOVERING. HE PROPOSED TO ME THIS MORNING."
Second Lady Doctor. "INDEED! HE WAS PROBABLY DELIRIOUS."

4. Woman's triumph in the professions, 1907

our faculties'.[185] Later, as more medical schools produced women graduates, and numbers within the profession increased, this sense of being part of a small, tightly knit group weakened. By the end of the period women were much more widely accepted by both colleagues and patients. A woman who trained in the 1940s commented that 'the pioneers had gone before us . . . they'd had more of a struggle than we'd had. We just had a struggle to get in [to medical school]. Once we were in we were all right.'[186] Both world wars had been catalysts in forcing that acceptance, because the absence of many male doctors in the forces had normalized the presence of women in general practice.[187]

Women in general practice operated professionally in a semi-separate sphere. Forced for much of the period to create their own training establishments, and to found hospitals and dispensaries so as to get clinical experience, medical women forged distinctive aspirations and values. In order to carve out economically viable niches women frequently had to found or pur-

---

[185] M. Scharlieb, *Seven Lamps of Medicine* (Oxford, 1888), 8.
[186] CMAC, GP 29/2/9, Elizabeth Clubb, MB, BS (London 1947).
[187] CMAC, GP 29/2/37, Hilda Cantrell; CMAC, GP29/2/15, Vera Gavin, MRCS Eng, LRCP (London 1943).; CMAC, GP29/2/50, Kathleen Norton.

chase women-only practices. Female partnerships also facilitated this. Women's professional and social solidarity was further cemented by their own medical organizations. Not that women remained entirely excluded from the wider world: eventually a few won recognition for their clinical skills, whilst a minority served on national insurance committees, or were involved in BMA activities. But male domination characterized most institutions as well as much medico-political activity. Male anxiety that women would make the medical market even more competitive, and hence threaten their own professional survival, were only partly fulfilled. Women doctors found their own niches in under-resourced areas of practice, but rarely earned comparable salaries to their economically more successful male colleagues. In part this lack of earning power may have been because of the success of their male colleagues' strategy of marginalization, but at least as important were the different values that women brought to general practice. Despite masculine fears that the non-commercial, social-service ethic of the typical medical woman would lead to undercutting in fees, this did not happen. However, the personal commitment of women GPs was conspicuous. One encapsulated this with her poignant statement that medicine 'has been an exacting mistress, and has taken thing after thing away from me; tethered me down, taken my freedom and liberty . . . and yet I love her and serve her with the same passion'.[188]

Patients appreciated medical women's commitment. As with American 'lady doctors',[189] it was at the level of individual family practice or local community that most medical women found a warm recognition for that professional skill, and personal worth which had frequently eluded them in national or élite circles. In their relationships with their patients particularly, medical women appear to have achieved an empathy, a personal closeness that was more rarely found (or at least acknowledged) amongst their male colleagues. And, by the 1930s, even male colleagues were prepared to recognize that children and old people preferred female to male doctors although, significantly, they did not concede the main area of professional contention—women patients.[190]

In specializing with female and child patients medical women became more proficient in areas such as paediatrics, as well as in gynaecological and family planning concerns, with which their male colleagues were reluctant to engage. In areas of work that were common to both male and female GPs, any attempt to outline major differences in their clinical work is more problematical because the variety of approaches was often as much a matter of individual style as of gender-based differences. However, women GPs seem to have been readier to examine their patients;[191] were noted for their

[188] Malleson, *Murdoch*, 37.

[189] R. M. Morantz-Sanchez, *Sympathy and Science. Women Physicians in American Medicine* (Oxford, 1985), 183.

[190] *Daily Mail*, 13 June 1936.

[191] CMAC, GP 29/2/6 and 37, Margaret Norton examined half her patients, and Hilda Cantrell examined all of hers.

willingness to do minor surgery; and customarily saw a patient's physical complaint within a wider social context, thus going beyond a symptomatic approach. Medical women's rejection of an economically driven maximization of throughput militated against their creation of large incomes. Their patient-focused attitudes naturally involved a more holistic view of health and illness, and the logical (if untheorized) outcome of this was a less circumscribed view of clinical work. One female GP commented about her patients:

I never was ruled by the clock . . . people are all so different, and this is what's . . . such fun about general practice. This is what's made the whole life. The people. . . . Half the work in general practice is living, advice about living . . . it's as much as being ill.[192]

---

[192] CMAC, GP 29/2/6, Margaret Norton (MB, Ch.B., Birmingham, 1939).

8

Medical Investigation and Treatment

'THERE are no real standards for general practice. What the doctor does and how he does it, depends almost wholly on his own conscience.'[1] This critical comment followed from an examination of GP's surgeries shortly after the inception of the NHS. To what extent is it valid? The following analysis discusses the methods of general practitioners in their clinical work. A sustained attempt has been made to locate clinical records from past GP's practices, although their cryptic entries, incomplete series, and cross-referencing to records no longer extant, can make their contents elusive. To the breadth of the chapter's general analysis I have added several case studies of individual doctors or practices to illustrate the diversity of general practice in greater depth.

The period from 1850 to 1948 straddles the traditional and the modern in medicine, and the considerable overlap between the two means that it is not possible to make a clear divide between them. Traditional medicine was centred in symptomatic diagnosis and a humane interaction with the patient, whilst modern medicine relied to a much greater extent on precise and mechanistic measurements achieved with instruments, together with powerful pharmaceuticals that cured rather than palliated disease. A portrait contrasting medicine in 1948 with that eighty years before, emphasized that then the:

Science of clinical observation stood high, but that pathology was confined to what is now known as morbid anatomy. Little was known of the causation of disease, and therapeutic blood-letting and the polypharmacy of the alchemist still persisted. Since that day the science of bacteriology has appeared, and the control of sepsis has enabled surgery to take over the treatment of many diseases . . . Precision methods of many kinds have made diagnosis more exact.[2]

Charting the adoption of modern instrumentation in general practitioners' surgeries is problematical, not least because there was substantial variety between individual doctors. Advances in instrumentation meant that even specialists, let alone GPs, found it difficult to accommodate the pace of new methods of measuring vital physical indicators. Even the eminent clinical physician and tutor at Guys, W. W. Gull (1815–1890), commented in 1872,

[1] J. S. Collings, 'General Practice in England Today. A Reconnaissance' in *Lancet*, i (1950), 555.
[2] Sir Henry Ogilvie, 'Then and Now', *Practitioner*, 161 (July to Dec. 1948), 1–2.

'I have more than once been tempted to lay aside my thermometer because it has contradicted my clinical knowledge. But it must be so at first with all new evidence: it takes time to bring it fairly into count.'[3] This may suggest that at all levels of the medical profession there were generational differences. Indeed, instrumentation that was used with ease by a later generation, may have been integrated with some difficulty into the clinical routine of an earlier one. Also influential was the type of practice, individual doctors' preferences or abilities, and generational differences, with traditional methods living on in the practices of older doctors. Retrospectively, doctors were scathing about the limitations of traditional medicine. 'There was so little one had in 1935 . . . there was very little one could do for them.'[4] 'Everything was symptomatic, none of it did any good.'[5] This may be too simplistic a view, because arguably something may have been lost. Earlier doctors were very aware that in their all-too-frequent absence of ability to cure they had a duty to care, whereas modern scientific medicine has extracted a price in a loss of personal sensibility, and an objectification of the patient that is very apparent in hospital practice, and may also be evident to a lesser extent in general practice. Equally, some of a patient's respect may have been diverted from the doctor to wonder drugs and technology.

Diagnosis and Prognosis

The date and location of the doctor's training influenced the nature of examination and diagnosis. 'The tradition of English clinical teaching is to learn everything possible by clinical observation alone; to call in diagnostic aids only when clinical observation fails to give the answer.'[6] The more clinically minded GP might use the stethoscope, thermometer, ear syringe and, in fewer cases, the sphygmomanometer,[7] ophthalmoscope and the speculum as aids to diagnosis. But prescriptive literature on furnishing the surgery gave an over-elaborate view of what was likely to be purchased, or used. Such a list in 1928 gave a microscope, sphygmomanometer, and perhaps a haemocytometer, and a haemoglobinometer.[8] But in the 1920s a Derbyshire branch practice had only a stethoscope and thermometer, and in the 1930s a Hampshire practitioner in a practice with a surgical bias remembered only the use of a stethoscope, opthalmoscope, and laryngoscope, although the local

---

[3] 'Address to Clinical Society', 1872 in T. D. Acland (ed.), *W.W. Gull Memoirs and Addresses* (1896), 100.

[4] CMAC, GP/29/2/59, Samuel Isaacs, born Merthyr Tydfil, B.Sc (Wales, 1935), MB, BCh (1935.), practised Newport, Monmouth.

[5] CMAC, GP/29/2/48, Bertie Dover, MB, Ch.B. (Liverpool, 1945), practised in Liverpool.

[6] S. Taylor, *Good General Practice* (Oxford, 1954), 11–12.

[7] CMAC, GP/29/2/49, Donald Gawith, , MRSC, Eng, LRCP (London 1945), DPH (Glasgow, 1952).

[8] I. G. Briggs, *How to Start in General Practice* (1928), 61–2.

cottage hospital could give the GP access to X-ray equipment.[9] Some doctors did urine testing, and took their patients' blood pressure, a process hastened by the insistence of assurance companies on their use in examinations for life insurance.[10] Yet patient expectation was generally attuned to a 'low-tech' encounter. A medical woman who had qualified in Germany, but practised in interwar England, soon found that the clinical standards of urine and blood testing, and X-rays she was accustomed to work with went unrewarded by her patients, and so discontinued them.[11]

In the immediate post-NHS years Collings gave a devastating—and in critics' view a biased—impression of a lack of even such basic equipment as an examination couch or a wash basin in some GPs' surgeries.[12] This was, as a defensive editorial in the *BMJ* commented, both 'depressing in the extreme' as well as 'inexact and unfair'.[13] But while it failed to give an adequate overall picture its findings did depict the situation in a sizeable minority of practices. Dr Lilly, for example, found no examination couch on taking up a practice in Long Buckby, Northamptonshire in 1947 so that he had to do his examinations in patient's houses.[14] In British practice more generally this kind of inadequacy may well have inhibited examination, since if this was to be conducted later in the patient's home it probably lowered its frequency. Hadfield's survey in 1951–2 found great variety in the practices surveyed. Only one in eleven practices were without what he termed 'basic' instruments (syringes, auriscope, ophthalmoscope, stethoscope, sphygmomanometer, and urine-testing equipment) whereas one in seven had more elaborate instrumentation. Possession, significantly, did not necessarily mean use, and much equipment was dusty and disused.[15]

With or without the help of equipment, the process of diagnosis implied dependence on careful examination, experience and intuition that culminated in a clinical judgement.[16] How much GPs examined their patients must remain speculative. It varied according to the class and gender of the patient. Lower rates for working-class patients arose both because of low patient payment and from the related pressure on the doctor of the time that could be afforded. Rates of examination were also less good for female patients because, in the earlier part of the period, delicacy inhibited the exposure of

[9] Unpublished 'Memoirs of Dr William Henry Harding', 22; Pers. comm., James E. Rankine, MB, Ch.B. (1930), MD (Glasgow, 1938) came to Romsey in 1938.

[10] CMAC, GP/29/2/63, Robert (Tony) Leake, BM, CH (1952, MRCGP, 1965). He started general practice in 1954; Norfolk RO, BR 224/11 Dr Speirs of Diss, day book 1896–9 shows urine testing being carried out. Hugh Meredith Speirs MB, Ch.B. (1900), MD (Edinburgh, 1904); M. Dupree, 'Other than Healing: Medical Practitioners and the Business of Life Assurance During the Nineteenth and Early Twentieth Centuries', *SHM*, 10 (1997).

[11] CMAC, GP/29/2/62, Margarete Samuel, LMSSSA (London, 1931).

[12] Collings, 'General Practice' *Lancet*, 25 Mar. 1950.   [13] *BMJ*, i (1950), 709.

[14] Personal communication, Richard G. Lilly, MB, BS (Durham, 1941).

[15] *BMJ*, i (1953), 701. Dr Stephen Hadfield, an assistant secretary of the BMA, investigated 188 practices between Feb. 1951 and Mar. 1952.

[16] M. Bligh, *Dr Eurich of Bradford* (Bradford, 1960).

more than modest portions of the female body to a male practitioner, while limited 'chaperoning' facilities by practice nurse or practitioner's wife might make later examination more a matter of last—rather than first resort. A field survey of general practice during the early years of the NHS indicated that as many as 93 per cent did some kind of examination of their patients, although it is likely that the artificial conditions of the survey themselves inflated the number of examinations performed. However, even under these conditions inspection and percussion of the chest was rarely done to a high standard, while patients' abdomens were often examined through the clothes and with the patient standing.[17]

At the end of the nineteenth century doctors had been urged to substitute a scientific diagnosis for a patient-centred one:

It is obviously to an increased perfection of physical diagnosis, aided by pathology, that we must look for the advancement of medicine. The feelings of the patient, the so-called symptoms, are of little value taken in themselves . . . they need the inter-pretation of physical inquiry.[18]

This professional prescription was not before its time. Much traditional med-ical diagnosis was imprecise and showed substantial overlap with that of lay people, as Victorian poor-law records reveal. In the Oxfordshire Bicester Union the returns of George Dew, a relieving officer without medical quali-fication, showed a very substantial similarity with the terminology of the medically qualified district medical officers with whom he worked.[19] The returns that the Bicester MO furnished for the guardians indicated that at mid-century six doctors were each using diagnostic categories with a remark-ably small degree of overlap. It might be argued that the lack of a standard-ized medical classification arose from the need to communicate with lay bureaucrats, whose task it was to monitor such statements. But it is remark-able to find, as late as the 1890s, a later generation of poor-law doctors using a range of diagnoses that were only a little more recognizably medical and scientific in the terminology employed.[20] This indicates a considerable time-lag in the diffusion of modern medicine, since the epistemological revolution that germ theory had introduced in the 1870s, was not at all evident in these provincial returns.

It is in this context that we need to view the Registrar General's attempts to frame consistent diagnostic categorizations from the death certificates issued by doctors. In 1875 William Farr considered that 'diagnosis, though

---

[17] *BMJ*, i (1953), 687.

[18] W. W. Gull, 'Clinical Observation in Relation to Medicine in Modern Times', in Acland, *Memoirs*, 58.

[19] Oxfordshire Archives, PLU2/RL/2A4/1–2 Requests to Medical Officers for medical attention to paupers, 1876–7 and PLU2/6/1A16, Bicester District Medical Officers returns of sick paupers attended, 1836, 1846, 1892.

[20] Oxfordshire Archives, PLU2/6/1A16, Bicester District Medical Officers returns of sick pau-pers attended, 1836, 1846, 1892.

still imperfect, has within 35 years made remarkable progress . . . among the body of medical practitioners all over the kingdom.'[21] Beginning in the 1880s, and continuing for four decades, the General Register Office began confidential enquiries of medical practitioners, who had given a vague categorization of cause of death (such as tumour or dropsy), so as to get a more precise and convenient diagnosis for the compilation of vital statistics. This also served to educate and improve doctors' diagnostic powers. In 1895 4 per cent of deaths certified by doctors were still so unsatisfactory as to be useless for classification. Local variation in levels of certification were quite large with Wales, Cornwall and Herefordshire having much higher levels of uncertified deaths.[22] And twenty-five years later a proposal that NHI doctors should insert diagnoses on their patients' 'Lloyd George' record cards was dropped because expert opinion considered that medical work was based on probability, not certainty, in the vast majority of cases.[23] This judgement was probably correct, in that a GP who started work shortly after the NHS, commented of his work as a primary diagnostician, that 'in perhaps 50 per cent of cases in general practice, you can't make a definite diagnosis, you can only sort of hazard a guess'.[24] Even at the end of the period Dr Jeger commented of his patients that 'when they go into the doctor's surgery . . . they do not know what is the matter with them, and often the doctor does not know, but has to give them an expectorant or a waiting treatment'.[25] The term 'GOK' was thus a trusty professional diagnostic shorthand for 'God Only Knows'.[26]

Prognosis was even less well developed than was diagnosis. Doctors needed to have had several years in general practice before they accumulated sufficient clinical experience to feel confident. James Mackenzie commented that 'as an examiner of life insurance . . . I had no real knowledge of the prospects for the candidate's life'. It was not taught in medical school and doctors needed to work out the kind of questions that they needed to ask patients if they were to do this at all adequately.[27] Then, as now, a spot diagnosis of the commoner medical conditions was found to be relatively easy, although there was criticism that a small minority of practitioners abused this by not examining their patient when it was in fact called for.[28] However, it is likely that the experience and intuition involved in making a spot diagnosis by one

[21] *35th Annual Report of Registrar General*, PP, 1875, xliii, part I, supplement, lxxx.

[22] A. Hardy, ' "Death is the Cure of all Diseases": Using the General Register Office Cause of Death Statistics for 1837–1920', *SHM*, 7 (1994), 475; *Report of the Registrar General*, PP, 1900, xv, 37.

[23] PRO, MH 62/130, Interdepartmental Committee, Jan. 1920.

[24] CMAC, GP29/2/63, Robert (Tony) Leake.

[25] *Hansard*, 470 (1948–9), col. 2242. S. W. Jeger MRCS, Eng, LRCP, Lond. (1923). He became MP for St Pancras, SE, but continued to practise in Clerkenwell.

[26] Pers. comm., Allan F. Granger MB, Ch.B. (Glasgow 1938) practised in Kimbolton, Huntingdonshire, now Cambridgeshire.

[27] J. Mackenzie, 'The Opportunities of the GP', *BMJ*, i (1921), 799.

[28] *BMJ*, i (1953), 687.

doctor might be construed by another as professional overconfidence. The large patient throughput of an industrial practice might make such concerns redundant. A doctor who had been a locum in a Newcastle practice in 1946 recollected that it 'was an enormous practice with no records at all . . . where the standards were really appalling. There were all sorts of undiagnosed things, lurking'.[29]

In industrial areas doctors found their surgeries filled by patients with pre-dictable illnesses such as upper respiratory complaints, amongst which were bronchitis, 'chronic chest', and emphysema. In mining areas these were often superimposed upon silicosis, or anthacosis.[30] Digestive and alimentary disor-ders were as prominent as cardiovascular ones.[31] Tuberculosis was prevalent in poorer districts, more especially those with sub-standard housing. In all areas serious infectious diseases, such as diphtheria and scarlet fever, were to be found, as well as more common childhood illnesses such as measles, chicken pox, and mumps. In addition, croup, whooping cough, acute rheumatism, chorea, and a later development of endocarditis were also likely to be present. The prevalence of colds, coughs, and influenza—sometimes leading to bronchitis or pneumonia—created a heavy professional workload in winter, whilst diarrhoea and typhoid were present in summer during the earlier part of the period. Gradually the pattern of morbidity was transformed by autonomous disease fluctuations in the severity of many diseases, improved standards of living, interventions in public health, as well as ther-apeutic and pharmaceutical advances. Table 8.1 indicates common infectious illnesses treated in general practice during the 1920s and 1930s. By the early years of the NHS, as one GP commented:

You didn't get diphtheria, scarlet fever wasn't as common, rheumatic fever was on the decline, but we still did get cases. Polio was still a worry when I started in practice, and until we got immunisation . . . [but] tuberculosis was getting under control then.[32]

The age profile of the general practitioner's patients had also changed. During the century expectation of life at birth for the doctors' patients had changed dramatically. In England and Wales it had risen from 40 years for a man or 42 for a woman (1838–54) to 66.4 and 71.5 respectively (1950–2). In Scotland it had increased from 40.3 years for a man and 43.9 years for a woman (1861–70) to 64.4 and 68.7 years respectively (1950–2).[33] A doctor in 1871 would have recruited patients from a population where 36 per cent were under 14 and only 5 per cent were aged 65 or over. But in 1951 children made up only 22 per cent of the population, whereas the elderly formed as much as 11 per cent.[34] Alongside changes in the demographic profile were

[29] CMAC, GP 29/2/44, Thomas McQuay, MB, BCH, BAO (Belfast, 1945).
[30] Ibid., 29/2/59, Samuel Isaacs.   [31] Hadfield, *General Practice*, 538–9.
[32] CMAC, GP 29/2/63, Tony Leake.
[33] A. H. Halsey (ed.), *British Social Trends since 1900* (1988), table 11.4, 406.
[34] D. C. Marsh, *The Changing Social Structure of England and Wales 1871–1961* (1958), 25. Age statistics are for England and Wales.

TABLE 8.1. Cases of infectious disease in a fifteen-year epidemiological investigation

Diseases	Number
Influenza	1112
Diarrhoea and vomiting	1018
Measles	510
Febrile catarrh	407
Chicken pox	318
Whooping cough	295
Tonsillitis	289
Mumps	233
German measles	175
Herpes zoster	140
Scarlet fever	117
Lobar pneumonia	41
Glandular fever	41
Bornholm disease	25
Diphtheria	12
Total	4855

Source: W. Pickles, 'Epidemiology in Country Practice', *New England Journal of Medicine*, 239 (1948).

the persistent class and gender differences, which showed up strongly in comparative mortality and morbidity experience.

Treatment

A statement from *The Practitioner* (a new journal for GPs that began in 1868) made challenging reading:

The present state of Medical Science is in one respect most unsatisfactory. While our knowledge of the facts of disease, as well as the facts of healthy physiological life has made great progress of late years, Therapeutics, or the science of healing, has not. . . . We know tolerably well *what* it is we have to deal with, but we do not so well . . . [know] *how* to deal with it.[35]

For much of the period practical utility and well-tried custom were useful guides for medical treatment although surgery might appear to offer fresher vistas. A GP commented:

As a student I always felt disappointed at the position of medicine, Progress seemed at a standstill, and the reasons for employing certain treatments seemed inadequate,

[35] *Practitioner*, 1 (1868), 1.

Bacteriology was in its infancy . . . Diagnosis may have been frequently correct, but
. . . treatment was empirical. I often think that if surgery had not shown definite signs
of advancement I should have changed my profession.[36]

In reality, the excitement of expanding frontiers in surgery was more theoretical than practical. If it was noticeable at all, it would have been in the
work of the GP-Surgeon in the local hospital operating theatre,[37] rather than
in the more limited kitchen-table surgery of much of the general practitioner's work.

Here procedures in minor surgery dominated and, although circumscribed
by limited equipment, were multifarious. Common procedures included:
dressing wounds, removing stitches, lancing a boil, syringing ears, taking out
sebaceous cysts, opening and evacuating ganglia, opening a quinsy or an
abscess, dressing a carbuncle or a whitlow, passing a catheter, giving a smallpox vaccination, setting a fracture, tapping a hydrocele, or reducing a hernia.
Surgical fashions and practices evolved over the period: early on a depletive
regime of blistering, bleeding, or applying a caustic or a plaster might be
practised;[38] by the early twentieth century an up-to-date doctor could be
found injecting ergotin, or electrolysing a wart;[39] during the interwar period
circumcisions were performed in people's homes or in a special surgery on
Sunday mornings,[40] and tonsillectomy came into vogue. Tonsils were usually
guillotined rather than the later practice of dissecting them out.[41] It should
be emphasized, however, that minor surgery for many doctors comprised
only one case, at most two, per week.[42] For example, Dr Noot, a Welsh practitioner, performed only forty cases of minor surgery during 1875.[43] Some
with prior surgical experience and habituated to self-reliance in the circumstances of a country practice, were more ambitious in their treatments—doing
all fractures, 'D and C's (temporary dilation of the cervix and curettage of
the lining of the uterus), amputations, or even an appendectomy.[44] Dentistry
was also practised, especially in country areas devoid of dentists, where tooth
extraction was a compassionate service.[45]

---

[36] E. R. Furbes, CBE, *London Doctor*, (1940), 16–17.

[37] J. M. Tait, a Sutton practitioner, who was 'for many years on the staff of the Carsholton War
Memorial Hospital and did much work as a general practitioner surgeon' (*BMJ*, ii (1960), 1244).

[38] Clwyd RO (Hawarden), D/DM/301/3 Ledger of Dr John Ingham, Ruabon, Denbigh, 1855.
John Ingman, MRCS Eng. and LSA (1847).

[39] Clwyd RO (Hawarden), D/DM/63/1/32, day book of Dr Edwards, 1911–12, entries 17–31
Aug. 1911. Roger B. Edwards, MB, BS (London, 1911) and MRCS, LRCP (London, 1910). For the
use of ergotin for haemorrhage, and that of electrotherapeutics in warts see *The Medical Annual*
(1898), 266, 354–5 and (1913), 72–3, 75.

[40] CMAC, GP 29/2/8, Frank Boon, MB, BS, Durham 1935, MRCGP, 1958.

[41] Pers. comm., Beryl J. Goff, MB, BS (1945), MRCS, LRCP (1944).

[42] Essex RO (Chelmsford), D/DU 509, Felstead day book, 1934; D/F 79 A 5637, Maldon practice books, 1946.

[43] National Library of Wales, NLW MS 12540, Dr Noott's ledger, 1876.

[44] Pers. comm., Allan Granger.

[45] National Library of Wales, NLW MS 12540, Dr Noott's ledger, 1876.

A minority of practitioners became remarkably adept at surgery, and thus made it into a minor speciality. One such was William Robinson who practised on Wearside in the 1870s and who would amputate limbs, excise growths for cancer or joints for tubercular disease, operate for club foot, hare lip, and even attempt a lateral cystotomy for stone, or an ovariotomy.[46] The creation of cottage and local general hospitals enabled more elaborate surgical operations to be performed by general practitioners. Thus Drs Speirs and Barrie removed a uterine polypus in the Nursing Hospital in Diss.[47] Practitioners might do quite major operations for private patients in the local cottage hospital as did Dr Herman from 1920 to 1948, in the Tonbridge Queen Victoria Cottage Hospital. His operations were mainly appendectomies, and hysterectomies for fibroids, but included curettage, hernia repairs, and also a colostomy. Predictably, he later became a hospital consulting surgeon.[48]

The treatment of chronic conditions assumed a basic, if unspectacular part of the doctor's work. Lack of effective drugs during the acute stage of an illness could lead to a long-term medical condition: for example, a failing heart after scarlatina meant the doctor attempting to combat dropsy by drawing fluid from the legs by inserting needles.[49] Certain common chronic conditions—such as leg ulcers, arising from varicose veins—were found 'frustrating' because of the GP's surgical inability to ameliorate the condition.[50] Doctors had to remember to include long-term patients in their schedule of visits. For instance, a Kimbolton doctor visited his rheumatoid arthritis, bronchial, and congestive heart failure patients once a month.[51]

A long-term decline in dispensing within many practices did however, simplify professional life. At the start of the period it was customary to dispense, not least because in England payment for medicine rather than for the doctor's skill and time was the basis for the economics of primary health care.[52] Dispensing in urban areas declined with the gradual substitution of alternative payment systems during the second half of the nineteenth century. The later reluctance of the NHI scheme to pay for dispensing as a matter of course, (rather than as a result of a case being made, most commonly for rural practices), accelerated this trend.

Until the late nineteenth century polypharmacy appears to have been the norm, and this custom shared the same cultural tradition as did herbal remedies with their mixtures of plants compounded for an individual client on a particular occasion. Doctors' accounts with the local chemist indicated the extent to which medicine looked to the past as well as to the future. In the

[46] W. Robinson, *Sidelights on the Life of a Wearside Surgeon* (Gateshead on Tyne, 1939), 47.

[47] Norfolk RO, BR224/11, Dr Speirs Day Book, 1896–9, folio 118.

[48] Warders Medical Centre, Tonbridge, record of private operations, 1920–48 by A. E. Herman, BA, B.Ch., 1911, MB, 1913 (Cambridge and London Hospital); MRCS and LRCP (London, 1911); LRCS, 1920 (Edinburgh).

[49] Pers. comm., James Rankine of Romsey.

[50] CMAC, GP 29/2/44, Thomas McQuay.

[51] Pers. comm., Allan Granger.

[52] A. Digby, *Making a Medical Living*, 150–1.

1870s, for example, Dr Williams of Denbigh was buying leeches and poppy heads, as well as more powerful remedies such as morphia and chlorodyne.[53] And leeches were still being used in Edwardian general practice, for instance in cases of deep-seated eye inflammation.[54] Individual prescription was a matter of professional pride, and a doctor's special mixtures were viewed as an important asset in building up local reputation and patients. For example, Dr Bullmore, who practised in Wisbech from 1904 until 1946, was famed for his fenland cough mixture of Mist. Sod.Chor.Co. made palatable when 'taken three times daily in half a glass of hot milk and a tablespoon of rum'.[55]

At the end of the nineteenth century a Norfolk GP kept a beautiful day book, written in copperplate and with headings done in red ink to compose individualized prescriptions for his patients. He then dispensed them, and might use the parcel post to send out his medicines (especially repeat ones) to more distant patients.[56] For another dispensing country practice, this time in the interwar period, dispensing continued under the capable hands of the dispenser: eight ounce bottles were utilized more frequently than four, three, two, one, or half ounce bottles, or two dram phials.[57] In a third country practice, just before the advent of the NHS, panel patients got their medicines unwrapped but private patients had theirs in white paper fastened neatly with sealing wax.[58] Generally at this time liquid medicines were much more in evidence than the pill, or its more modern equivalent, the tabloid.

The discriminatory nature of clinical practice was quite marked. 'I practised . . . at the workhouse, but I found it some time before I could do it efficiently', remarked one practitioner of his dry-cupping techniques as used with bronchial and other chest complaints.[59] Poorer patients were given only a restricted range of medicines by the 'sixpenny doctor' at the turn of the century, or thereafter the panel doctor under the NHI scheme. Stock mixtures, differentiated with different colours, were measured out of large Winchester bottles. 'I had three bottles, and aspirins of various colours . . . pink, red, green and white', recollected one interwar practitioner.[60] For panel patients' 8oz. bottles, filled from stock mixtures, were standard treatment. It was not just panel practices where medicines were simplified, however, since the therapeutic arsenal of a rural dispensing practice might also consist of a bottle of aspirin and four Winchesters. Typically one would contain the 'speciality' of the practice. Thus one Winchester might glow with a pink mixture (for instance, 'Dr Ellis's cough mixture') that was renowned for its efficacy locally.[61] A Lancashire doctor reflected of these mixtures:

[53] Clwyd RO, Ruthin, DD/HB/959, Account book of Dr Williams, 1873–1907.
[54] Interestingly, leeches have been found recently to be very useful after delicate surgery.
[55] F. E. Lodge, 'Reminiscences from a Fenland Practice', *BMJ*, 289 (1984), 1760–2.
[56] Norfolk RO, BR 224/11, Day book of Dr H.M. Speirs, folios 16, 840, 890, 900.
[57] Oxfordshire Archives, Misc Sq X/1–10, Squire practice invoices and receipts, 1912–53.
[58] Pers. comm., Allan Granger.   [59] Lodge, 'Reminiscences'.
[60] CMAC, GP 29/2/62, Margarete Samuel.
[61] Pers. comm., Allan Granger describing his predecessor, later partner, Dr Ellis's practice in 1947.

an awful lot of them were *placebos*. But, on the other hand, there were some very powerful things . . . the use of things that are illegal now, the use of kaolin and morphine, the old chlorodyne. It was a very powerful remedy [but] the stock mixtures which you diluted down into the bottle of medicine, were very, very poor stock, indeed, compared with present times.[62]

From the turn of the century modern medicine became more apparent in general practice, made visible by single substance drugs that targeted specific conditions or diseases. Positive developments included the use of Aspirin for pain relief; Salvarsan for venereal disease; Insulin for diabetes; and iron injections (instead of raw liver sandwiches) for pernicious anaemia. Also notable was the benefit of immunization, as in cases where laryngeal diphtheria had meant earlier that the GP could have to perform an emergency tracheotomy with a severely cyanosed patient—whose condition was indicated by their blue colour, sometimes already beginning to turn black.[63] But it was not until the mid-1930s that a new breed of powerful medicaments began to arrive, with the potential to transform the clinical scene in primary health care. Prominent amongst these were Sulphonamides, introduced in 1935/6, which were antibacterial agents. They were active against a range of serious diseases, including streptococcal and meningococcal infections. Now almost forgotten, they were the 'miracle drugs' of their day, saving thousands of lives. They were soon eclipsed by Penicillin which was introduced into general practice in 1944/5. The new drugs meant that doctors could revise their daily pattern of work by making fewer visits to patients' homes.

You give penicillin, and you give enough for a week, and the doctor doesn't bother to come for a week to see you. But we hadn't got any penicillin. And so, you see, if we had a measles, we went for the first five days, every day, because that's when they're going to get pneumonia, if they're going to get it, and you can, you know, make sure they're in bed, and properly looked after.[64]

The treatment of acute lobar pneumonia was the most striking example of the transition from traditional to modern medicine, in which changing medication led to a substantial alteration in the role of the doctor. Historically the doctor had spent eight to ten days in apprehensive and attentive management of the patient, visiting as much as four times a day,[65] while the patient's temperature hovered around 103 to 105 °F, and the GP waited for 'the crisis' which brought either a welcome decline in temperature, or else death from the extent of the inflammatory action, either from exhaustion, or from heart failure. With penicillin there were fewer visits, less uncertainty and—despite recurrences and relapses—a dramatically improved prognosis. Before penicillin doctors had thus played a heroic role in the eyes of patients' relatives

---

[62] CMAC, GP 29/2/44, Thomas McQuay.
[63] Pers. comm., R. E. Hope Simpson, OBE, MRCS, LRCP (St Thomas, London), FRS.
[64] CMAC, GP 29/2/50, Kathleen Norton, MA (Oxon, 1926), BM (1926), MRCS (Eng)., LRCP (London, 1925).
[65] Pers. comm., James Rankine.

as well as neighbourhoods, and this undoubtedly contributed to their stature in their local communities.

Prescription of medicine served functions other than a strictly clinical treatment of disease, and ones that illuminated the complex and overlapping roles played by general practitioners in their interactions with patients. The granting of medicine might signify to the patient that the doctor took their illness seriously and was actively doing something about it. For the doctor, medicine might 'buy' time whilst an illness either proved to be self-limiting and therefore disappeared or, if more serious, allowed the illness to develop to the point where an accurate diagnosis was feasible. The advent of powerful modern drugs led to criticism that these might be taking the place of diagnosis and thus were being over prescribed.[66] At the end of our period, one experienced doctor commented:

We all know that a good deal of unnecessary medicine is being prescribed and consumed . . . that medicine is often given to a patient to act purely as a mental poultice . . . People go to doctors either because they are ill or because they have perfectly natural fears about their health. These fears may be justified or unjustified. It is not always possible to eliminate their fears by words. He has to do something more, and it may be that part of what he has to do is to supply a prescription.[67]

And the NHS deepened the impression, possibly begun with the NHI, that the doctor acted increasingly as a supplier of medicaments, rather than as medical adviser.[68] Throughout the NHI period there had been official concern about over-prescription for panel patients; criticism was directed at the growing number of prescriptions per patient and the prescription of expensive drugs that were not in the National Formulary.

Class differentiation in treatment was an unfortunate feature of medicine before the NHS. Industrial practices for the working-class were geared to a rapid throughput of patients and thus necessarily to only a small clinical input. An interwar practice in Merthyr Tydfil with nearly 4,000 patients gave three minutes to each doctor–patient encounter in the surgery, and four to five minutes during a visit. Treatment was basic:

The amount of clinical work you did in practice was very small, because the main conditions you dealt with were chest pneumoconiosis for the miners, miners' accidents, and the influenza, and general infections. This is the days before antibiotics and the medicine used to be a black liquorice medicine for the chest.

A number of large bottles made up with stock mixtures supplied patients with their obligatory bottles of medicine. One was labelled 'Mist ADT' or 'Mist Any Damned Thing' which was given to 'somebody you thought there was nothing wrong with, and you could do nothing for'. Yet this practice was said

---

[66] The BMA sent a postal inquiry to 17,616 general-paractitioner principals and received a response from 12,657 or over 70% of the total. *BMJ Supplement*, 26 Sept. 1953, 151.

[67] *Hansard*, 470 (148–9), col. 2244, Dr S. Jeger, speaking during a debate on prescription charges.

[68] *BMJ Supplement*, 26 Sept. 1953, 134, 137.

to be a cut above others in the town in that patients could have their blood pressure taken, and could wait their turn to see the doctor in a waiting room rather than queuing in the street.[69] Another doctor remembered the problem of chronic chests amongst his patients. The 'great source of relief was "Mist. Tussis Nigra" '—a tincture of chloroform and morphine which was effectively 'a drug of addiction'.[70] Thrice daily surgeries (except on Sundays when there was only one), dispensing on the premises, and visits on foot to patients' houses meant over-worked practitioners and routinized, basic medicine.

Encounters between doctors and patients were well documented for the end of the period. Those with panel patients were of an almost ritualistic nature, in which a steady throughput of patients was necessary to ensure that a full waiting room was emptied within two hours. The patient was in the doctor's surgery for between three and five minutes. Expectations as to the outcome of the interchange were modest. Doctors were aware of the limited therapeutic arsenal they could draw from, and patients showed stereotypical British characteristics in a stoical reluctance to make a fuss, or show too intimate an interest in their own anatomies. Hence, as one doctor, with experience of working both in continental Europe and in Britain, commented:

The British patient is so disciplined, that he listens to the doctor without asking too many questions, and he accepts what the doctor says. In Czechoslovakia the patient is nosy, he wants to know, and the doctor tells him.[71]

Practitioners (sharing the same cultural assumptions as their patients), and being pushed for time in dealing with large numbers of patients, showed little interest in examining, although recognizing the need to do so for a minority of patients, who therefore had as much as ten minutes in the surgery. Most patients were content with a standard bottle of medicine, which in England and Wales they were accustomed to see as the appropriate outcome of a visit to the doctor, although less inclined to do so in Scotland.[72] Preventative work was neither formalized nor paid for, yet nevertheless might punctuate the doctor–patient encounter: 'get your weight down', 'don't drink too much'. But family planning did not figure very much at all, at least with male doctors—'nobody ever discussed that'.[73] Interaction with private patients was more leisurely, a greater range of medicines and instruments were used, whilst referrals to specialists and recourse to pathological laboratories to aid diagnosis also facilitated a more comprehensive service.

---

[69] CMAC, GP/29/2/59, Samuel Isaacs.

[70] Mid-Glamorgan RO, CMS 11, George Bathgate, 'Thirty Years of Change in General Practice'.

[71] CMAC, GP/29/2/16, Frederick Barber, MD (Brno, 1930), MRCGP, who set up a practice in Islington at the start of the NHS.

[72] J. Hogarth, 'General Practice' in G. McLachan (ed.), *Improving the Commonweal* (Edinburgh, 1987), 169.

[73] CMAC, GP29/2/44, Thomas McQuay. This reflected wider attitudes in the medical profession, which until the 1930s saw contraception as a fringe rather than mainstream medical area, and even in the 1930s still vigorously opposed it (P. W. J. Bartrip, *Mirror of Medicine. A History of the British Medical Journal* (Oxford, 1990), 232–5).

Occasionally, a practice's records enable the differentiation between panel and private patients to be discerned. In a Maldon practice, for example, private patients were seen by the senior partners, were given more elaborate medication, had minor surgery performed more often, had more frequent visits in their own homes, and might be the subject of laboratory tests, or an occasional referral or consultation. In contrast, the panel and club patients were treated by the most junior doctor in the practice. An unforeseen consequence of this was that s/he was clinically often the most up-to-date doctor in the practice! But since for the most part panel patients had only routinized medication (for which they paid twopence or threepence), this advantage over private patients was perhaps more nominal than real.[74]

Yet the personal element in accomplishing even a routine and modest result was important to the self-esteem of both parties. Prescriptive advice for GPs included the view that cheerfulness, sympathy and a hopeful demeanour were essential qualities.[75] Quite apart from any distinctively clinical input into the exchange, the doctor's interest in the patient's well-being itself possessed healing qualities. 'The laying on of hands was the important thing . . . medicine was 70 per cent art and 30 per cent science.'[76] The relative proportions of art and science varied over time. Penicillin and sulpha drugs were the most conspicuous scientific advances in treatment available in modern general practice. By the early years of the NHS GPs could 'cure in the home conditions which could formerly be dealt with only in the hospital'.[77]

Obstetrics

Art and science were differentiated within the range of activities undertaken by the doctor; arguably the scientific element was at the lower end of the range where obstetrics was concerned. Midwifery stagnated during the nineteenth century; obstetrics was perceived less as a medical specialism than as one activity within general practice, and a low status one at that. Except at Edinburgh, Glasgow, and Dublin's Rotunda there were notably poor training facilities, and we have seen that it was not until 1886 that the Medical Registration Amendment Act required practitioners to have passed an examination in midwifery as well as in physic and surgery. This requirement improved neither the standard of teaching in midwifery, nor expanded the training opportunities sufficiently to allow a realistic experience of the dozen labours now legally required. In this context standards of care might slip. One student wrote in 1905 of the exhaustion suffered during his month on dis-

---

[74] Essex RO, Chelmsford branch, D/F 79 A5637, Maldon practitioner's records, 1945–51.
[75] E. Ward, *General Practice (Some Further Experiences)* (1930).
[76] CMAC, GP29/2/48, Bertie Dover.
[77] *BMJ Supplement*, ii (1953). Summary of field survey and postal inquiry amongst general practitioners undertaken by the BMA during 1951–2.

trict midwifery, which meant that 'I did not know whether it was yesterday, today or tomorrow.'[78] One conscientious doctor recollected that in the early twentieth century, when he was a student at St Thomas's, London, 'it was usual to get the art of midwifery out of the way at the earliest possible moment. This custom led to our being sent out "on the district" in complete ignorance of the subject'.[79] But the careful notes which his uncle had taken before him while on the district indicates that some youthful practitioners did attempt to maximize their learning from these restricted encounters.[80]

In spite of these limited midwifery skills, the typical young practitioner was keen to book confinements, because these were perceived as giving the GP an entrée to a middle-class or a better-off working class household. Irvine Loudon's masterly analysis in *Death in Childbirth*[81] suggests that the impact of competition between GPs and midwives was to drive down midwifery fees, and this then led to a highly unfortunate tendency for doctors to hasten a poorly remunerated part of their work, and thus to intervene more actively in childbirth with forceps. From around 1885 the adoption of antisepsis and asepsis in domiciliary midwifery contributed to a decline in maternal mortality but, from 1910 to 1934 this was reversed, possibly because—as Loudon argues—puerperal fever became endemic. A more positive feature occurred between 1935 to 1950, in that there was a drop of one-fifth in the maternal mortality rate, as a result of the new sulpha drugs which successfully combated puerperal sepsis.

The record of general practitioners in midwifery appears to have been very mixed. Sir John Williams had seven deaths in 1,174 cases during five years in Swansea engaged in general practice between 1876 and 1872, and this was reckoned to be highly successful.[82] In Newark, between 1895 and 1916, Ernest Ringrose had no maternal deaths at all in his first thousand cases. Yet the general record contrasted markedly with this and had, by the 1920s, become a matter of national concern. As MOH to Rochdale, the town with the highest maternal mortality rate at this time, Andrew Topping analysed the factors that had led to this unhappy situation.[83] He criticized the record of the town's general practitioners:

[78] Quoted in L. Marks, 'Mothers, babies and hospitals: "The London" and the Provision of Maternity care in East London, 1870–1939', in V. Fildes, L. Marks, and H. Marland (eds.), *Women and Children First* (1992), 56.

[79] Wellcome MS 5415, 'Memoirs' of Martin Wentworth Littlewood (1888–1972), MB, BS, FRSA, 10.

[80] Wellcome Institute, WMS 7209, Obstetric casebook of C. K. Ackland, 1883.

[81] I. Loudon, *Death in Childbirth. An International Study of Maternal Care and Maternal Mortality, 1800–1950* (Oxford, 1992), chs. 12–13 *passim*. This section of my chapter is indebted to this definitive work.

[82] E. Wyn Jones, 'Sir John Williams (1840–1926): His Background and Achievement', in J. Cule (ed.), *Wales and Medicine. An Historical Survey* (Cardiff, 1975), 91. John Williams, MRCS, MB (London, 1866), MD, MRCP, London, 1873, FRCP, 1879.

[83] A. Topping, 'Prevention of Maternal Mortality: the Rochdale Experiment', *Lancet*, i (1936), 545–7.

The problem of the doctor, however, presented the greatest difficulty. The training he received was lamentably inadequate at most schools, and the average man went into practice with no practical experience. Many were extremely competent, but it was idle to deny that deaths were often due directly to lack of knowledge, errors of judgement, carelessness, hurry or unwillingness to call in expert assistance.

It has been estimated that nationally about one in three maternal deaths came from poor obstetric practice, in an appalling indictment of all those involved in obstetrics, including GPs. Full term puerperal sepsis was the most common cause of maternal death.[84]

Practitioners were aware that although successful midwifery established reputation, death in childbirth had a disastrous effect on a general practice. Attitudes to midwifery tended to be of three types: the practitioner who disliked it and did almost none, the one who did some as a financially necessary part of a mixed practice, and the one who was attracted to it for its professional and human satisfaction. For the middle group its time-consuming and anxious nature had to be weighed against the other demands of a busy general practice and this meant, as with Hugh Mair Davie of Manchester, that he might do about twenty cases a year.[85] For traditional wisdom was clear that midwifery was 'the keystone of a successful general practice', and that the 'midder' bag should be packed and ready to go into service. Thus, if the principal or senior partner disliked obstetrics then delegation of this onerous task to an assistant or junior partner would ensue. The positive economic contribution that booked confinements made to the otherwise fluctuating uncertainties of day-to-day medical finances is clear in every practice ledger and this made forgoing midwifery difficult to contemplate for all but the most prosperous practice. And the calls of humanity for a difficult labour meant, in any case, that the personal attitudes of the doctor had to be disregarded, whatever the economic outcome. Dr Gunn of Peebles acknowledged this:

A woman whom I had attended in a severe and protracted nocturnal confinement, and to whom I had paid five subsequent visits, driving several miles each way, arrived to settle her account. One guinea—the sum in question—was extorted with the utmost difficulty on my part and the maximum reluctance on hers. No wonder that a country doctor seldom leaves a penny.[86]

For other doctors decisions on midwifery involved not just its financial implications but its contribution to a fuller professional self-worth; since it was 'the family doctor's duty and privilege to see his patients through their pregnancy and childbirth.'[87] This was a source of great personal satisfaction. 'It was, well it's still an enduring miracle . . . one can still feel a little pricking

[84] Loudon, 'Death in Childbed from the Eighteenth Century to 1935', *MH*, 30 (1986), 26.
[85] Pers. comm., Hugh Mair Davie, (born 1903), MB, Ch.B. (Glasgow 1927).
[86] C. B. Gunn, *Leaves from the Life of a Country Doctor* (Edinburgh, 1947), 96.
[87] Postal inquiry among members of BMA (1951–2), *BMJ Supplement*, ii (1953), 109.

behind the eyes, to see . . . a girl, turn into a woman and a mother, and have a live baby'.[88]

Midwifery experience in general practice varied according to several factors: the number and type of cases that the doctor was called to attend, the division of work (or otherwise) with midwives or other practitioners, and the attitudes and experience of the doctor. Midwifery practice fluctuated in its amount since during the early years of practice there were few cases but, assuming midwifery was conducted successfully, cases grew until a high but steady number of confinements were attended. Advancing age then made doctors more reluctant to take on very many of these tiring events so that numbers then tapered off towards retirement.[89] Of course the mishaps, and thus the local reputation of the individual doctor, could alter this general pattern.

Although *post-partum* visits had long been a matter of routine, few doctors before the 1920s and 1930s showed much interest in *ante-natal* care, so that it was common for GPs to be called in to help women in labour whom previously they had never seen.[90] Indeed, *ante-natal* clinics were described as a 'comparatively new development' by the BMA in 1929, but one that should be encouraged. Its report on encroachments in the sphere of private practice suggested that:

There seems no reason why [those] . . . who are in a position to engage a doctor for their confinement should not be encouraged to come as a matter of course to their doctor for the advice their poorer neighbours may have to receive at the [infant and maternity] centres.[91]

These centres had been set up by local authorities, starting in 1914, developing in more areas after the Maternity and Child Welfare Act of 1918, but only becoming widespread in the 1930s, so that by 1937 more than one in two mothers-to-be attended them.[92] Some practices began their own private *ante-natal* clinics. In an interwar Felstead practice in Essex, for instance, there was a monthly clinic run on Tuesday in the fourth week of each month, while a Child Welfare Session was held monthly in the second week.[93] Apart from a formal clinic individual patients might have problems in pregnancy such that their doctor would take urine samples for examination.[94] Certain

[88] CMAC, GP29/2/26, Norman Paros, MB, BS (London, 1946).

[89] Cambridgeshire RO (Huntingdon), Accn. 4175, Maternity Attendances of Drs Lucas, Hicks and Hicks; Norfolk RO BR 23/26, Day book of Burnham GP [Dr Hamill], 1915–20. Samuel M. Hamill, BA, RUI (1877), MD, M.Ch. (Queen's College, Cork, 1882); Notts. RO DD/14440, 24,18, Dr Ringrose's Obstetric Case Book, 1895–1916.

[90] Mid-Glamorgan RO, CMS 11, Bathgate, 'Thirty Years'.

[91] *BMJ*, i (1929), 131.

[92] J. Lewis, *The Politics of Motherhood* (1980), 151–2.

[93] Essex RO, Chelmsford branch, D/DU 509, Felstead Day Book, 1934–41.

[94] For example, Essex RO, Chelmsford branch, D/F 79 A5637, Maldon practice, entry folio 401, 5 Feb. 1947.

ante-natal consultations or visits were paid to private patients' homes,[95] and some of these cases were then booked into private nursing homes for delivery by the GP. The extent of local differentiation makes generalization about the nature of midwifery provision unwise, but the more detailed records of three general practices do help to illustrate some of its variety.

A Dowlais practice in the Rhondda Valleys, South Wales had a local reputation for skilful surgical intervention. Here Dr Cresswell (or his assistant) used forceps in nearly half the births attended in a sample of 1892 that has been analysed (see Table 8.2).[96] Forceps were used for a 'delay' in the second stage of labour, and this was more a matter of subjective assessment by the doctor than of objective differences in women and their labours. Conventional professional wisdom on the appropriate amount and timing of intervention varied markedly over time; from the 1870s to the 1940s the use of forceps was very much greater than in the preceding period of early nineteenth-century conservative non-interference, and was also higher than in the mid-twentieth century period of moderate activity. Practical considerations that might affect the doctor's decision as to whether to 'put on the forceps' were that it not only expedited the woman's labour, and thus economized on the doctor's time, but also justified a higher fee. Another by-product of instrumental intervention was the creation of a local reputation for helping women in difficult childbirths, which again had financial implications for a practice.[97] Whether some of the non-clinical, and thus rather disreputable,

TABLE 8.2. Midwifery cases in the Cresswell Practice, Dowlais, January to July 1892

Features of Non-Normal Births	No.	Features of Ante- or Post-Natal Conditions	No.
Breech presentation	6	Abortion haemorrhage	1
Transverse presentation	1	Miscarriage	2
Face presentation	1	Ante natal care needed	1
Multipares	1	Albuminuria anasarca	1
Forceps used	30	Pyrexia	3
Craniotomy	1	Puerperal fever	2
Termis	1	High temperature after confinement	2
Induced (eclampsia)	1	Prolapsed uterus	2
Hindrance of labour	1	Debility after parturition	2
Rigid os	2		
Adherent placenta/membrane	2		
Pyrexia	2		
Chloroform used	3		

[95] Essex RO, D/F79 A5637, Maldon books, folios 190 and 194, July to Aug. 1946; Cambridgeshire RO (Cambridge), Dr S. H. de Pritchard, patient's ledger 1945–6 (Stephen H. De Pritchard, MRCS Eng., LRCP (London, 1917)); CMAC, GP 5/5, day book 1941–2, folios 228, 430, 522, practice of Drs Craig and O'Connor, High Wycombe; Private archive of Kimbolton practice of Dr Granger, Visiting books.

[96] Mid-Glamorgan RO, D/D X 83/1/1, Cresswell Surgery and Home Visiting Book, Dowlais Surgery 1892.

[97] I am grateful to Irvine Loudon for these professional and historical insights.

factors came into play in the Cresswell practice, or whether there was an unusual amount of clinical difficulty which justified these high rates of intervention, cannot be discerned from midwifery records alone. But for a later period, food supplements given to malnourished mothers in the Rhondda valleys did lead to a decline in maternal mortality, stillbirths and neonatal mortality.[98] And, since Cresswell's midwifery fee was a guinea, an amount that was two to three times higher than that of the midwife,[99] it is also likely that the doctor in any case saw mainly the difficult births that the local midwife or handywoman felt were beyond her powers of assistance.

The second practice selected was that of Dr Ringrose in Newark, Nottinghamshire, with data based on the slightly later period of 1895–1916 (see Table 8.3).[100] Here less than half the numbers of midwifery cases of the Dowlais practice were attended, with an average of about fifty cases annually.[101] Dr Ringrose showed himself to be a careful and caring obstetrician.[102] He used forceps with discrimination employing them in only one in ten of his cases. Predisposing factors for their use appeared to be: long labours, where the mother had weak pains, or the baby an unusual presentation, in cases of disproportion, where the os or perineum was rigid, or in cases of twins. He appears to have been a skilful operator, as was exemplified in case 337, a labour that took six hours. 'Severe labour. Instruments. Large head.

TABLE 8.3. Dr Ringrose's domiciliary obstetric cases, 1895–1916

Dr Ringrose's description	Number	Corresponding numbers in a 1,000 births in a GP maternity unit, 1960s
BBA [born before doctor's arrival]	299	
Vertex presentations include:	665	
Occipito-posterior	25	45
Twins	14	12
Breech presentation	19	28
Feet presentation	10	
Placenta praevia	5	4
Face presentation	1	
Transverse presentation	1	
Maternal deaths	0	
Perineum stitched	200	85 episiotomies done

Source: Notts. RO, DD/1440/24/18; Cavenagh, *The New General Practice* (1968), 64–8.

[98] S. Cherry, *Medical Services and the Hospitals in Britain, 1860–1939* (1996), 23; *Report on Maternal Mortality in Wales*, 1937.

[99] Digby, *Making a Medical Living*, 258.

[100] Ernest Ringrose, MD, MRCS, Eng., LRCP (London, 1890).

[101] Nottinghamshire RO, DD/1440/24/18, Dr Ringrose's Obstetric Case Book, 1895–1916.

[102] I am indebted to Helen Sweet, SRN, SCM, for insights into quality of care given by these GPs.

Forceps. Placenta adherent. No tear. Normal nam. Child's face rather crushed, massaged.' Little recourse was had to drugs although chloral was mentioned as being used in a few cases, as in cases 102, 140, 339. Dr Ringrose made systematic notes on the mother and baby: the mother's name and age, when the baby was expected, the date and time of its actual arrival, the baby's order in the family, the sex of the baby, duration of labour, and the state of the perineum. He was very thorough in monitoring the mother's later progress noting when the mother got up (from the tenth to the twelfth day), her lochia, temperature, the state of her breasts, her suckling, bowel movements, sleep, after pains, and also whether she was healing well. Ringrose placed midwifery—along with surgery[103]—at the centre of his practice. He worked hard to ensure that a new maternity wing was opened at the Newark General Hospital and, significantly, this was seen locally as 'Dr Ringrose's baby'.[104]

The third practice was based in Huntingdon.[105] When surviving records began in 1901/2 Dr Joseph Lucas was already doing three dozen midwifery cases per year, and this rose to four dozen, before declining again shortly before he stopped doing obstetrics in 1924, four years before his retirement. Dr Lucas seems to have believed in letting nature largely take its course; there were infrequent cases where forceps were used and rather more cases, after 1917, where chloroform was employed. A quite different style of obstetrics was introduced by his successor, Dr C. E. Hicks. For five years between 1924 and 1928 chloroform and/or forceps deliveries became fairly standard. Whether despite this, or because of this, by the time that Hicks took over the practice in 1928 numbers of mothers booking their confinements had shrunk by two-thirds from the number of cases attended by Lucas. A later incursion into the high-risk territory of caesareans in the autumn of 1937 resulted in no bookings at all for the doctor's ministrations in the following spring, although numbers then picked up a little. The long-term trend in this practice's midwifery cases was downwards, and in this it broadly reflected a national trend, where the demographic change to smaller families, together with institutional developments eroded domiciliary midwifery available in general practice. However, the steepness of the local decline in the numbers of confinements attended by Dr Hicks seems likely to have been associated with his own style of, and record in, obstetrics.

By the 1930s the role of the general practitioner in midwifery was under general pressure. The proportion of births in hospitals increased from 15 per cent in 1927, to 25 per cent in 1937, and 54 per cent by 1946. Within these averages there were wide variations: in 1938, for example, 50 per cent of

---

[103] Ringrose published articles on fractures and hernias in the *Lancet*, 4 Dec. 1897 and 15 Oct. 1904. The new operating theatre at Newark General Hospital was named after him in 1939.

[104] Nottinghamshire RO DD/1440/26/3, Scrapbook on Dr Ringrose.

[105] Cambridgeshire RO (Huntingdon), Accn. 4175, Maternity Attendances of Drs Lucas, Hicks and Hicks. The clinical outcome of the practice's midwifery has not been made available for public scrutiny.

Tottenham mothers but only 10 per cent of those in Oxfordshire, gave birth in hospital. Differential rates in recourse to hospitals for births were apparently class-related, since in London a greater proportion of affluent women were delivered in their own homes.[106] Not that hospital births necessarily excluded the general practitioner since they served as honorary obstetricians in provincial voluntary hospitals. For example, J. C. Gordon became medical officer to the maternity department of Salisbury General Hospital in 1931, a post which he held until his retirement in 1956.[107] The midwife's role in domiciliary midwifery was also expanding. Although class, race and geography had always influenced whether a general practitioner or midwife was employed in a family, the impact of the Midwives Act of 1902, and still more that of 1936, tilted the balance decisively in favour of the midwife being employed in domiciliary deliveries. After the Midwives Act of 1936 many more pregnancies in England and Wales benefited from the work of a trained midwife, who was now employed by every county council and county borough. It was this earlier legislation, and not the NHS (as is often believed), that reduced the role of the GP in domiciliary obstetrics. However, the midwife still had to call the GP in for difficult cases. A doctor's case book might refer to: 'Midwife's call. Mrs B-P. Breech and hydrocephalic still born child.'[108] An Oxfordshire midwife summoned the doctor when her patients had retained or adherent placenta, 'strong pain—no advance—patient hysterical'; arrest of head; or 'head too long on the perineum—slow progress',[109] and in South Wales there was a very similar list of cases, including 'rigors and pulse very quick and os not fully dilated' or 'os very rigid, strong pains, but very slow progress', and 'baby slight jaundice'.[110]

In Scotland there was a more integrated set of services which had been set up by the Maternity Services (Scotland) Act. Not only was a domiciliary midwives service created, but also a general practitioner and an obstetric service, and (at least for urban areas), a system of medical examination with appropriate treatment where necessary throughout a woman's pregnancy. Scottish GPs had to limit themselves within this service only to 'minor manipulative or instrumental interference' in normal labours. During the Second World War improvement in maternity services was also brought about in all areas of Britain by efficient institutional childbirth and maternal care under the wartime Emergency Maternity Scheme.

[106] E. Peretz, 'A Maternity Service for England and Wales: Local Authority Maternity Care in the Inter-War Period in Oxfordshire and Tottenham', in J. Garcia, R. Kilpatrick, and M. Richards (eds.), *The Politics of Maternal Care* (Oxford, 1990), 34, 40; L. V. Marks, *Metropolitan Maternity: Maternal and Infant Welfare Services in Early Twentieth Century London* (1996), 200–3.

[107] *BMJ* Obituary, iv (1970), 59, Obituary of James Campbell Gordon, MA, MB, B. Chir. (Cambridge and Barts., 1928).

[108] Essex RO D/DU 509, Felstead day book, entry 15 Oct. 1934.

[109] Oxfordshire Archives, Misc Savil 1/i/2, Dr R.W. Meikle of Banbury, medical diaries 1922–33. Robert W. Meikle, MB, CM (Glasgow, 1898).

[110] Mid-Glamorgan RO, D/D X 236/6 Mrs Ann Evans, Notifications for sending for medical help, 1938–9.

The overall changes that had taken place were summarized by the Goodenough Report of 1944. During the last twenty years 'maternity has tended to pass more and more into the hands of the obstetricians and the midwives'. At the same time the report criticized the 'serious lack of facilities' in many medical schools, indicting a considerable laxity in complying with the GMC ruling that a dozen labours should have been attended during training.[111] In an attempt to redress this situation under the NHS, local Obstetric Lists of GPs were instituted in England and Wales, whereby those general practitioners more highly trained in obstetrics qualified for higher payment. Even under this more selective system anxieties surfaced amongst practitioners who did not feel that they were doing sufficient confinements to keep up-to-date.[112] In Scotland, in contrast, a more inclusive list continued to operate whereby all practitioners who wished to regularly practice obstetrics put their name forward to do so.

Variety in Practice

British general practice was extremely diverse. Three practices have been selected for discussion; none could be called representative but together they exemplify some of this range. These are a Scottish panel practice in Glasgow; a Welsh industrial and mining practice in the Rhondda Valley, and a mixed practice with both private and panel patients in the rural south of England.

Unusually, one Glasgow practice retained the so-called 'Lloyd George' record cards for its national health insurance patients during the interwar period.[113] These give us a detailed insight into the clinical standards of insurance practice.[114] Given the amount of population mobility, some patients also had comments on their cards from doctors in other practices so that what follows perhaps may be taken as broadly indicative of Scottish panel practice more generally. These records can have represented only 'the tip of the iceberg' in terms of illnesses presented to the panel doctors, because the record cards show brief entries for most patients only every other few years, and, on occasion, intervals of as much as ten or twenty years intervened between entries. This was in line with a survey of 1922 in Fife, where only ten per

[111] *Report of Inter-Departmental Committee on Medical Education* (1944), 189–90.

[112] Postal inquiry among members of BMA (1951–2), *BMJ Supplement*, Sept. 1953, 110.

[113] Normally, these record cards were sent to the local practitioners committee on the death of a patient, where they were routinely destroyed. I am thus grateful to the present partners in the practice of McFarlane, Blair, Short, and McQueen for permission to analyse these records, now deposited at the Greater Glasgow Health Board Archives and catalogued as HB 57. I am much indebted to Alistair Tough, the GGHB Archivist, for meticulously sampling and photocopying the records. Patient confidentiality under the 100-year rule was maintained through the omission of personal names on the photocopies supplied to the author.

[114] The practice was run by Drs Black and McFarlane during the NHI period. Robert Black, MB, Ch.B. (Glasgow, 1924) and Daniel McFarlane, MB, Ch.B. (Glasgow, 1924).

cent of these record cards detailed the medical treatment given.[115] Numbers of male patients in the Glasgow practice vastly outnumbered female ones, thus reflecting membership of the insurance scheme itself.

It is clear that clinical notes were made *only* for the minority of more serious conditions that required certification off work, and then for certification of later fitness for work, signified by a marginal 'C' or 'F'. Also noted were more serious conditions that presumably required action other than medication, usually for referrals or for operations. Diagnoses were perceived overwhelmingly in physical terms, so that there were only three cases of 'neurasthenia', 'nervous debility', and what the consultant later termed 'anxiety hysteria'. Physical diagnoses by the general practitioners fell into well-defined categories. Influenza was the most common reason for certification, followed by a second grouping of gastritis, dyspepsia, together with bilious and heart burn conditions. These were usually suffered by those with sedentary or clerical occupations. A third diagnostic grouping was of rheumatism, lumbago, sciatica, or fibrositis. A fourth category (much less common than in the Rhondda practice below), were work-related conditions; accident, hernia, strain, or sprain were presented by those employed in industrial, mining, or transport occupations. Septic fingers and feet or abscesses were also diagnosed. Bronchial or pleurisy cases were less evident than might have been expected, probably because of their chronic rather than acute nature. Predictably, given the absence of children from the records, acute infectious cases—such as chicken pox or mumps—were unusual. A miscellany of conditions remained including neuritis, conjunctivitis, laryngitis, and tonsillitis. Tonsillectomies were among the very few surgical operations recorded as having taken place in the practice. Interestingly, diagnoses often paired conditions which suggests that, whilst treating the acute condition for which the patient sought certification, a more chronic condition—for example, rheumatism—was also brought to the doctor's attention. Prognoses on cases were not recorded, but the practice's doctors might make their own mental judgement, as is clear from a later note on one card. Encountering an erstwhile patient some thirty years after an earlier diagnosis of a cardiac condition with raised blood pressure, the doctor recorded:

Very interesting indeed to see an old friend . . . Frankly I thought [he] might easily have passed to his father by now. Heart sounds remarkably good, chest clear, B.P. [blood pressure] 130/90. Am afraid little or nothing we can do about him rather let him carry on an easy mode of life he has been leading up till now.

It is in this context of attending to more serious illness that it is remarkable to discover just how very few clinical measurements were made in this interwar surgery, although it is possible that normal readings were not recorded, so that the written record only minuted cause for concern. References there to taking the pulse, temperature, or blood pressure were

[115] Scottish RO (W. Register House), HH3 6/6, Minutes of Fife NHI Committee, 2 Sept. 1922.

certainly rare. Even a note on the (furred) state of the tongue stood out by its very infrequency. Yet while clinical measurement within the practice was at a low level, the GPs were sufficiently perspicacious to refer more serious cases for treatment elsewhere. Urine tests or X rays were not performed in the surgery, but were conducted on patients sent to the Royal Infirmary or the Western Infirmary in the city. Patients were sent there with a variety of serious illnesses including pneumonia, perforated ulcer, appendix, fistula, erysipelas, bladder calculus, and occupational dermatitis (a rubber worker). Other single referrals were made to the Eye Infirmary, and to the Psychiatric Unit of Killearn Hospital, Stirlingshire. There was, however, a very minimal use of pathological services, as when sputum from a suspected case of TB was sent to Glasgow's Public Health Department. This confirmed the diagnosis and the patient was sent to a sanatorium.

The Cresswell practice in Dowlais had both similarities and differences with this Glasgow practice. Although the Glasgow practice confirmed the stereotypical view of low standards of clinical range and treatment in a panel practice, the Dowlais practice was more distinctive in catering largely for an industrial, working-class population yet attempting to use up-to-date clinical methods. It was enabled to do so by having middle- as well as working-class patients. A family based practice that operated from the 1860s to the 1970s, we shall concentrate here on seventy years—from 1878 (when the first extant clinical records begin) to 1948. The founder of the practice was Pearson Robert Cresswell, made the Chief Surgeon of the Dowlais Iron Works in 1862; a founder, later Senior Surgeon, of the Merthyr General Hospital, a JP for Glamorgan, and a member of the Council of the BMA.[116] His son, partner and successor was Stuart Cresswell, a Surgeon both to Dowlais Collieries and Iron Works, and to Merthyr General Hospital.[117] And his partner and successor was Pearson Leonard Cresswell, Surgeon and Radiologist at the same hospital.[118]

There were two surgeries in the practice: one at Dowlais and a branch surgery at Penydarren. Colliery schemes and club practice formed the backbone of the practice and a very high proportion of surgery attendance was made by the male working-class patient. The industrial and mining environment in which the practice was situated produced many chronic chest conditions. The practice books show a phenomenal amount of bronchitis, a high incidence of bronchial pneumonia, and with much pleurisy, and catarrh as well. There were many accident cases, with badly bruised, crushed or fractured limbs and thighs; some being dealt with by the doctor *in situ*, some in the surgery, and some sent to hospital. Amongst the latter were fearful

---

[116] MRCS Eng., 1859; LSA, 1863; FRCS Ed., 1873. A contributor to the *Lancet* in 1868 and 1874 with papers on 'Treatment of gunshot wounds and compound comminuted fractures on the anti-septic principle', indicated his introduction of antisepsis principles to South Wales.

[117] MRCS, LRCP, Lond., 1893.

[118] MA, BM, B.Ch., Oxon 1935, MRCS Eng., LRCP, Lond., 1935.

patients. For example, '25 October 1900. Crushed foot. Refused to have fractured and shattered toe taken off. Sent into hospital.'[119]

Women were even less visible in this practice than in the Glasgow panel practice. Some were treated as part of their husband's contributory schemes, although others were excluded. They presented cases that included menorrhagia, dysmenorrhea, cystitis or, much more rarely, 'hysteria', 'climacteric', or cancer of the breast. Also of interest were cases arising from the high local consumption of alcohol. For example:

2 Sept 1900. Mrs W. 'Bruise over left mama [sic], also on abdomen and thigh. Inflammation of external genitals . . . Said to be 3 months pregnant. Slight prolapse of womb. Injuries said to be inflicted by husband. An alcoholic subject. Called in about 6 pm. Prescribed an opiate and ordered a hot hip bath and the use of local antiseptics . . .

4 September 1900. Mrs H. Intoxicated. Dressed [condition] last night. (9.00). To be seen on the 5th. Sprain of ankle. [She] Came on 6th at 8.30 pm to be dressed. Was impertinent and went away.[120]

Another more cryptic clinical note (more accurately a social commentary), gives scope to the reader to envisage the results for the doctor of a male drunkard's mishap. '1 February 1892. G. 32. Horse. Drunk?'[121]

During the interwar period the Dowlais practice had an increased number of private, middle-class patients visible by their running accounts and cheque payments. Equally, there were diagnoses for private patients which had not appeared earlier with a working-class clientele, such as 'nerves' or 'migraine', and treatments that included the injection of special vaccines.[122] The practice's surgical bent continued in evidence with operations for the excision of polyps, or the removal of a stone from the bladder, as well as the usual humdrum routine of syringing ears, or stitching wounds.[123] Accident or more serious surgical cases were sent into hospital. For the years immediately preceding the NHS the doctors included much more scientific terminology in their diagnoses. Cases described as 'cerebral embolism', 'auricular fibrillation', or 'mitral incompetence' were unremarkable,[124] whereas half a century earlier it would have been unusual to see an entry like this one in 1901—'Influenza. (Diastolic mitral murmur)'.[125]

Despite the high 'turnover' of patients in the surgeries, the practitioners apparently managed to retain their clinical curiosity, and keep up with modern methods of diagnosis and treatment. Effectively this was achieved by giving two standards of care. A higher standard of clinical practice was focused

[119] Mid-Glamorgan RO, D/D X 83/1/131, Dr Cresswell's Surgery at Penydarren, 1899–1901.
[120] Ibid.
[121] Ibid., D/D X 83/1/1, Dr Cresswell's Surgery and Home Visit Book, Dowlais, 1892
[122] Ibid., D/D X 83/1/17, Surgery and Home Visit Book, 1936–8, entries for 3 May and 26 Oct. 1936, 1 June 1937.
[123] Ibid., D/D X 83/1/17, for example, entries 21 Nov. 1936, 11 Feb., and 5 Mar. 1937.
[124] Ibid., D/D X 83/1/21, Surgery and Home Visiting Book, 1946–9.
[125] Ibid., D/D X 83/1/131, Dr Cresswell's Surgery at Penydarren, 1899–1901, entry, 17 May 1901.

particularly on private middle-class patients but it is significant that working-class club or colliery scheme patients were also recipients of high standards of clinical care when needed. Alongside this went a faster, frequently routinized medical throughput for patients with more trivial complaints. For example, during the 1890s nearly one-third of the prescriptions were of stock mixtures, although this also meant of course that the dispenser made up individual prescriptions for the majority of patients.[126] Significantly, the practice was the earliest I have found using a clinical record card for surgery visits by patients. These must have been issued to a largely working-class clientele, and directed them to call at the surgery at a given time in the week, to use it to get medicines dispensed through the practice, and for the doctor to make clinical notes about the patient. There is a surviving example from 1887 for Lizzie Ann Evans, a 23-year-old dressmaker, who suffered from epileptic fits, where an unusual number of contacts with Dr Cresswell, senior, meant that the space for her clinical notes became unduly crowded. Another indication of the standard of clinical practice was that on visits to more seriously ill patients during the early 1890s measurement of the patient's temperature was often taken. But it also seems to have been the case that the pulse was much less commonly taken, and that it was unusual for urine testing to be done.[127]

Dr Cresswell (senior) kept two case history books in which he recorded clinical histories of an interesting or puzzling nature. Some cases were referred to consultants. Interestingly, during the late Victorian era, details of the case might be inserted on to standard anatomical outlines of the body and sent alongside Dr Cresswell's account of the case.[128] In the second case history book, which covered the pre-First World War and interwar years, cases mainly of private patients were referred to consultants, predominantly to Cardiff, with only half as many sent to London consultants, together with a few cases referred to specialists in Chester or Liverpool. In addition there were details of two cases sent for spa treatment to Llandrindod Wells and to Droitwich, and a couple of instances of clinical material transmitted to pathological laboratories in Cardiff and London. Reflecting the regionality of medical practice the geographical spread of these referrals was quite different from the southern England practice in Wantage.

The Church Street Practice in Wantage contrasted with that in Dowlais in that it was a country practice centred in a market town but also including surrounding villages and hamlets.[129] The Wantage doctors therefore made many visits, often seeing as many patients on visits as they did in the surgery. The partnership had both panel and private patients, and thus covered the entire spectrum of society. A remarkable survival of bills and invoices,

[126] Ibid., D/D X 83/3/2, Prescription book, 1890–2.
[127] Ibid., D/D X 83/1/1, Dr Cresswell's Surgery and Home Visit Book, Dowlais, 1892.
[128] Ibid., D/D X 83/4/1, Dr Cresswell's Case Books, 1878–99 and 1906 onwards (2 vols.).
[129] Insights into this Wantage practice were given by Dr Irvine Loudon, later the Senior Partner.

together with some clinical notes enables a detailed picture to be built up of interwar clinical work in a mixed general practice.[130]

Clinical notes indicated the diagnoses that the doctor made of their patients' illnesses. Much that was presented showed relatively little difference from that in a modern GP's surgery, with a mix of acute and chronic conditions, and in which upper respiratory infections, dermatological conditions, and rheumatic disorders predominated. Influenza, bronchitis, and rheumatic complaints such as sciatica, lumbago, pleurisy, appeared frequently. The large amount of TB, together with *long-running* septic conditions (abscesses, boils, septic fingers and hands) stand out as obvious differences from the present day. Equally, cardiovascular, asthmatic, diabetic, psychiatric, and gynaecological cases appeared with much less frequency than in a modern surgery.[131] The predominance of adult male patients, and the paucity of women and children, indicated just how much economic pressures circumscribed the social groups who could afford to see the doctor here, as in the other two practices.[132]

In 1919 the Wantage surgery had a stock of drugs worth £40 and furniture and fittings valued at £28, which for a practice valued at £3,000 seems low, even allowing for the fact that general drug costs were much lower than they became from the mid-1930s.[133] It is possible that these had been run down during war-time. However, the situation soon changed and the early 1920s saw an updating of surgery equipment. The most expensive purchase was an X-ray machine in 1921; expenditure informed by both a clinical and financial rationale, as patients paid dearly for the privilege of having X-rays taken. An X-ray machine was a rarity in general practice, and its value may have been the reason for its first location in a partner's house in the 'X-ray room', from whence it was only moved to the main surgery building in 1938. That it was regularly serviced indicated a continued use, although its actual utility to the practice (as opposed to a certain status value accrued by its possession), is uncertain. In 1924 an ophthalmoscope, blood pressure testing equipment, and expensive lenses (for optical work) were purchased. At a more mundane level the thermometer, catheter, or hypodermic needle were also frequently deployed.

The survival of all the practice bills (with piles of accounts for each succeeding year growing remorselessly in extent), means that the extent of work involved in a dispensing practice becomes apparent. The practice was very fortunate in having a trained dispenser, 'Jock' Stewart to take charge of this aspect of the practice's activities. Pharmaceuticals were purchased from

[130] Oxfordshire Archives, Misc Sq XII/4, clinical notes 1921–2, Misc Sq X/1–7, Invoices and receipts, 1912–53.

[131] Ibid.; J. Fry, *General Practice. The Facts* (1993), 24–8.

[132] See Ch. 5 for discussion of the finances of the Dowlais and Wantage practices.

[133] Oxfordshire Archives, Misc Sq XIX, partnership document. See, for example, Dr Martin's accounts of 1895–1902 where average annual expenditure on drugs for a single-handed practice was £73 (W. Sussex RO MP 2011).

a varied and changing list of firms in Liverpool, Nottingham, Bristol, London, and Birmingham. Some were famous names—Allen and Hanbury in the 1920s, Burroughs Wellcome in the 1930s, Bayer and also Glaxo in the 1940s. An important means for the dissemination of knowledge about new medicine would have occurred through visits from travelling representatives of Burroughs Wellcome distributing samples of tabloids and other newer products,[134] as did 'reps' from other firms. Certainly, the practice kept up-to-date in its treatments: for example, Prontosil—a Sulphonamide—was employed in February 1937, very shortly after it became available to GPs.[135] Anti-diphtheria serum was used with children. For a very few private patients vaccines were deployed against a range of diseases which included influenza, typhoid, catarrh, rheumatism, scarlatina, cholera, and whooping cough. There were referrals for private patients to consultants in Oxford and, less frequently, London. And there was a steady use of pathological laboratories; the Camberwell Research Laboratories, London; the Royal Berkshire Hospital, Reading; the Radcliffe Infirmary, Oxford; and—latterly—the University of Liverpool. Samples of sputum, urine, faeces, uterine discharges, or specimens of growths were sent off to be tested for diphtheria, whooping cough, carcinomas, TB, etc.

Not only was the Church Street practice a dispensing practice, as were most rural practices at the time, but it was also one that did eye-testing and even some dental work. It was an unusually wide-ranging clinical practice because its partners were keen to practise surgically as well as medically. With justification it was regarded as an exceptionally good general practice by the local teaching hospital, the Radcliffe Infirmary. If viewed in conjunction with the partners' surgical work in the local cottage hospital, the practice was virtually a health centre in embryo, but sadly it was one whose economically based differentiation in treatment meant that its full clinical potential could only be enjoyed by more affluent social classes.

These three practices resembled each other in the largely class-differentiated medicine that was practised: invariably a higher standard of clinical medicine was made available for the private patient who paid individually for treatment, than for the working-class one whose treatment was circumscribed by the cost-cutting nature of collective schemes. The basis of these schemes also meant that there was a gender—as well as class—bias evident in the patchy availability of medical services for working-class women. But what a detailed scrutiny of the clinical records of these three practices has discovered is not well known. This research has revealed that there were striking differences between practices in the extent to which better clinical care was given to low-paying working-class patients. Admittedly the medical and surgical conditions that were presented to these selected general practitioners were influenced by the social composition of the local community, while treatment

[134] R. Rhodes James, *Henry Wellcome* (1994), 102, 113.
[135] Loudon, *Death in Childbirth*, 260 and appendix table 32.

was shaped to some extent by the geographical availability of clinical services. But even more influential, however, were the choices that practitioners themselves made about the standard of medicine that they wished to practise. It was this above all that made general practice so highly differentiated.

Investigation and Research

Although GPs might adopt an experimental stance in selecting medicines in their everyday prescribing, the abundance of patients it was necessary to treat meant that most doctors adopted a receptive rather than active stance towards formal research. This did not prevent them from having a 'special interest' in one area in general practice, and about half of GPs did so. In this context midwifery appeared to have been the most favoured area.[136] Some kept careful records in this subject whose purpose indicated a research orientation. A good example of this under-publicized breed was Dr Ringrose of Newark whom we have seen kept an obstetrics notebook including a statistical analysis. This was a continuous record of his first 1,000 cases, delivered from 1895 to 1916.[137] This twenty-year investigation compared well with an equivalent later formal investigation, when 1,000 deliveries were analysed in a general-practitioner maternity unit over a period of seven years, and the results seen as sufficiently noteworthy to be reproduced by the British Medical Association in a book on the 'New General Practice' of the 1960s.[138]

The researches of relatively few individual practitioners were well known, amongst them—Withering, Jenner, Abercrombie, and Budd.[139] As a country practitioner in Devon, William Budd utilized his detailed local knowledge to help pioneer field epidemiology and, in his *Typhoid Fever* (1873), argued that typhoid was a communicable disease in which the water supply was the 'infective principle'.[140] Most colleagues of these pioneers were preoccupied only with attempting to keep up-to-date with medical advances through reading the *Practitioner* or the *BMJ*, and this kind of activity was as much as was usually expected. However, once a case of unusual clinical interest had occurred in general practice it might be presented by a member to a local medical society and then perhaps written up in its transactions but,

[136] *BMJ Supplement*, 26 Sept. 1953, 130, 138.

[137] Nottinghamshire RO, DD/1440/24/18, Obstetric case book of Dr Ernest Ringrose, 1895–1933.

[138] A. M. Cavenagh, 'Role of the General-practitioner Maternity Unit: 1000 Deliveries Analysed', in *The New General Practice* (BMA, 1968), 64–8.

[139] W. Withering, *An Account of the Foxglove* (1785); E. Jenner, Inquiry into the Cause and Effect of the Variolae Vaccine (1798); J. Abercrombie, *Pathological and Practical Research on Diseases of the Brain and Spinal Cord* (Edinburgh, 1828); J. Abercrombie, *Pathological and Practical Research on Diseases of the Stomach* (Edinburgh, 1828).

[140] William Budd (1811–80), MD, Edinburgh, 1838, practised at North Tawton in Devon, before moving in 1842 to Bristol.

inevitably, the results reached a very restricted audience. Thus, relatively few research findings by general practitioners had been publicized to a more than local readership before 1850, although there were accounts of an early morbidity survey in 1842, and of an enquiry into burns in 1847.[141] Given an unusual case (or cases), the more enterprising individual would see this as a means of promoting their career by writing them up for a medical journal with a national readership, as did W. P. Thornton in 1886 for the *Practitioner*, with descriptions of six interesting cases he had encountered in general practice.[142] The habit of sending off a single contribution to the *BMJ* or *Lancet* appears to have become much more common during the second part of the nineteenth century, and this was often related either to the subject of the MD thesis, or to work as honorary physicians or surgeons at local hospitals.[143] Occasionally, something more ambitious professionally was attempted as when, in Manchester during the early 1880s, group investigations were instigated by local GPs into the diseases of old age, acute rheumatism, and chorea.[144]

By this time the climate of élite medical opinion had begun to change towards the role of the general practitioner, and there was professional recognition of the part that general practitioners' diagnoses could play in the early mapping of disease. Hospital clinicians tended to mistake the end for the beginning of a disease, it was suggested, so that clinical work in private practice could remove this bias, by supplying a corrective to 'a too exclusive mechanical pathology'.[145] However, it remained the case that the main *locus* of nineteenth century medical research was not in general practice, but in medical institutions; the hospital and later the laboratory. It was not until the first half of the twentieth century that general practitioners asserted that a privileged position in making medical advances was conferred on general practitioners by the position they occupied in society.

James Mackenzie, a GP in Burnley from 1879 to 1907, argued vigorously that the laboratory concept of research was imperfect, and that the part played by the clinical observer in research was not recognized. Whereas the laboratory focused on the advanced state of disease, a general practitioner saw its early state and could then follow the disease through all its stages. His path-breaking work on the irregular action known as heart block,[146] provided the world of the general practitioner with a shining example of this method-

---

[141] D. J. Pereira Gray (ed.), *Forty Years On. The Story of the First Forty Years of the Royal College of General Practitioners* (1992), refers to publicity in the *Journal of the Royal Statistical Society*, and in the *Transactions of the Provincial, Medical and Surgical Association*.

[142] *Practitioner*, 37 (1886), 265–70.

[143] H. Marland, *Medicine and Society in Wakefield and Huddersfield, 1780–1870* (Cambridge, 1987), 308.

[144] Pereira Gray, *Forty Years On*, 45.

[145] T. D. Acland (ed.), W. W. Gull, *Memoirs and Addresses* (1890), President's address to the Clincial Society, 1871, 87–8, and Address on 'The International Collective Investigation of Disease', in 1884, 156.

[146] J. Mackenzie, *Principles of the Diagnosis and Treatment of Heart Affections* (1916).

ology, and the insights into disease that it could produce.[147] Mackenzie's distinction led to his departure from general practice, first to Harley Street, but then to his own research institute in St Andrews, where investigations were carried out on patients by local general practitioners. In advice to general practitioners on how to carry out research in general practice Mackenzie suggested that they look for a sign or symptom of which a patient complains, and then investigate how and why this medical condition had come about. He felt strongly that this focus on disease process had been ignored both in medical training and in medical textbooks.[148]

A review of Mackenzie's *The Study of the Pulse* commented:

We often hear that in the bustle of general practice scientific work is impossible; if Dr Mackenzie had done no more than dispel this error he would have done good service . . . [But] this work must take a permanent place in the standard records of the subject.[149]

Reacting to the publicity surrounding Mackenzie's achievements, the BMA instituted a prize for research in general practice.[150] During the ensuing period it is evident that several doctors were doing research in their general practices. Amongst them were the Devonshire GP, Jackson who was investigating blood pressure in his Crediton patients, and Dimock who was analysing the effectiveness of bran in the treatment of habitual constipation amongst his patients. In each case a thesis for an MD followed that was based on the investigations based on general practice. After the war Charlotte Naish also gained her MD by a study of breast feeding that she had undertaken in an Islington practice, and which won her the Charles Hastings Prize for 1946.[151] Obituaries indicate that after doctors embarked on what was euphemistically called 'retirement' (but which was often energetic part-time practice), they found it possible to devote themselves more actively to a particular clinical interest. Thus, James Goodfellow of Chesterfield studied iodine and iodine deficiency.[152]

The stereotype of the general practitioner was not a particularly intellectual one. Yet this does less than justice to the GP's medical and surgical contribution. GPs *were* active in clinical investigation and in disseminating their findings. Our database on GPs indicates that until the 1900s more than two out of five had publications, although the proportion then declined, as Figure 8.1 indicates. GPs published more often in the *BMJ* than in the *Lancet*, although the difference was not very marked. Figure 8.1 also suggests that around half the GPs in the mid-nineteenth century had MDs, although the

---

[147] Sir James Mackenzie, 'The Opportunities of the General Practitioner are Essential for the Investigation of Disease and the Progress of Medicine', *BMJ*, i (1921), 797–804. (James Mackenzie, MD, FRCP, LL D, FRS, a GP in Burnley, later Director of the St Andrews Institute of Clinical Research).

[148] Letter, *BMJ*, i (1924), 598.
[149] Review by Clifford Allbutt, *BMJ*, 26 July 1902.
[150] *BMJ*, i (1924), 550.
[151] Pereira Gray, *Forty Years On*, 47.
[152] *BMJ*, i (1950), 1145, James Anderson Goodfellow (1865–1950), MB, CM (Glasgow, 1887).

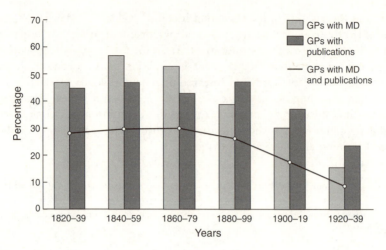

Fig. 8.1. Publications and MDs by GP cohort, 1820–1939

proportion then fell, no doubt as a result of the ending of the MD without examination. Those with an MD had a higher propensity to publish than other GPs, often on the basis of their MD dissertation. Arguably, the less academic orientation of GPs from the 1880s, evident both in qualification and publication, was a product of a more competitive medical market, in which it was more difficult to earn a living, and hence to find the time for investigation and writing up of results. It may also have resulted from the trend to a more specialized and laboratory-based medicine in which findings from general practice could appear insufficiently rigorous and scientific. That this did not necessarily marginalize the innovative researcher, who was attuned to the possibilities of general practice for advancing medical knowledge, was shown by William Pickles.

Pickles followed in the footsteps of his distinguished predecessor, William Budd, and in his later days was referred to as 'a second Budd'.[153] In 1913 Pickles had begun practice in Aysgarth, North Yorkshire, and was in partnership there for more than half a century. At the age of 41 he came across James Mackenzie's *The Principles of Diagnosis and Treatment in Heart Affections* and realized that 'even a GP' could contribute to medical knowledge.[154] Pickles came to believe that the country practitioner was privileged in standing 'on a strategic pinnacle for the investigation of infectious disease', more particularly in the 'determination of incubation period and the duration of infectiousness'. Indeed, an important objective of his classic *Epidemiology in Country Practice* (1939) was to stimulate his colleagues to keep records of epidemic disease.[155] The results of his epidemiological investigations in the

[153] Preface by John H. Hunt to W. Pickles, *Epidemiology in Country Practice* (RCGP edn., 1984).
[154] Obituary, *BMJ*, i (1969), 719.   [155] Pickles, *Epidemiology*, 3, 5, 7.

eight Wensleydale villages of his practice included an account of an infected pump that caused a typhoid fever epidemic in 1916, a discussion of epidemics of jaundice in 1910 and 1929, and an analysis of an influenza epidemic in 1935 during which a sick village schoolmistress infected seventy-eight school children. Pickles exploited the advantages that the stability and continuity in the life of a country doctor gave him, and which enabled him both to acquire an intimate knowledge of the village people from their early years, and to gain their cooperation in getting information not only about outbreaks of disease but also about heredity and consanguinity. In his researches he kept a pocket diary to note the date at which disease began, and these were then entered on to charts kept on a quarterly basis. His wife, Gertie, analysed and transferred the data on to neat coloured graphs that charted the incidence of disease. His wife's contribution was always acknowledged by her husband (see Table 8.1). Pickles's focus of enquiry on common infectious diseases (including measles, chicken pox, mumps, common colds, and influenza), in a domestic setting was also taken up by a friend and colleague in general practice, Edgar Hope-Simpson, in the Epidemiological Research Unit in Cirencester, from 1946. Interestingly, Hope-Simpson's inspiration was the doctor who had treated him when he was a child—James Mackenzie.[156]

Mackenzie had provided an attractive but largely unattainable role model for the family doctor in highlighting how a disease could be followed through from beginning to end. He has since become a professional icon, whilst on his eightieth birthday, the *Lancet* called Pickles 'The Grand Old Man of General Practice'.[157] Pickles had shown how an epidemic could be followed from the first to the last patient in tracing the spread of infection, and had publicized his work widely. In delivering a lecture on 'Epidemiology in Country Practice' (which in total he gave some 200 times), he modestly stated that 'I come to speak about very simple things, everyday happenings and elementary deductions drawn from them such as are within the scope of but a meagre intellectual equipment.'[158] But epidemiological work had not proved a simple component of professional life so that it was not widespread by 1948. A colleague (who had himself done a study of cholecystitis), put his finger on why this remained the case:

There's a lot of clinical material, you might say, available in general practice, which is untapped. But I think it is that GPs are just too busy, and they haven't got the funds, you know, to take time off from other work to do it.[159]

Research in general practice remained unrealistic for many but, for the enthusiast within the Royal College of General Practitioners, it was an enticing

[156] Pers. comm., R. E. Hope Simpson.
[157] Preface, *Epidemiology in Country Practice* (RCGP edn., 1984).
[158] W. Pickles 'Epidemiology in Country Practice', *New England Journal of Medicine*, 239 (1948), 419.
[159] CMAC, GP 29/2/63, Tony Leake.

ideal, and one that was embodied in the man whom they chose as their first President in 1952—William Pickles.

Conclusion

Before 1948 there had been a steadily widening range of clinical areas about which the general practitioner was supposed to be knowledgeable. Victorian books directed at the GP focused particularly on mainstream generalities (formularies, operations, or emergencies in general practice),[160] and those of the first two decades of the twentieth century on topics of notable current interest (for example, TB or VD).[161] Instead of a trickle of books on particular topics that had characterized the pre-war scene,[162] during the interwar years a steady stream of books reflected hospital specialism (ENT, obstetrics, skin diseases, fractures and dislocations, cardiovascular conditions, and so on),[163] as well as the promotion of an increasing range of treatments (such as insulin or radium treatments, X-rays, diathermy, dietetics, physiotherapy, medical gymnastics or massage).[164] In 1926 the *Lancet* feared that general practice might disappear under the weight of these growing specialisms.[165] The expectations and demands upon the GP in terms of an increasing amount of medical knowledge and professional competence were expanding, but the organization and resources of the practice were changing more slowly, while the education and training of the doctor was still not geared to the specific requirements of general practice. Some commentators therefore saw the future general practitioner being reduced to a mere sorting mechanism for more specialized services elsewhere. This did not happen. But clinical standards in a continued general medical practice were variable. How much did this impinge on the prosperity or survival of practitioners?

---

[160] *A Formulary of Selected Remedies for General Practice* (1884); E. M. Corner and H. Irving Pinches, *The Operations of the General Practitioner* (1903); J. W. Sluss, *Emergency Surgery for the General Practitioner* (1908 and 1910); P. Sargent and A. E. Russell, *Emergencies for General Practice* (1911).

[161] H. Hyslop Thomson, *Consumption in General Practice* (1912); L. W. Harrison, *Diagnosis and Treatment of Venereal Disease in General Practice* (1907).

[162] A. St Clair Brown, *Opthalmic Hints in General Practice* (1890); W. Bolton Thomas, *Electricity in General Practice* (1890); Corner, *Male Diseases in General Practice* (1910); P. Nicholson, *Blood Pressure in General Practice* (1914).

[163] G. Portman *Ear, Nose and Throat in General Practice* (1924); D. A. Crow, *Ear, Nose and Throat in General Practice* (1924); B. Solomons, *An Epitomy of Obstetrical Diagnoses and Treatment in General Practice* (1933); H. Davis, *Skin Diseases in General Practice* (1921); J. Hosford, *Fractures and Dislocations in General Practice* (2nd edn., 1939); R. McNair Wilson, *Clinical Study of . . . Circulating Diseases in General Practice* (1921); T. East, *Cardiovascular Disease in General Practice* (1938).

[164] A. Clark Begs, *Insulin in General Practice* (1924); A. J. Larkin, *Radium in General Practice* (1929); E. Payton Dark, *Diathermy in General Practice* (1934); L. Barrett Cole, *Dietetics in General Practice* (1938); E. Bellis Clayton, *Physiotherapy in General Practice* (1924); J. Arvedson, *Medical Gymnastics and Massage in General Practice* (1930).

[165] *Lancet*, ii (1926), 863.

The more positive clinical aspects of general practice included a widespread undertaking of minor surgical procedures, together with good clinical judgement—not least in the accurate spot diagnoses of common complaints. A minority of doctors practised opportunistic preventive care, or had an increasingly sensitized awareness of the psychological complexities of health care. There was some development from the person-centred traditional medicine, which was substantially dependent on social skills, to the clinically focused skills of modern medicine. This was evident in prescribing patterns with a transition from individualistic polypharmacy to standardized pharmaceutical drugs; a process which was most visible in the closing years of the period. Given limited resources and a heavy workload (arising from an increased demand for professional assessment and intervention), the typical GP managed to give continuity of care to some patients, as well as to provide reasonably efficient management of a large number of cases. The outcomes of general practice were cost-effective, if not always clinically very effective.

Offsetting more modern clinical practices were less progressive features. Increasingly the general record of obstetrics in general practice was indifferent. And the take-up of medical technology was frequently marked by conspicuous lags, as well as by some inclination to have instruments in the surgery as much for the display of scientific authority as for practical use. Examination of patients using medical technology might thus be under-utilized, with this kind of omission impeding accurate diagnosis or prognosis. In 1927 *The Conduct of Medical Practice* by the Editor of the *Lancet* complacently advised that, although accurate diagnosis was emphasized in hospital treatment, in general practice 'it is treatment which the average patient comes seeking'.[166] Overall, a standardization of clinical procedures was hardly a conspicuous characteristic of general medical practice. This was regrettable given that contemporary developments in the organization and delivery of health care in the community should have enabled GPs to focus more time and energy on improving the clinical treatment their patients experienced, not least through the organization of more patient contacts in the surgery rather than in house calls. A wider access to a range of hospital facilities should have resulted in fewer acute domiciliary cases for the GP to visit, while the growth of district nursing and of midwifery would also have reduced the load of home visits, and thus of time-consuming bedside vigils. However, it is difficult to discern any clear-cut gains to patients that resulted from these circumstances; Table 6.2 does not suggest any switch from time-consuming visits to surgery attendance during the interwar years. Did the static, conventional, even backward-looking, features in this provision matter to patients or potential patients?

A discussion of the status of the country doctor at the turn of the century had predicted that 'As the scientific basis of our position and practice is

166 Editor of the *Lancet*, *The Conduct of Medical Practice* (1927), 36.

developed our influence must be more and more unassailable . . . it must give us such advantage as to compel the growing respect of men and of communities.'[167] Such hopes were realized indirectly through the reflected glory from developments in medical science more widely, but in general practice the rhetoric of modern science was too often privileged over its practice. Why then did the forward-looking appeal of scientific credentialism not translate more rapidly into the adoption of scientific developments in general medical practice? It is salutary to remember that such omissions occurred within a wider cultural context in which there was a vigorous defence of the clinical *art* of British medicine.[168] And within general practice more specifically, individual GPs were aware that their authority with patients was created as much, or more, from individualistic social skills inherent in a traditional art of healing, than from any adoption of scientific advances. The manner in which the doctor worked—as much as what she or he did—strongly influenced the patient's view of the doctor's performance. Within middle-class private practice particularly the ideal of the family doctor had continued resonance, and hence possessed a strong pulling power in the recruitment of affluent patients. Here medicine was not yet a homogenized commodity to be consumed, but still an individualized encounter in which the patient's personal confidence in the doctor usually outweighed any suspicion of therapeutic deficiencies. Yet it would be facile to suggest that this healing art was *necessarily* antithetical to the exercise of scientific medicine.

The *BMJ* concluded that from the 1920s onwards 'rapid advances in medical science' had 'imposed stresses and strains on all types of practice'.[169] For GPs with an insurance or industrial practice—but few middle-class patients—there was a particularly obvious tension between a good clinical performance and a successful financial outcome. In many large cities, mining and industrial areas the deficiencies of clinical practice were very evident. Patients worked and lived in unhealthy conditions so that a high incidence of sickness, especially of a chronic type, had to be treated. But the economic rationale of such practices was a rapid surgery throughput, in which large numbers of patients were treated rapidly, and above all, cheaply. This was because patients had other cheap options in the corner chemist or the alternative practitioner so that their demand was sensitive to the prices that doctors charged for their services. Equally, practitioners might be constrained by low capitation payments from the friendly society or the NHI. That treatment was usually a bottle of medicine from a stock mixture satisfied both the patient's cultural expectations, and the doctor's need for economy. It was therefore mainly in suburban or rural areas—where economic conditions enabled a mixed social practice to be created that higher standards in clin-

---

[167] *Lancet*, i (1901), 797.

[168] C. Lawrence, 'Incommunicable Knowledge. Science, Technology and the Clinical Art in Britain, 1850–1914', *Journal of Contemporary History*, 20 (1985), 517.

[169] *BMJ*, ii (1953), 718.

ical routines could be achieved more easily. Here patients in a private or mixed practice had the financial resources to be able to respond to the doctor's modern medical technology. This was shown, for example, by the general practice in Wantage with its investment in an X-ray machine, which paid good dividends for its owners in the high fees that they could charge their patients for its use. Clinical standards were therefore strongly influenced by the economic resources available from private patients' fees or, after 1911, from the external input derived from public capitation fees for poorer patients under the national health insurance scheme. A more comprehensive attainment of this kind of cutting-edge performance was later made possible under the NHS when the 'Doctor's Charter' injected much-needed additional public funds into general medical practice in 1966.

'To do good medicine with compassion'[170] was an ideal with changing boundaries, and individual doctors measured up to it with varying degrees of competence. On the one hand, there was the lowest common denominator found amongst commercially minded doctors—from the club and shilling doctors of the late nineteenth century through industrial practitioners, to some panel doctors—who prioritized the business side of their practice above the clinical one.[171] On the other hand, there were practices where a core of private patients provided the resources which were a necessary, but not a sufficient, precondition to enable the practitioner to work to higher clinical standards. Whether to implement good standards of clinical practice, even in apparently unpromising circumstances, was the decision of the individual doctor—as has been illustrated in this chapter by the Drs Cresswell. But given widespread constraints in the doctor's economic resources the impact of the new scientific medicine was muted. Notwithstanding a number of doctors' indifferent clinical performance they were enabled to survive—if not necessarily to prosper—because of the poverty of expectation of their patients.

[170] CMAC, GP 29/2/26, Norman Paros.
[171] See, for example, the comment of a northern consultant on certain GPs in his area in Hadfield, *Good General Practice*, 29.

9

Patients

DISCUSSION of the dynamics of the patient–doctor encounter is a feature of the recent past. For the period covered by this volume, the nature of such meetings has to be teased out from a variety of records. Gaps and silences are conspicuous, and testimony on key topics tantalizingly elusive, so that inability to advance far with certain issues, but availability of evidence on others, has shaped the discussion. This chapter selectively explores aspects of doctor–patient encounters including patient choices and expectations, the financial implications of the patient–doctor encounter, and the doctor's evolving patient constituencies. The general practitioner's developing role—as a gatekeeper who controlled access to benefits of various types—is highlighted. The chapter begins with a discussion of the likely options facing sufferers in what was an unusually open market for health care. Professional survival in a situation where registered doctors had little, if any intrinsic competitive advantage in recruiting patients, meant that doctors needed to work at improving their accessibility to potential patients, whilst at the same time broadening their social appeal through effective communication, or a good 'bedside manner'.

Choices

In response to their aches, ailments, and afflictions sufferers had a range of choices: those within easy reach (such as household remedies), local ones (folk remedies from neighbours or patent medicines from the local shop); as well as possibly more distant encounters with practitioners, including herbalists, homeopaths, and registered doctors. We still know relatively little about sickness behaviour in the distant past—the characterizations of illness, the preferences of sufferers, and the conventions governing behaviour.[1] In the recent past, however, two out of three ailments were not taken by sufferers to the registered doctor, and nearly 30 per cent of the money spent on medicines in

---

[1] R. Porter, 'The Patient's View. Doing Medical History from Below', *Theory and Society*, 14 (1987), 167–74.

the UK was without such a doctor's prescription.[2] This was in a period when a free National Health Service was in operation, so that a reasonable presumption might be that the proportion of ailments treated without the professional intervention would be higher in the earlier period, before the NHS, with which we are concerned here. Was this in fact the case?

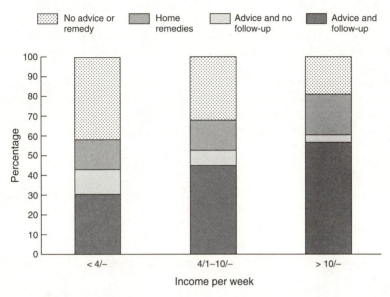

Fig. 9.1. Influence of income on treatment sought, 1933

We have an invaluable insight into how one class of women responded to illness in the relatively recent past—as a result of the findings of the Women's Health Inquiry of 1933. The objective of a health questionnaire was to collect information from women 'in widely differing districts, social conditions and occupations' but, since middle-class and unmarried women failed to respond, the sample actually consisted of 1,250 working-class married mothers' replies. These suggest some of the fascinating complexities of sufferers' responses to illness. On the one hand more than half had been prepared to seek professional advice of some kind, and on the other, one in six used home remedies. Nearly one in three sought no professional advice or remedy for their problems, but we can only speculate on whether this was because of lack of resources to do so, from stoicism, or perhaps cynicism about the utility of the help that middle-class doctors and others could give. Professional advice, when sought, was overwhelmingly from doctors, but might include other health care professionals in welfare clinics. Responses varied according to the

[2] *Without Prescription, a Study of the Role of Self-Medication* (Office of Health Economics, London, 1968), 3, 14.

type of medical condition and income of these women. The importance of income is shown very clearly in Figure 9.1. Whereas fewer than one in three sought advice and followed it amongst the poorest group (with income per head per week of under 4s.), three out of five did so in the top group (where income was over 10s. per head per week). And although only about one in five amongst the top income group sought neither professional advice, nor resorted to home remedies, two out of five women in the poorest group were in this category.[3] Home remedies were a resort of women in all income groups, but their use varied according to the type of medical condition. The six most frequent health problems reported were anaemia, headache, constipation and/or haemorrhoids (piles), teeth caries and toothache, rheumatism, gynaecological conditions, and bad legs. Women were least likely to seek professional help for constipation (seen as the province of home remedies) and most likely to consult a professional over serious conditions—rheumatism, gynaecological trouble, or bad legs (see Figure 9.2).

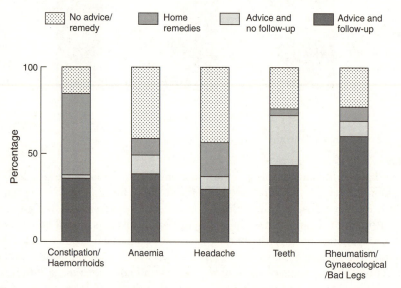

Fig. 9.2. Responses to medical conditions, 1933

These findings suggest that then as now, the sufferer would have made a preliminary physical (or perhaps psychological) self-diagnosis of the kind of complaint, its seriousness, and the likely cost of help in terms of money, time or distance. Stoicism and inaction may have followed if the complaint was deemed trivial or commonplace, or if the individual or household resources

[3] M. Spring-Rice, *Working-Class Wives* (1939), 57–63.

were insufficient to pay for assistance. For the self-limiting ailment traditional household remedies would frequently have been the first resort: perhaps rhubarb or senna for constipation, or goose grease for a cold. Until the mid-twentieth century working-class families might share favourite household remedies while certain women amongst them were relied upon to supply a herbal remedy for less serious afflictions.[4] As we have seen,[5] homeopathic remedies were also attracting their adherents from the mid-nineteenth century. One school of thought within homeopathy championed the God-given right of Everywoman to adopt homeopathic remedies in a domestic-centred medicine.[6] Patent medicines for self-medication might be another alternative, with the result that corn killers, cough balsams or blood purifiers found a flourishing market. Patent medicines were those with proprietary names protected by their trade name, and there was no hard-and-fast line between their ingredients and those in some herbal medicines. Herbal medicine was developing into a commercial variant known as medical botanism (alternatively as Coffinism or Thomsonianism) which also defended the individual's right to be his or her own doctor and found many adherents in the industrial towns of the north of England and Midlands.[7] Indeed, one of the major Midlands retail suppliers of patent medicines, Boots of Nottingham, had developed from a shop run by John Boot, a medical botanist, who in the mid-nineteenth century sold herbal medicines to town and country people. In 1874 his son, Jesse Boot, kept pace with a changing popular allegiance from herbal medicines to patent medicines by adding sales of proprietary medicines to those of herbal ones, advertising his wares heavily and cutting prices in an aggressive and very successful selling campaign to working people. Sufferers queued up at 'The People's Stores' to purchase 'Boots No Name Ointment', 'Boots Celebrated Bronchial Lozenges', or 'Boots Patent Lobelia Pills'.[8]

Resort to medicine was not just a narrow response to disease, pain, or suffering, but a more positive seeking after health as well. Perceptions of health as a commodity which could be purchased was not a new feature of the period,[9] although it seems likely that it had wider social appeal as general standards of living rose. One indication that this was the case was the availability of an increasingly wide range of cheap patent medicines, with numbers of retail outlets in chemists or grocery and general stores quadrupling in

[4] E. Roberts, *A Woman's Place*, 191. [5] See Ch. 2.

[6] G. Rankin, 'Professional Organisation and the Development of Medical Knowledge: Two Interpretations of Homeopathy', in R. Cooter (ed.), *Studies in the History of Alternative Medicine* (1988), 53–4.

[7] S. W. F. Holloway, 'The Regulation of the Supply of Drugs in Britain Before 1868', in R. Porter and M. Teich (eds.), *Drugs and Narcotics in History* (Cambridge, 1995), 83; U. Miley and J. V. Pickstone, 'Medical Botany Around 1850: American Medicine in Industrial Britain', in Cooter, *Alternative Medicine*, 140.

[8] S. Chapman, *Jesse Boot of Boots the Chemist* (1973), 11, 35, 37–41, 45.

[9] N. McKendrick, J. Brewer, and J. H. Plumb (eds.), *The Birth of a Consumer Society* (1982); Digby, *Medical Living*, 39–41.

number in the four decades after 1865. British sales of patent medicines increased from half a million pounds in the mid-nineteenth century to five millions by 1914, with a particularly rapid growth occurring from the 1870s. The sufferer's growing predilection for self-medication was shown clearly by the fact that expenditures on patent medicines increased twice as fast as real wages.[10] Evangelizing advertisements in the popular press exhorted the sufferer to embrace a healthy salvation, and the names of patent medicines both encouraged, and played on, suggestible states of mind. Potential consumers were beguiled by revitalizers and rejuvenators such as balsam of life, pills of health, and solar elixirs, while apparatus included electric body belts, loofah socks, and invigorator corsets. Advertisements targeted the popular psyche and the suggestibility of the sufferer by playing on hypochondria and, having stirred dormant anxieties, then befriended the consumer by selling satisfaction through testimonials which stressed the benefit of the product. Bile Beans promised to cure thirty-eight conditions and Beecham's pills thirty-one. Little wonder that by the early twentieth century a million pills of the latter were sold every day. These products, together with Eno's fruit salts, Parr's life pills, Holloway's blood purifiers, and Carter's little liver pills, became household names.[11]

In the eyes of sufferers, there was little distinction, if any, between patent medicines and those of the registered GP (see Plate 5). What there was might be blurred by the number of popular products promoted with a specious medical prefix. These included Dr Russell's cure for corpulence, Dr Gardner's celebrated worm medicine, Dr Hand's remedies for children, Dr Rooke's oriental pills, and Dr Sibly's re-animating pabulum of life. Old formulas were often recycled, with the result that ingredients of patent medicines (like those in traditional domestic or household remedies) overlapped with those in the *British Pharmacopoeia*.[12] Promoters of patent medicines thus attempted to stand within the medical mainstream in the eyes of their consumers—whether by means of the titles given the medicaments, their accompanying medical advice labels and booklets, or their quotations from medical authorities. But they also provided an oblique counterpoint of criticism of the medical profession that underlined their competitive edge. For example, the makers of Gower's Green Pills aimed to insinuate themselves into the consumer's confidence by claiming greater curative power. 'It is not your doctor's fault that he did not cure you, it was his misfortune. He had not these remedies in his possession.'[13]

In both Britain and the USA the medical profession felt sufficiently threatened by the competition of patent medicines (as well as motivated by the

[10] Chapman, *Boot*, 22–3, 26–7.

[11] Bodleian Western MSS, John Johnson collection, SJS/03.95, patent medicines; T. Richards, *The Commodity Culture of Victorian England. Advertising a Spectacle, 1851–1914* (Stanford, 1990), 172, 176.

[12] Richards, *Commodity Culture*, 180; M. Chamberlain, *Old Wives Tales* (1981), 174–5.

[13] Quoted in BMA, *Secret Remedies. What They Cost and What They Contain* (1909), 148.

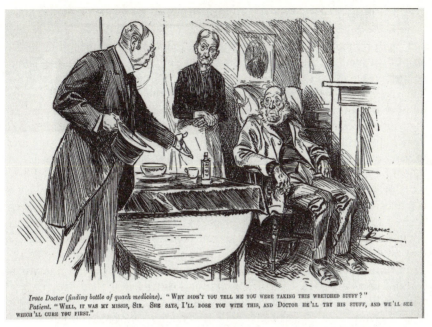

Irate Doctor (finding bottle of quack medicine). "WHY DIDN'T YOU TELL ME YOU WERE TAKING THIS WRETCHED STUFF?"
Patient. "WELL, IT WAS MY MISSIS, SIR. SHE SAYS, I'LL DOSE YOU WITH THIS, AND DOCTOR HE'LL TRY HIS STUFF, AND WE'LL SEE WHICH'LL CURE YOU FIRST."

5. 'Why didn't you tell me you were taking this wretched stuff?', 1909

public interest in regulating harmful medicines), to help stimulate public enquiry and/or restrictive legislation in the decade before the First World War.[14] This was also a response to the more general public concern about both quack and orthodox medicine which centred on a lack of a clear defining line between them. This anxiety was reflected in contemporary novels and plays whether it was R. L. Stevenson's genial quack Dr Jekyll whose *alter ego* was the infamous Mr Hyde; H. G. Wells's pharmacist, Edward Ponderevo, with his 'discovery' of the elixir of life; or G. B. Shaw's depiction of the medical profession as a conspiracy—'a huge commercial system of quackery and poison'—in *The Doctor's Dilemma*.[15]

In this pluralistic medical world where, if anywhere, did the registered doctors' market advantage lie, and how would patients be attracted to a general practitioner? An apparently authoritative contemporary statement suggested that the window of opportunity might only be small. William Farr, the Registrar General, wrote in 1875 that the working and middle classes 'trust to quacks; or do not call in aid for fear of medical bills at a time when the family may be earning nothing'.[16] For the trivial or self-limiting complaint

[14] J. H. Young, *The Toadstool Millionaires* (Princeton, 1961), 224, 242–4; BMA, *Secret Remedies* (1909) and *More Secret Remedies* (1912); *Select Committee on Patent Medicines*. PP, 1914, ix.
[15] R. L. Stevenson, *The Strange Case of Dr Jekyll and Mr Hyde* of 1886; H. G. Wells, *Tono-Bungay* of 1909; G. B. Shaw, *The Doctor's Dilemma (*1906) cited in T. Richards, *Commodity Culture*, 184–5.
[16] *Supplement to the 35th Annual Report of the Registrar General*, PP, 1875, xviii, part 1, lxxxi.

GPs had little, if any, obvious competitive appeal; the main stumbling block being widespread fear of the uncertain cost of a consultation. However, the fact that promoters of patent medicines had found it worth their while to use fraudulent medical titles to attest their utility in itself suggests that in popular perception the medical profession did have a certain medical authority. This had been considerably enhanced during the Victorian period by the number of official or public positions doctors occupied, which meant that their influence and control spread over a hinterland of everyday incidents. A monopoly existed for them as expert witnesses, as well as in the growing area of gatekeeping where their certification of ability/inability to go to work or school because of serious or infectious illness affected many families. Where acute or surgical conditions were concerned the doctor may also have held a competitive advantage because an enhanced scientific authority had been derived from hospital surgical advances. (To some extent this was offset by popular fear of surgery, so that patent medicine cancer cures might suggest they could cure without the knife.) A growth in medical appointments was also helpful in enhancing the GP's social visibility. Many general practitioners worked as poor-law medical officers for a district near their surgery, and thus might—as one young assistant described—go round the 'back slums'.[17] A legal change in 1885, whereby poor-law medical assistance no longer carried civic disability, and hence social stigma, resulted gradually in a more general recourse to the poor law by working people, thus bringing increased contact with the doctor.

Sale advertisements indicate the profession's contemporary awareness of the potentiality of the working-class market. For example, 'For disposal—Surgery, only been opened 3 months. At present doing little but good opening for man who can afford to wait a little time. It is situated in a thickly populated working class suburb of Manchester.'[18] If the individual doctor was to benefit from the developing working-class market for health, medical authority needed to be harnessed to easy geographical accessibility and modest, known financial cost. GPs trying to build up a practice nucleus in an urban working-class area used a bicycle, or else walked to patients, which made them familiar street figures in the neighbourhood of the surgery. 'I got lots of exercise by walking round the district trying to look as if I were very busy' recollected one doctor about starting his first practice in Gateshead in 1891.[19] Even those with more established practices, like Charles Grant in his Durham colliery practice, did most of his work on a bicycle, and was said to be always 'on his rounds'.[20] Some used a bicycle for ideological rather than commercial reasons, as did the Socialist Alfred Salter in Bermondsey, who considered that a car would distance him socially from his working-class

[17] Buckinghamshire RO, box 5, Diary of A. Blyth, 14 Oct. 1864.
[18] *BMJ* Supplement, 2 Dec. 1899.   [19] A. Cox, *Among the Doctors* (c.1949), 51.
[20] *BMJ*, i (1930), 1196.

patients.[21] In country areas the doctor on horseback also provided ready accessibility to patients, as did Dr Speiers on his rounds in Swaledale.[22] Adoption of everyday clothing by young late-Victorian doctors symbolized social and financial accessibility to working people, in contrast to the earlier medical 'uniform' of top hat and tails, which signalled only class distance and unaffordable expense. Those doctors who had themselves grown up in the same area as their practice undoubtedly found this a professional advantage in recruiting patients, while others built useful social bridges to the local community by regularly watching local football matches.

The convenient location, frequency, and regularity of surgery hours, and the low fees of the new branch surgeries were designed to draw in the sufferer for consultations. Dr Abbot, for example, set up in Carlisle in 1884 and sent out handbills advertising his charges as 1s. for a consultation, 1s. 6d. if medicine was required, and 10s. for a confinement, all strictly for cash payment only. His surgery was very accessible, being visible from the street (having been converted from a shop), and his surgery hours from 9 to 11 a.m., 2.30 to 4 p.m., and 6 to 9 p.m., meant that even long working hours did not disqualify the potential client. Twenty stock mixtures were used and patients soon came back for that 'bottle of medicine which did me so much good'.[23] Doctors thus gradually extended their customer base through working-class patients attending the surgery for a bottle of cough mixture for bronchitis, a tonic for their 'debility', or a stomach mixture for dyspepsia, so that the shilling doctor's white, pink or violet mixtures became successful competitors to the rival 'life pills', 'nervous drops', or 'sure cures' of patent medicines. Indeed the slum 'doctor's-shop' was not dissimilar in this respect from the general corner store, and in both cases proprietary mixtures were supplied over a counter, with accompanying advice being given in public.[24] Nor were remedies very different since an important element in the early twentieth-century general practitioner's therapeutic resources was aspirin supplied in a variety of colours. Practitioners were themselves aware that they needed to give a box of pills or a bottle of medicine to retain the confidence of patients. Spennymoor patients, for example, wanted value for money and had great faith in a bottle of their doctor's medicine.[25] Many were placebos or stock mixtures.[26] The small bottles in which medicine typically was given in working-class areas also meant that the 'Rep. Mist' (repeat mixtures) were the financial backbone of GPs' practices.[27] But highlighting clinical deficiencies— in that the encounter usually lacked a detailed case history taking from the

[21] F. Brockway, *Bermondsey Story. The Life of Alfred Salter* (1949), 36.
[22] Swaledale Folk Museum, N. Yorkshire, display on Dr Speiers.
[23] Cox, *Doctors*, 22–3.
[24] H. Roberts, 'A National Medical Service', *Nineteenth Century*, Aug. 1914, 404; H. Roberts, 'The Insurance Bill, the Doctors and National Policy', *Nineteenth Century*, July 1911, 155; CMAC, GP/29/7, Eric Grogono on his family's pre-First World War surgery in Stratford East, London.
[25] A. Mair, *Mackenzie*, 38.   [26] Roberts, 'Insurance Bill', 155.
[27] CMA, GP 29/2/71, E.B. Grogono.

patient, a physical examination, or costlier and individually prescribed medicines—misses an important point. In running successful practices in working-class areas doctors were—within stringent financial constraints—clearly
meeting their patients' cultural expectations of the doctor, and thus responding to what working-class patients wanted.

In broadening their appeal from their strengths amongst middle-class
patients to working-class ones, GPs might find themselves with gendered
lists. Not only did fewer women qualify as NHI patients, but many working-
class female patients preferred to deal with the medical women who
constituted only a small minority of the profession. Medical women characteristically created a following amongst poor women through their work in
free dispensary and hospital clinics, and later through Maternity and Infant
Clinics.[28] Where contact was not free, poorer women, preoccupied with balancing the meagre household budget, were just as—or perhaps more—likely
to patronize the local chemist because this was a cheaper alternative to the
doctor's fees. Where a male doctor was concerned, there was another disin-
centive to seeking help in that modesty might inhibit presentation of intimate
female complaints. A continued reluctance by male doctors to engage with
issues that became of pressing concern to women patients from all classes—
that of family limitation—further limited their appeal.[29] And, in the field of
midwifery, the female midwife gained an increasingly strong competitive
advantage over the male general practitioner, as the previous chapter has indicated.

Encounters

Class and gender circumscribed the kinds of patients that general practitioners recruited, and doctor–patient encounters differed according to the nature
of these clients. It was particularly in high fee-paying, middle-class households that the GP could focus on a patient in the context of family in gauging the impact of heredity factors or lifestyle on illness. It was mainly, if not
exclusively, with this kind of affluent clientele, that bedside medicine could
be practised, and the title of family doctor be earned. The frequency of a
rural doctor's visiting, also meant that a good knowledge and understanding
of patients' backgrounds would be built up. In contrast, in urban practices,
where reliance was placed to a greater extent on surgery attendances, a fast
throughput of surgery patients militated against much other than a brief
functional encounter. A continued emphasis on curative, rather than on preventive, medicine focused treatment on the individual, and only later did the

---

[28] See Ch. 7.
[29] Roberts, *Woman's Place*, 94; D. Gittins, *Fair Sex. Family Size and Structure, 1900–1939* (1982),
42; R. Porter and L. Hall, *The Facts of Life. The Creation of Sexual Knowledge in Britain, 1650–1950*
(1995), 237.

fuller development of social medicine begin to move the centre of gravity of the practitioner's work towards a wider concern with the individual and family within the community.

At the beginning of the period the transition from older views of holistic divine healing to those of specific scientific treatment was still incomplete. In 1854 a mother from a devout Quaker household, (the granddaughter of the Quaker reformer, Elizabeth Fry) suffered puerperal sepsis after giving birth to her fourth child. During her five days ordeal a nurse and two doctors responded to her physical needs; at first with soothing draughts and castor oil, later by leeches, finally by stimulants. Abel, her husband, and Ellen, her aunt, sought to raise her spirits by their devoted attentions and private prayer. Neither prayer nor prescription proved effective and—writing within the traditional conventions of a good death—Aunt Ellen recorded that Bessie 'fell asleep in Jesus'.[30] A clear example of the tensions involved in overlapping cultural belief systems, and thus of responses to mid-nineteenth-century illness was provided by Jane Richards—daughter of a minister, yet wife of a surgeon. She turned to the surgical remedy of her husband for immediate relief, but considered that the ultimate success of treatment depended on divine means. Her diary read:

5 April 1852. Very ill, not out of bed—but for Mr Richards to scarify my throat. . .

16 April 1852. If it is the will of providence that I am restored to health—I feel anxious to be of service to my neighbourhood in a spiritual as well as temporal sense.[31]

Personal entries ended here, as neither healing system proved efficacious, and she died within four months. Within this same context of belief in providential healing a letter from a male patient to his doctor indicated very clearly the respective perceived roles of divine healing relative to the doctor's more restricted ministrations. 'When I sent you first little did I think God would make you the instrument in His hands of the restoration of my health, it has pleased Him to do so, for which I feel very grateful.'[32]

A more important medical role has been assigned in recent interpretations which have viewed family doctors as the secular descendant of the priest or cleric in their roles as confidant and adviser in the sick room.[33] Like priests doctors had to believe in their own power because the psycho-dynamics of patient–doctor interaction were crucial to the healing process. Therapeutic activism helped practitioners by contributing to self-belief, which in turn assisted in the patient's confidence.[34] This has only been the formal subject

[30] Essex RO (Colchester), D/DU 353/4, Account of the death of Elizabeth Chapman, 1854.

[31] National Library of Wales, MS 7519B, Memoranda and diaries, Richards family of Merioneth.

[32] Wellcome Institute, WMS 5416, Henry Sanford to Dr William Ackland, 23 Oct. 1843.

[33] T. H. S. Escott, *Social Transformation of the Victorian Age* (1897), 388–97; R. Porter, *Disease, Medicine and Society in England, 1550–1860* (1987), 63.

[34] S. J. Kunitz, 'The Personal Physician and the Decline of Mortality', in R. Schofield, D. Reher, and A. Bideau (eds.), *The Decline of Mortality in Europe* (Oxford, 1991), 249–50.

of medical sociological inquiry or of medical-school teaching within the last few decades,[35] although other sources discussed later in the chapter indicate that its importance was earlier appreciated in the sick room.

To try to gain a longer-term historical perspective, material on doctor–patient relationships was analysed from the GP database. Interestingly, only a minority of the *BMJ* obituaries was found to have more than a brief comment about patients, who were often coupled with friends in a stereotyped comment such as 'much respected by his patients and greatly loved by his many friends'.[36] That this was the case is in itself perhaps a useful insight into professional values, since the brief format of a typical obituary forced the obituarist to highlight only what were perceived as the most important features of a life. Obituaries may obviously be read as a direct comment on a past doctor–patient relationship, but they also provide an oblique insight into the professional ideals of the obituarist, as well as a collective view of the way in which general practitioners perceived encounters with patients. Taken together the notices provided a model which was neatly complementary in featuring active doctors and passive patients. Significantly, this was similar to a modern theoretical attempt by doctors to model such encounters, which again gave active roles to professionals and passive ones to clients.[37]

Obituaries blended comment on the personal qualities that doctors brought to their relationships, with judgements on the professional skills that patients were said to appreciate. Although there was an anodyne, eulogistic character to many notices, this did not prevent some useful insights emerging. There was no major shift during the period in the personal, human qualities that obituarists commented on as being the mark of a good GP, which were painstaking attention or scrupulous care, together with sympathy, kindness, comfort, and generosity. These, it was inferred, then earned doctors the love, devotion, appreciation, or respect of patients. The affection of patients might also be shown by them turning out in large numbers for their doctors' funerals, particularly in the Victorian and Edwardian period, when a local doctor's funeral became a public event processing through the streets of the town.[38] Occasionally, a 'warts and all' obituary comment indicated an individual, rather than a more stereotypical, relationship. 'An outstanding family doctor . . . He was indeed loved by his patients, though some found him bluff, and he did not suffer fools, or those inclined to swing the lead, gladly.'[39] Less convincing were attempts to fit reality to conventional moulds as in the uneasy observation that his 'forceful and forthright personality inspired confidence in his patients'.[40] Comment on the professional skills applied by the

[35] See, for example, B. Bird, *Talking with Patients* (Philadelphia, 1955); A. Cartwright, *Patients and their Doctors* (1967).

[36] *BMJ*, i (1970), 753.

[37] T. S. Szasz and M. H. Hollender, 'A Contribution to the Philosophy of Medicine', *AMA Archives of Internal Medicine*, 97 (1956), 585–92.

[38] *BMJ*, 1910, i (1910), 1271; i (1930), 844; i (1940), 592–3.

[39] *BMJ*, i (1950), 193.   [40] *BMJ*, i (1950), 449.

doctor on behalf of patients was less usual but, when included, was expressed
in sufficiently specific terms to suggest an obituarist's good personal knowledge. 'His clinical skill was outstanding, and the sureness of his diagnosis
gave patients great comfort and confidence.'[41] Clinical comment also indicated some shifts in the nature of the doctor–patient encounter, as in 'from
his patients he expected, as did many doctors of his generation, obedience as
strict and meticulous as the care he lavished upon them'.[42]

One difference between early and late obituaries mirrored the changing
nature of society and of medicine. Victorian or Edwardian practitioners were
more likely to be commended for their interest in the poor or their tender-
hearted sympathy for their patients.[43] Later, this kind of intimate
doctor–patient involvement became less fashionable, apparently needing to be
balanced by more professionally detached qualities, as in 'that most priceless
characteristic of a good doctor—equanimity'.[44] Devotion to patients beyond
the usual call of duty continued to attract favourable comment, however, as
in the case of a GP who 'made frequent long journeys to visit them in hospital', another who tried to be present at his colliery patients' operations in
hospital, or a colleague who eschewed the phone, so that he could actively
'seek out his colleagues and bring them to the patient's bedside'.[45]

Other sources indicate that central to the patient–doctor encounter was
clinical history taking, which in importance continued to outweigh the physical examination, or the laboratory test that might follow it. History taking
was an art, and hence there was assumed to be flexibility in the sequence of
the general interrogation (on the family history, and the personal history—
including surroundings, home, exercise, food, sojourn abroad), and the special interrogation (on the organ affected and disease suspected).[46] The
importance of history taking was underlined:

There can be no question of the value of accurate and systematic case-taking. It trains
the beginner in habits of thoroughness and exactness at the bedside, and ensures that
no point of importance in the case is missed. To the more experienced clinician the
systematic record of cases . . . gives to his experience a concrete embodiment. . . .

It was suggested that the medical student on a ward round might find commercially supplied outline diagrams of the body, useful in taking notes of the
illness.[47] As was indicated in the previous chapter, these were also used by
practising doctors, for delineating the GP's view of the problem in correspondence with consultants.[48]

---

[41] *BMJ*, iv (1970), 691.   [42] *BMJ*, i (1950), 1207–8.
[43] *BMJ*, ii (1920), 225; i (1901), 121.   [44] *BMJ*, iv (1970), 373.
[45] *BMJ*, i (1960), 973; i (1960), 353; iv (1970), 372.
[46] A very well-tried training text was R. Hutchison and H. Rainy, *Clinical Methods* (1897), the 9th
edn. came out in 1929, by Hutchison and D. Hunter, and the 12th edn. in 1949. R. H. Major, *Physical
Diagnosis* (2nd edn., Philadelphia, 1940), and C. M. MacBryde, *Signs and Symptoms. Their Clinical
Interpretation* (Philadelphia, 1947) were key American texts but were less popular in Britain.
[47] Hutchison and Rainy, *Clinical Methods* (1897), 1–2.
[48] Mid-Glamorgan RO, D/DX 83/4/1. Dr Cresswell's Case Book, Dowlais, 1878–99.

The nature of clinical encounters between patients and practitioners was seldom illuminated by obituary notices of GPs, although some occasionally gave a useful insight. Dr Merriman's notice remarked on how he was 'particularly successful in conquering the fears of his juvenile patients by his kindly manner', and broke convention in that he 'actually laughed and smiled when he talked to a juvenile patient'.[49] And others indicated the healing quality of the doctor's presence: 'patients often remarked that they felt better as soon as they saw him' or he had such 'a wonderful bedside manner that his patients used to declare that his very presence made them feel better'.[50] This makes clear that the physician's personality was highly significant. Confidence in the doctor was crucial; physicians needed to believe in themselves and in their therapeutic interventions, otherwise they could not inspire their patients with hope.[51] That self-belief in turn was dependent on the confidence with which the patient regarded the doctor.[52] Hidden patient sensitivities on this crucial issue were exploited in contemporary humour, which pointed to only a qualified confidence. *Punch*, depicted a middle-class patient responding to a doctor's suggestion (in this case a consultant), that 'If this doesn't put you right, come to me again', with the rejoinder, 'How many guesses will you want?' (see Plate 6).[53]

Communication skills were also key elements in a successful encounter, and *Punch* may have been perspicacious in highlighting working-class patients (and their relatives) who misunderstood what the doctor was saying. Although the graphic depictions were crude—in showing ignorant patients who ate leeches, swallowed containers as well as pills, or used the barometer rather than a thermometer to take a temperature—they do not nullify the validity of the insight.[54] A subtler representation of a middle-class patient made the same point more effectively, in showing a doctor suggesting that 'What you need is to be taken out of yourself' and the patient apprehensively responding with, 'No. No, doctor, anything but an operation.'[55] The relationship with child patients was also perceived as being particularly problematical; linguistic pitfalls arising from a professional manner geared to talking to adult rather than young patients produced cartoons from the 1860s to the 1920s.[56] Apprehension, fear, the brevity of the encounter, as well as verbal difficulties arising from the use of technical language, contributed to misunderstanding in the daytime surgery. At night communication could also be fraught because the patient found the speaking tube (connecting the surgery door with the doctor's bedroom), puzzling, so that the doctor was irritated by being able only to elicit anxious breathing rather than pertinent information.[57]

[49] *BMJ*, i (1881), 621.   [50] *BMJ*, iv (1970), 311; ii (1979), 713.
[51] Kunitz, 'Personal Physician' 249–50.   [52] Roberts, 'Medical Service', 499.
[53] *Punch*, 28 July 1926, 91.   [54] For example, *Punch*, 1 Aug. 1906, 82; 3 May 1911, 329.
[55] *Punch*, 5 Mar. 1924, 253.   [56] Ibid., 6 Apr. 1861, 146; 1 Aug. 1863, 56; 27 Jan. 1926, 98.
[57] Pers. comm., Dr Henry W. Ashworth, B.Sc., MD, FRCGP, who practised at 306 Stockport Road, Ardwick, Manchester.

Distinguished Physician (handing prescription to patient). "IF THIS DOESN'T PUT YOU RIGHT, COME TO ME AGAIN."
Patient. "HOW MANY GUESSES WILL YOU WANT?"

6. 'How many guesses will you want?', 1926

Time pressures in general practice have meant that modern doctors usually worked within a narrow frame of reference, and thus might fail to see the consultation as a dynamic process, rather than a doctor-centred diagnosis of organic illness. They could be poor at picking up concealed patient offers of information, or oblique 'by the way' asides, which were the patient's attempt to introduce into the interview what he or she saw as their main purpose in coming to see the doctor.[58] It was not until the 1950s that Michael Balint's work publicized the need for practitioners to be alert to 'presenting symptoms'.[59] Doctors became more aware that conditions patients displayed to the doctor were not necessarily the real reason why they had come. Sometimes a patient made it easier for the practitioner to sieve the wheat from the chaff by belatedly disclosing their real anxiety. A medical woman briskly recounted a classic situation:

I remember one woman coming along, and she told me about the cold she'd got etc. etc., and then, just as she was going, she said, 'oh, by the way, I've got a lump on my breast.' And she'd really come [for that] but she hadn't liked to tell me. And I examined the breast, and discovered what it needed, and she had that off, and had treatment.

[58] P. S. Bryne and B. E. L. Long, *Doctors talking to Patients* (HMSO, 1976), 5, 8.
[59] See Ch. 9.

Balint encouraged doctors to use psychological approaches in their work, and his holistic approach of focusing both on mind and body in understanding illness is recognized as having helped to develop the concept of primary health care.[60] Balint's emphasis on the psycho-social is often credited with creating a distinctive doctor–patient relationship in which the patient was a subject rather than an object. However, it is more than likely that some general practitioners were already—at the very least intuitively—aware of the desirability of using this kind of approach.[61] Balint suggested that, at a superficial level, doctors usually helped patients to reorganize their 'illness' as a physical ailment, but that this was often more a result of the doctors' firmly held 'apostolic mission' to diagnose physical illness, than of the patient's actual problem(s).[62] GPs may have felt a shock of recognition at this perceptual clarification, whereas earlier there may have been only a niggling concern in the back of the mind that the patient's problem had not really been uncovered. Although patient–doctor interaction has recently been recognized to be a key element in the quality of care delivered,[63] converting the modern doctor from providing an illness-centred diagnosis to a patient-centred one has been difficult. Patients' deference towards doctors, together with nervousness and a sense of unease engendered by the doctor's authoritarian manner has tended to inhibit interaction.[64] Mass medicine has not fostered 'deep listening' whether this is the 'five minutes for the doctor' experienced by the NHS patients, or the 'three to four minutes for the doctor' given to those under the NHI.

Some doctors, like Jessie Murray or J. M. Craig, had had a natural facility for perceiving any psychological element in illness.[65] Patients' perspectives on good and bad doctoring included the need for professional psychological insight, and there was thus an appreciation of the doctor who took the psychological frailties of patients into consideration. After the inception of the NHS a very few doctors timetabled separate long interviews outside surgery hours with a few patients whom they considered to have a strong psychological component in their 'illnesses'. One such was Anthony Ryle because he was more interested in 'handling people's way of presenting or handling their way of being ill' rather than in treating physical illnesses.[66] When a doctor had more time, as in semi-retirement, psychological support for patients became easier.[67] A handful of practitioners also had some formal

[60] M. Jefferys and H. Sachs, *Rethinking General Practice. Dilemmas in Primary Medical Care* (1983), 326–9.

[61] See, e.g., Editorial, *BMJ*, ii (1938), 183.

[62] M. Balint, *The Doctor, his Patient and the Illness* (2nd edn., 1968), 123–4, 217.

[63] Editorial, *Journal of the Royal College of General Practitioners*, 24 (1974), 138.

[64] F. Fitton and H. W. K. Acheson, *Doctor/Patient Relationship. A Study in General Practice* (HMSO, 1979), 78–81.

[65] *BMJ* ii (1920), 723; ii (1960), 153–4.

[66] CMAC, GP 29/2/61, Anthony Ryle, BM, BCH (London, 1929), FRCP Psch, 1980.

[67] Harding, 'Memoir', 94.

training in psychology or psychiatry. One medical woman had specialized in psychiatry for her Halle MD and considered that this made her especially well 'qualified to listen and to hear and to make [a] very thorough history'. She added, 'My psychiatric background suited me well, it helped me particularly when 75 per cent of my patients were Jews, they are not easy to deal with.' More generally the focus remained on the physical rather than the mental state of the patient, so that there were few referrals to psychiatric services.[68]

Lacking therapeutic power the ratio of the art of healing to the science of medicine continued to be high in general practice, so that the humane and caring qualities of the doctors' personalities were important to their patients recovery. Years of doctoring often gave GPs good insight into human nature and into the needs of their patients. Thus functionally over-elaborate instructions for taking the medicine could be given, because 'it keeps the patient busy you see'. Presumably this gave patients a sense that their illness was being given due importance, and also gave them less opportunity to worry about it. Or a touch of humour sugared the pill of the side-effects of medication. In the case of valerian, 'If any lady complained that "it repeated" he [Dr Bullmore] would say that she should not complain as it was working a second time round at no extra cost.'[69] It was mainly, if not entirely, the private patients before 1948 who had a longer encounter, and who thus stood a better chance of having their physical problems adequately analysed. A doctor who had successively an interwar working class practice, and then a middle-class one, concluded that before the NHS he could look after only half as many patients in the second area because of the higher expectations of his middle-class patients.[70]

Towards a small minority of patients, doctors' overwhelming emotions might be helpless frustration or irritation. The 'human face to medicine' which had earlier attracted the entrant to general practice could be less than appealing in reality. One preoccupation before 1948, seldom aired publicly, was that concerning patients' cleanliness. In a mixed practice it was feared that the 'decent' folk might desert the practice if forced to sit next to a smelly individual in a cramped waiting room. An authoritarian line might be taken. 'I've given her two days to clean up the home, and if she hasn't cleaned up the house we can't take her. I've told her that. I can't have her sitting in my waiting room next to clean people.'[71] In maternity cases the practitioner was particularly vulnerable, and one recollected that the four and half hours spent being 'attacked by bugs' during a difficult childbirth as having been 'almost unbearable'.[72] Others maintained a *cordon sanitaire* on visits to vermin-infested homes, so that a doctor with a mixed practice that covered a range

[68] N. Bodkin, *et al.*, 'The General Practitioner and the Psychiatrist', *BMJ*, ii (1953), 723.
[69] Lodge, 'Reminiscences', *BMJ*, 289 (1984), 1760–2.
[70] CMAC, GP 29/1/71, Eric Grogono.
[71] Ibid., GP 29/1/20, Dr Margaret Hallinam of her father-in-law, in practice in Rotherham.
[72] Cox, *Doctors*, 54.

'from the sublime to the gor blimey' was careful in her bedside encounters. 'I always kept as far away from the bed as I could, because I knew that fleas can jump 14 inches.'[73]

There was another group of patients—the neurotics/hypochondriacs—for whom such simple tactics of avoidance were of limited utility. They engendered a sense of professional helplessness because GPs considered that they could do little for them, and had a number of private names, which indicates that they were a constant irritant. They were the 'backwards and forwards', 'the poor things' 'the never wells' or the 'heart-sinks'.[74] Doctors got them out of the surgery by telling them there was nothing the matter or by giving them a different bottle of medicine. Occasionally, the bolder practitioner would take more decisive steps as did Dr J. Adam who gave radical treatment to the *malade imaginaire*.[75] Another way of clearing a professional breathing space was referral to a consultant.

Practitioners in some industrial practices were afflicted by more general patient abuse. In a stubbornly non-deferential community drunken, inconsiderate, or non-compliant patients were conspicuous.[76] They prompted entries in the Dowlais surgery book in the Rhondda during 1900 such as:

Saturday 15 September. Mrs C. 22 Lower High Street. 12 midnight. Received a telephone message at night surgery for this man said to be injured. Found nothing wrong. The woman did not come for medicine. She was drunk.

Saturday 22 September. Jonah W. 182 High Street. Nothing at all the matter but laziness to come to the surgery for castor oil.

Sunday 21 October 8.15 p.m. 7 Tramroad Side. No necessity for sending for me.

Tuesday 11 December 8 p.m. Mrs P. Sent at 8 p.m. to come at once. Went at 8.30 p.m. All in bed.[77]

An assistant who had earlier worked in a similar practice in this area thought that patients showed little gratitude; recovery was attributed to luck but lack of recovery to the doctor's fault. As these contract patients 'never felt the payment of medical bills, medicine, and medical services, were never properly valued by them'.[78] The non-compliant patient was a problem in other types of practice as well. Amongst working-class female sufferers in the 1930s about one in six who had obtained health-care advice, admitted not following it (see Figure 9.1).[79] Arguably, the true rate of non-compliance was even higher than this. Where patients did not have to pay doctors for calling them out, because of being enrolled in a collective medical scheme, abuse was likely

---

[73] CMAC, GP 29/2/37, Hilda Cantrell, who had a mixed practice in interwar Liverpool.
[74] Ibid., GP 29/2/59, Samuel Isaacs.
[75] *BMJ*, ii (1940), 79–80
[76] R. Church, *The History of the British Coal Industry, volume 3, 1830–1913 Victorian Pre-eminence* (Oxford, 1986), 298.
[77] Mid-Glamorgan RO, D/D X 83/1/31, Dr Cresswell's Surgery Book at Penydarren, 1899–1901.
[78] Mullin, *Toiler's Life*, 153.   [79] Spring-Rice, *Wives*, 57–63

to occur, as in the Dowlais practice. Once the NHS supplied free treatment to all patients, the problem became a general one for the profession, rather than a specific one for the individual practitioner. A survey shortly after the inception of the NHS revealed that a 'recurrent complaint is that all over the country a persistent few [patients] harass the doctor with trivial complaints'. The doctor would be delighted to 'purge his list of this hard core of inconsiderate trouble-makers'.[80]

Cost

The economic aspect of the patient–doctor encounter was another common area of tension in general practice. Before 1948 the financial dimension of the patient–doctor relationship loomed large. Complaints by mid-Victorian doctors in the Highlands and Islands were particularly well-documented, and demonstrated the precariousness of a system of private medicine when many patients were destitute. The seriousness of the situation prompted the Royal College of Physicians in Edinburgh to conduct a detailed inquiry in 1852. This painted a bleak picture of the dire economic state of the medical profession in the region after the potato blight and depression in black cattle prices had reduced many, even in the *middle* ranks of cottars and crofters, to destitution. The inquiry revealed that only two out of five out of 155 parishes were adequately supplied with medical assistance, another one in three were partially supplied, while the remaining quarter were rarely, if ever, visited by a medical practitioner. There was thus an estimated 116,000 people with insufficient medical help to call on in time of need. Returns to seventy-one queries sent out to doctors in the area produced fifty-three returns. These showed in painful detail the problems of too few, ill-paid practitioners vainly attempting to meet the needs of patients who were scattered across a rugged terrain with poor communications.[81]

In many cases doctors had to subsidize their patients from their own pocket, and were paid neither for their extensive travel nor for medicine. Doctors also faced strong competition and complained that sufferers turned to the established clergy, to mercantile dealers, to itinerant irregulars, or chemists for aid. Impoverished patients, parochial boards which did not necessarily hand over to the doctor the government grant they received for medical assistance, and local subscriptions which did not materialize, meant that beleaguered doctors could themselves be reduced to penury. Dr Wood of Sanday, Kirkwall, for example, could not afford even to keep a horse to visit his patients. A litany of doctors' complaints suggests some of the financial

---

[80] *BMJ* i (1953), 718.
[81] Royal College of Physicians of Edinburgh, AD. 7.3, Statement regarding the Existing Deficiencies of Medical Practitioners in the Highlands and Islands, 3 Aug. 1852.

problems they were experiencing, as well as indicating the impact these then had on patients' care. The Argyllshire doctor, James Horne, focused on the doctor's predicament, 'The greatest hardship I have to suffer is non-payment for my services—I frequently undergo more toil in making an effort to obtain payment for my services than I had to endure in rendering them.' His experienced colleague, the Arran surgeon, Mr Stoddart, showed greater and more compassionate understanding of the source of the doctor's difficulties. 'The people are mostly poor and cannot pay for medical advice and the distance [is] so great that it is a hardship for a medical man to travel so far for nothing.' And Dr Coll Macdonald of Lockshiel linked the doctor's difficulties to the standard of care that he could provide for patients, 'The chief hardship is the want of an income which disables the practitioner from having medicines, instruments, or supplying medical comforts where required.' This was the bottom line in the economics of patient–doctor encounters.

Money matters and the bill were recurrent concerns with the middle classes as well, as contemporary humorous depictions of the doctor indicated in *Punch*.[82] Earlier medical bills usually itemized both visits and medicine; a practice dying out in the second half of the nineteenth century but sustaining a long tradition of cartoons with patients saying they would pay for the medicines but personally return the visits.[83]

Although we have seen that the centre of gravity of the British medical market was located in the middle-classes, areas of growth in urban working-class custom were evident by the turn of the twentieth century. A social cross-section was to be found amongst patients in individual rural practices. Thus an English country doctor—like Dr Speirs of Diss in Norfolk—recruited manual yet skilled workers (a mole catcher, gardener, carpenter, horseman, blacksmith, and gardener), alongside tradespeople (baker, butcher, dairy, miller, stationer, innkeeper), a growing 'service' class (schoolteacher, army officer, 'post office', 'station') as well as the traditional upper social echelons of inhabitants of rectory or manor.[84] Some collective provision existed for the working class (although almost entirely for males) in friendly societies and, after 1911 (mainly for males) in the NHI. Doctors came to appreciate the difficulty of translating need for medical treatment into an effective demand for it, more especially where women and children were concerned. Where household means were scarce the male worker's needs were usually privileged over those of his dependants. Expectations of average numbers of dependants of panel patients who would pay regular amounts for the benefit of the GP's attention had to be revised downwards.[85] Until the 1930s few women or children were recruited as patients for doctors' clubs.[86]

---

[82] For example, *Punch*, 10 June 1914, 21 Sept. 1921.

[83] These ranged from 'Paying in Kind', by W. Heath (1823) reproduced in Digby, *Making a Medical Living*, 219; to the *Tatler* 22 Mar. 1911.

[84] Norfolk RO, BR224/13/12, Dr Speirs' list of patients.

[85] Digby and Bosanquet, 'Doctors and Patients', 89.   [86] PEP *Report* (1937), 154.

Expedients might bridge a gap in a poor patient's resources so that medical attention could be given. Surviving letters to doctors from English patients and their friends illustrated how—by paying for impoverished fellow sufferers—more affluent individuals at the manor, vicarage, farm, or business might give paternalistic assistance to poorer people within a traditional country hierarchy. During 1901–2 a sample of letters proffering help, and thus mediating the patient–doctor relationship, read:

This man has had a bad foot for months will you kindly inform bearer what is best to be done for it, and charge this advise [sic] to me and oblige, John Kimber, College Farm, W. Hendred. [PS] You cannot rely on the old Man's word.[87]

Would you kindly go to see a child belonging to Private Norris . . . I told Mrs Norris I should ask you to call. It [sic] is a very delicate and evidently 'ricketty' and I should be glad if you would give it what is necessary and put it down to me, . . . The father is a discharged soldier and I am happy to say we have got him work as a Postman.[88]

The bearer is bringing a child who has very badly cut his arm. I thought a doctor ought to see him at once, so I will be responsible for [the] first charge, at any rate.[89]

The writers assumed personal direction of another through a self-assumed financial, as well as social, sense of responsibility, and revealed one way in which an informal medical welfare state operated in the local community. Another was through tacit agreement that the doctor should charge the affluent such high fees that they subsidized the low fees of the impoverished.[90] A third method was through the medical altruism practised by doctors in not charging patients whom they believed genuinely could not pay. Finally, consultants called in to operate on a wealthy patient in a local hospital might be persuaded to operate on a poorer one, at no cost to the latter.[91]

In poor households doctors were in any case likely to be called in only for serious afflictions or conditions, since their fees could upset the careful balancing of the household budget for months, if not years, at a time. The following letter from a heavily pregnant woman, asking for a doctor's attendance at her forthcoming confinement at the turn of the century, illustrated a lack of contact despite apparent need. The necessity of asking the price of assistance showed the mother's mental equation between cost and benefit:

To Dr Speirs, Dear Sir, Am writing to ask if you will come to me during my confinement which I expect in Jan[uary] if [I] go [to the] correct time, but [I] have been so sadly full of pain now for more than a week [that] I hardly know how to keep about, [so] that it may possibly occur at any time, as I have had two seven month children. This will make my seventh child [and] my husband would have me know

[87] Oxfordshire RO, Misc Sq X1/1, letter dated 1 Dec. 1901 to Drs Emerson and Woodhouse.
[88] Ibid., letter dated 17 Oct. 1902 to Dr Woodhouse.
[89] Ibid., bundles of correspondence from patients, letter from J. R. Holmes, bookseller and dealer of Hanney, Wantage to Dr Emerson, 22 Aug. 1902.
[90] F. Archer, *The Village Doctor* (Gloucester, 1986), 55.
[91] Unpubl. 'Autobiography' of Dr J. Richard of Stranraer.

if you will come, and [also] your fee. I have always had a doctor with each one. I hope you will attend me. I remain yours obediently, Mrs Ber.[92]

Cost–benefit analysis continued to be practised by poor sufferers in deciding whether to call in the doctor. It was also undertaken by patients in evaluating whether they had had value for money. Thus, a middle-class patient was shown in a cartoon looking at the (large) doctor's bill and ruminating 'Good Lord, Doctor, have I been as near death as that?' (see Plate 7).[93] The necessity of calculating clinical gain against financial pain was especially evident in working-class communities. During the interwar period one GP recollected that in S. E. London 'The poverty was extreme . . . [Patients] only sent for the doctor when they really needed you. You never got sent for nothing.' Patients, particularly poor patients, had their pride and this was important in maintaining their sense of self-esteem in what must have seemed an unequal social encounter with the doctor. 'On the corner of the table, and this was the unwritten law, you didn't see it until you'd finished the doctoring and, as you walked out, you picked up the sixpence off the corner of the table.'[94]

There was a large intermediate group located largely within the middle class, the upper ranks of the working class, and occasionally even in the upper class, where income should have meant that the practitioner could be paid. But lack of foresight in saving for a period when illness struck meant that there was no money to pay the medical bill. The doctor's calibration of the pressure that was needed to extract payment was both a matter of delicate social judgement, and a function of the economics of the practice itself, since doctors—as well as patients—might be in need of ready cash. Most of the time any professional pressure was felt by the patient to be justified, and aroused an apologetic response, although the form that this took was shaped by the relative social position of the patient. Thus, members of the local squirearchy might write with some embarrassment that, 'I am ashamed to add we do not want the family account now,'[95] or 'I am very sorry that the account has been standing so long and fully appreciate your kindness in not pressing the matter. I will send you some portion of the money as you suggest.'[96] A local post mistress used a more direct, commercial style. 'I am very sorry to keep you without your money so long, but I hope to come and settle with you in the course of a few days, as there is a little mistake in the bill which I want you to wright [sic].'[97] For a few others a code of honour existed, such that even if hard times forced them into debt, they would eventually clear their name. For example, a Liverpool Jewish family owed the doctor ten

[92] Norfolk RO, BR 224/13/5, Correspondence of Dr Speirs.
[93] *Punch*, 21 Sept. 1921.   [94] CAMC, GP 29/2/23 Margaret Norton.
[95] Abbey Mead Surgery, Hampshire (private archive), letter of 30 Sept. 1903 from S. A. Septima Hurst, pinned to folio 865 of day book and ledger (1897–1904).
[96] Oxfordshire RO, Misc Sq X1/1, A.L. Clement, Antwick's Manor, Letcombe, n.d.
[97] Ibid., Letter from M. Godfrey, Post Office, Charney, n.d.

Patient (receiving bill). "GOOD LORD, DOCTOR, HAVE I BEEN AS NEAR DEATH AS THAT?"

7. 'Good Lord, Doctor, have I been as near death as that?', 1921

pounds, managed to pay five before moving to Manchester, and sent the remainder five years later when times were better.[98]

Bad times and good times affected not just patients. Doctors also found themselves vulnerable to the fluctuating state of the local economy through unpaid accounts, as a surviving set of letters from a Berkshire farmer illustrates. These are a fascinating mix of temporizing pleas regarding his inability to pay the bill which was interspersed with more urgent missives asking for medical assistance in emergencies, thus indicating a tension between obligation and need. Also interesting was an offer (unusual in a British, if not an American, context) to pay interest on the bill. One letter read:

Dr Emerson. Dear Sir, I am much obliged to you for writing in the kind way you did respecting the payment of the account . . . if you will allow me a little while longer I have got some ricks ready for sale, for I [am] pleased to say I like others have had a good crop, and I shall be able to pay all or half my account at once. Thanking you for allowing the account to stand so long. I remain Dear Sir Yours faithfully N. Stratton.[99]

Correspondence to Dr Emerson from his patients was courteous in tone, and showed respect, even affection. Letters to a Norfolk practitioner, Dr Speirs,

---

[98] CAMC, GP 29/2/37, Hilda Cantrell, MB, ChB (Liverpool, 1923).
[99] Oxfordshire Archives, Misc Sq X1/1, letter dated 27 July 1902.

are similar in indicating that the level of unpaid doctor's bills was influenced by the state of the local economy. 'I have had no permanent employment' wrote one patient in apologizing for being unable to pay a bill of five guineas.[100] A keeper wrote regretting not settling his bill before moving, and stating that he would soon be able to, since 'I have a good situation here'.[101] This Norfolk correspondence had the same civility as that with Dr Emerson. 'I have every desire to be on good terms with you,' wrote a patient in promising to settle by cheque the following week.[102]

A more business-like note was evident in this practice's correspondence during the interwar era. Drs Birt and Squires—Emerson's successors—were far more aggressive in their entrepreneurial concerns. Their patients showed both awareness, and a matter-of-fact acceptance, of the financial aspects of their relationship.

Sir, I am writing in answer to your Bill this morning to say I am not in a circumstance to pay the bill all at once, as my Husband has been out of work a long time. I am sorry. But would you kindly take it in instalments which I will try my best [to pay] as I should not like you to sue me. Yours faithfully, Mrs E. Goodenough. I am sending 2/-.[103]

Correspondence during the 1920s and 1930s also indicated that economic worries were now afflicting the middle and upper classes to a greater extent, with erstwhile prosperous groups suffering from a failure of dividends or even from looming bankruptcy. The harshness of the times may have contributed to the more abrasive tone shown in a letter which began aggressively, before belatedly realizing the weakness of the patient's position relative to the doctor, if more treatment was needed:

To Dr Birt and Squires. I have today received a registered letter from you, asking for the payment of the bill I owe. I think [it] is to [sic] bad of you to keep on sending as I am willingly prepared to pay you but of course it will take time to do so as my wages are not extraordinarily high, and its much to my regret to still [be] owing but I am sure it would please me very much to come and pay you every penny . . . I am yours Truly, F. G. Wiggins. PS I hope this wont [sic] prevent you from attending if its nessary [sic].[104]

It is difficult to envisage such a communication being written three decades earlier to Dr Emerson. The tone of the letter was more egalitarian, while its brusque style points to the doctor's overtly mercenary stance having resulted in a loss of respect in the local community.

---

[100] Norfolk RO, BR 224/13/8, letter from Charles Crick, 14 June 1912, and BR 224/8, ledger (1906–12) folio 418.

[101] Ibid., BR 224/13/1, letter from R. Ward, 15 Feb. (year not given).

[102] Norfolk RO, BR 224/13/4, E. Fulcher(?) of Scole to H. Meredith Speirs, 4 Oct. 1911.

[103] Oxfordshire RO, Misc Sq XI/1, letter of 11 Apr. 1928.

[104] Ibid., Letter from F.G. Wiggins to Drs Birt and Squire, n.d.

Gatekeeping

Within the community the patient might gain or be denied access to services, employment or benefits because of the monitoring function of the medical profession. It has been well said that 'this gatekeeping role of physicians, though widespread, has been neither widely recognised nor extensively studied' and this part of the chapter aims to provide some historical case study material to extend the discussion.[105] Gatekeeping by the doctor could involve clinical decision-making as a rationing device, or act as a form of medical policing, thus creating a sense of alienation in the patient, and/or a loss of clientele for the doctor. Such work involved conflicts of interest and inescapable professional dilemmas. Was the doctor's prime loyalty to the patient or to the body employing the doctor? The doctor's financial relationship to the organization involved influenced this, as in whether the GP's structural role was as a private doctor, a salaried officer, or a consultant. So too did the functional nature of the role; whether it needed only data gathering or decision making as well.[106] A doctor's personal ethics and professional values also informed the gatekeeping process; the Hippocratic Oath stressed conduct that would benefit patients, with abstention from anything that would be deleterious or mischievous. However, this growing role by the doctor into allocative work, where clinical decisions had non-therapeutic consequences, was not part of the GP's education, nor did it receive much professional discussion.

The state's growing incursion during this period into health-related matters meant that doctors in public service performed a variety of gatekeeping roles, in attesting to patients' incapacity, and hence their eligibility for welfare or insurance-related benefits. In private practice, also, the GP could perform a similar function in relation to the growth in assurance work through examining an individual to gauge fitness for life insurance, assessing incapacity after industrial injury, or certifying fitness for employment. For example, in medical examinations for the Post Office conducted from the 1890s Tonbridge GPs looked at height, weight, chest, vision, vaccination record, and family history before certifying an individual as 'well developed and sound', 'physically sound' or, after 1911, merely as 'passed'.[107] Bureaucratic record keeping was less demanding for some private firms so that the doctor might take the clinical side less seriously. A woman, whose health was delicate, began work at a Lancashire mill in 1913 but recollected that the doctor only came to examine her after three or four weeks in the job.

---

[105] D. A. Stone, 'Physicians as Gatekeepers: Illness Certification as a Rationing Device', *Public Policy*, xxvii (1979), 227.

[106] A. Nugent, 'Fit for Work: the Introduction of Physical Examinations in Industry', *BHM*, 57 (1983), 587, 594; Stone, 'Physicians as Gatekeepers', 247–8.

[107] Warders Medical Centre Private Archive, Tonbridge, Post Office Medical Examination Book, 1890–1942.

'All I remember was him looking in your hair . . . He never sounded your chest or anything like that.'[108] Where industrial compensation cases were involved doctors showed greater awareness that they had to be stringent in assessing evidence of an individual's physical disability, no doubt because they were aware that their decisions would be scrutinized carefully, and possibly contested.[109]

Doctors varied in the degree to which they saw their responsibilities as clinical rather than moral, and thus whether they saw it as part of their responsibility to enquire closely into their patient's non-medical predicaments.[110] Some signed certificates on a routine basis. The laconic entries of the sick reports filled in by Wantage doctors during 1918 for the neighbouring POW camp at Compton, Berkshire appeared to fit this routinized category.[111] A few doctors might adopt a wider view of their responsibilities, taking the moral high ground if they thought they were being used for illicit certification of non-existent sickness, but thereby also running the risk of losing patients. Dr Norton, for instance, refused to sign certificates for the NHI scheme unless she was convinced of the patient's incapacity, and Dr Mackinnon had 'no patience with the malingerer', despite having an industrial practice at Murton, in the Durham Coalfield.[112] Some colliery doctors maintained a more equivocal stance since, although not convinced by a miner's alleged sickness, they were prepared to go along with it, and therefore recorded not an 'off' but 'a moot off'.[113] Interpretation is difficult in the absence of contextual documentation. This kind of response may have been a nod to professional conscience, alternatively it may have served as an *aide memoire* for future encounters with an individual's ambiguous symptoms. Perhaps it was prudent professional 'fence-sitting' in an era when diagnosis was less certain, or possibly it was dictated by their employment position because much of the doctor's remuneration depended on retaining the confidence of the workforce. Overall, this limited evidence showed a spectrum of attitudes, which suggests that the profession hardly deployed gatekeeping powers with any missionary fervour. However, survival of more detailed records of friendly societies, the poor law, and the NHI scheme enables the gatekeeping process to be scrutinized further.

Here we take the Oddfellows as an example of the processes involved for a doctor employed by a large friendly society. The Lodge Surgeon had successive gatekeeping roles because he first examined those who wished to join, and later might be called upon to certify incapacity, or a renewed capacity, for work. Applicants had to fill in a printed form declaring their previous

---

[108] Roberts, *Woman's Place*, 60.   [109] *General Practitioner*, ii (1910), 43.

[110] In the Netherlands doctors have less conflict of interest because they cannot write certificates for their own patients.

[111] Oxfordshire Archives, Misc. Sq X/1.

[112] CMAC, GP 29/2/23, Kathleen Norton; Obituary of Dr Mackinnon, *BMJ*, i (1960), 1686.

[113] Mid-Glamorgan RO, D/D X 83/1/31, Dr Cresswell's surgery at Penydarren, 1899–1901, entry 15 Jan. 1900.

record of sickness (itemized both by disease and by previous periods of sickness), stating whether they had been vaccinated, if they suffered from hereditary diseases, and asserting whether their spouse was in sound bodily health and of good constitution. (Any declaration later found to be false might invalidate the membership.)[114] The surgeon assessed these written applications whilst also physically examining the applicant. Given that the surgeon received only two shillings per head as late as the Edwardian period, little time can have been devoted to it. Nevertheless, the obviously unfit were excluded. For example, the 'runt in the litter', the young Bert, was taken by an elder sister to see the doctor and, alone among the family, was excluded from joining the Oddfellows. 'You can take him back and tell your mother she should have drowned him when he was young and I'm not going to do it.'[115]

The problems for sick members posed by these gatekeeping procedures were exemplified by an Oddfellow member, William Smith, who forwarded several letters to the Hope of Eynesford Lodge during the 1860s. These are written in a variety of hands, alternating between his unaided efforts and other more literate productions, perhaps written by a friend, brother, or the sick steward:

4 January 1864 Brothers i write these few lines to inform you that i had to give up wok . . . of January and i have [been] veary ill with a vilient cold . . . thinking i should get better but i have got worse and wish you all a happy new year. W Smith.

May 20 1864. To the NG the hope of Eynesford. I William Smith a brother of Wansforth and England Lodge residing at Eynesford feeling myself unable to follow my employment beg to declare on the funds of the Lodge. Yours William Smith.

Jan 27 1866 Eynesford to the NG the hope of Eynesford. I William Smith a brother of Wansford and England's Lodge residing at Eynesford feeling myself able to follow my employment beg to declare off the friends of the lodge. Your William Smith.

Eynesford January 20 1869. Sir, i write thies few lines to know the reason why i have not recived the sick money from the club for it is allmost a fortnight thince i sent the docter certificate. yours truly William Smith

Although the parallel certification from the lodge surgeon at this time has not survived, there are comparable certificates extant. Dr R. P. Turner stated in 1866 that 'I hereby certify that Josiah Redman is under my care suffering from rheumatism in the muscles of the chest', and again that 'I certify that Mr Fletcher leaves me cured and hereby signifies that he requires no more pecuniary help.'[116] During incapacity certification had to take place every week, the sick member apparently being visited both by brothers (who for a

---

[114] Norfolk RO, SO 59/63–146, Kenninghall Oddfellows Applications for Membership, 1871–1942.

[115] Quoted in Roberts, *Woman's Place*, 164.

[116] Cambridgeshire RO (Huntingdon), Wansford Lodge of Oddfellows, 2876/Q/8/23, surgeon's certificates and statements of health, 1845–1902, certificates for 4 Apr. and 29 Mar. 1866.

nominal payment served as sick stewards), as well as by the surgeon him-self.[117] But whilst the procedures were themselves rigorous, they were likely to have been undercut to some extent by the small amount of time that the GP would to be able to give, because of the meagreness of the remuneration. Payment of only 5s. per member per year was all that was made to their surgeon by the Wansford Lodge Oddfellows at this time (see also Table 5.5). A consequence of the meagre remuneration was that doctors examined recruits to a local club *en masse*.[118]

The attitudes that GPs brought to the role of gatekeeper are clearly illustrated by their work as poor-law medical officers. Here attempts to restrain public expenditures meant that the doctor was but one amongst several gatekeepers, and it is interesting to analyse the extent of medical, in relation to non-medical, authority. Sufferers amongst the poor who needed medical attention first applied to the union relieving officer or—in dire emergency—to their parish overseer. A rare survival of correspondence and official poor-law papers from the Bicester Union in Oxfordshire enables us to analyse the processes involved. A letter of 1875 by a poor woman to one of the Bicester relieving officers, George Dew, showed how strongly feelings about inaccessibility of medical help, were held:

To Mr Dew, Sir, I should feel obliged if you will give me A paper for the docters to attend my husband as he is very unwell and unable to work and when he is able to work he can scarcely earn enough to keep himself as i told you when i seen you last and i am not able to do anything myself as i am quit helpless. it is bad for me to sit and see my husband sinking away for want of medical assistance and canot aford to pay A docter for him. I shall feel thankfull to you if you will send me A paper by the Bearer and oblige, yours respectfully, A Andrews.[119]

If Dew, as the relieving officer, considered it appropriate to authorize medical treatment he filled in a form to be taken to the medical officer.

The union medical officer not only had to use his judgement in the grey area between medical and economic need, but also had to liaise with lay officials in order to arrange suitable options for patients, so as to treat them with as much consideration as general penny-pinching poor-law regulations, combined with a notably stringent local board of guardians, would permit. Life was inevitably untidier than bureaucratic procedures envisaged, so that in everyday practice a general practitioner was left with some professional discretion, as the following cases illustrate. Walter Wyke-Smith, a medical officer in the Bicester Union wrote to Dew in 1871 about a girl he had been summoned to see urgently by the parish Overseer at 10 p.m. on Saturday. 'I would not have gone had I not been told she was dying.' However, the doctor didn't think the case fell under his remit as a poor-law doctor, since the

---

[117] Norfolk RO, SO 59/208, Kenninghall Oddfellows Lodge minutes, 1904–11.
[118] Archer, *Village Doctor*, 38–9.
[119] Bodleian Library, Oxford, Dew MSS, box 3, official papers (I have inserted punctuation).

girl's father had good wages, 'I shall be glad if you will enquire into this', he wrote to Dew.[120] Four months later Dr Wyke-Smith was requested to visit a deranged person. On his arrival he found only an old lady with 'a very ill temper and a strong desire for mutton and porter', in other words for the 'medical extras' that the medical officer could prescribe for the sick. Wyke-Smith's sympathies were enlisted by the daughter who was caring for this difficult patient, and he concluded that the mother should be sent to the workhouse, because she was 'evidently a great nuisance to her daughter'.[121] In the following year a colleague, George McNair, was asked by a parish overseer to give a professional judgement on a Mary Smith's capacity to be moved to the workhouse. Having been found insensible, Mary was proving an expensive patient for the poor rate because fire, light, and women to watch over her, had to be paid for in her cottage. Dr McNair told Dew firmly that 'If she was moved to the workhouse, it would extinguish the little chance she has of rallying.'[122]

The poor-law doctor was a liberal gatekeeper, not least because of a professional appreciation of the relationship between poverty, poor diet, and sickness, so that the GP would attempt to privilege a patient's needs above the public purse. A sympathetic attitude might be evident even in a more strictly medical record, as another Bicester poor-law medical officer, Mr Knight showed in his empathetic comments of 'sadly' 'very sadly', or 'hopeless'.[123] Narrowly medical treatments given by the poor-law doctor to pauper patients were not subject to financial scrutiny and review by the board of guardians (not least because the cost of most medicines came from the doctor's own pocket), but nutritional supplements known as 'medical extras' did receive close attention. In the Bicester Union the guardians invariably approved the doctor's recommendations of mutton and wine (more unusually gin or brandy), but 'refused by Board' was their invariable response to the doctor's attempt to be more generous to paupers by making a triple recommendation such as mutton, wine, *and* cod liver oil. Equally, although guardians were prepared to sanction expenditure on a nurse recommended by the medical officer for a sick pauper, any extension of this nursing provision for the merely aged and infirm, was refused and an order for the '[work] House' was given. It was, however, open to the doctor to certify that the person was too infirm to be moved to the workhouse, and doctors might utilize this loophole to protect their patients, as had McNair above.[124] Contests of authority between the doctor and guardians were found in other unions, and

[120] Ibid., letter dated 27 Feb. 1871.

[121] Ibid., uncatalogued official papers, letter of 10 May 1871.

[122] Ibid., letter of 11 Sept. 1872.

[123] Oxfordshire Archives, PLU2/6/1A16, Bicester Union District Medical Officers Official Returns of Sick Paupers Attended, 1836, 1846, 1892.

[124] Oxfordshire Archives, PU2 RL/2A1/5, Bicester Poor Law Union Application and Report Book, 1865, especially for Reeve case of Lower Heyford, Rhyman case of Middleton Stoney, and Bayles case of Somerton.

centred on medical extras, which were suspected by lay administrators of being in aid-of-relief, rather than in-aid-of-sickness.[125]

There were later—and more publicized—contests of authority, this time between localities and central government, as a result of poor-law and NHI doctors certifying those on strike as ill. During and after the major Coal Mining Dispute of 1926 the government considered that poor-law medical officers in the Durham Union of Chester le Street, for example, were certifying single miners as sick, and therefore eligible for poor-law allowances when, as strikers, they would otherwise be ineligible. Equally, one panel doctor was thought to have been certificating patients without examination. While both 'offences' had occurred, their scale was very small.[126] And in South Wales sixteen insurance practitioners were interviewed at the Welsh Board of Health at the time of this Coal Dispute 'to explain the apparent freedom with which they were issuing medical certificates of incapacity'. They were warned that 'greater care should be taken in future'.[127] In Scotland, too, lax certification was officially perceived to be a problem. In Fife there were accusations that there had been an 'utter collapse from the normal standard of certification owing to the stress of industrial circumstances, involving an increase in the cost of sickness of two-thirds between May/June 1925 and May/June 1926'.[128]

Lax gatekeeping—whether real or alleged—had certainly become more of a public issue under the NHI. Whereas the Victorian poor law had customarily dealt only with patients in the poorest social groups, the later health and unemployment insurance schemes covered those commonly perceived to be 'salt-of-the earth' manual workers. Particularly during the 1920s and 1930s workers in the heavy industries experienced unprecedented levels of prolonged unemployment. In mining and industrial areas there might be intense local pressure on doctors to certify as sick, and therefore as eligible for health insurance benefits, those whose unemployed benefit had already expired. The official suspicion was that in areas where doctors were very dependent for income on panel patients lax gatekeeping would occur, because practitioners would fear that refusal to turn a blind eye to malingering would lead to patients deserting their lists. This problem was particularly acute under an arrangement where industrial premises such as collieries were deemed approved NHI institutions, so that they were able to administer the health insurance scheme for their workforce.

It was not just at times of crisis during major industrial disputes but throughout the NHI period that gatekeeping problems between doctors and

[125] A. Digby, *Pauper Palaces*, 176.

[126] Durham RO, U/CS/303, Chester le Street report of special guardians' meeting, 5 Aug. 1926; U/CS/321, Correspondence of Clerk to Chester le Street Guardians with Ministry of Health, 5 July 1928.

[127] PRO, MH 62/200, Report of Special Committee into Medical Certification in South Wales.

[128] Scottish RO, HH3 6/6, Minutes of Fife NHI Committee, 14 July 1926.

officials arose. Even at the beginning of the panel period the Welsh Insurance Commission feared that in industrial and mining areas panel doctors (who were usually also colliery doctors), were experiencing 'undue pressure' from their patients, and therefore that there were already excessive claims for sickness and disablement. It set up conferences to enquire into the matter, sent officials to visit Merthyr Tydfil in order to 'impress upon the panel doctors concerned the paramount importance of great care in the granting of certificates', and reprimanded doctors in some other areas for 'slackness in giving certificates'.[129] NHI commissioners attempted to stiffen doctor's resolve in all parts of Britain by monitoring returns of individual doctors, and by official medical referees examining patients for evidence of the disability and sickness certified by their insurance doctors. As a result of this the numbers of patients who were interviewed increased sevenfold between 1921 and 1931.[130] In 1931 a special committee was set up to look at NHI medical certification in South Wales. Four out of five doctors were either written to, or interviewed, about their unsatisfactorily high certification level.[131] In Scotland, the Department of Health for Scotland examined the comparative certification patterns of doctors in 1931–2, and concluded that there were a number of high certifying doctors, especially in Glasgow, Lanark, and to a much lesser extent in Dundee, or Fife. Regional Medical Officers were directed to address the problem, and reduced numbers deemed incapacitated by their doctors by two-fifths.[132] This policy of bureaucratic pressure seeking to erode nonconformist practice was the preferred official strategy for reducing panel doctors' lax gatekeeping, so that only small numbers of doctors were singled out for deterrent financial penalties.[133]

The extent of this practice of signing the well as sick was a complex issue which turned not only on the economy of doctors' practices, but also on their personalities. In areas where patients were socially more mixed doctors were financially freer to take an independent line, and one London medical woman was enabled to adopt a more unsympathetic stance. 'If you thought they were fit for work, you signed them off unemployment benefit, and they came back with a pain somewhere else, because they'd no intention of ever doing any work.'[134] Also relevant was the culture of the district so that even as late as the early years of the NHS, a doctor might stop his car outside the Miner's Institute in certain Scottish mining districts 'toot his horn like an ice-cream

---

[129] PRO, MH 49/12, Welsh Insurance Commisssion papers, 1911–15, minutes 26 June, 11 August, 14 and 28 Oct. 1913; MH 49/3 Welsh Insurance Commisssioners minutes, 15 May 1914.

[130] The sample increased from 0.6 to 4.4 per cent between 1921 and 1931 (Digby and Bosanquet, 'Doctors and Patients', 86).

[131] PRO, MH 62/200, Report of Special Committee into Medical Certification in South Wales.

[132] Scottish RO, HH3/18, Morbidity Statistics and Certification.

[133] PRO, MH 62/200, Medical Certification in South Wales. Between 1929 and 1932 these financial penalties affected 55 insurance doctors in England, 30 in Scotland, and 21 in Wales.

[134] CMAC, GP 29/2/23, Hilda Cantrell.

salesman, and hand out "lines" through the car window' certifying illness amongst miners whom the GP had not even seen.[135]

Conclusion

Doctors ran an increasing variety of Victorian and Edwardian practices which were variously described as old-established, family, mixed, town, industrial, colliery, country, or suburban. Panel practices were later added to this list. Each had distinctive patient constituencies. This conspicuous heterogeneity in general medicine suggests that practitioners would have had to construct a specific type of practice in order to ensure professional survival. How then did GPs attempt to gain a livelihood by interacting with, or perhaps more actively manipulating, a local environment in order to recruit the patients on whose fees their livelihood depended? Unburdened by very much prescriptive advice (either from professional manuals or from their medical schools) on the practicalities of making a medical living, GPs may well have imitated the well-tried models of older colleagues, but adjusted these by trial and error to suit their individual circumstances. Alternatively, they may have been skilful in transferring models of patient management from one context to another, as occurred after 1911 in the transmission of fast throughput methods from club to panel practice. More general strategies could have included a centrally placed surgery location, a highly polished brass plate attesting to medical qualification, and reliable but high-profile transport appropriate to their neighbourhood or social clientele. Each would serve to heighten professional visibility, while it would be hoped that their initial cost would soon be defrayed from the fees engendered. Plentiful surgery hours, and/or a willingness to undertake house calls also signalled the GP's ready accessibility to patients, a feature that was necessary in a competitive medical market encumbered not only by other registered doctors but by a variety of alternative practitioners, chemists, and druggists as well.

Responsiveness to the cultural expectations of discrete social groups of patients was also desirable—whether this was in meeting a working-class patient's desire for a bottle of medicine, or a middle-class patient's preference for a leisurely history-taking or examination. In each patient–doctor encounter the latter's confidence-inducing personality might constitute an important healing quality in an era when there was a high ratio of art to medical science. In practices with good resources the use of new medical technologies, adoption of procedures such as injections, or prescriptions of 'magic bullets' could arouse patient awareness of the GP's improved technical competence and therapeutic power. However the tension between the cost of such advances, and the limited ability of most patients to pay for them,

---

[135] R. E. Stewart, *Out of Practice. Memories of General Practice in Scotland During the 1950s* (Southport, 1996), 33–4.

circumscribed such initiatives. Shaping the practice to fit not only the needs—but the financial resources—of the neighbourhood was therefore the bottom line in adapting or assimilating a practice to its environment. In more fortunate localities the ability of the GP to access community resources (as in country areas with a cottage hospital or good district nursing service), would lead to improved standing with patients. In contrast, a growing range of gate-keeping functions, although adding to the authority of the doctor, might be more problematical in contributing tension to a patient–doctor relationship, since here the clinical acumen of the doctor was linked to a patient's eligibility for insurance or welfare benefits.

Patient–doctor relationships therefore showed occasional strain, but in many areas at most times were fairly harmonious. A later sense of alienation from the medical profession, stemming from a feeling that doctors treated the disease not the patient, was not yet apparent. Doctors often conciliated patients, not least because they needed to retain their custom, and patients were usually deferential to doctors, who were perceived to wield powers of life and death. This symmetry was upset when lay power challenged professional status, as in industrial practice, or where the patient as patron flexed financial muscle. 'Dear Doctor, I have much pleasure in enclosing my cheque for the amount of the fee, but that pleasure would have been proportionately greater had your account been 25 per cent less!'[136] Patients valued, but were not always prepared to pay for, the services of a general practitioner, who provided a varying measure of clinical effectiveness in an accessible way. In turn doctors engendered the kind of relationships with patients they found congenial: the short lists of country doctors facilitated a more friendly connection than that of urban doctors pressurized by a large clientele, while those with private practices had a closer association with patients than the routinized encounters of panel doctors. These personal styles were obvious to those who saw the doctor in action—as a 'a friend and guide' or 'a family friend and doctor'.[137] Personality as well as practice type thus dictated professional styles, and those doctors who emphasized that their patients were friends had a larger number of non-clinical encounters in which the doctor used bureaucratic or community contacts to help the patient. The differing roles of doctors within varied communities is explored further in the next chapter.

---

[136] Bligh, *Dr Eurich*, 224.   [137] *BMJ*, i (1970), 371; i (1960), 1510–11.

PART III

A Wider World

10

Public Duties and Private Lives

HEYWOOD Hardy's late-Victorian painting of an elderly country doctor, asking directions to a remote patient from a shepherd boy, depicted the GP riding across a barren, upland landscape under a lowering sky. Entitled 'Duty',
it provides us with a socially respectful view of the public face of a dedicated,
hardworking professional.[1] Luke Fildes's contemporary painting, *The Doctor*,
(reproduced on the cover) showed a more subtle blend of the GP's public
and private faces, which focused on personal feelings within a professional
encounter. In this artistic representation a GP could afford plentiful time for
a patient in the poorest family, so that a preoccupied doctor is shown gazing
with concern at a dying child, unable to save his patient despite his utmost
endeavours. This skilful blend of the authentic and the idealized appealed
both to the public, and to the GP's self-image.[2] The extent to which medical ideals and aspirations were constrained by therapeutic and economic realities was appreciated by contemporaries, as in Trollope's study of a
Barsetshire GP, *Dr Thorne* (1858), which the author considered was 'the most
popular book I have ever written'.[3] Literary representations of general practitioners produced by members of the medical profession themselves also
gave useful insights into public duties and private lives. A. J. Cronin, for
example, utilized his own experience as a young doctor in South Wales to
give, in *The Citadel* of 1937, a vivid picture of the hardships attached to a
young assistant's extensive duties in the Welsh valleys, as well as the personal
problems this caused.[4]

The lifestyles which doctors wished to live, as well as the interface between
public and private in the lives of doctors, were historically documented in the
sale advertisements of their practices which, whilst having a basis in reality,
also highlighted the kind of lives they wished to attain. Skilfully combining

---

[1] This was painted in 1888, and is reproduced in C. Wood, *Paradise Lost* (1988), 117.

[2] This painting of 1891 still adorns prominent positions in medical schools, while the American
Medical Association chose it for the postal stamp commemorating its centenary (V. Fildes, *Luke
Fildes, RA. A Victorian Painter* (1968)). Interestingly, GPs also chose to hang it in their waiting
rooms, as did Dr Harding in Faringdon.

[3] A. Trollope, *Dr Thorne* (World's Classics edn., Oxford, 1980)), pp. xi, 32.

[4] A. J. Cronin (1896–1981), studied medicine at Glasgow (MB, Ch.B., 1919), and first practised
in South Wales before moving to London.

utopian and practical elements in this ideal landscape were two Edwardian advertisements of attractive practices. The first was one for which many doctors would surely have applied, and the second would have attracted the small minority of practitioners with private income, where genteel lifestyle and leisure preferences could take precedence over financial needs:

S. Coast—Easily worked practice yields £900 a year. Beautiful country. Expenses light. Fees 2/6 to 10/6. Mild climate. Good society. Hunting and shooting. Plenty of scope for active man or a keen surgeon. Small hospital.

Cathedral City—Nice practice of about £450 a year. Unlimited scope. Good house, specially built, every modern convenience . . . Golf (10 minutes), tennis, boating, fishing, shooting, hunting and polo, all handy. No carriage required. Night work declined and midwifery discouraged . . . The house is situated in the best residential part.[5]

This was the ideal, but reality was not like this for many doctors, either in their public or their private lives.

From the point of view of doctors within specific communities, this chapter explores the kinds of pressures that were indicated in earlier discussion of the diversification of appointments which provided a very useful supplement to fee income in a competitive medical market.[6] The prosopographical or group biography approach which is adopted in this chapter is useful, in that it enables key factors to be investigated in individuals' lives, and gives enhanced visibility to the dynamics of career development within defined and evolving social environments.[7] In some contexts this was a struggle for survival but in others affluence and a desirable lifestyle resulted. Country, town and colliery practices have been selected for this kind of contextual discussion. These kinds of 'ecological niches' or 'medical habitats' within local communities might give the means to enable the doctor to survive or to prosper. The chapter also explores the conjunction of professional and private lives. In some contexts (or niches), the struggle for professional survival meant that private life was increasingly subsumed by public duties, but in others a greater affluence permitted a more desirable lifestyle for doctors and their families. A lynch pin between the public and the private was the doctor's house, which frequently served as both surgery and home, and within which the role of the doctor's wife was significant. The implications of making a medical living for the general practitioners' morbidity and mortality are later examined, as well as their connotations for retirement. The chapter ends with a reflection on the changing nature of the GP's values. Having sustained the heavy pressures of professional life before 1948, these appeared to later generations only as distinguishing (and dying) features of an 'old school' of practitioners.

[5] *BMJ Supplement*, 19 May and 2 Oct. 1909.   [6] See Ch. 4.
[7] L. Stone, 'Prosopography', *Daedalus*, 11 (1971).

Community Niches

Within an increasingly crowded medical market good prospects for professional survival were offered by the discovery and exploitation of local niches. Diversification of practices with adaptation to local environments were designed to ensure the survival of different species of practice. Key features here were assimilation to local circumstances, and manipulation of, or interaction with, central features of the community—as through social networking, and by appointments—in order to exploit its potential. This practice differentiation enabled a good 'fit' between practitioner and local community. The principle of territoriality operated by which—within these niches—doctors tried to monopolize as many professional openings as possible, and thus to keep out competitors from their practice area.[8] Especially during the Victorian and Edwardian eras general practitioners showed enterprise in developing the potential of their local environment by seeking out medically related appointments of varied kinds, and taking advantage of the new inventions of phone and car to extend the area within which they operated. Opportunistic strategies were dependent on the nature of the local communities in which doctors practised, and case studies within this chapter indicate their range and variety. To establish a reputation, and to foster the trust of local people through face-to-face contact in a range of activities was vital to professional success, and general practitioners worked hard to integrate themselves into community organizations and activities. Medical journals complacently recorded the growing social influence of medical men.[9] However, initiative in professional lives often imposed heavy duties on individuals, whilst skill or ingenuity in balancing personal and public obligations were less evident, so that penalties might accrue in private lives.

The contribution which general practitioners had made to their local societies through long service stimulated communities formally to recognize it by personal testimonials. More rarely the financial sacrifice made by the doctor through a life time's service (as in a country GP charging modest fees and sustaining a low income), was recognized by a retiring gift of a purse of sovereigns, a handsome cheque, or even by colliery patients having a levy taken from their wages to make a presentation.[10] More unusual recognition of a permanent nature was made when the doctor's portrait was hung in the local infirmary, or when a hospital ward was named after an individual.[11] Public bodies also recognized heroic exertion: for their dedicated service during cholera outbreaks GPs were given a gold watch or a silver snuff box by local

---

[8] Digby, *Making a Medical Living*, ch. 4 *passim*.

[9] For example, *Lancet*, 16 Mar. 1901, 797.

[10] *BMJ*, ii (1890), 1335–6; ii (1890), 251–2; i (1910), 607 and 1089–90; ii (1930), 983; i (1960), 353.

[11] J. H. Williams, *GPs of Barry, 1885–1979* (Barry Medical Society, 1979), 7; *BMJ*, i (1930), 671; ii (1950), 1063–4.

boards of guardians, or after a bad railway accident a handsome piece of plate was donated by railway directors.[12]

If fifty years of service or retirement marked important rites of passage in the doctor's relationship with the community, so too did the funeral of a beloved individual. 'We are here today lamenting the passing of "the Doctor", for as such he was known to all of us; he was a doctor *par excellence* who spent his life and himself without stint for those who he loved and willingly served.'[13] These words from the local vicar were said in 1940 of Dr Crawford of Swanley, Kent—but represented the kind of epitaph that many GPs had earned by a lifetime of devoted service. Professional encounters reflected the social composition of the local community: a doctor in a Yorkshire country town was consulted by operatives, farmers, clergy, and a few wealthy families; another in a rural Home Counties practice treated 'all classes from county families downwards', whilst a London doctor in suburban Clapham saw 'lower middle and better artisan class patients'.[14] That communities turned out to pay their last respects attested to the central role of the GP in local society. Dr Bucknill, for example, was a member of a family of GPs who had served the English Midlands town of Rugby for over a century, and who had himself acted as a GP for four decades. On his death over two thousand people gathered for his funeral procession.[15] And Dr G. A. Brown, who had been Chief Surgeon to the Tredegar Company's workmen, was laid to rest in Bedwellty churchyard:

amidst manifestations of profound grief, the long procession being headed by the police force and followed by representatives of the workmen, friendly societies, ministers, magistrates, county and district councillors, representatives of the South Wales and Monmouthshire Branch and Division of the British Medical Association, nurses of the union infirmary and cottage hospital and professional colleagues from all parts of the county.

That doctors were intimately involved *in* their community does not necessarily mean, however, that doctors were *of* the community, in the sense that their lives were closely integrated into all its social groups. The social landscape of Britain was fissured by differences in class, gender, and ethnicity. Barriers of language and lifestyle could militate against too close an identification of doctors with their local communities, in the sense of similitude, rather than through active leadership in communal activities. The type of practice, the class of patients, as well as the social background and aspiration of GPs themselves, determined the nature of the association. In the twentieth century particularly, more successful medical professionals marked their class distance from 'ordinary' people, so that the doctor's children might be sent away to be educated privately, rather than attending local state schools. The branch surgery in a working-class or mixed practice was usually some

[12] *BMJ*, ii (1881), 501; ii (1890), 252 and 110–11.   [13] *BMJ*, i (1940), 509–10.
[14] *BMJ Supplement*, 22 May, 21 Aug. and 11 Sept. 1909.   [15] *BMJ*, ii (1881), 1002.

geographical—and social—distance from the doctor's own house in a middle-class suburb. Professional dictates might conflict with personal needs, and these competing imperatives of inclusion and exclusion produced creative tension between the GP's public and private countenances. We turn first to the public world before later returning to the interface between public duties and private lives.

The range of appointments which *generational cohorts* of doctors cumulated has been explored earlier, and this economic individualism is investigated further in examining the distinctive medical habitats or environments that groups of GPs developed in contrasting *types* of practice. Heterogeneity of practice in upland and lowland, country and industrial, suburban and inner-city practices was conspicuous, but here we focus on three well-documented types of practice. Separating these practices into types necessarily involves some simplification, not only because there were mixed practices which possessed features of more than one practice type, but also because each individual practice within these general types was unique. Nevertheless, such analysis enables significant features to be highlighted of common ways in which doctors developed their practices through integrating themselves into key aspects of their local society, and furthered their careers by promoting new elements within it, thus attempting to ensure economic survival or prosperity.

Town Doctor

Both town and country doctors might have practices which were centred in urban settlements, but whereas the country doctor lived in a small town and travelled out to see patients over a wide rural hinterland, the town doctor lived in a larger community and practised mainly or entirely within an urban context. Office-holding proclivities, administrative capacity, not to speak of physical energy, were considerable professional assets for the town doctor. This kind of dedicated professional activism was clearly illustrated by the career and high public profile of Henry Aitchinson in the ship-building town of Wallsend on Tyne. His obituary is therefore worth quoting at length:

The death occurred suddenly of Dr Henry Hyslop Aitchinson of Wallsend on Tyne on January 17 at the age of eighty. Dr Aitchinson qualified at Edinburgh in the year 1880 as LRCP, LRCS, and graduated MB in 1881. He had been in active practice till the day of his death, in Wallsend for fifty-nine years, and his father, the late Dr James Aitchinson practised there before him. He had just been appointed deputy chairman of Northumberland Insurance Committee in Newcastle. A county magistrate and an ex-alderman, he was one of the first magistrates to sit on the Wallsend Bench, while for more than forty years he was vaccination officer for Wallsend, was medical officer to the Public Assistance Committee, and consulting surgeon to Wallsend and Willington Quay Infectious Diseases Hospital. Before the MOH was appointed he was in charge of the Wallsend and Willington Quay Infectious Diseases

Hospital. When the original Northumberland County Council was formed in 1889 Dr Aitchinson had the distinction of being a member; when he retired in 1930 he was the only remaining foundation member. Dr Aitchinson's other public duties included membership of the Wallsend Licensing Committee; he was a member of both Wallsend and Northumberland Probation Committees, and was at one time one of the visiting justices for the county under the Lunacy Act. He served as vice-chairman of Princess Mary Maternity Hospital in Newcastle, and of the Wallsend Infirmary and Maternity Hospital. Dr Aitchinson, a Presbyterian, was chairman of the management committee of Wallsend Presbyterian Church. Keenly interested in sport . . . He was president of the Wallsend Cricket Club and a foundation member of Wallsend Golf Club. He was also chairman of the Wallsend branch of the North of England Liberal Club.[16]

The range of non-medical attachments noted in his obituary was characteristic of Aitchinson's generation. English society in this period, in contrast to that of France, was rich in multiple membership of voluntary societies, so that the doctor's participation in many Wallsend associations was predictable.[17] And it may perhaps be inferred that the reason why Aitchinson was seldom merely a member, rather than an officeholder, was the result of being a middle-class professional in a predominantly working-class community. How far was the doctor narrowly instrumental in pursuing his career, and to what extent were many of his appointments the by-product of a convivial or multi-faceted personality? Unfortunately, the precise *motives* of Henry Aitchinson in cumulating such a range of appointments (as of other doctors in this chapter), is not documented, tentative inferences may be made, but much remains unresolved. In isolating appointments for analysis, it is possible that too instrumental an impression is given for what may well have come about naturally, and without much conscious forethought. The *effects* of such actions were, however, much more clearly discernible through their impact in advancing a professional career. Professional advantages would accrue to Aitchinson's practice from the changing public health, welfare, and maternity initiatives which occurred during his lifetime, and thus there were obvious advantages in holding infectious diseases, vaccination, public assistance, and maternity hospital appointments. Aitchinson's prominent non-medical offices, such as membership of the county council or of the magistracy, were likely to have given an indirect—rather than a direct—professional advantage, both through leading to a high public profile in the locality, and in the social networking with influential people, which would assist in the recruitment of affluent private patients, or facilitate nomination to other offices.

Starting shortly after Aitchinson had begun practice, this time in the east Midlands market town of Newark, was Dr Ernest Ringrose. Like Aitchinson,

    [16] *BMJ*, i (1940), 418.
    [17] J. Harris, *Private Lives, Public Spirit: A Social History of Britain, 1870–1914* (Oxford, 1993), 220.

Ringrose came from a medical family, being the fourth-generation of a medical dynasty. But this Newark practice was his own creation, rather than being based on earlier hard work by his family.[18] Starting from scratch during the late 1880s in a small town (of fourteen thousand people rising only to seventeen thousand by his retirement), a GP had perforce to be an active networker. Whereas in the larger world of Wallsend—within a wider hinterland of Newcastle—there were many institutions with appointments, a doctor in a small Midlands market town such as Newark, needed to be keen to spot an opportunity to develop acquaintance, and hence to expand the potential patient base of his practice.

Dr Ringrose was content slowly but steadily to further his participation in the town's institutions. Starting from scratch and without the advantage of name-recognition possessed by his northern contemporary, Ringrose operated more on the micro-level of the pluralistic institutions of urban civic society. He was active in a range of local groups: a keen churchman, school governor, chairman of a ward of the Unionist Party, president both of the Newark debating society and of the philatelic society, chairman of the Free Library, as well as being a captain in the volunteers, and a Vice-President of the British Legion. That this networking activity was successful is indicated by his eventual assimilation to the town's elite, manifested in his membership of the Newark bench, and the related chairmanship of the borough's juvenile court. Medically, he had an excellent reputation as an obstetrician, which was a sound basis for building up a successful family practice.[19] Ringrose was keen on both preventive and curative medicine having a high public profile in each sphere: giving lectures on health to his panel patients, and to other groups in the town; being particularly energetic as Surgeon and Lecturer in the St John Ambulance Brigade; and also campaigning for a Nottinghamshire Sanatorium. At the Newark Hospital long surgical service brought recognition and esteem. From the 1890s he closely observed activity in the wards, publishing his results in the *Lancet*. In 1903 he was appointed honorary surgeon, later was made a house surgeon, and in his final years in practice served as the hospital's vice-president. He had the unusual honour of having the new operating theatre named the Ringrose Theatre, before his retirement in 1939.[20]

Also retiring in that year was James Sinclair of Darlington who, like Ringrose, was sufficiently successful in the community to earn the distinction of having a hospital ward named after him.[21] Having a widowed mother and modest resources, Sinclair had to work his way through medical studies at Edinburgh, and was devoid of capital when he qualified in 1906. It took

[18] Ernest Ringrose, MD (Durham), MRCS (England), LRCP (London); publications in *Lancet* (4 Dec. 1897, 15 Oct. 1904), and *BMJ* (1910, 1673).
[19] See Ch. 8 for Ringrose's obstetrics.
[20] Nottinghamshire RO, DD 1440/26/3, scrapbook on Dr Ringrose.
[21] J. D. Sinclair, OBE, MRCS, LRCS (London, 1904).

another four years before he accumulated enough money to buy a practice in Darlington—a medium-sized, northern market and railway town. Visiting patients at first with a horse-drawn brougham, later a bicycle, he was sufficiently enterprising to be the first doctor in the town to buy a car, a single cylinder Wolseley. Saving time through faster transport meant more time with his patients, and one recollected that 'he never dashed in and hurried out, but he listened to what you had to say and always understood'. Sinclair's non-medical roles appear to have been more restricted than were Ringrose's, although he was President of the Rotary Club, as well as of the Aged People's Welfare Council, and was also active in the local Boy Scouts movement. Professionally, he was probably even more active in being President of the Red Cross in the town, an Officer Brother in St John Ambulance Brigade (taking ambulance classes for forty years), and Chairman of the Queen's Nursing Association. A Territorial before 1914, during the First World War he joined the Field Ambulance, was Honorary Anaesthetist and Radiologist at Greenbank Hospital, acted as MO to troops stationed in the town, and was in charge of the local Military Red Cross Hospital. For this energetic and high-profile war service he received wider public recognition through being awarded the OBE.

Sinclair's central medical interest was paediatrics. The doctor's obituarist in the *BMJ* was Dr Donald Robertson, who had been a childhood patient, and who remembered that 'the usual childhood ailments occasioned visits which were eagerly awaited for he had a wonderful way with a sick child.' Sinclair worked extremely hard to raise the funds to build a Children's Wing at Darlington Memorial Hospital. In a voluntaristic world this meant two years of energetic fund raising—of bring-and-buy sales, garden parties, competitions, sheepdog trials, as well as the proceeds of the railway's biennial Carnival—which successfully raised the £13,000 required. Revealingly, Sinclair told his wife that 'Darlington had been good to him and it behoved him to do what he could for Darlington'.[22] Deeper motivation in his calling came from his religion, for he was a staunch Presbyterian who lived by his faith. During the flu epidemic of 1918 he had the salutary experience (as had Mark Twain), of reading his own premature obituary in the local newspapers. Even after retirement his energy and commitment to the town enabled him to become a councillor for Cockerton Ward, and to serve for two years as the town's Deputy Mayor.

Beginning professional life in the increasingly overcrowded medical world of the late nineteenth and early twentieth centuries meant that Aitchinson, Ringrose and Sinclair needed energy, dedication and good fortune to succeed. Overall similarity in career profile, but a less obviously diverse counterpoint of activity, revealed how they cultivated ecological niches by exploiting, and benefiting from, the pluralistic life of urban communities. In contrast to the

---

[22] National Library of Scotland, Accn. 10334, no. 5, 'The Doctor on the Town.' Memoir of Dr James Donald Sinclair.

strategies available to the town doctor in seeking local appointments or the membership of local societies in order to gain a high community profile, rural doctors' tasks were both easier (in that they were immediately noticeable), but more taxing (in that chameleon-like they needed to take on local colour, and be assimilated into country life.)

Country Doctor[23]

An expert assimilationist was the country doctor, Dr D. A. Davies of Tregaron in Cardiganshire, west Wales. 'His was a life of service to the community as much as to the individual. . . . Be it funeral or carnival, eisteddfod or gymanfa, clinical meeting or prayer meeting' he would attend.[24] Other doctors had a comparable individual record but, in addition, came from families where successive generations of doctors had laid down roots and grown to be an integral part of their neighbourhoods. The Eminson family practised for four generations in Scotter in north Lincolnshire, amongst a scattered population in hamlets and farmsteads. Robert Eminson was the founder of the practice, obtaining a local appointment under the New Poor Law in the 1830s, and practising for the next fifty-six years, until cut down in an epidemic of pleuropneumonia. His grandson, T. B. F. Eminson joined the family general practice, and also practised for over half a century.

To drive with him on his long country rounds was an education in itself, as he seemed to know the names of every plant, bird and bush, one came across, and would discourse learnedly on any of them. Living among an intelligent race of farmers, he interested himself much in folk-lore and in the early history of his county. Later in life he took up the study of local place names. . . .[25]

In North Wales the personal flamboyance of the Denbigh doctor, Evan Pierce (1808–95) stood out from the understated general breed of North Wales country doctors, although displaying many typical characteristics as well.[26] Although Pierce was in mid-career by 1850 it is relevant to look at his earlier career in order to evaluate the kind of medicine he had developed. Pierce's earliest day book for 1833–6 has survived. Having served as an apprentice to practitioners in Denbigh, he studied in Edinburgh, London and Paris, then assisted Dr Mackintosh in Edinburgh during the cholera outbreak, before returning to Denbigh in time to deal with cholera cases there. This was an auspicious beginning in establishing a local reputation, which served to further what soon became a flourishing practice with patients drawn from near and far. His practice penetrated most social parts of the community—principally artisans, craftsmen, and traders—with poor-law contracts in

---

[23] See Chs. 5 and 8 for financial and clinical aspects of English country practice, and Chs. 9 and 12 for doctors in the Highlands and Islands.

[24] *BMJ*, iv (1970), 59.   [25] *BMJ*, i (1890), 1466; i (1940), 714.

[26] Evan Pierce, LSA (London, 1836), LRCS (1836, Edinburgh), LFPS (Glasgow, 1836) MD (1844, St Andrews) FRCS (1870, Edinburgh).

addition. Pierce thus quickly established a social and clinical practice that was general in character. The energetic young doctor travelled up to a radius of seven miles, and it was said of him that 'few men fitted a horse better across country, whether riding to hounds, or as a short-cut to his patient's bedside'. His accounting was as vigorous as were his medical treatments, as appears from the occasional comment beside the accounts, such as 'settled the above every farthing', or 'darn bad d[ebt]'—in the case of a rare unpaid account.[27] Pierce had a good eye for the market opportunity, and after the Denbigh Asylum was established in 1848, he diversified his medical concerns by developing (with a partner) the near-by fifteen-bed Salisbury Hall Retreat and Sanatorium. This was a place where 'men of good position desirous of overcoming habits of intemperance and of indulgence in narcotic drugs' could be treated. In line with the sporting interests of both doctors and patients, was the provision of stables, where patients could keep their own hunters.[28]

The doctor's vigour was directed beyond his practice to the local community where a high public profile ensued. Not only was he a member of the Town Council for almost half a century, but he served for five years as Mayor of Denbigh from 1866 to 1870. More mundane offices such as Captain of the Denbigh Fire Brigade were also held. He built a house for the Wesleyan minister at a cost of a thousand pounds, and gave two thousand pounds for a Memorial Hall dedicated to his mother's memory. Pierce was also prominent in acrimonious debates about public-health measures in the town.[29] He also achieved wider fame as the Coroner for North Denbighshire from 1848 to 1895. That Pierce continued to hold the Crown appointment of coroner into advanced old age (despite modest remuneration) suggests his continued liking for public position and influence.

Evan Pierce conducted the inquest into the crash of the Irish Mail in 1868, when a train travelling between Holyhead and Chester collided with wagons containing paraffin, and caused the deaths of thirty-three people. Dr Pierce, with twenty years of experience as a coroner under his belt, adopted a pragmatic approach. This was the subject of public controversy, with relatives of the victims vocal in their criticisms of him, but others, such as the *Morning Star*, thinking his behaviour characterized by 'wisdom, firmness and moderation.'[30] As Coroner for North Denbighshire, Pierce's Entry Book suggests a rather laid-back approach to his responsibilities; in more than two out of five cases he decided that 'Inquest not deemed necessary.' There were few medical explanations provided with any precision; such entries included 'probably heart disease', 'natural causes (pneumonia)', 'died from excessive

[27] National Library of Wales, MS 197033, day book of Dr Evan Pierce, 1833–6; 'Portrait of Evan Pierce, MD', *Provincial Medical Journal*, January, xii (1893); W.A. Evans, 'Dr Evan Pierce of Denbigh', *Transactions of the Denbighshire Historical Society*, 15 (1966), 158–68.

[28] Clwyd RO (Ruthin) DD/DM/266/32, Salisbury Hall Retreat and Sanitorium.

[29] Ibid., BD/A/567, removal of nuisances and protection against the Cholera, Jan. 1854.

[30] National Library of Wales, MS 19704, press cuttings on the Irish Mail Disaster.

drinking', or 'starvation from exposure'. Two in every five fatalities coming to his attention were accidents where the cause (frequently drink) and outcome were obvious: individuals were crushed in quarries, drowned, burned, or killed by horses, trains, and even by an omnibus. Almost one in ten deaths were deemed to have been suicides, and a handful were stated to have died by 'visitation of God'. No doubt general practitioners have seen many human predicaments in their professional lives, but serving as a coroner must surely extend the range, as in cases of children who had been worried to death by ferrets. [31]

Evan Pierce extended the usual sporting interests of the country practitioner to run his own pack of hounds, hunting with them twice weekly for fifteen years. Another arresting and unusual feature was his talent for self-publicity. He had a 72 ft. high limestone column erected in his honour, and that whilst he was still alive. The column was allegedly subscribed to by his grateful Denbigh patients, although local sceptics wondered whether he had paid for it himself!

North Wales doctors, of whom Pierce was an intriguing example, were a robust breed of stalwarts. A later portrait indicated that 'These men [sic] knew their patients, their personal and family history, their idiosyncrasies, their weakness and their strength. They were in return trusted, respected and revered.' This thumbnail sketch of a Welsh country doctor could have stood for the ideal rural doctor, wherever he or she practised. A country doctor needed to show initiative in all aspects of practice, but more particularly in the clinical sphere. A caesarean performed in a lonely farmhouse, or a child's neck opened with a penknife because choking for air during diphtheria, were some of the more heroic exploits of Edwardian hill practice in North Wales. Physical resilience was also needed since practices covered a far-flung hinterland, and most doctors still used horses. Attending confinements could therefore mean absence from home for up to twelve hours at a time. Henry Morris Jones, who had practised in North Wales, recollected—perhaps with some gilding of memory—what he saw as the quintessential characteristics of the Welsh country doctor. 'Sympathy with suffering, tenderness in dealing with the sick, imagination, tact, quickness of perception, and the power to recognise what others feel.'[32]

Comparable experiences were found amongst country doctors in Lowland Scotland. Dr David Huskie could well have been the model for Heywood Hardy's portrait of 'Duty' in so far as he had a practice area that stretched 23 miles into Selkirkshire, 20 miles into Peebleshire, and 23 miles into Lanarkshire. Beginning practice in Moffat in 1891, he recollected—in an address to colleagues over forty years later—that:

---

[31] Ibid., 19702E, coroner's entry book for North Denbighshire, 1874–95, kept by Dr Evan Pierce; Evans, 'Dr Evan Pierce of Denbigh', 62–4.

[32] H. Morris Jones, 'The Country Doctors of Fifty Years Ago', *Country Quest*, Autumn 1961, 22.

It has been a hard and strenuous life, and for years I seldom got to my bed on the same day that I left it; and frequently two or three nights in the week I never got to bed at all—arriving home only in time to have a bath and breakfast and start my rounds again . . . Still the life had its compensations. They were a kindly and grateful folk to work amongst, and very many of them staunch and loyal friends.[33]

Making friends included communication through acquiring dialect words. The doctor came to know that mumps was 'the branks' and whooping cough 'the kink-host', whilst parts of the body were similarly described in terms known to the local community but not at first to the Edinburgh-trained doctor, so that he learned that the stomach was 'the wame', and the tonsils 'the paps of the hass'.[34] When he had given the people of Moffat half a century of service, and came to retire, the community paid its 'tributes of affection and regard'. Amusing stories were told of patient–doctor encounters, the doctor's loud but comforting laugh was frequently mentioned, as was his disinterestedness and dedicated hard work. Responding to these eulogies Huskie said that:

He had now been at it for 52 years. At his old university of Edinburgh it had been impressed upon him that his first duty was self-effacement; his work in the first place was to relieve suffering, the first thing was the good of his patients, and [he was] at all times to keep himself in the background and to keep in touch with progress in his profession. He had tried to carry out these ideals to the best of his ability.[35]

Forty years after Huskie had begun his work as a Scottish country GP, Dr J. Richard, a prize-winning graduate of Glasgow University, began a single-handed country practice in the royal burgh of Stranraer.[36] He recorded that 'the people of Stranraer had a gift of hospitality and kindness to strangers', but that it definitely helped his practice that he was familiar both with local pedigrees and dialect, so that he was accepted as 'one of themselves'. Friendly relationships between Stranraer's practitioners also assisted work in the town, as in developing complementary surgical skills, or in raising money to extend the local Garrick Hospital.[37] The communitarian ethos of patient–doctor relationships in those pre-NHS years was congenial to this country doctor:

The poorer people of this area got the same crack of the whip as the more comfortably off. I think this has always been traditional in rural Scotland, and the purely commercial aspect of practice so appallingly evident in the cities did not enter to anything like the same extent. The old days were not nearly as bad as they are now represented to have been. I think the new [National] Health Service has destroyed something in the relationship of a doctor to his patient. I am happy to have been one of the 'old school.' One did the work first and at a later date hoped to Heaven that

---

[33] D. Huskie, 'Impressions and Experiences of a Country Doctor in the 'Nineties and After', *Transactions of the Medico-Chirurgical Society of Edinburgh* (1938), 12. (D. Huskie, MA, MB, FRCP Ed., died 1943).

[34] Huskie, 'Impressions', 4.   [35] *Moffat News*, 8 Aug. 1940.

[36] J. Richard (1904–83), OBE, MB, CHB (*BMJ*, 26 Nov. 1983).

[37] Id., unpublished 'Autobiography', 32–4.

enough patients would pay to keep one in bread and butter and maybe a bit of jam now and again.[38]

Colliery Doctor

Even more than rural communities, colliery ones were close-knit societies.[39] Doctors in mining areas, therefore had a particularly close relationship with the local community, even to the extent that Dr T. McFetridge of Edlington, near Doncaster, was reputed to have had a 'kind word for every child and a pat for every dog'.[40] Yet discussion of colliery practices contrasted with the golden haze which enveloped so much writing about country practice, and particularly towards the latter part of the period there was a distinctly greyer, grittier tone.[41] Colliery practice was the specialism of a small minority of general practitioners, so that there were many fewer mining than rural doctors. However, the two types of practice were not necessarily distinct. The Davies dynasty of colliery doctors had been founded in the eighteenth century by Welsh practitioners who combined doctoring with an agricultural calling, but had taken on a mining character when Evan Davies (1801–50) became medical officer to the first colliery in the Rhondda, and later attracted more than local fame with Henry Naunton Davies.

After graduating from Guys in 1854, Naunton Davies practised in Porth for the whole of his working life. In the course of this he became surgeon to eleven local collieries and works. The doctor was a foundation stone of the community—serving as Medical Officer of Health, Factory Surgeon, Public Vaccinator, Justice of the Peace, County Alderman, as well as becoming a founder of Porth Cottage Hospital. His example seems to have acted as an inspiration to his family, and by the interwar period there were twenty-seven members of the Davies clan in medical practice within the region.[42] This symbiosis between medical families and mining communities was also found with the smaller Armstrong medical dynasty. This included J. N. Armstrong and his younger brother, Fergus, who served successively as Surgeons to the Park and Dare Collieries at Cwmpare in the Rhondda.[43] The elder brother who won his appointment against 143 other applicants, went on to become parish doctor and vaccinator, surgeon-captain in the local volunteers, and brigade surgeon in the St John Ambulance Brigade. On his death the miners

[38] Ibid., 36.
[39] R. Church, *The History of the British Coal Industry, volume 3, 1830–1913 Victorian Pre-eminence* (Oxford, 1986), 283, 287, 292.
[40] *BMJ*, i (1930), 475. T. McFetridge, MB, Ch.B. (Edinburgh) also had a special interest in ambulance work.
[41] See Chs. 8 and 9 for the clinical side, as well as patient encounters of the colliery practice of the Cresswells, and Ch. 5 for financial aspects of two North Wales industrial and colliery practices.
[42] N. N. Davies, 'Two and a Half Centuries of Medical Practice. A Welsh Medical Dynasty', in J. Cule (ed.), *Wales and Medicine. An Historical Survey* (Cardiff, 1975), 217–20.
[43] J. N. Armstrong, MB and CM (Edinburgh, 1892); F. Armstrong, MB, Ch.B. (Edinburgh, 1909), MD, FRCS.

elected as his successor his brother Fergus, then running a practice in adjacent Ton Pentre.[44]

Naunton Davies's earlier career suggests that the colliery doctor might be bonded to the local community as much (or more), by stormy than by fair-weather days. He led a team of nine doctors at Tynewald Colliery Disaster after an extensive rock fall had resulted in heavy loss of life. Those long and agonizing nine days in April 1877, when four men and a boy were rescued by a team of doctors may well have brought them nearer to the hearts of the mining community than previous long years of doctoring. Such medical care was in any case a very active pursuit, because the South Wales coal mining industry had relatively high morbidity and mortality statistics, partly because of geological factors implicated in roof falls, but also because of a bad rate of accidents, and a comparatively high incidence of lung disease.[45] In this context local people had high regard for their doctor, as was shown by the illuminated address presented to a colleague, Dr Reidy of Llanbadrach, by 500 subscribers. Surrounded by hand-painted pictures of the doctor attending injured men underground, it read 'Assiduous attention to the call of duty and your readiness and fitness at all times and hours to respond to that call have secured to you the lasting confidence and gratitude of the community.'[46]

Colliery appointments could be combined with other responsibilities in the local economy—usually with industrial or railway appointments. In Mexborough, on the South Yorkshire Coalfield, John Gardner combined a partnership in a busy colliery practice with an appointment with the Great Northern Railway.[47] Table 10.1 indicates that dual appointments within industrialized areas were not uncommon, including doctors who were surgeon to more than one colliery. Other doctors in colliery districts were active in attempting to rebuild the community during the socially difficult interwar years, as did Francis Grant in Jarrow, on the Durham-Northumberland coal-field by helping to develop sporting facilities for the community.[48] Other contemporaries had similar concerns but focused more on the implications this had for health and sickness, as did Dr D. Elliot Dickson of Fife, with his interest in the 'morbid collier', or Dr MacFeat in Lanarkshire with the Miners Rehabilitation Centre.[49]

Dysfunctional elements were more conspicuous in later colliery practice, as the comfortable niches established earlier were disturbed by fractious social relationships in some areas. Contact between doctors' organizations and those of organized labour became embittered in South Wales and in Scotland, which might complicate the individual doctor's involvement with his community. Locally and nationally organized medicine was determined not to

[44] A. D. Morris, 'Two Colliery Doctors. The Brothers Armstrong of Treorchy', in Cule (ed.), *Wales and Medicine*, 209–11.

[45] Church, *Victorian Pre-eminence*, 588–9, 591–2.

[46] Mid-Glamorgan RO, D/D X 543/1, illuminated address to William Augustus Reidy, 1902.

[47] *BMJ*, i (1930), 844.   [48] *BMJ*, ii (1950), 1121.

[49] *BMJ*, ii (1940), 101; i (1960), 651.

TABLE 10.1. Colliery, railway, and industrial appointments, 1820–1939 (% of cohort)

Period when cohort qualified	1820–39	1840–59	1860–79	1880–99	1900–19	1920–39
Colliery Surgeon (coal mining)	—	1	2	4	1	—
Other quarries, works and mines	—	—	1	1	—	—
Railway or Canal Surgeon	4	1	2	3	1	1
Factory Surgeon	2	13	9	7	8	8
Individuals employed in collieries, quarries, works factories, rail or canal	6	15	20	19	12	10
N	53	103	138	243	234	168

Source: GP database

allow a 'cheapening of the medical service', so that the BMA opposed 'fixed salaries and control by [miners'] committees', and discussed 'ostracising medical men, who did not fall into line'. Glossing sectional occupational interests with wider social concerns, the BMA in South Wales declared that this type of conduct was 'not in the best interests of the public or the profession'.[50] In an almost continuous series of disputes during the first decade of the twentieth-century doctors who did not adhere to the professionally agreed position in their terms of appointment with miners in colliery schemes (as well as with railwaymen) were threatened with expulsion and professional blackballing.[51] Organized labour attempted forcefully, but ultimately unsuccessfully because of unexpected medical solidarity, to prohibit 'their' doctors from private practice (as in the Abergwynfi Colliery in 1905),[52] to try to reduce agreed rates of medical remuneration (as at Ammanford in 1907),[53] or to force doctors to set up additional branch surgeries (as in the Llanelli railwaymen dispute in 1907).[54] In the Ebbw Vale disputes of 1906–11 references to colleagues as 'blacklegs', or the expulsion of individuals from the BMA, indicated the bitterly contested nature of conflict with organized labour.[55] The BMA's expulsions, together with a blacklisting of appointments, suggests the professional 'can of worms' which these disputes had opened in the valleys of South Wales in the years immediately preceding the introduction of the NHI scheme.

[50] Mid-Glamorgan RO, D/D South Wales BMA Branch minute book, 1896–1908, minutes 28 Sept. 1904, 7 July and 1 Sept. 1905.
[51] Ibid., Monmouthshire BMA Division minutes, 1903–1914.
[52] Ibid., South Wales BMA Branch minutes, 18 Dec. 1905.   [53] Ibid., 21 Feb. 1907.
[54] National Library of Wales, BMA Collection of South Wales and Monmouthshire, newspaper cuttings.
[55] Mid-Glamorgan RO, S. Wales BMA Branch minutes, 13 Dec. 1906, 11 Apr. 1907.

In certain mining areas problems continued to bedevil relationships between doctors and important sections of their local communities even after 1911. In Scotland the militant Lanarkshire Practitioners Union was founded in 1913 to resist 'unfair encroachments' on their rights and interests.[56] With the largest membership on the Collieries and Public Work Surgeons Committee (Scotland), Lanarkshire stimulated medical militancy elsewhere, and provided leadership in confrontational meetings with the Miners Federation of Scotland. There were two main areas of dispute. The first concerned the terms under which the Medical Colliery Scheme operated with issues in contention such as remuneration for attendance at accidents, fees for examining members of rescue brigades, or the charges for certificates and reports in compensation cases.[57] The second set of arguments centred on the terms on which doctors would treat miners' dependants who were excluded from the scheme. Doctors wanted an increase in the flat rate fee, differential midwifery fees, and payment for the certification of school children's illness.[58] It is impossible to assess how much the abrasive nature of these collective confrontations led to a deterioration in an individual doctor's relationship with patients in miner's families, but an overly mercenary stance by doctors traditionally had led to loss of respect.

Not that colliery practice did not have a more positive side. Colliery doctors were pioneers in ambulance work and helped train miners to provide immediate first aid in this kind of situation. James Adamson, Surgeon to Hetton-le-Hole and North Hetton Collieries, for example, was a pioneer of ambulance work in County Durham, beginning the first course in 1877. A later keen ambulance man at Hetton-le-Hole was Dr MacLeod who lectured on ambulance work at Elemore colliery for thirty years.[59] And the Cornish doctor, William Blackwood, was 'horrified at the lack of facilities for dealing with injured tin miners' in the early twentieth century, so that he founded the Camborne St John Ambulance Division, and 'devoted an immense amount of time and work to the teaching of first aid'.[60] A Church Parade of the doctor with members in their uniforms might also highlight the importance of St John Ambulance activities to the colliery village, as at Blidworth in Nottinghamshire.[61]

This prosopographical (group biography) approach has been useful in highlighting similarities and differences between, and within, different kinds of practice. When the profile of prominent characteristics in these three sorts

---

[56] Glasgow Health Board Archives, HB 76, Lanarkshire Medical Practitioners Union minute, 19 Mar. 1913.

[57] Glasgow Health Board Archives, HB 76, 25 Nov. 1914.

[58] Ibid., 12 Mar., 15 June and 31 Dec. 1913, 28 June 1916.

[59] *BMJ*, i (1920), 313. J. Adamson, LRCS and LM (Edinburgh), MD (Glasgow); *BMJ*, ii (1950), 171, R. Macleod, MB, Ch.B. (Glasgow).

[60] *BMJ*, i (1960), 672. W. Blackwood, DSO, MBE, MB, Ch.B. (Edinburgh).

[61] Harding, 'Memoirs', 35. Involvement in ambulance work was by no means confined to the colliery doctor; the proportion of the GP database involved rose from one in ten to one in six.

of practices—town, country, and colliery—is considered then key differences emerge. In colliery practice driven professional lifestyles were the rule, unless an assistant was employed to take off some of the pressure.[62] A low leisure preference and pressurized work led to greater risks of ill-health, premature death, or early retirement. While the doctor was a very well-known figure in the mining community, relationships with varied interest groups may have been narrower, because of the importance of collectively negotiated medical agreements with collieries or works. Like their mining counterparts, successful town doctors experienced high workloads, low leisure preference but higher income. They could also be exposed to the same risk of ill-health from over-work. A greater distancing of work from home through the utilization of branch surgeries was increasingly likely. Offsetting this, however, was the town doctor's close involvement in community activities. The country doctor's public and private life was more closely integrated than was the case with either the mining or town practitioner; there was a higher leisure preference with time for sporting interests, gardening, and involvement in varied community activities. In country practices especially, but also for urban ones, there was considerable involvement by the doctor's wife in professionally-related activities. Running professional life from home also brought the doctor's children into intimate contact with medical vicissitudes. The relationship between public duties and private lives was therefore a close one.

Public/Private Lives

The connection between public and private in many practices was the doctor's wife. Women's contribution to Victorian family fortunes was substantial,[63] and that of the wives of doctors was no exception.[64] Jane, the wife of a Merioneth surgeon, Owen Richards, left an illuminating—if brief—account of her role in a country practice during the early 1850s. In the small communities of Bala and Llandderfel where her husband practised, her piety, public service and face-to-face encounters with her neighbours were a professional asset to her husband's medical work. She helped to create a high social profile which then enhanced public reputation and trust in 'the' doctor. Jane Richards's charitable activities were conspicuous; from collecting for the clothing club, through selling coal to the poor at substandard prices, helping at the workhouse, or buying blankets for the poor.[65] At home her housewifery was also important in cumulating assets (keeping honey bees, gardening, selling butter, making pies and sausages from the family pigs), and

---

[62] F. Maylett Smith, *The Surgery at Aberffrwd* (Hythe, 1981), 162.
[63] L. Davidoff and C. Hall, *Family Fortunes* (1987).   [64] See Ch. 6.
[65] National Library of Wales, MS 7519B, memoranda and diaries of Richards of Bala, Merioneth, entries 24 and 26 Dec. 1851. Jane Richards (1803–52), was daughter of Reverend Richard Lloyd of Beaumaris, and 'beloved wife' of Owen Richards, according to her Llanyed churchyard memorial.

in minimizing expenditures (through careful marketing, skilful housewifery, and incessant making and mending). Jane Richards also involved herself in the accounts of the practice. She recorded variously that a patient 'took tea and paid his account', and that another had 'sent a hobbet of oatmeal instead of his old balance' of account.[66] The custom of local doctors was to receive instalments on patients' accounts, so Jane's activities as collector and book-keeper were essential to the practice's viability.[67] And, if her husband fell sick, she nursed him back to health;[68] a function also performed by later medical wives, often at some cost to themselves.[69] Jane thus contributed very positively to making a family medical living.

Varied wifely activities could provide a crucial element in the success or failure of a practice. The wife of an unsuccessful practitioner might have to make a direct financial input into the household finances, in order to ensure professional survival. For example, William Cook's wife, Harriet, had always to supplement inadequate medical income with her own earnings as a successful journalist and writer.[70] A wife chosen from an elite family might strengthen the practice socially or financially.[71] Spouses could also make a valuable contribution through helping to manage the organization of the practice. Thus Mrs Mackinnon was said to be 'a very great help to him [Dr Mackinnon] in the business side of his practice'.[72] What was the nature of this kind of help? Mrs Ceely, wife of one of the partners in an Aylesbury practice, corresponded with new assistants in the practice, and wrote encouragingly to Alexander Blyth that 'There is full occupation, but I think I may tell you nothing that an active and intelligent young surgeon cannot actively accomplish.'[73] And Mrs Broughton, wife of a Gloucestershire GP undertook correspondence dealing with the sale of her husband's practice in 1884. Although for the most part she wrote formally as an intermediary between her husband and the purchaser, there is a revealing slippage in key sentences, such as 'unless we are paid', which suggests a more powerful female presence in the practice.[74]

[66] National Library of Wales, NLW, MS 7519B, Memoranda and diaries of Jane Richards of Merioneth, entries 11 Oct. and 19 Nov. 1851. The hobbet was a north Wales measure of two and a half bushels, and for oats amounted to £105. I am grateful to Professor Rees Davies for this elucidation.

[67] Ibid., MS 14135B, patient's ledger of Dr Owen of Llanbedr, Merioneth (1834–54), folios 351, 364, 377.

[68] Ibid., MS 7519B, 26–8 Nov. 1851. Jane's husband, Owen Richards (1813–86), LSA (1834, Barts); FRCS (Eng,. 1848), MD (Aberdeen, 1852) later became a JP for Merionethshire.

[69] *BMJ*, i (1960), 971; i (1960), 883–4; ii (1970), 609. Mrs Locket nursed her husband so devotedly in his terminal illness that she wore herself out, went down with pneumonia, and died two days before he did (*BMJ*, ii (1930), 984).

[70] W. D. Foster, 'The Finances of a Victorian General Practitioner', *Proceedings of the Royal Society of Medicine*, 66 (1973), 12–16.

[71] *BMJ*, i (1890), 272. Dr Pyle (1837–1890), married the eldest daughter of Sir George Elliot, Bart., MP.

[72] *BMJ*, i (1960), 1666.

[73] Bucks RO box 5, diary of A. W. Blyth, letter of Mrs E. P. Ceely to A. W. Blyth.

[74] Archer, *Village Doctor*, 20–1.

Until oral testimony the everyday activities of the doctor's wife were largely hidden from historical view, although rare glimpses emerge, such as the wife who always got up to make her husband a cup of tea when he was called out at night.[75] In the years preceding the NHS a daughter recollected her mother helping with her father's Faringdon practice, by acting as a part-time receptionist, telephonist, and secretary in the practice. In addition she acted like an assistant book-keeper in helping Dr Harding to transfer entries in the day book to the ledger every evening, and also sending out the bills periodically. Like many wives of busy professional men 'she made life very smooth for him domestically, looked after the children, looked after the house'.[76] Mrs Hendry, another GP's wife at this time, recollected that:

If you married a doctor in those days, it was quite *infra dig* for a doctor's wife to work, because a doctor's wife had to be 'on call' in the house. A doctor's house, a GP doctor's house, in those days was never left empty, so that it was 24 hours a day that you could call and ask the doctor to visit . . .[77]

Other wives were messengers for cases needing urgent attention, arranged the visiting list, or filed correspondence and records.[78] Clinically, they might act as informal gatekeepers, as able 'spot' clinicians for the less important ailment (more particularly if they had been nurses before marriage), as practice nurses doing bandaging or other simple surgical procedures, as wrappers of medicine bottles, or as dispensers. Sometimes the dispensing was amateur, in other cases the wife had trained and did this professionally, as did Mrs Granger in Kimbolton.[79]

For the mid-twentieth century period when maids were no longer available—but support staff had not yet been recruited—the life of the GP's wife was especially pressured because of the range of duties she performed. In competitive practice situations, doctors' wives were deployed to make calls on newcomers to the neighbourhood, effectively—if surreptitiously—'touting' for patients for their husband's practices.[80] Less contentiously, they could be engaged in public relations, as in paying courtesy visits to the wives of neighbouring doctors, or in supporting community activities. Wives were thus both marital and professional helpmeets, so that in a 'single-handed' practice she would effectively be a 'partner' in all but name. Occasionally, she might also act as research assistant in a clinical investigation, as did Gertie Pickles.[81] By 1948 the contribution of the wife was acknowledged financially in some practices, as when the wives of four partners in a Nuneaton practice, were each

---

[75] CMAC, GP 23/5, recollections of the wife of G.E. Hale, who practised in Eton from 1893 to 1905.

[76] Pers. comm., Mrs Sue Pope, daughter of Dr and Mrs Harding.

[77] Pers. comm., Mrs Emma Hendry of Nuneaton, wife of Duncan William Hendry, qualified Glasgow, 1922.

[78] *BMJ Supplement*, 26 Sept. 1953, 702.　　　[79] Pers. comm., Dr and Mrs A. Granger.

[80] J. E. Rankine, *150 Years in a Country Practice* (Romsey, 1982), 15.

[81] W. Pickles, *Epidemiology in Country Practice* (RCGP edn., 1984), preface.

paid £100 annually.[82] After the death of the doctor, his wife might perform a final service in memorializing her late husband by compiling memoirs or scrapbooks, as did Mrs Sinclair above. In contrast, the husbands of medical women seem seldom to have taken an active part in the practice, although occasionally their professional skills were deployed, as in the case of one who was an accountant and did the books of the practice.[83] In some practices the supportive role usually taken by a wife for a doctor-husband might be adopted by another female member of the family—a sister for a bachelor brother, or a daughter for a widowed father.[84] A well-founded estimate from the 1960s was that wives and other relatives contributed some five million pounds through their services.[85]

The doctor's house was usually both home and surgery so that the doctor's family necessarily shared in the life of the practice. From nights disturbed by the speaking tube connecting the front door to the bedroom, to days punctuated by patients' calls, the doctor's spouse and children were all too conscious that the term 'family doctor' had a second, more basic meaning. Particularly between the 1880s and the 1960s (that is between the demise of apprenticeship and the availability of government funding for auxiliary staff, and an increase in specialist premises away from the doctor's residence), the spouse assumed a central importance in contributing to the viability of the practice. The Hadfield Survey, conducted on behalf of the British Medical Association shortly after the inception of the NHS, found that more than eight out of ten wives helped their husbands in their practice to 'at least a moderate extent', whilst one in five 'took a considerable part in the administration of the practice'.[86] The survey's report commented sympathetically that '[The] wife has a considerable burden to bear.'[87] The typical doctor's wife played such an active role because in many practices there was no team of ancillary staff. She helped to manage the practice, yet her contribution was almost inevitably characterized by short-term, *ad hoc* improvisation, rather than being informed by a longer-term, more strategic vision.

Yet to focus solely on medical activity would be to give only a partial view of the lifestyles of general practitioners and their families. Some doctors lived only for their work having little time for hobbies, but others had well-developed leisure interests. Typically, the rural GP (having a less pressurized professional life), could participate in country pursuits; usually angling or shooting, but also hunting for some, and for others gardening or natural history. Wherever they practised growing numbers of doctors played golf. Some

[82] Private archive of Mrs E. Hendry, Receipts and Patients Acounts for Drs Forrest, Macdonald, Hendry, Bleakley, 1947–9.

[83] R. L. Bensusan-Butt, MB (1904), BS (1905), MD (1908). This marriage ended in divorce.

[84] *BMJ*, i (1910), 729; ii (1910), 1292; i (1940), 997.

[85] L. Dopson, *The Changing Scene in General Practice* (1971), 89.

[86] *BMJ Supplement*, 26 Sept. 1953, 141. These figures came from a field survey, and higher figures from an earlier postal survey have been disregarded as being likely to have been less accurate.

[87] *BMJ Supplement*, 26 Sept. 1953, 685.

Scottish doctors went in for curling. Sporting activity was perhaps a more conspicuous diversion from professional duties than were cerebral pastimes, although bridge was a popular leisure pursuit, and music, painting, or poetry were also widely enjoyed. Some practitioners had intriguing combinations of hobbies, as did Dr Clendon. 'Outside his work his main interests were in his home, photography, church architecture, caravanning, genealogy, literature and local history.'[88] Those who had a rounded lifestyle, with well-developed hobbies, were in the group who welcomed retirement, as did Dr Court, who retired on the morning of his sixtieth birthday so that he could devote himself to archaeology, angling and shooting.[89] But many more, however, were like Dr Crawford whose 'daily work [was] his sole hobby'.[90] Some who found complete fulfilment in their work managed to sustain this. The aptly named Dr W. Joy did not take a single day's holiday in fifty-five years of practice, for he considered that 'the pursuit of his profession furnished him with all the recreation he needed', and D. H. Stirling, also practised for fifty-five years, with 'a heavy burden of duty, which he always regarded as a pleasure'.[91] For others with less stalwart constitutions, this kind of unbalanced lifestyle was likely to have had repercussions on health, and on mortality.

Sickness, Retirement, Death

The Berwick doctor, George Johnston, recorded on reaching his fiftieth birthday 'advancing years lessen the love of labour, what was once recreation is now taken up with reluctance'. Three years later he wrote that 'I do not bear a doctor's business as well as I was wont.' Four years later he was forced through ill-health to take six months off work, and the following year he suffered a fatal stroke.[92] Robert Woods has done a valuable study of medical morbidity and mortality from 1860 to 1911 which highlighted the poor life chances of doctors. He concluded that until the second decade of the twentieth century, doctors suffered significant excess mortality, and general practitioners had a worse record in this respect than their colleagues who were physicians or surgeons. In terms of life expectancy, Fellows of the Royal College of Surgeons or of Physicians had a 74 per cent chance of what was possible, compared to only 65 per cent for the medical profession as a whole. The latter would be made up of large numbers of general practitioners, so that GPs had only a partial life expectancy. It was also estimated that GPs had two or three weeks annual loss of work through sickness at the start of their careers, an amount rising steeply after the age of 55. These are

[88] *BMJ*, iii (1970), 350–1. [89] *BMJ*, ii (1960), 1813.
[90] *BMJ*, i (1940), 509–10. [91] *BMJ*, ii (1880), 34; ii (1910), 1292.
[92] G. A. C. Binnie, 'Dr George Johnston, 1797–1855', in *Medicine in Northumbria* (Pybus Society, Newcastle-on-Tyne, 1993) George Johnston, LRCS (Edinburgh), MD (Edinburgh, 1819); FRCSE (Edinburgh, 1824).

sobering findings, and Woods concluded that 'general practice certainly was a dangerous trade'.[93] My study has indicated the professional pressures experienced by general practitioners, emphasizing that they were particularly intense during these years.

Death could occur as a direct result of medical activity, more especially in the middle part of the period, when part-time public health responsibilities were common. For example, one doctor contracted a fatal attack of scarlet fever whilst working at an Isolation Hospital, another succumbed to septic peritonitis after treating the septicaemia of a child patient at a Fever Hospital, and a colleague also died from septicaemia after conducting a post-mortem.[94] Work-related sickness was another hazard. There is a nice vignette of a Crewe doctor chasing a delirious smallpox patient who had escaped from isolation; the patient died of pneumonia, and the doctor caught smallpox, but was serenaded for his heroism by the town band playing under the window of his sick-room.[95] On a more mundane level the amount of visiting which doctors—especially country doctors—did in all weathers, made it predictable that many would suffer adverse consequences. The mid-nineteenth-century diaries of Dr Freer of Donington, in Lincolnshire show clearly this cause and effect, as when he minuted that he had got wet on horseback, this had then led to a fever, and that he had responded with self-medication.[96] Doctors usually privileged their patients' illnesses above their own, and hence might suffer accordingly, as when Dr Lavies saw a patient whilst suffering from a severe chill, contracted pneumonia, and died.[97] Jane Richards recorded a typical episode where her husband's health was damaged because of professional commitment:

November 16, 1851. Mr Richards ill with an attack of erysipelas in the face. He went out in the evening to see a patient and was very ill for several hours . . .

November 27 Rather better in the morning but the erysipelas was spreading until checked with caustic.

November 28 Mr Richards better—spent the day upstairs with him knitting and sewing.[98]

That a doctor's community also suffered the consequences of doctor's overwork in poor health, and/or early death is amply documented in obituaries.[99] One such notice spoke feelingly of Dr Aymer, who had been 'absorbed in his profession, and unsparing of himself', and of the town of Bervie in Kincardineshire along with the large surrounding district which, in conse-

[93] R. Woods, 'Physician Heal Thyself; the Health and Mortality of Victorian Doctors', *SHM*, 9 (1996), 9, 24–30.

[94] *BMJ*, i (1910), 484, 1208, and 1582.　　　　　　　　　　　　　　[95] *BMJ*, i (1940), 324.

[96] Lincolnshire RO, Misc 88/1–3, diaries of Dr Freer of Donington (1845–57), entries 14 and 16 Oct. 1846.

[97] *BMJ*, i (1900), 614.

[98] National Library of Wales, NLW, MS 7519B, memoranda and diaries of Richards family.

[99] *BMJ*, ii (1890), 988; i (1920), 523–4; i (1960), 1666.

quence of his sudden death, had 'suffered a severe loss'.[100] Amongst GPs who were 'over-workers' serious, sometimes fatal, attacks of influenza or pneumonia were not uncommon penalties.[101]

For cohorts of doctors who had war-time service, the injuries incurred might lead to chronic disabilities in general practice.[102] Service on the Home Front might also exact a physical toll, since particularly for elderly doctors, managing an understaffed practice with unprecedentedly large numbers of patients, caused strain. During the Second World War, especially, when to this kind of practice overload was added duty such as ARP casualty work, running a first aid post, acting as a part-time hospital anaesthetist, or working in an emergency hospital service, prolonged overwork resulted in illness, premature retirement or death.[103]

It was not only physical 'insults' that doctors cumulated, but also mental ones. Both as patients and as practitioners Victorian doctors featured prominently in analyses of male professionals, where prevalence of pecuniary anxiety and constant overwork allegedly had led to nervous exhaustion, depression, or breakdown. Predictably, in view of the then prevalent 'overwork and worry' interpretation, the BMA was informed in 1885 that one in every ten neurasthenic patients was a medical man.[104] The vulnerability of the professional to depression, as well as to suicide, was well-attested. Indeed, Victorian medics came fourth amongst all occupational groups in their tendency to suicide, with poison (from readily available drugs) the most common method employed.[105] Two of the doctors in the GP database committed suicide during depression: one from a fatal dose of morphia, the other through cutting his own throat.[106] Overstrain, a high rate of nervous disease, and a high suicide rate were attributed at the turn of the century to professional overcrowding.[107] Addiction to drugs or alcohol, then as now, was another not inconsiderable problem.[108] Hard drinking in practices in south Wales was conspicuous, and one doctor there was renowned for keeping his whisky bottle in a bottle marked 'POISON'.[109] Those so afflicted were not easy to assist, as was illustrated by the doctor—ruined by drink and drugs—who ended up, bereft of friends, in the Peebles Poorhouse.[110]

[100] *BMJ*, ii (1900), 961.   [101] *BMJ*, ii (1920), 874; ii (1930), 126; i (1940), 465.

[102] *BMJ*, i (1970), 242; iv (1970), 59.

[103] *BMJ*, i (1920), 588; i (1950), 1438; i (1970), 243.

[104] J. Oppenheim, '*Shattered Nerves*'. *Doctors, Patients and Depression in Victorian England* (Oxford, 1991), 153–5.

[105] O. Anderson, *Suicide in Victorian and Edwardian England* (Oxford, 1987), 70, 95, 419; Woods, 'Physician', 21.

[106] *BMJ*, ii (1881), 920; i (1890), 929.

[107] W. Gordon, 'The Overcrowding of the Medical Profession', *BMJ*, 16 May 1903, 1152–3.

[108] Woods, 'Physician', 17; V. Berridge and G. Edwards, *Opium and the People. Opiate Use in Nineteenth-Century England* (1981), 34. The Academy of the Medical Royal Colleges estimated that 15 per cent of present-day doctors had a drink or drug problem (*Independent*, 28 Jan. 1998).

[109] CMAC, GP 29/2/66, Walter Shaw.

[110] C. B. Gunn, *Lessons from the Life of a Country Doctor* (Edinburgh, 1947), 172.

The Hippocratic Oath's proscription of 'seduction' indicated awareness of another potential hazard in medical life. Within the restrictive, moralistic outlook of the late nineteenth and early twentieth centuries, professional self-censorship usually maintained a discreet public silence on this kind of issue, although a few cases of 'infamous conduct' involving sexual impropriety came before the General Medical Council. Although it did not issue any guidance on this issue until as late as 1914, the GMC held its first inquiry into sexual impropriety in 1863. During these early years there were a few cases where infamous conduct was proved: one in 1874 of a doctor's indecent assault on the 21-year-old housekeeper of a patient; a case of sodomy in 1877; and another in 1883 where a doctor committed adultery with a patient's wife.[111] That sexual advances might also be initiated by patients was not necessarily recognized by GPs. 'It was one of the surprises of the survey to find that most of the GPs visited were not at all concerned about being chaperoned when examining female patients . . . the occasional widely publicised case is a warning that the GP can take these risks too lightly.'[112] But that sexual activity, as opposed to attraction, between doctors and their patients concerned a small minority (even during a sexually more liberated era), was suggested in a recent survey.[113]

Some other risks in professional life included illness, accident, and consequent loss of earnings and these resulted in local societies being created (such as the West Riding Medical Charitable Society of 1828), as well as in more spontaneous gestures of medical benevolence. For example, when R. H. Cowan of Wigan died in 1900 his medical colleagues elected not to compete for any of the valuable colliery appointments he had held, so as to enhance the value of his practice (which presumably was up for sale), and so help his widow and children.[114] In 1884 the Medical Sickness Annuity and Life Assurance Society was formed on a national basis in order to help tide doctors over such ill-fortune. Interestingly, more assurance policies against accident than sickness were sold. As the *BMJ* suggested a decade later:

At all hours of the day and night the country practitioner is liable to be called upon to mount his horse or get into his trap and go along country lanes and roads as fast as he can. He is very often alone, and is liable to be thrown from his horse, or perhaps worse still, from his trap . . . and in a minute the country practitioner finds himself in much greater need of medical aid than most of those who send him night summonses.[115]

[111] R. Smith, 'The Development of Guidance for Medical Practitioners by the General Medical Council', *MH*, 33 (1993), 58–63.

[112] S. Taylor, *Good General Practice* (Oxford, 1954), 294–5.

[113] Although one-third of British doctors admitted to having been attracted to their patients, only 6 per cent had had sexual affairs with them (*Sunday Times*, 18 Jan. 1998, reporting on a nation wide survey in the *Doctor*).

[114] *BMJ*, ii (1900), 1222.

[115] Quoted in G.J. Knapman, *Care for the Caring. Medical Sickness Annuity and Life Assurance Society Limited, 1884–1984* (1984), 74.

Later, spills from bicycles, or fractures from starting up cars were also common accidents. But, as so often, people—not to speak of professional organizations—are poor judges of risks, and it is revealing that more claims for sickness than for accident were actually received by this society. Its membership, although growing steadily, represented only a small fraction of the medical profession.[116] Medical benevolent societies to some extent filled the gap.

They had been created to help those practitioners or their families whom illness, misfortune or old age had afflicted, leaving them uncovered by insurance, and with insufficient independent resources. For example, the Ladies Guild of the Medical Benevolent Fund at Glasgow gave grants of £20 per annum each to a doctor's widow left with five children, and to a doctor's daughter who had looked after her father to a very advanced age. They assisted in the case of a doctor dying with TB, and gave his widow a yearly grant, as well as help in moving to a smaller house. The organization's assistance embraced school or college fees for children, money for holiday or Christmas expenditure, parcels of clothes, grants for coal, and liaison with other charitable agencies in order to get additional resources.[117] The absolute dependence of some doctors' families on grants from medical benevolent societies such as these is well illustrated from the letter written by the wife of a doctor incapacitated by a stroke. She asked the Essex and Hertfordshire Benevolent Medical Society 'would it be troubling you too much to let us know what is decided. We feel miserably anxious.' Two years later she wrote effusively giving 'my most sincere thanks for the grant of £50 received this morning', and of 'your very great kindness in this matter which means so much to me'. That the wife was doing the correspondence was explained by her remark that 'his head is so affected that he cannot take any responsibility, he is as helpless as a child as regards any independent action'.[118]

The economic situation of many practices—where earnings were insufficient even to bridge the practitioner over a temporary period—reduced the numbers financially able to retire. Table 10.2 indicates that amongst general practitioners in the GP dataset fewer than half retired. Many of these did so only very shortly before death, and/or because they were so handicapped—by failing physique, defective hearing or imperfect eyesight—that professional life had become impossible.[119] That so many had an interval in retirement after professional life is an unexpected finding, given that the census did not distinguish between occupied and retired members of the

---

[116] Knapman, *Care for the Caring*, 28, 75.

[117] Royal College of Physicians and Surgeons of Glasgow, 16/2/6, Account book of beneficiaries of the Ladies Guild of the Medical Benevolent Fund, Glasgow, entries for Mrs Elizabeth McDonald, Miss Drysdale, and Dr and Mrs Jeffrey.

[118] Essex RO (Chelmsford), D/2 15/12, Colchester District Court of the Benevolent Medical Society of Essex and Hertfordshire (1909–19), letters from Clara Ivens, 23 June 1916 and 18 July 1918.

[119] *BMJ*, i (1930), 888; i (1950), 910.

medical profession until 1931, and that William Ogle (Statistical Superintendent of the General Register Office) had earlier indicated that being a general practitioner was generally for life.[120] In the years leading up to retirement fear of financial hardship, and a personal philosophy that saw professional activity as life itself, often led to problems, as professional capability dwindled after a lifetime of public duty. Responses varied. For the prudent the answer was a younger assistant recruited 'with a view to partnership', who could gradually take over the work of the practice, and whose share of practice assets grew in step with this. For the less well-organized doctor, a gradual running down of the practice happened imperceptibly, and without adequate economic safeguards. An elderly practitioner was stated in an advertisement of the sale of his practice to have 'taken matters very easily of late years', whilst another read 'Present income is over £600, but has been over £1,000 a year. There is ample scope for increase as, owing to age, the vendor has not pushed work in the last few years.'[121]

TABLE 10.2. Outcomes in later professional life, 1820–1939 (%)

Period when cohort qualified	1820–39	1840–59	1860–79	1880–99	1900–19	1920–39
Retired	47	46	29	40	50	46
Semi-retired	4	5	4	5	3	6
Death 'in harness'	38	42	62	46	38	46
Outcome unknown	11	7	5	9	9	2
N	53	103	138	243	234	168

Note: Members of the cohort of 1860–79 stayed in practice longer, because the economic pressures—arising from the greatly expanded numbers in medical practice—made retirement difficult if not impossible. Later generations benefited from the 1911 act.

Source: GP database

In contrast, some doctors were blessed with, if not boundless energy, at least sufficient professional vitality to desire to continue in practice to an advanced age. Seeing their role as a calling or vocation, rather than a mere job, they were loath to relinquish the occupational purpose that provided the central meaning in their lives. The physical topography of a home, which was also a workplace also buttressed this sentiment, by making it more difficult to withdraw from professional activity. So too did the fragmented set of responsibilities of the general practitioner, where appointments, and discrete sets of patients associated with them, meant that responsibilities could be gradually reduced to match dwindling physical energy, but where some part of a professional presence could long be preserved.

[120] W. Ogle, 'Statistics of Mortality in the Medical Profession', *Medico-Chirurgical Transactions*, 69 (1886), 222.
[121] *BMJ Supplement*, 12 Aug. 1899, 5 June 1909.

In this situation, although retired from full-time service in general practice, GPs were enabled to keep on part of their professional activities, typically retaining private patients but giving up some of their other professional
roles. In his semi-retirement Dr James Goodfellow, for instance, had duties
which were described as being 'only a little less after his retirement'.[122]
Another general practitioner, Dr W. D. Wright, was said to have 'retired
from general practice at the age of 80, but even after that was always willing
to take the occasional surgery or to make himself generally medically useful'.[123] A small minority (about one in twenty), continued to operate in this
manner until culled by Death the Reaper. A few were more adventurous and,
like Dr McGlashan of Guildford, developed a second career. He became a
ship's surgeon:

On one of his recent voyages a member of crew developed an acute appendix. They
were far from land. Should he give morphia and wait? Or should he send an SOS to
another ship? McGlashan had not touched a scalpel for twenty-five years but he
boiled up his instruments and got a voluntary anaesthetist and nurse. He operated,
saved his man and nursed him through a subsequent attack of pneumonia to complete recovery; almost at the cost of his own life, for his own exertions brought on
an anginal attack, and when the ship reached port it was the patient who walked
ashore, while the surgeon was carried off the ship on a stretcher![124]

'He died, as he wished, in full harness.'[125] As a result of this attitude a
small minority of GPs worked into their eighties: one of this resolute band
being 'greatly disappointed' when illness forced him to retire at the age of 87,
whilst another octogenarian was still conducting surgical operations.[126] The
frequent outcome of this philosophy—that one worked until one dropped—
was that cardiovascular conditions abruptly terminated lives. Thus, Dr
Gordon, who had 'worked hard and played hard', was said to have 'died of
the "doctor's complaint", angina pectoris'; Dr Lasnick survived two attacks
of coronary disease, but succumbed to the third, still professionally active;
and Dr Brien paid the ultimate penalty for professional misdiagnosis since,
in mistaking his own angina pectoris for rheumatic pain, he died in rushing
upstairs to fetch the day's visiting list.[127] Table 10.2 shows that a very sizeable proportion of doctors, varying from two- to three-fifths, literally dropped
down dead in the course of their work. Like Dr Brien they were still harnessed to the duties of a professional lifetime.

Conclusion

European commentators viewed medical professional life as relatively unattractive, as did Charton in 1851: 'There are few professions which demand

[122] BMJ, i (1950), 1145.   [123] BMJ, iv, (1970), 753.   [124] BMJ, i (1940), 509.
[125] BMJ, i (1920), 421.   [126] BMJ, ii (1930), 1067; ii (1900), 1472.
[127] BMJ, ii (1950), 51; i (1970), 825; ii (1910), 1895.

. . . such unremitting application, such complete sacrifice from day to day.'
He went on to say perceptively that the doctor 'is always at the command of
others, he does not belong to himself.'[128] The standard *BMJ* obituary phrase
'failing health compelled him to retire'[129] is indicative of comparably self-
denying attitudes in Britain during the period with which this volume is concerned.

A significant shift in the GP's own perceptions of a desirable lifestyle
evolved after the NHS. By the 1960s and 1970s doctors who had served
before the NHS were viewed critically by some of their successors, because
they saw their work as the absolute goal in life. A man who had qualified in
1907 was described as 'A GP of the *old school*, he was completely absorbed
in his work, and possessed a strong sense of duty',[130] whilst another, who had
qualified in 1925 was held to be 'almost defiantly proud of belonging to the
old school of general practitioners, which for him meant unlimited hours of
work, instant availability, and much moral and occasional surreptitious financial support to all the patients'[131] (my italics in both quotations). This change
in professional viewpoint developed gradually, being both cause and effect of
a number of key organizational changes in general practice including: a mid-
century growth in partnerships, the adoption from the 1950s of appointment
systems and the holding of fewer surgeries (which relieved the unremitting
demands of patients on the doctor); a growth in purpose-built premises from
the late 1960s (which enabled a physical separation of home from work); and
an accompanying increase in ancillary support staff (which freed the doctor's
spouse from a commitment to the practice that might be almost as great as
that of the doctor). All contributed to the development of a new, private
space, so that it was no longer the case that public duties were almost invariably prioritized over personal satisfactions—the doctor might 'belong to himself or herself' for part of the time at least. Underlying and informing this
slightly more relaxed lifestyle was a more stable public funding of primary
medical care, and a more secure role for the generalist relative to other members of the health care professions.

---

[128] E. Charton, *Dictionnaire des Professions* (2nd edn., Paris, 1851), 389–90.
[129] *BMJ*, ii (1970), 243.   [130] *BMJ*, i (1960), 1817.   [131] *BMJ*, ii (1970), 487.

11

Generalists, Specialists, and Others

WITHIN a wider medical world inter- and intra-professional disputes over medical terrain meant that the role of GPs, indeed their survival in a very competitive situation, became problematic. The GP was threatened by an expanding municipal health sector spearheaded by Medical Officers of Health, an increasing takeover of childbirth by midwives, and permeable, shifting boundaries relative to the specialist. Would the evolving division of labour leave the generalist in a contracting, residual position as was happening in some other countries? Alternatively, would the growing practice of referral stabilize the relationship of generalists and specialists?

A favourable, if patronizing, verdict on the generalist, was delivered by a distinguished specialist, Sir Clifford Allbutt:

His university was . . . nature; in his clinical experience he enriched the instruction, half empirical, half dogmatic, of his medical school by the shrewd, observant, self-reliant, resourceful qualities of the naturalist. His science, and practice were of the naturalist, not of the biologist. In my early days a country drive with such a doctor used to be one of the rewards of the consultant; and a bedside talk with him a lesson in quickness of wit and hand, and of instructive inference and prognosis; his rules of thumb were not without their efficacy, and his flair for the issues of disease marvellous.[1]

With the benefit of hindsight we can see that 1920, the date of this comment, marked something of a professional high point for the general practitioner, when previous integration into an expanded range of local medical services and institutions was still relatively unchallenged. Thereafter, the multiple roles of the generalist were increasingly threatened by: the growing speed of medical specialization, and with it the difficulty of keeping up-to-date or of buying expensive equipment; the financial insecurities of small local hospitals which earlier had provided opportunities to bridge the generalist/specialist divide; and the successful take-over of professional territory by rival practitioners. Compensating alternative opportunities for preventive or health work in health centres or municipal clinics were not viewed enthusiastically by most GPs. In failing to adopt a pro-active role 'the "all-rounder" of medical practice' was therefore left 'apprehensive of his fate'.[2]

[1] BMA, *Presidential Address* (1920).   [2] *BMJ Supplement*, 26 Sept. 1953, 132.

Why then had practitioners chosen general practice as a career at about the time when the NHS came into being? Oral testimony tells us about an individual's motivation in becoming a GP: 'As far back as I can remember, I'd always wanted to be a doctor. I don't know why'; 'just something I wanted to do', or 'never actively thought of anything else'.[3] These kind of deeply held, yet unreflective, statements were typical. On occasion a personal experience of sickness whilst young might impel someone into a medical career.[4] Or career aspiration could be related to the fact that a parent or other relative was a GP so that it just seemed an entirely natural process to grow up to be this kind of doctor. However, this personal imperative might conflict with parental views, more particularly if the aspirant was a woman:

I've come from a medical family. My father was a doctor, his father was a doctor, and his mother was a doctor's daughter . . . [but] Father didn't want me to be a doctor, because he said it was too hard. . . . when the War came . . . women came into their own, they did quite a bit replacing men . . . And then Father said if I really wanted to do medicine I could.[5]

In recalling the reasons for going into general practice, doctors illuminated the central importance of the personal element in their work. 'I don't like suffering.'[6] 'I liked people, and people interested me, and I wanted to help.'[7] The GP is 'a good listener, and compassionate', and a 'bit of a social worker too'.[8] Medical training might clarify this essentially humanitarian aim into a more specific professional objective, by developing a clear ideal of the personalized, holistic medicine an individual might wish to pursue in general practice, which contrasted with the narrow, and more impersonal nature of specialist medicine they had encountered in hospital or consultant medicine during their training. 'Being a general practitioner, being a whole doctor' was the objective.[9] Some also saw the variety in this occupation as being important, 'it combined study with practical work'.[10] For others general practice was less a matter of ability or of motivation than of economics: 'It seemed to be the sensible thing.'[11] Advisers took much the same realistic line. A headmaster advised that for a boy of moderate academic talents general practice gave a good income, whilst a north country GP gave some idea of what 'good' meant in this context. He counselled 'if you'd be satisfied with quite a good income, about a thousand a year', then general practice was the right opening.[12]

[3] CMAC, GP 29/2/22, Jack Ridgwick, MRCS Eng, LRCP (London, 1946); CMAC, GP/29/2/27, John Evans, MA (Cantab), MRCS Eng, LRCP, London, 1946, practised in Doncaster.

[4] Ibid., GP 29/2/20, Margaret Hallinan, MRCS Eng, LRCP (London, 1944); CMAC, GP/29/2/6, Margaret Norton, MB, CB (Birmingham, 1939).

[5] Ibid., GP 29/2/50, Kathleen Norton, MA, Oxford 1926, BM, 1926, MRCS Eng, LRCP (London, 1925).

[6] Ibid., GP 29/2/36, Emanuel Tuckman, MB, BS, 1944, MD, 1963.

[7] Ibid., GP 29/2/59, Samuel Isaacs.   [8] Ibid., GP 29/2/62, Margarete Samuel.

[9] Ibid., GP 29/2/48, Bertie Dover, qualified Liverpool, 1945.

[10] W. Robinson, *Sidelights on the Life of a Wearside Surgeon* (Gateshead, 1939), 17.

[11] CMAC, GP 29/2/37, Hilda Cantrell, MB, Ch.B. (Liverpool, 1923).

[12] Pers. comm., Dr Ashworth of Manchester, born 1921, qualified 1944 in Manchester.

Lord Moran's later dictum that GPs were those who had fallen off the ladder on the way to become consultants was well known to later cohorts of doctors.[13] Most who became GPs rejected the view in personal terms, but recognized that it reflected the low status in which general practice was held within the medical profession at that time. Teachers in medical schools were not themselves generalists but specialists, and they held an almost universally low opinion of general practice. One GP remembers being told by his specialist teacher in a Manchester medical school that it was 'diagnostically destitute and therapeutically sterile'.[14] Another reflected that 'general practice was considered to be a failure, you know, the drop outs went into general practice, in those days'. 'If you were top quality, you . . . became a consultant, you did hospital work.'[15] 'That general practice is, in itself, a speciality, and that you need proper training for it, as you would be trained to do consultant medicine, [that] you need to be trained in general practice, this is a comparatively modern view of general practice.'[16] It was one that the BMA wanted to foster during the early years of the NHS.[17] This was itself one indication of the continuously evolving structure of the medical profession, and of a changing balance during the century before the NHS between generalist and specialist/consultant.

There are several meanings given to the practice of consultancy. A doctor may call in colleagues in consultation in order to get a second opinion in a problematical case. Or a post may be prefixed by the term consulting, as in a consulting physician or a consulting surgeon; a title marking both the esteem in which the individual is held (usually towards the very end of a distinguished career), and of the part-time or occasional nature of the services to be expected from the position. Finally, the term 'consultant' was used for a specialist in a particular branch of medicine, and it is in this usage with which this chapter is concerned.

Generalists and Specialists

Although some have seen a new and divided professional structure based on a clearly defined difference between GP and consultant occurring even before 1850,[18] it is more accurately seen as a phenomenon confined mainly to London, where a small minority practised as specialists.[19] Indeed, the

[13] RC on Doctors' and Dentists' Remuneration (HMSO, 1958), QQ1220 and 1025.

[14] Pers. comm., Dr Ashworth.

[15] CMAC, GP 29/2/26, Norman Paros, MB, BS, London, 1946; ibid., GP 29/2/34, Jean Hugh-Jones.

[16] Ibid., GP 29/2/22, Jack Ridgwick.   [17] BMJ Supplement, 26 Sept. 1953, 140.

[18] I. Waddington, 'General Practitioners and Consultants in Early Nineteenth Century England: the Sociology of an Intra-Professional Conflict', in J. Woodward and D. Richards (eds.), Health Care and Popular Medicine in Nineteenth-Century England (1977), 164.

[19] Loudon, Medical Care and the General Practitioner, 188.

prejudice against specialism as an undesirable and inferior aspect of medicine continued into the early twentieth century.[20] During the second half of the nineteenth century consultants were found in a growing number of large provincial towns and cities, although it is important to appreciate that the demarcation between general practitioner and consultant remained far from clear cut.[21] Surgeons and physicians in Victorian voluntary hospitals saw it as desirable to be generalists rather than specialists within the institution, although they might also act as a general practitioner to a few elite families outside its walls. In defining the nature of a Victorian doctor's practice there were a number of grey areas, so that in marginal cases it is problematic whether to classify a doctor as a GP or a consultant. As late as 1937 an authoritative *Report* commented that specialist and consultant 'have no standard technical application'.[22]

This uncertain and unstable historical situation led to intra-professional disputes. Unlike the situation in the legal profession—where the distinctive respective roles of barrister and solicitor are legally and functionally defined—the ill-defined roles of generalist and specialist/consultant made conflict almost inevitable. Percival's enormously influential *Medical Ethics* of 1803 had focused mainly on this issue of intra-professional demarcation and, within this context, on the etiquette of professional behaviour.[23] Despite Percival's carefully enunciated ideals economic competition for patients meant that friction continued between general practitioners and consultants.[24] Indeed, in 1866 GPs formed an association to defend themselves against what they perceived to be the poaching of patients by consultants. This situation was considered to be especially bad in London, where consultants were found in greatest abundance.[25] But consultants themselves felt aggrieved, and made accusations of self-interest against general practitioners for failing to refer patients to consultants sufficiently quickly.[26] An indication that no *modus vivendi* had been reached was shown by the BMA's committee of inquiry in 1908. Interestingly, the committee was asked to report on whether a special class of practitioners should be recognized as consultants, who would be distinguished by treating patients only in cooperation with other practitioners.[27] Later, during the interwar period, there was a tendency by patients to refer

[20] Digby, *Medical Living*, 20.

[21] H. Marland, *Medicine and Society in Wakefield and Huddersfield, 1780–1870* (Cambridge, 1987), 274.

[22] PEP, *Report on the British Health Services* (1937), 159.

[23] Percival was concerned particularly with consultation in the sense of a second practitioner being called in (by the patient or someone acting on his or her behalf), to advise in special circumstances. This issue continued to exercise the profession (Digby, *Medical Living*, 59–61; E. M. Little, *History of the British Medical Association, 1832–1932* (1932), 293).

[24] J. Y. Simpson, 'On the Duties of Young Physicians', in *Physicians and Physic* (Edinburgh, 1851), 37; P. B. Granville (ed.), *Autobiography of A.B. Granville* (2 vols., 1874), 125; I. Waddington, 'The Development of Medical Ethics—A Sociological Analysis', *MH*, 19 (1975), 36–51.

[25] *BMJ*, 19 May 1886.

[26] *BMJ*, 10 Jan. 1866; *BMJ Supplement* (1910), 304, 323–6.   [27] Little, *History of BMA*, 292.

themselves straight to the specialist, without the intermediary of the family doctor. This indicated a growing public esteem for specialist relative to generalist, that was also evident in municipalities which opened specialist clinics.[28]

This suggests that by then the issue of referral had become the key issue. Earlier, general practitioners in London had been vexed by an enormous growth in out-patient attendance at hospitals during the second half of the nineteenth century. British GPs (like their American contemporaries),[29] had convinced themselves that this expansion of free treatment was harming their practices, not least because they considered (probably with little foundation), that many people were fraudulently claiming to be poor, and eligible for treatment, when they could perfectly well pay a GP for help. Only a very small percentage of these cases had been referred to the hospital consultant by general practitioners themselves, but the idea that medical referral should be the basis of admittance at first operated mainly in London, and gained growing support from the 1890s. This gave added security to the GP's livelihood.[30] Referral of patients by a general practitioner to a hospital specialist was a very important factor in giving British GPs a status and importance in medical care not enjoyed by those in the USA. 'The physician and surgeon retained the hospital, but the general practitioner retained the patient.'[31]

The economic condition of general practitioners continued to be a powerful influence on professional practice and attitude. After 1911 the NHI system of capitation payments, rather than payment per item of service, tended to discourage specialism amongst rank-and-file GPs. Patient numbers in a mixed public and private practice situation were now sufficiently large to generate an income which permitted doctors to survive financially as generalists. Part-time specialism amongst general practitioners was inhibited in Britain to a greater extent than in either the USA or in Germany where a breed of generalist with specialist interests was encouraged. In the USA doctors had access to a proportionately larger number of hospital beds for their patients, and in Germany an insurance system provided fees for each item of service.[32] It was not the case, however, that specialism amongst interwar British general practitioners was entirely absent. Specialism occurred, particularly amongst more ambitious individuals (usually among those who did not have an insurance practice), and this might lead to a consultancy practice.[33]

An interesting discussion on the definition of a specialist was put forward by the BMA in *Proposals for a General Medical Service for the Nation* of 1930.

[28] PEP, *Report*, 160.

[29] T. Goebel, 'American Medicine and the "Organizational Synthesis": Chicago Physicians and the Business of Medicine, 1900–1920', *BHM*, 68 (1994), 656–7.

[30] I. Loudon, 'Historical Importance of Outpatients', *BMJ*, i (1978), 3, 7–9. Except for St Thomas's Hospital, GP referrals were 6 per cent or less.

[31] R. Stevens, *Medical Practice in Modern England* (New Haven, 1966), 33.

[32] F. Honigsbaum, *The Division in British Medicine* (New York, 1979), 124, 304–7.

[33] Stevens, *Medical Practice*, 148–9.

Here a doctor's claim to specialist rank rested on three criteria. Special skill or experience was acquired either by hospital or similar appointment, or through special academic or postgraduate study. Alternatively, other practitioners in the area gave a general recognition to special proficiency and experience. The PEP *Report* of 1937, which summarized the BMA proposals went on to describe how a GP might, through length of experience or some other factor, gain a sufficient local reputation to be called in for consultation, and in some cases 'confines himself entirely to "consultation" work'. If this related to a particular part of the body, the *Report* continued, then the doctor might be called by the public, 'a specialist', or act as one on the staff of the local hospital.[34] The professional difference perceived between generalists and specialist was institutionalized in separate BMA committees during this decade.[35]

By 1939 there was a ratio of one consultant to six or seven GPs . The consultant was able to command a higher fee: in 1878 this was two guineas—one for the consultation, and one for writing the letter—and sixty years later it was three guineas.[36] Rewards for successful consultants could be great, as had been the case with the City of London consultant, William Coulson, who in 1877 had left an estate worth £110,000.[37] In 1938–9 average incomes of consultants were typically twice that of general practitioners—£2,000 compared to £1,000, although there was a very wide scatter of net incomes in both groups. But whereas fewer than ten per cent of GPs had a net income of £2,000 or more, nearly half the specialists were in this category.[38] Within the profession the status of the GP was also lower than that of the consultant. James Mackenzie, an icon of modern GPs, and one of the minority who had made the transition between the two, wrote revealingly in a private letter of 'the drudgery' of general practice, and referred to consultancy as 'higher things'.[39] His own late transition to specialist at first proved difficult, not least because of the elitist attitudes of London consultants, who found it difficult to credit that an ex-provincial GP had anything much to offer clinically.[40]

It was only over a considerable length of time that a mutually advantageous professional network developed between consultants and GPs. Consultants became more reliant on GP referrals than upon cultivating individual

[34] PEP, *Report*, 159.   [35] Honigsbaum, *Division*, 148–9.

[36] Stevens, *Medical Practice*, 56–7; Honigsbaum, *Division*, 124; PEP, *Report on the British Health Services* (1937) 160; *BMJ*, i (1878), 111.

[37] D. I. Williams, 'William Coulson: Victorian Virtues Handsomely Rewarded', *Journal of Medical Biography*, 2 (1994), 135–6.

[38] B. Hill, 'The Doctor's Pay and Day', *Journal of the Royal Statistical Society*, cxiv (1951), 30. The returns came from three-quarters of the consultants and specialists practising in 1938–9 and surviving until the post-war period when the statistics were compiled. See also *Report of the Inter-Departmental Committee on the Remuneration of Consultants and Specialists*, [Spens] PP, 1947–8, xi, for whom the figures were compiled.

[39] Letter of Dec. 1904 to his brother, Will, quoted in A. Mair, *Sir James Mackenzie* (1973), 191.

[40] Mair, *Mackenzie*, 241.

patients.[41] By the mid-twentieth century there was an expectation that young doctors who had been trained in the consultant's 'firm' would later send their patients needing specialist treatment to their old mentor. Thus links between the teaching hospital and the local community of general practitioners were maintained or strengthened. Contact between erstwhile students and the civic universities of northern England seem to have been particularly resilient, and this was a function both of local recruitment as well as of the strongly region-alized nature of later practice there. It contrasted with a situation in London or Edinburgh Universities where recruitment of students was on a national or, indeed, international basis, and consequent practice locations were corre-spondingly geographically far-flung.

In 1948 consultants were given a privileged status not least because Bevan saw them as essential to his aim of creating a public image of the NHS as a first class service. Consultants were allowed to practise privately under part-time contracts which had advantageous financial terms. The pay structure did nothing (indeed rather the reverse) to correct existing deficiencies in the distribution of consultants between regions, and between specialisms. Gynaecology, obstetrics, paediatrics, dermatology, nervous diseases, and psy-chiatry were especially deficient in consultants (see Table 11.1).[42] This meant that general practitioners continued to supply specialist services in hospitals some distance away from teaching hospitals. The NHS did, however, mark the demise of the GP-Surgeon and is discussed below. The *BMJ* commented characteristically that 'It is infinitely harder to be an able general practitioner

TABLE 11.1. Distribution of specialists among medical sub-disciplines, 1938–9*

Speciality	Percentage
Surgery	23
Medicine	18
Ophthalmology	15
Ear, nose and throat	10
Gynaecology	8
Radiology	8
Anaesthetics	5
Dermatology and psychiatry	5
Orthopaedics	4
Pathology	4

Source: B. Hill, 'The Doctor's Pay and Day', *Journal of the Royal Statistical Society*, cxiv (1951), p. 32.

Note: *Exclusively engaged as specialists.

[41] S. Sturdy, 'The Political Economy of Scientific Medicine and Science. Education and the Transference of Medical Practice in Sheffield, 1890–1922', *MH*, 36 (1992), 151.

[42] C. Webster, *The Health Services since the War*, vol. 1 (1988), 261–2, 305, 313.

than to be an able specialist. Yet in the NHS the bait is set to attract the latter and almost to repel the former.'[43] But for the GP's patients the free health
service was advantageous. It meant that the flow of referrals increased
markedly because their doctors no longer needed to worry lest the patient
could not afford the consultant's fee.[44] Overall, the long-term impact of the
NHS on the medical profession was to underline the difference between general practitioners and consultants, however, by increasing the difficulty of
crossing the divide between them.

GPs and Consultants

The difficulty of making generalizations about GPs and consultants was
exemplified by no less a person than the Editor of the *BMJ*, who stated in
1878 that he did not wish to make a hard and fast line between the two,
because essentially there was only a difference in the ability to command levels of fees.[45] In this section we shall use the life histories of GPs encapsulated in our obituary database to both illustrate, and attempt to clarify, the
dynamic and permeable nature of the interface between general and specialist practice. Obituaries give a good indication of the careers of individuals,
and of the terms which colleagues used to describe them, giving an insight
into a professional topography that is both complex and obscure. Between
1850 and 1948 there appear to have been five main categories within a spectrum of careers in general and specialist medicine. First there were the classic general practitioners who practised a general clinical medicine for a mixed
social clientele. Secondly, there was a distinct group of what were termed
'GP-Surgeons' who, whilst practising as general practitioners (in the sense
defined above), also held a significant, but part-time, appointment as a
hospital surgeon. Thirdly, there were general practitioners who developed a
specialist interest of some kind, and who were consulted in an expert capacity in it, becoming a hybrid GP/consultant. Fourthly, some general practitioners moved beyond this to practise only as specialists or consultants, often
taking new consulting rooms to signal the change. Finally, there was a group
(excluded from the database) who were purely consultants throughout their
careers. Typically they had several of the following characteristics: an FRCP
or FRCS, a prestigious hospital appointment, teaching responsibilities, a
private practice, or specialist publications.

Amongst the first group of generalists were a substantial minority who had
a special clinical interest. Most commonly these interests were obstetrics in
the Victorian or Edwardian period, and anaesthesia in the interwar period. In

---

[43] Editorial, *BMJ*, i (1950), 709.
[44] Norfolk RO, BR 218/7, correspondence with consultants by Dr Pearce (senior and junior) and
Dr Bowes, 1936 onwards.
[45] *BMJ*, i (1878), 197.

the earlier period a study of occupational diseases or TB and, in the later one, radiology or ENT also had a body of enthusiasts. From the 1920s the range of interests widened considerably with ophthalmology or dermatology fascinating some, but with a wide spectrum of expertise including orthopaedics and psychiatry, as well as some early interest evidenced in paediatrics or, during the 1930s, in geriatrics. Not every general practitioner could find the time, enthusiasm or energy to actively pursue a specialist interest. For example, Dr Lowenthal, who had done full-time research on neurophysiology with Sir Victor Horsley at University College, Liverpool, 'found no time' for further investigations after entering general practice.[46]

Some family doctors developed their clinical interest to the point where they became GP/consultants. Although continuing to practise as GPs they were recognized as having specialist expertise in a certain medical field. This was an essentially 'horizontal' division of medical labour partitioning off organs, diseases, or technical procedures as the basis for specialist work. Such expertise covered a wide variety of fields including gynaecology, rheumatism, forensic medicine, spa treatment, and ophthalmology.[47] The dilemmas and problems of practising both as a generalist and specialist were exemplified by A. Rabagliata:

More and more he was consulted in medical cases, especially with reference to diet. He published numerous books on this subject, and built up a large consulting practice on dietetic lines; he was often urged to give up all general practice and confine himself to consulting work. That he did not definitely take this step was thought by many to be a mistake, but he held strong views about the responsibility of medical practice, and believed that he could do more good by the general care and guidance of patients whose cases were well known to him than by occasional specialist advice. However, in spite of himself, his consulting work rapidly increased; he also had a heavy load of correspondence, and so the general practice side of his work was virtually squeezed out.[48]

Alternatively, the GP/consultant might have a high local profile as a hospital surgeon but also practise as a family doctor, as did Michael Beverley in Norwich, where he was known as a 'general practitioner-consultant'.[49] This role was crucially dependent on the esteem of colleagues, and of referrals from GPs. 'The large private surgical practice' of Robert Jackson of Oldham, for example, was attributed to 'the trust and confidence placed in him by his fellow practitioners'.[50] For a time this type of medic was labelled as a GP-Surgeon. However, the increasingly specialized nature of modern medicine meant that the combination often proved unsustainable. C. M. Pearce of

[46] *BMJ*, ii (1960), 1243.

[47] In the USA, a 'vertical' specialism was also developed based on a hierarchy of personnel (B. B. Perkins, 'Shaping Institution-based Specialism: Early Twentieth-Century Economic Organisation of Medicine', *SHM*, 10 (1997), 423–4).

[48] A. Rabagliata, MD, FRCS (*BMJ*, ii (1930), 1067).   [49] *BMJ*, ii (1930), 500.

[50] *BMJ*, i (1950), 495.

Blackburn, who died in 1960, described as 'a very able surgeon, was a true family doctor' but 'was of a dying race, the combination of consultant surgeon and general practitioner'.[51] Also undercutting the possibilities of combining specialist work with general practice was the increasing geographical range of consultants operating within an expanding hinterland of the large city. From the 1930s GPs in Kent and Sussex, for example, found gradually diminishing opportunities for specialist work in local hospitals, as the 'motors' of London consultants extended to a growing range of places.[52] Although the NHS potentially made the GP/consultant combination obsolete, the new service itself offered opportunities for some GPs to become full-time hospital consultants to a group of hospitals.[53]

Those general practitioners who did manage to become fully fledged consultants benefited from their earlier professional breadth. D. C. Wilson, for example, was thought to have had 'that extra experience that counts so much in a consultant' in his later specialist work on rheumatism.[54] Those who went on from general practice to consultancy fell into two broad camps. On the one hand there were those whose work almost accidentally assumed a specialist character and, on the other, those who saw general practice as only a first (temporary) step towards a carefully mapped out career.[55] In both cases a period of overwork often preceded the decision to ride one horse rather than two.[56] Financial anxiety may well have delayed the decision to become a consultant, although this problem was avoided by those whose part-time anaesthesia or radiology work in interwar hospitals gradually grew into full-time work. That private consultancy did carry an economic risk is evident from those who, like Conan Doyle, failed as a specialist, in his case as an ophthalmologist.[57]

Later social and professional relationships between consultants and general practitioners were generally good, although this amity depended on an unspoken understanding of their respective roles. The letters which GPs sent with their patients to hospital might be of a poor quality, and in the case of those sent to out-patients' departments might consist only of a visiting card with 'Please see and advise' scribbled on it, thus reinforcing the GP's image as the 'lowest form of medical life'.[58] On occasion, the consultant might have esteem for the work of the general practitioner, as had Sir Clifford Allbutt, for the work of the self-reliant Yorkshire Dales doctor, John Cockcroft.[59] Some general practitioners developed close relationships with consultants locally, more particularly as seniority in the local profession highlighted status. For example, it was said of Louis Gordon, 'Over the past 50 years he had been a close friend and on many occasions the "GP" of many Leeds consultants.'[60]

[51] *BMJ* ii (1960), 1743–4.

[52] *BMJ*, ii (1930), 983; ii (1960), 1960.

[53] *BMJ*, iii (1970), 229; iv (1970), 437.

[54] *BMJ*, i (1960), 1743.

[55] Obituary of H. S. Allen (*BMJ*, ii (1960), 470).

[56] Obituaries of G. A. Allan and J. Stirling (*BMJ*, ii (1950), 1121; i (1950), 909).

[57] *BMJ*, i (1930), 71.

[58] CMAC, GP 29/1/69A, David Kerr.

[59] *BMJ*, ii (1930), 502.

[60] Obituary, *BMJ*, ii (1970), 243.

Sydney Hunt was also respected by local consultants for having the 'best type of family practice'.[61] Indeed, one reason for the doctor personally taking a patient to the consultant was so that the GP could get to know the consultant better, and have a chance to discuss the case. Occasionally, a general practitioner was not prepared to defer to the consultant, perceiving his own expertise as equal or superior. One reason for this was that family doctors knew the history of the patient better than the consultant and in some cases this enabled them to arrive at a more accurate diagnosis.[62] H. J. McEvoy, was prepared to say if he did not agree with the consultant, and specialists 'had to pull up their socks' in order to justify their verdict to him![63] And T. A. S. Kinnerly was such an outstanding diagnostician in his general practice, that the consultant 'often did not seem to add very much to what was already known about the patient'.[64] Those consultants who earlier had been general practitioners might recognize that not much in the way of expertise separated these two medical estates of specialist and generalist, and adopted a less lofty stance. This endeared them to GPs, as did L. J. Barford who had become a specialist in rheumatism, and 'as a consultant advised, but did not dictate'.[65] Egalitarianism was taken further by Philip Ellman (another GP turned consultant), who gave family doctors open access to the facilities of his clinic for chest diseases.[66]

The choice of cases which were referred by GPs to consultants or retained within general practice constituted a changing medical frontier. One country practice in the decade before the NHS sent private patients predominantly to consultants at the hospital in the county town, although a few were directed to Harley Street or elsewhere. A variety of conditions was referred including cases of abscesses, incomplete abortion, arthritis, cataract, carcinomas, cysts, deafness, fractures, fibroids, grand mal (epilepsy), haemorrhoids, heart problems, hernia, hydrocele, mastoids, migraine, polypi, stone, and thyroid problems. There were also some children with, for example, asthma, psychological problems, suspected TB, or an undescended testicle. Consultants' letters revealed that in a significant number of cases assessment had either involved the use of instruments and/or technology which was unlikely to have been found in general practice, or the referred cases involved major surgery. Other cases appear to have been of a problematical nature (either clinically, or in terms of the psychology of the patient), and therefore, in more straightforward circumstances, might have been dealt with satisfactorily by the GP.[67]

Consultants' letters showed a breezy familiarity with 'nervous' or 'neurotic' patients that perhaps points to frequent 'psychological' referral by general practitioners who were weary of troublesome or difficult patients, and also concerned to know whether there was any underlying physical problem. A

[61] *BMJ*, ii (1960), 396.
[62] Unpubl. 'Memoir of Dr William Henry Harding', 56, 83.
[63] *BMJ*, ii (1950), 1396.
[64] *BMJ* iv (1970), 122.   [65] *BMJ*, iv (1970), 438.
[66] *BMJ*, i (1960), 1574–5.
[67] Norfolk RO, BR 218/7, correspondence with consultants.

male patient was sent in 1932 by an Essex doctor to a London consultant who recorded that 'he complains of various nervous symptoms and his indigestion I think is nervous in origin . . . He is worried about himself and I hope I was able to reassure him.'[68] Female patients seemed more likely to be labelled in a facile way: 'A textbook description of globus hystericus' wrote one consultant. However, another consultant later found that there were organic problems with this same individual.[69] Another female patient, this time in Norfolk, was sent by her doctor to consultants in Norwich, Rugby and London. One consultant scrawled 'These patients easily become "neurotic"—or even worse: you must get her fat!' A second consultant agreed with this label of neurotic, and wrote: 'It is much easier to tell what is the matter with Mrs C. than to promise to improve matters . . . I am afraid this will prove to be an unsatisfactory case.' In a referral with another patient the consultant dismissed Mrs D's symptoms as 'menopausal syndrome'. 'I suggest that she is put to bed with adequate sedation, and I think you will find that the symptoms will subside, or at least improve.' And the same consultant—in discussing Mrs D's daughter—wrote 'I am sure that the fussiness of her mother is a definite factor in prolonging the cough. The child has obviously learnt that it is a very good way to avoid going to school just to produce a few well spaced coughs at breakfast time!' A different consultant, who was consulted over Mr T's suspected TB, responded by stating that, 'This man seems rather neurotic . . . there were no definite physical signs to be detected in his chest.'[70] In their confident tone, and dismissal of a physical basis to long-term problems, these consultants' letters might clarify the situation for GPs, in some cases by confirming their existing suspicions that nothing very life-threatening was the matter. An authoritative stance could then be taken with a difficult or time-consuming patient, thereby giving at least a breathing space to the hard-pressed GP.

Towards the Professional Margin

Contention between generalists and specialists had centred on underlying financial issues in referral. A growing element of economic competition also soured relationships between GPs and other members of the medical or nursing professions. By the Midwives Act of 1936 midwives achieved ascendancy in domiciliary obstetrics, a process that had begun with legislation in 1902. This was illustrated by a register of cases attended by a Nottinghamshire midwife, between 1904 and 1911, which indicated that of 503 cases attended, she called in the doctor on only seven occasions.[71] Whereas it has been

---

[68] CMAC, GP2/1. Gray's practice, Essex, letter of 14 Jan. 1932 from G. Liddock to Dr McCarter.

[69] CMAC, GP2/1. Gray's practice, Essex, letter of 30 Nov. 1948 from Dr Sundell to Dr T. Stevenson.

[70] Norfolk RO, BR 218/7, correspondence with consultants, 1936–9, 1947–8.

[71] Nottinghamshire RO, DD/NA 13/3, register of midwifery cases of Sarah Eyre, 1904–14.

estimated that for England and Wales in 1880 half of home deliveries were attended solely by doctors, by 1938 only one-third of deliveries were attended by the doctor alone or acting with midwives.[72] Increasingly marginalized in midwifery general practitioners managed to achieve a more favourable balance of power with nurses in the community. Some general practitioners were actively supportive of their work: Dr Goyder founded the Bradford Nurses Institute, Dr Barber the Nurses Home in Sheffield, and Dr Oldham a branch of the District Nursing Association in Morecambe.[73] Doctors were active in local nursing associations, gave lectures to nurses in training, and acted as their examiners.

But general practitioners feared the competition posed by nurses' lower fees, although they felt least threat from village nurses, who typically had had little training.[74] Doctors used their standing in local communities to force through agreements with local nursing associations which privileged their sectional interests. Thus the nurse could attend only the poorer classes, or would not attend patients unless previously treated by the doctor.[75] District nurses employed in Newark, Nottinghamshire at first attended those who did not pay income tax, but later were employed only by order of a medical practitioner.[76] Queen's Nurses in Brighton were sent to every new case requesting help, but could only continue when a doctor was in attendance. They might not provide nursing care after childbirth except when the doctor considered that skilful nursing was essential.[77] The bottom line of this interprofessional rivalry was economic, as was shown by a Cornish document of 1908 marked 'strictly confidential', where it was reported that 'our nurses frequently attend cases, which a doctor ought to see . . . our district nurses were taking away a great deal of the doctor's practice and in consequence they found it hard to live.'[78] The interests of the local medical profession would have circumscribed wider professional aspirations by nurses were it not for clinical and pharmaceutical developments which, from the 1920s, offset this tendency by making the nurse a key player in giving insulin, diuretic and other injections to domiciliary cases.

In other areas of inter- or intra-professional rivalry general practitioners tended, as the period progressed, to find themselves disadvantaged. GPs were

[72] I. Loudon, 'Childbirth' in Loudon (ed.), *Western Medicine. An Illustrated History* (Oxford 1997), 213. See also Ch. 8.

[73] *BMJ*, i (1920), 204; ii (1890), 657; I (1930), 131–2.

[74] R. Dingwall, A. M. Rafferty, and C Webster, *An Introduction to the Social History of Nursing* (1988), 181–2.

[75] J. Donnison, *Midwives and Medical Men. A History of Inter-Professional Rivalries and Women's Rights* (1977), 141–2.

[76] Nottinghamshire RO, DD NA 14/1–2, Newark Borough District Nursing Association (1905–11), Reports of 1905 and 1907.

[77] E. Sussex RO, CHC 9/13, Brighton Hove and Preston District Queens Nurses Reports of 1925 (rule 5) and 1946.

[78] CMAC, SA/RNI/H8/1, Report from West Penrith Medical Society to the Penzance and Madron Nursing Association, May 1908. I am grateful to Helen Sweet for drawing my attention to this document.

at first heavily involved in sanitary work. When MOHs were first appointed (in a few areas in 1847, and then compulsorily in all sanitary authorities in 1872), it was customary to select those who were also engaged in private practice. Victorian GPs had seen it as their duty to tackle disease on all fronts. 'The coming of the Medical Officer of Health means a new sort of attack on the strongholds of disease.'[79] Involvement by local doctors in public health initiatives through public meetings gave them a high profile in the local community, although what it did to their medical authority through their public disagreements over epidemics is less certain.[80] On a more routine basis co-operation between a Victorian MOH and other local practitioners was usually better. For example, T. H. Walker, MOH to the Longtown Rural Sanitary District recorded in 1878:

Before going to the houses I visited Dr Graham and was informed by him that he had no cases of fever with the exception of 2 or 3 cases of bilious fever (not typhoid). He accompanied me to these and also to [the] Phillips [house] where the fever was first said to be, this turned out to be simply sciatica.[81]

Crusading moral vigour had marked the work of many who, like the Welsh MOH, E. Jones, wrote 'fearless reports' on the unsanitary conditions of Dolgelly and Barmouth.[82] Such missionary activity was certainly needed, since in North Wales the town of Denbigh was held to be still as disease ridden, dirty, and unscavenged in 1902, as seventy years earlier, when it had had its first Board of Health.[83] Indeed, a minority of GPs had been such active crusaders for preventive medicine that they had moved from part-time to full-time service as a Medical Officer of Health. Dr Moore became so enthused by his sanitarian mission that he perceived his duty to be 'to devote himself to preventive rather than curative medicine'.[84] In the case of Dr Benton of East Ham, earlier work as a GP might well inform later professional work as a full-time MOH. This background in general practice 'made him realize the need for the school medical services which he initiated, and inspired his pioneer activities in maternity and child welfare clinics'.[85]

Mid-nineteenth-century sanitarian enthusiasm was shown by a rising proportion of GPs in the GP dataset who became Medical Officers of Health. Numbers peaked amongst those who graduated during the 1860s and 1870s when one in four held such appointments, and almost as many in the succeeding twenty-year cohort, when nearly one in five did so. This intense interest was also evident in medical journals like the *Lancet* and *BMJ* of the time, but coverage of sanitary matters was sidelined later by clinical discus-

[79] G. Newman, *Public Opinion in Preventive Medicine* (HMSO, 1920), 10.

[80] Clwyd RO (Ruthin), BD/A/567, Removal of Nuisances and Protection against the Cholera, Jan. 1854.

[81] Cumbria RO (Carlisle), SPUL, 5/5, Medical Officer of Health Report for Longtown, 7 Oct. 1878.

[82] *BMJ*, i (1900), 548.

[83] *Free Press*, 11 Apr. 1902.

[84] *BMJ*, ii (1960), 1842.

[85] *BMJ*, i (1951), 254.

sions.[86] By 1900 public health had become only one of many specialisms, and that of low status.

Part-time appointments gave the Victorian and Edwardian GP a good opportunity to serve as an MOH. In Scotland particularly the existence of police burghs with very small populations (even after reforming legislation in 1889 and 1892), meant that part-time appointments gave continued opportunities to GPs, although salaries might be as little as one pound per annum.[87] In England and Wales only twenty-four urban sanitary authorities in England, and a further five in Wales, had a full-time position at this time. Part-time work was almost universal in rural sanitary authorities, although the newly formed county councils provided appointments on a full-time basis, assuming they bothered to make an appointment at all.[88] It was the county boroughs which gave huge professional scope for their full-time MOHs. Their responsibilities widened during the late nineteenth, and early twentieth, centuries to include infectious diseases, environmental services, maternity and child welfare clinics, tuberculosis and VD services, as well as responsibilities for some hospitals—notably those for infectious diseases and, after 1930, those transferred from the poor law authorities. Local authorities were effectively developing a municipal health care system with the MOH as a key player. Increasingly in other areas also, the logic of the situation demanded full-time officers; legislation specified in 1929 that future MOH appointments must not be of those engaged in private practice, whilst it was made obligatory four years later for them to hold a Diploma in Public Health. The impact was dramatic. Whereas in 1918 only one in five English and Welsh appointments as MOH were full-time, twenty years later the proportion had doubled.[89]

A widening gulf between general practice and public health ensued: full-time, career MOHs were distrusted by GPs because they were perceived as being dominated by the lay bureaucrats of towns and cities.[90] Yet it was municipal medicine which was an expanding area during the first half of the twentieth century, and the growing exclusion of general practitioners from this buoyant sector of health care was a serious professional loss. Admittedly variability in urban provision continued, with striking contrasts between the poorest areas of north-eastern England, and high-spending cities such as Bradford, Leeds, Manchester or Liverpool. Metropolitan boroughs led the way towards a new interwar form of delivery of primary health care.

Prominent here were purpose-built health centres in Peckham, Bermondsey, and Finsbury. Peckham had a different philosophy from the

[86] F. B. Smith, *The People's Health, 1830–1910* (1979), 417.

[87] *Fourth Annual Report. Local Government Board for Scotland*, 1897, 318–20.

[88] *Return on Appointments of MOH under Sanitary Acts*, PP, 1888, lxxxxvi; *Return on Appointments of MOH by County Councils*, PP, 1896, lxxii.

[89] *Some Notes on Medical Education by George Newman*, PP, 1918, xix; *Eighteenth Annual Report of Ministry of Health*, 1936–7, 48, 223; PEP, *Report*, 156–7.

[90] P. M. J. Bartrip, *Mirror of Medicine. A History of the BMJ* (Oxford, 1990), 259–60.

others in having a concept of a positive health centre which was distinct from the NHI 'sickness' service. It was predicated on the idea of a proposed parallel medical institution—the therapeutic centre—which would be run by general practitioners. The latter was stillborn, but had been conceived as a centre which would enable GPs to do research as had Mackenzie's innovative Research Institute at St Andrews.[91] The Peckham Centre has been interpreted as encapsulating what was termed the 'surveillance medicine' of the twentieth century. Here the normal was problematized in that an apparently healthy population was targeted, and monitoring of its condition then blurred the distinction between health and disease.[92]

Other health centres combined health and medicine, preventive and curative work along the lines promoted in the Dawson Report of 1920. The health centre had the potential to allow the general practitioner to win back some of the professional territory ceded either to the full-time MOH, or to the specialist. Bermondsey had a solarium for TB cases, dental clinics, foot clinics, and child welfare clinics, and by 1946 it also employed a psychologist, and had an additional orthopaedic clinic, an X-ray department, an electro-medical department, and consulting rooms for visiting specialists. This model health centre had been inspired by its Socialist councillor, sometime MP and GP, George Salter, and that in 'the People's Republic of Finsbury' by an Indian émigré, Dr Katial. Significantly, a picture of the Finsbury Health Centre was used in a war poster entitled 'Your Britain, Fight for it Now'.[93] Although exceptional doctors were active in health centres, the majority of general practitioners stood aloof. Even after the NHS had begun, only two-fifths of GPs surveyed were in favour of health centres, and this approval was rooted in personal rather than professional reasons, in that it was thought that centres would give more privacy for the doctor and the doctor's family. An important reason for opposing the idea amongst the remainder was that health centres 'would tend to take the patient away from the family doctor'. Even those favourable to the idea considered that, whilst it might raise standards of medical practice, this would be at the expense of the doctor–patient relationship.[94]

The professional horizons of interwar general practitioners remained rooted in a sickness service rather than in a health service. There were exceptions to this blanket generalization; medical women were very active in the maternity and child welfare clinics of local authorities. For many GPs, however, the revival of general practice through the financial blood transfusion of NHI meant that their aspirations remained limited—even contracted—ones.

[91] J. Lewis and B. Brookes, 'The Peckham Health Centre, "PEP", and the Concept of General Practice during the 1930s and 1940s', *MH*, 27 (1983), 152–3.
[92] D. Armstrong, 'The Rise of Surveillance Medicine', *Sociology of Health and Illness*, 17 (1995), 393–8.
[93] I. H. Pearse and L. H. Pearse, *The Peckham Experiment* (1947); 'A vision still worth fighting for', *Independent*, 29 Mar. 1996; F. Brockway, *Bermondsey Story* (1944), 168–9.
[94] *BMJ Supplement*, 26 Sept. 1953.

After 1911 many practitioners were less concerned with new professional alternatives, than with the limitations of NHI practice. A lack of cover for most wives and all children of insured patients stimulated their energies to develop Public Medical Services during the 1920s and 1930s, under which doctors in a locality agreed to give the usual services of a general practitioner to subscribers to a central fund. Weekly subscriptions, on BMA insistence, were fixed at a sufficiently high level to equal or exceed the NHI capitation fee. Equally, membership was limited to those of the same low-income range as NHI, and as under the insurance scheme, patients retained a choice of doctor. Founding members of Public Medical Services, tended to be active medico-politicos who were also energetic players in NHI administration, like C. J. Palmer in Mansfield, or C. H. Panting in Essex.[95] The Essex scheme began in 1923 and recruited not only the dependants of NHI patients, but also others who had been excluded from the NHI, such as older club members.[96] A rapid growth of the Public Medical Service meant that by 1937 it had a membership of 600,000.[97]

Despite this success the GP remained on the margin of other areas of practice. Brighton doctors, for example, viewed 'with considerable concern the insidious inroads continually being made on private medical practice under the auspices of the State, voluntary bodies and others'.[98] Sufficient anxiety existed to cause the BMA to issue a *Report on Encroachments on the Sphere of Private Practice*. Its proposals were that GPs should be involved in local authority clinics both through part-time appointments, and through the patients who were attending clinics being put in touch with local private practitioners. Despite this, anxieties continued. In 1937 the Medical Practitioners Union urged the Ministry of Health to appoint a Royal Commission to enquire into the health services 'in view of the encroachment of the Health Services of the Local Authorities into the realm of curative medicine usually undertaken by general practitioners'.[99] In the following year the President of the BMA commented that general practice had a tendency 'to sink lower and lower in the estimation both of the public and of the student body from which the profession itself is recruited'.[100] And looking back on his years in general practice, Dr A.W. Anderson of Ogmore Vale in South Wales commented sadly in 1943 on:

the gradual development and encroachment of organised clinics on the everyday work of the practitioner. There was the diminished contact with the homes through the lessening of obstetric work and the supervision of the school child by public

[95] *BMJ*, ii (1940), 135–6; ii (1950), 895.

[96] Essex RO (Colchester), D/F 135 C227, Wivenhoe Doctor's Club Book 1855–1935, entry for Mar. 1930.

[97] PEP, *Report*, 153–4. In London a PMS Extension Scheme catered for middle class families.

[98] *BMJ*, i (1929), 130.

[99] Modern Records Centre, University of Warwick, MSS/79/MPU/1/2/1, council minutes of MPU, 17 Nov. 1937.

[100] C. Lindsay, 'The Profession and the Public' (*BMJ*, ii (1938), 163).

authorities. Then there were the increased and easier facilities for treatment in hospitals made by improved transport, and its effect on small local hospitals.[101]

Finding themselves in the wings, rather than centre stage of so many interwar developments, may have prepared more thoughtful doctors to view proposals for a new post-war health service, if not necessarily more enthusiastically, at least with a more open mind. The BMA was itself moving slowly towards the idea of a reformed system of health care, but envisaged one with the central agency provided by the GP as a family doctor.[102] Interwar plans remained paper dreams since financial stringency coupled with strong ideological differences between devotees of socialized, voluntary or private medicine, meant that effective national reform was delayed until after the Second World War. Not that that reform followed through logically from the innovations of previous decades, because the dynamic which for half a century had created a municipally based health care system centred on the MOH, was abruptly terminated by the National Health Service.[103]

Conclusion

This chapter has discussed some of the principal institutional and social changes which altered the meaning of general practice within a wider medical context, sometimes as a result of the initiative of GPs, but more usually as a result of the enterprise of others. Modifications in the professional ideal of a general practitioner—as perceived by later generations—were significant. During the century between 1850 and 1948 a transition was perceived to have occurred from the social skills of the bedside manner to more scientific accomplishment. 'He was an ideal practitioner, combining the courtliness of the older generation with the keener scientific drive for accuracy of the later school.'[104] Earlier generations were recognized as having belonged to a more self-reliant breed of all-rounders. 'In an age of specialisation he prided himself on his wide range of skills, reflecting days when the family doctor had less help to call upon.'[105] Alternatively, 'He was one of that fast-disappearing band of general practitioners whose wisdom and experience led to their being accepted as of consultant status.'[106] In other words he was that paradox to later generations—a generalist who could be, and was, a specialist. Between the end of the Victorian age and the beginning of a new, universal health service there was incremental change in medical provision which cumulatively made a massive difference to the role of the GP. Institutionally, the first half of the twentieth century had signalled a gradual yet marked diminution of

[101] National Library of Wales, BMA South Wales Collection, minutes of BMA Branch Council of S. Wales and Monmouthshire (1942–52), Presidential Address, 1 July 1943.
[102] BMA, *Proposal for a General Medical Service for the Nation* (1930).
[103] McLachlan, *Improving the Common Weal*, 315.   [104] *BMJ*, ii (1910), 1568.
[105] *BMJ*, iii (1970), 290.   [106] *BMJ*, i (1960), 1962.

community involvement by the general practitioner. From the mid nineteenth century to the 1930s, appointment as a local Medical Officer of Health had been an important characteristic of general practice. The trend from part-time to full-time appointments was lamented by one practitioner:

Midwifery has gone, school inspection has gone, and the treatment of school children in many places has gone; vaccination will soon go, and all the Poor Law appointments will also follow the Medical Officerships of Health, and then the Public Medical Service of the British Medical Association will be . . . all that will be left to private practitioners.[107]

During the interwar years practice territory was threatened by other professionals colonizing what earlier had been the professional terrain of the general practitioner. The response of GPs was less than vigorous, apart from a collective wringing of hands. A significant reason for this failure to respond adequately was the earlier creation of the national health insurance scheme that had already secured a role for the GP in state-funded primary health care. And, since the National Health Service of 1948 was path-dependent on this earlier scheme, the generalist had effectively been given a secure long-term future.

---

[107] Letter from Henry Gough of Northleach (*General Practitioner*, 11 (1910), 8).

12

National Health Insurance

THE connection between the individual's health and that of the body politic was given a new political imperative in 1904, when the findings of the Interdepartmental Committee on Physical Deterioration suggested that the vigour of the imperial state depended upon the physical health of the citizen. The creation of the national health insurance (NHI) scheme seven years later was related to German precedents, and in this way great-power competition reinforced domestic pressures to achieve a healthy and economically productive people.[1] Through its response to a complex of wider concerns in society—notably those of labour efficiency and citizen's rights—the scheme provided a major and largely exogenous shock to general practice. Although attempting to meet wider social needs the scheme also recognized some of the incipient requirements of doctors then engaged in general practice. Indeed, the *BMJ* later commented that it had 'had a profound influence on general medical practice'.[2]

Earlier, the Victorian state's relationship with health and with individuals' access to health had been complex, usually being of an implicit rather than explicit character. Compared to welfare, health did not have a high profile, being the junior partner in an overlapping set of concerns. The negative right to refuse health-related measures (as in smallpox vaccination), or health-related topics which impinged on property rights (as in doctors' right to sell their practices), were much more clearly articulated than an individual's positive private right to health. Public health interventions drew on the traditional (collectivist) right of the community to safety, but in certain circumstances might be contested by (individualistic) claims to defend the integrity or autonomy of the human body—as in the *furore* over the Contagious Diseases Acts. This tension between collectivism and individualism was not resolved by the time of the national insurance scheme of 1911,

---

[1] E. P. Hennock, *British Social Reform and German Precedents. The Case of Social Insurance, 1880–1914* (Oxford, 1987), 20. The scheme differed in important respects from the German one, especially in its uniform, rather than graduated, contributions and benefits (E. P. Hennock, 'The Origins of British National Insurance and the German Precedent, 1880–1914', in W. J. Mommsen (ed.), *The Emergence of the Welfare State in Britain and Germany, 1850–1950* (1981), 84–109).

[2] 'The Profession of Medicine', *BMJ*, ii (1933), 411.

so that this legislation had elements of both traditions.[3] In this context it is instructive to note that, although the NHI involved an obvious extension of collectivist responsibility for working-class sickness, it was at the same time related to a desire to restrict public financial involvement, thus confining the state mainly to regulatory functions.

The National Health Insurance Act of 1911 established a system of free health care financed by tripartite payments from those in employment, from employers and from the state. Anyone was eligible who earned under £160 per annum. This was later raised to £250 p.a. in 1920.[4] They could receive free medical treatment from a doctor of their choice by joining the panel of an insurance practitioner. Half the working population were on the panel of insurance doctors by the end of the interwar period, although dependant wives and children were still excluded. The British insurance scheme was therefore socially less inclusive than in the pioneering country of Germany .[5]

The Transition to NHI

What were the economic conditions of medical practice in the preceding quarter of a century which help to explain why general practitioners joined this new scheme in such (unexpectedly) large numbers? A London doctor, F. H. Alderson, referred in 1886 to the profession's 'small incomes', to the 'crowded state' of the profession, and to the provident dispensaries and fever hospitals that he thought had contributed to this unfortunate situation.[6] The medical profession was confronted by organized patient-power that was able to drive down the doctor's capitation fee to three or four shillings per head, as an enquiry by the BMA indicated in 1905.[7] The BMA had long been fighting the 'battle of the clubs' in which attempts were made through collective action to raise the payment per head given to their doctors by friendly societies, and medical aid societies. Several problems interconnected: the low annual payment; the moral hazard incurred when contributors made frequent contact with practitioners, thus driving down remuneration further in relation to doctors' time; and the pervasive medical under-employment which led to undercutting between colleagues.[8] The BMA noted that 'Largely, no

---

[3] J. Harris, 'The Right to Health: Historical Frameworks', unpubl. paper given at the 'Right to Health' conference, Oxford, July 1997.

[4] The ages included were at first those from 16 to 70, but in 1928 the upper limit was reduced to 65.

[5] In Germany the insured population doubled from 5 to 10 per cent in 1883, nearly one-quarter of the population were covered by 1914 (half if dependants are included), and over three-quarters of the wage-earning population were included by 1925 (C. Huerkamp, 'The Making of the Modern Medical Profession, 1800–1914: Prussian Doctors in the Nineteenth Century', in G. Cocks and K. H. Jarausch (eds.), *German Professions, 1800–1950* (Oxford, 1990), 75–6).

[6] F. H. Alderson, *The Wants of the General Practitioner of the Present Day* (1886), 6, 10. This was an inaugural address to the West London Medico-Chirurgical Society.

[7] *R.C. on Poor Laws*, PP, 1910, liii, 814 (evidence of T. G. Acland).

[8] H. Nelson Hardy, *The State of the Medical Profession* (Dublin, 1901), 29–30; *BMJ*, ii (1907), 480.

doubt, owing to the close competition of its own members, medical men have contracted to give their services to the friendly societies at a lower rate than was desirable from any point of view. Some concordat on this question of remuneration is of pressing importance.'[9] A less serious problem, but one which caused many outbursts of righteous indignation amongst doctors, was free treatment in dispensaries or hospital outpatients departments. Although there had been an undoubted increase in outpatient numbers seeking free treatment from London hospitals (from 1.0 to 1.6 million between 1887 and 1910),[10] Victorian and Edwardian doctors had less justification for their belief that these institutions provided free care for patients who might otherwise have contributed to doctors' incomes.[11] The 'sixpenny' doctor—whose standardized bottles of medicine, non-examination of patients, and low fee were held to undercut colleagues—was also condemned by respectable members of the profession. Finally, the expectation of the reform of the poor-law medical service as part of a wider restructuring of the relief of the poor, following from the Royal Commission on the Poor Laws (1905–9), together with the flourishing competition from alternative medicine highlighted in a *Report* in 1910, deepened doctors' insecurities in the run up to the 1911 act.[12]

Professional overcrowding was not a peculiarly British phenomenon as was indicated by a number of complaints from other places. In Europe a Viennese doctor lamented in 1898 that doctors had become merely 'medical clerks' forced to take many patients at low fees.[13] Low-fee doctoring was also found, for example, in Berlin, the Netherlands, the British Empire, as well as in the USA.[14] To help counter the situation in the USA, American physicians produced a spate of books with titles such as *The Physician as Businessman*, *Building a Profitable Practice*, or even, *Dollars to Doctors*,[15] but in England a genteel professional ethic inhibited such overt entrepreneurial responses. The Editor of the *Lancet* revealingly summarized medical perceptions of the situation facing doctors as involving 'The gross imposition of the quack, the unfair tactics of the medical aid associations, the immoral use of hospitals, and the ill-instructed rivalry of the druggist and the optician.'[16] Rather than solidarity this situation produced professional disarray, as we have seen. A

---

[9] *Majority Report of the RC on the Poor Laws* (1909), part V, ch. 3, para. 235.

[10] These were casual attenders—hence the later coinage—casualty departments. This attendance has been estimated to be 280 per 1,000 population, compared to 240 per 1,000 in the first years of NHS hospitals, and 346 per 1,000 in 1974 (Sprigge, *Medicine*, 58; Loudon, 'The Historical Importance of Outpatients', *BMJ*, i (1978), 974–7).

[11] S. Squire Sprigge, *Medicine and the Public* (1905), 57–66.

[12] *Report as to the Practice of Medicine and Surgery by Unqualified Persons in the UK*, PP, 1910, XLII. See also Ch. 2.

[13] R. Gersuny, *Doctor and Patient. Hints to Both* (Bristol, 1898).

[14] P. Weindling, 'Medical Practice in Imperial Berlin: the case book of Alfred Grotjahn', *BHM*, 61 (1987); H. van der Velden, 'The Dutch Health Services before Compulsory Health Insurance, 1900–1914' *SHM*, ix (1996), 50; A. Digby, ' "A Medical El Dorado"? Colonial Medical Incomes and Practice at the Cape', *SHM*, 8 (1995), 469–71; T. A. Pensabene, *The Rise of the Medical Profession in Victoria* (1980); P. Starr, *The Transformation of American Medicine* (New York, 1982), 67–8; 110–11.

[15] Digby, *Making a Medical Living*, 135.   [16] Sprigge, *Medicine and the Public*, 79–80.

relentless struggle for patients led to acrimonious relationships in industrial practice especially, where backbiting among doctors was accompanied by unseemly contests and blackballing in which practitioners accused one another of 'touting, canvassing, and general cheap-jack tricks'.[17] In South Wales, the BMA resorted to expulsion of members on ethical grounds, after a series of professional inquiries into practitioners who broke ranks in canvassing for patients, or who negotiated unilaterally with organized labour in an unprofessional manner.[18] These harsh years of competition and under-employment, when individual exertion proved inadequate to transform many doctors' economic situation, forged a generally favourable, if cautious medical stance towards a national health insurance scheme, because its collectivist solution promised better remuneration.[19] It offered a financial lifeline to a profession, where the economic anxieties of the majority of GPs were magnified by the spectacle of a drowning minority, already drifting into professional insolvency.[20]

Several interests were involved within the national health insurance scheme, with the result that a reconciliation of contentious elements involved substantial changes during the years from 1908 and 1912 when it was being negotiated. The politics of poverty meant that the pressing need of the working population to have affordable treatment during sickness had to be addressed. Friendly societies (whose practice shaped the basic organizational model), had to be accommodated because of the scheme's reliance on their administrative expertise, not least in relation to their experience in dealing with malingerers. Friendly societies, together with industrial insurance companies and collecting societies, were deployed in the NHI scheme as approved societies. This was in order to minimize public bureaucratic involvement within the transitional social-service state, which constituted an interim stage in the transition towards the more fully fledged welfare state of the 1940s, with its comprehensive national health service. In turn, GPs wanted a scheme where they could both 'have their cake and eat it'—one which would optimize their income, *and* preserve their professional autonomy. But in contrast with Lloyd George's early contact with friendly societies and commercial insurance industry, medical involvement in negotiations occurred belatedly and on a minor scale.[21]

Medical perceptions of the initial terms offered by the government's NHI Bill of May 1911 were unfavourable. One GP recollected that the 1911 act

---

[17] National Library of Wales, BMA Collection, Dr Hartland to Dr Paterson, letter 19 Aug. 1903.

[18] Ibid., Monmouthshire Division minutes Special Meeting 23 Apr. 1906; Annual Report of Branch Council of South Wales and Monmouthshire, June 1906.

[19] See, e.g., the Council of the BMA's *Report on the Organisation of Medical Attendance on the Provident or Insurance Principle* (1911).

[20] Between one-third and one-fifth of GPs were making a gross income of under £400 in the decade before NHI (Digby, *Making a Medical Living*, 144).

[21] B. B. Gilbert, *The Evolution of National Insurance in Great Britain. The Origins of the Welfare State* (1966), 363.

had 'stirred up the medical profession as never before. Never before had so many GPs become acquainted with each other. Meetings galore, some full of sound and fury.'[22] The Border Branch of the BMA minuted, for example, that 'This question threatened the very existence of the membership of the Branch . . . the matter was one of grave importance.' Individual members of this branch showed suspicion of the proposed role of the friendly societies (the 'clubs') in the NHI Bill together with a fear that the income limit of proposed membership of the scheme would be so high as to harm private practice. In consequence there was a strong impulse towards medical solidarity in attempting to improve the terms under which doctors would participate.[23] On 1 June 1911 a Special Representative Meeting of the BMA formulated the 'Six Cardinal Points' or prerequisites of a satisfactory scheme. These included: a demand for an 'adequate' payment (later defined as an annual capitation fee of 8s. 6d. per patient—excluding the cost of drugs and extras—rather than the 6s. then being offered by the government); an upper income limit for NHI patients of two pounds per week; and the free choice of doctor by insurance patients, subject to the doctor being willing to act.[24] A total of 27,400 doctors' signatures were collected in support of these points, together with declarations that individuals would not sign up with any scheme which was not 'in accordance with the declared policy of the BMA'.

The scheme was due to start on 15 January 1913, and negotiations, tactical stand-offs, and adversarial publicity between the BMA and the Chancellor, Lloyd George, ensued until the end of 1912. Both the government and the professional association agreed in 1912 to an inquiry into the remuneration of general practitioners, although it was the government that found useful ammunition in its results. The Plender Report, in its inquiry into selected towns, revealed that the average annual payment per patient in all aspects of general practice was only 4s. 5d.[25] However, in order to buy off the doctors' opposition Lloyd George made a final offer in October 1912 of an inclusive package of 9s. per patient. This was made up of 7s. capitation, for those doctors not dispensing drugs, and 8s. 6d. for those who were, as well as the so-called 'floating sixpence'. The latter was for any additional drugs, but otherwise went towards general medical remuneration. In December 1912 a Special Representative Meeting of the BMA—in fact dominated by an unrepresentative minority—voted four to one to reject the government's revised terms. This intransigence by the BMA leadership did not reflect the rapidly changing views of a wider general practitioner membership.

[22] Dr Tylor in Lodge, 'Reminiscences', 1762. M.F. Tylor qualifed in 1903 (Oxford and St George's) and retired in 1936.

[23] Cumbria RO (Carlisle), DSO/38/1, minute book of BMA Border Counties, 26 May 1911, Annual Report 1911, 12 Oct. 1911.

[24] Other points included: the administration by local medical committees of issues of medical discipline, of methods of payment, and of medical and maternity benefits; and an adequate representation of the profession on NHI administrative bodies.

[25] Report on Medical Attendance and Remuneration, PP, 1912–13, lxxviii; Gilbert, National Insurance, 408.

The Plender Report's findings should have given BMA leaders an early warning that the professional posture of intransigence was 'a triumph of rhetoric over reality'.[26] Many general practitioners knew only too well from their own practice ledger that they had been offered very generous terms. Lloyd George also engineered skilful press publicity on the alternative policy to be pursued if the medical profession did not cooperate, under which the hated friendly societies (now termed approved societies under the 1911 legislation), would replace designated local medical committees in administering NHI medical benefit. The prospect of a perpetuation of a system under which doctors were subordinated to lay control—as they had under the unpopular club system—was potent medicine in purging professional reservations amongst the rank-and-file. An expectation of substantial economic betterment together with less obtrusive control, when contrasted with the detailed interventions of existing friendly societies, were material factors in changing doctors' minds. By early January in 1913 some 10,000, and by mid-January some 15,000, GPs had signed contracts with local insurance committees. Ignominiously, the BMA was forced to release doctors from their pledge not to join the new scheme.[27] A crushing verdict on the BMA's record that 'as a fighting machine for the profession [it had been] simply futile', was recorded by a Midlands doctor.[28] Certainly, the medical profession itself saw the outcome in terms of a humiliating defeat.[29] But it must also be recognized that the association had substantially increased the amount of public money paid to doctors. It had also ensured that public panel practice was conducted on the same lines as that of private practice, thus enshrining doctors' right to control their lists, and patients' right to choose their doctors.[30] Largely as a result of the medical profession's hostility to the friendly societies, medical and cash benefits were also separated, unlike provision in the German insurance scheme.

Panel Doctors and Patients

By 1938 over 19,000 British GPs were insurance practitioners.[31] From two-thirds to three-quarters of British general practitioners worked in the NHI, compared to a situation in Germany, where four-fifths of the medical

[26] P. Bartrip, *Themselves Writ Large. The British Medical Association 1832–1966* (1996), 160.

[27] Gilbert, *National Insurance*, 401–16.

[28] Nottinghamshire RO, DD/1440/23/40, letter from W. B. Hallowes of Newark on Trent to E. Ringrose (honorary Secretary to the Local Medical Committee), 27 Feb. 1913.

[29] Bartrip, *Themselves Writ Large*, 162.

[30] G. F. McLeary, 'The Influence of the Medical Profession in the English Health Insurance System', *Millbank Memorial Fund Quarterly*, xiii (1935), 7–8. McLeary had been Principal MO to the English NHI Committee.

[31] A. Digby and N. Bosanquet, 'Doctors and Patients in an Era of National Health Insurance and Private Practice', *Economic History Review*, 2nd ser., xli (1988), table 1.

profession were insurance doctors.[32] Professional involvement within the NHI varied according to type of practice, so that the unifying trajectory of the scheme had an uneven impact in smoothing out the diversity of practice niches.[33] In industrial areas it was virtually axiomatic that doctors had large panels, typically in large towns around two-thirds did so, and in the countryside rather more than half the doctors might have a small or medium panel. Doctors with suburban, or old-established family practices in small towns were less likely to join the panel. Numbers of female insurance practitioners were for several years unduly low, but medical women gradually perceived the financial benefits of insurance practice, even though in their all-women practices there were few female patients with the requisite insurance qualification. Whereas only one in five women GPs were panel doctors during the 1920s, by the 1930s this had become two out of five, and by the 1940s the proportion had risen to nine out of ten.[34]

The reasons why individuals joined, refused to join, or having once joined, later withdrew from, the NHI scheme are instructive in revealing its perceived attractions, as well as indicating professional reservations. Strong support for the new system was given by younger doctors who had graduated from universities in unprecedently large numbers. Those starting up (or who were assistants still only planning such a prospect), considered that it offered them a good chance of commencing in practice, not least because they could begin in undoctored or under-doctored areas which previously had not provided the effective demand from paying patients to sustain a medical living.[35] In Scotland, for example, a panel practice was reckoned to be 'a sound investment' for young doctors entering practice on their own account.[36] Additionally, the insurance scheme offered later career flexibility in giving a doctor the potential to change the balance between public and private practice.[37]

Critics of NHI usually came from an older generation. One club doctor, practising in an industrial area, wrote that 'I don't suppose it will be a very difficult matter for young men to recover from the present upheaval of their practice, but for one like myself—over three score years—it is a very different matter.'[38] Some critics, like Horace Potts, who had opposed contract practice, saw the NHI as little—if at all—different from the detested clubs,

---

[32] A. Newsholme, *International Studies on the Relation between Private and Official Practice of Medicine* (3 vols., 1931), vol. i, 154, 161–2.

[33] See Ch. 10.

[34] *Lancet* 5 May 1923; MWF survey, reported in *MWFQN*, 1945.

[35] B. N. Armstrong, *The Health Insurance Doctor. His Role in Britain, Denmark and France* (Princeton, 1939), 82.

[36] A. Newsholme, *International Studies on the Relation between the Private and Official Practice of Medicine* (3 vols., 1931), vol. 3, 456.

[37] Digby, 'The Economic Significance of the National Health Insurance Act of 1911', in K. Waddington and A. Hardy (eds.), *Financing British Medicine* (forthcoming, Amsterdam, 1999).

[38] Nottinghamshire RO, DD/1440/23/40, letter from W.B. Hallowes of Newark on Trent to E. Ringrose, 27 Feb. 1913.

and therefore rejected it.[39] D. J. Williams of Llanelly also refused to join, because he believed that the profession must be master in its own house if it was to fulfil its duty to the people.[40] A few doctors were sufficiently convinced that the NHI was a wrong turning for general practice for them to organize opposition to it. These included Dr Buttar who saw the panel as a threat to the individual, and to the position of the family doctor, carrying many London doctors with him in opposing the act.[41] Also prominent was Dr Stevens who helped organize the Scottish resistance to NHI in the Medical Guild of Scotland, and who remained an implacable opponent of a state medical service.[42] Others having tried panel practice later decided it was not for them. Dr Poole withdrew from the panel because he concluded that it compromised standards of practice, so that it was not possible to give patients the detailed attention they deserved.[43] And David Coutts resigned after a few years because he thought the scheme irksome in that a third party had come between himself and his patients.[44]

The massiveness of that third-party bureaucracy has been insufficiently appreciated by historians. Variation in the emphases initially given to the scheme by counties and boroughs was gradually eroded, but not entirely eliminated, by the cumulative pressure of NHI rules and regulations. Of course, general practitioners were not only on the receiving end of the NHI administration, but were also themselves part of it, frequently giving long-service on its medical committees. Some older doctors found it difficult as panel practitioners to accept NHI constraints because they had been used to operating as autonomous individuals who set their own standards of practice. Dr Bower, for example, although serving for a quarter of a century on a panel committee, disliked the panel 'scripts' and would 'rather make medicine than write it'.[45] The Bermondsey doctor and MP, Dr Salter, took a more resolute line in 1914 in declaring that 'I am a doctor, not a clerk.' Having refused to fill in the forms for the London Insurance Committee, he was removed from the London panel, but sued successfully for his reinstatement.[46] The previous custom of having the dispenser rubber-stamp a prescription was now ruled an inadmissible professional practice. Doctors were sternly instructed to sign for themselves in pen or indelible pencil, and to provide adequate details on the prescription forms.[47] They had to date the prescription, detail the medicine, and give some indication of the illness. Some panel doctors did

[39] *BMJ*, i (1950), 1377, conjoint diploma (UCH, 1893).

[40] *BMJ*, i (1920), 350–1. D.J. Williams, MRCS (1877), FRCS (1894).

[41] *BMJ*, ii (1930), 450, Charles Buttar, MA (Cantab), MB, CM (St Bartholomew's, 1892), DPH (1895), MD (1898).

[42] *BMJ*, ii (1930), 196. John Stevens, MA (Edinburgh, MB, CM (Edinburgh, 1884), MD (1887).

[43] *BMJ*, i (1950), 849. T. B. Poole, MB, BS (Durham, 1896), MD (1898).

[44] *BMJ*, i (1950), 964. D. Coutts, MB, CM (Glasgow, 1891).

[45] *BMJ*, i (1941), 139. H.E. Bower, MB, CM, (Edinburgh, 1887), MD, (Edinburgh, 1905).

[46] F. Brockway, *Bermondsey Story* (1949), 63.

[47] Lancashire RO, IC BA 17/1, correspondence of Barrow in Furness NHI Committee, 1921–2, 1933–4; Nottinghamshire RO, SO NH/1/1, minute 3 Dec. 1915.

not supply the records on which capitation was to be calculated, and therefore did not receive their remuneration.[48] Despite some resistance—more
particularly in earlier years—the sanctions of financial loss or penalty were
quite effective deterrents in inducing doctors' conformity. However, this was
often of a perfunctory kind directed at impressing the bureaucrat rather than
reflecting the clinical record, as with a recollection about a Dorset GP who
'sat with the National Health [Insurance] records on his knee upside down
and back to front and writing on the back of them visit, visit, visit'.[49] Another
recollects that in a country practice NHI records were kept in a cardboard
box under the sofa in the dining room. On getting notice that a visiting
inspector would be coming, these were dusted off, and records filled up for
the past year. The inspector complimented the practitioner for keeping
records at all.[50]

How well did doctors do economically under the NHI? Despite their initial hostility to the proposal to implement a scheme for social insurance in
health general practitioners benefited very substantially. They were able to
increase their incomes both absolutely and relatively during the interwar
period, experiencing greater income gains than other professional groups. A
major reason for this was the payment for panel patients which gave average
gross payments of £400–500 a year, from the 900–1,000 NHI patients on an
average panel. Within general practice the stable platform of panel receipts
contributed to a significant narrowing of income differentials, and together
with the buoyant income from private practice, this meant that a reasonable
income was attainable for most GPs. As we have seen, this was also likely to
have impacted on the growth of partnerships. It is important to recognize,
however, that the mix of panel and private patients varied a great deal
between practices: a few doctors obtained less than 10 per cent of their
income from the NHI, a quarter received from 10 to 30 per cent, and more
than two-fifths received from 30 to 50 per cent by this means.[51]

Certain practitioners also benefited from special public funds, apart from
their regular capitation-based NHI cheque. As we have seen, rural doctors
had a special allowance from 1914 to compensate them for their high mileage
costs, and from 1924 'unremunerative practice' payments could also be used
for their telephones, cars, branch surgeries, as well as for locums. In addition, practitioners in the Highlands and Islands Medical Service could benefit from a special grant to help subsidize doctors' salaries and expenses. An
added bonus for panel doctors in all areas was that the regular insurance
cheque reduced the labour of book-keeping, as well as obviating the bad debt

[48] Lancashire RO, IC BA 17/1, minute 15 Dec. 1916.

[49] Pers. comm., E. Hope Simpson remembering the visit of an NHI inspector to the practice and
of his principal's reaction to it.

[50] G. Barber, *Country Doctor* (1973), 46.

[51] E.g. Scottish RO, HH3 8/001, Kirkcaldy NHI Ledger (1914–48), folios 5, 55–6, 126; HH3
7/001, Dunfermline NHI Committee Ledger (1913–49), folios 2–3, 6, 57; Digby and Bosanquet,
'Doctors and Patients', 75–80.

problem. One Yorkshire panel doctor summarized common feelings about the insurance scheme when he said:

When I see the queue at my surgery door, and when I see the heap of papers on my consulting room table, all of which must be filled up and signed, I say 'Oh, damn Lloyd George', but when, at the end of the quarter, I handle the insurance cheque, it is 'Well, here's to Lloyd George, the doctor's friend.'[52]

A minority of get-rich-quick practitioners at first abused the system by recruiting as many as 4,000 patients so that in 1920 a maximum list had to be fixed at 3,000. This was reduced still further to 2,500 in 1925. When an assistant was employed, a further 1,000 to 1,500 patients could be placed on the practice's list, making a maximum of 3,500 to 4,000. Individual insurance committees varied these regulations a little for their own locality so that in Glasgow, for example, the maximum panel was 2,000 with an extra 1,000 patients permitted if an assistant was employed.[53] In fact only a minority of practices approached these sorts of numbers. In 1926 the Ministry of Health stated that 30 per cent had 600–1,200 patients, and 35 per cent had under 600 patients. Of the remainder, 14 per cent of practices had over 2,000 panel patients, and 21 per cent between 1,200 and 2,000.[54] It was almost entirely doctors in these large 'specialist' insurance practices who maximized the income potential of the NHI through employing assistants.[55]

Potential patients were less ambivalent about the NHI than were doctors, and wanted their doctors to join the panel quickly. Some became angry if this didn't seem likely, and in the sleepy fenland town of Wisbech there were even riots in 1913, when it was discovered that nearly all the local doctors had refused to take national insurance patients. One doctor recollected that our 'homes were besieged and . . . windows smashed'.[56] Eligibility in terms of insurance contributions, however, meant that there was pronounced gender, age and marital differentiation in membership of the scheme as Table 12.1 indicates.

Once enrolled as panel patients what might the patient expect? Model rules for the administration of medical benefit were issued, and their contents suggest that the framer was cognizant with patient abuse in industrial practice.[57] Patients were exhorted to obey the instructions of the medical practitioner, not to conduct themselves in a way that would retard recovery, 'not to make unreasonable demands' upon the doctor, to attend the surgery 'whenever the condition permits', and to give notice before 10 a.m. that a home visit was requested.[58] (Interestingly, this framework was also perpetrated in NHS practices.) Evidence that patients took any notice of these instructions, or that

[52] Quoted in H. W. Pooler, *My Life in General Practice* (1948), 56–7.

[53] Newsholme, *International Studies*, vol. 3, 458.

[54] H. Levy, *National Health Insurance. A Critical Study* (Cambridge, 1944), 131.

[55] Digby and Bosanquet, 'Doctors and Patients', 83; Digby, 'Economic Significance'.

[56] Dr Tylor in Lodge, 'Reminiscences', 1762.   [57] See Ch. 9.

[58] Nottinghamshire RO, SO NH/1/1, Nottinghamshire NHI Committee minute, 28 Oct. 1912.

TABLE 12.1.   Estimated composition of contributors
to the NHI, 1918–21

Ages	Men	Unmarried women
16–24	85	65
25–34	81	60
35–44	76	47
45–54	73	33
55–64	62	15
65–70	50	2

Source: PRO, PIN 1/1, Interdepartmental Committee
on Health and Unemployment.

they were fined for infringements, is lacking. An enforcement of rules seems
inherently unlikely in a situation where some doctors were so keen to recruit
that they might actually tout for patients.[59]

As with the NHS later an initial demand for free services was high, indicating a previously unmet need for medical treatment. In some areas there
was said to have been 'a big rush on the chemists' at the inception of the
NHI.[60] The rate of prescription rose fairly steadily thereafter in all areas,
despite an anti-prescription campaign from 1928 to 1930. In England this
increase was attributed to 'the intense love of the insured person for a bottle
of medicine'.[61] One Welsh insurance doctor also recollected that 'They came
to see the doctor, expected to have a little chat with him, and they expected
to have a bottle of medicine. Everybody went out with a bottle of medicine.'[62]

Table 6.2 shows the rapid growth of take-up of services, in this case of
attendances at the doctor's surgery, as well as visits made by the doctor to
the patient's home. Before the NHI, and presumably in ignorance of the frequent patient–doctor contacts previously experienced both in private practice[63] and in friendly societies and medical aid schemes, the government
actuary had predicted that there would be fewer than two doctor–patient contacts annually. Twenty years later there were actually five.[64] The Royal
Commission estimated in 1925 that from 40 to 50 per cent of panel patients
saw their doctor in the course of the year, but a later estimate put this higher
at 60 per cent.[65] How can such a marked rise in doctor–patient consultations

---

[59] Nottinghamshire RO, SO NH/1/1, Nottinghamshire NHI Committee minute, 23 Jan. 1913.

[60] *Burnley News*, 10 May 1913.

[61] National Association of Clerks to Insurance Meetings. Proceedings of the Conference at
Scarborough, contribution of Mr Abbott of Middlesex.

[62] CMAC, GP 29/2/59, Samuel Isaacs.

[63] Pers. comm. from Dr John Holden on an Earlestown doctor's daybook for 1901, which indicates seven or eight visits per household.

[64] Digby and Bosanquet, 'Doctors and Patients', 87.

[65] H. Levy, *National Health Insurance. A Critical Study* (Cambridge, 1944), 131; D. W. Orr and
J. W. Orr, *Health Insurance with Medical Care* (New York, 1938), 25.

be explained? An earlier growth in patients attending hospital outpatients departments was perhaps the result of working people, having subscribed their penny a week to the Saturday Hospital Fund, considering that they had a *right* to such treatment since they had paid for it.[66] It seems likely that the NHI was also perceived as belonging to the patients, because they had contributed to it. The central factor in the growing demand for medical services, however, was that at the point of access such contact was now free for those in the scheme. The positive feature of such rising demand for a free good was that working-class patients within the scheme were enabled to seek medical treatment at an earlier stage of their illness, and that they were no longer deterred by the economic costs of doing so.

Dependants of insured workers were not in the same fortunate position because they were excluded from national health insurance. In 1910 the *Report* of the government actuaries had included a stark assertion of the primacy of the male breadwinner:

Married women living with their husbands need not be included, since where the unit is the family, it is the husband's and not the wife's health which it is important to insure. So long as the husband is in good health and able to work, adequate provision will be made for the needs of the family, irrespective of the wife's health, whereas when the husband's health fails there is no one to earn wages.[67]

The Royal Commission on Health Insurance concluded in 1925 that the inclusion of dependants would involve a 'prohibitive' cost,[68] although the BMA's *Report on a General Medical Service for the Nation*, later pressed for such an extension.

Doctors were only too aware that the need for the doctor's services amongst the wives and children of the insured worker did not translate into equivalent effective demand.[69] They recollected that in those circumstances 'We were much more poverty conscious in those days.' A family would send for the doctor in a case of serious or worrying illness, but the practitioner knew that in many cases this put a strain on the household budget, and so got into the habit of introducing any further visits by saying I've 'just dropped in' because I 'happened to be passing'. This later attendance went unbilled. The more independent or discerning amongst their clientele might reject this, 'Oh, come on, doctor, we're not *that* poor.'[70] General practitioners might also run their own clubs for the wives and children of their panel patients. Alternatively, as we have seen, they might enrol them in the Public Medical Service. The service collected 6d. per week from each patient, who then was able to register with a doctor, and receive appropriate consultation, diagnosis, and medicine. Unfortunately, as in earlier poor-law medicine

[66] S. Squire Sprigge, *Medicine and the Public*, 61.

[67] *Report of the Actuaries in Relation to the Proposed Scheme of Insurance*, March 1910 (quoted in Gilbert, *National Insurance*, 315).

[68] *RC on Health Insurance*, PP, 1926, xiv, 162, 314.   [69] See Ch. 9.

[70] Hewetson, 'Before and after the appointed day', 1271.

where doctors effectively subsidized the medicine from their own pockets, some 'awful rubbish' was prescribed.[71] Other dependants, like some in colliery districts, might be covered by occupational provision. The South Wales Miners Federation, for example, levied a 6*d.* a week subscription, which would pay for the medical treatments of the wife and children of the male breadwinner, even if this involved expensive surgical operations for the removal of an appendix, or for corrective surgery on a hare-lip.[72]

Standards

Amongst key issues posed by the NHI was the question of whether panel patients were second-class citizens when compared to private patients. Informing discussion were implicit value judgements as to the appropriate standard to be sought in a public service catering for poorer patients. Class assumptions shaped the perceptions of bureaucrats as well as of doctors. English Insurance Committees were circulated on whether panel patients received as good a service as private patients, and the omissions and face-saving phraseology in their replies pointed to a divided system of medical care.[73] An obvious indication of the two-tier nature of practice could be readily observed in the differentiated physical accommodation and reception of patients. Panel patients frequently queued at a back door to enter a cramped, barely furnished surgery, there to wait their turn for the doctor during fixed surgery hours. In contrast, their middle-class counterparts chose personally convenient times for appointments, were greeted by a maid at the front door, and waited in a comfortable room in the doctor's house for more extended medical interviews.[74] Indeed, there was neither incentive for the panel doctor to improve accommodation, nor any effective coercion to do so, since although the rare insurance committee (such as Birmingham) inspected the surgery accommodation of insurance doctors several times, others (like London or Devonshire), did so only rarely or unsystematically.[75]

The usual divide between panel and private patients was narrower in the Manchester and Salford Scheme. A local newspaper commented that 'it is to the doctor's interests to treat his panel patients with the same consideration he treats his private patients. Otherwise he would speedily find himself without any panel patients.'[76] This local initiative was predicated on payment to doctors on the basis of patient attendance and not, as was the case elsewhere, on an annual capitation payment. Panel patients were therefore on the same

---

[71] CMAC, GP 29/1/69A, David Kerr who began practice in south London just before the NHS.
[72] Personal testimony of Glyndwr Lloyd, recollecting the years 1918–24.
[73] PRO, MH 62/151, Court of Enquiry into Insurance Practitioners Remuneration, 1923.
[74] See Ch. 6.   [75] Armstrong, *Insurance Doctor*, 27–8.
[76] Lancs RO, IC Bu/3, *Burnley News*, (*c.*1923).

footing as private ones. Running for only a dozen years, the scheme collapsed under the weight of the administrative work it had generated.[77]

Insurance doctors had to give all proper and necessary medical services except those requiring special skill. This meant *inter alia* that treatment of fractures or dislocation was expected but not an operation for piles or an operation on tubercular glands.[78] More serious cases were referred for treatment in the outpatients departments of hospitals. Practitioners were supplied with 'Lloyd George' record cards for their NHI patients. Panel doctors recorded brief but intermittent entries for patients, usually in relation to more serious conditions, and/or those requiring certification in relation to employment. Diagnoses were almost entirely for physical ailments, and few clinical measurements were recorded as having been made in reaching them.[79] Panel doctors seem to have shown little or no appreciation of the value of the NHI clinical record for their patients. The financial committee of one Scottish panel even minuted that 'the present medical record system is serving no useful purpose and in the interest of economy should be scrapped'.[80] Patient–doctor confidentiality in relation to NHI certification was an issue raised by one NHI practitioner, who was outraged by the local insurance committee's insistence that the precise illness suffered by the panel patient be inserted on a certificate of incapacity for work. Interestingly, the point was made that 'health and character are so closely bound together that the declaration of a malady may blight the fair face of a whole family'. The doctor won his case, and the word 'illness' was deemed sufficient thereafter.[81]

Doctors complained about the fluctuating composition of their panels, although this was usually articulated in a grouse about form filling, rather than in manifesting concern about its implications for the continuous care of patients—a defining characteristic of good general practice. Many panel patients moved on to a new doctor's list because of changes of address or of employment. Panel patients did have the right to choose their insurance practitioners, but only very small numbers (between 3 and 5 per cent) were estimated to have initiated a change in their doctor by giving notice at the end of a quarter.[82] This finding might indicate either satisfaction with the standard of service or low patient expectation. That there was only a small trickle of panel patients' grievances about their doctors does not resolve this ambiguity. Complaints were usually about the practitioner charging for a procedure without prior warning, or charging for one which it was thought should have been in the category of insurance treatment rather than private practice.

---

[77] G. F. McLeary, 'The Influence of the Medical Profession on the English Health Insurance Scheme', *Millbank Memorial Fund Quarterly*, xiii (1935), 26.

[78] The record of panel doctors in the treatment of fractures was so dismal that fractures were later excluded from their remit (F. Honigsbaum, *The Division in British Medicine* (1979), 159).

[79] See Ch. 8.

[80] Scottish RO, Fife NHI Committee, minute 19 July 1922.

[81] *Burnley News*, 17 May, and 16 July, 1913.

[82] W. L. Foster and F. G. Taylor, *National Health Insurance* (3rd edn., 1937), 161.

Also prominent were allegations that the doctor showed insufficient courtesy or did not respond promptly to a request for a visit. Discourtesy or incorrect charging were complaints which were far more likely to be upheld by insurance medical committees, and the patient vindicated, than were charges of medical negligence when doctors on NHI medical committees might feel impelled to salvage colleagues' professional reputations by finding face-saving rationales for their conduct. In some instances, however, a doctor was so clearly clinically negligent that he was severely censured, and a substantial fine was imposed. One Scottish doctor, for example, was fined £50. He had been sent for on a Saturday afternoon, failed to attend the panel patient until Sunday morning, when castor oil was prescribed, called subsequently on Monday morning, when the patient was sent to hospital, where death soon ensued from appendicitis.[83] Friendly societies also criticized panel doctors for supplying inadequate certification in cases involving society members as insured patients; their allegations were well substantiated, and were usually upheld.[84]

Standards of practice varied, not only (predictably) between individual doctors, but also in the standards laid down by insurance committees between different areas. Nottinghamshire, for example, debated the merits of a Local Formulary, such as that introduced into the City of Nottingham, by which a limited pharmaceutical range had been sanctioned for panel patients. It concluded that stock mixtures partook of club practice, would encourage hasty prescribing, lead to deterioration in the mixtures during storage and, although producing economies, would not be in the interest of the insured person.[85] Barrow in Furness, in contrast, was only too ready to sanction and introduce a local Formulary. Out of twenty-eight stock mixtures which the BMA and the Pharmaceutical Society of Great Britain listed as suitable for storing in bulk, the Barrow in Furness Insurance Committee selected only ten stock mixtures for use by its practitioners including cough mixtures, tonics, and digestive or laxative medicines.[86]

If panel doctors prescribed expensive drugs they might be vulnerable to accusations of over-prescription, and liable to subsequent surcharging.[87] The annual prescription cost of Fife panel doctors was continually singled out as having been well above the Scottish average. In 1925 nineteen local doctors there were even surcharged £100 each for their excessive prescription. The Fife insurance practitioners defended their expenditures on the grounds that they were due both to inexperienced panel doctors as well as to the pre-

[83] Scottish RO, HH3 6/7, Fife NHI Committee minute, 12 May 1943.

[84] Nottinghamshire RO, SO NH/1/1, Nottinghamshire NHI Committee minutes, 1912–27.

[85] Nottinghamshire RO, SO NH, Nottinghamshire NHI Committee minute, 29 Oct. 1915.

[86] These were Mistura Alba, Bismuthi, Cascarae Composita, Expectorans, Ferri Aperiens, Ferri Arsenicalis, Ferri et Strychninae, Gentianae Alkalina, Sodae e. Rhei, and Tussis. (Lancashire RO, IC Bo 17/1, Barrow in Furness NHI Committee correspondence, 15 Sept. 1916).

[87] For example, Scottish RO, HH3 7/001, Dunfermline NHI Committee ledger (1913–49), folios 52, 55, 68.

scription of new expensive drugs, such as extract of liver, which was 'of great therapeutic value'. Later, local doctors considered that this restrictive bureaucratic policy had been beneficially modified.[88] However, this issue of pharmaceutical expense was to explode under the NHS, when much more expensive drugs came onstream.

The calibre of NHI pharmaceutical practice has received little academic attention, but it is obvious that the predominance of small chemists, making up a few NHI prescriptions for a handful of doctors, was unlikely to encourage accurate dispensing. When the Nottinghamshire Insurance Committee inquired into panel prescriptions, the analyst they employed found that as many as one in three were substandard.[89] Generally, new drugs were not sanctioned for NHI use, because it was stated that 'as a specific it is still in question', but to the historian the suspicion lingers that its cost was the material factor.[90] Appliances which were sanctioned by the NHI authorities in each locality were listed. These might include cheaper alternatives to those which doctors were accustomed to use, and Burnley doctors protested, for example, about the cheaper grey bandages they were expected to substitute for white ones for their panel patients.[91]

For the patient the 1911 act brought real, if heavily qualified, blessings. A panel doctor concluded that 'the Insurance Act was a boon both to the insured patient and to their medical attendant.' The doctor was no longer involved in 'balancing the value of his services against the length of his patient's purses', while the patients were not faced with bills and debts.[92] But although access to a doctor undoubtedly improved after 1911, the quality of care given was generally mediocre. Club doctors before the NHI had reduced visits in favour of a swift throughput through the surgery,[93] and the panel doctor continued with this. The panel system therefore institutionalized a pre-existing tension between the club doctor and his patient in that it emphasized the quantity of care delivered rather than intervening to improve its quality. Routinization linked to a low standard of patient care: with overprescription; a reluctance to treat difficult cases rather than to refer them elsewhere; and under-investment in modern equipment and premises were thereby encouraged.[94] This trend was linked to the capitation system of British insurance practice. In Germany where doctors were paid through items of service, insurance practitioners were encouraged to offer specialist as well as generalist services to their patients.[95]

[88] Scottish RO, HH3 6/6 and 6/7, Fife NHI Committee minutes, 8 May and 18 Sept. 1915, 7 July 1917, 5 May 1920, 8 July 1925, 16 Apr. 1930, 15 Mar. 1931, 24 Dec. 1947.

[89] Nottinghamshire RO, SO NH, Nottinghamshire NHI Committee minutes, 29 Oct. 1915, 27 May 1921.

[90] Lancashire RO, IC La/1/1, Lancashire NHI Committee minute, 8 June 1914.

[91] Burnley Express, 7 Apr. 1923.

[92] A Panel Doctor, On the Panel. General Practice as a Career (1926), 2–3.

[93] S. and B. Webb, The State and the Doctor (1910), 139.

[94] Digby and Bosanquet, 'Doctors and Patients', 77–9, 90–2.

[95] Honigsbaum, British Medicine, 304.

It was almost inevitable that the pressure of treating large numbers of patients should have had an adverse impact on the range and quality of patient–doctor encounters. A reluctance by panel doctors to engage in clinical work for which no remuneration was likely, meant a readiness to refer patients to hospital outpatient clinics. Even Dame Janet Campbell (formerly in the Ministry of Health), admitted that 'Panel practice does not justify the keen doctor . . . Work is hard, hours are long'.[96] Plate 8 satirizes the assembly-line character of insurance health care by showing the 'Express Panel Doctor' on roller skates together with an assembly line of patients waiting with their tongues out. At that time the doctor gave on average three-and-a-quarter minutes to each insurance patient in the surgery, and four minutes when on a visit to the patient's home.[97] But perhaps we should not be too critical on this score: it was not very different from the five minutes that the NHS doctor later spent.[98]

Conclusion

In contrast to the results of an upswing in numbers of medical graduates which had produced a growing *diversity* amongst general practitioners in the sixty years before 1911, the economic and medical framework of the NHI provided powerful and growing pressure for increased *uniformity*. The huge practice differentiation—that a previous desperate search for financial survival had encouraged in an overcrowded Victorian and Edwardian medical market—was eroded but not entirely eliminated. The detailed rules and regulations administered by national insurance commissioners resulted in a convergence in panel practice and, following from that, in general practice, because the majority of practices ultimately recruited a panel of patients. Through substituting capitation payments for the previous uncertainties of fee income, the scheme provided a financial safety net. But the state's meagre capitation payment imposed similar pressures on the insurance doctor as had been experienced earlier by the club doctor, depressing the quality of medical service through encouraging a cost-cutting regime of high patient throughput, minimal patient record keeping, the use of stock mixtures, and the deployment of a restricted range of clinical procedures. This systematization and diffusion of the less desirable features of some earlier forms of general practice was reinforced by the growing work load arising from an increasing demand for services by panel patients themselves.

The reform of 1911 was thus a defining moment when certain key elements within modern general practice emerged. By their initially reluctant partici-

[96] Quoted in Levy, *Health Insurance*, 135.

[97] *Medical World*, 9 Apr. 1914. This calculation was made on the basis of large list sizes of panel doctors.

[98] Digby, *Medical Living*, 308.

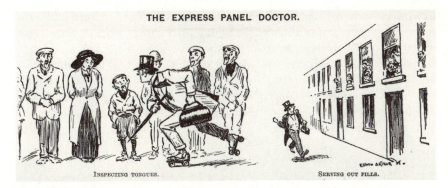

THE EXPRESS PANEL DOCTOR.

INSPECTING TONGUES.   SERVING OUT PILLS.

8. The express panel doctor, 1913

pation in the NHI British GPs acknowledged the need to temper Victorian individual commercialism with Edwardian social welfarism. Lloyd George later aptly commented that 'No scheme was ever more needed or less wanted.'[99] A widespread participation by GPs was important in helping to ensure a greater financial survival of general practice in Britain than in many other countries, despite the encroachments of specialism on the one hand, and of municipal medicine on the other. But, paradoxically, it was payment from the insurance scheme which tended to insulate some general practitioners from the need to effect clinical, technological or organization change. Response to the new technologies of car and phone, as well as a trend to partnership, was steady rather than dynamic, since although these might offer a better chance of meeting competition, panel income itself cushioned the GP from such challenges. After two decades of the NHI the *BMJ* commented that although 'medicine is a path to fortune only for the few' it was evident that 'no doctor who is willing or able to work need starve'.[100]

Seen from the sectional viewpoint of the general practitioner the NHI was perceived as constituting a greater break with what had gone before than was the later NHS of 1946/8. 'In fact the change [to the NHS] from the old NHI scarcely altered the daily pattern of general practice . . . To my father's generation of doctors it [the NHI] must have seemed far more revolutionary than its successor of 1948 did to us', reflected John Hewetson whose professional life spanned both the NHI and NHS. Thus, in 1948, GPs continued to treat 'panel' patients now re-labelled as 'NHS' patients, and signed up the dependants of erstwhile panel patients to their NHS patient list.[101]

Viewed from a longer term perspective—in charting an evolving right of the citizen to health—the national health insurance scheme appears as a major, but still interim, stage. Within the frame of reference of the then

[99] Speech at the 25th anniversary dinner of the NHI. (*BMJ*, 22 July 1933).
[100] *BMJ*, ii (1933), 412.
[101] Hewetson, 'Before and After the Appointed Day', 1271; Harding, unpubl. 'Memoir', 74.

Liberal government's political philosophy, health concerns were still subsidiary to welfare issues directed at labour productivity, so that health was linked to wealth creation. Insured workers were given a right of access to a limited range of health care providers (excluding hospitals) only when their health failed. Their dependants remained excluded. Under the NHI individuals were therefore recognized as having a *conditional right* to a health benefit which was dependent on their function in society.[102] It was left to the founders of the NHS to articulate health as an individual, *positive right* of citizenship.

---

[102] M. Freeden, 'The extension of Liberal rights: health, welfare, and community', unpubl. paper given at the 'Right to Health' conference, Oxford, July 1997.

13

The National Health Service

THE *Beveridge Report*'s blueprint for post-war welfare reform, of which the National Health Service was to be such a notable feature, was published in 1942, and two years later the wartime coalition government's White Paper, *A National Health Service*, was issued. A landslide Labour victory in the general election of 1945 then made possible a much more radical transformation of the health service. The interim Report of the Medical Planning Commission (1942)[1] and the Goodenough Report on Medical Education (1944) had also articulated the aspirations of the medical profession for this new health service. The latter gave a central role to general practitioners within it:

One of the principal aims of national policy should be to secure for everyone the highest possible standard of physical and mental health . . . By becoming advisers on health both to individuals and to the community, medical practitioners will have to bear much of the responsibility for ensuring this result.[2]

This chapter is concerned with the historical role that GPs played in shaping this new health service, and with the reception of the NHS by doctors and their patients.

A very extensive historiography on conflict or consensus in the formation of the NHS has given varied roles, alliances or animosities to socialist idealists, medical corporations, and paternalist bureaucrats.[3] In concentrating on the few years preceding the NHS historians have focused their attention on the state and the medical profession at a moment of high policy, but in doing so have tended to neglect the intervening period since the preceding high point—the national health insurance scheme of 1911, and thus have not brought the interwar years adequately into focus in order to explain the role of ideologies and interests in shaping these legislative watersheds. In a discussion of public policy Michael Freeden called this the 'on/off switch', and has also referred to the 'treeless wood', the tendency to assume that a piece

---

[1] The commission was set up by the Royal Colleges, the BMA, and the Scottish Royal Medical Corporation.

[2] *Goodenough Report*, 10.

[3] For an incisive discussion see C. Webster, 'Conflict and Consensus: Explaining the British Health Service', *Twentieth Century British History*, 1 (1990), 115–52.

of legislation (such as the National Health Service Act, 1946) is a manifestation of a single clear idea rather than 'a composite of multiple and parallel
motives and notions.'[4] To contextualize the development of the new health
service more satisfactorily a longer-run discussion of professional pressure
groups follows.

Professional Involvement in Change

The British Medical Association represented half of all doctors on the
Medical Register in 1901, and this had risen to three-quarters by 1948. The
BMA has been interpreted as becoming at that time 'the creature . . . of pub-
lic medical policies . . . engaged in constant co-operation' with the Ministry
of Health.[5] Politics thus became medicalized, and medicine politicized.[6] The
BMA clashed with government at moments of high policy at the start of the
NHI and NHS, but had also become enmeshed with the state in its admin-
istration of a growing range of public medical services, because it provided a
source of technical knowledge, a liaison agency and a means of mobilizing
GP's involvement.[7]

During the four decades before the NHS health-related matters were low
on the BMA's priorities in lengthy negotiations with the state. The Secretary
of the BMA did write to the Minister of Health, stating that 'the main point
at issue is not the money [but] . . . to maintain a good medical service for the
industrial population'.[8] Such disclaimers were rare. In 1930 the BMA published a *Report on a General Medical Service for the Nation*, and its *Essentials
of a National Health Service*, appeared in 1933, although these were more a
self-interested response to concerns in a wider society than a setting of a radical agenda. The health of the people it was noted was 'one of the most interesting and pressing public questions of the day', so that a national maternity
scheme was proposed, as well as an extension of NHI to dependants.
Predictably, GPs were to play a central role in each case. The need for a preventive orientation had been recognized even before the NHI. In 1910, for
example, the Webbs noted that, 'We do a great deal of State doctoring in
England . . . For the most part . . . instead of preventing the occurrence of
disease, we choose to let it happen, and then find ourselves driven to try
expensively to cure it.'[9] But the BMA missed this opportunity to work
towards a *social* health service.

---

[4] M. Freeden, 'The Stranger at the Feast: Ideology and Public Policy in Twentieth-Century
Britain', *Twentieth Century British History*, 1 (1990), 29, 31.
[5] H. Eckstein, *Pressure Group Politics. The Case of the British Medical Association* (1960).
[6] A. Cawson, *Corporatism and Political Theory* (1986), 114–116.
[7] Eckstein, *Pressure Group*, 46–8.
[8] PRO, MH 62/149, A. Cox to Sir W. Joynson Hicks, 27 Oct. 1923.
[9] S. and B. Webb, *The State and the Doctor* (1910), p. v.

Instead they privileged doctors' remuneration over other concerns. An indicator of an interest group's efficacy is its ability to get resources for its members,[10] but despite making this its principal concern the BMA had only limited success, as its record from 1911 to 1948 revealed. The previous chapter indicated that the BMA leaders were unable to carry its membership with it, in opposing the government's revised NHI offer, since many rank-and-file doctors were all too aware of the parlous state of their finances, the overcrowded state of the medical market, their limited ability to expand their market amongst the poorer patients catered for in the 1911 proposals, and thus recognized that they had been offered a substantial economic windfall. With diminished credibility the BMA had to ratify what individual members had already decided to do through joining the panel system.[11] During the interwar period the BMA was also ineffectual in its attempts to raise state payments to panel doctors.

Panel doctors recognized the need to organize a professional association which would be more exclusively focused on their needs. Shortly after the start of the NHI scheme the Medical Practitioners Union began its life as the Panel Medico-Politico Union in order to represent their interests.[12] Its records indicate how it gradually developed similar facilities for doctors to the BMA (a medical agency, a benevolent fund, and a pension, loan and insurance scheme), as well as producing a journal—the *Medical World*. A policy statement of 1928 indicated the union's exclusive focus on the role and responsibilities of general practitioners in relation *inter alia* to legal enactments, local authority health services, hospitals, medical schools, and the GMC.[13] The MPU's strongly economic orientation—together with its concern with an 'overcrowded' medical market—contributed to its violent antagonism to refugee doctors, and its pronounced anti-Semitic stance from the late 1930s onwards. Its view of doctors as 'employees', although under professional rather than lay control, was substantively not too distinct from the BMA's view of doctors as independent contractors. But the MPU's terminology of employee probably facilitated the MPU's controversial affiliation to the TUC in 1937/8. Members of the MPU thought that their more conservative colleagues would view the affiliation as if 'the Union dropped like Lucifer from Grace', and would see MPU members as 'striped trousered Bolsheviks'.[14] Indeed, the affiliation was too radical for some of its own members who resigned (not least because they had not been consulted on the move), but equally it attracted new members as a result. In the longer term,

[10] R. Klein, *The Politics of the National Health Service* (2nd edn., 1983), 55.

[11] N. R. Eder, *National Health Insurance and the Medical Profession in Britain, 1913–1939* (1982), 35–44.

[12] F. Brockway, *Bermondsey Story. The Life of Alfred Salter* (1944), 64.

[13] Modern Records Centre, University of Warwick, MSS 79/MPU/1/2/1, MPU council minute, 19 Jan. 1928.

[14] National Library of Scotland, accession. 6027, no. 19, Papers of the Medical Practitioners Union, Glasgow, third series of district meetings, n.d.

however, this action brought some benefit to the MPU in that the TUC ceded its single seat on the General Medical Council to the MPU.[15]

Membership of the MPU grew, in part as a result of active recruiting, with 'propagandising efforts' by a paid organizer, and through addresses to medical students. By 1944/5 a membership of 3,000 had been achieved.[16] There were branches in large towns in the north of England and in the west of Scotland. In Glasgow, for example, the MPU under the activist leadership of Dr T. Ross-Scott, first as its Secretary, and later as its Vice-President had a shrewdly chosen set of campaigning issues designed to attract interest and support by local panel doctors. These included the parsimony of the insurance drug fund, the increasing bureaucratic burden of doctors under the NHI, and the insufficient compensation for rising numbers of contacts between panel doctor and patient.[17] A radical, oppositional stance was taken against the established order, whether this was Glasgow's Medical Officer of Health, the local Insurance Committee (seen as dominated by the BMA), or the national BMA (referred to as the 'Lady Tavistock Square').

This classic outsider position was a reaction to the stance of other bodies. The MPU found itself marginalized professionally, as was shown by the refusal of the Editors of the *Medical Directory* to include notification of MPU membership in its entries.[18] This experience was not dissimilar to that of the Socialist Medical Association. Political and Economic Planning did not consult the SMA, for example, over its influential *Report on the British Health Services* in 1937.[19] From the late 1930s the MPU worked with the Socialist Medical Association in attempting to formulate a transition from what was considered an unsatisfactory panel scheme, to a more socially inclusive, free, and medically complete health service for the nation. Key elements in this MPU blueprint for a general practitioner service were health centres, professional team work by doctors within a salaried service, and state-provided equipment and support staff.[20]

The SMA was opposed to 'vested interests' in the health services, amongst which it numbered the BMA, whose attitudes were seen as inimical to medical progress. Founded in 1930, the SMA was formally affiliated with the Labour Party in the following year. Its membership came from all areas of the health services, but a public and municipal membership vastly outnumbered that of general practitioners. General practitioners with idealistic

---

[15] Modern Records Centre, University of Warwick, MSS 79/MPU/1/2/1, MPU council minute, 11 June 1941.

[16] Ibid., minutes, 8 July 1926, 30 Aug. 1939, 14 Nov. 1945; Fox, *Health Policies*, 112.

[17] National Library of Scotland, accession. 6027, no. 19, Papers of the Medical Practitioners Union, Glasgow. Dr T. Ross-Scott LRCP, LRCS (Edinburgh), LRFPS (Glasgow, 1915).

[18] Modern Records Centre, University of Warwick, MSS 79/MPU/1/2/1, MPU council minutes, 11 Sept. 1930.

[19] D. M. Fox, *Health Policies. Health Politics* (Princeton, 1986), 65.

[20] Modern Records Centre, University of Warwick, MSS 79/MPU/1/2/2, MPU council minutes, 23 Oct. 1940, 25 Feb. 1942, 1 Mar. 1944, 10 Apr. 1946.

and/or left-wing views were most likely to join the SMA. For example, members included Anthony Ryle and David Kerr who were also members of the Communist party.[21] Another member was the Stoke Newington doctor, D. S. Bryan Brown: a Christian Socialist and former medical missionary, who had a strong interest in public health, and was for a time 'an enthusiastic member,' and chair of the North London branch.[22]

By the 1940s membership was around the 4,000 mark, although the SMA wielded an influence disproportionate to its size.[23] Its growing strength on the London County Council, as well as on the health committees of the Labour Party, suggested that it would have an influential voice in shaping the NHS. Like the MPU the SMA believed that doctors should be encouraged to work in medical teams in health centres. An important reason for this in the case of the SMA, however, was the belief that general practitioners should not pursue their own vested interests in individual practices within a 'capitalistic medicine'. Reinforcing this was an advocacy of preventive rather than curative medicine, and a concern that doctors should not have a vested interest in sickness. In the event, although the SMA had worked hard for the NHS, which it viewed as a step in the right direction, the SMA's plan for a 'municipal, comprehensive and unified plan' was rejected, so that the association saw the health reform of 1946/8 as deeply flawed in its lack of democratic accountability, its non-adoption of a salaried GP service, and its inadequacies in respect to health centres.[24]

More idealistic GPs, such as those who joined the SMA, viewed the BMA leaders as 'very inward looking, very selfish . . . all they wanted was capitation rates to be increased'.[25] To its critics the BMA represented the 'petty bourgeois' of medicine—the traditional independent entrepreneur in general practice. Its anti-government and anti-NHS stance was thus predictable.[26] Like the American Medical Association the BMA used emotive language and dramatic posturing to whip up and sustain members' interest during a long campaign.[27] Some have seen the BMA as having been a vital part of policy-making. For example, Honigsbaum has highlighted the importance of doctors as decision-makers since civil servants could not match the influence of the BMA in the creation of the NHS.[28] Similarly, Eckstein has stressed the

---

[21] CMAC, GP 29/1/69A, David Kerr.

[22] *BMJ*, i (1960) 574. D. S. Bryan-Brown, MB. B.Ch. (St Thomas's 1914). He later switched allegiance, and became chair of the City Division of the BMA.

[23] C. Webster, 'Labour and the Origins of the National Health Service' in N.A. Rupke (ed.), *Science, Politics and the Public Good* (1988), 187.

[24] John Stewart, ' "Your Health, Mr Smith", British Socialist Doctors and Citizens Rights, *c*.1930–*c*.1970', unpubl. paper, 'Right to Health' Conference, Oxford, July 1997; 'Focus on the SMA', Oxford Brookes Research Forum, 4; J. Stewart, ' "For a Healthy London": The Socialist Medical Association and the London County Council in the 1930s', *MH*, 42 (1997), 432.

[25] CAMC, GP 29/2/6/1, Anthony Ryle.   [26] CMAC, GP 29/1/69A, David Kerr.

[27] D. M. Fox, *Health Policies. Health Politics* (Princeton, 1986), 140.

[28] F. Honigsbaum, *Health, Happiness and Security. The Creation of the National Health Service* (1989), 213–14, 217–18.

success of the BMA as an interest group in the period from 1911 to 1948.[29] But an important constraint on the BMA as a professional association was its inability to speak forcefully and monolithically for a unified profession. It represented non-elite GPs and was faced by a more powerful interest group, the consultants, whose interests were safeguarded by the Royal Colleges.[30] A convincing impression of the limitations in BMA negotiating muscle is given in the official history of the NHS by Charles Webster.[31]

'When devising means for translating the National Health Service legislation into practice the Government was entering a house haunted with ghosts from 1911.'[32] Aneurin Bevan, the Minister of Health, was anxious not to erode the hard-won settlement he had reached with some interested parties, which had been briefly debated in Parliament, and then enacted in the National Health Service Act of 1946. The BMA—fearing an equivalent humiliation to 1911—wished to compensate for what it regarded as uncongenial legislation, by forcing concessions over NHS regulations during the intervening period before the act came into effect on 5 July 1948. Amongst contested issues were: the government's aim of bringing about a long-term redistribution of GPs through closing off 'over-doctored' areas to new entrants; the relationship of partnership agreements to the proposed abolition of the sale and purchase of practices, as well as the amount of compensation envisaged; a 'tribunal' system for discipline; and the payment of GPs— whether with a basic salaried component or only through capitation payments. For much of this time relations between Bevan and the BMA were embittered by the government's unwillingness to raise GPs' capitation to the extent recommended by the Spens Report of 1946, an issue only fully resolved in May 1948.

Increasingly militant rhetoric was matched by an absence of movement in the stances of the two sides. In their plebiscites the medical profession continued to hold a generally hostile view of impending changes. Finally, with time running out until the Appointed Day, Bevan offered concessions, principally in minimizing the importance of salaries, by making them only a fixed element during the opening years of professional life. Opposition from general practitioners crumbled so that 8,000 changed sides between February and May 1948.[33] This 'roll-over' had been predicted three months earlier by Dr D. G. Morgan, the Branch Chairman for the BMA in South Wales, who represented his division at BMA Representative Meetings in London. His private diary entries recorded with ironic detachment that 'The BMA as usual was reactionary and unrealistic', 'the acrobatics of the [BMA] leaders are very amusing to watch', and 'the BMA are making fools of themselves', being

[29] Eckstein, *Pressure Group Politics*.

[30] R. Stevens, *Medical Practice in Modern England. The Impact of Specialisation and State Medicine* (New Haven, 1966), 77–9, 92–3; F. Honigsbaum, *The Division in British Medicine* (1979), 298–302.

[31] C. Webster, *The Health Services Since the War* (1988), 116–19.

[32] Webster, *Health Services Since the War*, 107.   [33] Ibid., 107–20.

driven not by 'principle but a deep-rooted fear or realisation that the high incomes now enjoyed from private practice will disappear'.[34] Divided against itself, and with even the *BMJ* critical of its stance, the BMA conceded defeat. The Chairman of the BMA Council pledged the support of the profession for the new service in a letter to *The Times* of 17 June, within three weeks of the Appointed Day on which the NHS was to take effect.[35]

Although the BMA had been consulted regularly by the Ministry of Health over routine matters, when high policy was created (as with the NHS), it became one of many interest groups involved. The state's own dynamic as an autonomous actor in the creation of policies was of key importance,[36] so that to only a limited extent did its growing interventionism mediate, translate, or more rarely incorporate those issues that had been put forward by an interest group such as the BMA. The government represented a wider constituency so that the 'power of the medical profession is in inverse relationship to the size of the stage on which a specific health care issue is fought out'.[37] Medical practitioners had influenced the creation of the NHI more strongly than that of the NHS, because in 1911 the public interest in developing primary care was more congruent with private practitioners' interests, whereas in 1948 the impact of war had moved the interests of citizens to a more central position in the creation of the classic welfare state. Nevertheless, the amended NHS legislation did embody a major campaigning issue of the BMA, in retaining capitation as the basis for the remuneration of GPs, although a salaried component was later to assume greater importance during reforms in the 1960s and 1990s.[38] The new service also mirrored many GP's individualistic and curative, rather than social and preventive, concerns.

Whether practitioners were in Scotland or in England and Wales made relatively little difference to the legal frameworks of the new service. As far as GPs were concerned there were no major differences between the National Health Service Act of 1946 of England and Wales, and the National Health Services (Scotland) Act of 1947, in contrast to the subsequent NHS reform of 1974. Minor differences in 1946–7 included the retention in the Scottish act of the provision in the Highlands and Islands Medical Service whereby houses could be provided for doctors.[39] The professional reception of these

[34] National Library of Wales, D.G. Morgan papers, 5 Apr. 1946 and 11 Feb. 1947, 4 Feb. 1948. Morgan was Medical Superintendent of Llandough Hospital. Interestingly, its well-known Pneumoconiosis Research Centre was visited by Bevan in Jan. 1948.

[35] P. Vaughan, *Doctors Commons. A Short History of the British Medical Assocation* (1959), 232–4. In the plebiscite 8,639 GPs voted in favour, and 9,588 against, the amended act.

[36] T. Skocpol, 'Bringing the State Back in: Strategies of Analysis in Current Research', in P. B. Evans, D. Rueschemeyer, and T. Skocpol (eds.), *Bringing the State Back In* (Cambridge, 1985), 3–37.

[37] Klein, *Politics*, 52.

[38] A. Digby, 'Medicine and the English State, 1901–1948', in S. J. D. Green and R. C. Whiting (eds.), *The Boundaries of the State in Modern Britain* (Cambridge, 1996), 228–30.

[39] Webster, *Health Services Since the War*, 104.

enactments was differentiated, however, with Scottish and Welsh GPs view-
ing the new service more positively than their English colleagues.[40]

The NHS and its Reception

A benign historiography on the socially desirable changes brought about by
the NHS, coupled with a critical view of the short-sightedly sectional way
that the BMA had handled the transition to a new system of health care, have
tended to obscure the very real, and widespread, uncertainties involved. Even
Bevan, the architect of the new service, commented later about patients that
'it was absolutely necessary that we should first of all allow people to behave
before we could form a view of what that behaviour pattern of the population would be in respect of spectacles, dentistry, drugs, and doctors'.[41]
Doctors whose professional lives spanned the watershed of 1948 have som-
bre recollections of this period of transition, because they felt generally
uncertain about what the NHS implied. Not all doctors had the time to go
to BMA meetings—especially if they had rural practices. 'We didn't know
what it was going to do . . . we didn't know [what] we were going to get paid.
And we didn't know whether we were going to get any compensation.'[42]
There was a prolonged period of waiting before the amount of compensation
for the goodwill of the practice was finalized. For example, almost a year after
the NHS had come into operation, a doctor might receive a standardized letter from the Ministry of Health as did Dr D. W. Hendry, which stated that
compensation for the goodwill of the Nuneaton practice in which he was a
partner had been calculated at £9,729, that with four partners his quarter
share was £2,432, but that this sum 'does *not* represent the amount of compensation to which you will be entitled, and a further communication will be
sent to you as soon as possible'.[43]

Medicine was a liberal profession. The BMA powerfully articulated issues
of 'professional freedom' and therefore played on the general practitioners'
anxiety that they would become like civil servants, and would lose their independence.[44] 'We were afraid of being taken into a salaried service, and
ordered about, and [of] getting a much smaller salary.'[45] There was also

[40] This is suggested by the fact that 37 per cent of Scottish doctors and 36 per cent of Welsh ones
had already signed up as individuals for the service, as against only 26 per cent of English doctors,
even before the BMA plebiscite of May 1948 (K. O. Morgan, *Labour in Power, 1945–1951* (Oxford,
1985), 160).

[41] *Hansard*, vol. 472, col. 1028, 14 Mar. 1950.

[42] CMAC, GP 29//2/32, Robert Clarke of Bolton.

[43] Private archive of Mrs E. Hendry, letter from Ministry of Health to Dr D. W. Hendry, 12 May
1949.

[44] Sir Henry Ogilvie, 'Then and Now', *Practitioner*, 161 (1948), 4; CMAC, GP 29/2/42, Arnold
Elliott.

[45] Pers. comm. from Dr Rankine of Romsey. The Labour Party's pamphlet, *A National Service
for Health* of 1943 (written by an SMA member), had stated that the medical profession should be
organized as a salaried service.

apprehension that the NHS would restrict prescribing freedom.[46] Trepidation was aroused that bureaucratic record keeping would grow although, retrospectively, there was disagreement about how much this had actually happened.[47]

The NHS had a strongly differentiated impact. Generational differences were highlighted amongst general practitioners with some older doctors going for early retirement rather than facing what they feared would be a radical change.[48] In contrast, the younger generation who had only recently come out of medical school, or who had served in the army, found the new health service reflected their ideals about practice. This was also the case amongst those with more left-wing politics, such as members of the Socialist Medical Association.[49] One such SMA doctor said, 'I wasn't a militant for commercialism, apart from the fact that I had to earn a living . . . I was interested in wanting to help people.'[50] Doctors in different sorts of practice experienced adjustment to the new conditions of the NHS with varied degrees of severity. This bore strong similarities to the situation experienced after 1911, when 'club' or 'sixpenny' doctors effortlessly adopted a fast throughput of national insurance or panel patients, because their prior conditions of practice were very similar. After 1948 those who had run a largely panel practice adjusted smoothly, and also benefited because the wives and children of their erstwhile male panel patients now came to them. But there was some generalized ill-feeling about the speed with which more entrepreneurial doctors signed up patients for the NHS, so that there was a redistribution of patients away from those doctors who were still holding out for a better deal under BMA leadership.[51] Interestingly, history was repeating itself in that this was comparable to complaints after the 1911 act that the 'sixpenny doctors' had signed up huge numbers of panel patients very quickly.

For those who had run a practice which was to a much greater extent—or wholly—composed of private patients, there was a longer period of adjustment; not least because it was unclear how many patients would remain private or opt for free treatment under the NHS. Doctors' own views showed some generational variation with older doctors tending to like private patients, while younger ones found them either uncongenial or else perceived their expectation of superior treatment to be uneconomic, and so often deliberately ran down, or ended, the private list.[52] In any case private patients disappeared much more rapidly than doctors envisaged before the NHS took effect. The swiftness and completeness with which the middle-class patient

[46] CMAC, GP 29/2/45, Arthur Griffiths.

[47] Ibid., GP 29/2/37, Hilda Cantrell thought it had; GP29/2/32 Robert Clarke of Bolton thought 'not a lot'.

[48] Ibid., GP 29/2/47, Clifford Aston of Allerton Bywater. It was also accepted wisdom amongst this cohort that NHS superannuation arrangements would make retirement impossible until after a further period of ten years of service. (I am indebted to Charles Webster for this insight.)

[49] Ibid., GP 29/2/42, Arnold Elliott.

[50] Ibid., GP/2/42, Arnold Elliott.

[51] Ibid., GP29/2/37, Hilda Cantrell.

[52] Pers. comm., Dr Granger of Kimbolton.

opted for the NHS found general practitioners unprepared. 'We were really quite surprised at the number of people in the really big houses who took advantage of the NHS right away.'[53] Dr Harding, a Faringdon general practitioner, recollected that 'My own former private patients lost no time in presenting their [NHS] cards. Very few remained aloof.'[54] The medical profession had grossly underestimated the prospective impact of the new health service. Rather than a socially inclusive and egalitarian new health service, many had envisaged it merely as an extension and enlargement of the national health insurance scheme for the working class. Nor have historians appreciated the unexpected scale and speed of this enormous change in the social character of primary care, in which private practice with the middle class all but disappeared overnight.

Some GPs were pro-active in accelerating these changes; they abandoned billing with no regret, and abolished their private practice, so running an entirely NHS practice.[55] But incorporating the better-educated patients into an NHS practice was not in itself unproblematic, with some GPs resenting their demands for more time and attention.[56] In the most common situation where there was a majority of NHS patients, but with an admixture of fewer middle-class patients, there was alleged to be no difference in the clinical treatment given to the practice's NHS and private patients, apart from preferential treatment over visiting.[57] In some partnerships greater differentiation was formalized by one partner—who liked private practice—retaining responsibility for the private patients. During parliamentary debates on the NHS, critics of a proposed bipartite system of free and paying patients had predicted that it would involve a two-tier system of care, and that this would then erode confidence in the new health service.[58] In the event, the concern was removed by this much smaller scale of surviving private practice.

Other practitioners were relieved by the loss of their private patients. 'This was actually a relief for me, as I had never found it easy to present adequate bills, particularly when I knew the family income was low.'[59] Others were heavily reliant on middle-class fees, and suffered financial loss if such patients opted for the NHS.[60] A few GPs actively mounted a campaign to retain their private patients, as did those in a Woodford practice. With a largely middle-class practice Eric Grogono told his patients that if they wished to be visited when they weren't very ill, they had better stay private patients, because in these circumstances NHS patients would be expected to come to the surgery. This salesmanship meant that a 'marginal' social class of patients, who otherwise would have turned to the NHS, remained as private patients for the next decade or so. He commented that this 'paid my school bills'.[61] And, in a few

[53] Pers. comm., Dr Rankine of Romsey.   [54] Harding, unpubl. 'Memoir', 74.
[55] Quoted in Collings Report, *Lancet*, i, (1950), 569; pers. comm., Dr Granger of Kimbolton.
[56] *Lancet*, 25 Mar. 1950.   [57] CMAC, GP 29/1/71, Eric Grogono.
[58] *Hansard*, vol. 442, col. 113, 30 Apr. 1946, Alice Bacon, MP for Leeds.
[59] Harding, unpubl. 'Memoir', 74.   [60] *Lancet*, 25 Mar. 1950.
[61] CMAC, GP/29/1/71, Eric Grogono.

areas, all-private practices remained, situated either in the residential centre of a large town (drawing on a substantial upper middle class), or in a country area (with an affluent resident gentry). These retained their clientele through offering high-quality service.[62] A Welsh medical woman, Dr Rosentyl Griffiths, explained why she and her sister (who were in partnership), concluded that the NHS was not for them although in principle they were generally in favour of the NHS

We felt that we wouldn't be able to give the necessary essential time to each patient in order to get good results and therefore informed our patients to register with a state doctor. We did not expect them to come to us. However, as it happened, contrary to expectation—and before we realised it—we were still practising, and so decided to carry on.[63]

GPs considered that the financial elements of the NHS settlement treated them illiberally. In this context compensation for the goodwill of practices was a major issue. Traditionally, doctors had been free to buy and sell practices; this was the main source of their capital and vital to their eventual retirement income. In 1945 Willink, the then Minister of Health, had stated that there would be no abolition of purchase and sale of practices. No doubt this shaped expectations, but was later falsified by events under his Labour successor, Aneurin Bevan. Some £66 million was allowed for compensation, based on assumptions of the average value of a practice at £4,000, and with compensation at retirement or death of the practitioner. Charles Webster, the official historian of the NHS, has interpreted the remuneration and compensation as 'generous', although John Horder considered that it devalued the doctor.[64] The BMA (in this case fully supported by the GPs), judged the compensation insufficient and campaigned unsuccessfully to augment the £66 millions.[65] Half a century later elderly GPs still considered their compensation terms to have been inadequate, with poor compensation value for the capital sunk in their practice, interest of 2.75 per cent and repayment deferred until retirement or death.[66] Over the years inflation and devaluation eroded the real values of the sums paid. 'We had a very poor deal', one GP concluded,[67] although another was more dismissive in stating that 'Many doctors kicked up an awful fuss about this.'[68] Sale of practices was prohibited and compensation therefore had to be paid, but Bevan's sleight of hand was in postponing payment. After retiring in 1969, one doctor commented bitterly that 'It was then I realised the extent of the confidence trick played on

[62] S. Taylor, *Good General Practice* (Oxford, 1954), 46.

[63] Pers. comm., Rosentyl Griffiths, B.Sc, MB, B.Ch., FRCGP. I am grateful to Angela John for letting me have a record of this interview.

[64] CMAC, GP/29/6, John Horder, 'The Reproduction of General Practice'.

[65] It is possible that the geographical location of the practice may have influenced whether compensation terms turned out to be generous or stingy.

[66] CMAC, GP 2/32, R. Clarke; National Health Service Act, 1948 sections 36–7.

[67] Pers. comm., Dr Lilly of Long Buckby.   [68] CMAC, GP 29/2/47, Clifford Aston.

the medical profession in 1948. . . . In my case, as with others of similar age, the sale value at retirement would have been at least three times greater than the amount I actually received.'[69] For a younger generation there were different problems, not least in acquiring a practice. It was no longer possible to buy into a practice, and the consent of the local executive council was needed to start. Entrants were supposed to be steered to 'under-doctored' areas, so that inequities in patients' access to doctors could be redressed but, as Table 13.1 suggests, progress effected towards giving geographical equity for patients was extremely slow.[70]

TABLE 13.1.   Regional distribution of general practitioners, 1952–63

Location	GPs per 100,000 population in 1952	Average list size in 1952	Average list size in 1963
Scotland	45.3	2,206	1,903
Wales	43.9	2,278	2,093
England	42.9	2,548	2,343
Northern	36.6	2,732	2,412
Yorks/Humberside	38.2	2,620	2,388
East Midlands	37.7	2,652	2,485
East Anglia	41.4	2,417	2,220
South Eastern	43.1	2,318	2,280
South Western	45.4	2,205	2,085
West Midlands	36.0	2,782	2,501
North Western	37.7	2,654	2,427

Source: Based on appendix 3.30 in C. Webster, *The Health Services Since the War, vol. ii* (1996), 829.

General practitioners were also dissatisfied about the initial NHS remuneration settlement. There had been a betterment value for remuneration above 1939 levels of only 20 per cent. The extent to which this undervalued their contribution was suggested by the Danckwerts Award of 1952, which raised GP's remuneration 100 per cent above the 1939 level, or 85 per cent above that of 1948.[71] GPs' evaluations of the NHS settlement differed. Essentially, this depended on how well a pre-NHS practice had done, with those having small lists of under 1,500 patients concluding that they had been advantaged.[72] Hence there was some disagreement as to whether

[69] Harding, unpubl. 'Memoir', 94.   [70] National Health Services Act, section 34.
[71] C. Webster, *The Health Services Since the War, vol. i, Problems of Health Care and the National Health Service before 1957* (HMSO, 1988), 71, 91, 96–7, 129, 198; C. Webster, 'Doctors, Public Service and Profit: General Practitioners and the National Health Service', *Transactions of the Royal Historical Society*, 5th series, 40 (1990), 212; J. S. Ross, *The National Health Service in Great Britain* (Oxford, 1952), 227, 387–8 suggest that the fine print (clarified in a ministerial letter of 1949) of the earlier Spens Award of 1948 of 20% on net income, in fact gave a betterment factor of some 70% over 1939.
[72] CMAC, GP 29/2/32, Robert Clarke.

the NHS was an economic boon. Dr H. Cantrell, for example, stated that in her opinion it had actually improved her income.[73] But there was a consensus that the NHS had made income more secure with guaranteed payments from the state, and with no more bad debts.[74] (Nevertheless, collection of pre-NHS debts run up by patients still continued for a couple of years.) 'I liked it, because it meant that I could just not worry about sending bills to patients', stated one medical woman.[75] Several reflected that the NHS was a boon because psychologically it was much easier to be a doctor, in that money did not come between you and the patient.[76] Another stated that despite the fact that—in anticipation—his feelings about the new service had been negative, once it had happened he felt that it had 'been very useful in many ways because you didn't have to bother about bills'. He implied that competition for patients had lessened after 1948 because 'there wasn't the same fear of people wandering'.[77] This was a rather optimistic view because capitation-based payments meant that competition for patients continued, although without the earlier extremes that had led to allegations of 'patient-pinching'.

Most doctors agreed that the main advantage gained had lain with patients—'everybody could have access to a doctor'. Professional opinion differed as to changes in the status of the doctor, or in the character of doctor–patient encounters. While some thought doctor–patient relationships had already become more egalitarian during the war, others considered that this had occurred after 1948. Again opinion was divided as to whether this involved a loss of respect.[78] One practitioner remarked that although 'You were still held in great respect, patients became more assertive, "I'm changing my doctor", if you didn't comply.'[79]

Before the NHS the health needs of many poorer women and children had fared worse than that of comparable adult males who were included in the panel system. Chapter 9 has indicated that nearly one in three working-class mothers in a Women's Health Inquiry of 1933 had sought no professional advice or remedy for their medical problems, with reluctance to seek help most obvious amongst those with low incomes. In 1948 previously untreated conditions, notably what were referred to as 'women's chronic internal complaints', together with cases of measles and whooping cough amongst children, were conspicuous amongst cases now taken for free treatment by the NHS doctor.[80]

[73] Ibid., GP 29/2/37, Hilda Cantrell.
[74] Ibid., GP 29/2/37, Hilda Cantrell; GP29/2/32, Robert Clarke.
[75] Ibid., GP 29/2/50, Kathleen Norton.
[76] Pers. comms., Dr Granger of Kimbolton, and Dr Davie of Stockport.
[77] CMAC, GP 29/2/45, Arthur Griffiths.
[78] Ibid., GP 29/2/37, Hilda Cantrell; GP29/2/50, Kathleen Norton.
[79] Ibid., GP 29/2/47, Clifford Aston.
[80] *Hansard*, vol. 422, col., 291, 1 May 1946, Dr Guest, MP, an SMA member who practised in Islington, London.

Meeting a backlog of need resulted in an unanticipated high rate of demand for health care, although its extent varied according to practice and area, a point obscured in general accounts. Doctors in an impoverished area detected a strong surge in demand. A doctor in a mining area remembered that 'What appalled me was . . . the demands of everybody. Oh, glasses free, teeth free. Everything was free.'[81] Another, with a practice in the East End of London, commented that people came to get a prescription from the doctor of Epsom Salts etc. that they could quite easily have got—and used to get—over the counter at the chemist.[82] Whilst free health care was undoubtedly a great boon to patients, the system militated against much individualized care, not least because a large maximum list size was permissible. For a single-handed practitioner this was at first 4,000, later reduced to 3,500. Both the NHI and NHS had a capitation system which gave doctors an incentive to spend as little as possible on their patients. How individual doctors translated this financial imperative into medical practice obviously varied a great deal. But, as one fondly recollected, 'Looking back, it seems to me that general practitioners deserve great credit for the devoted way they looked after their patients under this system of payment.'[83]

How substantive were clinical changes for patients after the NHS? A more efficient and coherent maternity service was one positive outcome, and the advent of the Obstetric List in England and Wales meant that fewer doctors did more confinements, thus facilitating greater experience in maternal care. In theory patients had rather better access to hospital pathological services through their GP, compared to the previous situation where this had been mainly channelled via consultants. However, the GP's access to laboratory facilities or X-rays could be frustrated by the uncooperative attitude of hospitals.[84] The overwork experienced by many general practitioners after 1948 led some to the conclusion that this may have led to too many referrals.[85] Clinically, a wider access to consultants was an obvious benefit of the NHS, as patients earlier had not been able to afford the three guineas fee.[86]

NHS doctors enjoyed their new-found freedom to prescribe without reference to the patient's ability to afford the medicine.[87] The availability of new drugs, especially of antibiotics, helped doctors with what they regarded as the 'old horrors' of TB, tonsillitis, sepsis, diphtheria, scarlet fever, or pneumonia. But an earlier generation of doctors, whilst welcoming these new drugs, also considered that they had phased out an age of heroic doctoring. Some felt that these eight-day titanic struggles with pneumonia had given them 'tremendous satisfaction', and had also earned them a hard-won respect in

---

[81] CMAC, GP 29/2/47, Clifford Aston.　　　　　　[82] Ibid., GP 29/2/50, Kathleen Norton.
[83] Hewetson, 'Before and After the Appointed Day', 1272.
[84] CMAC, GP 29/2/45, Arthur Griffiths.
[85] Mid-Glamorgan RO, CMS 11, Bathgate, 'Thirty Years'.
[86] CMAC, GP 29/2/37, Hilda Cantrell; CMAC, GP 29/2/45, Arthur Griffiths.
[87] Pers. comm., Dr Davie of Stockport.

the community that was no longer possible for their successors.[88] The advent of new pharmaceuticals transformed therapeutic potential in general practice, although take-up, and thus prescription costs, varied enormously between doctors. An imposition of a prescription charge in 1951 acted as some deterrent in numbers of prescriptions, but this was not sufficient to reverse a rising national drug bill.[89] In other respects the manner in which the new health service was financed contributed to a narrowing of service in general medical practice (the term now used to describe NHS general practice), with much less dispensing except for a few special cases in remote rural practices, and a steep overall decline in minor surgery performed. In certain practices patients were compensated by other kinds of attention. 'We encouraged everyone to become health-conscious, we raised the value of early diagnosis, and said that if people considered they had small ailments they should seek consultations, because small ailments if untreated often led to very serious diseases.'[90]

The received historical wisdom has been that GPs were cut off from hospitals with the NHS. A few years after the NHS one in every five or six GPs still had a hospital appointment of some kind, but the precise extent to which this was a decline on the earlier situation is unclear. Until the First World War generalists had occupied hospital positions, although since then the GP as consultant had become a rarer species. But the GP remained the backbone of the small country cottage hospitals with its limited range of surgical work, and the small voluntary hospital in the medium-sized town also relied heavily on the general practitioner, particularly in anaesthesia.[91] After 1948 the more defined administrative structures of the new health service did not make it easy for general practitioners to retain their position in tertiary care. A few were made full consultants, others became Senior Hospital Medical Officers, and some came to hold so-called '10B' part-time posts (named from the NHS regulation). GPs continued to do good work in local hospitals in general, maternity and geriatric units, while in GP or cottage hospitals they looked after patients in 'GP beds'. However, generalists in hospitals were heavily concentrated in the clinical areas of general medicine, general surgery, anaesthetics, midwifery and gynaecology, and (to a lesser extent) in geriatrics.[92] In the early days of the NHS general practitioners felt dissatisfaction with their evolving relationship with hospitals, considering their participation in them since 1948 to have declined in amount, and become restricted in range.[93]

[88] Pers. comm., Dr Lilly of Long Buckby.

[89] Webster, *Health Services Since the War*, ii, 13–14.

[90] *Hansard*, vol. 470, col. 2242 (Dr S. Jeger, MP, an SMA member, practised in Shoreditch, London).

[91] See Ch. 11.   [92] Taylor, *Good General Practice*, 332–43.

[93] *BMJ*, 26 Sept. 1953, (Hadfield Survey, 719).

Conclusion

The *BMJ* articulated the grievances of many GPs:

General practice is at the cross-roads. The general practitioner sees himself being elbowed out of the hospital, finds himself more isolated than ever before from his colleagues in specialist and consulting practice, is plagued with paper work, and sees little prospect of obtaining those pleasant conditions of work so alluringly offered to him by propagandists for the National Health Service during the years before July 1948.[94]

The incoming tide of health reforms in 1948 had buoyed up patients, but morale amongst general practitioners was left at a very low ebb. Professional dissatisfactions and economic disincentives meant that some later even considered the future of general practice itself to be in jeopardy.[95] Subjective feelings of being overworked and undervalued were not always supported by objective reality, although there was sufficient evidence to suggest that a partial indictment was justified. In the opening years of the NHS GPs' workloads worsened through an expanded take-up of free health services, involving an incorporation of many more children and women into patient lists. A poor financial settlement was not perceived as compensating for this, while its stark contrast with the very favourable treatment negotiated by consultants made things even worse. 'After three years of the NHS many GPs still thought of themselves as the Cinderellas of the new order.'[96] Nevertheless, about two-thirds of those in general medical practice accommodated themselves reasonably happily to the changes of the new health service,[97] while the substantial improvement in GPs' remuneration given by the Danckwerts Award in 1952 applied financial cement to the new structures. One doctor encapsulated the sentiments of many in remarking that 'My bank overdraft disappeared forever.'[98] But the year after the award a *BMJ* editorial expressed (perhaps injected?) some continuing professional malaise in giving vent to anxiety that general practice would evolve into 'a sort of glorified hospital out-patient department where intimate knowledge of the patient, continuity of treatment, and the idea of the doctor as guide, philosopher and friend are sacrificed to a hurried impersonal machine'.[99] However, in doing so the editorial was neatly contrasting the mythical virtues of a past golden age with a worst-case scenario for the present day. The reality of general practice was more prosaic, and more complicated, than this representation.

Within the NHS general medical practice was in key respects *path-dependent* on what had gone before, and so must be viewed from a longer-run

---

[94] *BMJ*, editorial, 25 Mar. 1950.
[95] M. Jefferys and H. Sachs, *Rethinking General Practice: Dilemmas in Primary Medical Care* (1983), 3–4.
[96] Taylor, *Good General Practice*, 446.
[97] *BMJ*, 26 Sept. 1953, 704.
[98] Harding, unpubl. 'Memoir', 74.
[99] *BMJ* editorial, 26 Sept. 1953.

perspective. A constructive working relationship between GPs and the state had long been delayed because of the economic conditions that had hitherto bedevilled an overcrowded medical profession. This had resulted in a deep-seated distrust of lay power, and a defence of professional independence. Lengthy negotiations between the Ministry of Health and the BMA during the interwar years had their central point in panel doctors' remuneration, so that health-related matters were usually peripheral. A restricted mind-set amongst the majority of BMA-led general practitioners resulted in a side-lining of more progressive elements involving radical changes in the NHS (notably through health centres or an emphasis on preventive rather than curative medicine), and meant that it remained a sickness rather than a health service. In reality, the NHS reorganized—but did not radically transform—general medical care. Several years into the new system an informed judge-ment was that 'Whereas the hospitals and specialist services were greatly altered by the coming of the NHS, general practice remained relatively unchanged.'[100] In the perceptions of general practitioners the NHS was an evolution of the preceding NHI.[101] Under both the NHI and NHS a capita-tion system operated, with the same disincentives for good patient care that such a system embodied. And it is insufficiently appreciated that many of the detailed regulations for the national health insurance scheme were merely transferred into the NHS.[102]

How has the idea of the NHS as a fundamental turning point occurred? As we have seen, there *were* substantive changes in the hospital sector and in specialist health services. But within general practice the major change was the extension (from the minority of insured working-class males who had been panel patients since 1911), of free-at-the-point-of-access health care to the whole population: to women and children as well as men, to the middle class as well as the working class. The standard of care and social ethos of the new health service was essentially a continuation of the old panel system. Charles Webster has concluded that 'general medical service under the NHS retained the characteristics of the old panel system. Essentially, the spirit of panel practice extended over the whole population.'[103] In compensating for any deficiencies in observed reality subjective perceptions assumed impor-tance in engendering a sense of a new world. In popular understanding at the time any discontinuities in 1948 were magnified because the NHS came to symbolize a more equitable social policy which contrasted with the post-war austerity then being endured.[104] As time passed, changes which in their tim-ing had pre-dated or post-dated the inception of the NHS, and which in any case had different rationales, tended to be aggregated with the NHS, thus

[100] Taylor, *Good General Practice*, 446.   [101] CMAC, GP 29/1/69A, David Kerr.
[102] McLachlan, *Improving the Common Weal*, 190.
[103] Webster, 'Doctors, Public Service and Profit', 213–14. See also J. Tudor Hart, *A New Kind of Doctor: The General Practitioner's Part in the Health of the Community* (1988), 9–10.
[104] Fox, *Health Policies*, 132.

helping to manufacture the sense of an historical watershed. General practitioners whose practice continued across the alleged divide of 1948 reflected that social changes in doctor–patient relationships that had actually *pre-dated* the NHS (in the greater social egalitarianism of the war years), or *post-dated* it therapeutically (with new drugs, especially antibiotics, coming onstream during the 1950s), were conflated in historical perception with 1948.

The NHS is usually seen as a major social and medical turning point, yet this volume's analysis of the preceding century has revealed substantial continuities with what had gone before, in which an evolutionary transition rather than a radical disjuncture occurred in general practice. However, in order to appreciate the full significance of the reforms of 1946/8, it is necessary to place primary health care within a wider medical context, and also to pose a counterfactual question. What kind of health care would have been available if the NHS had not come into existence? In particular, if free-at-the-point-of-access health care had not existed, would working-class patients have been able to benefit from the powerful but expensive new pharmaceuticals which transformed medical treatment in the post-war period? Without the NHS it seems highly likely that they would have been denied access to such drugs. Similarly, economic constraints would have become increasingly relevant beyond the frontiers of general medical practice, as more advanced—and ever more expensive—medical technologies also extended frontiers of specialist competence. In the absence of the NHS a deepening divide would have separated the affluent from the poorer British citizen, and an invidious two-tier system of health care would have existed, in which general practitioners would have been unable to provide many of the benefits of modern medicine to a substantial part of the population.

Select Bibliography

MANUSCRIPT SOURCES

BMA Archives, London
Ref. 2054 Details of practice accommodation and expenses.

Bodleian Library, Oxford
Dew MSS, box 3, Official papers, letter dated 27 February 1871.
Dew MSS, Uncatalogued official papers, letters of 1871–3.
John Johnson collection, SJS/03.95, patent medicines.

Buckinghamshire RO
Box 5, Diary of A. Blyth 1864.

Cambridgeshire RO (Cambridge)
Uncatalogued records of Dr S. H. de Pritchard, 1928–48.

Cambridgeshire RO (Huntingdon)
Accn. 4175, Maternity attendances of Drs Lucas, Hicks and Hicks.
Accn. 2876/Q/8/23, Wansford Lodge of Oddfellows, surgeon's certificates and statements of health, 1845–1902.

Cheshire RO (Chester)
NIB 9/1–2, Birkenhead NHI Committee register of payments to practitioners, 1924–30 and 1930–4.
NIB 10, Birkenhead NHI Committee register of sums credited to practitioners, 1914–19.

Clwyd RO (Hawarden)
D/DM/63/33, Ledger of Drs Edwards and Trubshaw, 1904–12.
D/DM/63/39, Correspondence of Dr Edwards, 1913–20.
D/DM/63/1/32, Day book of Dr Edwards, Mold, 1903–34.
D/DM/301/3, Ledger of Dr Ingham, Ruabon, 1855–61.
D/DM/337/12, Articles of partnership of John Owen Jones and Charles Edward Morris.
D/DM/337/15, Correspondence of Dr Morris, 1917.
D/DM/400/1–8, Papers of Dr H. Sparke Welton, Abermordu, 1930s and 1940s.

Clwyd RO (Ruthin)
BD/A/567, Removal of nuisances and protection against the Cholera, January 1854.
DD/HB/1959, Miscellaneous Accounts.
DD/HB/959, Account book of Dr Williams, 1873–1907.
DD/DM/266/32, Salisbury Hall Retreat and Sanitorium.
NTD/741, List of NHI medical practitioners in Denbighshire, 1911.

Cumbria RO (Carlisle)
DSO/38/1, Minute Book of BMA Border Counties, 1911.
DX 848/4, Transfer of panel practice in Workington, 1920.
SPUL, 5/5, MOH report for Longtown, 1878.

Cumbria RO (Kendal)
BMA Westmorland Branch Minutes, 1903–55.

Durham RO
U/CS/303, Chester le Street Poor Law Union, report of special guardians' meeting, 1926.
U/CS/321, Correspondence of Clerk to Chester le Street Guardians with Ministry of Health, 1928.

E. Suffolk RO
HD/177/DI/3, Indenture of apprenticeship to a surgeon, Robert Anderson of Sudbury, 1812.

E. Sussex RO
AMS 6315/5/1, E. Sussex Medico-Chirurgical Society minutes.
AMS 6315/9/2 Establishment of Medical Registration Committee, 1858/9.
AMS 6315/9/9, E. Sussex Medico-Chirurgical Society correspondence.
CHC 9/13, Brighton Hove and Preston District Queens Nurses Reports.

Essex RO (Chelmsford)
D/2 15/6 and 15/12, Benevolent Medical Society for Essex and Hertfordshire minutes.
D/DU 509, Felstead day book, 1934–41.
D/DT B4, Battersby, Jameson and Dobbyn articles of partnership, 1926.
D/DU 353/4, Account of the death of Elizabeth Chapman, 1854.
D/DDW B9/4, Draft article of partnership, 1882.
D/DWm T 39, Partnership document between George Eachus and Thomas Spurgin, 1831.
D/F 79 A5637, Maldon practice books, 1944–51.

Essex RO (Colchester)
D/DT B4, Articles of partnership of Griffith and Wells, 1926–9.
D/F 135 C227, Wivenhoe doctor's club book, 1855–1935.

Essex RO (Southend)
DZ/60/1–3, Southend NHI Committee minutes, 1915–38.

Greater Glasgow Health Board Archives (University of Glasgow)
HB 60, Testimonials of James Hill, of Glasgow, 1890.
HB 57 NHI Clinical records of Drs MacFarlane, Blair, Short and McQueen.
HB 76 1/1, Lanarkshire Medical Practitioners Union minutes, 1913–22.

Greater Manchester RO
Q 217/1, Medical Women's Federation scrapbook.

Lancashire RO
IC Ba /17/1, Barrow in Furness NHI Committee correspondence, 1913–34.
IC La /1/1, Lancashire NHI Committee minutes, 1912–16.

Lincolnshire RO
Misc 88/1–3, Dr Freer's diary, Donington, 1845–57.

Manchester RO
M134/1/2/8, Edmund Lyon's miscellaneous papers.

Mid-Glamorgan RO
D/D CMS/11, G. Bathgate, 'Thirty Years of Change in General Practice'.
D/DX 83/1/1, Dr Cresswell's surgery and home visiting book, Dowlais Surgery 1892.
D/DX 83/1/17, Dr Cresswell's surgery and home visit book, 1936–8.
D/DX 83/1/21, Dr Cresswell's surgery and home visiting book, 1946–9.
D/DX 83/1/131, Dr Cresswell's surgery at Penydarren, 1899–1901.
D/DX 83/3/2, Dr Cresswell's prescription book, 1890–2.
D/DX 83/4/1–2, Dr Cresswell's case books, 1878–99 and 1906–49.
D/DX 236/6 Mrs Ann Evans, Midwife, notifications for sending for medical help, 1938–9.
D/DS Wales BMA Branch minute book, 1896–1908.
D/DS/1–2 Monmouthshire BMA, Swansea Division minutes, 1903–14.

Modern Records Centre, University of Warwick
MS/79/MPU/1/2/1–2, Medical Practitioners Union, council minutes of, 1924–33, 1937–48.

National Library of Scotland
Accession 6027, no. 19, Medical Practitioners Union, papers.
Accession 10334, no. 5, 'The Doctor in the Town': scrapbook of the life of J. D. Sinclair.

National Library of Wales
BMA collection, S. Wales and Monmouth: correspondence, minute book of Branch, 1942–52 and newspaper cuttings.
D. G. Morgan papers.
NLW 10209A and 10210B, Diary of a medical student, 2 vols., 1856–9.
NLW, MS 12539 and 12540, W. M. Noot's ledgers, 1870 and 1876.
NLW, MS 21759D, Hugh Parry Jones's day book, 1880.
NLW, MS 19702E, Dr Evan Pierce's coroner's entry book for North Denbighshire, 1874–95.
NLW, MS 19703B, Dr Evan Pierce's day book, 1833–6.
NLW, MS 19704F, Press cuttings on the Irish Mail Disaster.
NLW, MS 7519B, Richards family of Merioneth, memoranda and diaries.

Norfolk RO
BR 23/26, Burnham GP's day book, 1915–20.
BR 218/1, Pearce, Robinson, and Bowes, deed of partnership, 1936.
BR 218/5, Pearce practice supplemental deed of partnership, 1947.
BR 218/6, Dr Pearce's annual statements of accounts, 1925–46.
BR 218/7, Drs Pearce and Bowes, correspondence with consultants.
BR 218/11, Dr Pearce's cash receipt book, 1936–9.
BR 224/8, Dr Speirs's ledger, 1906–12.
BR 224/11, Dr Speirs's day book, 1896–9.
BR 224/13/1–8, Dr Speirs's correspondence with patients.
BR224/13/12, Dr Speirs's list of patients.
SO 59/208, Kenninghall Oddfellows Lodge minutes, 1904–13.

SO 59/63–146, Kenninghall Oddfellows applications for membership, 1871–1942.

Nottinghamshire RO
DD/BW/215/26, Hill and Barham, articles of partnership, 1908.
DD/14440/24/18, Dr Ringrose's obstetric case book, 1895–1916.
DD/1440/26/3, Scrapbook on Dr Ringrose.
DD/NA 13/3, Sarah Eyre's register of midwifery cases, 1904–14.
DD/NA 14/1–2, Newark Borough District Nursing Association reports, 1905–11.
SO NH 1/1–3, Nottinghamshire NHI Committee minutes, 1912–48.
SO NH 1/6, Nottinghamshire NHI Finance and General Purposes Sub-Committee minutes, 1927–37 and 1937–48.
SO NH 1/10, Nottinghamshire NHI Medical Benefit Sub-Committee minutes, 1913–26.

Oxfordshire Archives
Misc Savil, I/i/1–6, Dr R.W. Meikle's medical diaries and visiting list, 1922–33.
Misc Savil, I/ii/1, Dr R.W. Meikle's medical notebook, 1922–33.
Misc Sq VII/1, Squire practice medical ledger, 1914–16.
Misc Sq VII/14, Squire practice ledger, 1941.
Misc Sq X/1–10, Squire practice invoices and receipts, 1912–53.
Misc Sq X1/1–3, Squire practice correspondence with patients 1898 to 1936.
Misc Sq XII/4, Squire practice clinical notes 1921–2.
Misc Sq XIX, Squire practice list of accounts with partnership document.
Misc Sq XIX, Revised partnership document for Drs Birt and Kennedy, 1919.
PLU2/G/1A16, Bicester Poor Law Union Medical District Officers' weekly returns of sick paupers attended, 1836, 1846, 1892.
PLU2/RL/2A1/5, Bicester Poor Law Union application and report book, 1865.
PLU2/RL/2A4/1–2, Bicester Poor Law Union requests to MO for medical attention, 1876–7.

Public Record Office
MH 49/3 Welsh Insurance Commisssioners minutes, 1914.
MH 49/12, Welsh Insurance Commisssion papers, 1911–15.
MH 62/151, Court of Enquiry into Insurance Practitioners Remuneration, 1923.
MH 62/130, Interdepartmental Committee, 1920.
MH 62/200, Report of Special Committee into medical certification in South Wales.
MH 77/175, Deans of medical schools' evidence to the Spens Committee, 1945.
PIN 1/1, Interdepartmental Committee on Health and Employment.

Rhodes House, Oxford
MSS British Empire, 4/1–3. P. A. Clearkin memoir.

Royal College of Physicians, London
MS 84, M. B. Webb's medical school letters, 1908.

Royal College of Physicians and Surgeons, Glasgow
RCPSG 1/10/6, Dr E. W. Pritchard's pocket journal of patients visited, 1862.
RCPSG 16/1/1, Ladies Guild of Royal Medical Benevolent Fund Glasgow minutes 1911–29.

Royal College of Physicians, Edinburgh
AD. 7.3, Statement regarding the existing deficiencies of medical practitioners in the Highlands and Islands, 1852.

Royal Free Hospital Archives, London
London Medical School for Women, reports.
London Medical School for Women, volumes of press cuttings.

Scottish RO
HH3 6/6–7, Fife NHI Committee Minutes.
HH3/18, NHI morbidity statistics and certification, Department of Health for Scotland.
HH3 7/001, Dunfermline NHI Committee Ledger (1913–49).
HH3 8/001, Kirkcaldy Insurance Ledger (1914–48).

Wellcome Institute for the History of Medicine, London
CMAC, GP 2/1, Gray's practice, Essex, correspondence.
CMAC, GP 5/4, Drs Craig and O'Connor, High Wycombe, annual income, 1935–59
CMAC, GP 5/5, Drs Craig and O'Connor day book 1941–2.
CMAC, GP 18, Drs Scrimgeour and E.V.Kuensberg West Granton practice records, 1947–79.
CMAC, GP 23/1, G.E. Hale's obituary notice.
CMAC, GP 23/2–3, G.E. Hale's cash books, 1893–1904.
CMAC, GP 23/5, Mrs Hale's notes on her husband's practice.
CMAC, GP 23/6, G. Hale and F.E.L. Phillips partnership agreement, 1933.
CMAC, 29/1/61, Anthony Ryle, London, tape of interview.
    29/1/71, Eric Grogono, London, tape of interview.
CMAC, GP 29/2 transcripts of interviews:
    29/2/01, John Hawkey, Wantage.
    29/2/06, Margaret Norton, Worcester.
    29/2/08, Frank Boon, Rotherham.
    29/2/09, Elizabeth Clubb, Oxford.
    29/2/15, Jean Gavin, Northampton.
    29/2/16, Frederick Barber, Islington.
    29/2/20, Margaret Joan Hallinam, Rotherham.
    29/2/22, Jack Ridgwick, Rotherham.
    29/2/26, Norman Paros, Colchester.
    29/2/27, John Evans, Doncaster.
    29/2/32, Robert Clarke, Bolton.
    29/2/34, Jean Hugh-Jones, St Helens.
    29/2/36, Emanuel Tuckman, Orpington.
    29/2/37, Hilda Cantrell, Liverpool.
    29/2/42, Arnold Elliot, Ilford.
    29/2/44, Thomas McQuay, Blackburn.
    29/2/45, Arthur Griffiths, Hove.
    29/2/47, Clifford Aston, Allerton Bywater.
    29/2/48, Bertie Dover, Liverpool.
    29/2/49, Donald Gawith, North Wales.
    29/2/50, Kathleen Norton, London.
    29/2/59, Samuel Isaacs, Merthyr Tydfil.
    29/2/62, Margarete Samuel, Manchester.
    29/2/63, Tony Leake, Bradford.
    29/2/66, Walter Shaw, Ebbw Vale.

CMAC, GP/29/6, John Horder, 'The Reproduction of General Practice', tape of seminar paper.
CMAC, SA/RNI/H8/1, West Penrith Medical Society Report to Penzance and Madron Nursing Association, 1908.
WMS 5415, M.W. Littlewood, Bideford, memoirs.
WMS 5416, W.H. Ackland, Bideford, correspondence.
WMS 7205, W.H. Ackland apprenticeship indentures.
WMS 7208, W.H. Ackland papers, 1859–88.
WMS 7211, C.K. Ackland correspondence, 1870–1921.

W. Sussex RO
NP 2011, Crawley practice accounts, 1895–1903

ADDITIONAL MANUSCRIPT SOURCES IN PRIVATE HANDS

Abbey Mead Surgery, Romsey
Day book, 1848–54.
Day book and ledger, 1897–1904.

Dr Granger of Kimbolton:
Visiting books, 1930s and 1940s.
Medical ledger and papers, 1947–61.

Mrs Hendry of Nuneaton
Financial records of Dr D.W.Hendry.

Warders Medical Centre, Tonbridge:
Post Office medical examination book, 1890–1942.
Record of private operations by A.E. Herman, 1920–48.

PARLIAMENTARY AND OFFICIAL PAPERS

RC into State of the Universities of Scotland, **1831**, XII.
S.C. on Medical Education, **1834**, XIII.
22nd Report of the Registrar General, PP, **1861**, 2897, XVIII.
Supplement to the 35th Report of the Registrar General, PP, **1875**, C1155, XLIII.
Correspondence on the Medical Registration of Women, PP, **1875**, LVIII.
Special Report from the SC on the Medical Act (1858), **1878–9**, C320, XII.
Report of RC to Enquire into Grant of Medical Degrees, PP, **1882**, C3251, XXIX.
Return on Appointments of MOH under Sanitary Acts, PP, **1888**, LXXXXVI.
Return on Appointments of MOH by County Councils, PP, **1896**, LXXII.
Third Annual Report. Local Government Board for Scotland, PP, **1897**, C8575, XXXVII.
Sixty-Second Report of the Registrar General, PP, **1900**, Cd. 323, XV.
RC into the Militia and Volunteers, PP, **1904**, Cd. 2061, XXV.
Report as to the Practice of Medicine and Surgery by Unqualified Persons in the UK, **1910**, Cd. 5422, XLIII.
Report of Sir William Plender in Respect of Medical Attendance and Remuneration in Certain Towns, PP, **1912–13**, Cd. 6305, LXXVIII.
Select Committe on Patent Medicines, PP, **1914**, IX.
Some Notes on Medical Education by George Newman, PP, **1918**, XIX.
Sixth Report of the Ministry of Health, PP, **1924–5**, Cmd. 2450, XIII.
Seventh Report of the Ministry of Health, PP, **1926**, Cmd. 2724, XI.

RC on Health Insurance, PP, **1926**, Cmd. 2596, XIV.

Eighteenth Report of Ministry of Health, **1936–7**, Cmd. 5516, X.

Joint Committee to Consider the Solicitor's Bill, **1938–9**, VIII.

Report of an Investigation into Maternal Mortality in Wales, PP, **1936–7**, Cmd. 5423, XI.

Report of Inter-Departmental Committee on Medical Education [Goodenough] **1944**.

Report of the Inter-Departmental Committee on Remuneration of General Practitioners, PP, **1945**, Cmd. 6810, XII.

Report of the Inter-Departmental Committee on the Remuneration of Consultants and Specialists [Spens], PP, **1947–8**, Cmd. 7420, XI.

Report of the Legal Committee on Medical Partnerships, PP, **1948–9**, Cmd. 7565, XVII.

RC on Doctors' and Dentists' Remuneration, [Pilkington], **1959–60**, Cmnd. 939.

PERIODICALS AND NEWSPAPERS

Birmingham Mail

British Journal of Homeopathy

British Medical and Chirurgical Journal

British Medical Journal

Burnley Express

Burnley News

Daily Chronicle

Daily Express

Daily Graphic

Daily Mail

Daily News

Daily Sketch

Fortnightly Review

Free Press

Friend

Gentlewoman

General Practitioner

Glasgow Herald

Hansard

Independent

Inverness Courier

Islington Daily Gazette

Journal of the Royal College of General Practitioners

Journal of the Royal Statistical Society

Lancet

Law Journal

Law Times

Liverpool Echo

Magazine of London

Manchester Evening News

Manchester Guardian

Medical Practitioner

Medical Press and Circular

Medical Women's Federation Quarterly Newsletter

Medical Women's Federation Quarterly Review
Medical Women's Journal
Medical World
Midland Free Press
Morning Leader
Morning Post
Observer
Pall Mall Gazette
Practitioner
Punch
Queen
Reynolds News
Royal Free Hospital Journal
Scotsman
South African Medical Journal
South African Medical Record
Star
Sunday Times
Tatler
The Times
Welsh Outlook
Western Morning News
Westminster Review
Women's Medical Journal
Young Woman

PRE 1949 PRINTED BOOKS AND ARTICLES

Note: The place of publication for books is London, unless otherwise stated.

A Formulary of Selected Remedies for General Practice (1884).

A London Physician, *Men-Midwives and Female Physicians* (1864).

A Panel Doctor, *On the Panel. General Practice as a Career* (1926).

Anon., 'The Recollections of a Welsh Doctor', *The Welsh Outlook*, xx (1933).

ABERCROMBIE, J., *Pathological and Practical Research on Diseases of the Brain and Spinal Cord* (Edinburgh, 1828).

—— *Pathological and Practical Research on Diseases of the Stomach* (Edinburgh, 1828).

ACLAND, T. D. (ed.), *W.W. Gull Memoirs and Addresses* (1896).

ALDERSON, F.H., *The Wants of the General Practitioner of the Present Day* (1886).

ALFORD, H., 'The Bristol Infirmary in my Student Days, 1822–28', *Bristol Medical and Chirurgical Journal*, September 1890.

ALLBUTT, Clifford, 'Review', *BMJ*, 26 July 1902.

ARMSTRONG, B. N., *The Health Insurance Doctor. His Role in Britain, Denmark and France* (Princeton, 1939).

ARVEDSON, J., *Medical Gymnastics and Massage in General Practice* (1930).

BARRETT COLE, L., *Dietetics in General Practice* (1938).

BELLIS CLAYTON, E., *Physiotherapy in General Practice* (1924).

BENNETT, A. H., *English Medical Women. Glimpses of their Work in Peace and War* (1915).

BILLINGTON, Miss, 'How can I Earn My Living?—As a Doctor', *Young Woman*, (1893).

BLACKWELL, E., *The Influence of Women in the Profession of Medicine* (1889).

BMA, *Secret Remedies. What They Cost and What They Contain* (1909).

—— *More Secret Remedies* (1912).

—— *Presidential Address* (1920).

—— *Proposal for a General Medical Service for the Nation* (1930).

—— *The Medical Practitioners Handbook* (1935).

—— *The Training of a Doctor* (1948).

BOLTON THOMAS, W., *Electricity in General Practice* (1890).

BRIGGS, I. G., *How to Start in General Practice* (1928).

BRODIE, B.C., *Autobiography* (1865).

—— *An Introductory Discourse on the Duties and Conduct of Medical Students and Practitioners* (1843).

CAMPBELL, R., *The London Tradesman* (1747).

CHARTON, E., *Dictionnaire des Professions* (2nd edn., Paris, 1851).

CLARK BEGS, A., *Insulin in General Practice* (1924).

COBBE, F. B., 'Medicine and Morality', *Modern Review*, 11 (1881).

COLLIER, A., 'Social Origins of a Sample of Entrants to Glasgow University, parts I and II', *Sociological Review*, 30 (1938).

CORNER, E. M., and IRVING PINCHES, H., *The Operations of the General Practitioner* (1903).

—— *Male Diseases in General Practice* (1910).

CROW, D. A., *Ear, Nose and Throat in General Practice* (1924).

DALE, W., *The State of the Medical Profession in Great Britain and Ireland* (Dublin, 1875).

DANIELS, G. W., and CAMPION, H., *The Distribution of National Capital* (Manchester, 1936).

DAVIS, H., *Skin Diseases in General Practice* (1921).

DE STYRAP, J., *The Young Practitioner*, (1890).

DUCKWORTH, SIR DYCE, 'Valedictory Address', *Lancet* (1889).

EAST, T., *Cardiovascular Disease in General Practice* (1938).

ESCOTT, T. H. S., *Social Transformation of the Victorian Age* (1897).

FAIRFIELD, L., 'Medical Women in a Combatant Country', *Journal of the American Medical Women's Association* (1946).

FLEXNER, A., *Medical Education* (1925).

FOSTER REANEY, M., *The Medical Profession* (Dublin, 1905).

FOSTER, W. L., and TAYLOR, F. G., *National Health Insurance* (3rd edn., 1937).

FULLER, H. W., *Advice to Medical Students* (1857).

FURBES, E. R., *London Doctor* (1940).

GALDSTON, I., 'Diagnosis in Historical Perspective' *BHM*, 9 (1941).

GORDON, W., 'The Overcrowding of the Medical Profession', *BMJ*, 16 May 1903.

GRANVILLE, P. B. (ed.), *Autobiography of A.B. Granville* (2 vols., 1874).

GREGORY, S., *Female Physicians* (1864).

GREGSON SLATER, J. J., *Should I Go To The Bar?* (1912).

GUNN, C. B., *Leaves from the Life of a Country Doctor* (Edinburgh, 1947).

HARRISON, L. W., *Diagnosis and Treatment of Venereal Disease in General Practice* (1907 and 1919).

HOLMES, T., *Introductory Address* (1868).

HOSFORD, J., *Fractures and Dislocations in General Practice* (2nd edn., 1939).

HUNTLEY, E. A., *The Study and Practice of Medicine by Women* (Lewes, 1886).

HUTCHISON, R., and RAINY, H., *Clinical Methods* (1897).

HYSLOP THOMSON, *Consumption in General Practice* (1912).

IVENS, FRANCES, 'Some of the Essential Attributes of an Ideal Practitioner', *Magazine of London*, ix, (1914).

JEAFFRESON, J. C., *A Book about Doctors* (2nd edn., 1861).

JENNER, E., *Inquiry into the Cause and Effect of the Variolae Vaccine* (1798).

KEETLEY, C. B., *The Student's and Junior Practitioner's Guide to the Medical Profession* (2nd edn., 1885).

KENEALY, A., 'How Women Doctors are Made', *Ludgate* (1897).

KERSHAW, R., *Special Hospitals* (1909).

LANCET, the editor of, *The Conduct of Medical Practice* (1927).

LARKIN, A. J., *Radium in General Practice* (1929).

LEYLAND, J., *Contemporary Medical Men and their Professional Work* (2 vols., Leicester, 1888).

LEVY, H., *National Health Insurance. A Critical Study* (Cambridge, 1944).

LINDSAY, C., 'The Profession and the Public', *BMJ*, ii (1938).

LITTLE, E. M., *History of the British Medical Association, 1832–1932* (1932).

MACBRYDE, C. M., *Signs and Symptoms. Their Clinical Interpretation* (Philadelphia, 1947).

MACKENZIE, J., *Principles of the Diagnosis and Treatment of Heart Affections* (1916).
—— 'The Opportunities of the GP', *BMJ*, i (1921).

MACKENZIE, SIR JAMES, 'The Opportunities for the General Practitioner are Essential for the Investigation of Disease and the Progress of Medicine', *BMJ*, i (1921).

McLEARY, G. F., *National Health Insurance* (1932).

McNAIR WILSON, R., *Clinical Study of Circulating Diseases in General Practice* (1921).
—— *The Beloved Physician* (1926).

MAJOR, R. H., *Physical Diagnosis* (2nd edn., Philadelphia, 1940).

MALLESON, H., *A Woman Doctor. Mary Murdoch of Hull* (1919).

MORRIS, MARY E. H., MD, 'A Plea for General Practice', *MWFQN*, November 1923.

MULLINS, J., *The Story of a Toiler's Life* (1921).

MURDOCH, MARY, 'Practical Hints to Students', *LMSW Report*, October 1914.

NEWMAN, G., *Some Notes on Medical Education* (1918)
—— *Public Opinion in Preventive Medicine* (1920).

NELSON HARDY, H., *The State of the Medical Profession in Great Britain and Ireland in 1901* (Dublin, 1901).

NEWSHOLME, A., *International Studies on the Relation Between the Private and Official Practice of Medicine* (3 vols., 1931).

NICHOLSON, P., *Blood Pressure in General Practice* (1914).

OGILVIE, SIR HENRY, 'Then and Now', *Practitioner*, 161 (1948).

ORR, D. W., and ORR, J. W., *Health Insurance with Medical Care* (New York, 1938).

PAYTON DARK, E., *Diathermy in General Practice* (1934).

PEARSE, I. H., and PEARSE, L. H., *The Peckham Experiment* (1947).

PEP, *Report on the British Health Services* (1937).

PICKLES, W., 'Epidemiology in Country Practice', *New England Journal of Medicine*, 239 (1948).

POOLER, H. W., *My Life in General Practice* (1948).

PORTMAN, G., *Ear, Nose and Throat in General Practice* (1924).

REANEY, FOSTER M., *The Medical Profession* (Dublin, 1905).

ROBERTS, H., 'A National Medical Service', *Nineteenth Century*, August 1914.

—— 'The Insurance Bill, the Doctors and National Policy', *Nineteenth Century*, July 1911.

ROBINSON, W., *Sidelights on the Life of a Wearside Surgeon* (Gateshead on Tyne, 1939).

ROGER, J., *Reminiscences of a Workhouse Medical Officer* (1889).

ST CLAIR BROWN, A., *Ophthalmic Hints in General Practice* (1890).

ST JOHN, C., *Christine Murrell. Her Life and Work* (1935).

SARGENT, P., and RUSSELL, A. E., *Emergencies of General Practice* (1911).

SCHARLIEB, M., *Seven Lamps of Medicine* (Oxford, 1888).

SHREWSBURY, W. J., *Christ Glorified in the Life, Experience and Character of J. B. Shrewsbury* (1850).

SIMPSON, A. R., *Address to the Medical Graduates in the University of Edinburgh* (Edinburgh, 1878).

SIMPSON, J. Y., *Physicians and Physic. Three Addresses* (Edinburgh, 1851).

—— 'On the Duties of Young Physicians', in *Physicians and Physic* (Edinburgh, 1851).

SHEFFIELD, G., *Simplex System of Book-Keeping* (1897).

SHEPHERD, A. B., *Introductory Address delivered at St Mary's Hospital* (1873).

SLATER, J. H., *A Guide to the Legal Profession* (1884).

SLUSS, J. W., *Emergency Surgery for the General Practitioner* (1908 and 1910).

SMYTHE, D. M., 'Some Principles in the Selection of Medical Students', *BMJ*, 14 September 1946.

SOLOMONS, B., *An Epitome of Obstetrical Diagnoses and Treatment in General Practice* (1933).

SPRING-RICE, M., *Working-Class Wives* (1939).

SQUIRE SPRIGGS, S., *Medicine and the Public* (1905).

STURGE, MARY D., 'The Medical Women's Federation, its Work and Aims', *MWFQN*, December 1921.

STERN, B. J., *American Practice in the Perspectives of a Century* (New York, 1945).

TAIT, L., 'The Medical Education of Women', *Birmingham Medical Review*, 18 (1874).

THOMSON, H. B., *Choice of a Profession* (1857).

THORNE, M., 'The Royal Free Hospital', *Medical Women's Journal*, April 1924.

TOPPING, A., 'Prevention of Maternal Mortality: the Rochdale Experiment', *Lancet*, i (1936).

TURNER, E. F., *The Organization of the Solicitor's Office* (1886).

WARD, E., *General Practice (Some Further Experiences)* (1930).

WEBB, S., and WEBB, B., *The State and the Doctor* (1910).

WEST, C., *The Profession of Medicine. Its Study and Practice. Its Duties and Rewards* (1896).

—— *Medical Women* (1878).

WITHERING, W., *An Account of the Foxglove* (1785).

WOODMAN, J. M., *Manual of Book-Keeping for Solicitors* (1888, 1906).

POST 1948 PRINTED BOOKS AND ARTICLES

Note: The place of publication for books is London, unless otherwise stated.

ABBOTT, A., *The System of Professions. An Essay on the Division of Expert Labour* (Chicago, 1988).

ABEL-SMITH, B., and GALES, K., *British Doctors at Home and Abroad* (1964).

—— and STEVENS, R., *Lawyers and the Courts* (1967).

ABLE, R. L., *The Legal Profession in England and Wales* (Oxford, 1988).

ADAMS, D. P., 'Community and Professionalization: General Practitioners and Ear, Nose and Throat Specialisms in Cincinatti, 1945–1947', *BHM*, 68 (1994).

ALEXANDER, W., *First Ladies of Medicine* (Wellcome Unit for the History of Medicine, Glasgow, 1987).

ANDERSON, O., *Suicide in Victorian and Edwardian England* (Oxford, 1987).

ARCHER, F., *The Village Doctor* (Gloucester, 1986).

ARMSTRONG, D., *Political Anatomy of the Body. Medical Knowledge in Britain in the Twentieth Century* (Cambridge, 1983).

—— 'The Rise of Surveillance Medicine', *Sociology of Health and Illness*, 17 (1995).

ARNOLD, D., 'Introduction', in Arnold, D. (ed.), *Warm Climates and Western Medicine; the Emergence of Tropical Medicine, 1500–1900* (Amsterdam, 1996).

BALINT, M., *The Doctor, his Patient and the Illness* (2nd edn., 1968).

BARBER, G., *Country Doctor* (1973).

BARTRIP, P. W. J., *Mirror of Medicine. A History of the British Medical Journal* (Oxford, 1990).

—— *Themselves Writ Large. The British Medical Association, 1832–1966* (1996).

BERRIDGE, V., and EDWARDS, G., *Opium and the People. Opiate Use in Nineteenth-Century England* (1981).

BIRD, B., *Talking with Patients* (Philadelphia, 1955).

BLIGH, M., *Dr Eurich of Bradford* (Bradford, 1960).

BODKIN, N. *et al*, 'The General Practitioner and the Psychiatrist', *BMJ*, ii (1953).

BONNER, T. N., 'Abraham Flexner as Critic of British and Continental Medical Education', *MH*, 33 (1989).

—— *Becoming a Physician. Medical Education in Britain, France, Germany, and the United States, 1750–1945* (Oxford, 1995).

—— *To the Ends of the Earth: Women's Search for Education in Medicine* (Cambridge, Mass., 1992).

BOWDEN, R. E. M., 'The Medical Women's Federation, 1917–87, Its Antecedents, Past Present and Future', *Medical Women*, 6 (1987).

BOYD, R., and RICHERSON, P. J., *Culture and the Evolutionary Process* (Chicago, 1985).

BRADFORD HILL, A., 'The Doctor's Pay and Day', *Journal of the Royal Statistical Society*, civ (1951).

BRADLEY, J., CROWTHER, A., and DUPREE, M., 'Mobility and Selection in Scottish University Medical Education', *MH*, 40 (1996).

BROCKLISS, L., 'The Professions and National Identity', in Brockliss, L., and Eastwood, D. (eds.), *A Union of Multiple Identities, The British Isles, c.1750–1850* (Manchester, 1997).

BROCKWAY, F., *Bermondsey Story* (1949).

BRYNE, P. S., and LONG, B. E. L., *Doctors talking to Patients* (1976).

BUTLER, S. V. P., 'A Transformation in Training: the Formation of University Medical Faculties in Manchester, Leeds and Liverpool, 1820–1884', *MH,* 30 (1986).

CARTWRIGHT, A., *Patients and their Doctors* (1967).

CAVENAGH, A. M., 'Role of the General-practitioner Maternity Unit: 1000 Deliveries Analysed', in *The New General Practice* (BMA, 1968).

CAWSON, A., *Corporatism and Political Theory* (1986).

CHADWICK, O., *The Victorian Church, Part II, 1860–1901* (1970).

CHAMBERLAIN, M., *Old Wives Tales* (1981).

CHAPMAN, S., *Jesse Boot of Boots the Chemist* (1973).

CHERRY, S., *Medical Services and the Hospitals in Britain, 1860–1939* (1996).

COCKRAM, J., 'The Federation and the BMA', *Journal of MWF,* (1967).

COLLINGS, J. S., 'General Practice in England Today, A Reconnaissance', *Lancet,* 25 March 1950.

COLLINS, K., *Go and Learn. The International Story of Jews and Medicine in Scotland* (Aberdeen, 1988).

COLLINS, R., 'Market Closure and the Conflict Theory in the Professions', in Burrage, M., and Torstendahl, R. (eds.), *Professions in Theory and History* (1990).

COPE, Z., 'The Influence of the Free Dispensaries upon Medical Education in Britain', *MH,* 13 (1969).

CORFIELD, P., *Power and the Professions in Britain, 1700–1850* (1995).

COX, A., *Among the Doctors* (c.1949).

CROWTHER, M. A., and DUPREE, M., 'The Invisible General Practitioner: the Careers of Scottish Medical Students in the late Nineteenth Century', *BHM,* 70 (1996).

CULE, J. (ed.), *Wales and Medicine. An Historical Survey* (Cardiff, 1975).

CUNNINGHAM, H., *The Volunteers* (1975).

DAVIDOFF, L., and HALL, C., *Family Fortunes* (1987).

DAVIES, N. N., 'Two and a Half Centuries of Medical Practice. A Welsh Medical Dynasty', in Cule, J. (ed.), *Wales and Medicine. An Historical Survey* (Cardiff, 1975).

DICKSON CARR, J., *The Life of Sir Arthur Conan Doyle* (1949).

DIGBY, A., *Pauper Palaces* (1978).

—— 'New Schools for the Middle Class Girl', in P. Searby (ed.), *Educating the Middle Classes* (1982).

—— and BOSANQUET, N., 'Doctors and Patients in an Era of National Health Insurance and Private Practice', *Economic History Review,* 2nd series, xli, (1988).

—— *Making a Medical Living. Doctors and Patients in the English Market for Medicine, 1720–1911* (Cambridge, 1994).

—— ' "A Medical El Dorado"? Colonial Medical Incomes and Practice at the Cape', *SHM,* 8 (1995).

—— 'Medicine and the English State, 1901–1948', in Green, S. J. D., and Whiting, R. C. (eds.), *The Boundaries of the State in Modern Britain* (Cambridge, 1996).

—— 'The Economic Significance of the 1911 Act', in Waddington, K. and Hardy, A. (eds.), *Financing British Medicine* (forthcoming, Amsterdam, 1999).

DINGWALL, R., RAFFERTY, A. M., and WEBSTER, C., *An Introduction to the Social History of Nursing* (1988).

DONNISON, J., *Midwives and Medical Men: A History of Inter-Professional Rivalries and Women's Rights* (1977).

DOPSON, L., *The Changing Scene in General Practice* (1971).

DUMAN, D., *The English and Colonial Bars* (1983).

DUPREE, M., 'Other than healing: Medical Practitioners and the Business of Life Assurance during the Nineteenth and Early Twentieth Centuries' *SHM*, 10 (1) 1997.

DYASON, D., 'The Medical Profession in Colonial Victoria', in MacLeod, R., and Lewis, M. (eds.), *Disease, Medicine and Empire. Perspectives on Western Medicine and the Experience of European Expansion* (1988).

DYHOUSE, C., *No Distinction of Sex? Women in British Universities, 1870–1939* (1995).

ECKSTEIN, H., *Pressure Group Politics. The Case of the British Medical Association* (1960).

—— *The English Health Service. Its Origins, Structure and Achievements* (Cambridge (Mass.), 1964).

EDER, N. R., *National Health Insurance and the Medical Profession in Britain, 1913–1939* (1982).

EIMERT, T. S., and PEARSON, R. J. C., 'Working Time in General Practice: How General Practitioners Use Their Time', *BMJ*, ii (1966).

ELLIOTT-BINNS, C., *The Story of a Northamptonshire Practice, 1845–1992* (Northampton, 1992).

ENGLISH, B. H., *Four Generations of a Whitby Medical Family* (Whitby, 1977) .

EVANS, B., *Freedom to Choose: the Life and Work of Dr Helena Wright, Pioneer of Contraception* (1984).

EVANS, E., 'Englishness and Britishness. National identities, 1790–1870', in Grant, A. and Stringer, K. J. (eds.), *Uniting the Kingdom? The Making of British History* (1995).

EVANS, R. J., *Rereading German History. From Unification to Reunification, 1800–1996* (1997).

EVANS, W. A., 'Dr Evan Pierce of Denbigh', *Transactions of the Denbighshire Historical Society*, 15 (1966).

FAIRFIELD, L., 'Medical Women in the Forces. Part 1. Women Doctors in the British Forces, 1914–18 War', *Journal of MWF* (1967).

FEINSTEIN, C. H., *Statistical Tables of National Income, Expenditure and Output of the U.K., 1855–1965* (Cambridge, 1972).

FITTON, F., and ACHESON, H. W. K., *Doctor/Patient Relationship. A Study in General Practice* (1979).

FLEETWOOD, J. F., *The History of Medicine in Ireland* (Dublin, 1983).

FOSTER, W. D., 'The Finances of a Victorian General Practitioner', *Proceedings of the Royal Society of Medicine*, 66 (1973).

FOX, D. M., *Health Policies Health Politics: The British and American Experiences, 1911–1965* (Princeton, 1986).

FRASER, F., *The British Postgraduate Medical Federation* (1967).

FREEDEN, M., 'The Stranger at the Feast: Ideology and Public Policy in Twentieth-Century Britain', *Twentieth Century British History*, 1 (1990).

FRY, J., *General Practice. The Facts* (1993).

GILBERT, B. B., *The Evolution of National Insurance in Britain* (1966).

GITTINS, D., *Fair Sex. Family Size and Structure, 1900–1939* (1982).

GOEBEL, T., 'American Medicine and the "Organizational Synthesis": Chicago Physicians and the Business of Medicine, 1900–1920', *BHM*, 68 (1994).

GLYNN, A., *Elinor Glynn—A Biography* (1955).

GRAY, D. PEREIRA (ed.), *Forty Years On. The Story of the First Forty Years of the Royal College of General Practitioners* (1992).

HAIG, A., *The Victorian Clergy* (1984).

HALE, G., and ROBERTS, N., *A Doctor in Practice* (1974).

HALL, D. L., *Science as Process* (Chicago, 1988).

HALLER, J. S., *American Medicine in Transition, 1840–1910* (Urbana, 1981).

HALSEY, A. H. (ed.), *British Social Trends since 1900* (1988).

HAMILTON, L., 'The Distribution of Capital among the Medical Profession in England and Wales, 1940–1', *Bulletin of the Institute of Statistics*, Oxford, 12 (1950).

HARDY, A., ' "Death is the Cure of all Diseases": Using the General Register Office Cause of Death Statistics for 1837–1920', *SHM*, 7 (1994).

HARRIS, J., *Private Lives, Public Spirit. A Social History of Britain, 1870–1914* (Oxford, 1993).

HAWKINS, M., *Social Darwinism and European and American Thought, 1860–1945* (Cambridge, 1997).

HAYNES, D. M., 'Social Status and Imperial Service: Tropical Medicine and the British Medical Profession in the Nineteenth Century', in Arnold, D. (ed.), *Warm Climates and Western Medicine; the Emergence of Tropical Medicine, 1500–1900* (Amsterdam, 1996).

HENNOCK, E. P., 'The Origins of British National Insurance and the German Precedent, 1880–1914', in Mommsen, W. J. (ed.), *The Emergence of the Welfare State in Britain and Germany, 1850–1950* (1981).

—— *British Social Reform and German Precedents. The Case of Social Insurance, 1880–1914* (Oxford, 1987).

HEWETSON, J., 'Before and After the Appointed Day', *BMJ*, 287 (1983).

HIGONNET, M. R. *et al.* (eds.), *Behind the Lines: Gender and the Two World Wars* (New Haven, 1987).

HILL, B., 'The Doctor's Pay and Day', *Journal of the Royal Statistical Society*, cxiv (1951).

HOLLIS, P., 'Women in Council', in Rendall, J. (ed.), *Equal or Different. Women's Politics, 1800–1914* (Oxford, 1987).

HOLLOWAY, S., 'The Apothecaries Act, 1815: A Reinterpretation. Part II The Consequences of the Act', *MH*, 10 (1966).

HOLLOWAY, S. W. F., 'The Regulation of the Supply of Drugs in Britain before 1868', in Porter, R., and Teich, M. (eds.), *Drugs and Narcotics in History* (Cambridge, 1995).

HONIGSBAUM, F., *The Division in British Medicine: A History of the Separation of General Practice from Hospital Care, 1911–1968* (1979).

—— *Health, Happiness and Security: The Creation of the National Health Service* (1989).

HUERKAMP, C., 'The Making of the Modern Medical Profession, 1800–1914: Prussian Doctors in the Nineteenth Century', in Cocks, G., and Jarausch, K. H. (eds.), *German Professions, 1800–1950* (Oxford, 1990).

HUTTON, I., *Memoirs of a Doctor in War and Peace* (1960).

INKSTER, I, 'Marginal Men: Aspects of the Social Role of the Medical Community in Sheffield, 1790–1850', in Woodward, J., and Richards, D. (eds.), *Health Care and*

Popular Medicine in Nineteenth Century England: Essays in the Social History of Medicine (1977).

JALLAND, P. (ed.), *The Autobiography of Octavia Wilberforce* (1989).

JARAUSCH, K. H., 'The German Professions in History and Theory', in Cocks, G., and Jarausch, K. H., *German Professions, 1800–1950* (Oxford, 1990).

—— *The Unfree Profession: German Lawyers, Teachers and Engineers, 1900–1950* (Oxford, 1990).

JEFFERYS, M., and SACHS, M., *Rethinking General Practice: Dilemmas in Primary Medical Care* (1983).

JENKINSON, J., 'The Role of the Medical Societies in the Rise of the Scottish Medical Profession, 1730–1939', *SHM*, 4 (1991).

JEWKES, J. and S., *The Genesis of the British NHS* (Oxford, 1962).

JOHNSON, T. J., *Professions and Power* (1972).

JONES, H., *Health and Society in Twentieth Century Britain* (1994).

KELLY, A., *The Descent of Darwin: The Popularization of Darwinism in Germany, 1860–1914* (Chapel Hill, 1981).

KING, L. S., 'Signs and Symptoms', *Journal of the American Medical Association*, 206 (1965).

KIRK, H., *Portrait of a Profession. A History of the Solicitor's Profession 1100 to the Present Day* (1976).

KITSON CLARK, G., *Churchmen and the Condition of England, 1832–1885* (1973).

KLEIN, R., *The Politics of the National Health Service* (2nd edn., 1983).

KNAPMAN, G. J., *Care for the Caring. Medical Sickness Annuity and Life Assurance Society Limited, 1884–1984* (1984).

KUNITZ, S. J., 'The Personal Physician and the Decline of Mortality', in Schofield, R., Reher, D., Bideau, A. (eds.), *The Decline of Mortality in Europe* (Oxford, 1991).

LANE, J., *Apprenticeship in England* (1996).

LAWRENCE, C., *Medicine in the Making of Modern Britain, 1700–1920* (1994).

LAWRENCE, S. C., 'Private Enterprise and Public Interest: Medical Education and the Apothecaries Act', in French, R. and Wear, A. (eds.), *British Medicine in an Age of Reform* (1992).

LEVINE, P., *Victorian Feminism* (1987).

LEWIS, J., *The Politics of Motherhood* (1980).

—— and BROOKES, B., 'The Peckham Health Centre, "PEP", and the Concept of General Practice during the 1930s and 1940s', *MH*, 27 (1983).

LEWIS, J. R., *The Victorian Bar* (1982).

LEWIS, R., and MAUDE, A., *Professional People* (1952).

LILLY, R. G., *An Account of Rural Medical Practice from the 18th Century Onwards in Long Buckby, Northamptonshire* (Dunton Bassett, 1993).

LINDSAY, A., *Socialized Medicine in England and Wales: The National Health Service, 1948–1961* (Chapel Hill, 1962).

LODGE, F. E., 'Reminiscences from a Fenland Practice', *BMJ*, 289 (1984).

LOUDON, I., 'The Historical Importance of Outpatients', *BMJ*, i (1978).

—— 'A Doctor's Cash Book: The Economy of General Practice in the 1830s', *MH* 27 (1983).

—— 'The Concept of the Family Doctor', *BHM*, 58 (1984).

—— *Medical Care and the General Practitioner* (Oxford, 1986).

—— *Death in Childbirth. An International Study of Maternal Care and Maternal Mortality, 1800–1950* (Oxford, 1992).

—— 'Death in Childbed from the Eighteenth Century to 1935', *MH*, 30 (1986).

—— 'Childbirth', in Loudon, I. (ed.), *Western Medicine. An Illustrated History* (Oxford 1997).

LOVEJOY, E. P., and REID, A. C., 'The Medical Women's International Association: an Historical Sketch', *Journal of the American Medial Women's Association* (1951).

McCLELLAND, C. E., *The German Experience of Professionalization* (Cambridge, 1991).

McKENDRICK, N., BREWER, J., and PLUMB, J. H. (eds.), *The Birth of a Consumer Society: the Commercialization of Eighteenth-Century England* (1982).

McLACHLAN, G. (ed.), *Medical Education and Medical Care* (Oxford , 1977).

—— (ed.), *Improving the Common Weal. Aspects of the Scottish Health Services, 1900–1984* (Edinburgh, 1987).

MADISON, D. L., 'Preserving Individualism in the Organisational Society: "Cooperation" and American Medical Practice, 1900–1920', *BHM*, 70 (1996).

MAIR, A., *Sir James Mackenzie, MD. General Practitioner* (1972).

MANTON, J., *Elizabeth Garrett Anderson* (1965).

MARLAND, H., *Medicine and Society in Wakefield and Huddersfield, 1780–1870* (Cambridge, 1987).

MARKS, L., 'Mothers, Babies and Hospitals: "The London" and the Provision of Maternity Care in East London, 1870–1939', in Fildes, V., Marks, L., and Marland, H. (eds.), *Women and Children First* (1992).

—— *Metropolitan Maternity: Maternal and Infant Welfare Services in Early Twentieth Century London* (1996).

MARSH, D. C., *The Changing Social Structure of England and Wales 1871–1961* (1958).

MILEY, U., and PICKSTONE, J. V., 'Medical Botany Around 1850: American Medicine in Industrial Britain', in Cooter, R. (ed.), *Studies in the History of Alternative Medicine* (Oxford, 1988).

MITCHELL, B. R., *Abstract of British Historical Statistics* (Cambridge, 1962 and 1988).

MOKYR, J., *The Lever of Riches: Technological Creativity and Economic Progress* (Oxford, 1990).

MORANTZ-SANCHEZ, R. M., *Sympathy and Science: Women Physicians in American Medicine* (Oxford, 1985).

MORGAN, K. O., *Labour in Power, 1945–1951* (Oxford, 1985).

MORRIS, A. D., 'Two Colliery Doctors. The Brothers Armstrong of Treorchy', in Cule, J. (ed.), *Wales and Medicine. An Historical Survey* (Cardiff, 1975).

MORRIS-JONES, H., 'The Country Doctor of Fifty Years Ago' *Country Quest*, Autumn (1961).

NEILL, J. G., 'Married Women Doctors' *Royal Free Hospital Journal*, xxvi, (1964).

NEWMAN, C., 'The History of Postgraduate Medical Education at the West London Hospital', *MH*, 10 (1966).

NICHOLLS, P. A., *Homeopathy and the Medical Profession* (1988).

NUGENT, A., 'Fit for Work: the Introduction of Physical Examinations in Industry', *BHM*, 57 (1983).

O'BOYLE, L., 'The Problem of an Excess of Educated Men in Western Europe, 1800–1850', *Journal of Modern History*, 42 (1970).

ODLUM, D., 'The Medical Women's International Association', *Journal of the MWF* (1958).

OFFER, A., *Property and Politics, 1870–1914: Landownership, Law, Ideology and Urban Development in England* (Cambridge, 1981).

—— 'Between the Gift and the Market. The Economy of Regard', *Economic History Review*, l (1997).

OGSTON, D., W. D., and C. M., 'Origins and Employment of the Medical Graduates of the University of Aberdeen, 1931–69', *BMJ*, iv (1970).

OPPENHEIM, J., *'Shattered Nerves'. Doctors, Patients and Depression in Victorian England* (Oxford, 1991).

OSWALD, N. T. A., 'A Social Health Service Without Doctors', *SHM*, 4 (1991).

PELLING, M., *Cholera, Fever and English Medicine, 1825–1865* (Oxford, 1978).

PEMBERTON, J., *Will Pickles of Wensleydale* (1970).

PENSABENE, T. A., *The Rise of the Medical Profession in Victoria* (1980).

PEREIRA GRAY, D. (ed.), *Forty Years On: The Story of the First Forty Years of the Royal College of General Practitioners* (1992).

PERETZ, E., 'A Maternity Service for England and Wales: Local Authority Maternity Care in the Inter-War Period in Oxfordshire and Tottenham', in Garcia, J., Kilpatrick, R., and Richards, M. (eds.), *The Politics of Maternal Care* (Oxford, 1990).

PERKIN, H., 'The Pattern of Social Transformation in England', in Jarausch, K. H. (ed.), *The Transformation of Higher Learning, 1860–1930* (Chicago, 1983).

—— *The Rise of Professional Society. England Since 1880* (1989).

PERKINS, B. B., 'Shaping Institution-based Specialism: Early Twentieth-Century Economic Organisation of Medicine', *SHM*, 10 (1997).

PERKINS, H. J., 'Middle-Class Education and Employment in the Nineteenth Century: A Critical Note', *Economic History Review*, xiv (1961).

PETERSON, M. J., *The Medical Profession in Mid-Victorian London* (Berkeley, 1978).

PICKLES, W., *Epidemiology in Country Practice* (RCGP edn., 1984).

PORTER, R., 'The Patient's View: Doing Medical History from Below', *Theory and Society*, 14 (1987).

—— *Disease, Medicine and Society in England, 1550–1860* (1987).

—— and HALL, L., *The Facts of Life. The Creation of Sexual Knowledge in Britain, 1650–1950* (1995).

RANKIN, G., 'Professional Organisation and the Development of Medical Knowledge: Two Interpretations of Homeopathy', in Cooter, R. (ed.), *Studies in the History of Alternative Medicine* (1988).

RANKINE, J., *150 Years in Country Practice* (Romsey, 1982).

REW, MABEL, 'Looking Back', *Journal of the MWF* (1967).

RHODES JAMES, R., *Henry Wellcome* (1994).

RICHARDS, T., *The Commodity Culture of Victorian England. Advertising a Spectacle, 1851–1914* (Stanford, 1990).

ROBBINS, K., 'Core and Periphery in British History', *Proceedings of the British Academy*, lxx, (1984).

—— *Nineteenth-Century Britain. Integration and Diversity* (Oxford, 1988).

—— 'An Imperial and Multinational Polity. The "scene from the centre", 1832–1922', in Grant, A., and Stringer, K. J. (eds.), *Uniting the Kingdom? The Making of British History* (1995).

ROBERTS, E., *A Woman's Place: An Oral History of Working-Class Women, 1890–1940* (Oxford, 1984).

RODIN, A. E., *Medical Casebook of Dr A. Conan Doyle* (Florida, 1984).

ROGERS HOLLINGSWORTH, J., *A Political Economy of Medicine: Great Britain and the United States* (Baltimore, 1986).

ROSS, J. S., *The National Health Service in Great Britain* (Oxford, 1952).

RUESCHEMEYER, D., *Power and the Division of Labour* (1986).

SANDERSON, M., *The Universities and British Industry, 1850–1970* (1972).

SIEGRIST, H., 'Public Office or Free Profession? German Attorneys in the Nineteenth and Early Twentieth Centuries', in Cocks, G., and Jarausch, K. H. (eds.), *German Professions, 1800–1950* (Oxford, 1990).

SINGER, C., and HOLLOWAY, S. W. F., 'Early Medical Education in England in Relation to the Pre-History of London University', *MH*, 4 (1960).

SKOCPOL, T., 'Bringing the State Back in: Strategies of Analysis in Current Research', in Evans, P. B., Rueschemeyer, D., and Skocpol, T. (eds.), *Bringing the State Back In* (Cambridge, 1985).

SMITH, F. B., *The People's Health, 1830–1910* (1979).

SMITH, R., 'The Development of Guidance for Medical Practitioners by the General Medical Council', *MH*, 33 (1993).

STAMP, W., *'Doctor Himself': An Unorthodox Biography of Harry Roberts, 1871–1946* (1949).

STARR, P., *The Social Transformation of American Medicine* (New York, 1982).

STAVERT, G., *A Study in Southsea: The Unrevealed Life of Dr Arthur Conan Doyle* (Portsmouth, 1987).

STEPHENSON, J., 'Women and the Professions in Germany, 1900–1945', in Cocks, G., and Jaurausch, K. H. (eds.), *German Professions, 1800–1950* (Oxford, 1990).

STEVENS, R., *Medical Practice in Modern England: The Impact of Specialization and State Medicine* (New Haven, 1966).

STEWART, J., ' "For a Healthy London": The Socialist Medical Association and the London County Council in the 1930s', *MH*, 42 (1997).

STEWART, R. E., *Out of Practice: Memories of General Practice in Scotland During the 1950s* (Southport, 1996).

STONE, D. A., 'Physicians as Gatekeepers: Illness Certification as a Rationing Device', *Public Policy*, xxvii (1979).

STURDY, S., 'The Political Economy of Scientific Medicine and Science: Education and the Transference of Medical Practice in Sheffield, 1890–1922', *MH*, 36 (1992).

SUPPLE, B., *The Royal Exchange Assurance: A History of British Insurance, 1720–1970* (Cambridge, 1970).

SZASZ, T. S., and HOLLENDER, M. H., 'A Contribution to the Philosophy of Medicine', *AMA Archives of Internal Medicine*, 97 (1956).

TAYLOR, S., *Good General Practice*, (Nuffield Hospitals Trust, Oxford, 1954).

THOMAS, J. R., and GRIFFITHS, M., 'Industrial Railways and Tramways of Flintshire', *Archives*, 14 (1997).

TUDOR HART, J., *A New Kind of Doctor: The General Practitioner's Part in the Health of the Community* (1988).

VAUGHAN, P., *Doctors Commons: A Short History of the British Medical Assocation* (1959).

VELDEN, H. VAN DER, 'The Dutch Health Services Before Compulsory Health Insurance, 1900–1914' *SHM*, ix (1996).

VROMEN, J. J., *Economic Evolution: An Enquiry into the Foundations of New Institutional Economics* (1995).

WADDINGTON, I., 'The development of Medical Ethics—A Sociological Analysis, *MH*, 19 (1975).

—— 'General Practitioners and Consultants in Early Nineteenth Century England: The Sociology of an Intra-Professional Conflict', in Woodward, J. and Richards, D. (eds.), *Health Care and Popular Medicine in Nineteenth-Century England* (1977).

—— *The Medical Profession in the Industrial Revolution* (1984).

WEBSTER, C., 'Labour and the Origins of the National Health Service', in Rupke, N. A. (ed.), *Science, Politics and the Public Good* (1988).

—— *The Health Services Since the War. Vol. 1. Problems of Health Care. The National Health Service Before 1957* (1988).

—— 'Conflict and Consensus: Explaining the British Health Service', *Twentieth Century British History*, 1 (1990).

—— 'Doctors, Public Service and Profit: General Practitioners and the National Health Service', *Transactions of the Royal Historical Society*, 5th series, 40 (1990).

—— *Government and Health Care. Vol. 2. Government and Health Care. The British National Health Service, 1958–1979* (1996).

WEINDLING, P., 'Medical Practice in Imperial Berlin: the case book of Alfred Grotjahn', *BHM*, 61 (1987).

—— 'The Contribution of Central European Jews to Medical Science and Practice in Britain, during the 1930s–1950s', in Carlebach, J., *et al.* (eds.), *Second Chance: Two Centuries of German-speaking Jews in the United Kingdom* (Tubingen, 1991).

—— 'A Transfusion of Medical Expertise: Medical Refugees in Britain, 1930–1950', *Wellcome Trust Review*, 4 (1995).

WEISZ, G., 'The Politics of Medical Professionalization in France, 1845–48', *Journal of Social History*, 12 (1978–9).

WHITESIDE, J. S., 'Private Agencies for Public Purposes: Some New Perspectives on Policy Making in Health Insurance Between the Wars', *Journal of Social Policy*, 12 (1983).

WILLIAMS, J. H., *G.P.s of Barry, 1885–1979*, (Barry Medical Society, 1979).

WILLIAMS, D. I., 'William Coulson: Victorian Virtues Handsomely Rewarded', *Journal of Medical Biography*, 2 (1994).

WINTER, J. M., *The Great War and the British People* (1986).

WITZ, A., *Professions and Patriarchy* (1992).

WOOD, C., *Paradise Lost* (1988).

WORSWICK, G. D. N., and TIPPING, D. G., *Profits in the British Economy* (Oxford, 1967).

WYN JONES, E., 'Sir John Williams (1840–1926) His Background and Achievement', in Cule, J. (ed.), *Wales and Medicine: An Historical Survey* (Cardiff, 1975).

YOUNG, J. H., *The Toadstool Millionaires* (Princeton, 1961).

ZELDIN, T., *A History of the French Passions, 1848–1945* (2 vols., Oxford, 1993).

ZWANENBERG, VAN D., 'The Training and Careers of those Apprenticed to Apothecaries in Suffolk, 1815–58', *MH*, 27 (1983).

UNPUBLISHED THESES, BOOKS, AND PAPERS

BENNETT, J., 'The British Army Medical Officer, 1900 to the Present Day', paper given at the 'Medicine and the Emergence of Modern Warfare Conference', Wellcome Institute, London, July 1995.

FREEDEN, M., 'The Extension of Liberal Rights: Health, Welfare, and Community', unpublished paper given at the 'Right to Health Conference', Oxford, July 1997.

ELSTON, M. A., 'Women Doctors in the Health Services: a Sociological Study of their Careers and Opportunities' (Ph.D., University of Leeds, 1986).

HARRIS, J., 'The Right to Health: Historical Frameworks', paper given at the 'Right to Health Conference', Oxford, July 1997.

HARDING, W. H., 'Memoirs'.

PALMER, D., 'Women, Health and Politics, 1919–1939. Professional and Lay Involvement in Women's Health Campaigns' (Ph.D., University of Warwick, 1986).

RICHARD, J.,'Autobiography'.

ROWOLD, K. J., 'The Academic Woman': Minds, Bodies, and Education in Britain and Germany *c.*1860–*c.*1914 (Ph.D., University of London thesis, 1996).

STEWART, J., ' "Your Health, Mr Smith", British Socialist Doctors and Citizens Rights, *c.*1930–*c.*1970', paper given at the 'Right to Health Conference', Oxford, July 1997.

WHITEHEAD, I., 'The British Medical Officer on the Western Front', paper given at the 'Medicine and the Emergence of Modern Warfare Conference', Wellcome Institute, London, July 1995.

PERSONAL COMMUNICATION/ORAL TESTIMONY

Sydney Adler of Brighton. (Interviewed by A. Digby).

Henry W. Ashworth of Ardwick, Manchester. (Interviewed by A. Digby).

Hugh Mair Davie of Manchester. (Interviewed by A. Digby).

Allan F. Granger of Kimbolton. (Interviewed by A. Digby).

Beryl J. Goff of Colchester. (Interviewed by H. Sweet).

Rosentyl Griffiths. (Interviewed by A. John).

Emma B. Hendry of Nuneaton. (Interviewed by H. Sweet).

Edgar Hope-Simpson of Cirencester. (Interviewed by H. Sweet).

Fred E. James of Cirencester. (Interviewed by H. Sweet).

Richard G. Lilly of Long Buckby. (Interviewed by A. Digby).

A. W. Maiden of Saxilby. (Tape supplied).

Susan Pope of Pencoyd, Herefordshire. (Interviewed by H. Sweet).

James E. Rankine of Romsey. (Interviewed by A. Digby).

Index of Medical Names

General Index